TRACTS FOR
THE TIMES

Volume One: 1833–1834
Tracts 1–46 and Records of the Church 1–18

SEMINARY STREET PRESS
The Library of Anglican Theology
Number 5.1

Published by Seminary Street Press, the Library of Anglican Theology seeks to provide newly typeset editions of important works from the Anglican tradition for a wide array of contemporary readers—Christian laypeople, historians of the Church, seminary students, bishops, priests, deacons, catechists, and theologians. The Library will provide a rich foundation on which to build as Anglicans continue to theologically engage with the pressing questions of our time.

Series Editor
CHRISTOPHER POORE

Tracts for the Times

Volume One: 1833–1834
Tracts 1–46 and Records of the Church 1–18

Written by
Members *of the*
University of Oxford

Edited by
Christopher Poore

SEMINARY STREET PRESS
GALESBURG, ILLINOIS

Galesburg, Illinois

2021 Paperback Edition
ISBN: 979-8-48-254300-9

facebook.com/SeminaryStreetPress
Twitter: @SeminaryStPress
Instagram: @SeminaryStreetPress
seminarystreetpress@gmail.com

All rights reserved.
While the work itself is in the public domain,
no part of this newly edited edition may be reproduced or transmitted
in any form or by any means, electronic or mechanical,
without the publisher's permission in writing.

Contents

Advertisement i

Tracts of 1833

1. Thoughts on the Ministerial Commission Respectfully Addressed to the Clergy 1
2. The Catholic Church 6
3. Thoughts Respectfully Addressed to the Clergy on Alterations in the Liturgy; The Burial Service; The Principle of Unity 10
4. Adherence to the Apostolical Succession the Safest Course 18
5. A Short Address to His Brethren on the Nature & Constitution of the Church of Christ and of the Branch of It Established in England. By a Layman 26
6. The Present Obligation of Primitive Practice 40
7. The Episcopal Church Apostolical 44
8. The Gospel a Law of Liberty; Church Reform 48
9. On Shortening the Church Services; Sunday Lessons 52
10. Heads of a Week-Day Lecture Delivered to a Country Congregation in ——shire 55
11. The Visible Church in Letters to a Friend: Letters I and II 60

12. Richard Nelson I: Bishops, Priests, and Deacons 69

13. Sunday Lessons: The Principle of Selection 84

14. The Ember Days 96

15. On the Apostolical Succession in the English Church 102

16. Advent 113

17. The Ministerial Commission: A Trust from Christ for the Benefit of His People 120

18. Thoughts on the Benefits of the System of Fasting, Enjoined by Our Church... 126

19. On Arguing Concerning the Apostolical Succession; On Reluctance to Confess the Apostolical Succession 152

20. The Visible Church, Letters to a Friend: Letter III 156

Tracts of 1834

21. Mortification of the Flesh a Scripture Duty 163

22. Richard Nelson II: The Athanasian Creed 168

23. The Faith and Obedience of Churchmen, the Strength of the Church... 185

24. The Scripture View of the Apostolical Commission 189

25. The Great Necessity and Advantage of Public Prayer, Extracted from Bishop Beveridge's Sermon on the Subject 199

26. The Necessity and Advantage of Frequent Communion, Extracted from Bishop Beveridge's Sermon on the Subject 207

27. The History of Popish Transubstantiation to Which Is Opposed the Catholic Doctrine of the Holy Scripture, the Ancient Fathers, and the Reformed Church by John Cosin, Bishop of Durham 227

28. The History of Popish Transubstantiation (Continued) 244

29. Christian Liberty, or, Why Should We Belong to the Church of England? 268

30. Christian Liberty, or, Why Should We Belong to the Church of England? (Continued) 279

31. The Reformed Church 288

32. The Standing Ordinances of Religion 292

33. Primitive Episcopacy 300

34. Rites and Customs of the Church 306

35. The People's Interest in Their Minister's Commission 313

36. Account of Religious Sects at Present Existing in England 317

37. Bishop Wilson's Form of Excommunication 323

38. Via Media, No. 1 331

39. Bishop Wilson's Form of Receiving Penitents 343

40. Richard Nelson III: On Baptism 347

41. Via Media, No. 2 361

42. Bishop Wilson's Meditations on his Sacred Office, Number 1: Sunday 372

43. Richard Nelson IV: Length of the Public Service 380

44. Bishop Wilson's Meditations on his Sacred Office, Number 2: Monday 394

45. The Grounds of Our Faith 402

46. Bishop Wilson's Meditations on his Sacred Office, Number 3: Tuesday 407

Records of the Church

1. Epistle of Ignatius to the Ephesians 413

2.	Epistle of Ignatius to the Magnesians	420
3.	The Apostle St. John and the Robber	424
4.	Epistle of Ignatius to Polycarp	428
5.	Epistle of Ignatius to the Trallians	431
6.	Account of the Martyrs of Lyons and Vienne	435
7.	Epistle of Ignatius to the Smyrnæans	447
8.	Epistle of Ignatius to the Romans	451
9.	The Martyrdom of Ignatius at Rome	455
10.	Epistle of Ignatius to the Philadelphians	461
11.	Account of the Martyrdom of St. James the Apostle	465
12.	The Martyrdom of Polycarp	468
13.	Justin Martyr, on Primitive Christian Worship	479
14.	Irenæus on the Rule of Faith	485
15.	The Temporal Condition and the Principles of Christians, from the Epistle to Diognetus	488
16.	Address of Clement of Alexandria to the Heathen	494
17.	Tertullian on the Rule of Faith	498
18.	Tertullian on the Rule of Faith (Continued)	504

Appendices

1.	Thematic Index of the Tracts, Volume 1	513
2.	Works Upholding the Doctrine Inculcated in the Tracts	517
3.	H.P. Liddon's Table of Tracts and Authors	520
4.	A Note on the Text	525

*If the trumpet gives an uncertain sound,
who shall prepare himself to the battle?*

1 CORINTHIANS 14:8

Advertisement

The following Tracts were published with the object of contributing something towards the practical revival of doctrines, which, although held by the great divines of our Church, at present have become obsolete with the majority of her members, and are withdrawn from public view even by the more learned and orthodox few who still adhere to them. The Apostolic succession, the Holy Catholic Church, were principles of action in the minds of our predecessors of the 17th century; but, in proportion as the maintenance of the Church has been secured by law, her ministers have been under the temptation of leaning on an arm of flesh instead of her own divinely-provided discipline, a temptation increased by political events and arrangements which need not here be more than alluded to. A lamentable increase of sectarianism has followed; being occasioned (in addition to other more obvious causes,) first, by the cold aspect which the new Church doctrines have presented to the religious sensibilities of the mind, next to their meagreness in suggesting motives to restrain it from seeking out a more influential discipline. Doubtless obedience to the law of the land, and the careful maintenance of "decency and order" (the topics in usage among us), are plain duties of the Gospel, and a reasonable ground for keeping in communion with the Established Church; yet, if Providence has graciously provided for our weakness more interesting and constraining motives, it is a sin thanklessly to neglect them; just as it would be a mistake to rest the duties of temperance or justice on the mere law of natural religion, when they are mercifully sanctioned in the Gospel by the more winning authority of our Saviour Christ. Experience has shewn the inefficacy of the mere injunctions of Church order, however scripturally enforced, in restraining from schism the awakened and anxious sinner; who goes to a dissenting preacher "because (as he expresses it) he gets good from him:" and though he does not stand excused in God's sight for yielding to the temptation, surely the Ministers of the Church are not blameless if, by keeping back the more gracious and consoling truths provided for the little ones of Christ, they indirectly lead him into it. Had he been taught as a child, that the Sacraments, not preaching, are the sources of Divine Grace; that the Apostolical ministry had a virtue in it which went out over the whole Church, when sought by the prayer of faith; that fellowship with it was a gift and privilege, as well as a duty, we could not have laid so many wanderers from our fold, nor so many cold hearts within it.

This instance may suggest many others of the superior *influence* of an apostolical over a mere secular method of teaching. The awakened mind knows its wants, but cannot provide for them; and in its hunger will feed upon ashes, if it cannot obtain the pure milk of the word. Methodism and Popery are in different ways the refuge of those whom the Church stints of the gifts of grace; they are the foster-mothers of abandoned children. The neglect of the daily service, the desecration of festivals, the Eucharist scantily administered, insubordination permitted in all ranks of the Church, orders and offices imperfectly developed, the want of Societies for particular religious objects, and the like deficiencies, lead the feverish mind, desirous of a vent to its feelings, and a stricter rule of life, to the smaller religious Communities, to prayer and bible meetings, and ill-advised institutions and societies, on the one hand,—on the other, to the solemn and captivating services by which Popery gains its proselytes. Moreover, the multitude of men cannot teach or guide themselves; and an injunction given them to depend on their private judgment, cruel in itself, is doubly hurtful, as throwing them on such teachers as speak daringly and promise largely, and not only aid but supersede individual exertion.

These remarks may serve as a clue, for those who care to pursue it, to the views which have led to the publication of the following Tracts. The Church of Christ was intended to cope with human nature in all its forms, and surely the gifts vouchsafed it are adequate for that gracious purpose.

There are zealous sons and servants of her English branch, who see with sorrow that she is defrauded of her full usefulness by particular theories and principles of the present age, which interfere with the execution of one portion of her commission; and while they consider that the revival of this portion of truth is especially adapted to break up existing parties in the Church, and to form instead a bond of union among all who love the Lord Jesus Christ in sincerity, they believe that nothing but these neglected doctrines, faithfully preached, will repress that extension of Popery, for which the ever multiplying divisions of the religious world are too clearly preparing the way.

OXFORD,
The Feast of All Saints
November 1, 1834

Tracts
of 1833

TRACT 1: AD CLERUM
Thoughts on the Ministerial Commission
Respectfully Addressed to the Clergy

I am but one of yourselves,—a Presbyter; and therefore I conceal my name, lest I should take too much on myself by speaking in my own person. Yet speak I must; for the times are very evil, yet no one speaks against them.

Is not this so? Do not we "look one upon another," yet perform nothing? Do we not all confess the peril into which the Church is come, yet sit still each in his own retirement, as if mountains and seas cut off brother from brother? Therefore suffer me, while I try to draw you forth from those pleasant retreats, which it has been our blessedness hitherto to enjoy, to contemplate the condition and prospects of our Holy Mother in a practical way; so that one and all may unlearn that idle habit, which has grown upon us, of owning the state of things to be bad, yet doing nothing to remedy it.

Consider a moment. Is it fair, is it dutiful, to suffer our Bishops to stand the brunt of the battle without doing our part to support them? Upon them comes "the care of all the Churches." This cannot be helped; indeed it is their glory. Not one of us would wish in the least to deprive them of the duties, the toils, the responsibilities of their high office. And, black event as it would be for the country, yet (as far as they are concerned) we could not wish them a more blessed termination of their course, than the spoiling of their goods, and martyrdom.

To them then we willingly and affectionately relinquish their high privileges and honors; we encroach not upon the rights of the

SUCCESSORS OF THE APOSTLES; we touch not their sword and crosier. Yet surely we may be their shield-bearers in the battle without offence; and by our voice and deeds be to them what Luke and Timothy were to St. Paul.

Now then let me come at once to the subject which leads me to address you. Should the Government and Country so far forget their God as to cast off the Church, to deprive it of its temporal honors and substance, *on what* will you rest the claim of respect and attention which you make upon your flocks? Hitherto you have been upheld by your birth, your education, your wealth, your connexions; should these secular advantages cease, on what must Christ's Ministers depend? Is not this a serious practical question? We know how miserable is the state of religious bodies not supported by the State. Look at the Dissenters on all sides of you, and you will see at once that their Ministers, depending simply upon the people, become the *creatures* of the people. Are you content that this should be your case? Alas! can a greater evil befal Christians, than for their teachers to be guided by them, instead of guiding? How can we "hold fast the form of sound words," and "keep that which is committed to our trust," if our influence is to depend simply on our popularity? Is it not our very office to *oppose* the world, can we then allow ourselves to *court* it? to preach smooth things and prophesy deceits? to make the way of life easy to the rich and indolent, and to bribe the humbler classes by excitements and strong intoxicating doctrine? Surely it must not be so;—and the question recurs, on *what* are we to rest our authority, when the State deserts us?

Christ has not left His Church without claim of its own upon the attention of men. Surely not. Hard Master He cannot be, to bid us oppose the world, yet give us no credentials for so doing. There are some who rest their divine mission on their own unsupported assertion; others, who rest it upon their popularity; others, on their success; and others, who rest it upon their temporal distinctions. This last case has, perhaps, been too much our own; I fear we have neglected the real ground on which our authority is built,—OUR APOSTOLICAL DESCENT.

We have been born, not of blood, nor of the will of the flesh, nor of the will of man, but of God. The Lord Jesus Christ gave His Spirit to His Apostles; they in turn laid their hands on those who should succeed them; and these again on others; and so the sacred gift has been handed down to our present Bishops, who have appointed us as their assistants, and in some sense representatives.

Now every one of us believes this. I know that some will at first deny they do; still they do believe it. Only, it is not sufficiently, practically impressed on their minds. They *do* believe it; for it is the doctrine of the Ordination Service, which they have recognised as truth in the most solemn season of their lives. In order, then, not to prove, but to remind and impress, I entreat your attention to the words used when you were made Ministers of Christ's Church.

The office of Deacon was thus committed to you: "Take thou authority to execute the office of a Deacon in the Church of God committed unto thee: In the name, &c.

And the Priesthood thus:

"Receive the Holy Ghost, for the office and work of a Priest, in the Church of God, now committed unto thee by the imposition of our hands. Whose sins thou dost forgive, they are forgiven; and whose sins thou dost retain, they are retained. And be thou a faithful dispenser of the Word of God, and of His Holy Sacraments: In the name, &c."

These, I say, were words spoken to us, and received by us, when we were brought nearer to God than at any other time of our lives. I know the grace of ordination is contained in the laying on of hands, not in any form of words;—yet in our own case (as has ever been usual in the Church), words of blessing have accompanied the act. Thus we have confessed before God our belief, that from the Bishop who ordained us, we received the Holy Ghost, the power to bind and to loose, to administer the Sacraments, and to preach. Now *how* is he able to give these great gifts? *Whence* is his right? Are these words idle (which would be taking God's name in vain), or do they express merely a wish (which surely is very far below their meaning), or do they not rather indicate that the Speaker is conveying a gift? Surely they can mean nothing short of this. But whence, I ask, his right to do so? Has he any right, except as having received the power from those who consecrated him to be a Bishop? He could not give what he had never received. It is plain then that he but *transmits;* and that the Christian Ministry is a *succession*. And if we trace back the power of ordination from hand to hand, of course we shall come to the Apostles at last. We know we do, as a plain historical fact; and therefore all we, who have been ordained

Clergy, in the very form of our ordination acknowledged the doctrine of the APOSTOLICAL SUCCESSION.

And for the same reason, we must necessarily consider none to be *really* ordained who have not *thus* been ordained. For if ordination is a divine ordinance, it must be necessary; and if it is not a divine ordinance, how dare we use it? Therefore all who use it, all of *us,* must consider it necessary. As well might we pretend the Sacraments are not necessary to Salvation, while we make use of the offices of the Liturgy; for when God appoints means of grace, they are *the* means.

I do not see how any one can escape from this plain view of the subject, except (as I have already hinted) by declaring, that the words do not mean all that they say. But only reflect what a most unseemly time for random words is that, in which Ministers are set apart for their office. Do we not adopt a Liturgy, *in order to* hinder inconsiderate idle language, and shall we, in the most sacred of all services, write down, subscribe, and use again and again forms of speech which have not been weighed, and cannot be taken strictly?

Therefore, my dear Brethren, act up to your professions. Let it not be said that you have neglected a gift; for if you have the Spirit of the Apostles on you, surely this *is* a great gift. "Stir up the gift of God which is in you." Make much of it. Show your value of it. Keep it before your minds as an honorable badge, far higher than that secular respectability, or cultivation, or polish, or learning, or rank, which gives you a hearing with the many. Tell *them* of your gift. The times will soon drive you to do this, if you mean to be still any thing. But wait not for the times. Do not be compelled, by the world's forsaking you, to recur as if unwillingly to the high source of your authority. Speak out now, before you are forced, both as glorying in your privilege, and to ensure your rightful honor from your people. A notion has gone abroad, that they can take away your power. They think they have given and can take it away. They think it lies in the Church property, and they know that they have politically the power to confiscate that property. They have been deluded into a notion that present palpable usefulness, produceable results, acceptableness to your flocks, that these and such like are the tests of your Divine commission. Enlighten them in this matter. Exalt our Holy Fathers the Bishops, as the Representatives of the Apostles, and the Angels of the Churches; and magnify your office, as being ordained by them to take part in their Ministry.

But, if you will not adopt my view of the subject, which I offer to you, not doubtingly, yet (I hope) respectfully, at all events, CHOOSE YOUR SIDE. To remain neuter much longer will be itself to take a part. *Choose your side; since side you shortly must, with one or other party, even though you do nothing. Fear to be of those, whose line is decided for them by chance circumstances, and who may perchance find themselves with the enemies of Christ, while they think but to remove themselves from worldly politics. Such abstinence is impossible in troublous times. HE THAT IS NOT WITH ME, IS AGAINST ME, AND HE THAT GATHERETH NOT WITH ME SCATTERETH ABROAD.

JOHN HENRY NEWMAN
September 9, 1833

TRACT 2
The Catholic Church

*No weapon that is formed against thee shall prosper,
and every tongue that shall rise against thee
in judgment* THOU SHALT CONDEMN.

It is sometimes said, that the Clergy should abstain from politics; and that, if a Minister of Christ is political, he is not a follower of Him who said, "My kingdom is not of this world." Now there is a sense in which this is true, but, as it is commonly taken, it is very false.

It is true that the mere affairs of this world should not engage a Clergyman; but it is absurd to say that the affairs of this world should not at all engage his attention. If so, this world is not a preparation for another. Are we to speak when individuals sin, and not when a nation, which is but a collection of individuals? Must we speak to the poor, but not to the rich and powerful? In vain does St. James warn us against having the faith of our Lord Jesus Christ with respect of persons. In vain does the Prophet declare to us the Word of the Lord, that if the watchmen of Israel "speak not to warn the wicked from his way," "his blood will be required at the watchman's hand."

Complete our Lord's declaration concerning the nature of His kingdom, and you will see it is not at all inconsistent with the duty of our active and zealous interference in matters of this world. "If My kingdom were of this world," He says, *"then would My servants fight."*—Here He has vouchsafed so to explain Himself, that there is no room for misunderstanding His meaning. No one contends that His Ministers ought to use the weapons of a carnal warfare;—but surely to protest, to warn, to threaten, to excommunicate, are not such weapons. Let us not be scared from a plain duty, by the mere force of a misapplied text. There is an unexceptionable sense in which a Clergyman may, nay must be *political*. And above all, when the Nation interferes with the rights and possessions of the Church, it can with even less grace complain of the Church interfering with the Nation.

With this introduction let me call your attention to what seems a most dangerous infringement on our rights, on the part of the State. The Legislature has lately taken upon itself to remodel the dioceses of Ireland; a proceeding which involves the appointment of certain Bishops over certain Clergy, and of certain Clergy under certain Bishops, without the Church being consulted in the matter. I do not say whether or not harm will follow from this particular act with reference to Ireland; but consider whether it be not in itself an interference with things spiritual.

Are we content to be accounted the mere creation of the State, as schoolmasters and teachers may be, or soldiers, or magistrates, or other public officers? Did the State make us? can it unmake us? can it send out missionaries? can it arrange dioceses? Surely all these are spiritual functions; and Laymen may as well set about preaching, and consecrating the Bread and Wine, as assume these. I do not say the guilt is equal; but that, if the latter is guilt, the former is. Would St. Paul, with his good will, have suffered the Roman power to appoint Timothy, Bishop of Miletus as well as Ephesus? Would Timothy at such a bidding have undertaken the charge? Is not the notion of such an order, such an obedience, absurd? Yet has it not been realized in what has lately happened? For in what is the English State at present different from the Roman formerly? Neither can be accounted members of the Church of Christ. No one can say the British Legislature is in our communion, or is even Christian. What pretence then has it for, not merely advising, but superseding the Ecclesiastical Power?

Bear with me, while I express my fear that we do not, as much as we ought, consider the force of that article of our Belief, "The one Catholic and Apostolic Church." This is a tenet so important as to have been in the Creed from the beginning. It is mentioned there as a *fact*, and a fact *to be believed*, and therefore practical. Now what do we conceive is meant by it? As people vaguely take it in the present day, it seems only an assertion that there is a number of sincere Christians scattered through the world. But is not this a truism? who doubt it? who can deny that there are people in various places who are sincere believers? what comes of this? how is it important? why should it be placed as an article of faith, after the belief in the Holy Ghost? Doubtless the only true and satisfactory meaning is that which our Divines have ever taken, that there is on earth an existing Society, Apostolic as founded by the Apostles, Catholic because it spreads its branches in every place; i.e. the Church visible with its Bishops, Priests, and Deacons. And this surely *is* a most important doctrine; for what can be better news to the bulk of mankind than to be told that Christ, when He ascended, did not leave us orphans but appointed representatives of Himself to the end of time?

"The necessity of believing the Holy Catholic Church," says Bishop Pearson, in his Exposition of the Creed, "appeareth first in this, that Christ hath appointed it as the only way to eternal life.... Christ never appointed two ways to heaven, nor did He build a Church to save some, and make another institution for other men's salvation. There is none other name under heaven given among men whereby we must be saved, but the name of Jesus; and that name is no otherwise given under heaven than in the Church. This is the congregation of those persons here on earth which shall hereafter meet in heaven ..... There is a necessity of believing the Catholic Church, because except a man be of that, he can be of none. Whatsoever Church pretendeth to a new beginning, pretendeth at the same time to a new Churchdom, and whatsoever is so new is none." This indeed is the unanimous opinion of our Divines, that, as the Sacraments, so Communion with the Church, is "generally necessary to salvation," in the case of those who can obtain it.

If then we express our belief in the existence of one Church on earth from Christ's coming to the end of all things, if there is a promise it shall continue, and if it is our duty to do our part in our generation towards its continuance, how can we with a safe conscience countenance the interference of the Nation in its concerns? Does not such interference tend to destroy it? Would it not destroy it, if consistently followed up? Now, may we sit still and keep silence, when efforts are making to break up, or at least materially to weaken that Ecclesiastical body which we know is intended to last while the world endures, and the safety of which is committed to our keeping in our day? How shall we answer for it, if we transmit that Ordinance of God less entire than when it came to us?

Now what am I calling on you to do? You cannot help what has been done in Ireland; but you may protest against it. You may as a duty protest against it in public and private; you may keep a jealous watch on the proceedings of the Nation, lest a second act of the same kind be attempted. You may keep it before you as a desirable object that the Irish Church should at some future day meet in Synod and protest herself against what has been done; and then proceed to establish or rescind the State injunction, as may be thought expedient.

I know it is too much the fashion of the times to think any earnestness for ecclesiastical rights unseasonable and absurd, as if it were the feeling of those who lived among books and not in the world. But it is our *duty* to live among books, especially to live by ONE BOOK, and a very old one; and therein we are enjoined to "keep that good thing which is committed unto us," to "neglect not our gifts." And when men talk, as they sometimes do, as if in opposing them we were standing on technical difficulties instead of welcoming great and extensive benefits which would be the result of their measures, I would ask them (letting alone the question of their beneficial nature, which *is* a question) whether this is not being wise above that is written, whether it is not doing evil that good may come. We cannot know the effects which will follow certain alterations; but we can decide that the means by which it is proposed to attain them are unprecedented and disrespectful to the Church. And when men say, "*the day is past* for stickling about ecclesiastical rights," let them see to it, whether they do not use substantially the same arguments to maintain their position, as those who say, "The day is past for being a Christian."

Lastly, is it not plain that by showing a bold front and defending the rights of the Church, we are taking the only course, which can make us respected? Yielding will not persuade our enemies to desist from their efforts to destroy us root and branch. We cannot hope by giving something to keep the rest. Of this surely we have had of late years sufficient experience. But by resisting strenuously, and contemplating and providing against the worst, we may actually prevent the very evils we fear. To prepare for persecution may be the way to avert it.

JOHN HENRY NEWMAN
September 9, 1833

TRACT 3

Thoughts Respectfully Addressed to the Clergy

On Alterations in the Liturgy

Attempts are making to get the Liturgy altered. My dear Brethren, I beseech you, consider with me whether you ought not to resist the alteration of even one jot or tittle of it. Though you would in your own private judgments wish to have this or that phrase or arrangement amended, is this a time to concede one tittle?

Why do I say this? because, though most of you would wish some immaterial points altered, yet not many of you agree in those points, and not many of you agree what is and what is not immaterial. If all your respective emendations are taken, the alterations in the Services will be extensive; and though each will gain something he wishes, he will lose more from those alterations which he did not wish. Tell me, are the present imperfections (as they seem to each) of such a nature, and so many, that their, removal will compensate for the recasting of much which each thinks to be no imperfection, or rather an excellence?

There are persons who wish the Marriage Service emended; there are others who would be indignant at the changes proposed. There are some who wish the Consecration Prayer in the Holy Sacrament to be what it was in King Edward's first book; there are others who think this would be an approach to Popery. There are some who wish the imprecatory Psalms omitted; there are others who would lament this omission as savoring of the shallow and detestable liberalism of the day. There are some who wish the Services shortened; there are others who think we should have far more Services, and more frequent attendance at public worship than we have.

How few would be pleased by *any given* alterations; and how many pained!

But once begin altering, and there will be no reason or justice in stopping, till the criticisms of all parties are satisfied. Thus will not the Liturgy be in the evil case described in the well-known story, of the picture subjected by the artist to the observations of passers-by? And, even to speak at present of comparatively immaterial alterations, I mean such as do not infringe upon the doctrines of the Prayer Book, will not it even with these be a changed book? and will not that new book be for certain an inconsistent one, the alterations being made, not on principle, but upon chance objections urged from various quarters?

But this is not all. A taste for criticism grows upon the mind. When we begin to examine and take to pieces, our judgment becomes perplexed, and our feelings unsettled. I do not know whether others feel this to the same extent, but for myself, I confess there are few parts of the Service that I could not disturb myself about, and feel fastidious at, if I allowed my mind in this abuse of reason. First, e.g. I might object to the opening sentences; "they are not evangelical enough; Christ is not mentioned in them; they are principally from the Old Testament." Then I should criticise the Exhortation, as having too many words, and as antiquated in style. I might find it hard to speak against the confession; but "the Absolution," it might be said, "is not strong enough; it is a mere declaration, not an announcement of pardon to those who have confessed." And so on.

Now I think this unsettling of the mind a frightful thing; both to ourselves, and more so to our flocks. They have long regarded the Prayer Book with reverence as the stay of their faith and devotion. The weaker sort it will make sceptical; the better it will offend and pain. Take, e.g. an alteration which some have offered in the Creed, to omit or otherwise word the clause, "He descended into *hell.*" Is it no comfort for mourners to be told that Christ Himself has been in that unseen state, or Paradise, which is the allotted place of sojourn for departed spirits? Is it not very easy to explain the ambiguous word, is it any great harm if it is misunderstood, and is it not very difficult to find any substitute for it in harmony with the composition of the Creed? I suspect we should find the best men in the number of those who would retain it as it is. On the other hand, will not the unstable learn from us a habit of criticising what they should never think of but as a divine voice supplied by the Church for their need?

But as regards ourselves, the Clergy, what will be the effect of this temper of innovation in us? We have the power to bring about changes in the Liturgy; shall we not exert it? Have we any security, if we once begin, that we shall ever end? Shall not we pass from non-essentials to essentials? And then, on looking back after the mischief is done, what excuse shall we be able to make for ourselves for having encouraged such proceedings at first? Were there grievous errors in the Prayer Book, something might be said for beginning, but who can point out any? cannot we very well *bear* things as they are? does any part of it seriously disquiet us? no;—we have before now freely given our testimony to its accordance with Scripture.

But it may be said that "we must conciliate an outcry which is made; that some alteration is demanded." By whom? no one can tell who cries, or who can be conciliated. Some of the laity I suppose. Now consider this carefully. Who are these lay persons? Are they serious men, and are their consciences involuntary hurt by the things they wish altered? Are they not rather the men you meet in company, worldly men, with little personal religion, of lax conversation and lax professed principles, who sometimes perhaps come to Church, and then are wearied and disgusted? Is it not so? You have been dining perhaps with a wealthy neighbour, or fall in with this great Statesman, or that noble Aristocrat, who considers the Church two centuries behind the world, and expresses to you wonder that its enlightened members do nothing to improve it. And then you get ashamed, and are betrayed into admissions which sober reason disapproves. You consider too that it is a great pity so estimable or so influential a man should be disaffected to the Church; and you go away with a vague notion that something must be done to conciliate such persons. Is this to bear about you the solemn office of a GUIDE and TEACHER in Israel, or to *follow a lead?*

But consider what are the concessions which would conciliate such men. Would immaterial alterations? Do you really think they care one jot about the verbal or other changes which some recommend, and others are disposed to grant? whether "the unseen state" is substituted for "hell," "condemnation" for "damnation," or the order of Sunday lessons is remodelled? No;—they dislike the *doctrine* of the Liturgy. These men of the world do not like the anathemas of the Athanasian Creed, and other such peculiarities of our Services. But even were the alterations, which would please them, small, are they the persons whom it is of use, whom it is becoming to conciliate by going out of our way?

I need not go on to speak against doctrinal alterations, because most thinking men are sufficiently averse to them. But, I earnestly beg you to consider whether we must not come to them, if we once begin. For by altering immaterials, we merely *raise* without *gratifying* the desire of correcting; we excite the craving, but withhold the food. And it should be observed, that the changes called immaterial often contain in themselves the germ of some principle, of which they are thus the introduction. E.G. If we were to leave out the imprecatory Psalms, we certainly countenance the notion of the day, that love and love only is in the Gospel the character of Almighty God and the duty of regenerate man; whereas that Gospel, rightly understood, shows His Infinite Holiness and Justice as well as His Infinite Love, and it enjoins on men the duties of zeal towards Him, hatred of sin, and separation from sinners, as well as that of kindness and charity.

To the above observations it may be answered, that changes have formerly been made in the Services without leading to the issue I am predicting now; and therefore they may be safely made again. But, waving all other remarks in answer to this argument, is not this enough, viz. that there *is* peril? No one will deny that the rage of the day is for concession. Have we not already granted (political) points, without stopping the course of innovation? This is a fact. Now, is it worth while even to *risk* fearful changes merely to gain petty improvements, allowing those which are proposed to be such?

We know not what is to come upon us; but the writer for one will try so to acquit himself now, that if any irremediable calamity befalls the Church, he may not have to vex himself with the recollections of silence on his part and indifference, when he might have been up and alive. There was a time when he, as well as others, might feel the wish, or rather the temptation, of steering a middle course between parties; but if so, a more close attention to passing events, has cured his infirmity. In a day like this there are but two sides, zeal and persecution, the Church and the world; and those who attempt to occupy the ground between them, at best will lose their labour, but probably will be drawn back to the latter. Be practical, I respectfully urge you; do not attempt impossibilities; sail not as if in pleasure boats upon a troubled sea. Not a word falls to the ground, in a time like this. Speculations about ecclesiastical improvements which might be innocent at other times, have a strength of mischief now. They are realized before he who utters them understands that he has committed himself.

Be prepared then for petitioning against any alterations in the Prayer Book which may be proposed. And, should you see that our Fathers the Bishops seem to countenance them, petition still. Petition *them*. They will thank you for such a proceeding. *They do not wish these alterations;* but how can they resist them without the support of their Clergy? They consent to them (if they do) partly from the notion that they are thus pleasing you. Undeceive them. They will be rejoiced to hear that you are as unwilling to receive them as they are. However, if after all there be persons determined to allow some alterations, then let them quickly make up their minds *how far* they will go. They think it easier to draw the line elsewhere, than as things now exist. Let them point out the limit of their concessions now; and let them keep to it then; and (if they can do this) I will say that, though they are not as wise as they might have been, they are at least firm, and have at last come right.

The Burial Service

We hear many complaints about the Burial Service, as unsuitable for the use for which it was intended. It expresses a hope, that the person departed, over whom it is read, will be saved; and this is said to be dangerous when expressed about all who are called Christians, as leading the laity to low views of the spiritual attainments necessary for salvation; and distressing the Clergy who have to read it.

Now I do not deny, I frankly own, it is sometimes distressing to use the Service; but this it must ever be in the nature of things, wherever you draw the line. Do you pretend you can discriminate the wheat from the tares? of course not.

It is often distressing to use this Service, because it is often distressing to think of the dead at all; not that you are without hope, but because you have fear also.

How many are there whom you know well enough to dare to give any judgment about? Is a clergyman only to express a hope where *he* has grounds for having it? Are not the feelings of relatives to be considered? And may there not be a difference of judgments? I may hope more, another less. If each is to use the precise words which suit his own judgment, then we can have no words at all.

But it may be said, "every thing of a *personal* nature may be left out from the Service." And do you really wish this? Is this the way in which your flock will wish their lost friends to be treated? a cold "edification" but no affectionate valediction to the departed? Why not pursue this course of (supposed) improvement, and advocate the omission of the Service altogether?

Are we to have no kind and religious thoughts over the good, lest we should include the bad?

But it will be said, that, at least we ought not to read the Service over the flagrantly wicked; over those who are a scandal to religion. But this is a very different position. I agree with it entirely. Of course we should not do so, and truly the Church never meant we should. She never wished we should profess our hope of the salvation of habitual drunkards and swearers, open sinners, blasphemers, and the like; not as daring to despair of their salvation, but thinking it unseemly to honor their memory. Though the Church is not endowed with a power of absolute judgment upon individuals, yet she is directed to decide according to external indications, in order to hold up the *rules* of God's governance, and afford a type of it, and an assistance towards the realizing it. As she denies to the scandalously wicked the Lord's Supper, so does she deprive them of her other privileges.

The Church, I say, does not bid us read the Service over open sinners. Hear her own words introducing the Service. "The office ensuing is not to be used for any that die unbaptized, or excommunicate, or have laid violent hands upon themselves." There is no room to doubt *whom* she meant to be excommunicated, open sinners. Those therefore who are pained at the general use of the Service, should rather strive to restore the practice of excommunication, than to alter the words used in the Service. Surely, if we do not do this, we are clearly defrauding the religious, for the sake of keeping close to the wicked.

Here we see the common course of things in this world. We omit a duty. In consequence our Services become inconsistent. Instead of retracing our steps we alter the Service. What is this but, as it were, to sin upon principle? While we keep to our principles, our sins are inconsistencies; at length, sensitive of the absurdity which inconsistency involves, we accommodate our professions to our practice. This is ever the way of the world; but it should not be the way of the Church.

I will join heart and hand with any who will struggle for a restoration of that "godly discipline," the restoration of which our Church publicly professes she considers desirable; but God forbid any one should so depart from her spirit, as to mould her formularies to fit the case of deliberate sinners! And is not this what we are plainly doing, if we alter the Burial Service as proposed? we are recognizing the right of men to receive Christian Burial, about whom we do not like to express a hope. Why should they have Christian Burial at all?

It will be said that the restoration of the practice of Excommunication is impracticable; and that therefore the other alternation must be taken, as the only one open to us. Of course it is impossible, if no one attempts to restore it; but if all willed it, how would it be impossible? and if no one stirs because he thinks no one else will, he is arguing in a circle.

But, after all, what have we to do with probabilities and prospects in matters of plain duty? Were a man the only member of the Church who felt it a duty to return to the Ancient Discipline, yet a duty is a duty, though he be alone. It is one of the great sins of our times to look to consequences in matters of plain duty. Is not this such a case? If not, prove that it is not; but do not argue from consequences.

In the mean while I offer the following texts in evidence of the duty. Matthew 28:15-17. Romans 16:17. 1 Corinthians 5:7-13. 2 Thessalonians 3:6, 14, 15. 2 Timothy 3:5. Titus 3:10, 11. 2 John 1:10, 11.

The Principle of Unity

Testimony of St. Clement, the associate of St. Paul (Phil. 4:3), to the Apostolical Succession.

> The Apostles knew, through our Lord Jesus Christ, that strife would arise for the Episcopate. Wherefore having received an accurate foreknowledge, they appointed the men I before mentioned, and have given an orderly succession, that on their death other approved men might receive in turn their office. Ep. i. 44.

Testimony of Ignatius, the friend of St. Peter, to Episcopacy.

> Your celebrated Presbytery, worthy of God, is as closely knit to the Bishop, as the strings to a harp, and so by means of your unanimity and concordant love Jesus Christ is sung. Eph. 4.
>
> There are who profess to acknowledge a Bishop, but do every thing without him. Such men appear to lack a clear conscience. Magn. 4.
>
> He for whom I am bound is my witness that I have not learned this doctrine from mortal man. The Spirit proclaimed to me these words: "Without the Bishop do nothing." Phil. 7.

With these and other such strong passages in the Apostolical Fathers, how can we permit ourselves in our present *practical* disregard of the Episcopal Authority? Are not we apt to obey only so far as the law obliges us? do we support the Bishop, and strive to move all together with him as our bond of union and head? or is not our every-day conduct as if, except with respect to certain periodical forms and customs, we were each independent in his own parish?

JOHN HENRY NEWMAN
September 9, 1833

TRACT 4: AD POPULUM
Adherence to the Apostolical Succession the Safest Course

We who believe the Nicene Creed, must acknowledge it a high privilege, that we belong to the Apostolic Church. How is it that so many of us are, almost avowedly, so cold and indifferent in our thoughts of this privilege?

Is it because the very idea is in itself overstrained and fanciful, apt perhaps to lay strong hold on a few ardent minds, but little in accordance with the general feelings of mankind? Surely not. The notion of a propagated commission is as simple and intelligible in itself, as can well be; is acted on daily in civil matters (the administration of trust property, for example); and has found a most ready, sometimes an enthusiastic, acceptance, in those many nations of the world, which have submitted, and are submitting themselves to sacerdotal castes, elective or hereditary. "Priests self-elected, or appointed by the State," is rather the idea which startles ordinary thinkers; not "Priests commissioned, successively, from heaven."

Or is our languor rather to be accounted for by the want of express scriptural encouragement to the notion of a divine ministerial commission? Nay, Scripture, at first sight, is express; whether we take the analogy of the Old Testament, the words of our Lord, or the practice of His Apostles. The Primitive Christians read it accordingly; and cherished, with all affectionate reverence, the privilege which they thought they found there. Why are we so unlike them?

I fear it must be owned, that much of the evil is owing to the comparatively low ground, which we ourselves, the Ministers of God, have chosen to occupy in defence of our commission. For many years, we have been much in the habit of resting our claim on the general duties of submission to authority, of decency and order, of respecting precedents long established; instead of appealing to that warrant, which marks us, *exclusively*, for GOD'S AMBASSADORS. We have spoken much in the same tone, as we might, had we been mere Laymen, acting for ecclesiastical purposes by a commission under the Great Seal. Waving the question, "was this wise? was it right, in higher respects?"—I ask, was it not obviously certain, in some degree, to damp and deaden the interest, with which men of devout minds would naturally regard the Christian Ministry? Would not more than half the reverential feeling, with which we look on a Church or Cathedral, be gone, if we ceased to contemplate it as the House of God, and learned to esteem it merely as a place set apart by the State for moral and religious instruction?

It would be going too deep in history, were one now to enter on any statement of the causes which have led, silently and insensibly, almost to the abandonment of the high ground, which our Fathers of the Primitive Church, i.e. the Bishops and Presbyters of the first five centuries, invariably took, in preferring their claim to canonical obedience. For the present, it is rather wished to urge, on plain positive considerations, the wisdom and duty of keeping in view the simple principle on which they relied.

Their principle, in short, was this: That the Holy Feast on our Saviour's sacrifice, which all confess to be "generally necessary to salvation," was intended by Him to be constantly conveyed through the hands of commissioned persons. Except therefore we can shew such a warrant, we cannot be sure that our hands convey the sacrifice; we cannot be sure that souls worthily prepared, receiving the bread which we break, and the cup of blessing which we bless, are Partakers of the Body and Blood of Christ. Piety, then, and Christian Reverence, and sincere, devout Love of our Redeemer, nay, and Charity to the souls of our brethren, not good order and expediency only, would prompt us, at all earthly risks, to preserve and transmit the seal and warrant of Christ.

If the rules of Christian conduct were founded merely on visible expediency, the zeal with which those holy men were used to maintain the Apostolical Succession, might appear a strange unaccountable thing. Not so, if our duties to our Saviour be like our duties to a parent or a brother, the unalterable result of certain known relations, previous to all consideration of consequences.[1] Reflect on this, and you presently feel what a difference it makes in a pious mind, whether ministerial prerogatives be traced to our Lord's own institution, or to mere voluntary ecclesiastical arrangement. Let two plans of Government, as far as we can see, be equally good and expedient in themselves, yet if there be but a fair probability of one rather than the other proceeding from our Blessed Lord Himself, those who love Him in sincerity will know at once which to prefer. They will not demand that every point be made out by inevitable demonstration, or promulgated in form, like a State decree. According to the beautiful expression of the Psalmist, they will consent to be "guided by" our Lord's "eye;"[2] the *indications* of His pleasure will be enough for them. They will state the matter thus to themselves: "Jesus Christ's own commission is the best external security I can have, that in receiving this bread and wine, I verily receive his Body and Blood. Either the Bishops have that commission, or there is no such thing in the world. For at least Bishops have it with as much evidence, as Presbyters without them. In proportion, then, to my Christian anxiety for keeping as near my Saviour as I can, I shall of course be very unwilling to separate myself from Episcopal communion. And in proportion to my charitable care for others, will be my industry to preserve and extend the like consolation and security to them."

Consider the analogy of an absent parent, or dear friend in another hemisphere. Would not such an one naturally reckon it one sign of sincere attachment, if, when he returned home, he found that in all family questions respect had been shewn especially to those in whom he was known to have had most confidence? Would he not be pleased, when it appeared that people had not been nice in enquiring what express words of command he had given, where they had good reason to think that such and such a course would be approved by him? If his children and dependants had searched diligently, where, and with whom, he had left commissions, and having fair cause to think they had found such, had scrupulously conformed themselves, as far as they could, to the proceedings of those so trusted by him; would he not think this a better

---

[1] Butler's Analogy, p. ii. c. 1.
[2] Psalm 32:9.

sign, than if they had been dextrous in devising exceptions, in explaining away the words of trust, and limiting the prerogatives he had conferred?

Now certainly the Gospel has many *indications*, that *our* best Friend in His absence is likely to be well pleased with those who do their best in sincerity to keep as near to His Apostles as they can. It is studiously recorded, for example, by the Evangelists, in the account of our Lord's two miraculous Feasts, that all passed through His Disciples' hands: (His *twelve* Disciples; as is in one instance plainly implied in the *twelve* baskets full of fragments.) I know that minute circumstances like this, in a Parable or symbolical act, must be reasoned on with great caution. Still, when one considers that our Blessed Lord took occasion from this event to deliver more expressly than at any other time the doctrine of communion with Him, it seems no unnatural conjecture, that the details of the miracle were so ordered, as to throw light on that doctrine.

But, not to dwell on what many will question (although on docile and affectionate minds I cannot but think it must have its weight), what shall we say to the remarkable promise addressed to the Twelve at the Pascal Supper? "Ye are they which have continued with Me in My temptation: and I appoint unto you a Kingdom, as My Father hath appointed unto Me; that ye may eat and drink at My table in My Kingdom, and sit on thrones, judging the twelve tribes of Israel." Thus much nobody will hesitate to allow, concerning this Apostolical Charter: that it bound all Christians whatever to be loyal and obedient to Christ's Apostles, at least as long as *they* were living. And do not the same words equally bind us, and all believers to the world's end, so far as the mind of the Apostles can yet be ascertained? Is not the *spirit* of the enactment such, as renders it incumbent on every one to prefer among claimants to Church authority those who can make out the best title to a warrant and commission from the Apostles?

I pass over those portions of the Gospel, which are oftenest quoted in this controversy; they will occur of themselves to all men; and it is the object of these lines rather to exemplify the occasional indications of our Lord's will, than to cite distinct and palpable enactments. On one place, however,—the passage in the Acts, which records, in honour of the first converts, that "they continued stedfastly in the Apostles' doctrine and fellowship,"—one question must be asked. Is it really credible, that the privilege so emphatically mentioned, of being in communion with the

Apostles, ceased when the last Apostle died? If not, who among living Christians have *so fair a chance* of enjoying that privilege, as those, who, besides Purity of Doctrine, are careful to maintain that Apostolical Succession, preserved to them hitherto by a gracious and special Providence? I should not much fear to risque the whole controversy on the answer which a simple unprejudiced mind would naturally make to these two questions.

Observe, too, how often those principles, which are usually called, in scorn, High-Churchmanship, drop as it were incidentally from the pens of the sacred writers, professedly employed on other subjects. "How shall they preach, except they be sent?"—"Let a man so account of us, as of the Ministers of Christ, and Stewards of the mysteries of God."—"No man taketh this honour to himself, but he that is called of God, as was Aaron." I do not think it possible for any one to read such places as these with a fair and clear mind, and not to perceive that it is better and more scriptural to have, than to want, Christ's special commission for conveying His Word to the people, and consecrating and distributing the pledges of His holy Sacrifice, if such commission be any how attainable;—better, and more scriptural, if we cannot remove all doubt, at least to prefer that communion which can make out the best probable title, provided always, that nothing heretical, or otherwise immoral, be inserted in the terms of communion.

Why then should any man here in Britain, fear or hesitate boldly to assert the authority of the Bishops and Pastors of the Church, on grounds strictly evangelical and spiritual: as bringing men nearest to Christ our Saviour, and conforming them most exactly to His mind, indicated both by His own conduct, and by the words of His Spirit in the Apostolic writings? Why should we talk so much of an *establishment,* and so little of an APOSTOLICAL SUCCESSION? Why should we not seriously endeavour to impress our people with this plain truth;—that by separating themselves from our communion, they separate themselves not only from a decent, orderly, useful society, but from THE ONLY CHURCH IN THIS REALM WHICH HAS A RIGHT TO BE QUITE SURE THAT SHE HAS THE LORD'S BODY TO GIVE TO HIS PEOPLE?

Nor need any man be perplexed by the question, sure to be presently and confidently asked, "Do you then unchurch all the Presbyterians, all Christians who have no Bishops? Are they to be shut out of the Covenant, for all the fruits of Christian Piety, which seem to have sprung up not scantily among them?" Nay, we are not judging others, but deciding on our own conduct. We in England cannot communicate with Presbyterians, as neither can we with Roman Catholics, but we do not therefore exclude either from salvation. "Necessary to Salvation," and "necessary to Church Communion," are not to be used as convertible terms. Neither do we desire to pass any sentence on other persons of other countries; but we are not to shrink from our deliberate views of truth and duty, because difficulties may be raised about the case of such persons; any more than we should fear to maintain the paramount necessity of Christian belief, because similar difficulties may be raised about virtuous Heathens, Jews, or Mahometans. To us such questions are abstract, not practical: and whether we can answer them or no, it is our business to keep fast hold of the Church Apostolical, whereof we are actual members; not merely on civil or ecclesiastical grounds, but from real personal love and reverence, affectionate reverence to our Lord and only Saviour. And let men seriously bear in mind, that it is one thing to slight and disparage this holy Succession where it may be had, another thing to acquiesce in the want of it, where it is (*if it be any where*) really unattainable.

I readily allow, that this view of our calling has something in it too high and mysterious to be fully understood by unlearned Christians. But the learned, surely, are just as unequal to it. It is part of that ineffable mystery, called in our Creed, The Communion of Saints: and with all other Christian mysteries, is above the *understanding* of all alike, yet *practically* alike within reach of all, who are willing to embrace it by true Faith. Experience shews, at any rate, that it is far from being ill adapted to the minds and feelings of ordinary people. On this point evidence might be brought from times, at first glance the most unpromising; from the early part of the 17th century. The hold which the propagandists of the "Holy Discipline" obtained on the fancies and affections of the people, of whatever rank, age, and sex, depended very much on their incessant appeals to their *fancied* Apostolical Succession. They found persons willing and eager to suffer or rebel, as the case might be, for their system; *because* they had possessed them with the notion, that it was *the* system handed down from the Apostles, "a divine Episcopate" so Beza called it. Why should we despair of obtaining, in time, an influence, far more legitimate and less dangerously exciting, but equally searching and extensive, by the diligent inculcation of our *true* and *scriptural* claim?

For it is obvious, that, among other results of the primitive doctrine of the Apostolical Succession, thoroughly considered and followed up, it would make the relation of Pastor and Parishioner far more engaging, as well as more aweful, than it is usually considered at present. Look on your Pastor as acting by man's commission, and you may respect the authority by which he acts, you may venerate and love his personal character; but it can hardly be called a *religious* veneration; there is nothing, properly, *sacred* about him. But once learn to regard him as "the Deputy of Christ, for reducing man to the obedience of God;" and every thing about him becomes changed, every thing stands in a new light. In public and in private, in church and at home, in consolation and in censure, and above all, in the administration of the Holy Sacraments, a faithful man naturally considers, "By this His messenger Christ is speaking to me; by his very being and place in the world, he is a perpetual witness to the truth of the sacred history, a perpetual earnest of Communion with our Lord to those who come duly prepared to His Table." In short it must make just all the difference in every part of a Clergyman's duty, whether he do it, and be known to do it, in that Faith of his commission from Christ, or no.

How far the analogy of the Aaronical priesthood will carry us, and to what extent we must acknowledge the reserve imputed to the formularies of our Church on this whole subject of the Hierarchy; and how such reserve, if real, may be accounted for;—these are questions worthy of distinct consideration.

For the present let the whole matter be brought to this short issue. May it not be said both to Clergy and Laity; "Put yourselves in your children's place, in the place of the next generation of believers. Consider in what way they will desire you to have acted, supposing them to value aright (as you must wish them) the means of communion with Christ; and as they will then wish you to have acted now, so act in all matters affecting that inestimable privilege."

On Alterations in the Prayer Book

The 36th Canon provides that "no person shall hereafter be received into the Ministry. . . . . except he shall first subscribe" certain "three Articles." The second of these is as follows.

> That the Book of Common Prayer, and of Ordering of Bishops, Priests, and Deacons, containeth in it nothing contrary to the Word of God, and that it may lawfully so be used; and that he himself will use the form in the said Book prescribed, in public Prayer, and administration of the Sacraments, and none other.

Now here is certainly a grave question to all who have subscribed this Article. We need not say, it precludes them from acquiescing in any changes, that are lawfully made in the Common Prayer; but surely it makes it most incumbent on them, to inquire carefully whether the Parties altering it have a right to do so; e.g. should any foreign Power or Legislature, or any private Nobleman or Statesman at home, pretend to reform the Prayer Book, of course we should all call it an usurpation, and refuse to obey it; or rather we should consider the above subscription to be a religious obstacle to our obeying it. So far is clear. The question follows; *where* is the competent authority for making alterations? Is it not also clear, that it does not lie in the British Legislature, which we know to be composed not only of believers, but also of infidels, heretics, and schismatics; and which probably in another year may cease to be a Christian body even in formal profession? Can even a Committee of it, ever so carefully selected, absolve us from our subscriptions? Whence do laity derive their power over the Clergy? Can even the Crown absolve us? or a commission from the Crown? If then some measure of tyranny be practised against us as regards the Prayer Book, HOW ARE WE TO ACT?

JOHN KEBLE
September 21, 1833

TRACT 5

A Short Address to His Brethren
On the Nature & Constitution of the Church of Christ
And of the Branch of It Established in England; By a Layman

> I believe one Catholic and Apostolic Church.
> THE NICENE CREED

There are many persons who have the happiness of being members of that pure and Apostolical branch of Christ's holy Church, which, as it is established in this our country, we call "the Church of England;" persons who attend with regularity and devotion to her services, and have participated in the benefits of her Sacraments; who may yet have no very clear idea either of the nature of that body which we call "the Church" in general, or of the peculiar circumstances and events which have led to the present position and constitution of that portion of it to which we belong.

To such persons it may not be unacceptable if we present them in these pages with a short account of "the Church;" of that institution which, previous to His return to the regions of His heavenly glory, our Lord bequeathed to the world, to be cherished and enjoyed as a precious legacy, until His coming again; of that body which He framed for the reception of the first gifts of His Almighty Spirit, and for the transmission of those precious gifts, from age to age, to the end of time. Such an account will naturally lead to a brief statement of the manner in which it has pleased Providence to bless us, in this our own island, with a branch of that holy institution; and thus to have established, and to continue among us, a body of men bearing a commission direct from Himself to admit us into His fold by the waters of Baptism, and to nourish us in the same, not only with the pure word of His doctrine, but with the spiritual nourishment of His most blessed body and blood.

It would have been in vain that the two Sacraments had been instituted, had no persons, no set of men, been appointed to administer them. You cannot suppose that you or I—(for he who thus addresses you is a layman like yourselves, that is, has never received the ordination of a clergyman)—you cannot, I say, suppose that any one of us might, with no other authority than his own good pleasure, proceed to baptize, or to administer the bread and wine in the Lord's Supper. Such a proceeding would, it is evident, involve the highest degree of arrogance and impiety, and would be nothing short of a mockery of that great and awful Being, of whose gifts these sacred ordinances are alike the appointed means and pledges.

And if, as men, as simple members of Christ's Church, we have not this power, the next question to ask is, who could give us this authority? If admission into the great Christian congregation, if the promise, confirmed to us in Baptism, of the assistance of Christ's Holy Spirit, cannot give it, is it to be supposed that any act emanating from men, from sinful creatures like ourselves, should be of force to convey it? Clearly not; no command of an earthly king, no ordinance of an earthly legislature, could invest us with power over the gifts of the Holy Ghost; for such may we well term the power duly to administer the Sacraments which Christ has ordained. No Act of Parliament, however binding the provisions of such Acts may be with regard to the temporal affairs of the nation, could make any one of us a Priest, or clothe us with one jot or one tittle of power over the things of the unseen world.

As little, surely, could popular election invest us with this power from on high. Men may express their readiness to receive the gifts of Heaven at our hands; but is it not absurd, that those who are to be the receivers from us of any boon whatsoever, should themselves be the persons to supply us with the means of bestowing it? It cannot be, then, that those to whom we are to administer the Sacraments should themselves confer upon us the power of their ministration.

To cut this inquiry short. He alone is evidently entitled to confer the power of conveying, by the appointed means, the gifts of His Spirit, who Himself gave, in the first instance, that Spirit to His Church. It is to Him that such commission must be traced in the case of every individual who would establish his right to this holy office.

Constitution of the Church of the Apostles

He appointed in the first place, as is well known to every reader of the Scriptures, the Apostles; to whom He at different periods entrusted all such powers as were necessary to the formation and continued protection of His Church, which they, under His Spirit, were to establish. He gave them the power of admitting members into it; and He put into their hands that power of expulsion from it, which it was necessary, for the well being of the society, should be vested somewhere: assuring them, at the same time, that their decrees in this respect should be ratified on high; that what they "bound on earth, should be bound in heaven." To them it was that he entrusted the power of baptizing all nations; and still more exclusively the power of celebrating the sacred rite which commemorates His passion.[1] They undertook the sacred trust, preached to all, and at first baptized all converts; though, when the number of these increased, when the Church could reckon its three thousand and its five thousand members, and when thus, to borrow the prophetic language of Daniel, the stone began to swell which was destined in time to become a great mountain, and to fill the whole world, it was plainly impossible that the small band of Apostles, employed as they were in the business of teaching the word, should suffice themselves to baptize all who should accept their offers of salvation. For this, among other purposes, the formation of a class of ministers, distinct from, and subordinate to, themselves, became necessary; a class, of the first establishment of which we read in the 6th chapter of the Acts of the Apostles. The members of this new class were called "Deacons:" they were at first only seven in number: they were chosen, at the suggestion of the Apostles, by the believers in general, or, in the language of the Church, by the laity; but they were ordained to the office by the Apostles themselves, by the laying of their hands on them, accompanied by prayer. A principal part of their office, when they were first appointed, was the distribution of the charitable gifts of the more wealthy believers among their poorer brethren: but that the power of administering baptism was a part of their commission is evident from the history of Philip the Deacon, contained in Acts 9. There were thus two

---

[1] "This do in remembrance of me," Luke 22:19; whereas the commission to baptize was apparently given to others besides the Apostles, though to them in the first place. Matthew 28:18, 19.

classes of guides and teachers to the Church of Christ, Apostles and Deacons; the first bearing authority over the general flock by the direct word of Christ Himself; the second by commission from those thus directly authorized; a commission given by them when the Holy Spirit was most abundantly poured out upon them, and solemnly ratified by that Holy Spirit Himself in the miraculous powers and graces vouchsafed to Stephen and his colleagues.

But as the limits of the Church began to extend, and the believers, instead of dwelling in one body in the city of Jerusalem, began to spread over the adjoining regions, the want was felt of another class, to superintend the scattered divisions of Christ's flock, to act in some measure as the substitutes of the Apostles in their absence, and as their deputies and subordinate officers in their presence. This class, of higher rank in the Church than the Deacons, and forming a connecting link between them and the Apostles, bears in Scripture the name of "Elders" or "Bishops," and is, by one or other of these names, the subject of frequent mention in the later books of the New Testament. The constitution of the Church was then, for the time being, complete. The Apostles, as, in the exercise of their high office, they founded congregations from city to city, ordained (always by the laying on of hands) Elders and Deacons; in whom each congregation recognised the ministers set over them by their Lord and Master in heaven; from whom they received the blessings conveyed in His Sacraments; and to whom they looked for guidance and example in the holy course on which they had entered, the Christian warfare which they had undertaken. The Apostle himself, however, who had planted each of these congregations, continued to exercise over it a general superintending authority, and to interfere, where the case required it, in the most solemn and decided manner. The nature and extent of the power thus assumed over each local Church, in virtue of his heavenly commission, by its Apostolic head, will be manifest from a study of the two Epistles written by St. Paul to the Church of the Corinthians; and from a comparison of the second of these Epistles with the first, it will be seen how fully this authority was recognised, and the directions thus sanctioned were obeyed, by the primitive believers.

It may not be amiss here to point out a circumstance from which we may most decidedly infer it to have been the will of the Holy Spirit that ordination, or the solemn ceremony above mentioned of the laying on of hands, should be the only mode of admission to the ministration of His gifts in the Church. Were there any one person who might, from the very peculiar circumstances of his call and conversion, have had grounds for conceiving himself entitled to dispense with this ceremony, that person was undoubtedly St. Paul; yet we find that, favoured as he had been, when it was seen meet to send him as an Apostle to the Gentiles, the Holy Ghost deigned to give express directions that he should be separated to the purpose; ordained, that is to say, to such ministry; and that, in compliance with those directions, the heads of the Church at Antioch, when they had fasted and prayed, and laid their hands on them,[2] sent him and Barnabas away.

The Apostolical Commission

The Church, under the government of its Apostles, Elders, and Deacons, was, as we have already stated, for the time being, complete. One thing, however, was still wanting to give perpetuity to its constitution, and that was, a provision for the supply of ordained ministers to distribute the gifts of the Spirit to the generations who should live when the Apostles themselves, and those who had received ordination from their hands, should have alike passed away from the scene of their labours. It was necessary that the Apostles should appoint successors to themselves; persons to be armed with at least all that portion of their authority which did not depend on their miraculous powers or extraordinary gifts of the Spirit; with neither of which was the power of ordination to any rank of the ministry necessarily connected. They felt this necessity, and they did appoint such persons; but from the altered condition of the Church, and the number of converts in each particular place, it became expedient, instead of giving to each person so appointed that species of general commission with which the Apostles themselves had commenced their labours, to fix the residence of each in some particular city, and to give him the peculiar superintendence of the Church therein and in the districts adjoining. It was thus that St. Paul appointed Timothy to preside (as what

---

[2] Acts 13:3.

we now call Bishop) over the Church at Ephesus; and Titus over that of Crete: and the Holy Spirit, by dictating to the Apostle those directions to them for the discharge of the duties of these offices which form the Epistles bearing their names, gave the fullest and most solemn ratification, not only to their individual appointment, but also to the establishment in perpetuity of the episcopal order in the Church.

Though this event in the history of the Church has been narrated as occurring subsequently to the appointment of the lower classes of ecclesiastical ministers, it must not be supposed that it was an after thought, or that the Apostles were not from the first aware that their office was to be perpetuated by succession. Our Lord ended the sentence in which He endued them with power to baptize, with the promise of His assistance in the discharge of their functions through all time: "Go," said He, "baptize all nations: and, lo, I am with you alway, even unto the end of the world:" a phrase which, as addressed to mortal men, must clearly have been understood as a promise of continual assistance to them and to their successors. We find, accordingly, that so far were they from understanding this gracious promise as applying solely to the individuals to whom the words were spoken, that one of their very first joint acts, when deprived of the presence of their Lord, was to select a person to be associated with themselves in the apostolic office, that the number originally named to that office by our Saviour might be complete. They did not, it is true, ordain him, in the manner afterwards adopted, by the laying on of hands; they were not, indeed, themselves consecrated to the exercise of this power till the descent upon them of the Holy Ghost; but in the pouring out of the gifts of Pentecost upon the head of Matthias, as well as upon those of the eleven, the Spirit bore a testimony, which could hardly be misunderstood, to the will of the Almighty that the Apostles should from time to time, as it became necessary, nominate such associates in their general apostolic toils and powers as they might select; associates on whom, as they themselves were gradually withdrawn from the world, the whole government of the Church, and the whole care of providing for its further continuance, must ultimately devolve.

The miraculous gifts and graces, which God in the first instance showered upon His Church, answered their purpose in giving it its first footing in the world; and, when no longer necessary for that purpose, were consequently withdrawn: but it should never be forgotten, that these, wonderful and striking as they must have been, were but secondary and subsidiary to those invisible spiritual gifts, which are the real fulfilment of God's promise of constant aid to his Church. With regard to these latter, it was indeed necessary that they should be her portion through all ages; but the others derived in truth their sole value from the evidence which they bore to the existence of these more precious boons; an evidence which, though immediately addressed to converts in the first ages, was intended to convince, not them alone, but all those to whom their report of these miraculous gifts should come, of the reality of God's promises with regard to those gifts which were not palpable to earthly senses; of the truth of Christ's saying, already quoted, that He would be with His Church even unto the end of the world; and of His declaration that the Comforter, whom He would send, should abide with that Church for ever.

What name was originally applied to the office borne by Timothy and Titus, of destined successors to the Apostles, is not very clear. There was perhaps at first no one name specially used to designate it. They may have sometimes been called Evangelists (see 2 Tim 4:5); sometimes, from their bearing in some measure the character of heavenly messengers to mankind, the Angels of their respective Churches. By this name, at least, the heads of the different Churches of Asia are addressed in the 2nd and 3rd chapters of the book of Revelations. Consecrated as they were by different Apostles in different parts of the world, some little time would necessarily elapse, before one general name would be applied by the whole Christian Church to the associates and successors of its first inspired governors.

Of the powers entrusted to these persons, a good idea may be formed from the study of the Epistles addressed to two of them. Timothy, it appears, had apostolic authority to superintend and arrange the celebration of divine service, to prescribe the nature of prayers to be used therein, and to give general directions for the decent and orderly behaviour of the congregation. (See 1 Tim 2) Copious instructions were given him as to the persons whom he should choose to ordain as Bishops (or Elders) and Deacons (chap. 3). He had power to select among the Elders such as should rule (ver. 17), probably over different portions of his congregation; and to hear and decide upon any accusations brought against them in the discharge of their office (ver. 19). He was reminded by St. Paul to stir up the gift that was in him by the putting on of his hands (2 Tim 1:6), and of the hands of the presbytery (1 Tim 4:14); to ordain no man suddenly (1 Tim 5:22), or without due examination into his character, but to commit the doctrine which he had learnt of St. Paul to faithful men, who should be able to teach others also (2 Tim 2:2).

Titus was left in Crete that he might set in order the things that were wanting, and ordain elders in every city, as St. Paul had appointed him (Titus 1:5). He was taught what sort of characters befitted those whom he should make Bishops—he was to exhort and rebuke with all authority, and let no man despise him (2:15). He was to be the general instructor of his flock, and to have the power of expelling thence obstinate heretics (3:10). But it is unsatisfactory to quote particular passages; the whole of these three epistles should be seriously studied by those who wish to form a good general idea of the powers with which the Apostles, or rather the Holy Ghost, by their means, invested those who were to bear rule in the Church in times when they themselves should have gone to their reward.

Those times came.—St. John, the last of the glorious company of the Apostles, entered into his rest, and the Church found itself committed, under Heaven, entirely to the charge of the three established orders of its ministers. To each of these a specific title was now ascribed, and applied with greater exactness than before. The title "Bishop," which had at first been used indifferently with "Elder," became the exclusive property of the highest class of functionaries, the colleagues of Timothy and Titus. The word "Elder" served to designate the second, and from its Greek equivalent, "Presbuteros," we have formed our English word "Priest," by which "Elder," is now, in common use, superseded. The third class preserved its original and appropriate name of "Deacons."

Such, then, was the constitution of which the Church, when first deprived of outward supernatural aid, found herself possessed; such the machinery at her disposal for the dispensation to mankind of those glorious gifts and privileges, which it was hers, and hers alone, to confer. As Priests or Deacons were required for the ministration of the Word and Sacraments to the different portions of her flock, the Bishops, in exercise of the heavenly gift confided to them, laid hands upon such individuals as they deemed suited to the charge, and as vacancies occurred among the angels of the churches, the successors of the Apostles themselves, or as additions were required to their number, the existing members of the sacred band, consecrated new individuals to the participation of their privileges, candidates for the office being presented to them by the laity for their approval, or fit and proper persons being selected by themselves.

The gift conferred by their ordination was now no longer confirmed by outward ocular demonstration; but, while they reverently complied with all the particulars and forms of these holy rites, as established under the guidance of inspiration by their predecessors, they would have held it a most guilty instance of want of faith, had they presumed to doubt the continued fulfilment of the Redeemer's promise, or the continued abiding, with the Church which he had framed, of the Almighty Comforter.

The Apostolical Succession

Since the Apostolic age seventeen centuries have rolled away—exactly eighteen hundred years have elapsed since the delivery of Christ's recorded promise; and, blessed be God, the Church is with us still. Amid all the political storms and vicissitudes, amid all the religious errors and corruptions which have chequered, during that long period, the world's eventful history, a regular unbroken succession has preserved among us ministers of God, whose authority to confer the gifts of His Spirit is derived originally from the laying on of the hands of the Apostles themselves. Many intermediate possessors of that authority have, it is true, intervened between them and these, their hallowed predecessors, but the gifts of God are without repentance; the same Spirit rules over the Church now who presided at the consecration of St. Paul, and the eighteen centuries that are past can have had no power to invalidate the promise of our God. Nor, even though we may admit that many of those who formed the connecting links of this holy chain were themselves unworthy of the high charge reposed in them, can this furnish us with any solid ground for doubting or denying their power to exercise that legitimate authority with which they were duly invested, of transmitting the sacred gift to worthier followers.

Ordination, or, as it is called in the case of Bishops, Consecration, though it does not precisely come within our definition of a sacrament, is nevertheless a rite partaking, in a high degree, of the sacramental character, and it is by reference to the proper sacraments that its nature can be most satisfactorily illustrated. And with respect to these, it would lead us into endless difficulties were we to admit that, when administered by a minister duly authorised according to the outward forms of the Church, either Baptism or the Lord's Supper depended for its validity either on the moral and spiritual attainments of that minister, or on the frame of mind in which he might have received, at his ordination, the outward and visible sign of his authority. Did the Sacraments indeed rest on such circumstances as these for their efficacy in each case of their ministration, who would there be of us, or of any Christian congregation, who could positively say whether he had been baptized or not; or what preparation or self-examination could give to a penitent the confidence that he had truly partaken of the body and blood of Christ, were the reality of that partaking to depend upon something of which he had no knowledge, and over which he could exercise no control; upon the spiritual state, not only of the officiating minister himself, but of every individual Bishop through whom that minister had received his authority, through the long lapse of eighteen hundred years? He who receives unworthily, or in an improper state of mind, either ordination or consecration, may probably receive to his own soul no saving health from the hallowed rite; but while we admit, as we do, the validity of sacraments administered by a Priest thus unworthily ordained, we cannot consistently deny that of ordination, in any of its grades, when bestowed by a Bishop as unworthily consecrated.

The very question of worth, indeed, with relation to such matters, is absurd. Who is worthy? Who is a fit and meet dispenser of the gifts of the Holy Spirit? What are, after all, the petty differences between sinner and sinner, when viewed in relation to Him whose eyes are too pure to behold iniquity, and who charges His very angels with folly? And be it remembered that the Apostolic powers, if not transmitted through these, in some instances corrupt channels, have not been transmitted to our times at all. Unless then we acknowledge the reality of such transmission, we must admit that the Church which Christ founded is no longer to be found upon the earth, and that the promise of His protection, so far from being available to the end of the world, is forgotten and out of date already.

The unworthiness of man, then, cannot prevent the goodness of God from flowing in those channels in which He has destined it to flow; and the Christian congregations of the present day, who sit at the feet of ministers duly ordained, have the same reason for reverencing in them the successors of the Apostles, as the primitive Churches of Ephesus and of Crete had for honouring in Timothy and in Titus the Apostolical authority of him who had appointed them.

The Church of England

A branch of this holy Catholic (or universal) Church has been, through God's blessing, established for ages in our island; a branch which, as has been already stated, we denominate the Church of England. Its officiating ministers are divided into the three original orders of Bishops, Priests, and Deacons, and into no other. In the exercise of that authority which is inherent in every society, of making salutary laws and regulations for its own guidance, it has been found expedient to vest in two of the principal members of the episcopal order in England a certain authority over the rest, and to style them Archbishops, but this is not by any means to be understood as constituting them another order in the Church. They are but, in strictness of language, the first and leading Bishops of our land.

The Priests and Deacons (whom we usually class together under the common name of Clergymen) who officiate in the Churches and Chapels of our Establishment, have each received ordination to the discharge of their holy office by the laying on of the hands of a Bishop, assisted, in the case of Priests, by members already admitted into the presbytery or priesthood, as was St. Paul in the ordination of Timothy (1 Tim 4:14).

And each Bishop of our Church has, at the hands of another Bishop (himself similarly called to the office) received in the most solemn manner the gift of the Holy Ghost, and that Apostolical power over the Church, for the support of which the Redeemer pledged Himself that His assistance should never be wanting to the end of time.

Wonderful indeed is the providence of God, which has so long preserved the unbroken line, and thus ordained that our Bishops should, even at this distance of time, stand before their flocks as the authorized successors of the Apostles;—as armed with their power to confer spiritual gifts in the Church, and, in cases of necessity, to wield their awful weapon of rejection from the fold of Christ;—as commissioned, like Titus, to bid, on heavenly authority, no man despise them, and to point out to those who, as a class, as Bishops of the Church, do despise them, the solemn words, "He that despiseth you, despiseth Me; and he that despiseth Me, despiseth Him that sent Me."

The mode in which new candidates for the episcopal station have been presented to existing Bishops for consecration, has differed in different ages and countries. They have sometimes been chosen by the laity, sometimes selected by other Bishops, and sometimes by civil magistrates. In our own country the latter mode has for some centuries prevailed, and the King of England has presented to the Prelates of its Church persons for their approval and consecration.

As the King and Legislature were the pledged defenders of the purity and integrity of that Church, this was perhaps a mode as unobjectionable as any which could have been substituted for it, and it possessed the advantage of being free from the turmoil and party feeling which have always been generated by proceedings in the way of popular election.

The mode, however, in which this presentation is made is, after all, of minor importance, it being understood that it is upon the responsibility of the Bishop himself that the solemn rite at last takes place. No earthly authority can compel him to lay his hands upon what he may conceive an unworthy head, or can presume to dispense with his concurrence, and arrogantly assume to itself the power to confer the Holy Ghost. The solemn words in which the offices of Bishop, Priest, and Deacon, are respectively conferred, are annexed to these pages, and from their perusal it will be seen how impious it would be, in any one but the deputed minister of Heaven, to utter them over a fellow-mortal, or to conceive that he, whatever his earthly rank or station, could bestow, or even aid in bestowing, the gifts imparted thereby.

Many ages ago the civil rulers of our country recognised the principle that a Christian nation should, as such, consider itself a branch of the Apostolical Church of Christ; they therefore acknowledged, and gave temporal dignity, and a voice in the general councils of the State to her ministers; privileges which they to the present day enjoy. And the Church, on her part, the above principle having been adopted by the State, acknowledged in the head of that State, the King, her temporal head; investing him with that general supremacy in ecclesiastical affairs, which he already possessed in civil. But we are not thence to infer that she gave, or that she could give, to an earthly monarch, or to his temporal legislature, the right to interfere with things spiritual, with her Doctrines, with her Liturgy, with the ministration of her Sacraments, or with the positions, relative to each other, of her Bishops, Priests, and Deacons.

When corruptions, prevalent among the professedly Christian world, render it necessary for her to state the substance of her faith in articles (as was done in A.D. 1562) or when circumstances appear to require any change or variation either in the forms of her Liturgy, or in her general internal government, the King has the constitutional power of summoning the houses of convocation, a sort of ecclesiastical parliament composed of Bishops or Clergy, from which alone such changes can fitly or legally emanate.

Such are the circumstances under which a branch of Christ's Church is domiciled among us, and claims over us, while acting according to His Spirit, the delegated authority of her Founder. She makes no pretensions to that immediate inspiration of the Spirit which, by positively securing her ministers from error, would clothe her decisions with absolute infallibility. She puts the Bible into the hand of every member of her communion, and calls upon us to believe nothing as necessary to salvation which shall not appear, upon mature examination, to be set down therein, or at least to be capable of being proved thereby; but shewing, at the same time, her authority as its appointed interpreter, she cautions him not rashly, or without having fully weighed the subject, to dissent from her expositions, the results of the accumulated learning and labour of centuries. She warns him not, without cause, to run the risk of incurring the fearful sin of schism, or unnecessary separation from, and violation of the unity of, Christ's fold; a sin of which, surely, none can think lightly, who remembers the Saviour's affecting and repeated prayer (see John 27) that His followers might be one, even as He and His Almighty Father were one. She bids him in that Bible itself read her credentials; she there exhibits, in the recorded indications of her Lord and Master's will, the rock on which she is built; the foundation which, whatever changes may convulse the globe around it, is to abide, unmoved and immoveable, till time shall be no more.

The duties which our knowledge of these things, Brethren of the Laity, makes incumbent upon us, are almost too clear to need recapitulation. Filial love and affectionate reverence toward the collective Church, and toward those, her Pastors and Masters, who are set in spiritual authority over us; a zeal for the inculcation of her pure doctrine and the extension of her heavenly fold; a determination in evil report and in good report to stand by her, and to approve ourselves her faithful members and children; these, and such feelings as these, are, by our bond of communion with her, peremptorily required of us; these let us make it the business of our lives to cultivate and comply with; and if tempted, as any one of us may be, hastily and needlessly to forsake her hallowed pale, let us reply to the temptation by addressing her in words somewhat similar to those of Peter to his Divine Master, "To whom shall we go? Thou hast the words of eternal life; and we believe and are sure that Thou art the" Minister and Representative of "Christ, the Son of the living God."

Appendix

The following are the words addressed respectively to Bishops, Priests, and Deacons, when their offices are conferred upon them by the laying on of hands.

To a Bishop: "Receive the Holy Ghost, for the Office and Work of a Bishop in the Church of God, now committed unto Thee by the Imposition of our hands; in the name of the Father, and of the Son, and of the Holy Ghost. Amen. And remember that thou stir up the grace of God which is given thee by this Imposition of our hands; for God hath not given us the Spirit of fear, but of power, and love, and soberness."

To a Priest: "Receive the Holy Ghost for the Office and Work of a Priest in the Church of God, now committed unto thee by the Imposition of our hands. Whose sins thou dost forgive, they are forgiven; and whose sins thou dost retain, they are retained. And be thou a faithful Dispenser of the Word of God, and of His holy Sacraments; in the name of the Father, and of the Son, and of the Holy Ghost. Amen."

To a Deacon: "Take thou authority to execute the office of a Deacon in the Church of God committed unto thee; in the name of the Father, and of the Son, and of the Holy Ghost. Amen."

JOHN WILLIAM BOWDEN
October 18, 1833

TRACT 6: AD POPULUM
The Present Obligation of Primitive Practice

When we look around upon the present state of the Christian Church, and then turning to ecclesiastical history acquaint ourselves with its primitive form and condition, the difference between them so strongly acts upon the imagination, that we are tempted to think, that to base our conduct now on the principles acknowledged then, is but theoretical and idle. We seem to perceive, as clear as day, that as the Primitive Church had its own particular discipline and political character, so have we ours; and that to attempt to revive what is past, is as absurd as to seek to raise what is literally dead. Perhaps we even go on to maintain, that the constitution of the Church, as well as its actual course of acting, is different from what it was; that Episcopacy now is in no sense what it used to be; that our Bishops are the same as the primitive Bishops only in name; and that the notion of an Apostolical Succession is "a fond thing." I do not wish to undervalue the temptation, which leads to this view of Church matters; it is the temptation of sight to overcome faith, and of course not a slight one.

But the following reflection on the history of the Jewish Church, may perhaps be considered to throw light upon our present duties.

1. Consider how exact are the injunctions of Moses to his people. He ends them thus: "These are the words of the covenant which the Lord commanded Moses to make with the children of Israel in the land of Moab, beside the covenant which He made with them in Horeb..... Keep therefore the words of this covenant, and do them, that ye may prosper in all that ye do..... Neither with you only do I make this covenant and this

oath; but with him that standeth here this day before the Lord our God, and also with him that is not here with us this day" (Deut 29:1, 9, 14-15).

2. Next, survey the history of the chosen people for the several first centuries after taking possession of Canaan. The exactness of Moses was unavailing. Can a greater contrast be conceived than the commands and promises of the Pentateuch, and the history of the Judges? "Every man did that which was right in his own eyes" (Judges 17:6).

Samuel attempts a reformation on the basis of the Mosaic law; but the effort ultimately fails, as being apparently against the stream of opinion and feeling then prevalent. The times do not allow of it. Again, contrast the opulent and luxurious age of Solomon, though the covenant was then openly acknowledged and outwardly accepted, more fully than at any other time, with the vision of simple piety and plain straightforward obedience, which is the scope of the Mosaic Law. Lastly, contemplate the state of the Jews after their return from the captivity; when their external political relations were so new, the internal principle of their government so secular, God's arm apparently so far removed. This state of things went on for centuries. Who would suppose that the Jewish Law was binding in all its primitive strictness at the age when Christ appeared? Who would not say that length of time had destroyed the obligation of a projected system, which had as yet never been realized?

Consider too the impossible nature (so to say) of some of its injunctions. An infidel historian somewhere asks scoffingly, whether "the ruinous law which required all the males of the chosen people to go up to Jerusalem three times a year, was ever observed in its strictness." The same question may be asked concerning the observance of the Sabbatical year;—to which but a faint allusion, if that, is made in the books of Scripture subsequent to the Pentateuch.

3. And now, with these thoughts before us, reflect upon our Saviour's conduct. He set about to fulfil the Law in its strictness, just as if He had lived in the generation next to Moses. The practice of others, the course of the world, was nothing to Him; He received and He obeyed. It is not necessary to draw out the evidence of this in detail. Consider merely His emphatic words in the beginning of Matthew 23 concerning those, whom as individuals He was fearfully condemning. "The Scribes and Pharisees sit in Moses' seat; all therefore whatsoever they bid you observe, that observe and do."—Again reflect upon the praise bestowed upon

Zacharias and his wife, that "they were both righteous before God, walking in all the commandments and ordinances of the Lord blameless."—And upon the conduct of the Apostles.

Surely these remarkable facts impress upon us the necessity of going to the Apostles, and not to the teachers and oracles of the present world, for the knowledge of our duty, as individuals and as members of the Christian Church. It is no argument against a practice being right, that it is neglected; rather, we are warned against going the broad way of the multitude of men.

Now is there any doubt in our minds, as to the feelings of the Primitive Church regarding the doctrine of the Apostolical Succession? Did not the Apostles observe, even in an age of miracles, the ceremony of Imposition of Hands? And are not we bound, not merely to acquiesce in, but zealously to maintain and inculcate the discipline which they established?

The only objection, which can be made to this view of our duty, is, that the injunction to obey strictly is *not* precisely given to us, as it was in the instance of the Mosaic Law. But is not the real state of the case merely this; that the Gospel appeals rather to our love and faith, our divinely illuminated reason, and the free principle of obedience, than to the mere letter of its injunctions? And does not the conduct of the Jews just prove to us, that, *though* the commands of Christ were put before us ever so precisely, yet there would not be found in any extended course of history a more exact attention to them, than there is now; that the difficulty of resisting the influence, which the world's actual proceedings exert upon our imagination, would be just as great, as we find it at present?

A Sin of the Church

> *Remember from whence thou art fallen, and repent, and do thy first works; or else I will come unto thee quickly, and will remove thy candlestick out of his place, except thou repent.*

The following extract is from Bingham, Antiq. xv. 9.

> In the primitive ages, it was both the rule and practice of all in general, both Clergy and Laity, to receive the Communion every Lord's day.... As often as they met together for Divine Service on the Lord's day, they were obliged to receive the Eucharist under pain of Excommunication.... And if we run over the whole history of the three first ages, we shall find this to have been the Church's constant practice.... We are assured farther, that in some places they received the Communion every day.

Is there any one who will deny, that the Primitive Church is the best expounder in this matter of our Saviour's will as conveyed through His Apostles?

Can a learned Church, such as the English, plead ignorance of His will thus ascertained?

Do we fulfil it?

Is not the regret and concern of pious and learned writers among us, such Bingham, at our neglect of it, upon record?

And is it not written, "THAT SERVANT WHICH KNEW HIS LORD'S WILL, AND PREPARED NOT HIMSELF, NEITHER DID ACCORDING TO HIS WILL, SHALL BE BEATEN WITH MANY STRIPES?"

And, putting aside this disobedience, can we wonder, that faith and love wax cold, when we so seldom partake of the means, mercifully vouchsafed us, of communion with our Lord and Saviour?

JOHN HENRY NEWMAN
October 29, 1833

TRACT 7

The Episcopal Church Apostolical

There are many persons at the present day, who, from not having turned their minds to the subject, think they are Churchmen in the sense in which the early Christians were, merely because they are Episcopalians. The extent of their Churchmanship is, to consider that Episcopacy is the best form of Ecclesiastical Polity; and again, that it originated with the Apostles. I am far from implying, that to go thus far is nothing; or is not an evidence (for it is) of a reverent and sober temper of mind; still the view is defective. It is defective, because the expediency of a system, though a very cogent, is not the highest line of argument that may be taken in its defence: and because an opponent may deny the fact of the Apostolicity of Episcopacy, and so involve its maintainer in an argument. Doubtless the more clear and simple principle for a Churchman to hold, is that of a *Ministerial Succession;* which is undeniable as a fact, while it is most reasonable as a doctrine, and sufficiently countenanced in Scripture for its practical reception. Of this, Episcopacy, i.e. *Superintendence*, is but an accident; though, for the sake of conciseness, it is often spoken of by us as synonymous with it. It shall be the object of the following tract to insist upon this higher characteristic of our Church.

My position then is this;—that the Apostles appointed successors to their ministerial office, and the latter in turn appointed others, and so on to the present day;—and further, that the Apostles and their Successors have in every age committed portions of their power and authority to others, who thus become their delegates, and in a measure their representatives, and are called Priests and Deacons. The result is an Episcopal system, *because* of the practice of delegation; but we may conceive their keeping their powers altogether to themselves, and in the same proportion in which this was done, would the Church polity cease to be Episcopalian. We may conceive the Order of Apostolic Vicars (so to call it) increased, till one of them was placed in every village, and took the office of parish priest. I do not say such a measure would be justifiable or pious;—doubtless it would be a departure from the rule of antiquity—but it is conceivable; and it is useful to conceive it, in order to form a clear notion of the Essence of the Church System, and the defective state of those Christian Societies which are separate from the Church Catholic. It is a common answer made to those who are called High Churchmen, to say, that "if God had intended the *form* of Church Government to be of great consequence, He would have worded His will in this matter more clearly in Scripture." Now enough has already been said to show the irrelevancy of such a remark. We need not deny to the Church the abstract right (however we may question the propriety) of altering its own constitution. It is not merely *because* Episcopacy is a *better or more scriptural form* than Presbyterianism (true as this may be in itself) that Episcopalians are right, and Presbyterians are wrong; but because the Presbyterian Ministers have assumed a power, which was never intrusted to them. They have presumed to exercise the power of ordination, and to perpetuate a succession of ministers, without having received a commission to do so. This is the plain fact that condemns them; and is a standing condemnation, from which they cannot escape, except by artifices of argument, which will serve equally to protect the self-authorized teacher of religion. If *they* may ordain without being sent to do so, *others* may teach and preach without being sent. They hold a middle position, which is untenable as destroying itself; for if Christians can do without Bishops (i.e. Commissioned Ordainers), they may do without Commissioned Ministers (i.e. the Priests and Deacons). If an imposition of hands is necessary to convey one gift, why should it not be to convey another?

1. As to the *fact* of the Apostolical Succession, i.e. that our present Bishops are the heirs and representatives of the Apostles by successive transmission of the prerogative of being so, this is too notorious to require proof. Every link in the chain is known from St. Peter to our present

Metropolitans. Here then I only ask, looking at this plain fact by itself, is there not something of a divine providence in it? can we conceive that this Succession has been preserved, all over the world, amid many revolutions, through many centuries, *for nothing?* Is it wise or pious to despise or neglect a gift thus transmitted to us in matter of fact, even if Scripture did not touch upon the subject?

2. Next, consider how *natural* is the doctrine of a Succession. When an individual comes to me, claiming to speak in the name of the Most High, it is natural to ask him for his authority. If he replies, that we are all bound to instruct each other, this reply is intelligible, but in the very form of it excludes the notion of a ministerial order, i.e. a class of persons set apart *from* others for religious offices. If he appeals to some miraculous gift, this too is intelligible, and only unsatisfactory when the alleged gift is proved to be a fiction. No other answer can be given, except a reference to some person, who has given him license to exercise ministerial functions; then follows the question, *how* that individual gained his authority to do so. In the case of the Catholic Church, the person referred to, i.e. the Bishop, has received it from a predecessor, and he from another, and so on, till we arrive at the Apostles themselves, and thence our Lord and Saviour. It is superfluous to dwell on so plain a principle, which in matters of this world we act upon daily.

3. Lastly, the *argument from Scripture* is surely quite clear to those, who honestly wish direction for *practice*. Christ promised He would be with His Apostles always, as ministers of His religion, even unto the end of the world. In one sense the Apostles were to be alive, till He came again; but they all died at the natural time. Does it not follow, that there are those now alive who represent them? Now who were the most probable representatives of them in the generation next their death? They surely, whom they have ordained to succeed them in the ministeral work. If any persons could be said to have Christ's power and presence, and the gifts of ruling and ordaining, of teaching, of binding and loosing (and comparing together the various Scriptures on the subject, all these seem included in His promise to be with the Church always), surely those, on whom the Apostles laid their hands, were they. And so in the next age, if any were representatives of the first representatives, they must be the next generation of Bishops, and so on. Nor does it materially alter the argument, though we suppose the blessing upon Ministerial Offices made,

not to the Apostles, but to the whole body of Disciples; i.e. the Church. For, even if it be the Church that has the power of ordination committed to it, still it exercises it through the Bishops as its organs; and the question recurs, *how* has the Presbytery in this or that country obtained the power? The Church certainly has from the first committed it to the Bishops, and has never resumed it; and the Bishops have no where committed it to the Presbytery, who therefore cannot be in possession of it.

However, it is merely for argument sake that I make this allowance, as to the meaning of the text in Matthew 28. At the same time, let it be observed what force is added to the argument for the Apostolic Succession, by the acknowledged existence in Scripture of the doctrine of a standing Church, or permanent Body Corporate for spiritual purposes. For, if Scripture has formed all Christians into one continuous community through all ages (which I do not here prove), it is but according to the same analogy, that the Ministerial Office should be vested in an Order, propagated from age to age, on a principle of succession. And, if we proceed to considerations of utility and expedience, it is plain, that, according to our notions, it is more necessary that a Minister should be perpetuated by a fixed law, than that the community of Christians should be, which can scarcely be considered to be vested with any powers, such as to require the visible authority which a Succession supplies.

JOHN HENRY NEWMAN
October 29, 1833

TRACT 8
The Gospel a Law of Liberty

It is a matter of surprise to some persons that the ecclesiastical system under which we find ourselves, is so faintly enjoined on us in Scripture. One very sufficient explanation of the fact will be found in considering that the Bible is not intended to teach us matters of *discipline* so much as matters of *faith;* i.e. those doctrines, the reception of which are necessary to salvation. But another reason may be suggested, which is well worth our attentive consideration.

The Gospel is a Law of *Liberty*. We are treated as sons, not as servants; not subjected to a code of formal commands, but addressed as those who love God, and wish to please Him. When a man gives orders to those who he thinks will mistake him, or are perverse, he speaks pointedly and explicitly; but when he gives directions to friends, he will trust much to their knowledge of his feelings and wishes, he leaves much to their discretion, and tells them not so much what he would have done in detail, as what are the objects he would have accomplished. Now this is the way Christ has spoken to us under the New Covenant; and apparently with this reason, to *try* us, whether or not we really love Him as our Lord and Saviour.

Accordingly, there is no part perhaps of the ecclesiastical system, which is not faintly traced in Scripture, and no part which is much more than faintly traced. The question which a reverend and affectionate faith will ask, is, "what is *most likely* to please Christ?" And this is just the question that obtains an answer in Scripture; which contains just so much as intimations of what is most likely to please Him. Of course different minds will differ as to the degree of clearness with which this or that practice is enjoined, yet I think no one will consider the state of the case, as I have put it, exaggerated on the whole.

Many duties are intimated to us by example, not by precept—many are implied merely—others can only be inferred from a comparison of passages—and others perhaps are contained only in the Jewish Law. I will mention some specimens to assist the reflection of the reader.

The early Christians were remarkable for keeping to the Apostles' *fellowship*. Who are *more likely* to stand in the Apostles' place since their death, than that line of Bishops which they themselves began? for that the Apostles *were* in some sense or other to remain on earth to the end of all things, is plain from the text, "Lo, I am with you," &c.

St. Paul set Timothy over the Church at Ephesus, and Titus over the Churches of Crete; i.e. as Bishops; therefore it is *safer* to have Bishops now, it is more likely to be pleasing to Him who has loved us, and bids us in turn love Him with the heart, not with formal service.

Our Lord committed the Administration of the Lord's Supper *to His Apostles;* "Do THIS in remembrance of Me"—therefore the Church has ever continued it in the hands of their Successors, and the delegates of these. On the other hand the command to baptize was given in the presence of the Disciples, and so indirectly to them; and therefore the Church has allowed lay-baptism, in cases where an ordained Minister could not be obtained.

From Christ's words, "Suffer the little children," &c. and from His blessing them, we infer His desire that children should be brought near to Him in baptism;—as we do also from St Paul's conduct on several occasions. Acts 16:15, 33; 1 Corinthians 1:16.

So also we continue the practice of Confirmation, from a desire to keep as near the Apostles' rule as possible.

Again, what little is there of express command in the New Testament for our meeting together in *public* worship! Yet we see what the custom of the Apostolic Church was from the book of Acts, 1 Corinthians, &c.

In like manner, the words in Genesis 2 and the practice of the Apostles in the Acts, are quite warrant enough for the Sanctification of the Lord's Day, even though the 4th Commandment were not binding on us.

For the same reason we continue the Patriarchal and Jewish rule of paying tithe to the Church. Some portion of our goods is evidently due to God;—and the ancient Divine Command is a *direction* to us in a case when reason and conscience have no means of determining.

These may be taken as illustrations of a general principle. And at this day it is most needful to keep it in view, since a cold spirit has crept into the Church of demanding rigid demonstration for every religious practice and observance. It is the fashion now to speak of those who maintain the ancient rules of the ecclesiastical system, not as zealous servants of Christ, not as wise and practical expounders of His will, but as *inconclusive reasoners,* and *fanciful theorists,* merely because, instead of standing still and arguing, they have a heart to obey. Are there not numbers in this day, who think themselves enlightened believers, yet who are but acting the part of the husbandman's son in the Gospel, who said, "I go, sir"—AND WENT NOT?

Church Reform

Surely, before the blessing of a Millennium is vouchsafed to us, the whole Christian world has much to confess in its several branches. Rome has to confess her Papal corruptions, and her cruelty towards those who refuse to accept them. The Christian communities of Holland, Scotland, and other countries, their neglect of the Apostolical Order of Ministers. The Greek Church has to confess its saint-worship, its formal fasts, and its want of zeal. The Churches of Asia their heresy. All parts of Christendom have much to confess and reform. We have our sins as well as the rest. O that *we* would take the lead in the regeneration of the Church Catholic on Scripture principles.

Our greatest sin perhaps is the disuse of "a godly discipline." Let the reader consider

1. The command. "Put away from yourselves the wicked person." "A man, that is a heretic, after the first and second admonition reject." "Mark them which cause divisions and offences, . . . and avoid them."

2. The example, viz. in the Primitive Church. "The Persons or Objects of Ecclesiastical Censure were all such delinquents, as fell into

great and scandalous crimes after baptism, whether men or women, priests or people, rich or poor, princes or subjects." Bing. Antiqu. xvi. 3.

3. The warning. "Whosoever . . . shall break one of these least commandments and shall teach men so, he shall be called the least in the kingdom of heaven."

JOHN HENRY NEWMAN
October 31, 1833

TRACT 9: AD POPULUM
On Shortening the Church Services

There is a growing feeling that the Services of the Church are too long; and many persons think it a sound feeling, merely because it *is* a growing one. Let such as have not made up their minds on the subject, suffer themselves, before going into the arguments against our Services, to be arrested by the following consideration.

The Services of our Church, as they now stand, are but a very small part of the ancient Christian worship; and, though people now-a-days think them too long, there can be no doubt that the primitive believers would have thought them too short. Now I am far from considering this as a conclusive argument in the question; as if the primitive believers were right, and people now-a-days wrong; but surely others may fairly be called upon, not to assume the reverse. On such points it is safest to assume nothing, but to take facts as we find them; and the facts are these.

In ancient times Christians understood very literally all that the Bible says about prayer. David had said, "seven times a day do I praise Thee;" and St. Paul had said, "pray always." These texts they did not feel at liberty to explain away, but complying with them to the letter, praised God seven times a day, besides their morning and evening prayer. Their hours of devotion were, in the day time, 6, 9, 12, and 3, which were called the Horæ Canonicæ; in the night, 9, 12, and 3, which were called the Nocturns; and besides these the hour of daybreak and of retiring to bed;—not that they set apart these hours in the first instance for public worship, this was impossible; but they seem to have aimed at praying with one accord, and at one time, even where they could not do so in one place. "The Universal Church," says Bishop Patrick, "anciently observed certain set hours of prayer, that all Christians throughout the world might at the same time join together to glorify God; and some of them were of opinion, that the Angelical Host, being acquainted with those hours, took that time to join their prayers and praises with those of the Church." The Hymns and Psalms appropriated to these hours were in the first instance intended only for private meditation; but afterwards, when religious societies were formed, and persons, who had withdrawn from secular business, lived together for purposes of devotion, chanting was introduced, and they were arranged for congregational worship. Throughout the Churches which used the Latin tongue, the same Services were adopted with very little variation; and in Roman Catholic countries they continue in use, with only a few modern interpolations, even to this day.

The length of these Services will be in some degree understood from the fact, that in the course of every week they go through the whole book of Psalms. The writer has been told by a distinguished person, who was once a Roman Catholic Priest, that the time required for their performance averages three hours a day throughout the year.

The process of transition from this primitive mode of worship to that now used in the Church of England, was gradual. Long before the abolition of the Latin Service, the ancient hours of worship had fallen into disuse; in religious Societies the daily and nightly Services had been arranged in groups under the names of Matins and Vespers; and those who prayed in private were allowed to suit their hours of prayer to their convenience, provided only that they went through the whole Services each day. Neither is it to be supposed that this modified demand was at all generally complied with. Thus in the course of time, the views and feelings, with which prayer had been regarded by the early Christians, became antiquated; the forms remained, but stripped of their original meaning; Services were compressed into one, which had been originally distinct; the idea of united worship, with a view to which identity of time and language had been maintained in different nations, was forgotten; the identity of time had been abandoned, and the identity of language was not thought worth preserving. Conscious of the incongruity of primitive forms and modern feelings, our Reformers undertook to construct a Service more in accordance with the spirit of their age. They adopted the

English language; they curtailed the already compressed ritual of the early Christians, so arranging it that the Psalms should be gone through monthly, instead of weekly; and, carrying the spirit of compression still further, they added to the Matin Service what had hitherto been wholly distinct from it, the Mass Service or Communion.

Since the Reformation, the same gradual change in the prevailing notions of prayer has worked its way silently but generally. The Services, as they were left by the Reformers, were, as they had been from the first ages, *daily* Services; they are now *weekly* Services. Are they not now in a fair way to become *monthly?*

Sunday Lessons

There are persons who wish certain Sunday Lessons removed from our Service, e.g. some of those selected for Lent,—nay, Jeremiah 5 and 22; and this, on the ground that it is painful to the feelings of Clergymen to read them.

Waving other considerations, which may be urged against innovation in this matter, may we not allow some weight to the following, which is drawn from the very argument brought in favour of the change? Will not the same feeling, which keeps men from reading the account of certain sins and their punishment from the *Bible,* much more keep them from mentioning them in the *pulpit?* Is it not necessary that certain sins, which it is distressing to speak of, should be seriously denounced, as being not the less frequent in commission, because they are disgraceful in language? And if so, is it not a most considerate provision of the Church, to relieve her Ministers of the pain of using their own words, and to allow them to shelter their admonitions under the holy and reverend language of Inspired Scripture?

R.H. FROUDE
October 31, 1833

TRACT 10

Heads of a Week-Day Lecture
Delivered to a Country Congregation in ——shire

Before we meet again, we shall have celebrated the feast of St. Simon and St. Jude, the Apostles. You will be at your daily work, and will not have the opportunity to attend the service in church. For that reason, it may be as well, you should lay up some good thoughts against that day; and such, by God's blessing, I will now attempt to give you.

As you well know, there were twelve Apostles; St. Simon and St. Jude were two of them. They preached the Gospel of CHRIST; and they were like CHRIST, as far as sinful man may be accounted like the blessed Son of GOD. They were like CHRIST in their deeds and in their sufferings. The Gospel for the festival shows us this (John 15:17). They were like CHRIST in their works, because CHRIST was a witness of the Father, and they were witnesses of CHRIST. CHRIST came in the name of GOD the Father Almighty; He "came and spoke," and "did works which none other man did." In like manner, the Apostles were sent "to bear witness of CHRIST, to declare His power, His great mercy, His sufferings on the cross for the sins of all men. His willingness to save all who come to Him."

But again, they were like CHRIST in their *sufferings*. "If the world hate you," He says to them, "you know that it hated Me, before it hated you. If ye were of the world, the world would love his own; but because ye are not of the world, but I have chosen you out of the world, therefore the world hateth you. Remember the word that I said unto you. The servant is not greater than his lord. If they have persecuted Me, they will also persecute you; if they have kept My saying, they will keep yours also."

Thus, they were like CHRIST in *office*. I do not speak of their holiness, their faith, and all their other high excellences, which GOD the Holy Ghost gave them. I speak now, not of their personal graces, but of their *office*, of preaching, of witnessing Christ, of suffering for being His servants. Men ought to have listened to them, and honoured them; some did; but the many, the world did not—they *hated* them; they hated them, for their office-sake; not because they were Paul, and Peter, and Simon, and Jude, but because they bore witness to the Son of GOD and were chosen to be His Ministers.

Here is a useful lesson for us at this day. The Apostles indeed are dead; yet it is quite as possible for men still to hate their preaching and to persecute them, as when they were alive. For in one sense they are still alive; I mean, they did not leave the world without appointing persons to take their place; and these persons represent them, and may be considered with reference to us, as if they were the Apostles. When a man dies, his son takes his property, and represents him; that is, in a manner he still lives in the person of his son. Well, this explains how the Apostles may be said to be still among us; they did not indeed leave their sons to succeed them as Apostles, but they left *spiritual* sons; they did not leave this life, without first solemnly laying their hands on the heads of certain of their flock, and these took their place, and represented them after their death.

But it may be asked, are these spiritual sons of the Apostles still alive? no;—all this took place many hundred years ago. These sons and heirs of the Apostles died long since. But then they in turn did not leave the world without committing their sacred office to a fresh set of Ministers, and they in turn to another, and so on even to this day. Thus the Apostles had, first, spiritual sons; then spiritual grandsons; then great grandsons; and so on from one age to another down to the present time.

Again, it may be asked, *who* are at this time the successors and spiritual descendants of the Apostles? I shall surprise some people by the answer I shall give; though it is very clear, and there is no doubt about it; THE BISHOPS. They stand in the place of the Apostles; and, whatever we ought to do, had we lived when the Apostles were alive, the same ought we to do for the Bishops. He that despises them, despises the Apostles. It is our duty to reverence them for their ofiice-sake; they are the shepherds of CHRIST's flock. If we knew them well, we should love them for the many excellent graces they possess, for their piety, loving-kindness, and other virtues. But we do not know them; yet still, for all this, we may honour them as the ministers of Christ, without going so far as to consider their *private* worth; and we may keep to their "fellowship," as we should to that of the Apostles (Acts 2:42). I say, we may all thus honour them even without knowing them in private, because of their high office; for they have the marks of Christ's presence upon them, in that they *witness* for Christ, and *suffer* for Him, as the Apostles did. I will explain to you how this is.

There is a temptation which comes on many men to honour no one, except such as they themselves know, such as have done a favour or kindness to them personally. Thus sometimes people speak against those who are put over them in this world's matters, as the King. They say, "What is the King to me? he never did me any good." Now, I answer, whether he did or not, is nothing to the purpose. We are bound *for* CHRIST'S sake, to honour him *because* he is King, though he lives far from us; and this all well-disposed right-minded people do. And so, in just the same way, though for much higher reasons, we must honor the Bishop, because he *is* the Bishop;—for his *office*-sake;—because he is CHRIST'S Minister, stands in the place of the Apostles, is the Shepherd of our souls on earth, while CHRIST is away. This is FAITH, to look at things not as seen, but as unseen; to be as sure that the Bishop is CHRIST'S appointed Representative, as if we actually saw upon his head a cloven tongue like as of fire, as you may read in the second chapter of the Acts of the Apostles.

But you will say, how do we know this, since we do not see it. I repeat, the Bishops are Apostles to us, from their *witnessing* CHRIST, and *suffering* for Him.

1. They witness CHRIST in their very *name,* for He is the true Bishop of our souls, as St. Peter says, and they are Bishops. They witness CHRIST in their *station;*—there is but one LORD to save us, and there is but one Bishop in each place. The meetingers have no head, they are all of them mixed together in a confused way; but we of CHRIST'S Holy Church have one Bishop over us, and our Bishop is the Bishop of ———. Many of you have seen him lately, when he confirmed in our church. That very *confirmation* is another ordinance, in which the Bishop witnesses CHRIST. Our LORD confirms us with the Spirit in all goodness; the Bishop is His figure and likeness, when he lays his hands on the heads of children. Then CHRIST comes to them, to confirm in them the grace of

Baptism. Moreover, the Bishop *rules* the whole Church here below, as CHRIST rules it above; and here again the Bishop is a figure or witness of CHRIST. And further, it is the Bishop who makes us Clergymen GOD'S Ministers. He is CHRIST'S instrument; and he visibly chooses those whom CHRIST chooses invisibly, to serve in the Word and Sacraments of the Church. And thus it is from the Bishop that the *news of redemption and the means of grace* have come to all men; this again is a witnessing CHRIST. I, who speak to you concerning CHRIST, was ordained to do so by the Bishop; he speaks in me,—as CHRIST wrought in him, and as GOD sent CHRIST. Thus the whole plan of salvation hangs together.— CHRIST the True Mediator above; His servant, the Bishop, His earthly likeness; mankind the subjects of His teaching; GOD the Author of Salvation.

2. But I must now mention the more painful part of the subject, i.e. the *sufferings* of the Bishops, which is the second mark of their being our living Apostles. The Bishops have undergone this trial in every age. As the first Apostles were hated and persecuted, so have they ever been. Time was, when they were cruelly slain by fire and sword. That time (though GOD avert it!) may come again. But, whether or not Satan is permitted so openly to rage, certainly some kinds of persecution are to be expected in our day; nay, such have begun. It is not so very long since the great men of the earth told them to *prepare for persecution;* it is not so very long since the mad people answered the summons, and furiously attacked them, and seemed bent on destroying them, in all parts of the country.

Yes! the day may come, even in this generation, when the Representatives of CHRIST are spoiled of their sacred possessions, and degraded from their civil dignities. The day may come, when each of us inferior Ministers—when I myself, whom you know—may have to give up our Churches, and be among you, in no better temporal circumstances than yourselves; with no larger dwelling, no finer clothing, no other fare, with nothing different beyond those gifts, which I trust we gained when we were made Ministers; and those again, which have been vouchsafed to us before and after that time, for the due fulfilment of our Ministry. Then you will look at us, not as gentlemen, as now; not as your superiors in worldly station, but still, nay, more strikingly so than now, still as messengers from Him, who seeth and worketh in secret, and who judgeth not by outward appearance. Then you will honor us, with a purer honor than you do now, namely, as those who are intrusted with the keys of heaven and hell, as the heralds of mercy, as the denouncers of woe to wicked men, as intrusted with the awful and mysterious gift of making the bread and wine CHRIST'S body and blood, as far greater than the most powerful and the wealthiest of men in our unseen strength and our heavenly riches. This may all come in our day; and I can hardly wish it should not come, painful as is the thought of the great wickedness, which those men must show forth, who persecute us; painful as is the thought of the sufferings, which that persecution will cause us. And, after all, if GOD'S loving kindness spares both us and you the trial, still it will have been useful to have steadily thought about it beforehand, and to have prepared our hearts to meet it.

JOHN HENRY NEWMAN
November 4, 1833

TRACT 11: AD SCHOLAS
The Visible Church
In Letters to a Friend

Letter I

MY DEAR——

You wish to have my opinion on the doctrine of "the Holy Catholic Church," as contained in Scripture, and taught in the Creed. So I send you the following lines, which perhaps may serve, through God's blessing, to assist you in your search after the truth in this matter, even though they do no more; indeed no remarks, however just, can be much more than an assistance to you. You must search for yourself, and God must teach you.

I think I partly enter into your present perplexity. You argue, that true *doctrine* is the important matter for which we must contend, and a *right state of the affections* is the test of vital religion in the heart; and you ask, "Why may I not be satisfied if my Creed is correct, and my affections spiritual? Have I not in that case enough to evidence a renewed mind, and to constitute a basis of union with others like minded? The love of CHRIST is surely the one and only requisite for Christian communion here, and the joys of heaven hereafter." Again you say, that —— and —— are constant in their prayers for the teaching of the HOLY SPIRIT; so that if it be true, that every one who asketh receiveth, surely they must receive, and are in a safe state.

Believe me, I do not think lightly of these arguments. They are very subtle ones; powerfully influencing the imagination, and difficult to answer. Still I believe them to be mere fallacies. Let me try them in a parallel case. You know the preacher at ——, and have heard of his flagrantly immoral life; yet it is notorious that he can and does speak in a moving way of the love of CHRIST, &c. It is very shocking to witness such a case, which (we will hope) is rare; but it has its use. Do you not think him in peril, in spite of his impressive and persuasive language? Why?—You will say, his life is bad. True; it seems then that more is requisite for salvation than an orthodox creed, and keen sensibilities; viz. consistent conduct.—Very well then, we have come to an additional test of true faith,—obedience to GOD'S word, and plainly a scriptural test, according to St. John's canon, "He who *doeth* righteousness is righteous." Do not you see then your argument is already proved to be unsound? It seems that true doctrine and warm feelings are not enough. How am I to know what is enough? you ask. I reply, *by searching Scripture.* It was your original fault that, instead of inquiring what God has told you is necessary for being a true Christian, you chose out of your own head to *argue* on the subject;—e.g. "I can never believe that to be such and such is not enough for salvation," &c. Now this is *worldly wisdom.*

Let us join issue then on this plain ground, whether or not the doctrine of "the Church," and the duty of obeying it, be laid down *in Scripture.* If so, it is no matter as regards our practice, whether the doctrine is primary or secondary, whether the duty is much or little insisted on. A Christian mind will aim at obeying the *whole* counsel and will of GOD; on the other hand, to those who are tempted arbitrarily to classify and select their duties, it is written, "Whosoever shall break one of these least commandments, and shall teach men so, he shall be called the least in the kingdom of heaven."

And here first, that you may clearly understand the ground I am taking, pray observe that I am not attempting to controvert any one of those high evangelical points, on which perhaps we do not altogether agree with each other. Perhaps you attribute less efficacy to the Sacrament of Baptism than I do; bring out into greater system and prominence the history of an individual's warfare with his spiritual enemies; fix more precisely and abruptly the date of his actual conversion from darkness to light; and consider that Divine Grace acts more arbitrarily against the corrupt human will, than I think is revealed in Scripture. Still, in spite of this difference of opinion, I see no reason why you should not accept heartily the Scripture doctrine of "the Church." And this is the point I wish to press, not asking you to abandon your present opinions, but to *add to them* a practical belief in a tenet which the Creed teaches and Scripture has consecrated. And this surely is quite possible. The excellent Mr. ——, of ——, who has lately left ——, was both a Calvinist, and a strenuous High-Churchman.

You are in the practice of distinguishing between the Visible and Invisible Church. Of course I have no wish to maintain, that those who shall be saved hereafter are exactly the same company that are under the means of grace here; still I must insist on it, that Scripture makes the existence of a Visible Church a condition of the existence of the Invisible. I mean, the *Sacraments* are evidently in the hands of the Church Visible; and these, we know, are generally necessary to salvation, as the Catechism says. Thus it is an undeniable fact, as true as that souls will be saved, that a Visible Church must exist as a means towards that end. The Sacraments are in the hands of the Clergy; this few will deny, or that their efficacy is not diminished by the personal character of the administrator. What then shall be thought of any attempts to weaken or exterminate that Community, or that Ministry, which is an appointed condition of the salvation of the elect? But every one, who makes or encourages a schism, *must* weaken it. Thus it is plain, schism must be wrong in itself, even if Scripture did not in express terms forbid it, as it does.

But further than this; it is plain this Visible Church is a *standing* body. Every one who is baptized, is baptized *into* an existing community. Our Service expresses this when it speaks of baptized infants being *incorporated* into GOD's Holy Church. Thus the Visible Church is not a voluntary association of the day, but a continuation of one which existed in the age before us, and then again in the age before that; and so back till we come to the age of the Apostles. In the same sense, in which Corporations of the State's creating, are perpetual, is this which CHRIST has founded. This is a matter of fact hitherto; and it necessarily will be so always, for is not the notion absurd of an unbaptized person baptizing others? which is the only way in which the Christian community can have a new beginning.

Moreover Scripture directly *insists* upon the doctrine of the Visible Church as being of importance. E.g. St. Paul says;—"There is *one body*, and one Spirit, even as ye are called in one hope of your calling; one LORD, one faith, one baptism, one GOD and Father of all" (Eph 4:4-6). Thus, as far as the Apostle's words go, it is as false and unchristian (I do not mean in degree of guilt, but in its intrinsic sinfulness) to make more bodies than one, as to have many Lords, many Gods, many Creeds. Now, I wish to know, how it is possible for any one to fall into this sin, if Dissenters are clear of it? What *is* the sin, if separation from the Existing Church is not it?

I have shown that there is a divinely instituted Visible Church, and that it has been one and the same by successive incorporation of members from the beginning. Now I observe further, that the word Church, as used in Scripture, ordinarily means this actually existing visible body. The exceptions to this rule, out of about 100 places in the New Testament, where the word occurs, are four passages in the Epistle to the Ephesians; two in the Colossians; and one in the Hebrews. (Eph 1:22; 3:10, 21; 5:23-32; Col 1:18, 24; Heb 12:23.)—And in some of these exceptions the sense is at most but doubtful. Further, our SAVIOUR uses the word twice, and in both times of the Visible Church. They are remarkable passages, and may here be introduced, in continuation of my argument.

Matthew 26:18: "Upon this rock I will build My Church, and the gates of hell shall not prevail against it." Now I am certain, any unprejudiced mind, who knew nothing of controversy, considering the Greek word ἐκκλησία means simply an *assembly*, would have no doubt at all that it meant in this passage a visible body. What right have we to disturb the plain sense? why do we impose a meaning, arising from some system of our own? And this view is altogether confirmed by the other occasion of our LORD'S using it, where it can *only* denote the Visible Church. Matthew 18:17: "If he (thy brother) shall neglect to hear them, tell it unto the Church; but if he neglect to hear the Church, let him be unto thee as a heathen man and a publican."

Observe then what we gain by these two passages;—the grant of *power* to the Church; and the promise of *permanence*. Now look at the fact. The body then begun has continued; and has always claimed and exercised the power of a corporation or society. Consider merely the article in the Creed, "The Holy Catholic Church;" which embodies this notion. Do not Scripture and History illustrate each other?

I end this first draught of my argument, with the text in 1 Timothy 3:15, in which St. Paul calls the Church "the pillar and ground of the Truth,"—which can refer to nothing but a Visible Body; else martyrs may be invisible, and preachers, and teachers, and the whole order of the Ministry.

My paper is exhausted. If you allow me, I will send you soon a second Letter; meanwhile I sum up what I have been proving from Scripture thus; that ALMIGHTY GOD might have left Christianity as a sort of sacred literature, as contained in the Bible, which each person was to take and use by himself; just as we read the works of any human philosopher or historian, from which we gain practical instruction, but the knowledge of which does not bind us to be Newtonians, or Aristotelians, &c. or to go out of our line of life in consequence of it. This, I say, He might have done; but, in matter of fact, He has ordained otherwise. He has actually set up a Society, which exists even at this day all over the world, and which (as a general rule) Christians are bound to join; so that to believe in CHRIST is not a mere opinion or a secret conviction, but a social or even a political principle, forcing one into what is often stigmatized as party strife, and quite inconsistent with the supercilious mood of those professed Christians of the day, who stand aloof, and designate their indifference as philosophy.

Ever yours,
* * *

Letter II

MY DEAR———

I am sometimes struck with the inconsistency of those, who do not allow us to express the gratitude due to the Church, while they do not hesitate to declare their obligation to individuals who have benefitted them. To avow that they owe their views of religion and their present hopes of salvation to this or that distinguished preacher, appears to them as harmless, as it may be in itself true and becoming; but if a person ascribes his faith and knowledge to the Church, he is thought to forget his peculiar and unspeakable debt to that SAVIOUR who died for him. Surely, if our

LORD makes man His instrument of good to man, and if it is possible to be grateful to man without forgetting the Source of all grace and power, there is nothing wonderful in His having appointed a company of men as the especial medium of His instruction and spiritual gifts, and in consequence of His having laid upon us the duty of gratitude to it. Now this is all I wish to maintain, what is most clearly (as I think) revealed in Scripture, that the blessings of redemption come to us through the Visible Church; so that, as we betake ourselves to a Dispensary for medicine, without attributing praise or intrinsic worth to the building or the immediate managers of its stores, in something of the like manner we are to come to that One Society, to which CHRIST has entrusted the office of stewardship in the distribution of gifts of which He alone is the Author and real Dispenser.

In the letter I sent you the other day, I made some general remarks on this doctrine; now let me continue the subject.

First, the Sacraments, which are the ordinary means of grace, are clearly in possession of the Church. Baptism is an incorporation into a body; and invests with spiritual blessings, because it is the introduction into a body so invested. In 1 Corinthians 12 we are taught first, the SPIRIT'S indwelling in the Visible Church or body; I do not say *in every member of it,* but generally *in* it;—next, we are told that the SPIRIT baptizes individuals *into* that body. Again, the Lord's Supper carries evidence of its social nature even in its name; it is not a solitary individual act, it is a joint communion. Surely nothing is more alien to Christianity than the spirit of Independence; the peculiar Christian blessing, i.e. the presence of CHRIST, is upon *two or three* gathered together, not on mere individuals.

But this is not all. The Sacraments are committed, not into the hands of the Church Visible assembled together (though even this would be no unimportant doctrine practically), but into certain definite persons, who are selected from their brethren for that trust. I will not here determine who these are in each successive age, but will only point out how far this principle itself will carry us. The doctrine is implied in the original institution of the LORD'S Supper, where CHRIST says to His Apostles, "Do this." Further, take that remarkable passage in Matthew 24:24-51, Luke 12:42-46, "Who then is that faithful and wise Steward, whom his Lord shall make ruler over His household, to give them their portion of meat in due season? Blessed is that servant, whom his Lord, *when He cometh,* shall find so doing!" &c. Now I do not inquire *who* in every age are the stewards spoken of (though in my own mind I cannot doubt the line of Bishops is that Ministry, and consider the concluding verses fearfully prophetic of the Papal misuse of the gift;—by the bye, at least it shows this, that bad men may nevertheless be the channels of grace to GOD'S "household"), I do not ask who are the stewards, but surely the words, *when He cometh,* imply that they are to continue till the end of the world. This reference is abundantly confirmed by our LORD'S parting words to the eleven; in which, after giving them the baptismal commission, He adds, "Lo! I am with you *always,* even unto the end of the world." If then He was with the Apostles in a way in which He was not present with teachers who were strangers to their "fellowship" (Acts 2:42), which all will admit, so, in like manner, it cannot be a matter of indifference in any age, what teachers and fellowship a Christian selects; there must be those with whom CHRIST is present, who are His "Stewards," and whom it is our duty to obey.

As I have mentioned the question of faithfulness and unfaithfulness in Ministers, I may refer to the passage in 1 Corinthians 4 where St. Paul, after speaking of himself and others as "*Stewards* of the mysteries of God," and noticing that "it is required of Stewards, that a man be found faithful," adds, "With me it is a very small thing that I should be judged of you or of man's judgment. . . . therefore *judge nothing before the time.*"

To proceed, consider the following passage: "Obey them that have rule over you, and submit yourselves" (Heb 13:17). Again I do not ask *who* these are; but whether this is not a duty, however it is to be fulfilled, which multitudes *in no sense* fulfil. Consider the number of people, professing and doubtless in a manner really actuated by Christian principle, who yet wander about from church to church, or from church to meeting, as sheep without a shepherd, or who choose a preacher merely because he pleases their taste, and whose first movement towards any clergyman they meet, is to examine and criticize his doctrine, what conceivable meaning do they put upon these words of the Apostle? Does any one *rule over* them? do they in any way *submit themselves?* Can these persons excuse their conduct, except on the deplorably profane plea (which yet I believe is in their hearts at the bottom of their disobedience) that it matters little to keep CHRIST'S "least commandments," so that we embrace the peculiar doctrines of His gospel?

Some time ago I drew up a sketch of the Scripture proof of the doctrine of the Visible Church; which with your leave I will here transcribe. You will observe, I am not arguing for this or that form of Polity, or for the Apostolical Succession, but simply the duties of order, union, and ecclesiastical obedience; I limit myself to these points, as being persuaded that, when they are granted, the others will eventually follow.

I. That there was a Visible Church in the Apostles' day.
1. General texts. Matt 16:18, 18:17; 1 Tim 3:15; Acts passim, &c.
2. Organization of the Church.
    (1) Diversity of ranks. 1 Cor 12; Eph 4:4-12; Rom 12:4-8; 1 Pet 4:10, 11.
    (2) Governors. Matt 28:19; Mark 16:15, 16; John 20:22, 23; Luke 22:19, 20; Gal 2:9, &c.
    (3) Gifts. Luke 12:42, 43; John 20:22, 23; Matt 28:18.
    (4) Order. Acts 8:5, 6, 12, 14, 15, 17; 11:22, 23; 11:2, 4; 9:27; 15:2, 4, 6, 25; 16:4; 18:22; 21:17-19; conf. Gal 1:1, 12; 1 Cor 14:40; 1 Thess 5:14.
    (5) Ordination. Acts 6:6; 1 Tim 4:14; 5:22; 2 Tim 1:6; Titus 1:5; Acts 13:3; cf. Gal 1:1, 12.
    (6) Ecclesiastical obedience. 1 Thess 5:12, 13; Heb 13:17; Tim 5:17.
    (7) Rules and discipline. Matt 28:19; Matt. 28:17; 1 Cor 5:4-7. Gal 5:12. &c. 1 Cor 16:1, 2; 1 Cor 11:2, 16, &c.
    (8) Unity. Rom 16:17; 1 Cor 1:10, 3:3, 14:26; Col 2:5; 1 Thess 5:14; 2 Thess 3:6.

II. That the Visible Church, thus instituted by the Apostles, was intended to continue.
1. Why should it not? The onus probandi lies with those who deny this position. If the doctrines and precepts already cited are obsolete at this day, why should not the following texts? e.g. 1 Pet 2:13 or, e.g. Matt 7:14, John 3:3.
2. Is it likely so elaborate a system should be framed, yet with no purpose of its continuing?

3. The objects to be obtained by it are as necessary now as then. (1.) Preservation of the faith. (2.) Purity of doctrine. (3.) Edification of Christians. (4.) Unity of operation. Vid. Epists. to Tim. & Tit. passim.
4. If system were necessary in a time of miracles, much more is it now.
5. 2 Tim 2:2; Matt 28:20, &c.

Take these remarks, as they are meant, as mere suggestions for your private consideration, and believe me, &c. &c.

JOHN HENRY NEWMAN
November 11, 1833

TRACT 12
Richard Nelson
I: Bishops, Priests, and Deacons

> *It is evident unto all men diligently reading the Holy Scripture and ancient authors, that from the Apostles' time there have been these orders of Ministers in Christ's Church; Bishops, Priests, and Deacons.*
> —Pref. to the Ordination Service.

In the course of this last summer of 1833, I had the pleasure of a visit from an old and valued friend, one of the most respectable merchants in the city of Bristol (and this, in my opinion, is no small praise).

We were discussing one day the subject of National Schools, their merits and demerits. He was pleading strenuously for them; and to confirm his arguments, "I will mention," said he, "a circumstance which happened to me when I was in this part of the world about eleven or twelve years ago. I was travelling on a coach somewhere between Sheffield and Leeds, when we took up a lad of fourteen or fifteen years of age; a rough country-looking boy, but well-mannered and of an intelligent countenance.

"I found upon conversation with him, that he belonged to a National School in the neighbourhood, which he was, he said, on the point of leaving. This gave me occasion to ask him various questions, which he answered with so much readiness and vivacity, yet without any self-conceit in his manner, that when the coach stopped (I think it was at Barnsley) for a short time, I took him with me into a bookseller's shop, and desired him to select some book which I might give him as a testimony of my approbation. After looking at a few which the bookseller recommended, he fixed on a "Selection from Bishop Wilson's Works," whose name, he said, he had often heard. He begged me to write his name in it, which I did, and we parted with mutual expressions of good-will; and I will be bold to prophesy that that boy (or young man as he must now be, if he is still alive) is giving by his conduct stronger testimony in favour of the National School System than a thousand of your speculating philosophers can bring against it."

"Well," said I, "you are apt to be sanguine in your views, but as I must confess they are very often right, so I will hope you may not have been deceived in this instance."

It so happened that two or three days after this conversation we were taking a walk together, and discussing various topics, such as the present state of things might well suggest, when we met a young man, a neighbour of mine, a mason, who detained us two or three minutes, while he asked my directions about some work he was doing for me.

After he was out of hearing,—"That," said I, "is one of the most respectable young men I know. Soon after I came here, more than four years ago, he married a young woman of a disposition similar to his own; and they live in that cottage that you see there, to the right of that row of beeches."

"I see it, I believe," said he, hardly looking the way I pointed, and not altogether seeming pleased at having our conversation thus interrupted.

"He has two or three little children, and I believe sometimes it goes hard with them, as in the winter work is short hereabouts, and he does not like beating about far from home. I sometimes tell him he ought to look farther; but he is so fond of his home, his wife and children, that I verily think he would rather live on potatoes seven days in the week with them, than have meat and beer by himself. And besides, I know he does not relish the companions he must work with at the town. However, on the whole, they do tolerably well, as they have a garden of a fair size, and he never spends an unnecessary penny."

"I am glad to hear it," said he; "but we were talking about the value of an apostolical succession in the ministry, were we not? and of the great ignorance and neglect now prevailing on the subject."

"We were," said I; "but to tell you the truth, though I have bestowed considerable attention on the subject, and examined the various opinions which have been put forth on it, yet I have scarcely learned so much hereon from the works of learned theologians, as I have from repeated conversations with that very young man we just now met."

"You surprise me," said he.

"You may be surprised, but it is however true, and (if you have no objection) I will tell you how it was."

"By all means," he answered.

"When I first came to the parish I looked about for some person to take charge of the Sunday School, as the master was old, and so deaf as to be unequal to the work. I was recommended to apply to Richard Nelson (that is the man's name),"—Here my friend interrupted me, saying, "Richard Nelson? why, now I remember, that was the very name of the boy I travelled with." "Indeed!" said I, "then doubtless it is the same person: for his age will agree with your account very well, and I know he was bred at —— National School." "Well," said he, "I am quite delighted to find myself a true prophet in this instance." "Perhaps," said I, "you will be still more pleased, when you have heard all I have to tell you: you will find that your little present was by no means thrown away." "Go on," said he, "I am all attention."

"I was telling you, I believe, that I requested Nelson to become master of the Sunday School. After some little hesitation, he declined my offer, under the plea that he could not give constant and regular attendance; though he was willing to attend occasionally, and render what assistance he could. So it was arranged that the old master should still remain; and I afterwards discovered that an unwillingness to deprive him of the little emolument, was Nelson's real reason for declining my offer. As the Sunday School is nearly three-quarters of a mile from my house, in a direction beyond Nelson's, along the Beech Walk, as we call it, it frequently happened that we joined in company as we went to and fro. We generally talked over such subjects as had reference to the School, or to the state of religion in general: and, amongst other topics, that on which you and I are conversing,—the authority of Christian ministers. I remember it was on the following occasion that the subject was started between us. I thought that I had observed one Sunday, that he was making the boys of his class (our School professes to be on the Bell System) that he was, I say, making his boys read the nineteenth and some other of the Thirty-nine Articles relating to the ministerial office: and that afterwards he was explaining and illustrating them, after his usual manner, by referring them to suitable parts of Scripture. On our walk homewards, I enquired if I was right in my conjecture. He said, Yes: and that, in the present state of things, he could not help thinking it quite a duty to direct the minds of young persons to such subjects. And on this and many subsequent occasions, he set forth his opinions on the matter, which I will state to you, as far as I can remember, in his own words.

"My good mother," he said, "not long before her death, which happened about half-a-year before I came to live here, said to me very earnestly one day, as I was sitting by her bed side.—'My dear Richard, observe my words: never dare to trifle with GOD ALMIGHTY.' By this I understood her to mean, that in all religious actions we ought to be very *awful,* and to seek nothing but what is right and true. And I knew that she had always disapproved of peoples' saying, as they commonly do, 'that it little matters what a man's religion is, if he is but sincere;' and 'that one opinion or one place of worship is as good as another.' To say, or think, or act so, she used to call 'Trifling with GOD'S truth:' and do you not think, sir (addressing himself to me), that she was right?"

"Indeed I do," said I.

"And," he said, "I was much confirmed in these opinions by constantly reading a very wise, and, as I may say to you, precious book, which a gentleman gave me some years ago, whom I met by chance when I was going to see my father in the infirmary. It is called a Selection from Bishop Wilson's Works, and there are many places in it which shew what his opinions were on this subject; and I suppose, sir, there can be no doubt that Bishop Wilson was a man of extraordinary judgment and piety."

"He has ever been considered so," I answered.

"I could not think much of any one's judgment or piety either, who should say otherwise," he replied; "and what Bishop Wilson says, is this, or to this effect:—That 'to reject the government of Bishops, is to reject an ordinance of GOD.'"[1]

That "our salvation depends, under God, upon the ministry of those whom JESUS CHRIST and the HOLY GHOST have appointed to reconcile men to GOD."[2]

That "the personal failings of ministers do not make void their commission."[3]

---

[1] Sacr. Priv.
[2] Serm. 88.
[3] Ibid.

That "if the Unity of the Church is once made a light matter, and he who is the centre of Unity, and in CHRIST'S stead, shall come to be despised, and his authority set at nought, then will error and infidelity get ground; JESUS CHRIST and His Gospel will be despised, and the kingdom of Satan set up again here as well as in other nations."[4] With many other expressions like these.

"And yet, Sir," he continued, "the gentleman who lives over there (pointing to a great house in sight four or five miles off down the valley), who is said to be a person of much learning, and who does a great deal of good, he does not take the matter in the same light. For he told a man of —— whom I was working with, that if a person preached what was right and good, that was the best sign of his being ordained a minister, without the ceremony of laying on a Bishop's hands upon his head. And the man that told me, very much admired the opinion, in regard (he said) of its being so very *liberal,* or some such word. Though I confess I could not exactly see what there was so much to admire. Because, if the opinion were true, it was good, and if it were false, it was bad, equally as much (to my thinking) whether it were called liberal or bigotted."

"Doubtless you were right," said I. "And," he proceeded, "it seemed to me (and I told the man so) like going round and round in a wheel, to say, If he is GOD'S minister, he preaches what is good; and if he preaches what is good, he is GOD'S minister. For still the question will be, what *is* right and good? and some would say one thing and some another; and some would say there is nothing right nor good at all in itself, but only as seems most expedient to every person for the time being. So for my own satisfaction, and hoping for GOD'S blessing on my endeavour, I resolved to search the matter out for myself as well as I could. My plan was this. First, to see what was said on the subject in the Church Prayer Book, and then to compare this with the Scriptures; and if, after all, I could not satisfy myself, I should have taken the liberty of consulting you, Sir, if I had been here, or Mr. ——, who was the minister at ——, where I came from."

"Yours was a good plan," I said; "but I suppose you had forgotten that the chief part of the Church Services which relate to these subjects, is not contained in the Prayer Books which we commonly use."

---

[4] Charge 1721.

"I was aware of that," he answered, "but my wife's father had been clerk of —— parish, and it so happened that the churchwarden had given him a large Prayer Book in which all the Ordination Services were quite perfect, though the book was ancient, and in some parts very ragged. This book my wife brought with her when we came here, and indeed she values it very highly on account of her poor father having used it for so many years. Thus you see, Sir, with the Bible and Prayer Book, and (as I hoped) GOD'S blessing on my labours, I was not, as you may say, unfurnished for the work."

"Indeed, Richard, you were not," I replied.

"Well then," he proceeded, "I first observed, that the church is very particular in not allowing any administration of the Sacraments, or any *public* service of ALMIGHTY GOD to take place, except when there is one of her Ministers to guide and take the lead in the solemnity. Thus not only in the administration of Baptism, and of the Lord's Supper, but in the daily Morning and Evening Prayers, in the Public Catechizing of Children, in the Solemnization of Marriage, in the Visitation of the Sick, and in the Burial of the Dead;—in all these cases the Christian congregation is never supposed complete, nor the service perfect, unless there be also present a minister authorized to lead the devotions of the people. And yet I also observed that neither minister nor people, not even with the leave of the Bishop himself, had power or authority given them to alter or vary from the Rules set down in the Prayer Book. And often have I thought how well it would be if Ministers and people too would be more careful to keep to the rules."

"Yes," said I, "it is too true; we are all to blame."

"But," he proceeded, taking a small Prayer Book out of his pocket, "the question I had next to ask was,—who are meant by these Ministers so often referred to in the Church Service. To this question I found a general answer in the Twenty-third, Twenty-sixth, and Thirty-sixth Articles; where the judgment of the Church is thus plainly given:—

1st. "That it is not lawful for any man to take upon him the office of public preaching, or ministering the Sacraments in the Congregation, before he be lawfully called and sent to execute the same."

2ndly. "That those *are* lawfully called and sent, who are chosen and called to the work by men who have public authority given them in the Congregation to call and send Ministers into the LORD'S vineyard."

3rdly. "That though sometimes evil men may have chief authority in the ministration of the Word and Sacraments; yet, forasmuch, as they do not the same in their own name but in CHRIST'S, and do minister by His commission and authority, we may use their ministry with full hope of GOD'S blessing."

4thly. "That whosoever are consecrated and ordained according to the Rites there prescribed, are rightly, orderly, and lawfully consecrated and ordained."

"But here, Sir, I will take occasion to ask you whether it would not have been better, instead of calling the second order of Ministers Priests, to have used the word which is frequently found in the New Testament applied to them, "Elders," or "Presbyters."

"Why," I said, "I have no doubt the wise and good men who framed the Prayer Book had a good reason for retaining the title of Priests. But in truth it is one of the very words you mentioned, only somewhat shortened by our forefathers in their pronunciation of it—Presbyter was made Prester, and that by degrees became Prest, or Priest."

"That," said he, "is very remarkable, and proves that we ought to enquire before we find fault. But to go on with what I was saying—I next proceeded to read over, and I assure you, Sir, I did it with great care, the three Services in our Great Prayer Book—namely, for Consecration of Bishops, Ordaining of Priests, and Making of Deacons. And I must confess to you that I could not but greatly admire them; and at the same time feel much astonishment at two considerations which they brought to my mind."

"What were they, Richard?" I enquired.

"The one was," he said, "to think that after such a solemn dedication to the ministry, there should be such a thing as a careless or a wicked Clergyman. And yet, Sir, is it not also astonishing that after such a solemn dedication of ourselves as we all make to GOD in Baptism, there should be such a thing as a careless or a wicked Christian?"

"So it is," I said, "when we judge others we condemn ourselves. But what was the other ground of your surprise?"

"Why, it was this; that there should be any doubt what the opinion of the Church is respecting the Christian Ministry. Comparing the Ordination Service with the Liturgy and Articles, it seems to me quite clear, that in the judgment of the Church, none can shew themselves duly authorized Ministers of CHRIST, who do not belong to one or other of the three orders, of Bishops, Priests, or Deacons.

"But, said I to myself, other Churches have erred, why may not this then be the misfortune of the Church of England also? and this very opinion may be one of her errors. You see then, Sir, the next thing I had to do was to consult the Scriptures on the subject, and (if it be not too bold in such a one as I to say so) to try the Prayer Book by the Bible."

"Your method was the best possible," I said. "But, if you please, do not use the expression, the Church *of* England, but the Church *in* England."

"Why indeed, Sir," said he, "in the present state of things perhaps it would be more proper. But to proceed with my enquiry. I first observed, that in the History of the Jews, as contained in the Old Testament, as well as in that of Christians in the New, the ALMIGHTY seems almost or quite always to have communicated His will to mankind through some chosen Minister; some one, whether it were angel or man, who could give suitable evidence of the authority by which he spoke or acted. But there seemed to me to be this great difference between Jews and Christians, in this as in other cases; that in the Jews' religion, all the rules and regulations were set down so plainly and distinctly, that no one could mistake their meaning; for instance, in the Levitical laws concerning the priesthood; of what family and tribe the Priests and High Priest should be, what their respective duties, and what their dress, &c. Whereas in the Christian religion, the rules and regulations, however important, and even necessary, are yet not so exactly set down. And I remember hearing a very good and wise Clergyman say in a Sermon at —— Church, that this is probably what St. James means, when he calls the Gospel 'a Law of Liberty;' namely, that its rules and directions are *not* so plainly set down, *on purpose,* that Christians might have freer space (I remember that was his expression) and opportunity, to exercise their Faith and Love for their Redeemer. And I have sometimes thought myself, that what St. Paul says about the difference between walking by faith and by sight, seems to suit the different cases of Jews and Christians. *They* walked by sight, *we* must walk by faith; and faith, in this world, we are told, can see but as through a glass darkly."

"It seems, so," I said.

He proceeded.

"With this view I went on to examine the New Testament, expecting to find therein some *general* instruction respecting the institution and authority of Ministers in the Christian Church. But I did not expect that these rules should be as particular and distinct as those on the same subject in the Old Testament, any more than I should expect to find a command to Christians to observe the LORD'S Day set down as distinctly as the command to observe the Sabbath was set down for the Jews. And yet, Sir, I suppose all will agree, that no one who wilfully neglects the LORD'S Day can be a true Christian."

"There are strange opinions now afloat," said I; "and if many despise the LORD'S Ministers, it is no wonder if many also despise the LORD'S Day."

"Indeed, Sir," said he, "it is not to be wondered at. But to go on with my statement. On carefully perusing the New Testament History, I remarked that our LORD did not grant ministerial authority to His disciples in general, but first to twelve, and then to seventy; that of those twelve, one was among the wickedest of mankind, and that our LORD knew his character when he appointed him (John 6:64, 13:18); that possibly some of those seventy also might be unworthy persons; that our LORD, just before His departure, gave what may be called a fresh commission to His Apostles, which they should act upon after His ascension; that after that event, the twelve Apostles were the leading persons in the Christian Church, having under them two orders or degrees, viz. Bishops (sometimes called Elders) and Deacons; that this threefold division of Ministers in the Church lasted as far as the New Testament History reaches, the Apostles having set men over different Churches with Apostolical authority, to preside during their absence, and to succeed them after their decease. This sufficiently appears from places in St. Paul's Epistles to Timothy and Titus."

"Do you remember any of the passages?" I asked him.

"I cannot," he said, "call to mind chapter and verse, but I have with me a little paper of memorandums which I use at the school, and which, if it be not too much trouble, I will thank you to look at,"

The paper was as follows:—for I thought it well to copy what he had written into my pocket memorandum-book.

It appears that Timothy had authority at Ephesus to check false or unedifying Teachers. 1 Timothy 1:3, 4;—to select persons proper to be ordained Bishops, 3:1-7;—and also Deacons, 3:8-13.

That he should have particular regard to the Elders who rule well, 5:17.

That he should be cautious of receiving accusations against Elders, 5:19.

That if any [Elders] were convicted it was his duty to reprimand them publicly, 5:20.

That in his decisions he should be strictly impartial, 5:21.

That he should be very cautious on whom he laid his hands, 5:22.

That Timothy was in a station, which even the rich and great might respect, 6:17.

That Timothy had been ordained by St. Paul himself, once, if not twice, 2 Timothy 1:6.

That at his ordination or consecration there was something remarkable in the *Sermon*, 1 Timothy 4:14, 1:18.

That he was to commit what he had heard from St. Paul to faithful men, who should be able to pass it on to others, 2 Timothy 2:2.

That Titus had authority to set in order what was wanting in the Cretan Church; Titus 1:5: and to ordain Bishops in every city; 1:5, 7.

That he was to be cautious whom he selected for this office, 1:6-9.

That he should rebuke false teachers sharply, 1:13.

That if Titus *himself* was a pattern of good works and a teacher of truth, *the whole Church* would gain credit, 2:7, 8.

That he should rebuke with all authority, 2:15.

That he should suffer no man to despise him, 2:15.

That after one or two admonitions he should reject heretical persons, 3:10.

"Now, Sir, it seems to me evident, from these and others similar passages, that there were certainly in the Church, *as far as the Testament History reaches,* 3 different ranks or orders of Ministers, one above the other."

"It is plainly so," I said.

"But," said he, "there was one point which rather perplexed me, and I was some time before I could make out such an explanation of it as was satisfactory to myself."

"What was that?" I asked.

"Why," said he, "it was this. I considered that any person to whom the Apostles granted apostolical authority (Timothy, for instance) was from that time higher than a Presbyter or Bishop, and yet could not properly be called an Apostle. What then could he be called? I at last remembered a place in Bishop Wilson's little book, which led me to reflect, that surely as there were Angels (whether it might mean guardians, or heavenly messengers, or missionary Bishops, as we might say) of the seven Churches in Asia,—so Timothy might have been called the Angel of the Ephesian Church; and Titus, of the Church of Crete; and the same in other cases. And it came into my thoughts, that, perhaps, after St. John's decease, whether out of humility, or because (the Churches being settled) the ministers need no longer be missionaries, the title of Apostles or Angels was laid aside, and that of Bishops limited to the highest of the three orders.

Thus I seemed to myself every where to have traced the three-fold order, down from the beginning of the Gospel; the authority and distinction peculiar to each being preserved, a difference in name only taking place.

Thus at first they were..............Apostles, Elders, Deacons.
After the decease of some of the
    Apostles or at least while
    St. John was yet living............Angels, Bishops, Deacons.
At some period, after St. John's
    decease...................................Bishops, Priests, Deacons.

"I do not see how, what you have said, can be contradicted," I replied.

"But," he proceeded, "there is one thing I must, Sir, confess to you, and it is this;—that I have often said to myself, what a comfort it would be, if it had pleased GOD to preserve to us some few writings of the good men who lived close after the Apostles, that so we might have known their opinion on matters of this kind: and we might have known, too, by what names *they* distinguished the different orders of Ministers, one from another. For, surely, what they would think most proper in such cases, must be safest of all rules for us to follow; unless (which is a thing not to be supposed) *their* rules should be contrary to those of the Apostles, as set down in Scripture. So, Sir, I have often thought, if any such writings could be found, what a precious treasure they would be."

"What," said I, "Richard, did you never hear of those who are called the Apostolic Fathers: Clement, Polycarp, Ignatius?"

"I believe I have heard of them," he answered; "but I observed, that you, Sir, and other Clergymen, scarcely ever notice them in your Sermons; and the man I mentioned just now told me that, Mr. Cartwright, who is the minister of the Independent Chapel at the Town, and who is reckoned to be a very learned man and an admired preacher,—that he should say in a Sermon, that the works of the Fathers were very imperfect, and their opinion not much to be trusted to."

"But," said I, "Richard, if a person, whose word you could take, were to shew you an old book written by persons who had seen our SAVIOUR; who had heard St. John and St. Paul preach, and had been well acquainted with them; should you not value such a book, and wish to know whether there was any thing in it, which could throw light on the history of those early times of the Church, and especially with reference to the subjects you and I have been now conversing on?"

"Indeed, Sir, I should," he said. "But if what Mr. Cartwright said is true, it is too much to expect that any such treasure should be found by us."

"No, Richard," I said, "it is not too much. The kind Providence of GOD has permitted some of the writings of those good men to be preserved to this day. And there is no more doubt that they are their genuine writings, than that Bishop Ken wrote the Evening Hymn, or Bishop Wilson that little book you like so much."

"If this is indeed as you say," he replied, "we have great reason to be thankful for such a proof of GOD'S care for His Church. But I beg you, Sir, to tell me, whether there is any thing in these writings you speak of, which confirms what I have been venturing to state to you as my opinion gathered from Scripture, concerning the threefold distinction of Christian Ministers."

"Next Sunday," said I, "you shall see and judge for yourself."

As we came home from Church in the afternoon of the following Sunday, he reminded me of my promise; and I gave him a written paper, containing a few extracts, which I had translated from the works of the Apostolical Fathers, telling him, that I might possibly have made a mistake here and there in the rendering, but that he might depend on such being the general force and meaning of the passages.

The Extracts I gave him were the following:—

"Clement, with other my fellow labourers." —*Phil. 4:3.*

"Ignatius and the holy Polycarp, the Bishop of the Smyrmæans, had formerly been disciples of the holy Apostle John." —*Martyrdom of S. Ignatius.*

※

"The Apostles, preaching throughout countries and cities, used to appoint their first fruits, after they had proved them by the Spirit, to be Bishops and Deacons of those who should hereafter believe." —*S. Clement to the Cor.*

"The Apostles knew that there will be dispute about the name of Bishoprick or Episcopacy, wherefore they appointed the aforementioned, and gave them authority beforehand, in order that if themselves should fall asleep, other approved men might succeed to their ministerial office." —*The same.*

"All of you follow the Bishop as JESUS CHRIST followed the Father; and the Presbytery as the Apostles; and reverence the Deacons as GOD'S ordinance. Let no man do any of those things which pertain to the Church without the Bishop. He that honoureth the Bishop, is honoured of GOD; he that doeth any thing without the privity of the Bishop, doeth service to the Devil." —*S. Ignat. to Smyrm.*

"Have regard to the Bishop, that GOD also may regard you. My soul for theirs who are subject to the Bishops, Elders, and Deacons; and may it be my lot to have a portion with them in God." —*S. Ignat. to Polycarp.*

"The Bishops who were appointed in the farthest regions are according to the will of JESUS CHRIST; whence it becometh you to go along with the will of the Bishop." —*S. Ignat. to the Ephes.*

"That ye may obey the Bishop and the Presbytery, having your mind without distraction, breaking one bread." —*The same.*

"Some indeed talk of the Bishop, yet do every thing without him: but such persons do not appear to me conscientious; on account of their congregations not being assembled strictly according to the commandment." —*S. Ignat. to the Magnes.*

"I exhort you to be zealous to do all things in divine concord: the Bishop presiding in the place of GOD, and the Presbyters in the place of the council of Apostles, and the Deacons (in whom I most delight) intrusted with the service of JESUS CHRIST." —*The same.*

"For as many as are GOD'S and JESUS CHRIST'S, these are with the Bishop." —*S. Ignat. to the Philadelph.*

"Be ye earnest to keep one Eucharist, for the flesh of our LORD JESUS CHRIST is one, and there is one cup in the unity of His blood, one altar, as one Bishop, together with the Presbytery, and Deacons, my fellow-servants." —*The same.*

"Hold to the Bishop, and to the Presbytery, and Deacons. Without the Bishop do nothing." —*The same.*

"When you are subject to the Bishop as to JESUS CHRIST, ye appear to me as living not according to man's rule, but according to JESUS CHRIST." —*S. Ignat. to the Trail.*

"He that without the Bishop, and Presbytery, and Deacon, doeth ought, that person is not pure in his conscience." —*The same.*

"Polycarp, and the Presbyters, who are with him, to the Church of GOD, sojourning at Philippi."—*S. Polyc. to the Philipp.*

"Being subject to the Presbyters, Deacons, as to GOD and CHRIST."—*The same.*

Two or three weeks afterwards, as we were walking homewards after Evening Service, he gave me back the paper, with expressions of great satisfaction and thankfulness; and added, that he blessed GOD for having led him to make the enquiry; and that he was sure, if many religiously-disposed persons, who now think little of such matters, would turn their minds to them without partiality, they would fear to separate from a Church like ours, which, whatever may be its imperfections, is substantially pure in its doctrine, and in the Apostolical Succession of its Ministry.

"Sir," said he, "I am a poor hard-working man, as you know: but the interests of my soul and of those dear to me, are of as great importance in the sight of ALMIGHTY GOD, and ought to be to me also, as if my lot had been cast in a higher station. It is to me, therefore, no matter of indifference (as many have told me it should be) what is the truth on these great subjects; but I am more and more sure that it is a Christian duty first to enquire into them, and, when we have found the truth, to act up to it, humbly but resolutely.

"The times are bad, I confess; but yet, young though I am, I do not expect, as the world now goes, to see them much better.

"What our LORD said about iniquity abounding, and love growing cold, seems to be but too suitable to our present slate. I have often thought it and said it, though I have seldom met with anyone who would agree with me in the opinion. The Church *of* England I can plainly see, more plainly perhaps than a person in a higher station, is in a manner gone. The Church *in* England, God be thanked, however afflicted, remains, and ever will, I trust,—whether the world smiles or frowns upon her.

"I have therefore determined, Sir, by GOD'S grace, to look to myself, my wife, and children; and not to trust the world to do us any good, either in time, or in Eternity.

"And if by following THE TRUTH now, we shall all be together hereafter in the Society of Prophets, Apostles, Saints, and Martyrs, you know then, Sir, we shall have nothing more to wish for, nothing more to fear; every doubt will be satisfied, every difficulty removed. And I assure you, Sir, it is the very comfort of my life to spend a portion of every Sunday, in looking forward to that happy time."

"God bless you, Richard," said I, as we parted at his garden gate. And, when I came home, I could not but fall on my knees and thank GOD for having given me such a Parishioner.

THOMAS KEBLE
December 4, 1833

TRACT 13: AD POPULUM
Sunday Lessons
The Principle of Selection

Among projected alterations in the Liturgy, not the least popular seems to be a very considerable change in the selection of the Sunday Lessons. People do not see, first of all, why such and such chapters are chosen out of the Old Testament, in preference to others, which they think more edifying. Secondly, they see no reason why the Church should not assign Proper Lessons to every Sunday from the New Testament, as well as from the Old.

One who hopes that he should not be found froward, were a change to be made by competent Spiritual Authority, begs leave, nevertheless, to submit, to all considerate lovers of the Prayer-Book, the following remarks on the two points specified above.

1.

Before people find fault with the selection of particular chapters, they ought to be tolerably certain that they understand the principle, on which the Lessons in general were selected. It is to be regretted, that we have remaining little, if any, historical evidence, touching the views of the Compilers of the Liturgy in that portion of their task. What we do know, amounts to this:—

In King Edward's Prayer-Books no distinction was made, as to appointing Lessons, between Sundays and other days of the week. The chapter of the Old Testament set down for the day of the month was read in course for the Sunday Lesson; as is the case still in regard of the New Testament. With a view to this, probably, the well-known notice was prepared, which now stands prefixed to the Second Book of Homilies, but in Strype's opinion belongs rather to the First Book.[1] "Where (i.e. whereas) it may so chance, some one or other chapter of the Old Testament to fall in order to be read upon the Sundays or Holidays, which were better to be changed with some other of the New Testament for more edification, it shall be well done to spend your time to consider well of such chapters before-hand." This came out first, as it seems, in 1560; and about the same time a Commission was given to Archbishop Parker, Bishop Grindal, and others; "to peruse the order of the Lessons, throughout the whole year, and to cause new Calendars to be printed." In pursuance of which the present Table of Sunday Lessons was prepared, and came out the same year. We may then consider it as Archbishop Parker's; and surely not one among the Reformers might be more thoroughly depended on for a sound practical view of things. Farther than this, we have no direct information. We must be guided, therefore, entirely by the internal evidence of the Lessons themselves.

The series begins from Septuagesima Sunday, because it was the custom of the early Church to read the Book of Genesis in Lent.[2] Let us examine them in their order, ending with the 6th Sunday after Epiphany in the following year. We shall find, if I mistake not, that the selection may be accounted for on this supposition, viz. That the arrangers desired to exhibit GOD'S former dealings with His chosen people *collectively,* and the return made by them to GOD, in such manner as might best illustrate His dealings with each *individual,* chosen now to be in His Church, and the snares and temptations most apt to beset us *as Christians.*

Certainly, there does exist a very wonderful analogy between these two cases, that of the Jewish nation delineated in the Bible, and that of a baptized Christian, as known by daily experience: an analogy most striking in itself, most clearly pointed out more than once in the New Testament, and very serviceable, if rightly understood, in many great points of faith

---

[1] Life of Parker, i. 167. 8vo.

[2] See Wheatley on the Common Prayer, ch. iii. sect. x. §. 4.

and practice. This analogy arises out of the fact, that Christians severally are, what the Jews collectively were, partakers of an especial Covenant.

It is to be supposed, that the Great Enemy has his peculiar way of dealing with souls placed in such a relation, as with parents, children, subjects, and others, according to *their* several relations. To exhibit such his purpose and proceedings, and to exemplify also the counteracting methods of Providence, seems to be one especial purpose of the historical portions of the Old Testament: in which the prophetical are here included.

To give an instance of what is here meant. One of the most prevailing temptations to unbelief and careless practice is the daily experience we have, of Christians behaving so very differently from what one should expect, *à priori,* in GOD'S elect. It does not seem as if, left to ourselves, we should have any adequate idea of the kind of hypocrisy described by Bishop Butler, in his Sermon on Self-deceit, and elsewhere; I mean, the temper which leads men to act towards GOD ALMIGHTY (whom, in theory and understanding, they own) as if it were in their power to deceive Him. To explain this for the benefit of those most in danger, seems one great purpose of the Old Testament: to explain it, I say, for the benefit of unworthy Christians, who may discern themselves, by anticipation, in the faithless demeanour of the Jews.

It is conceivable, that a series of extracts might be made, to illustrate this matter more particularly; i.e. on a principle of *admonition.* Would not such a series coincide, very nearly, with the Sunday Lessons?

Thus, the first and second chapters of Genesis represent man as at first placed in covenant with his Maker; the third, sixth, and ninth represent his fall, and the wonderful mixture of judgment and mercy which prepared him for the recovery, which God had in store for him, by virtue of a New Covenant. Then, follows the first definite step towards the establishment of that New Covenant: the call of Abraham, to be the select pattern and spiritual progenitor of all who shall ever be saved by it (Gen 12). And here again judgment is shewn mingled with mercy, and thorough probation accompanying both, by the two selected chapters of Abraham's history; the fall of Sodom, and the sacrifice of Isaac.[3] Then begins the account of Jacob and his family, the other great section of the

---

[3] Genesis 14, 22.

Patriarchal History; displaying on the one hand, the great danger of taking liberties with moral duty, under the notion of being favourites with God (for the subsequent misfortunes of Jacob's family are clearly traceable to that first want of faith); on the other hand, the mysterious ways of Providence, turning those misfortunes and errors into means for the great purpose of preparing a covenanted nation to take the place of the covenanted family.[4]

With Exodus begins the history of that nation, which may perhaps not improperly be styled the appropriate type of each *backsliding* Christian, as Abraham we know was the type of the *faithful*. The chapters selected shew, first, GOD preparing the way for their election;[5] then their reluctant acceptance of the favour,[6] next, the actual process of their deliverance;[7] the whole being so arranged, that this latter shall correspond with the season of Easter; which is indeed (so to speak) the *point of sight* of the whole Christian Calendar, as the passover is of the Jewish.

But to proceed:—The Lessons from Easter to Whit-Sunday (taking into account the great days of Easter-week and Ascension) are so many specimens of the transgressions of the elect people, and of the methods taken to chastise or reclaim them.[8] The case of Balaam, most evidently, needs not to be excepted from this account; for never was a clearer analogy than between him and the Jewish people; they murmuring and rebelling with the Shechinah before their eyes; he coveting the reward of iniquity, perhaps plotting seduction in his heart, while he heard the words of GOD, and saw the vision of the ALMIGHTY. No analogy can be more exact; except it be that between the same miserable man and a Christian baptized, sinning against faith and knowledge.

The Lessons for Trinity-Sunday, as was natural, interrupt for one week the progress of the history, for the purpose of reviewing the whole course. The mind is carried back, first, to GOD'S original intent in creating man after His own image;[9] next, to the appointed condition or mean, by which that image is to be regained; viz. the imitation of Abraham's faith.[10]

---

[4] Genesis 27, 24, 29, 42, 43, 45.
[5] Exodus 3.
[6] Exodus 5.
[7] Exodus 9, 10, 12, 14.
[8] Exodus 16, 17, 20, 32; Numbers 16, 22-25; Deuteronomy 4-10, 12-13, 16, 30.
[9] Genesis 1.
[10] Genesis 18.

In effect, they rehearse to us both Covenants; that of Paradise, and that of the Gospel.

Resuming our view of the covenanted *people,* we contemplate them first victorious,[11] peaceful, and comparatively innocent, renewing their engagements with their Maker in the days of Joshua;[12] in the days of the Judges backsliding and factious, but not yet deliberately unbelieving;[13] next, trained by Eli's sons to irreverence for holy things;[14] and so, not ill-prepared to apostatize, by choosing a king on principles of accommodation and worldly policy.[15]

The gradual degeneracy and downfall of that unhappy king[16] (the emblem of the Jews of his time, as Balaam had been of a former generation), and the substitution of one of better mind, are continued through a chain of Lessons, to the excision, long after his death, of almost all that remained of his family.[17]

But, in the mean time, a new source of sin and misery had arisen in the family of David himself. His personal sins, indeed, were fast followed by sincere repentance, and therefore obtained speedy pardon;[18] but *because* they were the sins of one with whom a peculiar covenant had been made,[19] they drew down the severest temporal judgments; the sword never departed from his house; and, by the dissentions which arose in his time,[20] a way was prepared for the schism and two-fold apostasy, first heretical and afterwards infidel, of the greater part of the chosen people. These, with GOD'S endeavours to reclaim them by the warnings of Elijah and Elisha,[21] and by the sword of Jehu,[22] are traced in the chapters taken from the Books of Kings, from the first curse on Jeroboam's schismatical altar, till the final reprobation and captivity of the ten tribes.[23] In the course of which history, especial emphasis is laid, first on the misfortunes incurred by the nameless prophet from Judah, by king Jehoshaphat and others, for their licentious communication with the heretical and idolatrous tribes,[24] secondly, on the extension of GOD'S favour to the Gentiles, in two

---

[11] Joshua 10.
[12] Joshua 23.
[13] Judges 4-5.
[14] 1 Samuel 2-3.
[15] 1 Samuel 12.
[16] 1 Samuel 13, 15, 17.
[17] 2 Samuel 21.
[18] 2 Samuel 12, 24.
[19] Psalm 89, 2 Samuel 12:14.
[20] 2 Samuel 19.
[21] 1 Kings 13, 17-19, 21-22.
[22] 2 Kings 9-10.
[23] 2 Kings 18.
[24] 1 Kings 13, 22; 2 Kings 9-10.

instances[25] for ever memorable; which extension, we may believe, was virtually a signal warning to His then elect people.

At length we arrive at the last sad scene of the history; the downfall of the Church of Judah also. We behold a temporary amendment in the days of Hezekiah, occasioned by the combination of miraculous mercy to herself, with judgment on Samaria in her sight.[26] But we presently read of her thorough relapse; of her resistance to the example and efforts of good Josiah;[27] of her sensuality[28] and oppression,[29] her neglect[30] and contempt[31] of warnings, all accompanied with high pretences to civilization, and a certain kind of orthodoxy. All these, *her dealings with GOD,* are delineated at large by Jeremiah. In the Lessons from Ezekiel we have revealed more of *GOD'S dealings with her.* He peremptorily orders his message to be delivered, whether men will hear, or whether they will forbear.[32] He denounces the false prophets, preaching peace where there was no peace; and discovers their secret and vulgar artifices.[33] He answers pretences from feigned conformity, from reliance on the remnants of good in the land;[34] and again, from an affected perplexity at the supposed inequality of his proceedings.[35] He recapitulates, by special message, all their past conduct, *as* His chosen people:[36] a summary, answering with marvellous exactness to the sad experience of the Christian world. When all these had failed, He utters, in two fearful parables, a final sentence of direct reprobation.[37] All this we have set before us from Ezekiel. The Lessons from Daniel[38] serve to show that the chosen people were not yet abandoned; they keep alive hope, and exemplify faith, triumphing in the worst of times; which is also the drift of the prophecy selected from Joel. Then Micah is introduced, like Samuel and Ezekiel, recapitulating the whole course of the probation of the elect;[39] and Habakkuk,[40] extending the judgment to their oppressors, and reasserting the condition required on their part to make their election not a curse but a blessing. "The just by his faith shall live."

---

[25] 1 Kings 17; 2 Kings 5.
[26] 2 Kings 18-19.
[27] 2 Kings 23.
[28] Jeremiah 5.
[29] Jeremiah 22.
[30] Jeremiah 35.
[31] Jeremiah 36.
[32] Ezekiel 2.
[33] Ezekiel 13.
[34] Ezekiel 14.
[35] Ezekiel 18.
[36] Ezekiel 20.
[37] Ezekiel 24.
[38] Daniel 3, 6; Joel 2.
[39] Micah 6.
[40] Habakkuk 2.

Finally, the readings from the Proverbs[41] of Solomon bring the warning home, so to speak, to every man's own door. Taken in connexion with all that had gone before, they turn GOD'S miraculous proceedings with the Jews into an available sanction of righteousness, for the meanest man's use on the slightest occasion.

And now, the year drawing to a close, and the mysterious time of Christmas approaching, our Mother, with true parental anxiety, takes up, as it were, the thread of her instructions anew, at that point of the fortunes of Israel, to which the circumstances of civilized and Christian Europe, especially those of our own country, during the comparatively few years which have passed since the arrangement of the Prayer-Book, may reasonably be thought to correspond most nearly. The Church reverts to the time of Hezekiah, and selects the prophecy of Isaiah as the fittest to prepare the mind for Christ's two Advents. By the confession of some, who are most apt to find fault, her selection here has been most appropriate. Witness the sins reproved in the Jews; their formality,[42] pride,[43] oppression, drunkenness, presumption, sophistical self-deceit;[44] their impatience of primitive truth, and reliance upon mere worldly expedients.[45] Witness again the wonderful mixture of triumph and desolation, judgments and mercies, *foretold;*[46] such as might seem impossible to be accomplished together, at one and the same time, among one and the same people. Yet we seem to behold both accomplished; the one in the *tendencies* of the Gospel, and what it performs for the faithful privately; the other, in men's ordinary way of receiving it, and what may be called its public failure. The very denunciations against idolatry,[47] by some, perhaps, accounted an outward sin, how well do they apply to the various apostasies, which men contrive for themselves now, and say, to one after another, Deliver me, for thou art my GOD! The summaries of past *national* mercies,[48] how truly do they represent what is now done for each redeemed and sanctified soul! And as to the anticipation of mercies and judgment *to come*,[49] they do not only *correspond* to the revelations of the New Testament, but we have the express authority of our LORD and St.

---

[41] Proverbs 1, 3, 6-17, 19.
[42] Isaiah 1.
[43] Isaiah 2.
[44] Isaiah 5.
[45] Isaiah 30.
[46] Isaiah 24, 26, 32, 41, 43, 49, 55, 60, 64-66.
[47] Isaiah 44, 46.
[48] Isaiah 43, 51.
[49] Isaiah 65-66.

Paul[50] for believing, that, of both, language was purposely used (in the purpose, I mean, of the Holy Spirit) which *literally refers* to the life and death everlasting, the sanctions of GOD'S covenant with every Christian singly.

This hasty and brief sketch may serve to point out the thread of warning, which, it is conceived, runs through the Sunday Lessons, and renders it very improper to deal with them as if they had been taken at random, or might fitly be changed at will, for others supposed in themselves more edifying.

Whether Archbishop Parker and his coadjutors had this connexion in view, as it is not, perhaps, possible to ascertain, so neither is it very material. But that they must have had *some special* rule of selection in their minds is plain, from the fact mentioned above, that they had just before authorized the Clergy, provisionally, to read what each thought, *prima facie*, most edifying.

The idea, therefore, according to which it is now wished to new-model the Lessons, had occurred to them, and the result shows that they did not think it, on the whole, the most instructive way. Perhaps the fact of its spontaneous evolution (if such an expression may be allowed) would make it appear so much the more delicate, and tampering with it so much the more perilous. For, on that supposition, it must be more than humanly interwoven with the very staple of the Scripture History. But, supposing it designed, it may have been suggested by the tenour of the Invitatory Psalm, commonly called, *Venite exultemus;* which Psalm had been used daily in the Church quite down from primitive times. Many persons, probably, have asked themselves, why that Psalm in particular should be preferred above the many of the same general tenour, for unremitting use in the Church daily. The answer probably may be found in the grave monitory warnings at the end; which, by the case of the Jews in the wilderness, describe so forcibly the position and peculiar danger of a *chosen* people. That one Psalm may, on reflection, give the key to the arrangement of the Lessons; allowing, of course, for the interruption

---

[50] St. Mark 9:44. comp. Isaiah 66:24.
1 Corinthians 2:9 comp. Isaiah 64:4.

sometimes caused by the special matter of some great Christian Festival. In general, however, the course of the Lessons will be found adapting itself, with exquisite felicity, to the course of the Festivals also.

Occasionally, the Archbishop's choice may have been influenced (in subordination, however, to the great principle) by the connexion of the portion of history with some offence which required warning, but, from the weakness of human nature, was very likely to pass unnoticed. The thirty-fourth of Genesis, and the fifth of Jeremiah, are instances. When men shrink from reading those chapters, they bear witness instinctively to the wisdom and kindness of the Church in ordering them to be read.

Whatever may be one's private opinion, it is not necessary here to maintain, that the general principle suggested above was the very best on which selection might proceed, or that the very aptest chapters of all have been selected in each instance. But clearly, if such a principle be at all recognized, it ought to be most carefully kept in view, whatever insertions or omissions are proposed. Many persons seem to think, that questions of this sort are settled, if on merely comparing the present Lesson with the proposed substitute, it appear that the one, taken singly, is more edifying than the other. But this will not hold, if it be a mistake altogether to take any one singly and apart. The quantity of edification may be greater on the whole by completing the proposed narrative or argument, though on this or that particular day the impression made may be less. To neglect this consideration partakes of the same error, as if one should reckon all preaching nugatory, which did not expressly place the highest matters of faith in the most affecting point of view. If Christianity be a great *system,* such a test of preaching must be incorrect: and if the Sunday Lessons be a *series,* it will never do to censure any one chapter as unedifying, except you can produce one more edifying, which would come in equally well at the same point of the series.

I will take the example which appears to myself the most doubtful in the whole Calendar. At first sight, almost any one would say, that 2 Samuel 21 might with great advantage be changed for 1 Kings 3 or 8, the dream of Solomon, or the dedication of the Temple. Not so, perhaps, when we come to recollect, that the melancholy tale of the ruin of Saul's family is completed in the first-mentioned chapter, and with it the denunciation of such perverse conduct as drew down the curse upon him.

The other chapters, however instructive in themselves, can hardly with so much propriety be said to make part of the system of *warning*.

And surely those who, in whole or in part, are for disturbing that system, should look to it, that they be well provided with somewhat, *on the whole,* more edifying, in its room. Else they may go far towards depriving the Church of a great help to practical knowledge, and to the true use of the Old Testament. Inadequate views of that portion of God's Word have ever been found fruitful in heresy, filling men's hearts with perplexity and irreverence. Can it be denied, that our own times show fearful symptoms in that quarter? There is room for not a little anxiety, surely, lest a clue to many Scripture difficulties, so necessary to the people's welfare, and (may we not say?) so providentially put into the Pastor's hands, should be let drop, because some of us do not always clearly see which way it is leading them.

It may be said, the alterations proposed would not amount to a disturbance of the general system. This the writer begs leave to doubt; since it is conceived a very moderate alteration, which shall include all the following particulars, "some (at least three I suppose) of the Proper Lessons for the Sundays in Lent, five chapters in Deuteronomy, two in Jeremiah, four in Ezekiel," and the principles on which these are made specimens of "omittenda," would as well justify the omission of at least twenty more. Either, therefore, the rule of selection adopted by Archbishop Parker must be renounced, or other chapters must be found, completing his idea as accurately as these do: which latter, it is imagined, would prove a difficult task.

2.

The other matter proposed for enquiry is less important, and may be dismissed in a few words. Why, it is asked, should there not be Lessons from the New Testament *proper* for every Sunday in the year, as well as for a few great days? In answer to which it may be observed, first, that there *are,* generally, two such Lessons, always one, read in the Communion Service. Only that which is called The Second Lesson, varies with the day of the month. Of the reasons which, in point of fact, led to the continuance of this latter arrangement, I am not aware that any record remains. But it appears to be accompanied with two incidental advantages, which some may think considerable enough to render alteration unadviseable, without very clear proof of greater benefit likely to arise from it.

One of these advantages is, the standing memorial thus afforded to the people, that there was once such a thing as a Daily Service; that such is the system and wish of our Church, and the theory on which the Prayer-Book is constructed. It is an intelligible hint, that a Churchman's devotion was not meant to be all narrowed into the Sunday. The Services of that holy day were but to be a continuance and an expansion of those due on the other days; not a totally distinct thing. This we are weekly reminded of, by the very place in the Calendar, where we must look for the Second Sunday Lesson. The value of the hint people of course will estimate more or less highly, according to their sense of the importance of a *Daily Service,* and of the responsibility which Churchmen have incurred by letting it drop so very quietly in almost every parish of the kingdom.

The other advantage of these varying Second Lessons (and it will be found in practice a very considerable one) is this; that it presents the Old and New Scriptures in endless variety of mutual combinations, the more striking because they are unforeseen, and in a certain sense casual. The thought is happily expressed by Herbert, thus addressing Holy Scripture:—

> "O that I knew how all thy lights combine,
> And the configurations of their glory;
> Seeing not only how each verse doth shine,
> But all the constellations of the story!"

Very much help, both for pastors and people, both for giving and receiving instruction, may be gathered (if the writer deceive himself not concerning the results of his own experience) by attending to this hint yearly, as the *varying* Psalms and Second Lessons come successively into conjunction with the *unvarying* First Lessons, Epistles, and Gospels. To note and collect the scattered lights will be found in itself a most engaging and interesting task, and it will serve in no slight degree to impress considerate minds, from time to time, more deeply with the fulness, the harmony, the condescension, of the Word of Life.

These reasons are respectfully addressed to those, who, in their anxiety for immediate visible edification, appear somehow to overlook the fact, that the Church Lessons are a *series,* arranged according to certain general principles. Scruples, and feelings of different kinds, occurring to this or that person as to the use of *particular* passages, must be met, of course, on their own grounds; except so far as they ought to be silenced by the overpowering advantage, which may appear to arise by adhering to the general principle of selection.

At any rate, it is much to be wished, that *very free talking,* and *very cheap publishing,* in behalf of such changes, were carefully avoided. Is there not something even *cruel,* in raising scruples and niceties, and unpleasant associations of various kinds, among those who as yet happily have never dreamed of criticising the Bible? If change is wanted, let proper reasons be *quietly* submitted to *competent* authorities. But let us not appeal lightly, and at random, to the sense of an irreverent presumptuous age, on one of the most sacred of all subjects.

JOHN KEBLE
December 5, 1833

TRACT 14: AD POPULUM

The Ember Days

In reading the Epistles of St. Paul we cannot but observe how earnestly he presses upon those to whom he was writing, the duty of praying for a blessing on himself and his ministry. We not only find his request contained in general terms, "Brethren, pray for us" (1 Thess 5:25), but when he feels he stands in need of any particular support, he mentions it as an especial subject of prayer for the Churches. For instance, in writing to the Romans, at a time when he was looking forward to trouble from Jewish unbelievers, he says to them, "Strive together with me in your prayers to GOD for me, that I may be delivered from them that do not believe in Judæa" (15:30), and in Philippians 1:19 he expresses a confidence that the very opposition he was meeting with would, through the intercession of the Saints, be turned into a good to himself. "I know that this shall turn to my salvation through your prayer." It is the same when he has any object at heart, which he desires to see accomplished. He longs much for the spread of the Gospel, and therefore, in 2 Thessalonians 3:1 he says, "Finally, Brethren, pray for us, that the word of GOD may have free course and be glorified." And feeling his own weakness to discharge the sacred trust committed to him, he asks the Ephesians to make supplication in his behalf, "that utterance might be given unto him, that he might open his mouth boldly, to make known the mystery of the Gospel" (6:15, 19). I shall mention but one passage more, that in 2 Corinthians 1:11; for here not only the duty of praying for their Apostle is pressed upon the people, but they are bidden to do so for the express purpose that they might also join in expressing thanks that their prayer had been graciously heard. "Ye also helping together by prayer for us, that, for the gift bestowed on us by the means of many persons, thanks may be given by many on our behalf" (Compare Col 2:4; Heb 13:19; Phlm 22).

These texts show clearly, that it is the Christian's duty to pray at all times for the Ministers of the Gospel. There are other texts which teach that supplication ought particularly to be made for them at the time of their Ordination. We find, that, when our LORD was about to send forth His twelve Apostles to preach His kingdom, "He went out into a mountain to pray, and continued all night in prayer to God" (Luke 6:12). And when one of those Apostles had by transgression fallen from his Ministry, the whole Church united in supplication to God, that He would shew whom He had chosen to succeed him (Acts 1:24, 25). The same is observable in the Ordination of the first Deacons, where it is said, the multitude set them before the Apostles, and "when they had prayed, they laid their hands on them" (Acts 6:6). Again, when Paul and Barnabas are sent forth on their special mission, "the Church fasted and prayed" for them (Acts 13:3). And St. Paul in turn observed the same practice, when he ordained Elders in the Churches where he had preached. "They prayed with fasting, and commended them to the LORD, on whom they believed" (Acts 14:23).

In conformity to this Apostolical custom, the Church of England views with peculiar solemnity the times at which her Ministers are ordained; and invites all her members to join, at these sacred seasons, in prayer and fasting in their behalf. It is the object of these pages to bring this subject especially before the reader's notice; for the observance of this ordinance of the Church has fallen so generally into disuse, that few comparatively feel the value of it; and some perhaps are not even aware of its existence. To those who may be in this case, I would say briefly that the Ordination Sundays occur four times a year, and that the days of fasting, or Ember days (as they are called) are in the week immediately before those respective Sundays. These days are as follows; the Wednesday, Friday, and Saturday after the first Sunday in Lent; after the Feast of Pentecost; after September 14; after December 13; as may be seen by referring to the Prayer-Book. And particular prayers are ordered during the whole of the weeks, in which these days occur; that the Bishops may make a wise and faithful choice, and that those who are to be called to the Ministry, may especially be blessed with GOD'S grace and heavenly benediction.

That such a practice is good and right in itself, and could not fail to produce a large benefit, cannot be doubted by those, who believe that prayer is the appointed channel whereby GOD is pleased to send mercies on mankind. He that feels the truth of "Ask, and it shall be given you," cannot deny, that he is losing a great privilege, whenever he neglects this duty. And if there is any Order of men who more especially need the help of others' supplications, it is that of those, who are called to the high office of ministering the Word of Life to their fellow-creatures, and of being labourers together with their Divine Master in bringing men to salvation. I would go further than this, and say, that if there is any time when the Ministers of the Gospel more particularly call for the prayers of the Church, it is at these seasons of Ordination. Whether we consider the solemn office which the Bishops are performing, or the solemn vows which the Priests and Deacons are taking on themselves, we must allow that it is an occasion of the greatest importance. Here are a number of men going forth for the great work of winning back to Christ souls which have gone astray from the right path, and of fighting in the first ranks against the world, the flesh, and the devil; and in most cases going forth young and inexperienced in their work, not knowing (for who can know till he has tried?) the dangers and difficulties which beset them. Surely it is the duty of every Christian to give them what help he can, and send them forth strengthened for the labours of their journey.

I doubt not that there are many in this kingdom, who are in the habit of making supplication to GOD for their Ministers; many who join heartily in the several prayers of the Church Services, where mention is made of them, as well as remember them in their private devotions. And some of these may ask, of what advantage it is to appoint particular days for such intercession. They may say, "we pray daily for the Clergy, and not unfrequently for those who are just entering their Ministerial life. Why should one day be fixed upon as better than another for this purpose? Let each do as he finds opportunity." I would answer, first, that if it was the custom of the Apostles to set apart the times of Ordination for especial prayer, as well as the regulation of our own Church, it is no longer a matter of indifference to us whether we adopt this method or not. The example of the one, and the injunction of the other, mark plainly for us what we ought to do. But, secondly, there will be advantages to ourselves in taking the course so recommended; I would mention one or two which appear to be of importance.

1. When men have been at all careless and indifferent about any duty (and how few are there who can say that they have not been careless in this matter?), it is very useful to have some settled way for beginning it aright. What has long been put off from time to time is seldom properly attended to, if we leave the performance of it to any chance opportunity that may be offered. The convenient season will seldom come, or at least will not come to us in so profitable a way. For setting apart a particular occasion for solemn prayer, brings with it more seriousness and attention, and makes us think far more of the value of the blessing for which we ask.

2. And, secondly, I would remind all those who value the promises of the Bible, that there is an especial blessing promised to *united* prayer. Our Lord says, "If two of you shall agree on earth, as touching any thing they shall ask, it shall be done for them of MY FATHER which is in Heaven" (Matt 18:19). And when a good is sought for all, all ought to be seeking for it, and "striving together," that it may be obtained. Now this could not be done, except days were appointed, which all may know of as a standing Ordinance; and to be able to join together in spirit, however far apart they are in body. We might thus not only in all parts of this kingdom, but in distant lands, wherever our Brethren are residing, unite in sending up supplications, which our common FATHER would not fail to hear and answer abundantly. And when engaged in prayer we should have the great comfort and support of knowing that we are not single, but that others are perhaps mentioning what we are leaving out; and that others have more earnestness and devotion than we feel in ourselves.

Should this paper fall into the hands of any who have never before heard or thought seriously of this Institution, it may be useful to offer a few hints for its better observance. Let each consecrate the days as much as possible to prayer and holy meditation, adding to them religious Fasting, if health permit. The true end of fasting is beautifully expressed in the Collect for the first Sunday in Lent; "using such abstinence, that our Flesh being subdued to the Spirit, we may ever obey our LORD'S godly motions in righteousness and true holiness." It is to give the mind liberty and ability to consider and reflect while it is actually engaged in Divine Service, or preparing for some solemn part of it; to humble ourselves before GOD under a sense of our sins, and the misery to which they expose us; to deprecate His anger, and to supplicate His mercy and favour.[1] We must use it in the same spirit in which Daniel did, when he set himself to pray for pardon for his own and his brethren's sins, and sought "the LORD GOD with prayer and supplication, and fasting, and sackcloth, and ashes" (Dan 9:3).

The subjects for prayer on the Ember days will be the Church of GOD of which we are members; especially those who are called to bear office in the same; and of these more particularly those who are either ordaining or being ordained. But our Petitions need not stop with these. These are seasons, in which every Minister should be remembered before the throne of grace, in which every Bishop, Priest, and Deacon, claim the prayers of the People. We may ask for them, that their doctrine may be sound and pure, and may come to the hearts of their hearers; that they may diligently labour in their several spheres of action, for the glory of GOD and the good of mankind; above all, that they may themselves lead holy lives, such as are consistent with their high profession. And, because we are so much more earnest in prayer when we are asking for particular things, and those which we feel to need ourselves, we may make especial mention of our own Clergyman, and our own Bishop, praying that the light, which shines on them, may be reflected on our own neighbourhood. For the same reason, if we happen to know of any trouble or trial, to which the Sacred Ministry near us is exposed, we may mention this also. Additional subjects of meditation will arise according to the particular Ember days which we are celebrating. In those in Lent, we shall have more particularly before us our LORD'S example of prayer and fasting, and ask for His Ministers, that they may be like Him, in retiring from the world and overcoming worldly snares and temptations. In those in Whitsun-week, we shall remember our SAVIOUR'S words, that His disciples would fast when He was taken from them, think much of the HOLY SPIRIT, which is vouchsafed to them to supply His absence, and implore GOD that on us in our day this precious Blessing may be given abundantly. And again in those in Advent, we shall reflect on the near approach of the anniversary of our LORD'S birth, reflect on His forerunner, the self-denying Baptist, who was filled with the Holy Ghost from His mother's

---

[1] Nelson's Festivals and Fasts, p. 358.

womb, and pray that the "ministers and stewards of His mysteries may like him prepare the way for CHRIST'S second coming."

The times in which we live will furnish additional ground for supplication. We cannot but see, that there is a great struggle going on between good and evil; and that, while we trust true Religion is increasing, it cannot be denied that Infidelity and Opposition to lawful authority, whether of GOD or man, is increasing likewise. And, especially, as regards our own Church, we cannot shut our eyes to the fact, that she has many and powerful enemies, both visible and invisible, and that wicked spirits and wicked men are seeking to undermine and overthrow her. The thought of these evils on all sides will naturally lead us to Him, who alone can protect us from them.

These remarks are written, in the hope that those who read them will ask themselves honestly, whether they have not been guilty of neglecting the proper observance of the Ember days; and whether the revival of the primitive custom of keeping them might not be attended with a great national blessing; whether it might not be a means under GOD of averting the dangers which surround us. Many are now lamenting that we have in some respects lost sight of that "godly discipline," which the Church orders for the good of her members. But ought we not to seek a restoration of what is lost, as well as lament for it; and seriously set ourselves to the most effectual way of gaining what we need? And again, many are crying out against the faults of the Church, but have any a right to do so, till they themselves have tried every means in their power of amending what they feel to be an evil? And can we say, that we have tried every means, as long as an Institution like that of which I have been speaking, so edifying, and so likely to gain a blessing, is so generally neglected?

ALFRED MENZIES
December 12, 1833

TRACT 15

On the Apostolical Succession in the English Church

When Churchmen in England maintain the Apostolical Commission of their Ministers, they are sometimes met with the objection, that they cannot prove it without tracing their orders back to the Church of Rome; a position, indeed, which in a certain sense is true. And hence it is argued, that they are reduced to the dilemma, either of acknowledging they had no right to separate from the Pope, or, on the other hand, of giving up the Ministerial Succession altogether, and resting the claims of their Pastors on some other ground; in other words, that they are *inconsistent* in reprobating Popery, while they draw a line between their Ministers and those of Dissenting Communions.

It is intended in the pages that follow, to reply to this supposed difficulty; but first, a few words shall be said, by way of preface, on the doctrine itself, which we Churchmen advocate.

The Christian Church is a body consisting of Clergy and Laity; this is generally agreed upon, and may here be assumed. Now, what we say is, that these two classes are distinguished from each other, and united to each other, by the commandment of God Himself; that the Clergy have a commission from GOD ALMIGHTY through regular succession from the Apostles, to preach the gospel, administer the Sacraments, and guide the Church; and, again, that in consequence the people are bound to hear them with attention, receive the Sacraments from their hands, and pay them all dutiful obedience. I shall not prove this at length, for it has been done by others, and indeed the common sense and understanding of men, if left to themselves, would be quite sufficient in this case. I do but lay before the reader the following considerations.

1. We hold, with the Church in all ages, that, when our LORD, after His resurrection, breathed on His Apostles, and said, "Receive ye the HOLY GHOST,—as My FATHER hath sent Me, so send I you;" He gave them the power of sending *others* with a divine commission, who in like manner should have the power of sending others, and so on even unto the end; and that our LORD promised His continual assistance to these Successors of the Apostles in this and all other respects, when He said, "Lo I am with you," (that is with you, and those who shall represent and succeed you,) "alway, even unto the end of the world."

And, if it is plain that the Apostles left Successors after them, it is equally plain that the Bishops are these Successors. For it is only the Bishops who have ever been called by the title of Successors; and there has been actually a perpetual succession of these Bishops in the Church, who alone were always esteemed to have the power of sending other Ministers to preach and administer the Sacraments. So that the proof of the doctrine seems to lie in a very small space.

2. But, perhaps it may be as well to look at it in another point of view. I suppose no man of common sense thinks himself entitled to set about teaching religion, administering Baptism and the LORD'S Supper, and taking care of the souls of other people, unless he has *in some way* been called to undertake the office. Now, as religion is a business between every man's own conscience and GOD ALMIGHTY, no one can have any right to interfere in the religious concerns of another with the authority of a teacher, unless he is able to shew, that God has in some way called and sent him to do so. It is true, that men may as *friends* encourage and instruct each other with consent of both parties; but this is something very different from the office of a Minister of religion, who is entitled and called to exhort, rebuke, and rule, with all authority, as well as love and humility.

You may observe that our LORD Himself did not teach the Gospel, without proving most plainly that His FATHER had sent Him. He and His Apostles prove their divine commission by miracles. As miracles, however, have long ago come to an end, there must be some *other* way for a man to prove his right to be a Minister of religion. And what other way can there possibly be, except a regular call and ordination by those who have succeeded to the Apostles?

3. Further, you will observe, that all sects think it necessary that their Ministers should be ordained by other Ministers. Now, if this be the case, then the validity of ordination even with *them* rests on a *succession;* and is it not plain that they ought to trace that succession to the Apostles? Else, why are they ordained at all? And, any how, if *their* Ministers have a Commission, who derive it from private men, much more do the Ministers of our Church, who actually do derive it from the Apostles. Surely those who dissent from the Church have *invented* an ordinance, as they themselves must allow; whereas Churchmen, whether rightly or wrongly, still maintain *their* succession not to be an invention, but to be GOD'S ordinance. If Dissenters say, that *order* requires there should be some such *succession*, this is true, indeed, but still it is only a testimony to the mercy of CHRIST, in having, as Churchmen maintain, *given us* such a succession. And this is *all* it shows; it does nothing for *them;* for, their succession, not professing to come from God, has no power to restrain any fanatic from setting up to preach of his own will, and a people with itching ears choosing for themselves a teacher. It does but witness to a need, without supplying it.

4. I have now given some slight suggestions by way of evidence for the doctrine of the Apostolical Succession, from Scripture, the nature of the case, and the conduct of Dissenters. Let me add a word on the usage of the Primitive Church. We know that the Succession of Bishops, and ordination from them, was the invariable doctrine and rule of the early Christians. Is it not utterly inconceivable, that this rule should have prevailed from the first age, everywhere, and without exception, had it not been given them by the Apostles?

But here we are met by the objection, on which I propose to make a few remarks, that, though it is true there was a continual Succession of pastors and teachers in the early Church who had a divine commission, yet that no Protestants can have it; that we gave it up, when our communion ceased with Rome, in which Church it still remains; or, at least, that no Protestant can plead it without condemning the Reformation itself, for that our own predecessors then revolted and separated from those spiritual pastors, who, according to our principles, then had the commission of JESUS CHRIST.

Our reply to this is a flat denial of the alleged facts on which it rests. The English Church did *not* revolt from those who in that day had authority by succession from the Apostles. On the contrary it is certain that the Bishops and Clergy in England and Ireland remained the same as before the separation, and that it was these, with the aid of the civil power, who delivered the Church of those kingdoms from the yoke of Papal tyranny and usurpation, while at the same time they gradually removed from the minds of the people various superstitious opinions and practices which had grown up during the middle ages, and which, though never formally received by the judgment of the whole Church, were yet very prevalent. I do not say the case might never arise, when it became the duty of private individuals to take upon themselves the office of protesting against and abjuring the heresies of a corrupt Church. But such an extreme case it is unpleasant and unhealthy to contemplate. All I say here is, that this was not the state of things at the time of the Reformation. The Church then by its proper rulers and officers reformed itself. There was no new Church founded among us, but the rights and the true doctrines of the Ancient existing Church were asserted and established.

In proof of this we need only look to the history of the times. In the year 1534, the Bishops and Clergy of England assembled in their respective Convocations of Canterbury and York, and signed a declaration that the Pope or Bishop of Rome had no more jurisdiction in this country by the word of God, than any other foreign Bishop; and they also agreed to those acts of the civil government, which put an end to it among us.[1]

The people of England, then, in casting off the Pope, but obeyed and concurred in the acts of their own spiritual Superiors, and committed no schism. Queen Mary, it is true, drove out after many years the orthodox Bishops, and reduced our Church again under the Bishop of Rome, but this submission was only exacted by force, and in itself null and void; and, moreover, in matter of fact it lasted but a little while, for on the succession of Queen Elizabeth, the true Successors of the Apostles in the English Church were reinstated in their ancient rights. So, I repeat, there was no revolt, in any part of these transactions, against those who had a

---

[1] Vid. Collier, Eccl. Hist. v. ii. p. 94.

commission from God; for it was the Bishops and Clergy themselves, who maintained the just rights of their Church.

But, it seems, the Pope has ever said, that our Bishops were bound by the laws of God and the Church to obey *him;* that they were subject to him; and that they had no right to separate from him, and were guilty in doing so, and that accordingly they have involved the people of England in their guilt; and, at all events, that *they* cannot complain of their flock disobeying and deserting them, when they have revolted from the Pope. Let us consider this point.

Now that there is not a word in *Scripture* about our duty to obey the Pope, is quite clear. The Papists indeed say, that he is the Successor of St. Peter; and that therefore he is Head of all Bishops, because St. Peter bore rule over the other Apostles. But though the Bishop of Rome was often called the Successor of St. Peter in the early Church, yet every other bishop had the *same* title. And though it be true, that St. Peter was the *foremost* of the Apostles, that does not prove he had any *dominion* over them. The eldest brother in a family has certain privileges and a precedence, but he has no power, over the younger branches of it. And so Rome has ever had what is called the *primacy* of the Christian Churches; but it has not therefore any right to interfere in their internal administration; not more of a right, than an elder brother has to meddle with his younger brother's household.

And this is plainly the state of matters between us and Rome, in the *judgment of the Ancient Church* also, to which the Papists are fond of appealing, and by which we are quite ready to stand or fall. In early times, as is well known, all Christians thought substantially alike, and formed one great body all over the world, called the Church Catholic, or Universal. This great body, consisting of a vast number of separate Churches, with each of them its own Bishop at its head, was divided into a number of portions called Patriarchates; these again into others called Provinces, and these were made up of the separate Dioceses or Bishopricks. We have among ourselves an instance of this last division in the Provinces of Canterbury and York, which constitute the English Church, each of them consisting of a number of distinct Bishopricks or Churches. The Head of a Province was called Archbishop, as in the case of Canterbury and York; the Bishops of those two sees being, we know, not only Bishops with Dioceses of their own, but having, over and above this, the place of precedence among the Bishops in the same Province. In like manner, the Bishop at the head of a Patriarchate was called the Patriarch, and had the place of honour and certain privileges over all other Bishops within his own Patriarchate. Now, in the early Christian Church there were four or five Patriarchates; e.g. one in the East, the Head of which was the Bishop of Antioch; one in Egypt, the Head of which was the Bishop of Alexandria; and, again, one in the West, the Head of which was the Bishop of Rome. These Patriarchs, I say, were the Primates or head Bishops of their respective Patriarchates; and they had an order of precedence among themselves, Rome being the First of them all. Thus the Bishop of Rome, being the first of the Patriarchs in dignity, might be called the honorary Primate of all Christendom.

However, as time went on, the Bishop of Rome, not satisfied with the honours which were readily conceded to him, attempted to gain *power* over the whole Church. He seems to have been allowed the privilege of *arbitrating* in cases of appeal from other Patriarchates. If, e.g. Alexandria and Antioch had a dispute, he was a proper referee; or if the Bishops of those Churches were at any time unjustly deprived of their sees, he was a fit person to interfere and defend them. But, I say, he became ambitious, and attempted to *lord it* over God's heritage. He interfered in the internal management of other Patriarchates; he appointed Bishops to sees, and Clergy to parishes which were contained within them, and imposed on them various religious and ecclesiastical usages illegally. And doing so, surely he became a remarkable contrast to the Holy Apostle, who, though inspired, and an universal Bishop, yet suffered not himself to control the proceedings even of the Churches he founded; saying to the Corinthians, "not for that we have dominion over your faith, but are helpers of your joy; for by faith ye stand" (2 Cor 1:24). This impressive declaration, which seems to be intended almost as a prophetic warning against the times of which we speak, was neglected by the Pope, who, among other tyrannical proceedings, took upon him the control of the Churches in Britain, and forbade us to reform our doctrine and usages, which he had no right at all to do. He had no right to do so, because we were altogether independent of him; the English and Irish Churches, though in the West, being exterior to his Patriarchate. Here again, however, some explanation is necessary.

You must know, then, that from the first there were portions of the Christian world, which were not included in any Patriarchate, but were governed by themselves. Such were the Churches of Cyprus, and such were the British Churches. This need not here be proved; it is confessed by Papists themselves. Now, it so happened, in the beginning of the 5th century, the Patriarch of Antioch, who was in the neighbourhood of Cyprus, attempted against the Cyprian Churches, what the Pope has since attempted against us; viz. took measures to reduce them under his dominion. And, as a sign of his authority over them, he claimed to consecrate their Bishops. Upon which the Great Council of the whole Christian world, assembled at Ephesus, A.D. 431, made the following decree, which you will find is a defence of England and Ireland against the Papacy, as well as of Cyprus against Antioch.

"An innovation upon the Rule of the Church and the Canons of the Holy Fathers, such as to affect the general liberties of Christendom, has been reported to us by our venerable brother Rheginus, and his fellow Bishops of Cyprus, Zeno, and Evagrius. Wherefore, since public disorders call for extraordinary remedies, as being more perilous, and whereas it is against ancient usage, that the Bishop of Antioch should ordain in Cyprus, as has been proved to us in this Council both in words and writing, by most orthodox men. We therefore decree, that the Prelates of the Cyprian Churches shall be suffered without let or hindrance to consecrate Bishops by themselves; and moreover, that the *same rule shall be observed also in other dioceses and provinces every where, so that no Bishop shall interfere in another province, which has not from the very first been under himself and his predecessors;* and further, that, if any one has so encroached and tyrannized, he must relinquish his claim, that the Canons of the Fathers be not infringed, nor the Priesthood be made an occasion and pretence for the pride of worldly power, nor the least portion of that freedom unawares be lost to us, which our Lord JESUS CHRIST, who bought the world's freedom, vouchsafed to us, when He shed His own blood. Wherefore it has seemed good to this Holy Ecumenical Council, that *the the rights of every province should be preserved pure and inviolate, which have always belonged to it, according to the usage which has ever obtained,* each Metropolitan having full liberty to take a copy of the acts for his own security. And, should any rule be adduced repugnant to this decree, it is hereby repealed."

Here we have a remarkable parallel to the dispute between Rome and us; and we see what was the decision of the General Church upon it.

It will be observed, the decree is past *for all provinces in all future times*, as well as for the immediate exigency. Now this is a plain refutation of the Romanists on their own principles. *They* profess to hold the Canons of the Primitive Church; the very line they take, is to declare the Church to be one and the same in all ages. Here then they witness against themselves. The Pope *has* encroached on the rights of other Churches, and violated the Canon above cited. Herein is the difference between his relation to us, and that of any civil Ruler, whose power was in its origin illegally acquired. Doubtless we are bound to obey the Monarch under whom we are born, even though his ancestor were an usurper. Time legitimises a conquest. But this is not the case in spiritual matters. The Church goes by *fixed laws;* and this usurpation has all along been counter to one of her acknowledged standing ordinances, founded on reasons of universal application.

After the Canon above cited, it is almost superfluous to refer to the celebrated rule of the First Nicene Council, A.D. 325, which, in defending the rights of the Patriarchates, expresses the same principle in all its simple force and majesty.

"*Let the ancient usages prevail,* which are received in Egypt, Libya, and Pentapolis, relative to the authority of the Bishop of Alexandria; as they are observed in the case of the Bishop of Rome. And so in Antioch too, and other provinces, let the prerogatives of the Churches be preserved."

On this head of the subject, I will but notice, that, as the Council of Ephesus controlled the ambition of Antioch, so in like manner did St. Austin rebuke Rome itself for an incroachment of another kind on the liberties of the African Church.

Bingham says,

"When Pope Zosimus and Celestine took upon them to receive Appellants from the African Churches, and absolve those whom they had condemned, St. Austin and all the African Churches sharply remonstrated against this, as an irregular practice, *violating the Laws of unity,* and the settled rules of ecclesiastical commerce; which required, that no delinquent excommunicated in one Church should be absolved in another, without giving satisfaction to his own Church that censured him. And therefore, to put a stop to this practice, and check the exorbitant power which Roman Bishops assumed to themselves, they first made a Law in the Council of Milevis, That no African Clerk should appeal to any Church beyond sea, under pain of being excluded from communion in all the African Churches. And then, afterwards, meeting in a general Synod, they dispatched letters to the Bishop of Rome, to remind him how contrary this practice was to the Canons of Nice, which ordered, That all controversies should be ended in the places where they arose, before a Council and the Metropolitan."[2]

Thus I have shown, that our Bishops, at the time of the Reformation, did but vindicate their ancient rights; were but loyal, grateful, and therefore jealous champions of the honour of the old Fathers, and the sanctity of their institutions; were but acting in the magnanimous spirit of that Apostle, who bade us "stand fast in the liberty wherewith Christ hath made us free."—For true magnanimity consists in neither encroaching nor submitting to encroachment: in taking our rights as we find them, and using them; or rather in regarding them altogether as trusts, the responsibility of which we cannot avoid. As the same Apostle says, "Let every man abide in the same calling, wherein he is called." And, if England and Ireland had a right to assert their freedom under any circumstances, much more so, when the corruptions imposed on them by Rome even made it a duty to do so.

I shall answer briefly one or two objections, and so bring these remarks to an end.

1. First, it may be said, that Rome has withdrawn our orders, and excommunicated us; therefore we cannot plead any longer our Apostolical descent. Now I will not altogether deny, that a Ministerial Body might become so plainly apostate, as to lose its privilege of ordination. But, however this may be, it is a little too hard to *assume*, as such an objection does, the very point in dispute. *When* we are proved to be heretical in doctrine, then will be the time to begin to consider, whether our heresy is of so grievous a character as to invalidate our orders; but, *till then*, we may fairly and fearlessly maintain, that our Bishops are still invested with the power of ordination.

2. But it may be said, on the other hand, that, if we do not admit ourselves to be heretic, we necessarily must accuse the Romanists of being such; and that therefore, on our own ground, we have really no valid orders, as having received them from an heretical Church. True, Rome is

---

[2] Bingh. Antiq. xvi. 1. §14.

heretical now; but she was not an heretical Church in the primitive ages. She has apostatized, but it was at the time of the Council of Trent. Then it was that the whole Roman Communion bound itself by a perpetual bond and covenant to the cause of Antichrist.[3] But before that time, grievous as were the corruptions in the Church, no individual Bishop, Priest, or Deacon, was bound by oath to the maintenance of them.[4] Extensively as they were spread, no Clergyman was shackled with obligations which prevented his resisting them; he could but suffer persecution for so doing. He did not commit himself in one breath to two vows, to serve faithfully in the Ministry, and yet to receive all the superstitions and impieties which human perverseness had introduced into the most gracious and holiest of God's gifts. On the contrary, we may say with the learned Dr. Field, "that none of those points of false doctrine and error which Romanists now maintain, and we condemn, were the doctrines of the Church before the Reformation constantly delivered or generally received by all them that were of it, but doubtfully broached, and devised without all certain resolution, or factiously defended by some certain only, who as a dangerous faction adulterated the sincerity of the Christian verity, and brought the Church into miserable bondage."[5] Accordingly, acknowledging and deploring all the errors of the dark ages, yet we need not fear to maintain, that after all they were but the errors of individuals, though of large numbers of Christians; and we may safely maintain, that they no more interfere with the validity of the ordination received by our Bishops from those who lived before the Reformation, than errors of faith and conduct in a priest interfere with the grace of the Sacraments received at his hands.

---

[3] The following is from the Life of Bernard Gilpin, vid. Wordsworth's Ecclesiastical Biography, vol. iv. p. 94. "Mr. Gilpin would often say that the Churches of the Protestants were not able to give any firme and solid reason of their seperation besides this, to wit, that the Pope is Antichrist.... The Church of Rome kept the rule of faith intire, untill that rule was changed and altered *by the Council of Trent, and from that time it seemed to him a matter of necessitie to come out of the Church of Rome,* that so that Church which is true and called out from thence might follow the word of God . . . . . . But he did not these things violently, but by degrees."

[4] The Creed of Pope Pius IV, in which every Roman Priest professes and promises to maintain all the errors of Popery, was only imposed *after* the Council of Trent.

[5] See Field on the Church, Appendix to book iii. where he proves all this. See also Birkbeck's Protestant's Evidence.

3. It may be said, that we throw blame on Luther, and some of the foreign Reformers, who *did* act without the authority of their Bishops. But we reply, that it has been always agreeable to the principles of the Church, that, if a Bishop taught and upheld what was contrary to the orthodox faith, the Clergy and people were not bound to submit, but were obliged to maintain the true religion; and if excommunicated by such Bishops, they were never accounted to be cut off from the Church. Luther and his associates upheld the true doctrine of the Church; and though it is not necessary to defend *every* act of fallible men like them, yet we are fully justified in maintaining, that their conduct generally in defending the truth against the Romish party, even in opposition to their spiritual rulers, was worthy of great praise. At the same time it is impossible not to lament, that they did not take the first opportunity to place themselves under orthodox Bishops of the Apostolical Succession. Nothing, as far as we can judge, was more likely to have preserved them from that great decline of religion, which has taken place on the Continent.

WILLIAM PALMER
revised and completed by
JOHN HENRY NEWMAN
December 13, 1833

TRACT 16: AD POPULUM
Advent

The name Advent, which means Coming, is given to the four Sundays immediately before Christmas-day, the feast which celebrates our LORD'S coming in the flesh to suffer for us. This season, then, is set apart by the Church, in accordance with ancient and venerable usage, in the first place, to prepare the minds of her children, by holy meditation, for welcoming with more devout and heartfelt joy that great day, the day of CHRIST'S Nativity. But her services at this solemn time are also directed to another object, very closely connected with the former; viz. to lead our thoughts onward to that *second* coming of our Lord and Master "in His glorious Majesty to judge the quick and the dead," which the Church is still expecting and anxiously looking for. These two subjects are very closely blended in the services of this season, as indeed there is much naturally to unite them in our thoughts and feelings; for the promise of Christ's *second* coming is to *us*, what the hope of His *first* coming was to *the Jews*. And therefore, while we go back in our thoughts to the time when Christ appeared in the flesh, and to the state of the Jewish Church at that time, we must apply all to the searching out of our own spirits, whether we are like holy Simeon and Anna, and the faithful few, who "waited for redemption in Jerusalem," or rather like the great mass of the people, who thought only of worldly and temporal things, and so rejected their King when He appeared among them. Let us here examine, what help the Church will give us in comparing our own privileges and condition with those of GOD'S ancient people.

The Collects for the Sundays in Advent, those at least for the first three Sundays, are very much formed upon the language of the Epistles, with more or less reference to the Gospels. It will be right, then, to look first to the Epistles, and from them try to learn, how, as members of the Christian Church, we are to prepare for the second awful coming of our Lord and Master.

1. We are awakened, then, in the Services of the first Sunday, by the warning voice of an Apostle, that "now it is high time to awake out of sleep;" that "the night is far spent,—the day is at hand;" that we must therefore, without delay, "cast off the works of darkness, and put on the armour of light." Just so the Jewish Church was awakened by the voice of one crying in the wilderness, "Prepare ye the way of the LORD;" the message of John the Baptist was the same as the Apostle's to us—"*Repent ye*, for the kingdom of heaven is *at hand*." He was to "turn the heart of the fathers to the children, and the disobedient to the wisdom of the just;" he was to be the Elias who was "to restore all things;" and accordingly the prophecy in which his mission was foretold, after vehement rebukes and warnings to the Jewish people, concluded with a solemn exhortation to them to "*remember the law* of GOD'S servant Moses, which he commanded in Horeb for all Israel, with the *statutes and the judgments*" (Mal 4). In like manner St. Paul urges upon *us* the solemn *Law* which has been given to the *Christian Church*, the "*new commandment*," by which *we* shall be tried, when the Messenger of the Covenant comes again to His Temple. The Apostle has been giving many precepts of Christian practice (ch. 12, 13), but it seems as if he heard his Master's voice, "Behold, I come quickly," and so the more anxiously sounded in our ear the simple commandment which He left us, to "love one another." "He that *loveth* another, hath *fulfilled* the Law. *Love* is the *fulfilling of the Law*. And that, knowing the time; the day is at hand; let us therefore walk honestly as in the day, *not in strife and envying*. But put ye on the LORD JESUS CHRIST." And now, having seen and felt *what* CHRIST will seek for, when He comes into His temple, we may profit duly by the awful lesson which we learn in the Gospel. The Jews had long been looking impatiently for the promised Deliverer (Mal 2:17, 3:1), and when they saw Him riding into Jerusalem as the Prophet had foretold, they cried, saying, "Hosanna to the Son of David, Blessed is He that cometh in the name of the LORD; Hosanna in the highest!" Meanwhile, what were the thoughts of the "meek and lowly"

King? His forerunner had been despised, the Law of Moses had not been "remembered," the hearts of the fathers were not turned to the children, nor the hearts of the children to the fathers;—and He was now coming to "smite with a curse" (Mal 4:6). And when He came near, He beheld the city and wept over it; He went into the temple, and cast out the buyers and the sellers and the money changers, as a type and signal of that still more fearful clearing of His Temple, when He laid Jerusalem even with the ground, and her children within her, and gave the privileges of His chosen to the Gentile world. Such fearful vengeance was taken of those who "refused Him that spake on earth;" how then "shall we escape if we turn away from Him that speaketh from heaven?"—we, who have "received the kingdom which cannot be moved;" who are come not to Horeb, but unto *Mount Sion,* "unto the city of the living GOD, the *heavenly Jernsalem.*" Surely it becomes *us* to listen to the affectionate warnings of the Church, as she awakens us from our slumber, and recounts our high duties and our inestimable privileges.

2. In the services of the Second Sunday we have the first great privilege of the Church brought before us, viz. that in the Church we have preserved to us those Holy Scriptures, in which is set before us "the blessed hope of everlasting life." "The promises made to the fathers" have now been fulfilled; and as they "through patience and comfort of the Scriptures" had "hope" of CHRIST'S first coming, and through Him of life and immortality, so we, having the same sure word of prophecy, may look onward to the day of the Church's final redemption, and anticipating that coming of Christ's kingdom for which we daily pray, and that "life everlasting," in which we daily profess our belief, may "abound in hope through the power of the HOLY GHOST." Meanwhile the influence which Holy Scripture is intended to have upon the Christian Church, is strikingly put before us in the *context* of the Epistle. St. Paul has been enforcing the duty of mutual forbearance by the argument of CHRIST'S example; "for even CHRIST pleased not Himself . . . . Now the GOD of patience and consolation grant *you* to be *like-minded one towards another, according to* CHRIST JESUS; that ye may with *one mind and one mouth* glorify GOD, even the Father of our LORD JESUS CHRIST. *Wherefore receive 'ye one another, as* CHRIST *also received us,* to the glory of GOD.'" The faith of the Holy Catholic Church, grounded upon GOD'S "Holy Word," is the bond of unity; a link which so binds together the

congregation of the faithful every where, that there is but "one body and one spirit." And in that Christian Temple the worshippers so speak "as one, to make one sound to be heard in praising and thanking the Lord,"—the "Holy, Holy, Holy LORD GOD of Sabaoth;"—that "the house is filled with a cloud," the special presence of the Great Author of peace and Lover of Concord, "the Father of our LORD JESUS CHRIST, our only Saviour, the *Prince of peace*."[1] And when we recollect the deep and earnest tones of CHRIST'S last solemn prayer before He suffered, that the Church might be one in itself and in Him through the faith which He had given it; and when again we remember, that the sentence of His judgment-seat, when He shall come the second time in His glory, will be grounded on the relation between Himself as the Head of the Church, and His brethren as its members,—a relation so close, that what has been done unto them, He considers as done unto Him; and what has been denied to them, as denied to Him (Matt 25); we shall surely return with a feeling of deeper humiliation to the Church's Advent Prayer, that we may have "grace to cast off the works of darkness, and to put on the armour of light;" that so, when "He shall come again in His glorious Majesty to judge the quick and the dead," those Holy Scriptures, which were given to His Church for our learning, may not rise up in judgment against us for our neglect of that new and great commandment, the observance of which was to be the distinctive characteristic of His disciples.

    3. But fresh privileges and responsibilities are brought before us in the services of the Third Sunday in Advent. For we have in the Church not merely "Holy Scriptures written for our learning," but Ministers of Christ and Stewards of the mysteries of GOD, sent to prepare and make ready the way for His second coming, that we may then be found an acceptable people in His sight. We might have been left to derive from Scripture by our own unaided efforts its rich and glorious contents "for doctrine, for reproof, for correction, for instruction in righteousness;" but our merciful FATHER has dealt otherwise with His Church under each dispensation. For the Baptist, who heralded CHRIST at His coming, though "more than a prophet," was but the successor of a "goodly company," whom GOD had raised up from time to time to vindicate the Law and to foreshew the Gospel. "But he that is least in the kingdom of

---

[1] Prayer for Unity.

GOD is greater than he." The prophet of *the ancient Church* had for his main office to enforce the Law, to shew GOD'S people their transgression and their sin; if he spoke of the Gospel, it was in prospect only, and seen afar off. The Messengers sent to *us* are a "Ministry of reconciliation," Ministers and Stewards of the mysteries of redemption, with power and commandment, as ambassadors of CHRIST, to declare and pronounce to GOD'S people, being penitent, the blessed tidings of forgiveness, and in the preaching of His word and the distribution of His sacraments to convey and apply its benefits to each individual member of CHRIST'S body. And does not this great blessing entail upon us a heavy responsibility? Let us learn from the Church how such a gift should be received; she instructs us in the words of St. Paul's admonition to the proud and schismatical Church of Corinth. The Apostle bids them look upon himself and his fellow-labourers as *Ministers of CHRIST*, responsible to their own Master, and to be judged by Him alone; as men who thought it a very small thing that even their own consciences acquitted them, or that in man's judgment they were preferred and made the head of a party; who were Stewards, and therefore required to be faithful to Him who gave them their commission; and who sought to have "praise" not of man but "of GOD," in that solemn day of His appearing, when He should "bring to light the hidden things of darkness and make manifest the counsels of the heart." And if we had imbibed more deeply St. Paul's spirit, we should less resemble than (it is to be feared) we sometimes do, the contentious Corinthians, or the multitudes who flocked to the wilderness to the Baptist's preaching, as if it had been some spectacle for idle curiosity (Matt 11). Wisdom would be justified of all her children, even in our judgment; we should see them all to be Ministers and Ambassadors of GOD, and our commendations and censures would be turned into prayers on their behalf, such as the Church has taught us, that like the Baptist they "may likewise so prepare and make ready the way of CHRIST, by turning the hearts of the disobedient to the wisdom of the just, that at His second coming to judge the world, we may be found an acceptable people in His sight." And in this way too, as well as in faith in the inspired Word, we should promote the fulfilment of CHRIST'S commandment of love; for it was for this purpose that He has commissioned the Ministers and Stewards of His word and sacraments. St. Paul tells us, "He gave some, apostles; and some, prophets; and some, evangelists; and some, pastors and teachers; for the *perfecting of the saints*, for the work of the ministry, for the *edifying of the body of* CHRIST; *till we all come* in the *unity of faith* and of the knowledge of the SON of GOD unto a perfect man, unto the measure of the stature of the fulness of CHRIST; that we henceforth be no more children, tossed to and fro, and carried about with every wind of doctrine, but, speaking *the truth* in *love*, may grow up unto Him in all things which is the Head, even Christ; from whom *the whole body*, fitly *joined together* and *compacted* by that which every joint supplieth, according to the effectual working in the measure of every part, maketh increase of the body unto the edifying of itself in love" (Eph 4:11-16).

4. And now, having reviewed the privileges with which we are favoured in CHRIST'S Holy Church, until His coming again, we are solemnly warned in the Epistle of the fourth Sunday, as before in that of the first, of His near approach; "The LORD is at hand." And if we indeed lived answerably to our privileges as members of CHRIST'S Church and household, we should be able to await the fulfilment of the promise in the spirit of calm confidence and joy, which St. Paul describes in the verses that follow; "the peace of GOD which passeth all understanding," "keeping our hearts and minds by CHRIST JESUS." The passage which is chosen for the Gospel, places us at the point of time when CHRIST was on the eve of appearing as "the Lamb of GOD which taketh away the sin of the world." He had been baptized, and was now returning from the wilderness; for it was "the next day," we read, that the Baptist pointed Him out to the notice of His disciples. He was already standing among them, though they knew Him not, ready to baptize them with the HOLY GHOST and with fire. And so now, in these latter days, the Heralds of CHRIST'S second coming are warning the people that He is at hand, and like the Baptist, referring to the Scripture for a proof that they are duly commissioned to prepare His way before Him. Like Him they tell the Church of a "salvation ready to be revealed," of "times of refreshing" to come "from the presence of the LORD," of times "of the restitution of all things," and of the more glorious establishment of CHRIST'S kingdom; and in earnest looking for the promise, they offer up the prayer of the Church that GOD would be pleased to raise up His power and come among us, and with great might succour us. But, while we hope for the *promise*, we must not forget the *threatening;* the Baptist spoke of CHRIST'S coming with His fan in His hand, and of the separation which

He would make between the chaff and the wheat (comp. Mal 4); but what were the days of vengeance upon the Jewish Church compared with those which *we* must expect, when the time is at length come that judgment must begin at the house of GOD, and the heavenly Reaper thrusts in His sharp sickle and reaps the earth? "The LORD, *whom ye seek*, shall suddenly come to His temple; behold He shall come, saith the LORD of HOSTS; but *who* may abide the day of His coming, and *who* shall stand when He appeareth?" We find that when JESUS was coming nigh to Jerusalem, on the day of His triumphant entry, because they thought that the kingdom of GOD should immediately appear, He added and spake a parable; it was the parable of the talents (Luke 19). And so, when we are disposed to indulge in bright anticipations of coming glory to the Church, let us rather turn our thoughts inward to our own individual privileges and individual responsibility, remembering that the kingdom of GOD is *within* us, and that to whomsoever much is given, of him will be much required. And especially let us remember that among the gifts given to us, for which we must give account, are, the New Commandment of love, the Inspired Word of GOD, written for our learning, and His duly appointed Ministers sent before Him to prepare us for His coming.

BENJAMIN HARRISON
December 17, 1833

TRACT 17: AD POPULUM
The Ministerial Commission
A Trust from Christ for the Benefit of His People

It will be acknowledged by all who have followed the Jewish Church through her days of suffering, and who have learnt the deep feeling of our own impressive Litany, that the main strength of the Church of GOD, in her times of trial and danger, is in the lowliness of her humiliation before her heavenly Guardian, for her many imperfections and sins. But there is another element of her strength, which, it is to be feared, is sometimes forgotten, though not less essential to her character; I mean, her firm and unshaken reliance upon the promises of GOD made to her. Thus in Daniel's prayer there are the most heart-broken confessions of sin in the name of his Church and people; but, at the same time, there is throughout a stedfast hope of God's mercy, as pledged to His holy city and temple. "O LORD, righteousness belongeth unto Thee, but unto us confusion of face, as at this day; to our kings, to our princes, and to our fathers, because we have sinned against Thee." "O LORD, *according to all Thy righteousness*, I beseech Thee, let thine anger and thy fury be turned away from Thy *city Jerusalem,* Thy *holy mountain;* because for our sins, and for the iniquities of our fathers, *Jerusalem* and Thy *people* are become a reproach to all that are about us. O LORD, hear; O LORD, forgive; LORD, hearken and do; defer not, for *Thine own sake,* O my GOD: for *Thy city and Thy people are called by Thy Name.*" It can scarcely be necessary to remind the members of our own Church, how beautifully the close of her Litany breathes the spirit of Daniel's prayer; how, in the midst of reiterated supplications for GOD'S forgiveness and mercy, now addressed more especially to the SON, now to the FATHER, now to every Person of the Blessed and Holy Trinity, now in the prevailing words which CHRIST Himself has taught us; supplications so deeply expressive of "the sighing of a contrite heart, the desire of such as be sorrowful,"—there still break in a gleam of faith and hope in the memory of the noble works which we have heard with our ears, and our Fathers have declared unto us, a strong yet humble confidence, that GOD will yet again arise and help us, and deliver us for His Name's sake, and for His Honour.

Now this is a point which it is of great importance to have strongly impressed upon our minds; because it is to be feared, that there are many of our brethren in the present day, who allow the thoughts of present and past transgressions, of our own sins, and those of our Fathers, to banish entirely the remembrance of the glorious promises and privileges which belong to us. They see so much neglected, and so much to be done, that they think it would become us each to work in lonely humiliation, "in fear and in much trembling," instead of endeavouring to magnify our office, and cheer one another with the songs of Zion. Now, I would ask, if this notion exist in any of our brethren, whether, under the semblance of good, it does not argue something of mistaken feeling, and that in more than one essential point.

1. Does not this opinion seem to imply the supposition that the dignity conferred on the Ministerial Office is something given for the exaltation of the Clergy, and not for the benefit of the people? as if there were a different interest in the two orders, and, in maintaining their Divine appointment, the Clergy would make themselves "lords over GOD'S heritage?" I do not now enter upon the point, that to magnify the *office* is not necessarily to exalt the *individual* who bears it; nay, that the thought which will most deeply humble the individual, most oppress him with the overwhelming sense of his own insufficiency, is the consciousness "into how high a dignity, and to how weighty an office and charge" he has been called; an office "of such excellency, and of so great difficulty." I would now rather ask, *for whose benefit* this high and sacred Office has been instituted? For the Clergy, or for the people? The Apostle will decide this point: "He gave some, Apostles; and some, Prophets; and some, Evangelists; and some, Pastors and Teachers; for the *perfecting of the saints*, for the work of the ministry, *for the edifying of the body of CHRIST*" (Eph 4:11-12). "All things are *yours*, whether Paul, or Apollos, or Cephas"

(1 Cor 3:22). And this, it should be well observed, the Apostle says on purpose to put an end to that *exaltation* of individuals, which the Church of Corinth had fallen into from forgetting that their pastors and teachers were all *"Ministers of* CHRIST;*"* Ministers by whom they believed *"even as the* LORD *gave to every man."* And so again to the same Church, and in reference to the same subject, St. Paul says, "All things are *for YOUR sakes,* that the *abundant grace* might, through *the thanksgiving of many*, redound to the glory of GOD" (2 Cor 4:15). Scripture then is express upon this point, that whatever power and grace CHRIST has given to His Ministers, He has given them for the good of His people, and the glory of His heavenly FATHER. And do not our own understandings and consciences bear witness to the same truth? For what is our commission? Is it not a "Ministry of reconciliation?"—"to wit, that GOD was in CHRIST, reconciling the world unto Himself;" and hath committed to us the proclamation of the pardon? Let us put the case on which the Apostle's language is founded; the case, I mean, of people in rebellion against their Sovereign, visited with the news that their King is willing, nay, even anxiously desirous to give them forgiveness and favour. In such a case, would not the first question be, what authority does this report go upon? who are the persons who bring it? is it merely a matter of their individual belief, or are they duly *authorized* and *commissioned* from the Court? are they come as volunteers, or have they been *sent* by their Master? "Now then WE are *Ambassadors for CHRIST*;" we are sent to "bring good tidings and to publish *peace*," "to preach deliverance to the captives, and the opening of the prison to them that are bound;" and, if we allow our commission to be questioned, nay, if we do not most unequivocally and prominently assert it, whom are we robbing? not ourselves of honour, but the people, to whom we are sent, of the blessedness and joy of knowing, that GOD "desireth not the death of a sinner, but rather that he should turn from his wickedness and live;" and that, in token of this desire, He "hath given power and commandment to His Ministers to declare and pronounce to His people, being penitent, the absolution and remission of their sins." We are sent to preach good tidings unto the *meek*, to bind up *the broken-hearted*, to comfort *all that mourn;* and it is the meek, and the broken-hearted, and the mourners, which will feel the loss, if our blessed Office be set at nought, or disregarded. Let us well consider this point. There is a humble and fearful member of CHRIST'S flock, who desires to

strengthen and refresh his soul by the Body and Blood of Christ; but he cannot quit his own conscience; he requires further comfort and counsel. Surely it is to *his* comfort, that there is a duly commissioned Minister of GOD'S Word at hand; to whom he may come and open his grief, and receive the benefit of the sentence of GOD'S pardon, and so prepare himself to approach the holy Table "with a full trust in GOD'S mercy, and with a quiet conscience;" and so draw near with faith, and take that holy Sacrament to his comfort. And then, again, when he lieth sick upon his bed, does not his SAVIOUR "make all his bed in his sickness," when he sends His Minister to him, to receive the confession of his sins, and to relieve his conscience of the "weighty" things which press it down; and then ("if he humbly and heartily desire it") by virtue of the power which He has left to His Church, assures him of the pardon of his sins, that so, as his sufferings abound, his consolation also may abound through CHRIST; and as his outward man perisheth, the inward man may be renewed day by day. How then ought we to look upon the power which has been given us by CHRIST, but as a sacred treasure, of which we are Ministers and Stewards, which it is our duty to guard for the sake of His little ones; for whose edification (2 Cor 13:10) the LORD Himself has left the powers with His Church. And if we suffer it to be lost to the Christian Church, how shall we answer it, not merely to those who might now rejoice in its holy comfort, but to those also that are to come after us? "For the promise is unto you and to your children, and unto all that are afar off, even as many as the LORD our GOD shall call."

2. But if we are thus bound by our duty to the Christian flock, are we not also still more solemnly bound by our obligation to its Chief Shepherd, and Bishop? For we are Ministers of CHRIST and Stewards of the mysteries of GOD; and "in Stewards it is required that a man be found faithful." It becomes us, therefore, well to consider and ask, what is the full amount of the riches which have been committed to our care; what is the height and depth of the Mysteries which have been entrusted to our keeping; for we serve a Master who will strictly require at our hands every talent which He has left with us, and rigorously examine whether we have been afraid and hid it in a napkin, or have diligently put it out to usury and turned it to full account. Let us turn our thoughts again to the representation, which St. Paul gives us, of our character and calling. "We are Ambassadors for CHRIST." Now what should we think of the

Ambassador of an earthly King, who when he came among the people to whom he was sent, should seem to regard it as a matter of slight importance, whether he were indeed commissioned or not, or seem willing to conceal the full powers with which he was vested, and speak only as an individual? Would this be to be *faithful* to him that appointed him? would his Master own him as a good and faithful servant? And if we are Ambassadors for CHRIST, His "deputies for the reducing of man to the obedience of GOD," we must follow the example which our Master has set us, and, as he was, so must we be in this world. For He has Himself declared to us, "as My FATHER hath sent Me, even so send I you."[1] How then did CHRIST fulfil the office which the FATHER had committed to Him? Let us look to His discourses as recorded in St. John's Gospel, and to the solemn prayer with which He concluded His earthly Ministry. We there find Him again and again proclaiming that He had been sent from the FATHER; it was with this in view He prayed so earnestly for the unity and holiness of His Church, that the world might believe that the FATHER had sent Him; it was because His chosen disciples *had* believed that the FATHER had sent Him, that He poured forth such fervent thanksgivings on their behalf.[2] "I am *not come of Myself,* but *He sent Me.*" "I have not spoken of Myself, but the Father *which sent Me, He gave Me a commandment,* what I should say and what I should speak." "They have known that all things *are of Thee;* they have known that *I came out from Thee;* they have believed *that Thou didst send Me.*"[3] Thus did CHRIST stand in the midst of His generation as an Apostle, as one sent from GOD; and so must His deputies likewise stand among their brethren; as men sent to a rebellious house, whether they will hear or whether they will forbear, speaking with authority, "*as though GOD did beseech you by us,* we pray you *in CHRIST'S* stead, be ye reconciled unto GOD." And if we are asked by what authority we speak, and who gave us this authority, we have our credentials at hand; "whose soever sins ye remit, they are remitted, and whose soever sins ye retain, they are retained." "Verily I say unto you, whatsoever ye shall bind on earth shall be bound in heaven; and

---

[1] Comp. John 17:18. "As Thou hast sent Me into the world, so have I also sent them into the world."

[2] John 12:8, 21, 23, 25.

[3] John 12:49, 50. Comp. 14:10, 24. vid. also our LORD'S remarkable words, 5:31, 43.

whatsoever ye shall loose on earth shall be loosed in heaven." "He that heareth you, heareth Me; and he that despiseth you, despiseth Me; and he that despiseth Me, despiseth Him that sent Me" (see Matt 18; Luke 10; John 20).

If ever, then, we are tempted to be ashamed of CHRIST and of His words, or to allow His high and heavenly mission to be thought lightly of in the person of His Deputies and Ministers, let us remember, that it is no matter of personal consideration, that two sacred interests are involved, the glory of GOD and the edifying of His people. Let us remember that, as CHRIST received of the FATHER "a commandment," so we too have received a commandment from Him, the "*commandment*" as well as the "power" to declare to His people the message of forgiveness; that CHRIST has commanded us to teach all nations to observe *whatsoever* He has *commanded* us, and then He will be with us alway, even to the end of the world. And above all, let us not be silenced by the sense of past unworthiness and neglect, whether in ourselves individually, or in the Church at large; this would be but to add sin to sin. Rather, seeing we have this Ministry, this glorious ministration of righteousness (2 Cor 4:1; comp. chp. 3), let us not faint, but strive how we may shew ourselves "dutiful and thankful to that LORD who hath placed us in so high a dignity." The world would fain silence our glorying, and would have CHRIST rebuke His disciples, but let us not be ashamed of the good confession; for with such powers and graces, given to us by CHRIST Himself, as Ambassadors for Him, and Workers together with GOD, if we should hold our peace, the very stones would immediately cry out.

BENJAMIN HARRISON
December 20, 1833

TRACT 18
Thoughts on the Benefits of the System of Fasting,
Enjoined by Our Church

To a person but little accustomed to observe any stated Fasts, the directions given by our Church on this subject, would probably occasion two very opposite feelings. On the one hand, he would be struck by the practical character and thoughtfulness evinced by some of the regulations; on the other, he would probably feel repelled by the number of days, and the variety of occasions, which the Church has appointed so to be hallowed. Most Christians, who really loved their SAVIOUR (unless prevented by the habits of early education) would probably see something appropriate and affectionate in the selection of the Friday, for a weekly commemoration of their SAVIOUR'S sufferings, and of humiliation for their own sins, which caused them; or, at all events, they would feel that there was some thoughtfulness in the direction annexed, that this weekly Fast should not interfere with the Christian joyousness brought back by the Festival of their LORD'S Nativity, when these should in the cycle of years coincide. Again, if they should fail to appreciate the wisdom of appointing certain days to be kept sacred in memory of the holy men who left all to follow Christ, and consequently should be rather deterred than attracted, by observing that many of these days were ushered in by a preceding Fast; still they would hardly fail to be struck by the provision, that this previous Fast should not interfere with the Christian's weekly Festival of his LORD'S Resurrection, but that "if any of these Feast-days should fall upon a Monday, then the Fast-day should be kept on the

Saturday, not upon the Sunday next before it."[1] Again, he must observe, that during certain periods of the Church's year, which are supposed to be times of especial joy to the Christian, those, namely, following the Nativity and the Resurrection, these preparatory Fasts are altogether omitted. Some or other of these regulations would probably strike most thoughtful minds, as instances of consideration and reflection in those who formed them. The Clergy more especially would appreciate, abstractedly at least, the imitation of the Apostolic practice of Fasting, when any are to be ordained to any holy function in the Church; and some probably will feel mournfully, that if the Church were now more uniformly to observe those acts of Fasting and Prayer, which were thought needful, before even Paul and Barnabas[2] were separated for GOD'S work, we should have more reasonable grounds to hope, that many of our Clergy would be filled with the spirit of Barnabas and Paul.

On the other hand, it is naturally to be expected, that one not accustomed to any outward restraint in this matter, would feel indisposed to ordinances so detailed; that, although he could reconcile to himself the one or the other of these observances, which most recommended themselves to his Christian feelings, he would think the whole a burthensome and minute ceremonial, perhaps unbefitting a spiritual worship, and interfering with the liberty, wherewith CHRIST has made him free. This is very natural; for we are by nature averse to restraint, and the abuse of some maxims of Protestantism, such as the "right of private judgment," has made us yet more so: we are reluctant to yield to an unreasoning authority, and to submit our wills, when our reason has not first been convinced; and the prevailing maxims of the day have strengthened this reluctance: we have been accustomed to do, "every one that which was right in his own eyes," and are jealous of any authority, except that of the direct injunctions of the Bible: we have, I fear also, so untruly spiritualized our religion, that we have almost lost sight of that part of it, which is adapted to us, as being yet in the flesh: in our zeal for the blessed truths of the cross of CHRIST, and of our sanctification by the HOLY SPIRIT, we have begun insensibly to disparage other truths, which bring us less immediately into intercourse with

---

[1] See Tables prefixed to the Common Prayer-book.
[2] Acts 13:2-4; 4:23.

God, to neglect the means and ordinances, which touch not upon the very centre of our faith.

The practical system of the Church is altogether at variance with that which even pious Christians in these days have permitted themselves to adopt; much which she has recommended or enjoined would now be looked upon as formalism, or outward service: in our just fear of a lifeless formalism, we have forgotten that every Christian feeling must have its appropriate vehicle of expression; that the most exalted acts of Christian devotion, that our closest union with our SAVIOUR, is dependant upon certain forms; that the existence of forms does not constitute formalism; that where the Spirit of CHRIST is, there the existence of forms serves only to give regularity to the expression, to chasten what there might yet remain of too individual feeling, to consolidate the yet divided members "in the unity of the faith, and of the knowledge of the SON of GOD, unto a perfect man, unto the measure of the stature of the fulness of CHRIST."

Yet, as in every case in which the current of prevailing opinions, either in faith or practice, has for some time set in one direction, there have not been wanting indications, that Christians have felt their system incomplete; that there was something in the tranquil piety of former days, which they would gladly incorporate into the zealous excitement of the present; that although religion is in one sense strictly individual, yet in the means by which it is kept alive, it is essentially expansive and social; that the only error here to be avoided, is a reliance upon forms; that the forms themselves, as soon as they are employed to realize things eternal, and to cherish their communion with their SAVIOUR, become again spiritual and edifying.

It is accordingly remarkable in the present day to observe, in how many cases individuals have been led back by their own Christian experience to observances, in some respect similar to those which the Church had before suggested and provided for them. In the more advanced period of their Christian course, or amid the respite from the unceasing circle of active duty, which GOD has granted them through an interval of sickness, they have seen the value of those rites, the scrupulous adherence to which they once regarded as signs of lifelessness. In either case they would willingly own, that the union provided by the Church is not only more ordered, and less liable to exception, than one which individuals could frame; but also, that, as being more comprehensive, it would more effectively realize their objects.

It is granted, then, that the proportion of the Fast Days enjoined by the Church will, to persons unaccustomed to observe them, appear overlarge, and the variety of the occasions for which they are adapted, overminute and arbitrary. The question however occurs, whether we ought to be influenced by such considerations to reject the entire system, or whether we ought not rather to be moved by the indications of a practical character evinced in some regulations, to make the trial of those, whose benefit we do not at present discern. Now it would seem plain that, in a *practical* matter, he who from the traces of wisdom or thoughtfulness in one regulation should infer the probable wisdom and reasonableness of others emanating from the same source, would act more wisely than one, who, on account of the *apparent* unreasonableness and superfluity of some provisions, should proceed to condemn the whole. For in practical matters, the great test of the expediency of any habit, for which we have not direct divine authority, is *experience:* they only who have tried a line of conduct, or narrowly watched its effects upon others, can speak with certainty as to its result. Of all the lesser courses of action, which tend so powerfully to form our moral habits, it would be impossible, probably, for one who had not tried their effect, to predict certainly what that effect would be; or if we could guess the nature of the effect, certainly we should not be able to foresee its degree and amount. With the exception of gross and flagrant sins, whose character and wages we know from *authority,* there is probably no one line of action, with regard to which we might not beforehand prove very plausibly to ourselves, that it would not have the effects, to which it is in fact tending, and which we afterwards perceive to have been its natural results. Yet such abstract reasonings about the possibilities or tendencies of things would not be listened to in any other case. When sick, men eagerly listen to the means, however improbable, by which any disease, resembling their own, was removed. Be it a poison, which they are bidden to take, yet if it be proved satisfactorily that, in cases like their own, that poison has been the messenger of health, they would not hesitate. They would listen to no abstract reasonings, that it was improbable that what had been an instrument of death could be their life; they would look to those, whom it had restored to health, and would do the like. The sight of one person, undeniably raised from death to life, would affect men more than any à priori demonstration that the medicine was pernicious or deadly. Much more then, since this medicine has been recommended to us by the great Physician of our souls; since it has been beneficial, wherever it has not been substituted for all other means of restoring or maintaining our spiritual health. The only question is,—not whether Fasting be in itself beneficial, but—whether certain regulations concerning it tend to promote or to diminish its efficacy; and in this case, the testimony of those who have proved their value, is manifestly of primary importance; the preconceived opinions of such as have not tried them, are but mere presumptions. If then either in the regulations or the histories of those holy men, through whom these recommendations have become part of the system of our Church, we find indications that they themselves knew from experience the value of what they recommended, we have evidence of the value of their advice, which we may not, without peril of injury to our souls, neglect.

It was in part, by some such process as the preceding, that the writer of these pages was led to consider what one may be allowed to term the less solemn Fasts of the Church, those which Christians now ordinarily pay less regard to; for the first day of Lent and the annual commemoration of our SAVIOUR'S sufferings are, I suppose, still very commonly observed. As the history of every mind is, under some modifications, the mirror of many others, it may to some be useful to see by what course of reflection or experience an individual was brought to feel the value of the regulations of the Church in this respect.

It will perhaps to some seem strange to find placed among the foremost of these advantages, the *Protection* thereby afforded—protection against one's self; protection against the habits and customs of the world, which sorely let and hinder one in systematically pursuing what one imagines might be beneficial. I speak not of course of any known duty; in that case the opinion or practice or invitations of the world were nothing; but with regard to those indefinite duties or disciplines, which one thinks may be performed as well at one period as at another, and which, on that very account, are frequently not performed at all, or at best occasionally only, and superficially. No thoughtful Christian will doubt of the propriety and duty of fasting, whatever he may understand by the term. "The bridegroom is taken away from us, and so we must fast in these days:"[3] our Blessed SAVIOUR has given us instructions *how* we ought to fast,[4] and therefore implied that His disciples would fast: the Apostles were "in fastings often:"[5] in fastings,[6] as well as in sufferings for the Gospel, or by pureness, by knowledge, by all the graces which the HOLY GHOST imparted, they approved themselves the Ministers of GOD. "Our LORD and SAVIOUR," says Hooker, "would not teach the manner of doing, much less propose a reward for doing that which were not both holy and acceptable in GOD'S sight."[7] And yet, after all the allowances which can be made for that fasting, which is known to our FATHER only who seeth in secret, one cannot conceal from one's self that this duty is in these days very inadequately practised. It is, in fact, a truth almost proverbial, that a duty which may be performed at any time, is in great risk of being neglected at all times. The early Christians felt this, and appointed the days of our Blessed SAVIOUR'S crucifixion and murder, the Wednesday and Friday of each week,[8] to be days of fasting and especial humiliation. Those days, in which especially the bridegroom was taken away, the days, namely, in which He was crucified and lay in the grave, were besides early consecrated as Fasts by the widowed Church. Nor was it because they were in perils, which we are spared; because they were in deaths oft, that they practised or needed this discipline. Quite the reverse. Their whole life was a Fast, a death to this world, a realizing of things invisible. It was when dangers began to mitigate, when Christianity became (as far as the world was concerned) an easy profession, it was then that the peril increased, lest their first simplicity should be corrupted, their first love grow cold![9] Then those who had spiritual authority in the Church increased the stated Fasts, in order to recall that holy earnestness of life, which the recentness of their redemption, and the constant sense of their SAVIOUR'S presence, had before inspired. Fasts were not merely the voluntary discipline of men, whose

---

[3] Matthew 9:15; Mark 2:20; Luke 5:35.
[4] Matthew 6:16-18.
[5] 2 Corinthians 11:27.
[6] 2 Corinthians 6:5.
[7] Eccl. Pol. B. V. §. 72. Bp. Taylor, Rule of Conscience, B. ii. c. 3. rule O.
[8] See Bingham, Antiq. of the Christian Church, B. xxi. c. 3.
[9] Cassian. Collat. xxi. c. 30. ap. Bingham, B. xxi. c. 1.

conversation was in heaven; they were adopted and enlarged in periods of ease, of temptation, of luxury, of self-satisfaction, of growing corruption.

To urge that Fasts were abused by the later Romish Church, is but to assert that they are a means of grace committed to men; that they would subsequently be unduly neglected, was but to be expected by any one, who knows the violent vacillations of human impetuosity. It was then among the instances of calm judgment in our Reformers, that cutting off the abuses which before prevailed, the vain distinctions of meats, the lucrative dispensations, and, above all, the subtle poison of the intrinsic acceptableness of Fasting, and (which was closely allied to it) the monstrous doctrine of human merit, they still prescribed Fasting "to discipline the flesh, to free the spirit, and render it more earnest and fervent to prayer, and as a testimony and witness with us before God of our humble submission to His high Majesty, when we confess our sins unto Him, and are inwardly touched with sorrowfulness of heart, bewailing the same in the affliction of our bodies."[10]

They omitted that, which might be a snare to men's consciences, they left it to every man's Christian prudence and experience, *how* he would fast; but they prescribed the days upon which he should fast, both in order to obtain an unity of feeling and devotion in the members of CHRIST'S body, and to preclude the temptation to the neglect of the duty altogether. Nor is the interference in this matter any thing insulated in our system, or one which good men would object to, had not our unhappy neglect of it now made it seem strange and foreign to our habits. In some things we are accustomed to perform a duty, which is such independently of the authority of the Church, in the way in which the Church has prescribed, and because she has so appointed. We assemble ourselves together on the Lord's day, because GOD has directed us by His Apostle not to forsake such assemblies; but we assemble ourselves twice upon that day rather than once, not upon any reason of the abstract fitness of so doing, but because the Church has prescribed it. And probably at an earlier period of our lives, perhaps even later, when indisposition or indolence or any prevailing temptation has beset us, there are few amongst us who have not owed their regular perseverance in public worship to this ordinance of the Church; there is no one assuredly who having broken this

---

[10] First Part of the Homily on Fasting.

ordinance, has afterwards by GOD'S mercy been brought back to join more uniformly in the public worship of his God and Saviour, who has not been thankful for this restriction. This then is protection.[11]

The like has undoubtedly taken place even in the celebration of the Supper of our Lord. Individuals have been induced to join, and that beneficially to themselves, in the Communion even of their SAVIOUR'S body and blood, just so often in the year as their Church has prescribed to them. This is not so unusual a case as it might seem. One cannot doubt, that in many cases, where the Holy Communion is celebrated but three times in the year, this is so done, because such is the smallest number, of which the Church admits, and the Minister supposes that his flock would not join with him more frequently. Had the Church made no such regulation, many probably, who now partake three times a year, might not have joined even thus often; yet would it not be true to say that such persons in all cases partook without real devotion, or any love to their SAVIOUR. Again, where there are opportunities of a monthly Communion, there may be some, who would not have desired the privilege unless the provision had been made for them, and they had been invited by the Church so to do; yet will it not of necessity follow that they partake coldly or unacceptably. A warmer love would indeed lead the one to a more frequent, the other to a more glad Communion; nor have such persons well understood the principles of their Church; still, GOD forbid that we shall judge that they had not partaken worthily and devotionally.

Here again then is protection; in either case, we have a command of GOD, obeyed in such wise as is prescribed by the Ministers, whom He has

---

[11] "No doubt but penitency is as prayer, a thing acceptable to God, be it in public or in secret. Howbeit, as in the one, if men were only left to their own voluntary meditations in their closets, and not drawn by laws and orders unto the open assemblies of the Church, that there they may join with others in prayer, it may soon be conjectured what Christian devotion would that way come unto in a short time; even so in the other, we are by sufficient experience taught, how little it booteth to tell men of washing away their sins with tears of repentance, and so to leave them altogether to themselves. O Lord, what heaps of grievous transgressions have we committed, the best, the perfectest, the most righteous amongst us all, and yet clean past them over unsorrowed for, and unrepented of, only because the Church hath forgotten utterly how to bestow her wonted times of discipline, wherein the public example of all was unto every particular person a most effectual mean to put them often in mind, and even in a manner to draw them to that, which now we all quite and clean forget, as if penitency were no part of a Christian man's duty." Hooker, l.c.

made the Stewards of His Word and Sacraments; and since we in these cases admit their regulation, why should we think it strange or incongruous, that they have given us their godly admonitions in another ordinance of God?

Nor is it to the undecided, or the timid, or the hesitating, or the novice only, that this protection is beneficial; although no reflecting Christian will speak lightly of the value of any mean, which tends to strengthen the broken reed or to kindle anew the smouldering flax. The comparison of our own times with those of the Reformers were proof enough of the benefit of authoritative interposition in these matters. Is human nature changed? or have we discovered some more royal road, by which to arrive at the subjugation of the body, the spiritualizing of the affections? or have we, even from, without, fewer temptations to luxury and self-indulgence? or will not even the more pious and decided Christians among us confess, upon reflection, that they had probably been now more advanced, had they in this point adhered to the Ancient Discipline of our Church? Our Reformers kept and enjoined one hundred and eight days in each year, either entirely or in part, to be in this manner sanctified; two sevenths of each year they wished to be in some way separated by acts of self-denial and humiliation. Let any one consider what proportion of each year he has himself so consecrated, and whether, had he followed the ordinances of the Church, his spirit would not probably have been more chastened and lowly, more single in following even what he deems his duty, whether self would not have been more restrained, whether he would not have walked more humbly with his GOD.

Yet authority is a valuable support against the world, even to minds who yet are not inclined to compromise with the world unlawfully. There are many situations in life, in which it were almost impossible to continue without observing a system of habitual and regular Fasting, certainly not one, attended with those accompaniments, which the Fathers of our Church thought it desirable to unite with it. It is true, that every Fast may be made a Feast, and every Feast a Fast, that as far as self-denial is concerned, if there be a stedfast purpose, the objects may perhaps be better accomplished in the midst of plenty and luxury, than by the purposed spareness of a private board; it is possible also, that the acts might be in some measure concealed; still there are very many minds, and those such as one would be the most anxious to protect, to whom the very suspicion that they might be observed, would be matter of pain and a species of profanation; they would shrink from any thing which might be construed into Pharisaic abstinence, or which would seem to pretend to more than ordinary measures of Christian prudence. To such mild and unobstrusive spirits, the recommendation or direction of the Church is an invaluable support; they may now adopt the line of conduct which they love, unimpeded by any scruple, lest their good should be evil spoken of; they are acting under authority; they pretend to nothing more than the Founders of their Church have deemed expedient for every one; their conduct involves no lofty pretensions; they follow in simplicity and faithfulness an old and trodden track, which has been marked out for them as plain and safe.

The first advantage then which may result from the authoritative interposition of the Church in regulating this duty, is the securing of greater regularity and more uniform perseverance in its performance; not undoubtedly as in itself an end, but as leading to great and important ends; for as those pious men, who laid so much stress thereon, themselves say, "when it respecteth a good end, it is a good work; but the end being evil, the work is also evil."[12] "Fasting is not to be commended as a duty, but as an instrument; and, in that sense, no man can reprove it, or undervalue it, but he that knows neither spiritual acts, nor spiritual necessities."[13]

But further, it is not even true, that all the purposes of Fasting can be attained by mere self-denial in the midst of luxury. For the acquisition of the habit of self-denial, although an important object, is by no means the sole end of Fasting.[14] The great purpose, in connection with which it

---

[12] First Part of the Homily on Fasting.
[13] Bishop Taylor, Works, iv. 212.
[14] "Much hurt hath grown to the Church of God through a false imagination that Fasting standeth men in no stead for any spiritual respect, but only to take down the frankness of nature, and to tame the wildness of the flesh. Whereupon the world being bold to surfeit, doth now blush to fast, supposing that men, when they fast, do rather bewray a disease, than exercise a virtue. I much wonder what they, who are thus persuaded, do think, what conceit they have, concerning the Fasts of the Patriarchs, the Prophets, the Apostles, our Lord Jesus Christ himself." Hooker's Eccl. Pol. B. v. §. 72.

"If the Church intends many good ends in the Canon, any one is sufficient to tie the law upon the conscience, because, for that one good end, it can be serviceable to the soul; and indeed Fasting is of that nature, that it can be a ministry of repentance by the affliction, and it can be a help to prayer, by taking off the loads of flesh and a full stomach;

is chiefly mentioned in Holy Scripture, is prayer. The influences of Society, rightly chosen, *may* dispose the mind to more fervent (possibly only more excited) prayer; it is solitude generally, or communion with a single friend, which brings us to a humble, contrite, lowly, intercourse with our God. In the present day, the first paramount evil which destroys its tens of thousands, is probably self-indulgence; the second, which hinders thousands in their progress heavenwards, is the being "busy and careful about many things," whether temporal or spiritual. "We have kept the vineyards of our mother's children, but our own vineyards have we not kept." The tendency of the age is to activity, and we have caught its spirit; if we be but active about our Master's calling we deem ourselves secure; we think not, until we are precluded from active exertion, "how much activity belongs to some (ages and some) natures, and that this nature is often mistaken for grace."[15] Meanwhile an activity, which leads us not inwards, has taken place of that tranquil retiring meditation on the things of the unseen world which formed the deep, absorbing, contemplative, piety of our forefathers; even the conception of the joys of heaven, which very many of us form, is but a glorified transcript of our life here; we look, when through GOD'S mercy in CHRIST we shall be delivered from the burthen of the flesh, to be like the "Ministers of His, who do His pleasure;" but we look not, comparatively at least, to that which our Fathers longed for, to be with CHRIST and to see Him as He is. Our age is in general too busy, too active, for deep and continued self-observation, or for thoughtful communion with our GOD. It would not be too broad or invidious a statement to say, that for real insight into the recesses of our nature, or for deep aspirations after GOD, we must for the most part turn to holy men of other days: our own furnish us chiefly with that which they have mainly cherished, a *general* abhorrence of sin, they guide us not to trace it out in the lurking corners of our own hearts: they teach us to acknowledge *generally* the corruption of our nature, the necessity of a Redeemer, and the love we should feel towards Him; but they lead us not to that individual and detailed knowledge of our own personal sinfulness,

---

and it can be aptly ministerial to contemplation. Now, because every one is concerned in some one or more of these ends of Fasting, all people are included within the circles of the law, unless by some other means they be exempted." Bp. Taylor, Rule of Conscience, B iii. c. 4. rule 19.

[15] A Fragment, written in illness, by the Rev. Richard Cecil.

whence the real love of our Redeemer can alone flow. A religious repose and a thoughtful contemplation would be a second advantage of complying in this respect with the instructions of our Church.[16]

Braced and strung by retirement into ourselves, and tranquil meditation upon GOD, we should return to our active duties with so much more efficiency, as we ourselves had become holier, humbler, calmer, more abstracted from ourselves, more habituated to refer all things to GOD. Were human activity alone engaged on both sides, then might we the rather justify the prevailing notions of the day, that energy is to be met by counter-energy alone: but now, since "we wrestle not against flesh and blood, but against principalities, against powers, against the rulers of the darkness of this world," it especially behoves us to look wherein our great strength lies, and to take heed that "the weapons of our warfare be not carnal." It is tempting to adopt into the service of GOD the weapons or the mode of warfare, which in the hands of His enemies we see to be efficacious; but the faithful soldier of CHRIST must not go forth with weapons which he has not proved; the Christian's armoury, as the Apostle continues to describe it, is mainly defensive; and when he has urged his brethren to assume it, he exhorts them to add that whereby alone it becomes effectual—a duty in which again we appear to ourselves to be inactive—"praying always with all prayer and supplication in the Spirit, and watching thereunto with all perseverance and supplication for all saints." Fasting, retirement, and prayer, as they severally and unitedly tend to wean us from ourselves and cast us upon God, will tend to promote singleness of purpose, to refine our busy and over-heated restlessness into a calm and subdued confidence in Him, in whose strength we go forth. Nor shall we until the day of judgment know how much of the victory was granted to those, who in man's sight took no share in the conflict; how far the "unseen strength" of Fasting, humiliation, prayer, put forth by those of whom the world took no account, was allowed by GOD to prevail. The world saw only that the Apostle whom they had imprisoned, escaped their power;

---

[16] "It is best to accompany our Fasting with the retirements of religion and the enlargements of charity; giving to others what we deny to ourselves." Bp. Taylor, Works, iii. 102. "Fasting, saith Tertullian, is an act of reverence towards God. The end thereof, sometimes elevation of mind; sometimes the purpose thereof clean contrary. The reason why Moses in the Mount did so long fast, was mere divine speculation; the reason why David, humiliation." Hooker, l.c.

they knew not that the prayer of the Church had baffled their design.[17] In the present conflict throughout the world, in which the pride of human and Satanic strength seems put forth to the utmost, humility and a chastened dependent spirit would seem to have an especial efficacy. On these, as the graces most opposed to the world's main sin, we might look the more cheerfully for GOD'S blessing; thus shall we at least be saved from augmenting the evil we would oppose. "Fasting directly advances towards chastity, and by consequence and indirect powers to patience, humility, and indifference. But then it is not the fast of a day that can do this; it is not an act, but a state of fasting, that operates to mortification."[18]

A third benefit, which might be hoped to result from the more assiduous practice of this duty, would be a more self-denying extensive charity. "Fasting without mercy, is but an image of famine; Fasting without works of piety is only an occasion of covetousness;"[19] and an Apostolic Father gives us this excellent instruction, "A true Fast is not merely to keep under the body, but to give to the widow, or the poor, the amount of that which thou wouldest have expended upon thyself; that so he who receives it may pray to GOD for thee."[20]

It may perhaps seem strange to some that the present age should be thought wanting in self-denying charity. And yet let men but consider with themselves not what they give only, but what they retain; let them enquire a little further, not only what wants are relieved, but what remediable misery remains unabated; or let them but observe generally the glaring contrasts of extremest luxury and softness, and pinching want and penury; between their own cieled houses, and the houses of GOD which lie waste; or let them only trace out one single item in the mass of human wretchedness, disease, insanity, religious ignorance, and picture to themselves what a Christian people might do, what the primitive Christians would have done to relieve it,—and then turn to what is done, to what themselves do, and say whether means to promote self-denying charity can well be spared.

---

[17] Acts 12:5.
[18] Bp. Taylor, Works, iii. 97.
[19] Chrysologus Serm. 8. de Jejun. ap. Bingham, Book xxi. c. 1. §. 18.
[20] Hermas Pastor, Lib. iii. c. 3, p. 105. ed. Coteler. Fasting without alms-giving, says Augustine, is a lamp without oil.

A further important object of the stated and frequent recurrence of the prescribed Fasts of our Church, is the public recognition of the reality of things spiritual. Here also very many have felt (and it is a feeling whose strength is daily increasing) that some public protest is needed against the modes of acting, tolerated (would one must not say, reigning!) in our nominally Christian land: that the Church, or the body of believers, ought to have some recognized mode of distinguishing themselves from those, who manifest by their deeds, that although "amongst us, they are not of us;" and who, on the principles of our Church, would have gone out or been removed from us. It has been with a right view of what the ideal of the Christian Church should be, its holiness, and its purity, although not, I must think, with a just conception of the nature of the Church, that men jealous for the honour of their GOD and their REDEEMER, have in some measure formed Churches within the Church. The plan has, I think, been defective, sacred and praiseworthy as was the object contemplated. It is true, that the mere union in the celebration of the weekly festival of our LORD'S Resurrection does not, as things now are, furnish a sufficient condemnation of the maxims and offences of the world; that the Church and the world are too much amalgamated; that while the light of the Church has in part penetrated the gross darkness of the world, there is yet danger, lest that light itself should be obscured. Yet the remedy for this, under GOD'S blessing, is not to be sought in rescuing or concentrating some scattered rays of that Church, while the Church itself is abandoned to the world. The Ordinances of the Church itself afford the means of its own restoration. Not to speak of those ulterior and fearful powers, committed to it (and which other communions exercise) of ejecting from its bosom "the wicked person," the observance of its own other institutions would virtually eject them. Not indeed at once (as indeed GOD Himself has thought fit to allow even His own Blessed Spirit but gradually to leaven our corrupted mass), not at once, for at present, long continuance in opposed habits would prevent many from receiving the Ordinances of the Church, but yet, one should trust, steadily and increasingly; the mists which now encircle the Church, would disperse, and its glorious elevation on Zion's hill would more effectually be seen. Those, whom the easy Service of the Lord's Day repels not, who would fain serve GOD on the seventh day, and Mammon on the remaining six, would be brought to some test of what spirit they were; and if the Church, like Him, who is its Head, and because joined to that Head, becomes a stone of stumbling, if some shall more openly fall back unto perdition, still it will have performed its office; many, one may be sure (for our assurance rests on GOD'S Word) would also be awakened from their lethargy of death; and if it be to some a savor of death, it will, by GOD'S mercy, be to many more a savor of life, unto life. Yet the result of any system, built upon GOD'S Word, belongs not to us. Were the consequences of more Apostolic practice a great apparent defection and desolation, we dare not hesitate. "It must be made manifest that they are not all of us." Meanwhile a beacon will be held out to those, who would wish to see their path: the plea, that every shew of religion, which the world tolerates not, is the mere excess and badge of a party, could no longer be held; those, who shrink from what might seem a voluntary or ostentatious forwardness, would no longer be deterred from uniting in observances, which, if authorized, they would love; and there might again be no separation but between those who serve GOD, and those who serve Him not. The world has seen that its own principles are leading to its own destruction; it acknowledges that its increased laxity has fearfully increased its corruption; offences, which even it abhors, are multiplied; vices, which disturb even its peace, stalk more openly; yet while it reaps the bitter fruits of its own ways, it dares not strike the root.

The Fasts, appointed by our Church, appear eminently calculated, not in truth as a panacea of all evil, but as one decided protest against the "corruption which is in the world by lust," as one testimony to the conviction of men of the reality of things eternal.

Men may "fast for strife and to smite with the fist of wickedness," as they may also "for pretence make long prayers;" yet will not men, in general, submit to inconvenience and privation, except for a real and substantial object; the world has easier paths for its followers: he, who suffers hardship for an unseen reward, at least gives evidence to the world of the sincerity and rootedness of his own conviction; he attests that he is a pilgrim journeying to a better country, and however men may for a while neglect his testimony, it cannot be silenced.

Such are some of the advantages, which a recurrence to the system of our Church in respect of Fasting might, in dependance upon GOD'S blessing, tend to realize: a more uniform, namely, and regular observance of an injunction of our Blessed SAVIOUR; a deeper humiliation, and a more chastened spirit in carrying on His will; a more thorough insight into ourselves, and a closer communion with our GOD; a more resolute and consistent practice of self-denying charity; a more lively realizing of things spiritual; a warning to the world of GOD'S truth and its own peril. I have spoken with reference to prevailing habits and general character only, partly because they are these habits which the regulations of a Church must mainly contemplate;[21] in part also, because, in whatever degree, they will probably form a portion of our own. The evil or defective character of any period is not formed by, nor will it exist in, those only who are evil; it encompasses us, is within us; we also contribute in our degree to foster and promote it; nay, it is from us probably that it receives its main countenance and support. Our own standard is insensibly lowered by the evil, with which we are environed. A self-indulgent age is not a favourable atmosphere for the growth of self-denial; nor an age of busy and self-dependant activity for that of a calm and abiding practical recognition, that every thing is in GOD'S hands; nor a period absorbed in the things of sense for thoughtful meditation on things eternal. The predominant evils will indeed appear in the Christian in a subdued form; yet whether the temptation be to an unconscious compliance with them, or unwittingly to oppose evil with evil, the danger lies nearer here than in any other part of duty. And if the salt in any wise lose its savour, wherewith shall the self-corrupting world be preserved? wherewith the salt itself be salted?

The benefits above named are such as depend on the increased degree of Fasting, exercised in compliance with the directions of the Church, independently of the consideration of the days or seasons selected for that purpose. The results to be anticipated from a more general adherence to these rules appear, however, to be heightened by that selection. The general objects of the Church were, 1. to impress upon the mind and life the memory of her SAVIOUR'S sufferings; 2. to prepare the mind for different solemn occasions, which recur in her yearly service. The first, or the Friday Fast, as above stated, was universally adopted in the early Church, and in all probability was coeval with the Apostles; it was

---

[21] "We must observe all that care in public Fasts, which we do in private; knowing that our private ends are included in the public, as our persons are in the communion of saints, and our hopes in the common inheritance of sons." Bishop Taylor, Works, iv. 103.

continued uninterruptedly, alike in the Eastern and the Western Church, and preserved in our own, through the respect which she bore to primitive antiquity, and the experience of the elder Church. It was perhaps at the first adopted, as the natural expression of sorrow for the loss of their LORD and for His bitter sufferings. With this would soon connect itself, almost to the exclusion of the former, sorrow for the sins, which caused those sufferings. "We do not fast," says Chrysostom, "for the Passion or the Cross, but for our sins;—the Passion is not the occasion of fasting or mourning, but of joy and exultation.—We mourn not for that, God forbid, but for our sins, and therefore we fast."[22] As then the LORD'S day was the weekly festival of their SAVIOUR'S resurrection, a weekly memorial of our rising again, in Him and through Him, to a new and real life; so was the Friday's fast a weekly memorial of the death to sin, which all Christians had in their SAVIOUR died, and which, if they would live with Him, they must continually die. Thus each revolving week was a sort of representation of that great week, in which man's redemption was completed; the Church never lost sight of her SAVIOUR'S sufferings; each week was hallowed by a return of the "good Friday."[23] One need scarcely insist upon the tendency of such a system deeply to impress on men's hearts the doctrine of the Atonement, by thus incorporating it into their ordinary lives, and making them by their actions confess this truth. In the early Church its efficacy was probably increased by the accession of the Fast of the Wednesday, or fourth day of the week; so that no portion of the week was without some memorial of the Saviour of the Church. There is however another object, which, although not originally contemplated,

---

[22] Ap. Bingham, b. xxi. c. 1. §. 14. Chrysostom is there speaking of the Lent Fast, but the application is the same.

[23] "Forasmuch as Christ hath foresignified that when Himself should be taken from them, His absence would soon make them apt to fast, it seemed that even as the first Festival Day appointed to be kept of the Church was the day of our Lord's return from the dead, so the first sorrowful and mournful day was that which we now observe, in memory of His departure out of this world. It came afterwards to be an order, that even as the day of Christ's resurrection, so the other two, in memory of his death and burial, were weekly. The Churches which did not observe the Saturday's fast, had another instead thereof, for that when they judged it meet to have weekly a day of humiliation, besides that whereon our Saviour suffered death, it seemed best to make their choice of that day especially, whereon the Jews are thought to have first contrived their treason together with Judas against Christ." Hooker, l. c.

was in fact attained by this institution, the holier celebration, namely, of our most solemn day, that of our SAVIOUR'S death. Most Christians, probably, who have endeavoured to realize to themselves the events of that day, have been painfully disappointed in so doing; instead of

> "Touching the heart with softer power
> For comfort than an angel's mirth,"

it has been to them an oppressive day; its tremendous truths overwhelmed rather than consoled; it was so unlike all other days, that the mind was confounded by its very greatness; it seemed unnatural to do any thing, which one would do even on any other holy day, and the heart was equally unsatisfied with what it did or did not do. Something of this kind has taken place in very many minds; and the reason probably was, that the solemnity of that day was too insulated; that (if one may use the expression) it was out of keeping with the religious habits of the rest of the year. This then the weekly Fast and solemn recollection recommended by the Church are calculated to remedy; as indeed, had they been observed, these feelings would never have found place. In whatever degree its advice is adhered to, Good Friday becomes a day of more chastened, and yet, probably, of intenser feeling; it is connected with a train of the like emotions, affections, and resolves; insulated no longer, but the holiest only among the holy. "Neither in moral or religious, more than in physical and civil matters," says a very acute observer of human nature, "do people willingly do any thing suddenly or upon the instant; they need a succession of the like actions, whereby a habit may be formed; the things which they are to love, or to perform, they cannot conceive as insulated and detached: whatever we are to repeat with satisfaction, must not have become foreign to us."[24] The principle is of important application in the whole range of

---

[24] Goethe aus meinem Leben, tom. ii. p. 179. The author is there lamenting "the nakedness which, Jeremy Taylor says, the excellent men of our sister Churches complained to be among themselves," and which our own happily avoided. In the contrast there drawn, it is not a little remarkable to see, that the doctrine of Apostolical Succession which has of late been by some regarded as cold and unpractical, is put forward as that which gives to the Romish Sacraments a warmth, which the Lutheran Church does not possess. He sums up thus; "All these spiritual miracles spring not, like other fruits, from the natural soil; there can they neither be sown, nor planted, nor nurtured. One must obtain them by prayer from another country; and this cannot every one do, nor at all times. Here then we are met

our duties; nor could it be too often repeated, in warning, "that what is not practised frequently, can never be performed with delight." We are sensible of the value of habits in moral action, and are not surprised that one, who makes only desultory efforts, should never succeed in acquiring any habit; we feel it in some degree in our public worship of GOD, and think it natural that one who does not diligently avail himself of all his opportunities of attending it, should join in it but coldly and lifelessly; it is strange to him, and therefore at best a stiff and austere service: and yet, in other matters, we act in defiance of this maxim; we have allowed our Fasts to become rare, and therefore it has come to pass, that so many never fast at all; our holy days have passed for the most part into neglect, and therefore the few that remain excite but little comparative feeling; our daily service is well nigh disused, and therefore our weekly is so much neglected; we have diminished the frequency of our communions, and therefore so many are strangers to the LORD'S Table, so many formal partakers. Not so the Apostles, nor the Primitive Church, nor our own in its Principles, or in its most Apostolic days: they knew human nature better; or, rather, acting from their own experience and self-knowledge, they ordained what was healthful for men of like nature with themselves; what was a duty at any period of the year, must needs be performed

---

by the highest of these symbols derived from an old venerable tradition. We hear that one man can be favoured, blessed, consecrated from above more than others. Yet, in order that this may appear no mere natural gift, this high favour, united as it is with a weight of duty, must be transmitted from one commissioned individual to another; and the greatest good which man can attain, and yet cannot possess himself of by any exertions or power of his own, must be preserved and perpetuated upon earth by a spiritual inheritance. Nay, in the consecration of the Priest, every thing is united, which is necessary for effectually joining in those other holy ordinances, whereby the mass of Believers is benefitted, without their having any other active share therein, than that of Faith and unconditional confidence. And thus the Priest is enrolled in the succession of those who have preceded or shall come after him, and in the circle of those anointed to the same office, to represent Him, from whom all blessings flow; and that the more gloriously, because it is not Himself whom we respect, but His office; it is not before His bidding that we bow the knee, but before the benediction which he imparts, and which seems the more sacred, the more immediately derived from Heaven, because the earthly instrument cannot, by any sinfulness or viciousness of his own, weaken it, or render it powerless." The author manifestly speaks of the value of the Sacraments, with the feelings with which a spectator might be inspired, but still as one, in whom great powers of observation could supply every thing but the warmth of actual experience.

throughout; each portion had its Festivals and its Fasts, and the varying circle formed one harmonious whole of Christian humiliation and Christian joy.[25]

The Church was in those days consistent; its ministers derived their commission not of man, but of GOD, who called them inwardly by His Spirit, and outwardly through those to whom, through his Apostles, He had delegated this high office. The admission into Holy Orders was no mere outward consecration or ceremony, but an imparting of GOD'S Spirit to those who were separated to this work through the prayers of the congregation, and the delegated authority of the Bishop. Christian edification was not left to each man's private judgment, but each was taught by those who had authority and experience, what was good and expedient for his soul's health. We also have been in these days becoming consistent; if we fast, we fast for ourselves; if we keep a holy day, or select a portion of the weekly service, it is because we of our own minds deem it convenient; we have become in all things the judges of the Church, instead of reverently obeying what has been recommended to us; we judge beforehand what will be useful to us, instead of ascertaining by experience whether that recommended by elder Christians be not so.

Yet I would fain hope that there will not long be this variance between our principles and our practice; but that, instead of examining what is the present practice of any portion of our Church, and enquiring how this may be amended, men would first investigate, in the Canons and the Rubrics,[26] what the real mind of the Church is, and see whether adherence to these would not remove the regretted defect.

One only objection can, I think, be raised by any earnest-minded Christian to this weekly Fast, namely, that the means employed, mere self-denial in so slight a matter as one's food, is so petty and trifling a thing, that it were degrading the doctrine of the Cross to make such an observance in any way bear upon it. One respects the feelings of such a person and his love for the Cross; but the objection probably proceeds from inex-

---

[25] "We are more apt to Calendar Saints' than sinners' days, therefore there is in the Church a care not to iterate the one alone, but to have frequent repetition of the other." Hooker, l.c.

[26] In respect to the ordinance of Fasting, it might contribute to regularity, if Clergymen were to observe the direction of their Church as contained in the Rubric after the Nicene Creed.

perience in the habit of Fasting. For let any one consider from his childhood upwards by what the greater part of his habits have been formed and by what they are continued: not by any great acts or great sacrifices (as far as any thing might be relatively great), but by a succession of petty actions, whose effect he could not at the time foresee, or thought too minute to leave any trace behind them, and which have in fact, whether for good or for evil, made him what he is. Practice will universally shew, that the motive ennobles the action, not that the action dishonours the motive. "True it is," says Bishop Taylor, "that religion snatches even at little things; and as it teaches us to observe all the great commandments and significations of duty, so it is not willing to pretermit any thing, which, although by its greatness it cannot of itself be considerable, yet by its smallness it may become a testimony of the greatness of the affection, which would not omit the least minutes of love and duty."[27] He who pronounced a blessing upon the gift of a cup of cold water to a disciple in His name, will also bless any act of sincere self-denial practised in memory of Him. Only let us not mock GOD, let us deny ourselves in something which is to us really self-denial; let us, in whatever degree we may be able to bear it without diminishing our own usefulness, put ourselves to some inconvenience, in sorrow and shame for those sins, "the lust of the flesh, and the lust of the eye, and the pride of life," which made our SAVIOUR a man of sorrows, and exposed him to shame, and we shall not afterwards think the practice degrading to Him, or without meaning. The Fast of the early Christians during Lent was an entire abstinence until evening, on the Friday, until three o'clock; unused as we for the most part are to any such discipline, many of us would at the first not be well able to endure it; the difference also of climate might render that *degree* of abstinence oppressive to us, which in more southern latitudes would recruit only and refresh the spirit:[28] the

---

[27] Life and Death of the Holy Jesus, Works, t. iii. p. 96. Of Fasting.
[28] Yet, in what seem to have been *standing* 'orders for the Fast' in our Church in the 17th cent. (at least the orders during the plague in 1636 and 1665, agree to the very letter), the most rigid of the Fasts of the early Church was prescribed. The direction is, 2. "All persons (children, old, weake, and sicke folkes, or the like excepted) are required to eat upon that day but one competent Meal, and that towards night after Evening Prayer, observing sobrietie of diet, without superfluitie of riotous fare, respecting necessitie and not voluptousnesse." This additional Fast was ordered to "bee held everie weeke upon the Wednesday."

weak and sickly again have always been exempt from those more rigid abstinences: they might not beneficially be able to deprive themselves of an early or an entire meal: yet doubtless many of them will have been enabled to trace in themselves the evils of even a necessary softness and indulgence of the body; and the mind which shall have become alive to these, will not be slow in discovering some mode of "keeping under the body, and bringing it into subjection." The early Church, besides its more rigid Fasts, admitted also of the substitution of less palatable and of diminished nourishment; and our own has, in insulated directions accompanying her occasional Fasts, recognized the same principle: in general, she has left the mode of observing her Fasts free to the conscience of each; only let them consist in real self-denial, and be accompanied by charity, retirement, and prayer.

The early Church acted, as it supposed, upon our Blessed SAVIOUR'S own authority, in connecting these acts of bodily abstinence with the memory of His death. The Bridegroom was taken away! Yet if any one should find in himself any abiding repugnance to associate matters, necessarily humiliating, with the doctrine of the Cross, let him not endeavour to force his feelings; the Church wished to lay no yoke upon her members; let him perform the acts in mere compliance with the advice of the Church, and the experience of elder Christians; when he shall have attained the habit of self-denial and self-humiliation, the doctrine of the Cross will, without effort, connect itself with each such performance.

The other Fasts of the Church require the less to be dwelt upon, either because, as in Lent, her authority is yet in some degree recognized, although it be very imperfectly and capriciously obeyed; or, as in the case of the Ember Weeks, the practice has direct scriptural authority; or in that of the other Festivals, because when we shall again value the privilege of having the blessed examples of Martyrs and Saints set before us to

——— ——— Remind us, how our darksome clay
May keep the ethereal warmth our new Creator brought;

we shall feel also the advantage of ushering in each such day by actions which may remind us how they entered into their glory, by taking up their SAVIOUR'S cross and following Him.[29]

---

[29] The only case in which the preparatory Fast is omitted (besides those already alluded to,

Only with regard to the Ember Weeks, it may be permitted to observe, how this institution yet more fully embraces the objects which some good men are endeavouring, by voluntary association, to attain. For the solemn period of the four Ember Weeks is obviously calculated for prayer, not for those only who are to be ordained to any holy function, but for all who shall have been so called, that GOD "would so replenish them with the truth of this doctrine, and endue them with innocency of life, that they may faithfully serve Him;" and thus, not only some few individuals, more nearly known to each other, but all the Ministers and all the people of Christ should, with one mind and one mouth, implore a blessing upon the Ministry, which He has appointed.

And this also is an especial privilege of the whole public Fasting of our Church, beyond the voluntary discipline adopted by individuals, that it presents the whole Church unitedly before GOD, humbling themselves for their past sins, and imploring Him not to give His heritage to reproach. The value of this united humiliation and prayer GOD only knoweth; yet, since He hath promised to be present where two or three are gathered together in His name, how much more when His Church shall again unite before Him "in weeping, fasting, and praying;" how much more shall he spare, though we deserve punishment, and in His wrath think upon mercy. He who spared the Ninevites, how much more may we trust that He will spare us, for whom He has given His well-beloved Son.

"Let us, therefore, dearly beloved, seeing there are many more causes of fasting and mourning in these our days, than hath been of many years heretofore in any one age, endeavour ourselves both inwardly in our hearts, and also outwardly with our bodies, diligently to exercise this godly exercise of fasting, in such sort and manner, as the holy prophets, the apostles, and divers other devout persons for their time used the same. God is now the same God that he was then; God that loveth righteousness, and that hateth iniquity; God which willeth not the death of a sinner, but rather that he turn from his wickedness and live; God that hath promised to turn to us, if we refuse not to turn to him: yea, if we turn our evil works from before his eyes, cease to do evil, learn to do well, seek to do right, relieve the oppressed, be a right judge to the fatherless, defend the widow,

---

pp. 1, 2), is the Festival of St. Michael and all Angels, in which this ground for the Fast also ceases. See Wheatley.

break our bread to the hungry, bring the poor that wander into our house, clothe the naked, and despise not our brother which is our own flesh; *Then shall thou call*, saith the prophet, *and the Lord shall answer; thou shalt cry, and he shall say. Here am I:* yea, God, which heard Ahab, and the Ninevites, and spared them, will also hear our prayers, and spare us, so that we, after their example, will unfeignedly turn unto him: yea, he will bless us with his heavenly benedictions, the time that we have to tarry in this world, and, after the race of this mortal life, he will bring us to his heavenly kingdom, where we shall reign in everlasting blessedness with our saviour Christ, to whom with the Father and the Holy Ghost be all honour and glory, for ever and ever. Amen." Homily on Fasting, part 2.

"Lord have mercy upon us, and give us grace, that while we live in this miserable world, we may through thy help bring forth this and such other fruits of the Spirit, commended and commanded in thy holy word, to the glory of thy name, and to our comforts, that, after the race of this wretched life, we may live everlastingly with thee in thy heavenly kingdom, not for the merits and worthiness of our works, but for thy mercies sake, and the merits of thy dear Son, Jesus Christ, to whom, with thee and the Holy Ghost, be all laud, honour, and glory, for ever and ever. Amen." Homily on Fasting, part 1.

Postscript

In the preceding remarks, the observance of the Fasts enjoined by the Church has been recommended on the ground of the practical wisdom and spiritual experience of the Holy Men, by whose advice they were adopted, rather than on that of the direct authority of the Church. And this has been done, not because the writer doubted of the validity of that authority in this instance, but because it involved a question, which would to many appear distant and abstract; whether, namely, the Church's Laws on this subject were by long disuse virtually abrogated. For I am persuaded that many excellent men, who would shrink from contravening a distinct command of their Church, do in fact neglect these, from some notion that the Church herself has tacitly abandoned them. This notion does indeed appear to me to rest on a wrong supposition.

For, 1st. Since the Church has not annexed any censures to the neglect of this Ordinance (which may correspond to the penal provisions of a civil law), the mere silence of the Church, or of her Spiritual Authorities, is no proof of her acquiescence in the breach of its directions.

2. It would be admitted in any other case, that the mere multitude of those who broke any law, did not alone abrogate that law; that the intrinsic sanctity of the law cannot depend upon the obedience which men may yield to it; that the laxity or remissness of men, at one period, cannot annihilate the authority by which that remissness was to be controlled. The disobedience of others, be they many or few, nay, though they should be even the majority, can have no force in absolving us from the law by which we are in common bound. It is true that observances, which the Church has at one time on her own authority ordained, she may at another abrogate; yet, until she do this, it is to be presumed that she wishes them to be retained in force. And it has already happened, that ordinances have for a time fallen into disuse, which yet were never intended to be abrogated, and which afterwards have been very beneficially revived. It is within the memory of man, that the yearly Commemoration of our Blessed SAVIOUR'S death was in country congregations very generally omitted. This is now, I trust, almost universally observed; nor is there any apparent reason, why this other ordinance of the Church, whereby we humble ourselves for the sins which caused that Death, should not, if men once came seriously to consider it, be promptly, and with very wholesome results, restored. I doubt not, that if the question were formally proposed to the Spiritual Authorities of our Church, whether they would think it adviseable that our stated Fasts should be abolished, they would earnestly deprecate it. Their silence therefore on this subject is rather to be ascribed to the supposed hopelessness of attempting to bind our modern manners to Ancient Discipline, than to any disparagement of the institutions themselves. Our institutions in many cases sleep, but are not dead; nay, one has reason to hope, that although the many neglect them, a faithful few have ever been found, who have experienced and could testify the value of those, which the world seems most entirely to neglect.

Yet, although these grounds of Church authority appear to myself perfectly valid, and I doubt not that many others will feel their weight, as soon as they shall reflect upon them, the other argument, drawn from the practical wisdom and experience of the enacters of these regulations, seems to lie nearer to men's consciences. The argument lies in a narrow compass. Regular and stated Fasts formed a part of the Discipline, by which all Christians of old (if health permitted) subdued the flesh to the spirit, and brought both body and mind into a willing obedience to the Law of GOD. They thought this Discipline necessary as an expression and instrument of repentance, as a memorial of their SAVIOUR, to "refrain their souls and keep them low," to teach them to "trust in the LORD," and seek communion with Him. The value of this remedy for sin has come to us attested by the experience, and sealed by the blood of Martyrs; who having learnt thus to endure hardships, like good soldiers of CHRIST, at last resisted to the blood, striving against sin. Shall we untried pronounce that to be needless for ourselves, which the Goodly Company of the Prophets, the Noble Army of Martyrs, the Holy Church throughout all the world, found needful?

I can hardly anticipate other than one answer. Only let not any one be deterred by the irksomeness, or perplexities, or harassing doubts, which every one must find in resuming a neglected portion of duty. It were scarcely a discipline, if its practice brought with it an *immediate* reward; and we have besides to pay the penalty of our sloth and diseased habits. "Patiently to lack what flesh and blood doth desire, and by virtue to forbear what by nature we covet, this no man attaineth unto, but with labour and long practice."[30] And if it be that blessed instrument of holiness, which they who have tried it assure us, it will not be without some struggle with our spiritual enemy, that we shall recover the ground which we have lost. Only let us persevere, not elated with the first petty victories over ourselves, which may be perhaps conceded to us, in order to produce over-confidence and carelessness; nor dejected by the obstacles which a luxurious and scoffing age may oppose; nor by the yet greater difficulties from within, in acquiring any uniform or consistent habit. Men, aided by God, have done the like; and for us also, His grace will be sufficient.

EDWARD BOUVERIE PUSEY
The Feast of St. Thomas • December 21, 1833

---

[30] Hooker, l.c.

TRACT 19
On Arguing Concerning the Apostolical Succession

Men are sometimes disappointed with the proofs offered in behalf of some important doctrines of our religion; such especially as the necessity of Episcopal Ordination, in order to constitute a Minister of Christ. They consider these proofs to be not so strong as they expected, or as they think desirable. Now such persons should be asked, whether these arguments they speak of are in their estimation weak as a guide to their own practice, or weak in controversy with hardheaded and subtle disputants. Surely, as Bishop Butler has convincingly shown, the faintest probabilities are strong enough to determine our *conduct* in a matter of duty. If there be but a reasonable likelihood of our pleasing Christ more by keeping than by not keeping to the fellowship of the Apostolic Ministry, this of course ought to be enough to lead those, who think themselves moved to undertake the Sacred Office, to seek for a licence to do so from it.

It is necessary to keep this truth distinctly in view, because of the great temptation, that exists among us, to put it out of sight. I do not mean the temptation, which results from pride,—hardness of heart,—a profane disregard of the details and lesser commandments of the Divine Law,—and other such like bad principles of our nature, which are in the way of our honestly confessing it. Besides these, there is a still more subtle temptation to slight it, which will bear insisting on here, arising from an over-desire to convince others, or, in other words, a desire to out-argue others, a fear of seeming inconclusive and confused in our own notions and arguments. Nothing, certainly, is more natural, when we hold a truth strongly, than to wish to persuade others to embrace it also. Nay, without reference to persuasion, nothing is more natural than to be dissatisfied in all cases with our own convictions of a principle or opinion, nay suspicious of it, till we are able to set it down clearly in words. We know, that, in all matters of thought, to write down our meaning is one important means of clearing our minds. Till we do so, we often do not know what we really hold and what we do not hold. And a cautious and accurate reasoner, when he has succeeded in bringing the truth of any subject home to his mind, next begins to look round about the view he has adopted, to consider what others will say to it, and to try to make it unexceptionable. At least we are led thus to fortify our opinion, when it is actually attacked; and if we find we cannot recommend it to the judgment of the assailant, at any rate we endeavour to make him feel that it is to be respected. It is painful to be thought a weak reasoner, even though we are sure in our minds that we are not such.

Now, observe how these feelings will affect us, as regards such arguments as were alluded to above; viz. such as are open to exception, though they are sufficiently strong to determine our conduct. A friend, who differs from us, asks for our *reasons* for our own view. We state them, and he sifts them. He observes, that our conclusions do not necessarily follow from our premises. E.g. to take the argument for the Apostolical Succession derived from the ordination of St. Paul and St. Barnabas (Acts 13:2, 3), he will argue, that their ordination *might* have been an accidental rite, intended merely to commission them for their Missionary journey, which followed it, in Asia Minor; again, that St. Paul's direction to Timothy to "lay hands suddenly on no man" (1 Tim 5:22), *may* refer to confirmation, not ordination.

We should reply (and most reasonably too) that, *considering the undeniable fact* that ordination has ever been thought necessary in the Church for the Ministerial Commission, our interpretation is the most probable one, and therefore the safest to act upon; on which our friend will think awhile, then shake his head, and say, that "at all events this is an *unsatisfactory* mode of reasoning, that it does not convince him, that he is desirous of clearer light, &c."

Now what is the consequence of such a discussion as this on ourselves? not to make us *give up* the doctrine, but to make us afraid of *urging* it. We grow lukewarm about it; and, with an appearance of judgment and caution (as the world will call it) confess that "to rest the claims of our Clergy on an Apostolical Descent is an unsafe and inexpedient line of argument; that it will not convince men, the evidence not being sufficient; that it is not a practical way of acting to insist upon it, &c."—whereas the utmost that need be admitted, is, that it is out of place to make it the subject of a speculative dispute, and to argue about it on that abstract logical platform which virtually excludes a reference to conduct and duty. And indeed, it would be no unwise caution to bear about us, wherever we go, that our first business, as Christians, is to address men as responsible servants of CHRIST, not as antagonists; and that it is but a secondary duty (though a duty) to "refute the gainsayers."

And, as on the one hand it continually happens, that those who are most skilled in debate are deficient in sound practical piety, so on the other it may be profitable to us to reflect, that doctrines, which we believe to be most true, and which are received as such by the most profound and enlarged intellects, and which rest upon the most irrefragable proofs, yet may be above *our* disputative powers, and can be treated by us only with reference to our conduct. And in this way, as in others, is fulfilled the saying of the Apostle, that "the preaching of the Cross is to them that perish foolishness; but unto us, who are saved, it is the power of GOD. . . Where is the wise? where is the scribe? where is the disputer of this world? hath not GOD made foolish the wisdom of this world? . . . The foolishness of GOD is wiser than men; and the weakness of GOD is stronger than men."

On Reluctance to Confess the Apostolical Succession

If a Clergyman is quite convinced that the Apostolical Succession is lost, then of course he is at liberty to turn his mind from the subject. But if he is not quite sure of this, it surely is his duty seriously to examine the question, and to make up his mind carefully and deliberately. For if there be a chance of its being preserved to us, there is a chance of his having had a momentous talent committed to him, which he is burying in the earth.

It cannot be supposed that any serious man would treat the subject scoffingly. If any one is tempted to do so, let him remember the fearful words of the Apostle. "Esau, a *profane person*, who for one morsel of meat, sold his birthright."

If any are afraid, that to insist on their commission will bring upon them ridicule, and diminish their usefulness, let them ask themselves, whether it be not cowardice to refuse to leave the event to GOD. It was the reproach of the men of Ephraim that, though they were "harnessed and carried bows," they "turned themselves back in the day of battle."

And if any there be, who take upon them to contrast one doctrine of the Gospel with another, and preach those only which they consider the more essential, let them consider our SAVIOUR'S words, "These things ought ye to have done, and not to leave the other undone."

JOHN HENRY NEWMAN
December 23, 1833

TRACT 20: AD SCHOLAS
The Visible Church
Letters to a Friend

Letter III

MY DEAR———

You have some misgivings, it seems, lest the doctrine I have been advocating "should lead to Popery." I will not, by way of answer, say, that the question is not, whether it will *lead to Popery*, but whether it is *in the Bible;* because it would bring the Bible and Popery into one sentence, and seem to imply the possibility of a "communion" between "light and darkness." No; it is the very enmity I feel against the Papistical corruptions of the Blessed Gospel, which leads me to press upon you a doctrine of Scripture, which we are sinfully surrendering, and the Church of Rome has faithfully retained.

How comes it that a system, so unscriptural as the Popish, makes converts? because it has in it an element of truth and comfort amid its falsehoods. And the true way of opposing it is, not to give up to them that element, which GOD'S providence has preserved to us also, thus basely surrendering "the inheritance of our Fathers," but to claim it as our own, and to make use of it for the purposes for which GOD has given it to us. I will explain what I mean.

Before CHRIST came, Divine Truth was, as it were, a pilgrim in the world. The Jews excepted, men who had portions of the SPIRIT of GOD, knew not their privilege. The whole force and current of the external world was against them, acting powerfully on their imagination, and tempting them to set sight against faith, to trust the many witnesses who prophesied falsehood (as if) in the name of the LORD, rather than the still small voice which spoke within them. Who can undervalue the power of this fascination, who has had experience of the world ever so little? Who can go at this day into mixed society, who can engage in politics or other active business, but finds himself gradually drifting off from the true Rock on which his faith is built, till he begins in despair to fancy, that solitude is the only safe place for the Christian, or, (with a baser judgment) that strict obedience will not be required at the last day of those who have been engaged in active life? If such is now the power of the world's enchantments, surely much greater was it before our SAVIOUR came.

Now what did He do for us, in order to meet this evil? His merciful Providence chose means which might act as a counter influence on the imagination. The visible power of the world enthralled men to a lie; He set up a Visible Church, to witness the other way, to witness for Him, to be a matter of fact, as undeniable as the shining of the sun, that there *was* such a principle as conscience in the world, as faith, as fear of GOD; that there were men who considered themselves bound to live as His servants. The common answer which we hear made every day to persons who engage in any novel undertaking, is, "You will get no one to join you; nothing can come of it; you are singular in your opinion; you do not take practical views, but are smit with a fancy, with a dream of former times," &c. How cheering is it to a person so circumstanced, to be able to point to others elsewhere, who actually hold the same opinions as himself, and exert themselves for the same objects! Why? because it is an appeal to a *fact*, which no one can deny; it is an evidence that the view which influences him is something external to his own mind, and not a dream. What two persons see, cannot be an ideal apparition. Men are governed by such facts, much more than by argumentative proof. These act upon the imagination. Let a person be told ten times over that an opinion is true, the *fact* of its being said becomes an argument for the truth of it; i.e. it is so with most men. We see from time to time the operation of this principle of our nature in political matters. Our American colonies revolt; France feels the sympathy of the event, and is revolutionized. Again, in the same colonies, the Episcopal Church flourishes; we Churchmen at home hail it as an omen of the Church's permanence among ourselves. On the other hand, what can be more dispiriting than to find a cause, which we advocate, sinking in some other country or neighbourhood, though there be no reason for concluding, that, *because* it has fallen elsewhere, therefore it will among ourselves. In order then to supply this need of our minds, to satisfy the imagination, and so to help our faith, for this among other reasons CHRIST set up a visible Society, His Church, to be as a light upon a hill, to all the ends of the earth, while time endures. It is a witness of the unseen world; a pledge of it; and a prefiguration of what hereafter will take place. It prefigures the ultimate separation of good and bad, holds up the great laws of GOD'S Moral Governance, and preaches the blessed truths of the Gospel. It pledges to us the promises of the next world, for it is something (so to say) in hand; CHRIST has done one work as the earnest of another. And it witnesses the truth to the whole world; awing sinners, while it enspirits the fainting believer. And in all these ways it helps forward the world to come; and further, as the keeper of the Sacraments, it is an essential means of the realizing it at present in our fallen race. Nor is it much to the purpose, as regards our duty towards it, what are the feelings and spiritual state of the individuals who are its officers. True it is, were the Church to teach heretical doctrine, it might become incumbent on us (a miserable obligation!) to separate from it. But, while it teaches substantially the Truth, we ought to look upon it as one whole, one ordinance of GOD, not as composed of individuals, but as a House of GOD'S building;—as an instrument in His hand, to be used and reverenced for the sake of its Maker.

Now the Papists have retained it; and so they have the advantage of possessing an instrument, which is, in the first place, suited to the needs of human nature; and next, is a special gift of CHRIST, and so has a blessing with it. Accordingly we see that in its measure success follows their zealous use of it. They act with great force upon the imaginations of men. The vaunted antiquity, the universality, the unanimity of their Church puts them above the varying fashions of the world, and the religious novelties of the day. And truly when one surveys the grandeur of their proceedings, a sigh arises in the thoughtful mind, to think that we should be separate from them; Cum talis esses, utinam noster esses!—But, alas, AN UNION IS IMPOSSIBLE. Their communion is infected with heresy; we are bound to flee it, as a pestilence. They have established a lie in the place of GOD'S truth; and, by their claim of immutability in doctrine, cannot undo the sin they have committed. They cannot repent. Popery must be destroyed; it cannot be reformed.

Now then what is the Christian to do? Is he forced back upon that cheerless atheism (for so it practically must be considered) which prevailed in the world before CHRIST'S coming, poorly alleviated, as it was, by the received polytheims of the heathen? Can we conceive a greater calamity to have occurred at the time of our Reformation, one which the Enemy of man would have been more set on effecting, than to have entangled the whole of the Church Catholic in the guilt of heresy, and so have forced every one who worshipped in spirit and in truth, to flee out of doors into the bleak world, in order to save his soul? I do not think that Satan could have desired any event more eagerly, than such an alternative; viz. to have forced Christians, either to remain in communion with heresy, or to join themselves in some such spontaneous union among themselves, as is dissolved as easily as it is formed. Blessed be GOD! his malice has been thwarted. I do believe it to be one most conspicuous mark of GOD'S adorable Providence over us, as great as if we saw a miracle, that Christians in England escaped in that evil day from either extreme, neither corrupted doctrinally, nor secularized ecclesiastically. Thus in every quarter of the world, from North America, to New South Wales, a Zoar has been provided for those who would fain escape Sodom, yet dread to be without shelter. I hail it as an omen amid our present perils, that our Church will not be destroyed. He hath been mindful of us; He will bless us. He has wonderfully preserved our Church as a true branch of the Church Universal, yet withal preserved it free from heresy. It is Catholic and Apostolic, yet not Papistical.

With this reflection before us, does it not seem the most utter ingratitude to an astonishing Providence of GOD'S mercy, to be neglectful, as many Churchmen now are, of the gift? to attempt unions with those who have separated from the Church, to break down the partition walls, and to argue as if religion were altogether and only a matter of each man's private concern, and that the State and Nation were not bound to prefer the Apostolical Church to all self-originated forms of Christianity? But this is a point beside my purpose. Take the matter merely in the light of human expedience. Shall we be so far less wise in our generation than the children of this world, as to relinquish the support which the Truth receives from the influence of a Visible Church upon the imagination, from the energy of operation which a well disciplined Body ensures? Shall we not foil the Papists, not with their own weapons, but with weapons which are ours as well as theirs? or, on the other hand, shall we with a melancholy infatuation give them up to them? Depend upon it, to insist on the doctrine of the Visible Church is not to favour the Papists, it is to do them the most serious injury. It is to deprive them of their only strength. But if we neglect to do so, what will be the consequence? Break down the Divine Authority of our Apostolical Church, and you are plainly preparing the way for Popery in our land. Human nature cannot remain without visible guides; it chooses them for itself, if it is not provided for them. If the Aristocracy and the Church fall, Popery steps in. Political events are beyond our power, and perhaps out of our sphere; but ecclesiastical matters are in the hands of all Churchmen.

But my letter has run to an unusual length.—Excuse it.

And believe, &c.

JOHN HENRY NEWMAN
December 24, 1833

Tracts of 1834

TRACT 21: AD POPULUM
Mortification of the Flesh
A Scripture Duty

If we take the example of the Holy Men of Scripture as our guide, certainly bodily privation and chastisement are a very essential duty of all who wish to serve GOD, and prepare themselves for His presence.

First, we have the example of Moses. His recorded Fasts were miraculous; still they were Fasts, and the ordinance was recommended to the notice of all believers afterwards, by the honour put upon it. "I abode in the mount forty days and forty nights; I neither did eat bread nor drink water." Again; "I fell down before the LORD, as at the first, forty days and forty nights; I did neither eat bread nor drink water, because of all your sins" (Deut 9:9, 18). Fasting is in the former instance subservient to divine contemplation, in the latter to humiliation and intercession for sinners.

Elijah. "He said unto him. What manner of man was he which came up to meet you, and told you these words? And they answered him, He was an hairy man, and girt with a girdle of leather about his loins. And he said, It is Elijah the Tishbite" (2 Kgs 1:7, 8). It is indeed needless to show the ascetic character of him, who was in fact the chief and type of those who "wandered about in sheepskins and goatskins," "in deserts, and in mountains, and in dens and caves of the earth." He too fasted by the power of God for forty days and nights; "He arose and did eat and drink, and went in the strength of that meat forty days and forty nights, unto Horeb the mount of GOD" (1 Kgs 19:8).

Daniel. "I set my face unto the LORD GOD, to seek by prayer and supplications, with fasting, and sackcloth, and ashes; and I prayed unto the LORD my GOD, and made my confession" (Dan 9:3, 4). It must be observed, that Daniel was not bound by any vow, as Samson and Samuel. Moreover, it would appear the gift of prophecy was given him in reward for his self-chastisements, as the following passage shows. "In those days I Daniel was mourning three full weeks; I ate no pleasant bread, neither came flesh nor wine in my mouth; neither did I anoint myself at all, till three whole weeks were fulfilled. . . . . . And he said unto me, O Daniel, a man greatly beloved, understand the words that I speak unto thee, and stand upright; for unto thee am I now sent. . . . . . Fear not, Daniel; for *from the first day* that thou didst set thine heart to understand, and *to chasten thyself* before thy GOD, thy words were heard, and I am come for thy words" (Dan 10:2, 3, 11, 12; vide also Luke 2:37, Acts 10:30).

2. Now here it will be objected, perhaps, that these instances are taken from the Old Testament, and belong to the Law of Moses, which is not binding on Christians.

I answer;

(1.) That in the above passages Fasting is connected with moral acts, humiliation, prayer, meditation, which are equally binding on us as on the Jews. Man is now what he was then; and if affliction of the flesh was good then, it is now.

(2.) In matter of fact, *private* Fasting, such as instanced in the passages above quoted, was no special duty of the Mosaic Law. Public Fasting, indeed, was on one occasion enjoined by Moses himself, and on others by subsequent Rulers; but this was in part a ceremonial act, not a moral discipline, and was doubtless abolished with the other rites of the Law.

"Of Fasts," says Lewis, "there was no more than one appointed by the Law of Moses, called the Fast of Expiation. . . . . The great day of Expiation was a most severe Fast, kept every year upon the tenth day of the month Tizri, which answers to our September. . . . . . This solemnity was observed with fasting and abstinence, not only from all meat and drink, but from all other pleasure whatsoever; insomuch that they did not wash their faces, much less anoint their heads, nor wear their shoes, ... nor (if their Doctors say true) read any portion of the Law which would give them delight. They refrained likewise not only from pleasure, but from labour, nothing being to be done upon this day but confessing of sins and repentance."¹

Nay, it may rather be said, that the Jewish Law, as such, was rather opposed than otherwise to austerities. The Nazarites and Rechabites, being exceptions to the rule, are evidence to it. Vide, on the other hand, Deuteronomy 12, Ecclesiastes 5:18.²

Such then being the character of the Law in its formal letter, it tells just the contrary way to that which superficial reasoners might expect. For it is most remarkable, first, that the greatest prophets under it, such as Elijah, and Daniel, were without express command singularly austere and self-afflicting men, in the midst of a people, who from the first went lusting after "the fish which they eat in Egypt freely; the cucumbers, and the melons, and the leeks, and the onions, and the garlick, and said, Who shall give us flesh to eat?" Next, there is something of a very startling and admonitory nature in the *miraculous* fasts of Moses and Elijah, under this same imperfect dispensation. The miracle evidently was for some purpose; yet it did not sanction, in any direct way, any injunction of the Law. Was it not an admonition to the Israelites, that there was a more excellent way of obedience than that which ALMIGHTY GOD as yet thought fit to promulgate by solemn enactment? Is it not an intimation serviceable for Christian practice, as much as Moses' announcement of the destined "Prophet like unto him" is intended for the comfort of Christian faith?

Surely the duty of bodily discipline might be rested on the answer to this plain question, *Why* did Daniel use austerities not enjoined by the Law?

3. Now turn to the New Testament, and observe what clear light is therein thrown upon the duty already recommended to us by the Old Testament Saints.

First, there is the instance of St. John the Baptist. "John came neither eating nor drinking" (Matt 11:28); and his disciples fasted (Matt 9:14).

Our SAVIOUR did *not* stately fast; but here also the exception proves the rule. He who did not fast, was the only one born of woman

---

¹ Lewis, Hebrew Republic, iv. 14.
² Vid. Spencer de Legg. Hebræor. lib. 3. diss. 1. ii. 3. diss. 4. i. 5. &c.

who was untainted by sinful flesh; which seems to imply, that all who are natural descendants of guilty Adam ought to fast.

He bade His disciples to fast. Consider His implied precept, which is an express command to those who obey the Law of Liberty. "When thou fastest, anoint thine head and wash thy face, that thou appear not unto men to fast" (Matt 6:17, 18).

Consider, moreover, the *general austere character* of Christian obedience, as enjoined by our LORD;—a circumstance much to be insisted on in an age like this, when what is really self-indulgence is thought to be a mere moderate and innocent use of this world's goods. I will but refer to a few, out of many texts, which I am persuaded are now forgotten by numbers of educated and amiable men, who are fond of extolling what they call the mild, tolerant, enlightened spirit of the Gospel. Matthew 5:29, 30; 7:13, 14; 10:37-39. Mark 9:43-50; 10:25. Luke 14:12, 26-33.

And reflect, too, whether the spirit of texts, such as the following, will not move every true member of the Church Militant, "The ark, and Israel, and Judah abide in tents; and my lord Joab, and the servants of my lord, are encamped in the open fields; shall I then go into mine house, to eat and to drink?...... as thou livest, and as thy soul liveth, I will not do this thing" (2 Sam 11:11).

Now take the example of the Apostles. St. Peter was fasting, when he had the vision which sent him to Cornelius (Acts 10:10). The prophets and teachers at Antioch were fasting, when the HOLY GHOST revealed to them His purpose about Saul and Barnabas (Acts 3:2, 3; vide also Acts 14:23; 2 Cor 6:5, 11:27).

Weigh well the following text, which, I am persuaded, many men would deny to be St. Paul's writing, had not a gracious Providence preserved to us the epistle containing it. "I keep under my body, and bring it into subjection; lest that by any means, when I have preached to others, I myself should be a cast-away" (1 Cor 9:27).

Lastly, Consider the practice of the Primitive Christians.

The following account of the early Christian Fasts, is from Bingham, Antiq. lib. xxi.

THE QUADRAGESIMAL OR LENT FAST.—"The Quadragesimal Fast before Easter," says Sozomen, "some observe six weeks, as the Illyrian and Western Churches, and all Libya, Egypt, and Palestine; others make it seven weeks, as the Constantinopolitans and neighbouring nations as far as Phœnicia; others fast three only of those six or seven weeks, by intervals; others the three weeks next immediately before Easter."

The manner of observing Lent among those that were piously disposed to observe it, was to abstain from all food till evening, for anciently a change of diet was not reckoned a fast; but it consisted in perfect abstinence from all sustenance for the whole day till evening.

THE FASTS OF THE FOUR SEASONS.—The next Anniversary fasting days were those which were called *Jejunia quatuor temporum*, the Fasts of the Four Seasons of the Year. . . . . These were at first designed. . . . .to beg a blessing of God upon the several seasons of the year, or to return thanks for the benefits received in each of them, or to exercise and purify both body and soul in a more particular manner, at the return of these certain terms of stricter discipline and more extraordinary devotion. [These afterwards became the Ember Fasts.]

MONTHLY FASTS.—In some places they had also Monthly Fasts throughout the year; except in the two months of July and August. . . . because of the sickness of the season.

WEEKLY FASTS.—Besides these they had their Weekly Fasts on Wednesday and Friday, called the Stationary Days, and Half-Fasts, or Fasts of the Fourth and Sixth Days of the Week. . . . These Fasts, being of continual use every week throughout the year, except in the Fifty Days between Easter and Pentecost, were not kept with that rigour and strictness which was observed in the time of Lent. . . . . [but] ordinarily held no longer than 9 o'clock, i.e. 3 in the afternoon."[3]

JOHN HENRY NEWMAN
The Feast of the Circumcision
January 1, 1834

---

[3] [The original tract was signed "J.H.N., Oxford, *The Feast of the Circumcision*."]

TRACT 22

Richard Nelson

II: The Athanasian Creed

> ...Athanasius's Creed...ought thoroughly to be
> received and believed; for [it] may be proved by
> most certain warrants of holy Scripture.
> —Article VIII

I look back with much pleasure to the visit I had from my friend Mr. Woodnot, the Bristol Merchant I before spoke of.

He staid with me some days, and we had many agreable rambles and discussions together, which were to me peculiarly interesting, from the wide experience he had had of men and things, and of places too, as he had been often abroad, in Switzerland, in Turkey, and on different parts of the American Continent, where he had spent some years.

Two or three days after our meeting with Richard Nelson, as stated before, we took our walk (it being a pleasant evening towards the end of August) along the side of a little stream, which we traced for a mile or two down the valley, returning by a kind of natural terrace, which terminated in my favourite beech-walk. The sun was low when we got here; and we stood still (it was not far from Nelson's garden hedge) to admire its rich glow on the opposite side of the valley. I was pointing out to my friend a bold and almost mountainous outline of hills rising in the distance, far to the west in Lancashire, Pendle-hill, as I fancied, and other lofty tracts in the neighbourhood of Clitheroe; and we were speculating on the distance they might be from us.

"Sir," said a voice, which startled me, from my not observing that any one was near; "Pendle-hill must be full fifty miles off; what you see is most likely some of the high ground beyond Halifax."

"Why, Richard," said I, "What are you doing down there?" for I could scarcely see more than his head—"You seem to be making a strong entrenchment round your castle."

"I dare say, Sir," he answered, "you may wonder what I am about; but at this time of year, when the springs are low, I generally spend an hour, when I have leisure in an evening, in repairing the garden-mound, that it may be fit to stand against the assaults of what I call my two winter enemies."

"What can they be?" I asked; "I did not know that you had any enemies."

"Yes, Sir, I have," he replied; "at least my garden had two, land-floods, and Scotch ponies. Almost every winter, once, if not twice, there is a violent land-flood from the high ground behind the house; and if this ditch were not kept clear, to take the water off immediately, the garden would not recover the damage all the next year. To be sure, this kind of flood does not commonly last many hours; but that is long enough, you know, Sir, to spoil the labour of weeks and months."

"That I can understand," I answered; "but how you can be in any alarm about Highland ponies, I cannot imagine."

"Why," said he, "you know, Sir, that there is a fair at the town every year, early in the Spring, where a great many of these ponies are bought and sold; and for many years past, Mr. Saveall, the owner of this field, has let it for one day and night to the horsedealer (a well-known man out of Lincolnshire) to turn those ponies into, as well as other horses he may have purchased at the fair. The first year I was here, I was not aware of this custom, and had taken no precaution against it; so these little mountaineers got in at a weak place in the hedge during the night, and trod the garden, as one may say, to a mummy. So, to protect myself for the future against such mischievous visitors, I put this fence along, which I was now repairing. And if you will please to look at it, I think you, Sir, will allow that it was not badly contrived, though I say it, who should not say it."

All along the whole length of the garden (which might be perhaps nearly one hundred yards) on that side which was next the foot-path, he had fixed very neatly, about half way up the slope of the ditch on the opposite side, a double indented line of sharp strong stakes, pointing upwards, presenting a sort of *chevaux de frise;* an impenetrable barrier, which no pony, highland or lowland, could possibly get through or over.

We said something in commendation of his skill and precaution: on which he observed; "I am glad, Sir, you approve of what I have done; for it has cost me a good deal of labour. And my neighbour, Farmer Yawn, who has been standing by me for the last three quarters of an hour, and went away just as you came up, he says, I am taking a deal of trouble, and very likely for nothing; how can I be sure there will be a land-flood, or that the man will turn in the ponies? and besides (says he) neither land-flood nor ponies would stay twelve hours. But I know better, Sir, than to take Mr. Yawn's advice; for if my bit of garden should be ruined for a twelvemonth, it would be no comfort afterwards to think, that perhaps it might not have happened, or that the mischief was quickly done, or that with timely caution it might have been prevented."

After a few more words we wished him a good evening, and walked on for some little way in silence, which my companion put an end to by saying, "It must be confessed that our friend Nelson is a sensible man; and not the less so (added he, with a smile) because I am sure he will agree with me in opinion."

For in the course of our walk we had been discussing rather earnestly the subject of the Athanasian Creed; the question between us not being as to the doctrines contained in it, but as to the expediency of retaining it in the Liturgy, supposing any changes should take place in that also, as in every thing else. Not that there was any real difference of opinion between us on that point either; but wishing to know his views on the subject, I had been urging the various objections, such of them at least as are most plausible, and had been gratified with observing how little weight he attached to them; and my satisfaction was the greater, because, from his education and profession, as a layman and a merchant, he could not be accused of what have been scornfully designated as "academical and clerical prejudices."

In the course of our conversation he had expressed himself most earnestly in favour of the Athanasian Creed; alleging, for this his opinion, various reasons, and among others the following; "that he regarded this Creed in the light of a fence or bulwark set up to protect the Truth against all innovations and encroachments; and that to take it away, particularly in times when popular opinion, or rather feeling, was against it, would be almost high treason against GOD (that was his Word): would be, so far as in us lies, wilfully to expose the Truth to be trodden down by its enemies."

"Now," said he, "whilst you were talking to our friend Nelson, it struck me that his care about his garden very aptly expresses our duty in respect of this very subject. For why is this Creed so obnoxious? simply because it is so strongly and sharply worded; because it leaves no opening for a semi-socinian or a five-quarter latitudinarian to creep in at; because it presents an insurmountable obstacle to every intruder who would trample under foot the LORD'S vineyard.

"And even if the aspect of things were more favourable, even if there were no sign of danger at hand, I should much rather advise that, like Nelson, we should look forward to probable or possible inroads, than venture to neglect, much less to remove, our fences.

"But," he continued, "in the present condition of what is by courtesy (or one might almost say, facetiously) called the Christian world, it were in my judgment little less than madness to yield so strong a position,—one too, which if once lost can never be recovered."

And then he referred to what he had before been insisting on, the great mistake made by the American Church in rejecting the Athanasian Creed from her Liturgy; and how, from personal observation during his residence first at New York, and afterwards at Charleston, he was sure the time would come when its loss would be felt and acknowledged by the true sons of that Church. "And I wish," added he, as we concluded our walk and our discussion together, "you would endeavour to ascertain what are the sentiments of our friend Nelson on this subject, for I have no doubt he has turned it over in his mind; and his opinion must certainly be of value, because happily for himself he has not been, I suppose, in the way of hearing the profane absurdities that are daily written and spoken against this inestimable Creed."

"Yes," said I, "whatever his opinions are, I doubt not they will be found candid, and free from unreasonable prejudice; and I will take an early opportunity of ascertaining them."

Soon after this my friend left me, and I promised to communicate to him the result of my enquiries. The Sunday following, it being a serene autumnal morning, according to the description of the Divine Poet—"most calm, most bright"—I proceeded earlier than usual towards the school.

When I came up to Richard's cottage, he was standing at the gate, with his infant child in his arms, looking as if he could envy no man; as if

Sunday were to him what it should be to us all, "the couch of time, care's balm and bay."

"You are rather earlier, Sir, than usual," he said.

"Yes," I answered, "the morning is so lovely, so Sunday-like, I could not endure to stay any longer within doors."

After some few observations had passed between us,—in which he expressed with an unaffected solemnity of manner peculiar to himself, his sense of the value of each returning LORD'S day, calling it (and I think he used, though unconsciously, Isaac Walton's very words) "a step towards a blessed eternity,"—I asked him if he would have any objection to take two or three turns with me in the beech-walk, as it still wanted a considerable time to school.

He answered that he would gladly accompany me, especially as it might be better for the child to be taken under the shade of the trees.

"Richard," said I, "my friend Mr. Woodnot, and I may call him your friend too, was much amused with your plan for keeping off the enemies of your garden. He commended it highly, and thinks you therein set a good example to all true Churchmen, and especially to us of the Clergy."

"In what respect, Sir?" he asked. "Why," I replied, "in keeping your fences strong and sharp, and contrived in the best possible way to serve the purpose *of* fences; namely, to preserve one's property from injury. For we understood you to say, that, were it not for a little observation and foresight, however well all might be for three hundred and sixty-four days in the year, in one twenty-four hours all might be laid waste, either by the torrent from the high ground above you, or by the cattle from your neighbour's field."

"Indeed, Sir," he answered, "that is no more than the truth. But I confess I do not exactly see how in acting thus I have set any particularly good example. No person of common sense could do otherwise."

"As to that," I replied, "perhaps what some witty man said of common honesty, he might too have said of common sense, that it is a very *uncommon* thing. But be that as it may, it certainly would appear to me to be no mark of sense nor of honesty either, if we Christians who are 'put in trust (as St. Paul speaks) with the Gospel,' were to draw back from our strong advanced positions, in the vain hope that the Enemy would be content with this success, and encroach no further."

"May I ask, Sir," he said, "what it is you refer to?"

"Why, Richard," I replied, "of course you have heard that a great many people think the Church Prayer Book ought to be altered; and that first and foremost the Athanasian Creed ought to be put out of it."

"Sir," said he, "I have heard more than one person make this observation, but I never took much account of it till about a year or eighteen months ago, when a brother-in-law of mine, who is fond of poring over the newspapers, told me he had been reading extracts from the works of a famous preacher, one Dr. Hoadley, which I am sorry to say he was inclined to admire. For in these extracts there were objections made to other parts of the Church Service, and particularly to the Athanasian Creed, which (the Dr. said) was a great blot in the Prayer Book, and that he wished we were well rid of it, with other such disrespectful expressions. Now, Sir, it seemed to me such a thing, for a Clergyman who had signed the Articles and the Prayer Book, and had his maintenance from the Church, and had taken an oath before God and man to teach the truth to his flock, *according to the Prayer Book;* that a Church Minister should take upon him to omit so remarkable a portion of the Church Service; nay more, should speak so slightingly of what he had solemnly assented to, and was even sworn to; this seemed to me to be astonishing; and, I must confess to you, even shocking. And, Sir, I thought of what my mother had said to me in her last illness, about the danger of trifling with GOD ALMIGHTY. I thought too, if there should be many such Clergymen as this Dr. Hoadley, what confusion and perplexity they would throw people's minds into, driving some perhaps into downright infidelity. And then I went on to reflect, what if *my* poor children should hereafter fall into the way of some such false teachers, and learn to deny the LORD that bought them, and to despise the SPIRIT of Grace.

"This thought I could not endure; so I resolved, that with GOD'S gracious help, I would search the matter out for myself; for surely, Sir, it is a matter in which not the Clergy only, but we all are deeply interested."

"You say right," I replied; "the knowledge of GOD'S truth must be the greatest earthly treasure to us all. It unquestionably concerns the Laity full as much as it does the Clergy, to ascertain the Truth and to keep it; also to hand it on pure and uncorrupted to their children after them."

He proceeded; "My plan was this; first to endeavour to make out what was the intention of the Church in appointing this and the other two

Creeds to be occasionally used; and then to try this Athanasian Creed by Scripture rules; and if I could not reconcile it to them, why then certainly, however unwillingly, I should have joined in opinion with those who wish to have it left out of the Prayer Book."

"A very good plan," said I, "but you must recollect that the enemies of this Creed would ask, what possible reason you could have for being *unwilling* to part with it, especially when you know that great numbers of people have so vehement a dislike to it."

"Sir," said he, "I have long made up my mind, that on questions of this kind relating to GOD and Eternity, people's likings and dislikings are not much in the scale either way. But I think, Sir, I can offer one or two good excuses for my being unwilling to have this Creed laid aside. In the first place, it would give me pain to have any great alterations made in such a book as the Prayer Book; which I have been used to from my infancy; which as a child I was always taught to reverence; and which (I am not ashamed to say) I do reverence from my heart more and more the older I grow. In the next place, I am sure all must allow that some parts of the Athanasian Creed are very noble and beautiful to hear, especially when they are well read or repeated. And again, even a child may see that if this Creed be put away, great encouragement will be given, not only to protest infidels, but also to many wild thoughtless persons, who would fain believe that Religion, like every thing else, needs to be radically reformed."

"But, Richard," I said, "you are not, I suppose, so vain as to imagine that our Church Reformers will be willing to keep the Prayer Book just as it is, merely because you and I and a few more admire some of the clauses in this Creed."

"Sir," said he, "you may be sure I never imagined such a thing. I was not presuming to give an opinion, whether or not the Prayer Book is likely to be improved by any alterations which may be made in it. I was only excusing myself for being lothe to part with the Athanasian Creed."

"But," said I, "will you now tell me what conclusion you came to in your enquiry into the intention of the Church in appointing this and the other two Creeds to be used."

"I remembered," he said, "that I had heard you, Sir, or some one whose opinion I could take on these subjects, make an observation, that the three Creeds were not written all at the same time, but at three different periods. That the Apostles' Creed was made first, either in the time of the Apostles, or very soon after. That the Nicene Creed came next, after an interval of two hundred years or more. And that then again, after another considerable space, I think I understood more than a century, followed the Creed of St. Athanasius, as it was called.

"So it came into my thoughts that the Church seemed to act like a tender mother very anxious for her children, from the very first; but growing still more and more anxious as they grow older, are more exposed to dangers, and yet less and less willing to yield themselves to her control.

"Thus it may seem, that in the most ancient, the Apostles' Creed, a plain simple rule of faith is given.

"In the next, the Nicene Creed, *the same rule is laid down*, but more at length, and in a tone of anxiety and caution as if the enemy were at hand.

"But in the last, the Athanasian Creed, where still *the very same rule of faith is laid down*, the alarm is loudly sounded, there is throughout an expression of urgent warning, as needful for persons in the very midst of foes, some open, and more secret foes, who would rob GOD of His honour, and man of the everlasting inheritance, purchased for him by his SAVIOUR'S Blood.

"Indeed," said I, "it is fearful to think to what lengths the pride of human reason will draw those who yield to it. But before you proceed with your statement, I should wish to know what opinion you have come to respecting what are so falsely, not to say profanely, called 'the damnatory clauses' in the Athanasian Creed. You are doubtless aware that many good sort of persons, who profess not to disapprove of the other parts of the Creed, are (or at least fancy themselves) much offended and hurt in their feelings by these clauses.

"Observe, I am not now exactly referring to persons who speak harshly or disrespectfully of this Creed, but rather to persons of piety and learning, who with all reverence for it as an ancient and true confession of faith, have yet thought that some of the expressions in it are unnecessarily strong, and what they cannot endure to repeat or to hear."

"Sir," he replied, "if it is not presumptuous in me to pass my opinion on the conduct of such persons as you represent, I should say to them, if you can endure to believe these things, you may also endure to acknowledge such your belief, and to hear it confirmed by the voice of the Church.

"The parent who *cannot endure* to correct his child, will doubtless live to repent his mistaken tenderness, as we are taught in Scripture.

"And if the Church or her Ministers through like false pity should no longer endure to hold out to our consciences the terrors of the LORD, we of the people shall no doubt have cause to lament *their* mistaken tenderness; even though now, like over-indulged Christians, we may many of us be impatient of strict restraint or of warnings seemingly severe; yet, *if the Church will be but firm to her sacred trust,* many souls will doubtless in the end bless God for these very warnings and threatenings, which now they fancy to be almost intolerable.

"But as to persons who scruple not to speak scornfully and reproachfully of this Creed, or any part of it, I must think such language of theirs shows rashness, and ignorance too, very unbecoming a Christian. For, it may well be asked, is a mother to be blamed who, seeing her child in imminent danger, warns him of it in language the most powerful her tongue can give utterance to?

"*If the Gospel of* CHRIST *be indeed our only hope*, is not the Church a true friend to us, in telling us so; in making us confess it, as one may almost say, whether we choose or no?

"*If* the Gospel of the LORD JESUS be our only hope; is not this kind?"

"Indeed," said I, "your argument is most just; it is the truest kindness to warn people of their danger. But as it is too often a thankless office; so in the present instance. For, as you know, these which may fitly be called 'The Warning Clauses,' or 'The Monitory Clauses,' are especially reviled; as, in fact, the tendency of the whole Creed is accounted to be unscriptural and uncharitable, even by some who think themselves, and desire to be thought by others, very serious Christians."

"Sir," said he, "to any *Christian* who was disposed to think so ill of it, I should like just to mention a conversation I had some time last year with a man of our parish, Edmund Plush, the man that has set up the new beer-house. You know. Sir, I dare say, that he was once a gentleman's servant."

"I have heard so," I answered; "but as I see some of the boys coming, it is time for me to leave you, and make the best of my way to the school."

"And I," said he, "will take the child back, and be after you in a quarter of an hour; but in the evening I shall hope, Sir, to have some further conversation with you."

"I hope so too," I answered. But, as it happened, I was called to go after the Evening Service to visit a sick person in a distant part of the parish; and a week or two passed away before we again met. He then happened to come to my house one evening to settle an account; I desired he might come to me into my Study; and when we had concluded our business, I told him I wished he would stay half an hour, that we might finish the conversation which we had broken off so abruptly before.

He said, if I were disengaged he would be glad to stay; and not without some difficulty I prevailed on him to sit down.

"Richard," said I, "if you recollect, you were going to tell me of a conversation you had with Edmund Plush."

"Yes, Sir," he replied; "I had two or three days' work, pointing his garden wall (for Edmund is very curious about his fruit, especially about some favourite Orlean plums); and one day, as he was standing by me, and running on with his talk about alterations and reforms, he said, among other observations not very moderate, that the Church Prayer Book wanted to be altered and reformed as much as any thing."

To this I replied, that "alteration was one thing, and reform was another; and that if the Prayer Book was altered, it did not follow that it would be reformed."

"He then went on to say, that while he was footman at Squire Martingal's, over in Cheshire, one day, when he was waiting at table, and there were four or five gentlemen at dinner, they were talking about the Prayer Book, and whether it was not now time for it to be altered.

"And the Squire gave it as his opinion that there was one word in particular which he wished very much to see put entirely out of the Book; and that was, the word 'damnation.' Such words as that, he said, ought not to be in a book, which gentlefolks were expected to sit and hear.

"Edmund went on to say, that there was a gentleman at the table, who observed, it would be better to alter the word to 'condemnation:' of which the company very much approved, though (as Plush himself remarked), it was not easy to see what was gained by the alteration.

"Now, Sir, it does seem to me, that Squire Martingal and his friends forgot, when they made such short work with the Prayer Book, that there was the Bible still in their way, quite as much needing to be corrected and amended.

"And I told Edmund so; and I also told him, that if I were in his place, I should not like to go about repeating private conversations which he might have overheard at his master's table; especially when they were so little calculated to be of use.

"However, Edmund must do as he pleases; but for myself, Sir, I do assure you, that after giving the subject the best consideration in my power, the objections which people make against the Athanasian Creed, are, to my thinking, not at all more substantial than Squire Martingal's against the Prayer Book and Bible. Indeed, Sir, it is my opinion, that there is nothing in that Creed either unscriptural or uncharitable, but quite the very contrary; that it is essentially (as I once heard you call the Commination Service) 'in its matter, Christian Truth; and in its manner, Christian Love.' And, Sir, if you will not be weary of me, I will try to show you how I came to this conclusion."

"Richard," said I, "you need not fear that you will tire me."

"Well, Sir," he proceeded; "it seemed to me plain from the Scriptures (what no one indeed will deny or question) that the Great ALMIGHTY GOD should be the object of all our Love and Adoration. From the same Scriptures it also appeared, that the LORD JESUS CHRIST, our only Saviour and Hope, is entitled to all our Love and Adoration.

"And again, from the same Scriptures, it appears that the HOLY SPIRIT of GOD, the only Sanctifier, Guide, and Guardian of His Church, is entitled to all our Love and Adoration."

"Certainly," I replied; "no one, who believes the Scriptures, can doubt this."

"And is not this," he said, "the very doctrine of the first part of the Creed; 'that the Father is GOD, the Son is GOD, and the Holy Ghost is GOD; and yet they are not three GODS, but one GOD?' In like manner, if any man enquire for the very foundation of Christian hope and consolation, surely it is the doctrine that GOD our SAVIOUR took on Him our frail and mortal nature; that He was 'perfect man,' as well as 'perfect GOD.' Without this doctrine, the *peculiar* hopes and consolations of the Gospel fade away and disappear. Now this is the great truth prest on our thoughts in the *second* part of the Athanasian Creed, where we are taught boldly to maintain that 'the right faith is, that we BELIEVE AND

CONFESS,—not believe only, but believe and confess,—that our LORD JESUS CHRIST, the Son of GOD, is GOD AND MAN.'"

"Yes," I answered, "it is difficult to imagine how any one who acknowledges the truth of the Scriptures, can deny and question this. But you must, I am sure, be aware, that many people object, that this doctrine is not simply stated, and so left to every one's own conscience to approve, but that attempts are made to draw out distinctions and explanations, which are not in the Scripture, and which no one can understand; and then, after all, people are made to say, that whoever does not believe all this, has no chance of salvation."

"Sir," he replied, "there is a verse in the Psalms, which seems to give an answer to such objectors; 'If I should say like them, I should condemn the generation of GOD'S children.' No one will dare deny that those who framed this Creed, and those who put it into our Prayer Book, were good and holy men, sincerely anxious for the honour of ALMIGHTY GOD, and for the salvation of men's souls. It was surely not their fault that these distinctions and explanations (if they are to be so called) became necessary, but the fault of rash or loose-minded people, who attempted to corrupt the hearts of the simple with their *false* distinctions and *false* explanations.

"Against such, the Church, as a good parent should, warns her sons in the strongest terms; and if stronger terms could have been found, no doubt she would have used them.

"And it seems to me, that it is not at all the intention of the Church, in this Creed or anywhere else, to endeavour to explain what is above human comprehension; but only to warn us that quibbled and pretended distinctions have been made of old, and will be again, against the essential doctrines of the Gospel; and that, come in whatever shape they may, they are to be opposed at once with a sharp and strong denial; to be at once, and as the Article says, 'thoroughly' rejected.

"And the absolute need of some such strong impenetrable fence appears from what I have heard, that there have been Church people, and even Clergymen, who denied these doctrines, and (as might be expected) scorned this Creed. How they could reconcile their conduct to their consciences, it is not for me to say; but it is plain, that if the fence were taken away and weakened, the danger to the fold would be much increased."

"I fully agree with you," was my reply; "but you know those who dislike this Creed assert, that the 'Fence,' as you call it, is much sharper and stronger than it need be; and that it would be better to have no 'Monitory Clauses' at all, than any exprest in such strong and, as they call them, violent terms."

"Sir," he answered, "you know that in different places in the New Testament we are taught that adultery, fornication, drunkenness, and other such crimes, are entirely unsuitable to the Christian Profession, and that persons who are guilty of them do in practice renounce the Gospel.

"Now supposing it should be thought well by the Governors of the Church to set forth a solemn warning to profligates thus worded:—

"'Whosoever will be saved, before all things it is necessary that he avoid the crimes of adultery, whoredom, drunkenness, and blasphemy; which crimes, unless every one do carefully abstain from, without doubt he shall perish everlastingly;'

"And if then were to follow some solemn admonitions, setting forth (according to the sense, though not in the very words of Scripture) the necessity of self-denial, mortification, and constant communion with ALMIGHTY GOD in prayer and at His holy table, so that the affections may be kept set on high and heavenly things; and all concluding thus:—

"'This is the rule of Christian Purity, which except a man observe faithfully he cannot be saved;'

"Do not you, Sir, think such warnings would be quite agreeable to Scripture and to Christian Charity?"

"Indeed I think so," I replied.

"And yet," he proceeded; "supposing such an admonition as this were to be made by authority, and ordered to be printed in all the Prayer Books, and to be read twelve times a year in every Church in England, do you not think there would be a great outcry against it; and that many people, when it was going to be read, would shut their books, or perhaps go out of the Church?"

"It is too probable," I replied, "considering how little account is now made of crimes of this kind, even by many who are thought religious people. Indeed, I have understood from a person I can rely upon, otherwise I could not have credited it, that one of the objections which Mr. Cartwright himself brought against the Prayer Book was, that in the Litany, fornication is termed 'a deadly sin.'"

"It is strange, indeed, Sir," said he, "and sad to think that any one who believes the Scriptures could offer such an objection. But it confirms an opinion I was going to express to you. For if a good kind of man, as Mr. Cartwright is said to be, objects to the Litany on such grounds, how much more is it to be expected that such an admonition as that which I have spoken of would be frequently scorned and hooted at.

"And then," continued he, "supposing such an admonition as this had been made and used in the Church for hundreds of years, and it were now to be left out in the reformed Prayer Book, would not such a measure give great satisfaction and encouragement to all the loose dissolute people throughout the country?"

"That cannot be doubted," I answered. "But there is one objection (absurd enough to be sure) which people offer against the Athanasian Creed, which you have not noticed, perhaps because you had never heard of it.

"The objection I mean is, that this Creed leaves no allowance for unavoidable ignorance, or bad education; nor any chance even for persons of weak doubting minds, no not for idiots, or children, to escape from its heavy censures.

"It is, obviously, an absurd objection, yet it is what people do urge, and people too who make pretension to reason and religion."

"Sir," said he, "I can never suppose that any really conscientious person, whose mind was free from prejudice, could offer such an objection.

"It must be quite plain to all candid minds, that as in the Scripture itself, so in the Church Prayer Book, we are always instructed to believe that our merciful GOD makes allowance for our weakness and blindness in matters of knowledge and faith, as well as in other things. As in the Scriptures, so in the Church Prayer Book we are always taught, that occasional doubt and perplexity are no proof of want of Faith; that he truly believes who *acts* (if I may so say) *upon trust*, who like Abraham, the father of the faithful, 'obeys and goes on' obeying, 'not knowing whither he goes;' knowing only that if he follow GOD'S guidance, he must be right.

"It is too always taught, as in the Scriptures, so in the Prayer Book, that upon true repentance, sincere faith in the Blood and Mediation of the One Redeemer, and entire submission to the guidance of the One Sanctifier, it is, I say, *always* taught, that the door of mercy is open even to the most inveterate sinners, whatever the nature of their sins might have been; unless indeed the sin against the HOLY GHOST be considered an exception; to guard Christians against which, may be supposed one great and surely charitable purpose of this Creed.

"How then," he proceeded, "can the Church with any show of reason be called 'uncharitable,' which, with this evangelical doctrine implied *in all her Services*, uses occasionally the strongest language of warning (or even of threatening) against fatal sins and errors, if by any means she may preserve the souls committed to her charge stedfast in the faith, 'the faith which was once delivered unto the Saints?'"

"Yes," said I, "*once for all*, never to be changed or frittered away in base compliance with the ever-varying customs and fancies of worldly and self-conceited men."

"And Sir," he proceeded, "I put it to myself in this way. What a fearful thing it would be for a person on his death-bed to deny the SON of GOD, the only Redeemer, and the SPIRIT of GOD, the only Comforter! Now the Church Prayer Book considers us all as it were on our death-beds, or at least but a little way from them. The Services for the Visitation of the Sick, and the Burial of the Dead, come very close after Baptism and the Catechism. As we should wish to *die*, so the Church would have us *live*. If it be an awful thought to pass into *Eternity* in wilful ignorance or negligence of the essential truths of the Gospel; is it not also an awful thought that people should spend this their probationary *time* in such ignorance or negligence? And again, I would ask, can the Church be called 'uncharitable,' which earnestly and incessantly, and in the plainest, strongest words that the English language can supply, warns her members of their danger in this respect?"

"Certainly, Richard," I replied, "what you say is most worthy to be thought on by all persons who find fault with this Creed. But I wish you to recollect, that many of them take what they call 'high ground' in their argument. They confidently assert that it is 'bigotted,' 'unscriptural,' 'unchristian,' and other such hard names, to pretend that 'modes of faith' (that is their term) are of any great importance, or indeed of any importance at all; that if a man's life is in the right, his faith can't be wrong; that *of course* adultery and those kind of things are forbidden in the Testament, but that there are few passages or (as some of them say) none at all, which can be brought forward in support of the opinions put forth in the Athanasian Creed; much less (they assert) can any passages be found, denouncing so heavy a woe against those who reject these opinions."

"Sir," he replied, with more than even his usual energy, "I will be bold to say, that there are as many passages in the New Testament, distinctly proving and supporting the great doctrines put forth in the Athanasian Creed, as there are passages expressly forbidding adultery, and other such crimes. But supposing it were otherwise, it really does not appear to me, that the case would be different. *Gambling* is not *in words* forbidden (so far as I can recollect) in any part or passage of the Old or New Testament; yet no one doubts, I mean, no serious thinking person, that it is one of the most fatal habits a person can get into; not because it is expressly forbidden in any part or passage, but because it is against the whole Gospel; *utterly inconsistent with a Christian's practice.*

"Now, Sir, it really does appear to me, that to deny the great doctrines contained in this noble Creed, is not merely to go against express passages of Scripture; passages, I mean, wherein our LORD JESUS, and the Blessed SPIRIT, are spoken of as GOD; but more than this, it is against the whole Gospel, *utterly inconsistent with a Christian's faith.*"

"Well, Richard," I said, "the considerations you have suggested are certainly such as should lead all Christians to pause before they encourage in themselves or others any dislike of this ancient, and as you justly call it, this noble Creed."

"Sir," he replied, "in my poor judgment it is indeed a noble, a magnificent confession.

"But still, noble and magnificent as it is, if it, or any part of it, were against Scripture, or against Christian Charity, I, for one, should not be easy till it were put out of the Prayer Book.

"How happy then am I to think that it breathes the very spirit of pure Christian Charity; of Love, more than parental; of Love like His, Sir, who '*so often* would have gathered His children together, as a hen gathereth her chickens under her wings, BUT THEY WOULD NOT!'"

"Yes, Richard," I said; "and often as this tender yearning anxiety for men's souls is displayed in the conduct and words of our adored Master, I have frequently thought it nowhere more strikingly appears, than in that pathetic chapter of warnings to which you refer, the 23rd of St. Matthew; a chapter truly of 'monitory clauses.'"

"Sir," he answered, "it might almost be expected of those who rashly accuse the Church of uncharitableness for retaining the Athanasian Creed, that they should also wish to have that chapter left out of the Calendar; as indeed I have heard that they do wish many of the Psalms to be omitted on some such ground.

"But it is now time for me to wish you good evening; hoping, Sir, that I have not taken too great a liberty in thus speaking out my opinions, or wearied you by staying too long."

"Richard," said I, "once for all, believe me it is one of the chief comforts and encouragements I have, to be with you at Church and at School, and to talk with you on these great subjects."

THOMAS KEBLE
The Feast of the Epiphany
January 6, 1834

TRACT 23

The Faith and Obedience of Churchmen, the Strength of the Church

"And Simon Peter answered and said, Thou art the CHRIST, the Son of the Living God. And JESUS answered and said unto him, Blessed art thou, Simon Bar-jona: for flesh and blood hath not revealed it unto thee, but My Father which is in heaven. And I say also unto thee, That thou art Peter; and upon this rock I will build My Church; and the gates of hell shall not prevail against it" (Matt 16:16-18).

The rock, then, upon which the Church is built, is the confession, that JESUS is the CHRIST, the Son of the Living GOD; a truth set forth and shadowed by the Prophets, but openly and plainly taught by the Apostles. St. Paul uses a similar expression, when he speaks of the body of Christians being "*built* upon the foundation of the Apostles and Prophets;" (i.e. resting in the sound and true doctrine which they taught;) "JESUS CHRIST Himself being the chief corner-*stone*" (Eph 2:20);—our very spiritual existence depending upon our adherence to this great truth, that JESUS was the anointed SON of GOD, GOD and Man, the promised SAVIOUR of the world;—He, who by taking man's nature upon Him in the womb of the Blessed Virgin, fulfilled the prophecy, that the SAVIOUR should be of the seed of Abraham, in whom "all the nations of the earth should be blessed" (Gen 22:18), and the seed of the woman, who should "bruise the serpent's head" (Gen 3:15);—and who, inasmuch as He was "the Only-begotten SON of GOD" (John 3:18), "GOD of GOD," "Very GOD of very GOD" (Nicene Creed), fulfilled the prophecy, that the SAVIOUR should be "the mighty GOD" (Isa 9:6);—He, of whom it was said, "Let all the Angels of GOD worship Him" (Heb 1:6);—and of whom it was likewise said, "Thy throne, O GOD, is for ever and ever" (Ps 45:6).

I said, that our very spiritual existence depends upon our adhering to this great and fundamental truth; and this I said, not of us as individuals only, but as Members of the Church of CHRIST, and of that portion of CHRIST'S Church in this Kingdom which is usually called the Church of England. It is true of us individually, as appears by the words of St. John; "He that hath the SON, hath life; and he that hath not the SON of GOD, hath not life" (1 John 5:12); by which we learn, that as long as we slight or disbelieve, or deny this sacred truth, we have no spiritual life in us. It is also true of us, as Members of the Church of CHRIST, and of that portion of CHRIST'S Church in this Kingdom which is usually called the Church of England, as appears from the passage before us; "Upon this rock, (i.e. upon this firm confession of faith in JESUS as the CHRIST, the Son of the Living GOD) I will build My Church; and the gates of hell shall not prevail against it." For from this we learn, that the Church, and any given portion of that Church, is only then able to defy the assaults of the Devil, that she can only then look forward with confidence to get the victory, so long as she adheres firmly to this faith and belief in CHRIST. When she departs from that foundation, then she ceases to have a claim for the continuance of the promised aid. This is a matter which it behoves Christians at all times to place before their eyes, and to keep in remembrance; but, especially, at the present time, does it behove us, who are Members of the Church of CHRIST in England, to do so; because of the unceasing endeavours which are being made by men who are either careless of religion altogether, or who have embraced false views of it, to overthrow our Church; endeavours, which we have reason to regard either with fear, or not, according as we have reason, or not, to suppose that the Members of the Church have departed from the true faith and fear of GOD, and of the LORD JESUS CHRIST. If there is reason to believe that many or most of the Members of our Church are regardless of that true faith, and of the honour of Him in whom we believe, that by their lips, or by their lives, they set at nought His Majesty, neglect His Sacraments, despise His Word, forsake His Worship, obey not His Voice, or look for redemption and salvation by any other means than by His Cross and Blood, then we have every reason to fear, that these endeavours of our enemies will be successful; that the light of

GOD'S presence will be withheld from us; and that, as He withdrew from the Jews, when they neglected CHRIST, the LORD of Glory, so He will withdraw from our Nation also, and leave it to the wretchedness of its own chosen ways; to the enjoyment of those idols, the world, the flesh, and the Devil, for which it will have forsaken the HOLY ONE of Israel, and refused to hearken to the voice of the LAMB of GOD, who died to take away the sins of the world. But if not, if we have reason to hope that there are many true Servants of GOD still to be found; that there are many who, not with their lips only, but in their hearts and with their lives acknowledge Him the only true GOD, and JESUS CHRIST whom He has sent; acknowledge Him so as to obey His voice, and keep and do what He has commanded; then may we regard the attempts of our enemies without dismay; then may we have firm and stedfast hope, that the gates of Hell shall not prevail against us: that though it may please GOD that we should suffer for a while;—as we suffered, together with good King Charles, at the hands of the Dissenters; as we suffered, in the days of bloody Queen Mary, at the hands of the Roman Catholics; as we suffered during the first three hundred years after CHRIST, at the hands of the Heathens and the Jews;—yet that eventually triumph will await us; that He will bring our Church out of the trial, like gold out of the fire, more pure and of greater worth ("I will purely purge away thy dross, and take away all thy tin;" Isa 1:25), that "all things will work together for good" to us; and that the purpose aimed at by the affliction is, that He "may present our Church to Himself as a glorious Church, not having spot, or wrinkle, or any such thing; but that it should be holy and without blemish" (Eph 5:27).

It will hence appear, that it is in the power of every individual, by a holy and religious life in the true faith and fear of GOD and our LORD JESUS CHRIST, to promote not only his own salvation, but the welfare and stability of the Church of CHRIST; or by an unholy, careless, and irreligious life, not only to secure his own damnation, but to assist the enemies of GOD and man, who are purposed to overthrow that Church.

If times of confusion and trouble shall come, where can we seek for comfort but in the love of CHRIST, in the love of GOD to man for CHRIST'S sake? But how can we *then* take comfort in that love, if *now* we take no account of it? Let me entreat you, then, Christian Brethren, while the days of peace are vouchsafed to you, to give more and more heed to all religious duties. The days may come, when your Churches will be shut up, or only filled by men who will not teach the whole truth as it is in JESUS; when you will be deprived of Ministers of Religion; or have only such as are destitute of GOD'S Commission. Do not, I beseech you, by your neglect now, add to your misery then the bitterness of self-reproach, when you will have to say, "I had once the opportunity of worshipping GOD aright, but I neglected it, and He now has withheld it from me. I had once the means of receiving the Body and Blood of my SAVIOUR, at the hands of His own Minister; but I refused it, and now He has placed it out of my power."

ARTHUR PHILIP PERCEVAL
The Feast of the Epiphany
January 6, 1834

TRACT 24: AD POPULUM

The Scripture View of the Apostolical Commission

In referring to the Epistles of the New Testament for proof of the duty of submission to Spiritual Authority, we are sometimes met by the objection, that the case is very much altered since the days of the Apostles, and since the extraordinary gifts of the SPIRIT have been withdrawn from the Church. Now it will readily be admitted, on all hands, that the state of the Church *is* very greatly altered since these miraculous powers have ceased; but at the same time we must not allow a general principle of this sort to set aside the authority of Holy Scripture, as far as regards our own practice, until, by a diligent and careful study of the Apostles' writings, we have found that the principle *does* really apply to the case in question; as, for instance, that the Apostolic Authority is grounded in Scripture upon the possession of miraculous powers, and therefore necessarily ceased when those powers were withheld. Let us then examine this point more particularly.

Have we then considered, in reference to this matter, that the extraordinary gifts of the SPIRIT were not confined to the appointed teachers of the Church, but were shed abroad upon the congregation at large, upon the young and the old alike, upon the servants, and upon the handmaidens? (Comp. Joel 2:28, 29.) It was the promise of the Old Testament, that, under the dispensation of the New Covenant, GOD would write His Law in the hearts of His people, so that they should teach no more every man his neighbour, and every man his brother, saying; Know the LORD, "for they shall all know Me, from the least of them unto the greatest of them, saith the LORD" (Jer 31:33, 34). This promise, we are told in the Epistle to the Hebrews, was fulfilled in the Gospel; and St. John, in his First General Epistle, expressly acknowledges the accomplishment of the Prophet's words. He says to his "little children," "Ye have an *unction from the Holy One,* and ye *know all things.* I have not written unto you because ye know not the truth, but *because ye know it.* These things have I written unto you concerning them that seduce you. But the anointing which ye have received from Him abideth in you, and ye *need not that any man teach you;* but as *the same anointing teacheth you of all things,* and is truth, and is no lie, and even as it hath taught you, ye shall abide in Him" (1 John 2:20, 21, 27). Such general illumination by GOD'S Holy Spirit might seem to make any authoritative Apostolic declarations altogether unnecessary for the converts; but we still find St. John writing to them, and declaring his testimony to the Christian doctrine with much earnestness; and why? Let us hear his own words at the beginning of his Epistle; "That which *we* have seen and heard declare *we* unto *you,* that *ye also may have fellowship with us;* and truly OUR fellowship is with the FATHER, and with His Son JESUS CHRIST. And these things write we unto you, that your *joy may be full."* Here we have the object of the Apostle's affectionate address fully and clearly stated. He and his Fellow-Apostles, the witnesses of their Master's Life and Death and Resurrection, had received from Him a glorious revelation to communicate to the world; they had seen and did testify, that the FATHER sent the SON to be the Saviour of the world; upon this foundation they were commissioned to build the Christian Church; and it was their holy and blessed office to "stablish, strengthen, settle" the faith of their "little children" in the Gospel; to tell them how they might keep themselves from the spirit of error; and continuing "stedfast in *the Apostles' doctrine and fellowship,"* might *through them* have fellowship with the FATHER and the SON, and so "rejoice with joy unspeakable and full of glory." Here we learn the full force of St. John's authoritative language. He was marking the lines of "the foundation of the Apostles and Prophets," in order that his disciples might duly be built upon their most holy faith into a temple meet for the habitation of GOD through the SPIRIT; *they* were GOD'S building, and the Apostle was one of the "wise master-builders," whom CHRIST had appointed to build His Spiritual House. And this view of the matter will become still clearer, if we study well the prayer which CHRIST offered for His Church at the solemn moment when He was just about to purchase it to Himself by the shedding of His precious Blood. We there find our Blessed LORD, having first declared that His work was finished on earth, and having earnestly besought the FATHER now to glorify Him, proceeds to pray for His Apostles, that His FATHER would preserve them in *unity,* and *truth,* and *holiness.* He says, "I have manifested Thy name unto *the men which Thou gavest Me out of the world;* I have given unto *them* the words that Thou gavest Me, and they have received them; Holy FATHER, keep through Thine own name *those whom Thou hast given Me,* that they may be *one* as We are. Sanctify them through Thy *truth;* Thy word is truth. As Thou hast sent Me into the world, even so *have I also sent them into the world.* And for their sakes I sanctify Myself, that they also might be *sanctified* through the truth." Thus did CHRIST lay the foundations of His *One Holy, Catholic, Apostolic* Church; in the remainder of His prayer He intreats like blessings for all who should be built on this sure foundation, that they might be so joined together in *unity of spirit by the Apostles' doctrine,* as to be made an holy temple acceptable to GOD through Him. (Coll. for St. Simon and St. Jude.) "Neither pray I for these alone, but *for them also which shall believe on Me through their word;* that they *all* may be *one,* as Thou FATHER art in Me and I in Thee, that they also may be one in Us, that the world may believe that Thou hast sent Me." Accordingly we read that when, on the day of Pentecost, three thousand were brought to believe on Christ through St. Peter's word, they were baptized into that holy communion, "and they continued stedfast in *the Apostles' doctrine and fellowship"* (according to a text already quoted), and the LORD daily added fresh members to this Church. And in later times, when false teachers were gone abroad seducing the disciples, the Apostles wrote to them, declaring and reminding them what the Apostolic doctrine was, that they might have the joy fulfilled in themselves of knowing that they were in the unity of the Apostolic Church, one in CHRIST and in the FATHER. And so St. Paul explains why he wrote to the Corinthians, "not for that *we* have dominion over your faith, but are *helpers of your joy;* for *by faith ye stand"* (2 Cor 1:14).

St. Peter, again, in his Second Epistle, uses exactly the same language with St. John. He writes as "a servant and an *Apostle* of JESUS CHRIST, to them that have obtained *like precious faith with US;* according as His divine power hath given unto us all things that pertain unto life and godliness; exceeding great and precious promises, that by these *ye* might be partakers of the Divine nature;" i.e. he does not draw any line of difference between himself and his brethren, as if he had miraculous powers which they had not; but rests his teaching on the plain fact of his being commissioned, and commissioned with the simple object of communicating the doctrine which had been disclosed to him. He addresses his converts just as St. John does, not as though they were ignorant or unmindful of the truth, but in order to strengthen their conviction of those holy facts and doctrines to which he and his Brother-Apostles were commissioned to bear witness. "I will not be negligent," he says, "to put you always in remembrance of these things, *though ye know them, and be established* in the present truth. Yea, I think it meet, as long as I am in this tabernacle, to stir you up by putting you in remembrance. Moreover, I will endeavour that after my decease ye may have these things always in remembrance. For we have not followed cunningly devised fables, when we made known unto you the power and coming of our LORD JESUS CHRIST, but *were eye-witnesses* of His Majesty, ... and this voice which came from heaven *we* heard, when we were with Him in the Holy Mount." Again he says, "This Second Epistle, beloved, I now write unto you; in both which I stir up your pure minds by way of remembrance, that ye may be mindful of the words which were spoken before by the holy Prophets, and of *the commandment of us the Apostles of the* LORD *and* SAVIOUR." For by adherence to the commandment of the Apostles, and the doctrine of the Prophets, it might be known that Christians were building themselves up on the only true foundation, even JESUS CHRIST.

But it is in St. Paul's writings that we shall find the fullest and clearest view of Apostolical Authority; and it is well worthy of our observation, that the Church upon which the Apostle most strongly enforces that Authority, is the very Church which is most distinguished in the New Testament for the abundance of its Spiritual gifts; so that clearly it was not an exclusive possession of miraculous powers, which constituted the distinction between Apostles and private Christians. He begins his First Epistle to the Corinthians by thanking GOD on their behalf "for the grace of GOD which was given them by JESUS CHRIST, that *in every thing* they were enriched by Him *in all utterance* and *in all knowledge,* so that *they came behind in no gift.*" But the Apostle goes on immediately to reprove them for their want of unity; it had been declared to him, that there were contentions among them. And how did these contentions arise? in low views of Apostolical Authority. They had forgotten that there was but One Foundation; One Building of GOD; One Rule, according to which the several builders must carry up the structure which Apostles had founded. And how did the Apostle endeavour to drive out the spirit of schism? by asserting and enforcing his own authority over them, as the *one* only father whom they had in the Gospel (though they might choose for themselves ten thousand instructors), and by sending Timothy to bring into their remembrance his *ways which were* in CHRIST, as *he taught every where in every Church*. Thus were they to be brought back to the blessed unity of spirit of the One Catholic and Apostolic Church.—And here, by the way, we have light thrown upon the doctrine contained in the Epistles of Ignatius. Remarkable and consolatory to the inquirer after truth as is the evidence therein afforded to the divine appointment of Episcopacy, perhaps there is mingled with his satisfaction some surprise at the earnestness and frequency with which the Holy Martyr urges the doctrine. But it is plain, what the Apostles are in St. Paul's Epistles, such the Bishops are in those of Ignatius, centers of unity; and as St. Paul, when denouncing schism, magnifies the Apostolic Office, in just the same natural, or rather necessary way, does Ignatius oppose the varieties of opinion in his own day by the doctrine of Episcopacy.—To return: the same Apostle writes to the Church of Rome; "I myself am persuaded of you, my brethren, that ye *also* are full of goodness, filled with all knowledge, able also to admonish one another. Nevertheless, brethren, I have written the more *boldly* unto you in some sort, as putting you in mind, *because of the grace that is given to me of GOD, that I should be the Minister of JESUS CHRIST to the Gentiles, ministering the Gospel of GOD"* (Rom 15:14-16). The passage which follows is worthy of especial notice, as shewing that the Apostles marked out for themselves distinct provinces, so that each had his own Diocese, as it were, his own peculiar sphere of duty and authority. St. Paul tells us he strove to preach not where CHRIST was named, lest he should build upon another man's foundation (Rom 15:20). Each laid down for himself his own "measure," and would not stretch beyond it (2 Cor 10:14). And this will perhaps help to explain the fact which early tradition hands down to us of the wide dispersion of the Apostolic Body. At all events, it is certain from History, that the different Churches claiming Apostolic Descent, were very careful to maintain the practices which they had each derived from their respective Founders. To the Church of Corinth accordingly St. Paul writes as *its* sole Founder and Father, claiming upon this ground Supreme Authority over it in the name of JESUS CHRIST. And with this Epistle before us, we cannot doubt of the conclusion which we have already seen may be clearly enough deduced from other Epistles of the New Testament, viz. that the Authority which the Apostles claim for themselves, they claim, not on the ground of high supernatural endowments (for these were the possession of the Church at large) but on the ground of "the Grace and Apostleship" which they had received from CHRIST, the Head of the Christian Church, "for *obedience to the faith among all nations* for His name." That is, they refer directly to their Commission as His Apostles, to go into all the world and preach the Gospel to every creature; they refer to the Authority with which He invested them when He stood in the midst of them, and said unto them, "as My FATHER *hath sent Me,* even so SEND I you;" and bade them receive the HOLY GHOST, to be with them in the prosecution of their High and Holy Office. This point is very strikingly exhibited in the First Epistle to the Corinthians, because there the possession of extraordinary gifts, and the possession of Spiritual Authority, are brought into immediate contrast with each other. The Corinthians, proud of the gifts of other teachers, had raised parties in opposition to St. Paul, and questioned his authority. How then did he maintain it? not by claiming higher gifts and graces for himself (though he spoke with tongues more than they all) but by referring to his *Office,* as a Minister and an Apostle of CHRIST, whose One Spirit governs the whole body of the Church, appointing divers orders, and dividing to every man severally as He will. That he *was* an Apostle he proved by the fact, that he had been equally favoured with the Twelve; that he had seen our LORD JESUS CHRIST in the flesh; and had received the doctrines of His Gospel, and grace to preach them to the world. This was the simple ground on which he claimed Authority; it was not, because of the gifts or graces which he as an individual possessed; nor was it because he had laboured more abundantly than all the other Apostles; nor because of his signal labours and afflictions for CHRIST'S sake. He mentions these in his Second Epistle, to show, that if he chose to adopt the language of his adversaries, he had a better right than they to glory; but all the while he tells the Corinthians that he was "become a fool in glorying;" that *they* had compelled him; that he could show the *signs of an Apostle,* and needed no epistles of commendation. It was in *right* of his *Office* that he claimed Authority; it was for the *sake* of that Office that he endeavoured to give no offence in any thing, but in all things to approve himself as the Minister of GOD.

Now, perhaps some persons may be disposed to think that this Apostolical Authority would terminate with the Apostles themselves, with the favoured men who had been "eye-witnesses and ministers of the word," and could declare to others what they had themselves heard and seen. This might appear probable, if we had only our own reasonings to go upon, but Scripture teaches us a very different lesson. When St. Paul felt that his time was now nearly come, he writes to Timothy, his "dearly beloved son," giving him his last solemn charge, as to one who was henceforth to occupy the post which he had hitherto, by GOD'S grace, maintained in the battles of his LORD. He earnestly commands him, "watch THOU in all things, endure afflictions, do the work of an Evangelist, make full proof of thy ministry. *For* I am now ready to be offered, and the time of my departure is at hand. I have fought the good fight, I have finished my course, I have kept the faith." This faith which St. Paul had so anxiously kept, was now to be committed to Timothy's charge; he had already been put in trust with the Gospel by the HOLY GHOST and the imposition of the Apostles' hands; and now upon *Him* was to devolve the solemn responsibility of being left in charge of the Apostles' testimony, and of handing it down to future ages. "Be not thou therefore ashamed," says the Apostle, "of the *testimony of our LORD, nor of me His prisoner; Hold fast the form of sound words which thou hast heard of me* in faith and love which is in CHRIST JESUS. *That good thing which was committed unto thee, keep* by the HOLY GHOST which dwelleth in us." And, in reminding him of this indwelling of the HOLY GHOST, the promise of CHRIST to His Ministers, the Apostle endeavours, with evident anxiety, to embolden Timothy, by filling him with a sense of the authority and power committed to him. "I put thee in remembrance, that thou *stir up the gift of God which is in thee by the putting on of my hands.* For GOD hath not given us the spirit of fear, but of *power,* and of love, and of a sound mind."[1] "Thou, therefore, my son, be *strong* in the *grace* that is in CHRIST JESUS. And *the things that thou hast heard of me among many witnesses, the same commit thou to faithful men, who shall be able to teach others also.*"[2] This last passage is very important, because it shows so clearly that the testimony which the Apostles bore to CHRIST did not cease with their ministry, but was to be transmitted along the sacred line of those whom they ordained, and so handed down to those who were to come after. And where does this line end? Blessed be GOD, it has not ended yet; and CHRIST's promise gives us the comfortable assurance that it shall last "even to the end of the world." Down to our days, the Church has been "a witness and keeper of Holy Writ" (Article 20), and so faithful a witness, and so watchful a keeper, that we can feel as certain of the facts of the Gospel History, and so of the glorious doctrines which rest upon them, as if we heard them from the Apostles' own lips. And how beautifully are we reminded of St. Paul's dying charge to Timothy, when we see the Fathers of our own Church laying their hands on the heads of their sons in the faith, bidding them receive the HOLY GHOST for their high office and work in the Church of GOD, and charging them to be faithful dispensers of the Word of GOD and His Holy Sacraments; and then delivering into their hands that Holy Book which the Church has preserved and handed down, with authority to preach it in the congregation! Thus is the testimony of the Apostles still delivered in the Church, which is "the pillar and ground of the truth;" and thus do their Successors declare it with authority, "GOD also bearing them witness," not indeed now, "with signs, and wonders, and divers miracles," but still according to His own most true promise with invisible "gifts of the HOLY GHOST."

Let us now return to see how St. Paul *exercised* his Apostolical Authority. He had been consulted by the Church of Corinth upon several questions which had caused difference of opinion among them; how then does he decide these questions? In the first place, he draws a broad line of distinction between the points on which he had an express commandment of his LORD to go upon, and those on which he had to give his own

---

[1] So, writing to the Corinthians, St. Paul joins Timothy with himself, and claims for him like authority. "If Timotheus come, see that he may be with you *without fear;* for he worketh the work of the LORD, as I also do. Let no man therefore despise him."
[2] Comp. 1 Timothy 1:18.

judgment. In some cases he says, "I command;" in others, "not I, but the LORD." As a Minister and Steward of CHRIST'S household, his first consideration was, whether in the course of His ministry his Master had left him any explicit *commandment;* if he found no such commandment, his next duty was to decide the question by the *principles* of CHRIST'S Gospel. In this case, he gave his "judgment, as one that had obtained mercy of the LORD to be faithful," as having been "allowed of GOD to be put in trust with the Gospel;" and in such decisions he felt assured that he had the SPIRIT of GOD. Accordingly he says with confidence, "If any man think himself to be a prophet or spiritual, let him acknowledge that the things that I write unto you are the commandments of the LORD;" referring at the same time to his Apostolical Authority, "What? came the word of GOD out from you? or came it unto you only? is it nothing to you that the Apostles have so ordained, and the Catholic Church so received and practised?" And now I would ask, where is the essential difference between the Apostolic age and our own, as to the relation in which GOD'S Ministers and His people stand to each other? I do not say that the Ministers of His word in these days can feel so sure as the Apostles could, that in the commandments which they give they have the SPIRIT of GOD; very far from it. But I do say, that neither can the people feel so sure as in those days of miraculous gifts, that *they* have the SPIRIT of GOD with *them*; and thus the *relation* between the two parties remains the same. Since the times of the Apostles and of miracles, the City of GOD is, as it were, come down from heaven to earth; the scene is changed, but the city remains the same. The Corner-stone is the same, its foundations are the same; if it be not built up by the same heavenly rule, it will not be the city that is at unity in itself, the city of Him, who "is not the Author of confusion, but of *peace, as in all Churches of the Saints.*" His HOLY SPIRIT works at sundry times in divers manners according to His own Almighty wisdom; sometimes He descends upon His Ministers with an audible sound and in a visible form; and sometimes invisibly, amidst the deep silence and the prayers of His faithful congregation. Outward appearances may be changed, yet His Mighty Agency remains the same; and it will be our wisdom and our blessedness to feel and acknowledge His presence in the "still small voice," as well as in the "mighty and strong wind," and in "the fire." For though miracles and tongues may have ceased, He has never ceased to send forth Apostles, and Prophets, and Evangelists, and Pastors, and Teachers; nor will He cease to send them until the work of their ministry is accomplished in "the edification of the body of CHRIST;" "till we all come in the unity of the faith, and of the knowledge of the SON of GOD, unto a perfect man, unto the measure of the stature of the fulness of CHRIST."

The question to which these few observations refer, is one, it must be allowed, of much importance. Our Blessed LORD declares to His Apostles, "As My FATHER hath sent Me, even so send I you." Again He says, "He that heareth you, heareth Me; and he that despiseth you, depiseth Me." It becomes then a grave question, to whom did CHRIST address these words? To the Twelve Apostles exclusively, or to them and their Successors to the end of the world? It is surely worth our while carefully to search the Scriptures with a view to ascertain this point. And while we do this, let us bear constantly in mind that slight *intimations* of our LORD'S Will are in their degree as much binding upon us as express commands; that he who knows what *probably* his LORD'S Will is, will be judged as one who had *probability* to guide him; that he who knew not through negligence or slothfulness, will have his negligence or slothfulness to answer for. It will not be a sufficient excuse for us that we thought all that was said in the New Testament of Apostolical Authority *could* apply only to the Apostolic age. Let us remember, as a solemn warning to us, how it came to pass that the Jews despised and rejected CHRIST. They saw no sign from heaven, and therefore thought He could not be the Prophet, like unto Moses. Their fault was, that they did not humbly and heartily "search the Scriptures."

BENJAMIN HARRISON
The Feast of the Conversion of St. Paul
January 25, 1834

TRACT 25

The Great Necessity and Advantage of
Public Prayer
Extracted from Bishop Beveridge's Sermon on the Subject

Besides our praying to, and praising GOD in the midst of other business, we ought to set apart some certain times in every day wholly for this. The Saints of old were wont to do it three times a day, as we learn from Daniel. For when King Darius had signed the decree, "That whosoever should ask a petition of any god or man for thirty days, except of the king, should be cast into the den of lions," it is written, "That when Daniel knew that the decree was signed, he went into his house; and, his windows being open in his chamber toward Jerusalem, he kneeled upon his knees three times a-day, and prayed, and gave thanks unto his God, as he did aforetime" (Dan 6:10). *As he did aforetime;* which shows that this had been his constant practice before, and he would not leave it off now, though he was sure to be cast into the den of lions for it. But what times of the day these were, which were anciently devoted to this religious purpose, we may best gather from King David, where he saith, "Evening, and morning, and at noon, will I pray, and cry aloud; and He shall hear my voice" (Ps 55:17). He begins with the evening, because day then began, according to the Jewish account; but he observed all these times of prayer alike. And so questionless did other devout people as well as he. The Jews have a tradition that those times were ordained to that use, the morning by Abraham; noon, by Isaac; and evening by Jacob. But whether they have any ground for that or no, be sure this custom is so reasonable and pious, that the Church of Christ took it up, and observed it all along from the very beginning. Only to distinguish these times more exactly, the Christians called them (as the Jews also had done before) by the names of the *third,* the *sixth,* and the *ninth* hours. Of which Tertullian saith, "Tres istas horas ut insigniores in rebus humanis, ita et solenniores fuisse in orationibus divinis; 'as they were more famous than others in human affairs, so they were more solemn in divine prayers'" (Tertul. de Jejun. c. 10).

I know the Primitive Christians performed their private devotions at other times as well as these; but at these set times every day, especially at the *third* and *ninth* hour, they always performed them *publicly,* if they could get an opportunity. And if we would be such Christians as they were, we must follow their pious example in this, as well as in other things.

As the Jewish Church had by GOD'S own appointment the Morning and Evening Sacrifice every day in the year; so all Christian Churches have been used to have their Morning and Evening Prayers *publicly* performed every day. As might easily be shewn out of the Records of the Church, from the beginning of Christianity.

Not to insist upon other Churches, I shall instance at present only in our own; which, as in all things else, so particularly in this, is exactly conformable to the Catholic and Apostolic Church. In the First Book of Common-Prayer, made by our Church at the beginning of the Reformation, there was a Form composed both for Morning and Evening Prayer: the title of that for the Morning ran thus; *An Order for Mattins daily through the Year;* and of that for the Evening, *An Order for Even Song throughout the Year:* and accordingly there were Psalms and Chapters appointed both for the Morning and Evening of every day. About three or four years after, the same book was revised and put forth again. And then the Church taking notice that *Daily Prayers* had been in some places neglected, at the end of the Preface she added two new Rules, or, as we call them, Rubrics; which are still in force, as ye may see in the Common-Prayer Books which we now use.

The first is this:

> *And all Priests and Deacons are to say daily the Morning and Evening Prayer, either privately or openly, not being let by sickness, or other urgent cause.*

By this, every one that is admitted into Holy Orders, although he be neither Parson, Vicar, nor Curate of any particular place, yet he is bound to say both Morning and Evening Prayer every day, either in some Church or Chapel where he can get leave to do it, or else in the House where he dwells, except he be hindered by some such cause which the Ordinary of the place judges to be reasonable and urgent.

The other Order is this:

> *And the Curate that ministereth in every Parish-Church or Chapel, being at home, and not being otherwise reasonably hindered, shall say the same in the Parish-Church or Chapel where he ministereth, and shall cause a bell to be tolled thereunto, a convenient time before he begin, that people may come to hear God's Word, and pray with him.*

Here we have a plain and express command, that the Curate, whether he be the Incumbent himself, or another procured by him to do it; whosoever it is that ministereth GOD'S Holy Word and Sacraments in any Parish-Church or Chapel in England, shall say the same Morning and Evening Prayer daily in the Parish-Church or Chapel where he ministereth, and shall take care that a bell be tolled a convenient time before he begins, that people having notice of it, may come to GOD'S House to hear his Holy Word read, and join with the Minister in performing their *public* devotions to him. This every Minister or Curate in England is bound to do every day in the year, if he be at home, and be not otherwise reasonably hindered. And whether any hinderance be reasonable or no, the Minister himself is not the ordinary judge; for in all such cases that is referred by the common laws of the Church to the Bishop of the Diocese, or the Ordinary of the place where he ministereth.

The law hath made this the duty of every Minister, and the Bishop or Ordinary is to see he doeth it; and whether any have reasonable cause ever to omit it, or whether the cause they pretend for it be reasonable or no; this is left by the law to him. He may allow or disallow of the pretence, as he upon the full hearing of it shall see good; and may punish with the *censures* of the Church any Minister within his jurisdiction that doth not read the Prayers of the Church, or take care they be read every Morning and Evening in the Year, except at such times when the Minister can prove that he had such a reasonable hinderance or impediment as will justify him before GOD and His Church.

This care hath our Church taken, that Public Prayers be read every Morning and Evening throughout the Year in every parish within her bounds, that all who live in her communion, may after the example of the Apostles . . . . , go every day into the Temple or Church at the Hour of Prayer. She hath not appointed the hour when either Morning or Evening Prayer shall begin; because the same hour might not be so convenient in all places. So that in some places it might be pretended that there was a reasonable hinderance; that it could not be done just at the time. Wherefore to prevent any such plea, and to make the duty as easy and practicable, both to the Minister and people, as it could be, the Church hath left that to the Ministers themselves, who considering every one his own and his peoples' circumstances, may, and ought to appoint such hours both for the Morning and Evening Prayer in their respective places, as they in their discretion shall judge to be most convenient. Only they ought to take care in general that Morning Prayers be always read before, and Evening after Noon. And it is very expedient that the *same hours* be every day, as much as it is possible, observed in the same place, that people knowing it beforehand, may order their affairs so as to be ready to go to the Church at the *hour of prayer*.

But notwithstanding this great care that our Church hath taken to have *daily Prayers* in every parish, we see by sad experience, they are shamefully neglected all the kingdom over; there being very few places where they have any Public Prayers upon the Week-days, except perhaps upon Wednesdays and Fridays; because it is expressly commanded, that both Morning and Evening Prayers be read *every day* in the Week, as the Litany upon those. And why this commandment should be neglected more than the other, for my part I can see no reason. But I see plain enough that it is a great fault, a plain breach of the known laws of CHRIST'S Holy Catholic Church, and particularly of that part of it, which by his blessing is settled among us. But where doth this fault lie? I hope not in the Clergy. For I dare not suppose or imagine, but that every Minister in England that hath the care of souls committed to him, would be willing and glad to read the Prayers every day, for their edification, if the people could be persuaded to come to them. I am sure there is never a Minister but is *obliged* to read them *daily;* and never a parish in England, but where the people may have them so read, if they will; for they may *require* it by the *laws* both of our *Church* and *State*, except at such times when their Minister is reasonably hindered from the execution of his office, in the sense before explained.

But the mischief is, men cannot, or rather will not be persuaded to it. They think it a great matter to come to Church upon the LORD's day, when they cannot openly follow their particular callings if they would. Upon other days they have other business to mind of greater consequence, as they think, than going to Prayers. To some it is a great disturbance to hear the bell sounding in their ears, and calling them to their duty, which they being resolved not to practise, it makes them very uneasy to be so often put in mind of it. Others can make a shift to bear that pretty well, as not looking upon themselves concerned in it. For they take it for granted, that Prayers were intended only for such as have nothing else to do. As for their parts, they have a great deal of work upon their hands, and must mind that, without troubling their heads about any thing else. This is the plain case of some; but not of all. Blessed be GOD, He hath opened the eyes of many, especially in this city, who now see "the things that belong to their everlasting peace," and therefore are as constant at their *public devotions*, as they are at their *private business*. And I trust in His infinite Goodness and Mercy, that He who hath "begun so good a work among us," will one day perfect it, that we may all meet together "with one heart, and with one mouth to pray unto him," and praise and glorify His great name *every day* in the week, both in this city, and all the kingdom over. What a *happy* city, what a *glorious* kingdom would it then be! And how happy should I think myself, if it would please GOD to make me, the unworthiest of all His Servants, an instrument in His Almighty hand towards the effecting of it in *this place!* It is too great a felicity for me to flatter myself with the least hopes of. Howsoever I must do my duty, and leave the issue to Him who hath the hearts of all men in His hand.

That it is His [CHRIST'S] pleasure that we should constantly use *that Form* of Prayer, which He, as our Great LORD and MASTER, was pleased to compose for all his Disciples is so plain, that I wonder how any can doubt of it; there being no *command* in all the Bible more plain than that, "When ye pray, say, Our Father, which art in Heaven," &c. (Luke 11:2).

But it is as plain that He designed *this* Prayer should be used *publicly*, and in *common* by his Disciples when met together in their public assemblies: in that he hath drawn it up all along in the *plural number,* that many may join together in it, and say, "Our Father, which art in Heaven. Give us this day our daily bread. And forgive us our trespasses, as we forgive them that trespass against us. And lead us not into temptation; but deliver us from evil." So that there is not *one* petition, nor *one* expression in it, but what a *whole congregation* may jointly use. From whence St. Cyprian truly observed, that this is *Publica et communis Oratio;* a *Public* and *Common* Prayer. Not but it may, and ought to be used also privately by every single Christian apart by himself; because every Christian is a member of CHRIST'S Catholic Church, and should pray as such in *private* as well as in *public*; and for all his fellow-members, as well as for himself, they being all but one body. But however, it must be acknowledged, that, it being so exactly fitted to a *public* congregation, it was primarily and chiefly intended for that purpose. And that our SAVIOUR would have us say this Prayer every day, appears most plainly from that petition in it, "Give us this day our daily bread." For this shews, that as we depend upon GOD every day for our necessary food, so we ought to pray unto Him every day for it. And if we must put up this petition every day, we must put up all the rest with it. For CHRIST hath *joined* them together, and therefore we must not *put them asunder.* Neither is there any part of the Prayer but what is as necessary to be said every day as this.

Wherefore seeing our Blessed SAVIOUR Himself was most graciously pleased to compose *this* Prayer so as to suit it to our *daily public* devotions, and hath plainly commanded us to use it, according as He had composed it; we may reasonably from thence infer, that it is His divine will and pleasure that we should *publicly* pray to our Heavenly FATHER *every day*, as His Church had all along before done it, *Morning* and *Evening*. Be sure His Apostles thought so, when they had received His Holy Spirit, "to lead them," according to His promise, "into all truth," and to "bring into their remembrance all things that He had said unto them." For after the day of Pentecost, on which the HOLY GHOST came upon them, the next news that we hear of any of them is, that "Peter and John went up together into the Temple at the hour of Prayer, being the *ninth* hour," or the hour of *Evening Prayer;* which they would not have done, if they had not believed it to be agreeable to the doctrine which He had taught them.

The more pleasing any duty is to GOD, the more profitable it is to those who do it. And therefore He having so often, both by word and deed, manifested Himself well-pleased with the *public* or common Service which His people perform to Him, we cannot doubt but they always receive proportionable advantage from it. The Jews call *stated public* Prayers מעמרוה, *Stations;* and have a saying among them, "That without such Stations the world could not stand." Be sure no people have any ground to expect *public* peace and tranquillity, without praising and praying *publicly* unto Him, who alone can give it. But if all the people (suppose of this nation) should every day with *one* heart and mouth join together in our *common* supplications to ALMIGHTY GOD, how happy should we then be? how free from danger? how safe and secure under His protection? This is the argument which CHRIST Himself useth, why "Men ought always to pray, and not to faint;" in the Parable of the unjust Judge, who was at last prevailed with to grant a widow's request, merely by her importunity in asking it. "And shall not GOD," saith He, "avenge His own elect, which cry *day and night* unto Him, though He bear long with them? I tell you that He will avenge them speedily." But then He adds, "Nevertheless, when the SON of MAN cometh, shall He find faith on the earth?" (Luke 18:7, 8). As if He had said, GOD will most certainly avenge and protect those who cry day and night, *morning* and *evening*, to Him. But men will not believe this; and that is the reason why there are so few who believe that He will hear their prayers, according to His promise. But blessed be GOD, though they be but few, there are some, who really believe GOD'S Word, and accordingly *pray* every *morning* and *evening*, not only for themselves, but for the country where they live, for all their Governors both in Church and State, and for all sorts and conditions of men among us. To these the whole kingdom is beholden for its support and preservation. If they should once fail, I know not what would become of us. But so long as there are pious and devout persons crying day and night to GOD for aid and defence against our enemies, we need not fear any hurt they can ever do us; at least according to GOD'S ordinary course of dealing in the world. I know that He is sometimes so highly incensed against a people, that He will hearken to no intercessions for them. As when he said of the idolatrous and factious Jews; "Though Moses and

Samuel stood before Me, yet My mind could not be towards this people" (Jer 15:1). Moses had before diverted His wrath from them (Exod 32:11, 12, 14); and so had Samuel (1Sam 7:9); but at this time He saith, Though both of them stood before Him, and besought Him for it, yet He would not be reconciled to this people. Which plainly implies, that this was an *extraordinary* case, and that He *ordinarily* used to hearken to the prayers which His faithful servants, such as Moses and Samuel were, made to Him in behalf of the people among whom they dwelt: according to that of the Apostle St. James, "The effectual fervent prayer of a righteous man availeth much" (Jas 5:16). To the same purpose is that parallel place in the Prophet Ezekiel, where GOD saith, "That if a land sin grievously against Him, and He send the famine, the sword, the pestilence, or the like punishment, to cut off both man and beast from it; though these three men, Noah, Daniel, and Job were in it, they should deliver none but their own souls" (Ezek 4:14, 16, 18, 20). But here we may likewise observe, that in such an *extraordinary* case as this (which GOD grant may not be our own ere long!), although such righteous persons by all their prayers and tears can deliver none else, yet they themselves shall be delivered. As Lot was out of Sodom, and the Christians at the final destruction of Jerusalem, when eleven hundred thousand Jews perished (Joseph. de Bel. Jud. l. 7. c. 17), and not one Christian, they being all, by the secret providence of God, conveyed out of the city before the siege began (Euseb. Hist. Eccl. l. 3. c. 5). Which shews the particular care that GOD takes of all that believe and serve Him. And that one would think is enough to prevail with all that consult their own and others' welfare, to neglect no opportunities which they can get of serving so great and good a Master, all the ways they can, and particularly by performing their daily devotions to Him. In that they have good ground to hope that He will hear their prayers for *others* but may be sure He will take care of *them*, whatsoever happens.

Reprinted January 25, 1834
The Feast of the Conversion of St. Paul

TRACT 26

The Necessity and Advantage of
Frequent Communion
Extracted from Bishop Beveridge's Sermon on the Subject

I have done what I could; I have taken all occasions to convince you of your sin and danger in neglecting this *Blessed Sacrament,* and to persuade you to a more frequent receiving of it; but I see nothing will do: indeed nothing can do it but the Almighty Power of GOD, whom I therefore beseech of His Infinite Mercy to open men's eyes, that they may "see the things that belong to their everlasting peace, before they be hid from them." And then I am sure this Sacrament would be as much *frequented,* as it hath been hitherto *neglected.* But seeing He is usually pleased to do this great work by the Ministry of His Word, I shall make it my business at this time, in His name, to put you in mind of your *duty* and *interest* in this particular, and so set before you such reasons why you ought to take all opportunities of receiving the Mystical Body and Blood of CHRIST your Saviour, as I hope by His blessing may prevail with many to do it: GOD grant that it may do so with all that hear me at this time.

For this purpose, therefore, I desire you to consider, First, that this is CHRIST'S *own Institution and Command.* He, "who being in the form of GOD, thought it no robbery to be equal with GOD, and yet made Himself of no reputation for your sakes." He, who loved you so, as to *give Himself for you,*—He, who *laid down His own life* to redeem and save you,—He, the very night before He died for you, He then instituted this Holy Sacrament; and He then said to all that hoped to be saved by Him, and to you among others, "Do this in remembrance of Me;" and, "do this as oft as ye drink it, in remembrance of me." What? and will you that hope to be saved by Him, will you never do this at all? Or only now and then, when perhaps you have nothing else to do? How then can ye hope to be saved by Him? Do you think that He will save you, whether ye observe His *commands* or no? And which of all His commands can ye ever observe, if ye do not observe this, which is so *plain,* so *easy,* so *useful,* and so *necessary* for you? No, deceive not yourselves. He that came into the world, and died on purpose to save you, you may be confident would never have required you to do this, and *as often as* you do it, to remember Him, but that it is necessary for your salvation that ye do it, and that ye do it *as often as ye can, in remembrance of Him.* And if it had been necessary in no other, as it is in many respects, yet His very commanding it, makes it so to you, and to your salvation. For as He is the only "Author of eternal salvation," He is so only to "those who obey Him" (Heb 5:9); that is, "to those who observe all things whatsoever He hath commanded" (Matt 28:20). But this is one of those things which He hath commanded; and therefore unless you *do this,* you do not *obey* Him, and so have no ground to expect salvation from Him. He Himself hath told you in effect, that He will not save you; in that He said, "Except ye repent, ye shall all likewise perish" (Luke 13:3, 5). But ye all know, that he who lives in any wilful and known sin, or in the wilful neglect of any known duty, he hath not yet *repented,* and turned to GOD, but is still in his natural estate, in a state of sin and damnation. And if he happens to do so, he must inevitably perish; there is no help in the world for it.

Wherefore, my brethren, ye had need look about you. CHRIST your Saviour hath expressly *commanded* you often to receive the Sacrament of His Body and Blood *in remembrance* of Him. And therefore you, who never yet received it, have lived all this while in the wilful breach of a known Law, and by consequence in a wilful and known sin: and you who receive it but *seldom,* do not fully *obey* or come up to the Law, which plainly requires you to do it *often;* at least if it may be had. It is true, should GOD in His Providence cast you upon a place where you could not receive it if ye would, I do not doubt but He would accept of your earnest desires of it, as well as if ye did receive it; and would make up the great losses you sustained in your spiritual estate for want of it, some other way. But blessed be His Great Name, this is not your case; for He in His good Providence hath so ordered it, that you live in a place where this Holy

Sacrament is actually celebrated every *LORD'S Day*, and may be so, if there be occasion, *every day* in the year. Our Church requires the *first*, and hath provided for the *other*, by ordering that the *same Collect, Epistle*, and *Gospel* which is appointed for the Sunday, shall serve all the week after; and by consequence the whole *Communion Service*, of which they are a part. And therefore, unless you *receive* it, and receive it *often* too, you will live in the gross neglect, if not in a plain contempt of CHRIST'S *command*; as you will one day find to your shame and sorrow; for how well soever ye may otherwise live, this one sin is enough to ruin and destroy you for ever. "For," as St. James saith, "whosoever shall keep the whole law, and yet offend in one point, he is guilty of all" (Jas 2:10). And therefore, whatsoever else ye do, if ye do not this, but *offend in this one point,* you are liable to all the punishments that are threatened in the Law of GOD. Neither is there any way to avoid them, except you repent, and turn from this as well as from all other sins.

And that ye may not think that the receiving of this Blessed Sacrament only now and then, as perhaps two or three times a year, will excuse you from the imputation of living in the neglect of CHRIST'S *command;* I desire you to consider how the Apostles themselves and the Primitive Christians understood it. Which they sufficiently declared by their practice. For when our LORD was gone to Heaven, and had, according to His promise, sent down the HOLY SPIRIT upon His Apostles, and by that means brought into His Church about three thousand souls in one day, it is said of them, that "they continued stedfastly in the Apostles' doctrine and fellowship, and in breaking of bread, and in prayers" (Acts 2:42); and of all that believed, it is said, that "they, continuing daily with one accord in the Temple, and breaking bread from house to house, did eat their meat with gladness and singleness of heart" (2:46). Where we may observe, first, that by *breaking of bread* in the New Testament, is always meant the *Administration of the LORD'S Supper*. Secondly, this they are said to have done, κατ' οἶκον, *from house to house,* as we translate it; or rather *in the house,* as the Syriac and Arabic versions have it, and as the phrase κατ' οἶκον is used by the Apostle himself (Rom 16:5; 1 Cor 16:19); that is, they did it either in some *private* house where there was *a Church*, or more probably in some of the *houses* or *chambers* belonging to the Temple, where they daily continued. Thirdly, as they continued *daily* in the Temple at the hours of prayer, to perform their solemn devotions there, so they *daily* received the Holy Sacrament, and ate this spiritual food "with gladness and singleness of heart." This being indeed the chief part of their devotions, whensoever they could meet together to perform them. Especially upon the LORD'S Day, as the HOLY GHOST Himself informs us, saying, "And upon the first day of the week, when the disciples came together to break bread, Paul preached unto them, being ready to depart on the morrow" (Acts 20:7); where we see, they did not only *break bread,* or *administer the Sacrament of our LORD'S Supper* upon the first day of the week, which we, from St. John, call the LORD'S Day; but upon that day they came together for that end and purpose. It is true, St. Paul being to go away next day, he took that opportunity when they were met together for that end, to give them a Sermon. But that was not the end of their meeting together at that time. They did not come to hear a Sermon, though St. Paul himself was to preach, but they *came together* to *administer* and *receive* CHRIST'S Mystical Body and Blood; which plainly shews, that this was the *great work* they did every LORD'S Day: and that they came together then on purpose to meet with CHRIST, and to partake of Him at His own table. And seeing that the Law itself required, "that none should appear before the LORD empty" (Exod 23:15); therefore St. Paul requires, that upon the *first day* of the week, when Christians thus met together to receive the Sacrament, "every one should lay by him in store, as God prospered him, for pious and charitable uses" (1 Cor 16:2). And hence proceeded that custom which is still continued in our Church, and ought to be so in all. That whensoever we appear before the LORD at His own table, we, every one, according to his ability, offer up something to Him, of what He had bestowed upon us, as our acknowledgment of His *bounty* to us, in giving us whatsoever we have, and of His infinite *mercy* in giving Himself for us.

Now seeing the Apostles themselves, and such as they first converted and instructed in the faith of CHRIST, usually received this Holy Sacrament *every day* in the week, and *constantly* upon the LORD'S Day; it cannot be doubted, but that they looked upon themselves as obliged by CHRIST'S *command* to do so: and that when He said, "Do this, as often as ye do it, in remembrance of Me," His meaning and pleasure was, *that they should often do it, so often as they met together to perform their public devotion to Him, if it was possible, or at least upon the* LORD'S *Day*. And as this was the sense wherein the Apostles understood our SAVIOUR'S words; so they transmitted the same together with the Faith, to those who succeeded them. For Tertullian, who lived in the next century after the Apostles, saith, that the Sacrament of the Eucharist, "in omnibus mandatum à Domino, etiam Antelucanis cœtibus," was commanded by our Lord, to be celebrated in *all Christian assemblies,* even those which were held before day (Ter. de cor. mil. cap. 3). And before him Pliny the Second, who was contemporary with St. John, in the account he gave of the Christians' manners to the Emperor Trajan, saith, among other things, "that they were wont upon a certain day, to meet together, before it was light, and to bind themselves by a Sacrament, not to do any ill thing" (Plin. Ep. 1. 10. cap. 97). Which can be understood only of the *Sacrament of the LORD'S Supper,* as *administered* and *received* by them upon the LORD'S Day. And Justin Martyr himself, who lived in the next age after, in the Apology he wrote to Antonius Pius in behalf of the Christians, giving a particular account of what they did in their public congregations, saith, that τῇ τοῦ ἡλίου λεγομένῃ ἡμέρᾳ, upon that which is called the *day* of the *Sun,* or *Sunday,* all Christians that live either in the cities, or in the country, meet together; where they hear the writings of the Prophets and Apostles read, and an exhortation made to them; and then they having all joined together in their common prayers, bread and wine is brought and consecrated, or blessed by the President or Minister; and distributed to every one there present, and carried by Deacons to such as were absent. Καὶ ἡ διάδοσις καὶ ἡ μετάληψις ἀπὸ τῶν εὐχαριστηθέντων ἑκάστῳ γίνεται. And the distribution and participation of the consecrated elements is made to every one (Just. Mart. Apol. 2). And this food, saith he, Καλεῖται παρ' ἡμῖν Εὐχαριστία, is called by us the Eucharist. From whence it appears, that in *these* days, every one that was at Prayers and Sermon, received also the Holy Sacrament, at least upon the LORD'S Day. None offered to go out until that was over; or if they did so, they were cast out of the Church, as not worthy to be called Christians: as appears from the Apostolical Canons made or collected much about that time, or soon after. One whereof runs thus, Πάντας τοὺς εἰσιόντας πιστοὺς, etc. All believers that come to Church, and hear the Scriptures, but do not stay to join in the *Prayers,* and the *Holy Communion,* ought to be *excommunicated,* as bringing confusion into the Church (Can. Apostol. 9). It was then, it seems, reckoned a great *disorder* and *confusion* for any to go out of the Church, as they now commonly do, until the *whole Service,* of which the

Communion was the principal part, was all over: and if any did so, they were judged unfit to come to Church, or keep company with Christians any longer. This was the *discipline* of the *Primitive* and *Apostolic* Church. This was the *piety* of the *first Christians:* and it continued in a great measure for some ages, as might easily be shown. But this may be sufficient at present to prove, that the Apostles and Primitive Christians did not think that they observed our LORD'S *command* in the institution of this Holy Sacrament aright, by receiving it only *now* and *then.* For, as they would never have done it at all, but only in obedience unto that *command;* so in obedience to that *command,* they took all opportunities they could get, of doing it; at least they never omitted it upon the LORD'S Day. But upon *that day,* whatsoever they did besides, they always did this in remembrance of what their Great LORD and SAVIOUR had done for them. And if we desire to be such Christians as they were, we must do as they did. We must, after their pious example, observe our LORD'S command, by *eating this bread,* and *drinking this cup as often* as we can; lest otherwise we lose the benefit of that death He suffered for us, by our neglecting to do what He hath *commanded* in *remembrance* of it.

What effect they [my arguments] will have upon those that hear them, I know not; but fear that it will be much the same that reason and argument usually have upon the greatest part of mankind; that, very little, or none at all. But for my own part, when I seriously consider these things, I cannot but wonder with myself, how it comes to pass, that this Holy Sacrament, instituted by CHRIST Himself, is so much neglected and disused as it is, in a place where His religion is professed and acknowledged to be, as really it is, the *only true religion* in the world. And after all my search, I can resolve it into nothing else but the degeneracy of the age we live in, and the great decay of that most Holy Religion among us. I am sure, *from the beginning it was not so.* For some ages after the Establishment of the Christian Religion by CHRIST our Saviour, so long as they who embraced it gave themselves up to the conduct of that HOLY SPIRIT which He sent down among them, and were inspired by it with true zeal for GOD, and enflamed with love to their ever blessed REDEEMER, so as to observe all things that He had commanded, whatsoever it cost them; then they never met together upon any day in the week, much less upon the LORD'S Day, for the Public Worship of GOD, but they all received this Holy Sacrament, as the principal business they met about, and the most proper Christian service they could perform. And it is very observable, that so long as this continued, men were endowed with the extraordinary gifts as well as the graces of GOD'S Holy Spirit, so as to be able to do many wonderful things by it; yea, and suffer too whatsoever could be inflicted on them for CHRIST'S sake. But in process of time men began to leave off their first love to Him, and turn His religion into *dispute* and *controversy;* and then as their piety and devotion grew cooler and cooler, the Holy Sacrament began to be neglected more and more; and the Priests who administered it, had fewer and fewer to receive it, until at length they had sometimes none at all. But still they mistook themselves to be obliged in *duty* and *conscience* to consecrate and receive it themselves, although they had none to receive with them. And this mistake, I suppose, gave the first occasion to that multitude of *private masses* which have been so much abused in the Church of Rome; where the priest commonly receives himself, although he hath never a one to communicate with him; and so there can be *no communion* at all. And as that *abuse,* so the *disuse* of the Holy Sacrament, sprang first from men's *coldness* and *indifferency* in religion, which hath prevailed so far in our days, that there are many thousands of persons who are baptized, and live many years in the profession of the Christian religion, and yet never receive the Sacrament of CHRIST'S Body and Blood in all their lives. And but very few that receive it above once or twice a year; which is a great reproach and shame to the age we live in; but none at all to the *Church:* for she is always ready to administer it, if *people* could be persuaded to come to it. But that they cannot, or rather will not be; they have still one *pretence* or other to excuse themselves, but none that will excuse them before GOD and their own consciences another day.

What their *pretences* are, I shall not undertake to determine. They are so many, that they cannot easily be numbered. And many of them so *vain* and *trifling,* that they are not worth rehearsing. But the bottom of them all is this; men renounced the world, the devil, and the flesh in their baptism, but they are loth to do it in their lives: they then promised to serve GOD, but now they find something else to do. They have all one *sin* or other that reigns over them, and captivates their hearts and affections, so that they cannot endure the thoughts of parting with it. And they think, as they ought to do, that if they come to the Holy Sacrament, they must *first examine themselves,* repent of all their sins, turn to GOD, renew their baptismal vow, and resolve to lead a new life. But this they are resolved not to do. And if they should come to the Sacrament, it would but disturb their quiet, make them uneasy in their minds, and hinder them from enjoying the pleasure they were wont to take in all their sins. And for their part, they had rather displease GOD than themselves; and neglect their duty rather than leave their sins. And so add sin to sin, and "treasure up to themselves wrath against the day of wrath, and the revelation of the righteous judgment of GOD." This is plainly the case of most of those who live in the neglect of His Holy Commandment. And what can be said to such men? so long as such, they are not fit to come to the Communion. And therefore all that can be said to them, is only to beg of them to consider their condition before it be too late, and repent as soon as they can: lest they die, as they have lived, in sin, and so be punished with "everlasting destruction from the presence of the LORD, and from the glory of His power."

But there are others who do receive the Sacrament of CHRIST'S Body and Blood sometimes, as perhaps *two* or *three* times in a year; and my charity prompts me to believe, that they would do it *oftener,* if they thought it to be their *duty.* But there are some things which at first sight may seem, at least to them, to plead their excuse; and therefore deserve to be duly considered by us. As first, they say, our Church requires them only to receive *three* times a year: and they do not question but she would oblige them to receive it *oftener,* if it was necessary. This is a mistake that a great many have fallen into, and by that means have been kept from the Sacrament more than otherwise they would have been. I call it a mistake; for it is so, and a very great one. For as in all things else, so particularly in this, our Church keeps close to the pattern of the Apostolic and Primitive Church; when, as I have before observed, the LORD'S Supper was administered and received commonly *every day* in the week, but most constantly upon the LORD'S Day. And our Church supposeth it to be so still, and therefore hath accordingly made provision for it. Which, that I may fully demonstrate to you, it will be necessary to enquire into the sense and practice of our Church in this point all along from the beginning of the Reformation, or, to speak more properly, from the time when she was restored to that Apostolical form which she is now of, as she was at first; which we date from the reign of King Edward VI.

For in the first year of that pious prince, the Liturgy, or Book of Common Prayer, was first compiled; and in the second it was settled by act of parliament. In which book it is ordered, that the Exhortation to those who are minded to receive the Sacrament, shall be read; which is there set down, much the same that we read now. But afterwards it is said, "in Cathedral Churches, or other places where there is daily Communion, it shall be sufficient to read this Exhortation above written once in a month. And in Parish Churches upon the week-days it may be left unsaid" (Fol. 123). Where we may observe, first, that in those days there was daily Communion in Cathedral Churches, and other places, as there used to be in the Primitive Church. And accordingly I find, in the records of St. Paul's, that when the plate, jewels, &c. belonging to the said Cathedral, were delivered to the King's Commissioners, they, upon the Dean and Chapter's request, permitted to remain, among other things, "two pair of basyns for to bring the Communion Bread, and to receive the offerings for the poor; whereof one pair silver, for every day, the other for festivals, &c. gilt." (Dugdal Hist. of St. Paul's, page 274). From whence it is plain, that the Communion was then celebrated in that Church every day. And so it was even in Parish Churches. For otherwise it needed not to be ordered as it is in the Rubric above mentioned, that in Parish Churches upon the week-days the said Exhortation may be left unsaid. And to the same purpose it is afterwards said, "when the Holy Communion is celebrated on the work-day, or in private houses, then may be omitted the Gloria in Excelsis, the Creed, the Homily and the Exhortation" (Fol. 132).

Next after that we quoted first, this Rubric immediately follows; "And if upon the Sunday or Holy-day, the people be negligent to come to the Communion, then shall the Priest earnestly exhort his parishioners to dispose themselves to the receiving of the Holy Communion more diligently, saying," &c. Which shews, that upon all Sundays and Holy-days people then generally received; the Church expected and required it of them. And if any Minister found that his parishioners did not always come, at least upon those days, he was to exhort and admonish them to dispose themselves more diligently for it; and that by the command of the Church itself; whereby she hath sufficiently declared her will and desire, that all her members should receive the Communion as they did in the Primitive times, every day in the week if possible; and if that could not be, yet at least every Sunday and Holy-day in the year.

In the Rubric after the Communion Service, there are several things to the same purpose; for it is there ordered, that upon Wednesdays and Fridays, *although there be none to communicate,* the Priest shall say all things at the Altar appointed to be said at the celebration of the LORD'S Supper, until after the Offertory. And then it follows: "And the same order shall be used whensoever the people be customably assembled to pray in the Church, and none disposed to communicate with the Priest" (Fol. 130). Whereby we are given to understand, that upon *what day soever* people came to Church, the Priest was to be ready to celebrate the *Holy Sacrament* if any were disposed to *communicate* with him. And if there were none, he was to shew his readiness, by reading a considerable part of the Communion Service.

There is another Rubric in the same place, that makes it still plainer. Which I shall transcribe, because the book is not commonly to be had; neither can it be expressed better than in its words, which are these: "Also, that the receiving of the Sacrament of the Blessed Body and Blood of CHRIST, may be most agreeable to the Institution thereof, and to the usage of the Primitive Church, in all Cathedral and Collegiate Churches there shall always *some* communicate with the Priest that ministereth. And that the same may be also observed every where abroad in the country, some *one* at the least of that house in every *Parish,* to whom by course, after the ordinance herein made, it appertaineth to offer for the charges of the Communion; or some other whom they shall provide to offer for them, shall receive the Holy Communion with the Priest; the which may be the better done, for that they know before when their *course* cometh, and may therefore dispose themselves to the worthy receiving of the Sacrament. And with him or them, who doth so offer the charges of the Communion, all other who be then godly disposed thereunto, shall likewise receive the Communion. And by this means the Minister having always some to communicate with him, may accordingly solemnize so High and Holy Mysteries, with all the suffrages and due order appointed for the same. And the Priest on the week-day shall forbear to celebrate the Communion, except he have some that will communicate with him."

Here we see what care the Church took that the Sacrament might be daily administered, not only in Cathedral, but likewise in *Parish Churches.* For which purpose, whereas every Parishioner had before been used to find the Holy Loaf, as it was called, in his *course;* in the Rubric before this, it is ordained that every Pastor or Curate shall find sufficient Bread and Wine for the *Communion;* and that the Parishioners every one in his course, shall offer the charges of it at the Offertory to the Pastor or Curate; and in this it is ordained that every such Parishioner shall then in his course communicate, or else get some other person to do it, that so the Communion may be duly celebrated; and all there present that were godly disposed might partake of it. Which one would have thought as good a Provision as could have been made in the case. But notwithstanding, through the obstinacy or carelessness of some, in not making their said offering as they were commanded, it sometimes failed; as appears from the Letter written about a year after by the Privy Council, and subscribed by the Archbishop of Canterbury and others, to the Bishops, to assure them that the King intended to go on with the Reformation, wherein among other things they say: "And farther, whereas it is come to our knowledge that divers froward and obstinate persons do refuse to pay towards the finding of Bread and Wine for the Holy Communion, according to the order prescribed in the said book, by reason whereof the Holy Communion is many times omitted upon the Sunday; These are to will and command you to convent such obstinate persons before you, and them to admonish and command to keep the order prescribed in the said book. And if any such shall refuse so to do, to punish them by suspension, excommunication, or other censures of the Church" (Hist. of Reform. Part II. Coll. p. 192). From whence we may also learn how much they were troubled to hear that the Holy Sacrament was any where omitted even upon the Sunday, upon any Sunday; how great a *fault* and *scandal* they judged it to be, and what care they took to prevent it for the future.

This was the state of this affair at the beginning of the Reformation, and it continues in effect the same to this day. About three or four years after the aforesaid Book of Common Prayer first came out, it was revised, and set forth again with some alterations in the form, but none that were material in the substance of it. Only the former way of the Parishioners finding Bread and Wine for the Communion every one in his *course,* being now found not so effectual as was expected; that was now laid aside, and it was ordered to be provided at the charges of the Parish in general, in these words; "The Bread and Wine for the Communion shall be provided by the Curate and Churchwardens, at the charges of the Parish; and the Parish shall be discharged of such sums of money or other duties, which hitherto they have paid for the same, by order of their houses, every Sunday." Where we may take notice, that as hitherto it had been provided every Sunday by the houses of every Parish, as they lay in order, it was now to be provided by the Minister and Churchwardens, at the charges of the whole Parish, but still every Sunday, as it was before; which being the most certain way that could be found out for it, it is still continued. The first part of this Rubric, whereby it is enjoined, being still in force. But the latter part, from these words, "and the Parish shall be discharged," &c. is now left out, as it was necessary it should be after the former course had been disused for above an hundred years.

Now this Book of Common Prayer, which was thus settled by Act of Parliament, in the fifth and sixth year of Edward the VI, was that which was afterwards confirmed in the beginning of Queen Elizabeth's reign, with one alteration or addition of certain lessons to be used on every Sunday in the year, and the form of the Litany altered, and corrected, with two sentences only added in the delivery of the Sacrament to the Communicants. These were all the alterations that were then made, or indeed that have been ever made since that time to this, except it be in words or phrases, in the addition of some prayers, and in some such inconsiderable things, as do not at all concern our present purpose. For the care of our Church, to have the Holy Communion constantly celebrated, hath been the same all along, from the time that the Book of Common Prayer before spoken of, was first settled. As may be easily proved from that which was established by the last Act of Uniformity. Which therefore I shall now briefly consider, so far as it relates to the business in hand; that we may understand the sense of our Church at present concerning it.

For this purpose therefore we may first observe that the Communion Service is appointed for the Communion itself, and therefore called the Order for the Administration of the LORD'S Supper, or Holy Communion. Now our Church supposing, or at least hoping that some of her members will receive this Holy Communion every day, hath taken care that this service may be used every day in the week, as appears from the Rubric immediately before the proper lessons, which is this: "Note also, that the Collect, Epistle, and Gospel appointed for the Sunday, shall serve all the week after, where it is not in this book otherwise ordered." But the Collect, Epistle, and Gospel are part of the Communion Service, for which there is no occasion on the week-days; neither can it be used except the Communion be administered, which therefore is here supposed to be done *every day* in the week. And so it is also in the celebration of the Communion itself, where there are proper prefaces appointed to be used upon certain days. Upon Christmas-day and seven days after. Upon Easter-day and seven days after. Upon Ascension-day and seven days after. Upon Whit-Sunday and six days after (the next day being Trinity Sunday, which hath one peculiar to itself). Now to what purpose are these prefaces appointed to be used seven days together, or six, none of which can be a Sunday, if the Sacrament ought not to be administered upon all those days, and so upon week days as well as Sundays? They are all, as I intimated before, to be used in the actual Administration of it, and therefore plainly suppose it to be actually administered upon each of those days, which being for the most part neither Sundays nor Holy-days, they most evidently demonstrate, that according to the mind and order of our Church, as well as the Primitive, the LORD'S Supper ought to be administered *every day*, that all who live as they ought, in her Communion, may be daily partakers of it.

In the rules and orders (which we call the Rubric) after the Communion Service, there are several things that deserve to be considered in this case. It is there ordered, that there shall be no celebration of the Communion, except there be a convenient number; that is, *four*, or *three* at the least, to communicate with the Priest. According to which rule, although the Priest have all things ready, and desires to consecrate and receive the Holy Sacrament himself, yet he must not do it, unless he have such a number to communicate with him, that it may be properly a Communion. But, as it is there ordered, "Upon the Sundays and other Holy-days (if there be no Communion) shall be said all that is appointed at the Communion until the end of the general prayer (for the good estate of the Catholic Church of CHRIST);" where we may observe, that the Church, as I have shewn, appoints the Sacrament to be administered *every day*. But if it so fall out, that there be not in any place a convenient number to communicate with the Priest, and by consequence according to the order before mentioned, no Communion; yet nevertheless upon Sundays and other Holy-days so much of the Communion Service shall be said as is there limited. Why only upon Sundays and Holy-days, but to distinguish them from other days, on which if there be a sufficient number of

Communicants, the whole Communion Service is to be used; but no part of it, except there be so; but upon Sundays and Holy-days, although there be not such a number, and therefore no Communion; yet, however, the Priest shall go up to the Altar, and there read all that is appointed to be said at the Communion, until the end of the prayer for CHRIST'S Catholic Church; whereby the people may see, that neither *he* nor the *Church* is to be blamed, if the Holy Sacrament *be* not then administered. For as much as he is there ready by the order of the Church to do it, and goes as far as he can in the Service appointed for it, without the actual administration of it; and therefore that the fault is wholly in themselves that it is not *actually* administered, because they will not make up a convenient number among them to communicate with him. Which is a most excellent order; for the people hereby have not only GOD'S Holy Commandments solemnly proclaimed, the Epistle and Gospel for the day, the Nicene Creed, and prayers proper for that occasion read to them; but they are likewise put in mind of their duty to their SAVIOUR in receiving His most Blessed Body and Blood, and upbraided with their neglect of it. For which purposes also, I think it very expedient, that the order of the Church for the reading that part of the Service at the Communion Table, even when there is no Communion, be duly observed.

The next Rubric, in the same place, that concerns our present business, is this; "And in all Cathedral and Collegiate Churches and Colleges, where there are many Priests and Deacons, they shall all receive the Communion with the Priest every Sunday at the least, except they have a reasonable cause to the contrary." Where we see that the Church doth not command, but supposes that the Sacrament is constantly administered in all such places; taking it for granted, that it is never omitted there, where there are so many persons devoted to the service of God; but that there is always a sufficient number to *communicate*. But she absolutely commands, that all Priests and Deacons that belong to such foundations, shall receive the *Communion* with the *Priest* every *Sunday* at the least, except any of them have a reasonable cause to the contrary (which the Ordinary of the place, I suppose, is to be judge of): they are bound therefore, all and every one of them, to receive it every Sunday, which notwithstanding they cannot do, unless it be administered every Sunday among them. Wherefore if there be any such places where it is not so *administered,* or any such persons who do not, without just cause to the contrary, *receive* it every *Sunday* in the year, I do not see how they can answer it to God, to the Church, or to their own *consciences*. Neither are they bound to receive it only every *Sunday*, but *every Sunday at the least:* which plainly supposeth that it is administered upon *other* days as well as *Sundays*. For otherwise they could not receive it *oftener*, if they would. And it is to be hoped, that all such persons *receive* it as often as it is administered among them. But the Church expressly requires them to *receive* it at least every Sunday, so as never to omit it at least upon *that* day, except they have a reasonable, or such a cause to the contrary as will justify their omission of it before the Church, and CHRIST Himself at the last day. These things being thus briefly explained, we shall easily see into the meaning of the words that gave us the occasion to discourse of them, which are these, in the place last quoted; *And note, that every parishioner shall communicate at the least three times in the year, of which* EASTER *to be one*. From whence some have been tempted to think, that the Church doth not look upon it as necessary that they should communicate above *thrice* a year. I say, tempted to think so. For no man surely in his right wits can of himself draw such an inference from these words, which is so directly contrary to the sense of the Church, and hath no foundation at all in the words themselves. For the Church, as I have shown, hath taken all the care she can, that the Holy Sacrament should be every where administered, if it was possible, every day, at least every Sunday and Holy-Day in the year; which she would never have done, if she had thought it sufficient for any one to receive only *thrice* a year. For then all her care about the *frequent* administration of it, would be in vain, and to no purpose. And besides, she hath drawn up an excellent exhortation to be read by the Minister of every parish, in case he sees the people negligent to come to the Holy Communion, beginning thus: "Dearly beloved, on —— I intend by GOD'S Grace, to celebrate the LORD'S Supper." Where we may observe, that it is not said on such a Sunday, but on —— with a blank, to shew that the Minister may appoint the Communion on any day of the week, when he can have a sufficient number to communicate with him; and so it is in the other exhortation; only there is *day* put in, which may be understood of Tuesday or Wednesday, or any other day as well as Sunday, for the same reason. In that first mentioned, the Minister, in the words, and by the order of the Church, invites all there present, and beseecheth them for the LORD JESUS CHRIST'S sake to come to the LORD'S *Supper*. And among other things, he saith to them all, "I bid you in the name of God, I call you in CHRIST'S behalf, I exhort you as you love your own salvation, that ye will be partakers of this Holy Communion." There are several such pathetical expressions in that Exhortation, wherewith the Church most earnestly exhorts, adviseth, admonisheth all persons to come to this Holy Sacrament. And this Exhortation every Minister is to read publicly before all his congregation, whensoever he sees them negligent to come to it; as all are, who come but *two* or *three* times a year, where they may have it oftener if they will. They plainly live in the *neglect* of it, and therefore ought to have this Exhortation read to them, according to the order of the Church. Whereby she hath sufficiently demonstrated, that she doth not think it enough for people generally to receive it only *three* times in a year; but that it is her opinion, that they ought, and her hearty desire they would receive it as often as it is, or, according to her order, ought to be administered among them.

But then she wisely considers withal, that being a *National* Church, made up of all sorts of persons, it is necessary that her general *Rules* and *Orders* should be accommodated as much as possible, to the several conditions and circumstances that many of them may be sometimes in. And therefore, although she exhorts all her members to *frequent* and *constant* Communion, yet she does not think fit to command, and oblige them all, under the pain of *excommunication*, to receive oftener than *three* times a year, lest some might be thereby tempted to come sometimes without that preparation and disposition of mind that is requisite to the worthy partaking of so great a Mystery. I say, under pain of *excommunication;* for that is the meaning and the effect of this law, that they who do not communicate at least *three* times in a year, may, and ought to be cast out of the Communion of CHRIST'S Church, as no longer fit to be called Christians, seeing they live in such a gross neglect of CHRIST'S own command, and of that duty whereby Christians are in an especial manner distinguished from other men. Other men, as Jews, Turks, and Heathens, may fast and pray and hear Sermons, in their way; but to receive the Sacrament of CHRIST'S Supper, is proper and peculiar only to Christians, or such as profess that religion which JESUS CHRIST hath settled in the world. And therefore they who receive the Sacrament, do thereby manifest themselves to be Christians. They who do it not, make it at least doubtful whether they be Christians or no; for although they were baptized, and so made Christians once, who knows whether they have not renounced their baptism and apostatized from the Christian religion? They themselves perhaps may profess they have not; but the Church can never know it, but hath just cause to suspect the contrary, so long as they refuse to renew the vow they made in the Sacrament of Baptism, by receiving that of the LORD'S Supper. And the least that can be required of them for that purpose, is to do it *three* times a year; which therefore the Church absolutely requires; not that it is not necessary for them to receive it *oftener,* in order to their salvation; but because it is necessary they should do it at least so *often,* that the Church may be satisfied that they continue in their communion, and constant to that religion wherein alone salvation can be had.

And hence it is, that in the rule itself, it is not said that *every person,* but *every parishoner,* shall communicate at the least *three* times in the year; which therefore is required of all, not as they are members only of the *Catholic,* but as they are members of a *Parochial* Church; and they are bound by this law to do it at least so often in their own *Parish Church,* where they are parishioners: otherwise they do not do it as *parishioners,* as the law requires. So that although a man communicates an hundred times in any other place; as in the Cathedral, which is free to all of the Diocess, or in a Chapel of Ease, or in any other *Church,* when he can have it at his own, this does not satisfy the law. But he must communicate at least *three* times in the year, as a parishioner, in his own *Parish Church,* where there are officers called Churchwardens, appointed on purpose to take notice of it, and to inform the *Church* against him, if he neglect to do it so often as she requires. That she may use the most effectual means to bring him to repentance for his sin, and to make him more careful for the future to perform so great and necessary a duty as this is; or if he continue obstinate, cut him off from the Body of CHRIST, as no longer worthy to be called a member of it. And therefore all that can be reasonably inferred from this law, is, that the *Church* doth not think them fit to communicate at all, who will not communicate at least *three* times in the year. But as for her opinion of the *necessity* of communicating oftener, in order to men's obtaining eternal salvation by the Blood of CHRIST, that she hath sufficiently declared, by the great care she hath taken, to have this *Holy Sacrament* administered constantly, as *often* as it was in the *Apostles'* and *Primitive* time of Christianity; that is, *as often* as any Christian can desire to have it. For according to the order and discipline of our Church, if a sufficient number of *parishioners,* against whom there is no just exception, desire to receive it every *Sunday,* or *every day* in the year, the Minister of their parish not only may, but, as I humbly conceive, is bound to *consecrate* and *administer* it to them. The want of such a number being, as far as I can perceive, the only reason that can ever justify the omission of it.

 I have endeavoured to set this matter in as clear a light as I could, because it will discover to us, several things very observable concerning the *Church* we live in. For hereby we see how exactly she follows the pattern of the *Primitive* and *Apostolic Church* in this particular, as well as others; what great care she hath taken that the Bread and Water of Life may be duly distributed to all her members whensoever they *hunger and thirst* after it. With how great prudence she hath so ordered it, that all may have it *as often* as they will, and yet none compelled to receive it oftener than it is absolutely *necessary,* in order to their manifesting themselves to continue in the faith of CHRIST. How desirous she is that all would receive it *constantly*, and yet how careful that none may receive it *unworthily*. How *uniform* she hath been in her orders about it all along; and by consequence what cause we all have to bless GOD, that we live in the *communion* of such a Church; and how much it behoves us to receive the Holy Communion of her; not only *as often* as she strictly commands all to receive it under the pain of *excommunication,* but *as often* as she adviseth and exhorteth us to do it in order to our Eternal Salvation, and as she is ready and desirous to communicate it to us. And then we should be sure to receive it *as often* as we are bound, either in duty to GOD, or by our own interest to do it.

The Blessed Body and Blood of CHRIST, received, as it ought to be, with a quick and lively faith, will most certainly have its desired effect. But it operates, for the most part, upon our *souls,* as our ordinary food doth upon our *bodies,* insensibly and by degrees. We *eat* and *drink* every day, and by that means our bodies grow to their full stature, and are then kept up in life, health, and vigour, though we ourselves know not how this is done, nor perhaps take any notice of it. So it is with this spiritual meat and drink, which GOD hath prepared for our souls. By eating and drinking frequently of it, we grow by degrees in grace, and in the "knowledge of our Lord and Saviour JESUS CHRIST," and still continue steadfast and active in the true faith and fear of GOD; though after all, we may be no way sensible how this wonderful effect is wrought in us, but only as we find it to be so by our own experience. And if we do that, we have no cause to complain that we get nothing by it; for we get more than all the world is worth; being strengthened in the inward man, and so made more fit for the service of GOD, more constant in it, and more able to perform it; or at least are kept from falling back, and preserved from many sins and temptations, which otherwise we might be exposed to; and this surely is enough to make any one that really minds the good of his soul, to *hunger* and *thirst* after this Bread and Water of Life, and to *eat and drink* it as *often* as he can, although he do not presently feel the happy effect of it, as some have done, and as he himself sometimes may, when GOD seeth it necessary or convenient for him. In the meanwhile he may rest satisfied in his mind, that he is in the way that CHRIST hath made to Heaven; and thank GOD for giving him so *many opportunities* of partaking of CHRIST'S Body and Blood, and also grace to lay hold of them, to improve them to his own *unspeakable* comfort, such as usually attends the *worthy receiving* of the LORD'S *Supper:* whereby we are not *only* put in mind of the great *Sacrifice* which the SON of GOD offered for our sins, but likewise have it actually *communicated* unto us, for our *pardon* and *reconciliation* to the ALMIGHTY GOVERNOR of the world, which is the greatest comfort we can have on this side Heaven; so great, that we shall *never* be able to express it unto others, how deeply soever we may be affected with it in ourselves. And though we be not always thus *sensibly* cheered and refreshed with it, as we could wish to be, howsoever we can *never* receive the Blessed Sacrament, but we have the *pleasure* and *satisfaction* of having *done* our *duty* to our MAKER and REDEEMER, which far exceeds all the comforts of this life, and therefore may well stay our stomachs till GOD sees good to give us more.

The oftener we do it [partake the LORD'S Supper], the more expert we shall be at it, and the more *benefit* and *comfort* we shall receive from it. It is very difficult, if not impossible, for those who do it only now and then (as once or twice a year) ever to do it as they ought; for every time they come to it, they must begin as it were again; all the impressions which were made upon their minds at the last Sacrament, being worn out before the next; and it being a thing they are not accustomed to, they are as much to seek how to do it now, as if they had never done it before. It is by frequent acts that habits are produced. It is by often eating and drinking this spiritual food, that we learn how to do it, so as to digest and convert it into proper nourishment for our souls. And therefore I do not wonder that they who do it seldom, never do it as they ought, nor by consequence get any good by it; I should rather wonder if they did. But let any man do it often, and always according to the directions before laid down, and my life for his, he shall never lose his labour; but, whether he perceives it or not, he will grow in grace, and gather spiritual strength every time more and more.

If such considerations as these will not prevail upon men, to lay aside their little excuses for the neglect of so great a duty, and to resolve for the future upon the more constant performance of it; for my part I know not what will: and therefore shall say no more, but that I never expect to see our Church settled, Primitive Christianity revived, and true piety and virtue flourish again among us, till the Holy Communion be oftener celebrated, than it hath been of late, in all places of the Kingdom: and am sure, that if people were but sensible of the great advantage it would be to them, they would need no other arguments to persuade them to frequent it as often as they can. For we should soon find, as many have done already, by experience, that this is the great means appointed by our Blessed REDEEMER, whereby to communicate Himself, and all the merits of His most precious Death and Passion to us, for the pardon of all our sins, and for the "purging our consciences from dead works to serve the Living GOD." So that by applying ourselves thus constantly unto Him, we may receive constant supplies of grace and power from Him to live in His true faith and fear all our days; and by conversing so frequently with Him at His Holy Table upon earth, we shall be always fit and ready to go to Him, and to converse perpetually with Him at His Kingdom above, where we shall have no need of Sacraments, but shall see *Him face to face*, and adore and praise Him for ever; as for all His other blessings, so particularly for the many opportunities he hath given us, of partaking of His most Blessed Body and Blood.

Reprinted February 2, 1834
The Feast of the Purification

TRACT 27

The History of Popish Transubstantiation
To Which Is Opposed the Catholic Doctrine of the Holy Scripture, the Ancient Fathers, and the Reformed Church

BY JOHN COSIN, BISHOP OF DURHAM

Chapter 1
The Spiritual Presence of Christ in the Sacrament of the Lord's Supper

Those words which our Blessed SAVIOUR used in the institution of the blessed Sacrament of the Eucharist, "This is My Body which is given for you; this is My Blood which is shed for you, for the remission of sins;" are held and acknowledged by the Universal Church to be most true and infallible: and if any one dares oppose them, or call in question CHRIST'S veracity, or the truth of His words, or refuse to yield his sincere assent to them, except he be allowed to make a mere figment, or a bare figure of them, we cannot, and ought not, either excuse or suffer him in our Churches; for we must embrace and hold for an undoubted truth whatever is taught by Divine Scripture. And therefore we can as little doubt of what CHRIST saith, John 6:55, "My Flesh is meat indeed, and My Blood is drink indeed;" which, according to St. Paul, are both given to us by the consecrated Elements; for he calls the Bread, "the Communion of CHRIST'S Body," and the Cup, "the Communion of His Blood."

Hence it is most evident, that the Bread and Wine (which according to St. Paul are the Elements of the holy Eucharist) are neither changed as to their substance, nor vanished, nor reduced to nothing, but are solemnly consecrated by the words of CHRIST, that by them His blessed Body and Blood may be communicated to us.

And further it appears from the same words, that the expression of CHRIST and the Apostle, is to be understood in a sacramental and mystic sense; and that no gross and carnal presence of body and blood can be maintained by them.

And though the word Sacrament be no where used in Scripture to signify the blessed Eucharist, yet the Christian Church, ever since its Primitive ages, hath given it that name, and always called the presence of CHRIST'S Body and Blood therein, Mystic and Sacramental. Now a Sacramental expression doth, without any inconvenience, give to the sign the name of the thing signified; and such is as well the usual way of speaking, as the nature of Sacraments, that not only the names, but even the properties and effects of what they represent and exhibit, are given to the outward Elements. Hence (as I said before) the Bread is as clearly or positively called by the Apostle, the Communion of the Body of CHRIST.

This also seems very plain, that our Blessed SAVIOUR'S design was not so much to teach, what the Elements of Bread and Wine are by nature and substance, as what is their use and office and signification in this mystery; for the Body and Blood of our SAVIOUR are not only fitly represented by the Elements, but also, by virtue of His institution really offered to all, by them, and so eaten by the faithful mystically and sacramentally; whence it is, that "He truly is and abides in us, and we in Him."

This is the spiritual (and yet no less true and undoubted than if it were corporal) eating of CHRIST'S Flesh, not indeed simply as it is flesh, without any other respect (for so it is not given, neither would it profit us) but as it is crucified and given for the redemption of the world; neither doth it hinder the truth and substance of the thing, that this eating of CHRIST'S body is spiritual, and that by it the souls of the faithful, and not their stomachs, are fed by the operation of the HOLY GHOST; for this none can deny, but they who being strangers to the Spirit and the divine virtue, can savour only carnal things, and to whom, what is spiritual and sacramental, is the same as if a mere nothing.

As to the *manner* of the presence of the Body and Blood of our LORD in the Blessed Sacrament, we that are Protestant and Reformed according to the ancient Catholic Church, do not search into the manner of it with perplexing inquiries; but, after the example of the Primitive and purest Church of CHRIST, we leave it to the power and wisdom of our LORD, yielding a full and unfeigned assent to His words. Had the Romish maintainers of Transubstantiation done the same, they would not have determined and decreed, and then imposed as an article of faith absolutely necessary to salvation, a manner of presence, newly by them invented, under pain of the most direful curse, and there would have been in the Church less wrangling, and more peace and unity than now is.

Chapter 2
Illustrated from Protestant Authorities

So then, none of the Protestant Churches doubt of the real (that is, true and not imaginary) presence of CHRIST'S Body and Blood in the Sacrament; and there appears no reason why any man should suspect their common confession, of either fraud or error, as though in this particular they had in the least departed from the Catholic faith.

For it easy to produce the consent of Reformed Churches and authors, whereby it will clearly appear (to them that are not wilfully blind) that they all zealously maintain and profess this truth, without forsaking in any wise the true Catholic faith in this matter.

I begin with the Church of England . . . . . It teacheth therefore, "that in the Blessed Sacrament, the Body of CHRIST is given, taken, and eaten; so that to the worthy receivers, the consecrated and broken Bread is the communication of the Body of CHRIST; and likewise the consecrated Cup the communication of His Blood; but that the wicked, and they that approach unworthily the Sacrament of so sacred a thing, eat and drink their own damnation, in that they become guilty of the Body and Blood of CHRIST." And the same Church, in a solemn prayer before the consecration, prays thus; "Grant us, gracious LORD, so to eat the Flesh of thy dear Son JESUS CHRIST, and to drink His Blood, that our sinful bodies may be made clean by His body, and our souls washed through His most precious blood; and that we may evermore dwell in Him, and He in us." The Priest also, blessing or consecrating the Bread and Wine, saith thus; "Hear us, O merciful FATHER, we most humbly beseech Thee, and grant that we receiving these Thy creatures of Bread and Wine, according to Thy

Son our Saviour JESUS CHRIST'S holy institution, in remembrance of His Death and Passion, may be partakers of His most blessed Body and Blood." . . . . The same, when he gives the Sacrament to the people kneeling, giving the bread, saith; "The Body of our LORD JESUS CHRIST which was given for thee, preserve thy body and soul unto everlasting life." Likewise when he gives the cup, he saith, "The Blood of our LORD JESUS CHRIST which was shed for thee, preserve thy body and soul to everlasting life." Afterwards, when the Communion is done, follows a thanksgiving; "Almighty and everliving GOD, we most heartily thank Thee, for that Thou dost vouchsafe to feed us, who have duly received these holy mysteries, with the spiritual food of the most precious Body and Blood of Thy Son, our Saviour JESUS CHRIST;" with the Hymn, *Glory be to God on high,* &c. Also in the public authorised Catechism of our Church, appointed to be learned of all, it is answered to the question concerning the inward part of the Sacrament, that "it is the Body and Blood of Christ which are verily and indeed taken and received by the faithful in the LORD'S Supper." And in the Apology for this Church, writ by that worthy and Reverend Prelate Jewel, Bishop of Salisbury, it is expressly affirmed, "that to the faithful, is truly given in the Sacrament the Body and Blood of our LORD, the life-giving Flesh of the SON of GOD which quickens our souls, the Bread that came from Heaven, the Food of immortality, grace and truth, and life; and that it is the Communion of the Body and Blood of CHRIST, that we may abide in Him, and He in us; and that we may be ascertained that the Flesh and Blood of CHRIST is the food of our souls, as bread and wine is of our bodies."

The right Reverend Doctors, T. Bilson, and L. Andrews, Prelates both of them, thoroughly learned, and great defenders of the Primitive Faith, ... made it most evident by their printed writings, that the Faith and Doctrine of the Church of England is in all things agreeable to the holy Scriptures, and the Divinity of the Ancient Fathers. And as to what regards this mystery, the first treats of it, in his Answer to the Apology of Cardinal Alan, and the last in his Answer to the Apology of Cardinal Bellarmine, where you may find things worthy to be read and noted as follows. "CHRIST said this is My Body; in this, the object, we are agreed with you, the manner only is controverted. We hold by a firm belief, that it is the

Body of CHRIST, of the manner how it comes to be so, there is not a word in the Gospel; and because the Scripture is silent in this, we justly disown it to be a matter of faith; we may indeed rank it among tenets of the school, but, by no means, among the Articles of our Christian Belief. We like well of what Durandus is reported to have said, 'We hear the word, and feel the motion, we know not the manner, and yet believe the presence;' for we believe a real presence no less than you do. We dare not be so bold as presumptuously to define any thing concerning the manner of a true presence; or rather, we do not so much as trouble ourselves with being inquisitive about it; no more than in Baptism, how the Blood of CHRIST washeth us; or in the Incarnation of our Redeemer, how the divine and human nature were united together. We put it in the number of sacred things, or sacrifices (the Eucharist itself being a Sacred Mystery) whereof the remnants ought to be consumed with fire; that is (as the Fathers elegantly have it) adored by faith, but not searched by reason."

As for the opinion and belief of the German Protestants, it will be known chiefly by the Augustan Confession, presented to Charles the Fifth by the Princes of the Empire, and other great persons. For they teach, that "not only the bread and wine, but the Body and Blood of CHRIST is truly given to the receivers;" or, as it is in another edition, that "the Body and Blood of CHRIST are truly present, and distributed to the communicants in the LORD'S Supper;" and refute those that teach otherwise. They also declare, "that we must so use the Sacraments, as to believe and embrace by faith, those things promised which the Sacraments offer and convey to us." Yet we may observe here, that faith makes not those things present which are promised; for faith, as it is well known, is more properly said to take and apprehend, than to promise or perform; but the Word and Promise of God, on which our faith is grounded (and not faith itself) make that present which is promised; as it was agreed at a conference at St. German, betwixt some Protestants and Papists; and therefore it is unjustly laid to our charge by some in the Church of Rome, as if we should believe, that the presence and participation of CHRIST, in the Sacrament, is effected merely by the power of faith.

The Saxon Confession, approved by other churches, seems to be a repetition of the Augustan. Therein we are taught, that "Sacraments are actions divinely instituted; and that, although the same things or actions in common use, have nothing of the nature of Sacraments, yet when used according to the divine institution, CHRIST is truly and substantially present in the Communion, and His Body and Blood truly given to the receivers; so that He testifies that He is in them; as St. Hilary saith, 'these things taken and received make us to be in CHRIST, and CHRIST to be in us.'"

The Confession of Wittemberg, which in the year 1552, was propounded to the Council of Trent, is like unto this: for it teacheth that "the true Body and Blood of CHRIST are given in the Holy Communion;" and refutes those that say, "that the Bread and Wine in the Sacrament are only signs of the absent Body and Blood of CHRIST."

Luther was once of opinion, that the Divines of Basil and Strasbourg did acknowledge nothing in the LORD's Supper besides Bread and Wine. To him Bucerus, in the name of all the rest, did freely answer; "That they all unanimously did condemn that error; that neither they, nor the Switzers, ever believed or taught any such thing; that none could expressly be charged with that error, except the Anabaptists; and that he also had once been persuaded, that Luther in his writings, attributed too much to the outward symbols, and maintained a grosser union of CHRIST with the bread than the Scriptures did allow; as though CHRIST had been corporally present with it, united into a natural substance with the bread; so that the wicked as well as the faithful were made partakers of grace by receiving the Element; but that their own doctrine and belief concerning that Sacrament was, that the true Body and Blood of CHRIST was truly presented, given, and received together with the visible signs of Bread and Wine, by the operation of our LORD, and by virtue of His institution, according to the plain sound and sense of His words; and that not only Zuinglius and Œcolampadius had so taught, but they also, in the public confessions of the Churches of the Upper Germany, and other writings, confessed it; so that the controversy was rather about the manner of the presence or absence, than about the presence or absence itself." All which Bucer's associates confirm after him. He also adds; "That the magistrates in their Churches had denounced very severe punishments to any that should deny the presence of the Body and Blood of CHRIST in the LORD's

Supper." Bucerus did also maintain this doctrine of the blessed Sacrament in presence of the Landgrave of Hesse and Melancthon, confessing, "That together with the Sacrament we truly and substantially receive the Body of CHRIST." Also, "That the Bread and Wine are conferring signs, giving what they represent, so that together with them the Body of CHRIST is given and received." And to these he adds; "That the Body and Bread are not united in the mixture of their substance, but in that the Sacrament gives what it promiseth, that is, the one is never without the other; and so they agreeing on both parts, that the Bread and Wine are not changed, he holds such a Sacramental Union." Luther having heard this, declared also his opinion thus; "That he did not locally include the Body and Blood of CHRIST with the Bread and Wine, and unite them together by any natural connexion; and that he did not make proper to the Sacraments that virtue whereby they brought salvation to the receivers; but that he maintained only a sacramental union betwixt the Body of CHRIST and the Bread, and betwixt His Blood and the Wine; and did teach, that the power of confirming our faith, which he attributed to the Sacraments, was not naturally inherent in the outward signs, but proceeded from the operation of CHRIST, and was given by His SPIRIT, by His words, and by the Elements." And finally, in this manner he spake to all that were present; "If you believe and teach, that in the LORD'S Supper the true Body and Blood of CHRIST is given and received, and not the Bread and Wine only; and that this giving and receiving is real and not imaginary, we are agreed, and we own you for dear Brethren in the LORD." All this is set down at large in the twentieth tome of Luther's Works, and in the English Works of Bucer.

The next will be the Gallican Confession, made at Paris in a National Synod, and presented to King Charles IX at the Conference of Poissy. Which speaks of the Sacrament on this wise; "Although CHRIST be in Heaven, where He is to remain until He come to judge the world, yet we believe that by the secret and incomprehensible virtue of His Spirit, He feeds and vivifies us by the substance of His Body and Blood received by faith. Now we say that this is done in a spiritual manner; not that we believe it to be a fancy and imagination, instead of a truth and real effect, but rather because that mystery of our union with CHRIST is of so sublime a nature, that it is as much above the capacity of our senses, as it is above the order of nature." *Item;* "We believe that in the LORD'S Supper GOD gives us really, that is, truly and efficaciously, whatever is represented by the Sacrament. With the signs we join the true profession and fruition of the thing by them offered to us; and so, that Bread and Wine which are given to us, become our spiritual nourishment, in that they make it in some manner visible to us that the Flesh of CHRIST is our food, and His Blood our drink. Therefore those fanatics that reject these signs and symbols are by us rejected, our blessed SAVIOUR having said, 'this is My Body, and this cup is My Blood.'" This Confession hath been subscribed by the Church of Geneva.

Now because great is the fame of Calvin (who subscribed the Augustan Confession, and that of the Switzers), let us hear what he writ and believed concerning this sacred mystery. His words in his Institutions and elsewhere are such, so conformable to the style and mind of the Ancient Fathers, that no Catholic Protestant would wish to use any other. "I understand," saith he, "what is to be understood by the words of CHRIST; that He doth not only offer us the benefits of His Death and Resurrection, but His very body, wherein He died and rose again. I assert that the Body of CHRIST is really (as the usual expression is), that is truly given to us in the Sacrament, to be the saving food of our souls." Also in another place; *Item*, "That word cannot lie, neither can it mock us; and except one presumes to call GOD a deceiver, he will never dare to say, that the symbols are empty, and that CHRIST is not in them. Therefore if by the breaking of the bread our SAVIOUR doth represent the participation of His Body, it is not to be doubted but that He truly gives and confers it. If it be true that the visible sign is given us, to seal the gift of an invisible thing, we most firmly believe that receiving the signs of the Body, we also certainly receive the Body itself. Setting aside all absurdities, I do willingly admit all those terms that can most strongly express the true and substantial Communication of the Body and Blood of CHRIST, granted to the faithful with the symbols of the LORD'S Supper; and that, not as if they received only by the force of their imagination, or an act of their minds, but really, so as to be fed thereby unto Eternal Life." Again, "We must therefore confess that the inward substance of the Sacrament is joined with the visible sign, so that, as the bread is put into our hand, the Body of CHRIST is also given to us. This certainly, if there were nothing else, should abundantly satisfy us, that we understand, that CHRIST, in His Holy Supper, gives us the true and proper substance of His Body and Blood, that it being wholly ours, we may be made partakers of all His benefits and graces." Again, "The Son of GOD offers daily to us in the Holy Sacrament, the same Body which He once offered in sacrifice to His FATHER, that it may be our spiritual food." In these he asserts, as clearly as any one can, the true, *real,* and substantial Presence and Communication of the Body of CHRIST, but how, he undertakes not to determine. "If any one," saith he, "ask me concerning the manner, I will not be ashamed to confess that it is a secret too high for my reason to comprehend, or my tongue to express; or to speak more properly, I rather feel than understand it: therefore without disputing I embrace the truth of GOD, and confidently repose on it. He declares that His Flesh is the food, and His Blood the drink of my soul; and my soul I offer to Him to be fed by such nourishment. He bids me take, eat, and drink His Body and Blood, which in His holy Supper He offers me under the symbols of Bread and Wine: I make no scruple, but He doth reach them to me, and I receive them." All these are Calvin's own words.

I was the more willing to be long in transcribing these things at large, out of Public Confessions of Churches, and the best of Authors; that it might the better appear, how injuriously Protestant Divines are calumniated by others unacquainted with their opinions, as though by these words, *Spiritually* and *Sacramentally,* they did not acknowledge a true and well-understood *real* Presence and Communication of the Body and Blood of CHRIST in the Blessed Sacrament; whereas, on the contrary, they do professedly own it, in terms as express as any can be used.

Chapter 3
How the Papists Understand the Doctrine of the Spiritual Presence

Having now, by what I have said, put it out of doubt, that the Protestants believe a *spiritual* and *true* presence of Christ in the Sacrament, which is the reason, that according to the example of the Fathers, they use so frequently the term *spiritual* in this subject, it may not be amiss to consider, in the next place, how the Roman Church understands that same word. Now they make it to signify, "That CHRIST is not present in the Sacrament, either after that manner which is natural to corporal things, or that wherein His own body subsists in heaven, but according to the manner of existence proper to spirits, whole and entire in each part of the host: and though by Himself He be neither seen, touched, nor moved, yet in respect of the species or accidents joined with Him, He may be said to be seen, touched, and moved; and so the accidents being moved, the Body of CHRIST is truly moved accidentally, as the soul truly changeth place with the body; so that we truly and properly say, that the Body of CHRIST is removed, lifted up, and set down, put on the Paten, or on the Altar, and carried from hand to mouth, and from the mouth to the stomach; as Berengarius was forced to acknowledge in the Roman Council under Pope Nicholas, that the Body of CHRIST was sensually touched by the hands, and broken and chewed by the teeth of the Priest." But all this, and much more to the same effect, was never delivered to us, either by holy Scripture, or the ancient Fathers. And if souls or spirits could be present, as here Bellarmine teacheth, yet it would be absurd to say that bodies could be so likewise, it being inconsistent with their nature.

Indeed Bellarmine confesseth with St. Bernard, that "CHRIST in the Sacrament is not given to us carnally, but spiritually;" and would to God he had rested here, and not outgone the holy Scriptures, and the doctrine of the Fathers. For endeavouring, with Pope Innocent III and the Council of Trent, to determine the manner of the presence and manducation of CHRIST'S Body, with more nicety than was fitting, he thereby foolishly overthrew all that he had wisely said before, denied what he had affirmed, and opposed his own opinion. His fear was lest his adversaries should apply that word *spiritually*, not so much to express the manner of presence, as to exclude the very substance of the Body and Blood of CHRIST; "therefore," saith he, "upon that account it is not safe to use too much that of St. Bernard, 'the body of CHRIST is not corporally in the Sacrament,' without adding presently the above-mentioned explanation." How much do we comply with human pride, and curiosity, which would seem to understand all things! Where is the danger? And what does he fear, as long as all they that believe the Gospel, own the true nature, and the real and substantial presence of the Body of CHRIST in the Sacrament, using that explication of St. Bernard, concerning the manner, which he himself, for the too great evidence of truth, durst not but admit? and why doth he own that the manner is spiritual, not carnal, and then require a carnal presence, as to the manner itself? As for us, we all openly profess with St. Bernard, that the presence of the Body of CHRIST in the Sacrament, is spiritual, and therefore true and real; and with the same Bernard, and all the Ancients, we deny that the Body of CHRIST is carnally either present or given. The thing we willingly admit, but humbly and religiously forbear to enquire into the manner.

We believe a presence and union of CHRIST with our soul and body, which we know not how to call better than sacramental, that is, effected by eating; that while we eat and drink the consecrated Bread and Wine, we eat and drink therewithal the Body and Blood of CHRIST, not in a corporal manner, but some other way, incomprehensible, known only to GOD, which we call spiritual; for if with St. Bernard and the Fathers a man goes no further, we do not find fault with a general explication of the manner, but with the presumption and self-conceitedness of those who boldly and curiously inquire what is a spiritual presence, as presuming that they can understand the manner of acting of GOD'S Holy Spirit. We contrariwise confess with the Fathers, that this manner of presence is unaccountable, and past finding out, not to be searched and pried into by reason, but believed by faith. And if it seems impossible that the flesh of CHRIST should descend, and come to be our food, through so great a distance; we must remember how much the power of the Holy Spirit exceeds our sense and our apprehensions, and how absurd it would be to undertake to measure His immensity by our weakness and narrow capacity; and so make our faith to conceive and believe what our reason cannot comprehend.

Yet our faith doth not cause or make that presence, but apprehends it as most truly and really effected by the word of CHRIST: and the faith whereby we are said to eat the flesh of CHRIST, is not that only whereby we believe that He died for our sins (for this faith is required and supposed to precede the Sacramental Manducation), but more properly, that whereby we believe those words of CHRIST, *This is My Body;* which was St. Austin's meaning when he said, "why dost thou prepare thy stomach and thy teeth? believe and thou hast eaten." For in this mystical eating by the wonderful power of the HOLY GHOST, we do invisibly receive the substance of CHRIST'S Body and Blood, as much as if we should eat and drink both visibly.

The result of all this is, that the Body and Blood of CHRIST are sacramentally united to the Bread and Wine, so that CHRIST is truly given to the faithful; and yet is not to be here considered with sense or worldly reason, but by faith, resting on the words of the Gospel. Now it is said, that the Body and Blood of CHRIST are joined to the Bread and Wine, because, that in the celebration of the Holy Eucharist, the Flesh is given together with the Bread, and the Blood together with the Wine. All that remains is, that we should with faith and humility admire this high and sacred mystery, which our tongue cannot sufficiently explain, nor our heart conceive.

Chapter 4
The Popish Doctrine of Transubstantiation

It is an Article of Faith in the Church of Rome, that in the blessed Eucharist the substance of the Bread and Wine is reduced to nothing, and that in its place succeeds the Body and Blood of CHRIST . . . . . The Protestants are much of another mind; and yet none of them denies altogether but that there is a conversion of the Bread into the Body (and consequently the Wine into the Blood) of CHRIST; for they know and acknowledge, that in the Sacrament, by virtue of the words and blessing of CHRIST, the condition, use, and office of the Bread is wholly changed, that is, of common and ordinary, it becomes our mystical and sacramental food; whereby, as they affirm and believe, the true Body of CHRIST is not only shadowed and figured, but also given indeed, and by worthy communicants truly received. Yet they believe not that the bread loseth its own, to become the substance of the Body of CHRIST; for the holy Scripture, and the ancient interpreters thereof for many ages, never taught such an essential change and conversion, as that the very substance, the matter, and form of the bread should be wholly taken away, but only a mysterious and sacramental one, whereby our ordinary is changed into mystic bread, and thereby designed and appointed to another use, end, and office than before. This change, whereby supernatural effects are wrought by things natural, while their essence is preserved entire, doth best agree with the grace and power of GOD.

There is no reason why we should dispute concerning GOD's Omnipotency, whether it can do this or that, presuming to measure an Infinite Power by our poor ability, which is but weakness. We may grant that He is able to do beyond what we can think or apprehend, and resolve His most wonderful acts into His absolute will and power, but we may not charge Him with working contradictions. And though GOD's Almightiness were able in this mystery to destroy the substance of Bread and Wine, and essentially to change it into the Body and Blood of CHRIST, while the accidents of Bread and Wine subsist of themselves without a subject, yet we desire to have it proved that GOD will have it so, and that it is so indeed. For, that GOD doth it because He can, is no argument; and that He wills it, we have no other proof but the confident assertion of our adversaries. Tertullian against Praxeas declared "that we should not conclude GOD doth things because He is able, but that we should enquire what He hath done;" for GOD will never own that praise of His Omnipotency, whereby His unchangeableness and His truth are impaired, and those things overthrown and destroyed, which, in His Word, He affirms to be; for, take away the Bread and Wine, and there remains no Sacrament.

They that say, that the matter and form of the Bread are wholly abolished, yet will have the accidents to remain. But if the substance of the Bread be changed into the substance of CHRIST's Body by virtue of His words, what hinders that the accidents of the Bread are not also changed into the accidents of CHRIST's Body? They that urge the express letter, should show that CHRIST said, "This is the substance of My body without its accidents." But He did not say, that He gave His Disciples a phantastic body, such a visionary figment as Marcion believed, but that very body which is given for us, without being deprived of that extension and other accidents of human bodies, without which it could not have been crucified; since the maintainers of transubstantiation grant that the Body of CHRIST keeps its quantity in Heaven, and say it is without the same in the Sacrament; they must either acknowledge their contradiction in the matter, or give over their opinion.

Protestants dare not be so curious, or presume to know more than is delivered by Scripture and antiquity, they firmly believing the words of CHRIST make the form of this Sacrament to consist in the union of the thing signified with the sign, that is, the exhibition of the Body of CHRIST with the consecrated Bread, still remaining bread; by divine appointment these two are made one; and though this union be not natural, substantial, personal, or local by their being one within another, yet it is so straight and so true, that in eating the blessed Bread, the true Body of CHRIST is given to us, and the names of the sign and thing signified are reciprocally changed, what is proper to the Body is attributed to the Bread, and what belongs only to the Bread, is affirmed of the Body, and both are united in time, though not in place. For the presence of CHRIST in this mystery is not opposed to distance but to absence, which only could deprive us of the benefit and fruition of the object.

From what has been said it appears, that this whole controversy may be reduced to four heads; 1. Concerning the Signs; 2. Concerning the thing signified; 3. Concerning the union of both; and 4. Concerning their participation. As to the first, the Protestants differ from the Papists in this; that according to the nature of Sacraments, and the doctrine of the holy Scripture, we make the substance of Bread and Wine, and they accidents only to be signs. In the second, they not understanding our opinion, do misrepresent it, for we do not hold (as they say we do) that only the merits of the death of CHRIST are represented by the blessed Elements, but also that His very Body which was crucified, and His Blood which was shed for us, are truly signified and offered, that our souls may receive and possess CHRIST, as truly and certainly as the material and visible signs are by us seen and received. And so in the third place, because the thing signified is offered and given to us, as truly as the sign itself, in this respect we own the union betwixt the Body and Blood of CHRIST, and the Elements, whose use and office we hold to be changed from what it was before. But we deny what the Papists affirm, that the substance of Bread and Wine are quite abolished, and changed into the Body and Blood of our LORD in such sort, that the bare accidents of the Elements do alone remain united with CHRIST'S Body and Blood. And we also deny that the Elements still retain the nature of Sacraments when not used according to divine institution, that is, given by CHRIST'S Ministers, and received by His people; so that CHRIST in the consecrated bread ought not, cannot be kept and preserved to be carried about, because He is present only to the communicants. As for the fourth and last point, we do not say, that in the LORD'S Supper we receive only the benefits of CHRIST'S death and passion, but we join the ground with its fruits, that is, CHRIST with those advantages we receive from Him; affirming with St. Paul, "That the bread which we break is κοινωνία, the Communion of the Body of Christ, and the cup which we bless, the Communion of His Blood" (1 Cor 10:16); of that very substance which He took of the blessed Virgin, and afterwards carried into Heaven; differing from those of Rome only in this, that they will have our union with CHRIST to be corporal, and our eating of Him likewise; and we on the contrary maintain it to be, indeed as true, but not carnal or natural. And as he that receives unworthily (that is, with the mouth only, but not with a faithful heart) eats and drinks his own damnation; so he that doeth it worthily, receives his absolution and justification; that is, he that *discerns,* and then receives the LORD'S Body as torn, and His Blood as shed for the redemption of the world. But that CHRIST (as the Papists affirm) should give His Flesh and Blood to be received with the mouth, and ground with the teeth, ... this our words and hearts do utterly deny.

So then (to sum up this controversy by applying it to all that hath been said), it is not questioned whether the Body of CHRIST be absent from the Sacrament duly administered according to His institution, which we Protestants neither affirm nor believe; for it being given and received in the Communion, it must needs be that it is present, though in some manner veiled under the Sacrament, so that of itself it cannot be seen. Neither is it doubted or disputed whether the Bread and Wine, by the power of GOD and a supernatural virtue, be set apart and fitted for a much nobler use, and raised to a higher dignity than their nature bears; for we confess the necessity of a supernatural and heavenly change, and that the signs cannot become Sacraments but by the infinite power of GOD, whose proper right it is to institute Sacraments in His Church, being able alone to endue them with virtue and efficacy. Finally, we do not say that our Blessed SAVIOUR gave only the figure and sign of His body; neither do we deny a Sacramental Union of the Body and Blood of CHRIST with the sacred Bread and Wine, so that both are really and substantially received together: but (that we may avoid all ambiguity) we deny that after the words and prayer of Consecration, the Bread should remain bread no longer, but should be changed into the substance of the Body of CHRIST, nothing of the bread, but only the accidents continuing to be what they were before; and so the whole question is concerning the Transubstantiation of the outward Elements; whether the substance of the Bread be turned into the substance of CHRIST'S Body, and the substance of the Wine into the substance of His Blood; or, as the Romish Doctors describe their Transubstantiation, whether the substance of bread and wine doth utterly perish, and the substance of CHRIST'S Body and Blood succeed in their place, which are both denied by Protestants.

The Church of Rome sings on Corpus Christi day, *This is not bread, but GOD and Man my SAVIOUR.* And the Council of Trent doth thus define it; "Because CHRIST our Redeemer said truly, that that was His body, which He gave in the appearance of bread; therefore it was ever believed by the Church of God, and is now declared by this sacred Synod, that by the power of Consecration the whole substance of the bread is changed into the substance of CHRIST'S Body, and the whole substance of the wine into the substance of His Blood; which change is fitly and properly called Transubstantiation by the holy Catholic (Roman) Church. Therefore if any one shall say, that the substance of Bread and Wine remains with the Body and Blood of our Saviour JESUS CHRIST, and shall deny that wonderful and singular conversion of the whole substance of the Bread and Wine into the substance of the Body and Blood of CHRIST, the only appearance and outward form of the Bread and Wine remaining, which conversion the Catholic (Roman) Church doth fitly call Transubstantiation,—let him be accursed."

Now we leave inquiring what GOD is able to do, for we should first know His will in this matter, before we examine His power; yet thus much we say, that this Roman Transubstantiation is so strange and monstrous, that it exceeds the nature of all miracles. And though GOD by His Almightiness be able to turn the substance of bread into some other substance, yet none will believe that He doth it, as long as it appears to our senses, that the substance of the Bread doth still remain whole and entire. Certain it is, that hitherto we read of no such thing done in the Old or New Testament, and therefore this tenet, being as unknown to the Ancients as it is ungrounded in Scripture, appears as yet to be very incredible, and there is no reason we should believe such an unauthorised figment, newly invented by men, and now imposed as an article of Christian Religion. For it is in vain that they bring Scripture to defend this their stupendous doctrine; and it is not true, what they so often and so confidently affirm, that the Universal Church hath always constantly owned it, being it was not so

much as heard of in the Church for many ages, and hath been but lately approved by the Pope's authority in the Councils of Lateran and Trent.
To be continued.

Reprinted February 24, 1834
The Feast of St. Matthias

TRACT 28

The History of Popish Transubstantiation
To Which Is Opposed the Catholic Doctrine of the Holy Scripture, the Ancient Fathers, and the Reformed Church (Continued)

BY JOHN COSIN, BISHOP OF DURHAM

Chapter 5
The Doctrine of Transubstantiation Is Contained Neither in Scripture nor in the Writings of the Fathers

The word Transubstantiation is so far from being found either in the Sacred Records, or in the Monuments of the Ancient Fathers, that the maintainers of it do themselves acknowledge that it was not so much as heard of before the twelfth century. For though one Stephanus, Bishop of Autun, be said to have once used it, yet it is without proof that some modern writers make him one of the tenth century; nor yet doth he say, that the Bread is transubstantiated, *but as it were* transubstantiated, which well understood might be admitted.

Nay, that the thing itself without the word, that the doctrine without the expression, cannot be found in Scripture, is ingeniously acknowledged by the most learned Schoolmen, Scotus, Durandus, Biel, Cameracensis, Cajetan, and many more, who finding it not brought in by the Pope's authority, and received in the Roman Church, till 1200 years after CHRIST, yet endeavoured to defend it by other arguments.

And indeed, the words of institution would plainly make it appear to any man that would prefer truth to wrangling, that it is with the Bread that the

Lord's Body is given (as His Blood with the Wine), for Christ, having taken, blessed, and broken the Bread, said, "This is My Body;" and St. Paul, than whom none could better understand the meaning of Christ, explains it thus; "The Bread which we break is the κοινωνία, Communion or communication of the Body of Christ," that whereby His Body is given, and the faithful are made partakers of it. That it was Bread which He reached to them, there was no need of any proof, the receiver's senses sufficiently convinced them of it; but that therewith His Body was given, none could have known, had it not been declared by Him who is the Truth itself. And though, by the divine institution and the explication of the Apostle, every faithful communicant may be as certainly assured that he receives the Lord's Body, as if he knew that the Bread is substantially turned into it; yet it doth not therefore follow, that the Bread is so changed, that its substance is quite done away, so that there remains nothing present, but the very natural Body of Christ, made of Bread; for certain it is, that the Bread is not the Body of Christ any otherwise than as the Cup is the New Testament, and two different consequences cannot be drawn from those two not different expressions. Therefore as the Cup cannot be the New Testament but by a Sacramental figure, no more can the Bread be the Body of Christ, but in the same sense.

As to what Bellarmine and others say, that it is not possible the words of Christ can be true, but by that conversion, which the Church of Rome calls Transubstantiation, that is so far from being so, that if it were admitted, it would first deny the Divine Omnipotency, as though God were not able to make the Body of Christ present, and truly to give it in the Sacrament, whilst the substance of the Bread remains. 2. It would be inconsistent with the Divine Benediction which preserves things in their proper being. 3. It would be contrary to the true nature of the Sacrament, which always consisteth of two parts. And lastly, it would in some manner destroy the true substance of the Body and Blood of Christ, which cannot be said to be made of Bread and Wine by a Priest, without a most high presumption. But the truth of the words of Christ remains constant, and can be defended, without overthrowing so many other great truths. Suppose a testator puts deeds and titles in the hand of his heir, with these words, 'Take the house which I bequeath thee;' there is no man will think that those writings and parchments are that very house which is made of wood or stones, and yet no man will say that the testator spake falsely or obscurely. Likewise our blessed SAVIOUR, having sanctified the Elements by His words and prayers, gave them to His Disciples as seals of the New Testament, whereby they were as certainly secured of those rich and precious legacies which He left to them, as children are of their father's lands and inheritance, by deeds and instruments signed and delivered for that purpose.

To the Sacred Records we may add the judgment of the Primitive Church. For those orthodox and holy Doctors of our holier religion, those great lights of the Catholic Church, do all clearly, constantly, and unanimously conspire in this, that the presence of the Body of CHRIST in the Sacrament is only mystic and spiritual. As for the entire annihilation of the substance of the Bread and the Wine, or that new and strange tenet of Transubstantiation, they did not so much as hear or speak any thing of it; nay, the constant stream of their doctrine doth clearly run against it, how great soever are the brags and pretences of the Papists to the contrary. And if you will hear them one by one, I shall bring some of their most noted passages only, that our labour may not be endless by rehearsing all that they have said to our purpose on this subject.

I shall begin with that holy and ancient Doctor, Justin Martyr, who is one of the first after the Apostles' times, whose undoubted writings are come to us. (A.D. 144.) What was believed at Rome and elsewhere in his time, concerning this holy mystery, may well be understood out of these his words: "After that the Bishop hath prayed and blessed, and the people said Amen, those whom we call Deacons or Ministers give to every one of them that are present a portion of the Bread and Wine; and that food we call the Eucharist, for we do not receive it as ordinary bread and wine." They received it as bread, yet not as common bread. And a little after; "By this food digested, our flesh and blood are fed, and we are taught that it is the Body and Blood of JESUS CHRIST." Therefore the substance of the bread remains, and remains corruptible food, even after the Consecration, which can in no wise be said of the immortal Body of CHRIST; for the Flesh of CHRIST is not turned into our flesh, neither doth it nourish it, as doth that food which is sacramentally called the Flesh of CHRIST. But the Flesh of CHRIST feeds our souls unto eternal life.

After the same manner, it is written by that holy Martyr Irenæus, Bishop much about the same time. (A.D. 160.) "The bread which is from the earth is no more common bread, after the invocation of GOD upon it, but is become the Eucharist, consisting of two parts, the one earthly, and the other heavenly." There would be nothing earthly if the substance of the bread were removed. Again: "As the grain of wheat falling in the ground, and dying, riseth again much increased, and then receiving the word of GOD becomes the Eucharist (which is the Body and Blood of CHRIST); so likewise our bodies, nourished by it, laid in the ground and dissolved, shall rise again in their time." Again; "We are fed by the creature, but it is He Himself that gives it. He hath ordained and appointed that Cup which is a creature, and His Blood also, and that Bread which is a creature, and also His Body. And so when the Bread and the Cup are blessed by GOD'S word, they become the Eucharist of the Body and Blood of CHRIST, and from them our bodies receive nourishment and increase." Now that our flesh is fed and encreased by the natural Body of CHRIST, cannot be said without great impiety by themselves that hold Transubstantiation. For naturally nothing nourisheth our bodies but what is made flesh and blood by the last digestion, which it would be blasphemous to say of the incorruptible Body of CHRIST. Yet the sacred Elements, which in some manner are, and are said to be the Body and Blood of CHRIST, yield nourishment and encrease to our bodies by their earthly nature, in such sort, that by virtue also of the heavenly and spiritual food which the faithful receive by means of the material, our bodies are fitted for a blessed Resurrection to immortal glory.

Tertullian, who flourished about the two hundreth year after CHRIST, when as yet he was Catholic, and acted by a pious zeal, wrote against Marcion the Heretic, who, amongst his other impious opinions, taught that CHRIST had not taken of the Virgin Mary the very nature and substance of a human body, but only the outward forms and appearances; out of which fountain the Romish Transubstantiators seem to have drawn their doctrine of accidents abstracted from their subject hanging in the air, that is, subsisting on nothing. Tertullian, disputing against this wicked heresy, draws an argument from the Sacrament of the Eucharist, to prove that CHRIST had not a phantastic and imaginary, but a true and natural body, thus: the figure of the Body of CHRIST proves it to be natural, for there can be no figure of a ghost or a phantasm. "But," saith he, "CHRIST having taken the Bread, and given it to his Disciples, made it His Body by saying, 'This is my Body, that is, the figure of my Body.' Now, it could not have been a figure except the Body was real, for a mere appearance, an imaginary phantasm is not capable of a figure." Each part of this argument is true, and contains a necessary conclusion. For, 1. The bread must remain bread, otherwise Marcion would have returned the argument against Tertullian, saying as the Transubstantiators; it was not bread, but merely the accidents of bread, which seemed to be bread. 2. The Body of CHRIST is proved to be true by the figure of it, which is said to be bread, for the bread is fit to represent that Divine Body, because of its nourishing virtue, which in the bread is earthly, but in the Body is heavenly. Lastly, the reality of the Body is proved by that of its figure; and so if you deny the substance of the Bread (as the Papists do), you thereby destroy the truth and reality of the Body of CHRIST in the Sacrament.

Origen also, about the same time with Tertullian, speaks much after the same manner. "If CHRIST," saith he, "as these men (the Marcionites) falsely hold, had neither Flesh nor Blood, of what manner of Flesh, of what Body, of what Blood did He give the signs and images when He gave the Bread and Wine?" If they be the signs and representations of the Body and Blood of CHRIST, though they prove the truth of His Body and Blood, yet they being signs, cannot be what they signify; and they not being what they represent, the groundless contrivance of Transubstantiation is overthrown. Also upon Leviticus he doth expressly oppose it thus: "Acknowledge ye that they are figures, and therefore spiritual, not carnal; examine and understand what is said, otherwise if you receive as things carnal, they will hurt, but not nourish you. For in the Gospel there is the Letter, which kills him that understands not spiritually what is said; for if you understand this saying according to the Letter, 'Except you eat My Flesh and drink My Blood,' the Letter will kill you." Therefore as much as these words belong to the eating and drinking of CHRIST'S Body and Blood, they are to be understood mystically and spiritually.

St. Cyprian, Bishop of Carthage, a glorious Martyr of CHRIST (A.D. 250), wrote a famous Epistle to Coecilius concerning the sacred Chalice in the LORD'S Supper, whereof this is the sum; "Let that cup which is offered to the people in commemoration of CHRIST be mixt with wine," (against the opinion of the Aquarii, who were for water only,) "for it cannot represent the Blood of CHRIST when there is no wine in the cup, because the Blood of CHRIST is exprest by the Wine, as the faithful are understood by the

Water." But the patrons of Transubstantiation have neither Wine nor Water in the Chalice they offer; and yet without them (especially the Wine appointed by our Blessed SAVIOUR, and whereof Cyprian chiefly speaks), the Blood of CHRIST is not so much as sacramentally present. *So far was* the Primitive Church from any thing of believing a corporal presence of the Blood, the Wine being reduced to nothing (that is, to a mere accident without the substance), for then they must have said, that the Water was changed into the people, as well as the Wine into the Blood. But there is no need that I should bring many testimonies of that Father, when all his writings do plainly declare that the true substance of the Bread and Wine is given in the Eucharist; that that spiritual and quickening food which the faithful get from the Body and Blood of CHRIST, and the mutual union of the whole people joined into one body may answer their type, the Sacrament which represents them.

Those words of the Council of Nice (A.D. 325) are well known, whereby the faithful are called from the consideration of the outward visible Elements of Bread and Wine, to attend the inward and spiritual act of the mind, whereby CHRIST is seen and apprehended. "Let not our thoughts dwell low, on that Bread and that Cup which are set before us, but lifting up our minds by faith, let us consider, that on this sacred Table is laid the Lamb of GOD which taketh away the sins of the world. And receiving truly His precious Body and Blood, let us believe these things to be the pledges and emblems of our resurrection; for we do not take much, but only a little (of the Elements) that we may be mindful, we do it not for satiety, but for sanctification." Now, who is there, even among the maintainers of Transubstantiation, that will understand this, *not much, but a little*, of the Body of CHRIST; or who can believe that the Nicene Fathers would call His Body and Blood symbols in a proper sense? when nothing can be an image or a sign of itself. And therefore, though we are not to rest in the Elements, minding nothing else (for we should consider what is chiefest in the Sacrament, that we have our hearts *lifted unto the* LORD, who is given together with the signs), yet Elements they are, and the earthly part of the Sacrament, both the Bread and the Wine, which destroys Transubstantiation.

St. Athanasius, famous in the time, and present in the Assembly of the Nicene Council, a stout Champion of the Catholic faith, acknowledgeth none other but a spiritual manducation of the Body of CHRIST in the

Sacrament. "Our LORD," saith he, "made a difference betwixt the Flesh and the Spirit, that we might understand that what He said, was not carnal, but spiritual. For how many men could His Body have fed, that the whole world should be nourished by it? But therefore He mentioned His ascension into heaven, that they might not take what He said in a corporal sense, but might understand that His Flesh whereof He spake is a spiritual and heavenly food given by Himself from on high; for the words that I spake unto you they are spirit, and they are life, as if He should say, My Body which is shown and given for the world, shall be given in food, that it may be distributed Spiritually to every one, and preserve them all to the resurrection to eternal life." Cardinal Perron having nothing to answer to these words of this holy Father, in a kind of despair, rejects the whole Tractate, and denies it to be Athanasius's, which nobody ever did before him, there being no reason for it.

Likewise St. Ambrose (A.D. 380), explaining what manner of alteration is in the Bread, when in the Eucharist it becomes the Body of CHRIST, saith, "Thou hadst indeed a being, but wert an old creature, but being now baptized or consecrated, thou art become a new creature." The same change that happens to man in baptism, happens to the Bread in the Sacrament: if the nature of man is not substantially altered by the new birth, no more is the Bread by consecration. Man becomes by baptism, not what nature made him, but what grace new-makes him; and *the Bread becomes by consecration, not what it was by nature, but what the blessing consecrates it to be.* For nature made only a mere man, and made only common bread; but Regeneration, of a mere man, makes a holy man, in whom CHRIST dwells spiritually; and likewise the Consecration of common Bread makes Mystic and Sacramental Bread. Yet this change doth not destroy nature, but to nature adds grace; as is yet more plainly exprest by that holy Father in the fore-cited place. "Perhaps thou wilt say," saith he, "this my bread is common bread; it is bread indeed before the blessing of the Sacrament, but when it is consecrated it becomes the Body of CHRIST. This we are therefore to declare, how can that which is Bread be also the Body of CHRIST? By Consecration. And Consecration is made by the words of our LORD, that the venerable Sacrament may be perfected. You see how efficacious is the Word of CHRIST. If there be then so great a power in the Word of CHRIST to make the Bread and Wine to be what they were not, how much greater is that power which still preserves them to be what they were, and yet makes them to be what they were not? Therefore, that I may answer thee, it was not the Body of CHRIST before the Consecration, but now after the Consecration, it is the Body of CHRIST; He said the word and it was done. Thou thyself went before, but wert an old creature; after thou hast been consecrated in Baptism thou art become a new creature." By these words St. Ambrose teacheth how we are to understand that the Bread is the Body of CHRIST, to wit, by such a change that the Bread and Wine do not cease to be what they were as to their substance (for then they should not be what they were), and yet by the blessing become what before they were not. For so they are said to remain (as indeed they do) what they were by nature, that yet they are changed by grace; that is, they become assured Sacraments of the Body and Blood of CHRIST, and by that means certain pledges of our Justification and Redemption. What is there, can refute more expressly the dream of Transubstantiation?

St. Chrysostom (A.D. 390) doth also clearly discard and reject this carnal Transubstantiation and eating of CHRIST'S Body, without eating the Bread. "Sacraments," saith he, "ought not to be contemplated and considered carnally, but with the eyes of our souls, that is, spiritually; for such is the nature of mysteries;" where observe the opposition betwixt *carnally* and *spiritually*, which admits of no plea or reply again. "As in Baptism the spiritual power of Regeneration is given to the material water; so also the immaterial gift of the Body and Blood of CHRIST is not received by any sensible corporal action, but by the spiritual discernment of our faith, and of our hearts and minds." Which is no more than this, that sensible things are called by the name of those spiritual things which they seal and signify. But he speaks more plainly in his Epistle to Cæsarius; where he teacheth, that in this mystery there is not in the bread a substantial, but a Sacramental change, according to the which, the outward Elements take the name of what they represent, and are changed in such a sort, that they still retain their former natural substance. "The Bread," saith he, "is made worthy to be honoured with the name of the Flesh of CHRIST, by the consecration of the Priest, yet the Flesh retains the proprieties of its incorruptible nature, as the Bread doth its natural substance. Before the Bread be sanctified we call it Bread; but when it is consecrated by the divine grace, it deserves to be called the LORD'S Body, though the substance of the Bread still remains." When Bellarmine could not answer this testimony of that great Doctor, he thought it enough to deny, that this Epistle is St. Chrysostom's; but both he and Possevin do vainly contend that it is not extant among the works of Chrysostom. For besides that at Florence and elsewhere it was to be found among them, it is cited in the Collections against the Severians which are in the version of Turrianus the Jesuit, in the 4th tome of Antiq. Lectionum of Henry Canisius, and in the end of the book of Joh. Damascenus against the Acephali.

Which also hath been said by St. Austin (A.D. 400) above a thousand times; but out of so many almost numberless places, I shall choose only three, which are as the sum of all the rest. "You are not to eat this Body which you see, nor drink this Blood which My crucifiers shall shed; I have left you a Sacrament which, spiritually understood, will vivify you." Thus St. Austin, rehearsing the words of CHRIST again; "If Sacraments had not some resemblance with those things whereof they are Sacraments, they could not be Sacraments at all. From this resemblance they often take the names of what they represent. Therefore as the Sacrament of CHRIST'S Body is in some sort His Body; so the Sacrament of Faith, is faith also." To the same sense is what he writes against Maximinus the Arian. "We mind in the Sacraments, not what they are, but what they show; for they are signs, which are one thing, and signifies another." And in another place, speaking of the Bread and Wine; "Let no man look to what they are, but to what they signify, for our LORD was pleased to say, 'this is My Body,' when He gave the sign of His Body.'"

And the same kind of expressions . . . . were also used by venerable Bede, our countryman, who lived in the eighth century, in his Sermon upon the Epiphany; of whom we also take these two testimonies following: "In the room of the Flesh and Blood of the Lamb, CHRIST substituted the Sacrament of His Body and Blood, in the figure of Bread and Wine." Also, "At Supper He gave to His Disciples the figure of His holy Body and Blood." These utterly destroy Transubstantiation.

In the same century Charles the Great wrote an Epistle to our Alcuinus, wherein we find these words. "CHRIST at Supper broke the Bread to His Disciples, and likewise gave them the Cup, in figure of His Body and Blood, and so left to us this great Sacrament for our benefit." If it was the figure of His Body, it could not be the Body itself; indeed the Body of CHRIST is given in the Eucharist, but to the faithful only, and that by means of the Sacrament of the consecrated Bread.

But now, about the beginning of the ninth century, started up Paschasius, a Monk of Corbie, who first (as some say whose judgment I follow not) among the Latines, taught that CHRIST was consubstantiated, or rather inclosed in the Bread, and corporally united to it in the Sacrament; for as yet there was no thoughts of the Transubstantiation of Bread. But these new sorts of expressions not agreeing with the Catholic doctrine, and the writings of the ancient Fathers, had few or no abettors before the eleventh century. And in the ninth, whereof we now treat, there were not wanting learned men (as Amalarius, Archdeacon of Triars; Rabanus, at first Abbot of Fulda, and afterwards Archbishop of Ments; John Erigena, an English Divine; Waldfridus Strabo, a German Abbot; Ratramus or Bertramus, first Priest of Corbie, afterwards Abbot of Orbec in France; and many more), who by their writings opposed this new opinion of Paschasius, or of some others rather, and delivered to posterity the Doctrine of the Ancient Church. Yet we have something more to say concerning Paschasius, whom Bellarmine and Sirmondus esteemed so highly, that they were not ashamed to say, that he was the first that had writ to the purpose concerning the Eucharist; and that he had so explained the meaning of the Church, that he had shown and opened the way to all them who treated of that subject after him. Yet in that whole book of Paschasius, there is nothing that favours the Transubstantiation of the Bread, or its destruction or removal. Indeed, he asserts the truth of the Body and Blood of CHRIST'S being in the Eucharist, which Protestants deny not; he denies that the consecrated Bread is a bare figure, a representation void of truth, which Protestants assert not. But he has many things repugnant to Transubstantiation, which, as I have said, the Church of Rome itself had not yet quite found out. I shall mention a few of them. "CHRIST," saith he, "left us this Sacrament, a visible figure and character of His Body and Blood, that by them our spirit might the better embrace spiritual and invisible things, and be more fully fed by faith."

Again, "We must receive our spiritual Sacrament with the mouth of the soul, and the taste of faith." Item, "Whilst therein we savour nothing carnal, but we being spiritual, and understanding the whole spiritually, we remain in CHRIST." And a little after, "The Flesh and Blood of CHRIST are received spiritually." And again, "To savour according to the Flesh, is death; and yet to receive spiritually the true Flesh of CHRIST, is life eternal." Lastly, "The Flesh and Blood of CHRIST are not received carnally, but spiritually."

As for the opinion of Bertram, otherwise called Ratramnus, or Ratramus, perhaps not rightly, it is known enough by that book which the Emperor Charles the Bald (who loved and honoured him, as all good men did, for his great learning and piety) commanded him to write concerning the Body and Blood of our LORD. For when men began to be disturbed at the book of Paschasius, some saying one thing, and some another, the Emperor being moved by their disputes propounded himself two questions to Bertram. 1. Whether, what the faithful eat in the Church, be made the Body and Blood of CHRIST in figure and in mystery. 2. Or whether that natural Body which was born of the Virgin Mary, which suffered, died, and was buried, and now sitteth on the right hand of GOD the Father, be itself daily received by the mouth of the faithful in the mystery of the Sacrament. The first of these Bertram resolved affirmatively, the second negatively; and said, that there was as great a difference betwixt those two bodies, as betwixt the earnest and that whereof it is the earnest. "It is evident," saith he, "that that Bread and Wine are figuratively the Body and Blood of CHRIST. According to the substance of the Elements, they are after the Consecration what they were before. For the Bread is not CHRIST substantially. If this mystery be not done in a figure, it cannot well be called a mystery. The Wine also which is made the Sacrament of the Blood of CHRIST by the Consecration of the Priest, shews one thing by its outward appearance, and contains another inwardly. For what is there visible in its outside but only the substance of the Wine? These things are changed, but not according to the material part, and by this change they are not what they truly appear to be but are something else besides what is their proper being; for they are made spiritually the Body and Blood of CHRIST; not that the Elements be two different things, but in one respect they are, as they appear, Bread and Wine, and in another the Body and Blood of CHRIST. Hence, according to the visible creature they feed the body; but according to the virtue of a more excellent substance they nourish and sanctify the souls of the faithful." Then having brought many testimonies of holy Scripture and the ancient Fathers to confirm this, he at last prevents that calumny which the followers of Paschasius did then lay on the orthodox, as though they had taught that bare signs, figures, and shadows, and not the Body and Blood of CHRIST were given in the Sacrament. "Let it not be thought," saith he, "because we say this, that therefore the Body and Blood of CHRIST are not received in the mystery of the Sacrament, where faith apprehends what it believeth, and not what the eyes see; for this meat and drink are spiritual, feed the soul spiritually, and entertain that life whose fulness is eternal." For the question is not simply about the real truth, or the thing signified being present, without which it could not be a mystery, but about the false reality of things subsisting in imaginary appearances, and about the carnal presence.

All this the Fathers of Trent, and the Romish Inquisitors could not brook, and therefore they utterly condemned Bertram, and put his book in the Catalogue of those that are forbidden.

Chapter 6
Romish Objections Considered,
As Drawn from the Writings of the Fathers

. . . . Let us see what props these new builders pretend to borrow from Antiquity to uphold their castle in the air, *Transubstantiation*. They use indeed to scrape together many testimonies of the Fathers of the first and middle age, whereby they would fain prove, that those Fathers believed and taught the *Transubstantiation* of the Bread and Wine into the natural Body and Blood of CHRIST, just as the Roman Church, at this day, doth teach and believe. We will therefore briefly examine them, that it may yet more fully appear that Antiquity and all Fathers did not in the least favour the new tenet of Transubstantiation; but that, that true doctrine which I have set down in the beginning of this book, was constantly owned and preserved in the Church of CHRIST.

Now, almost all that they produce out of the Fathers will be conveniently reduced to certain heads, that we may not be too tedious in answering each testimony by itself.

1. To the first head belong those that call the Eucharist the Body and Blood of CHRIST. But I answer, those Fathers explain themselves in many places, and interpret those their expressions in such a manner, that they must be understood in a mystic and spiritual sense, in that Sacraments usually take the names of those things they represent, because of that resemblance which they have with them; *not by the reality of the thing, but by the signification of the mystery;* as we have been shown before out of St. Austin and others. For nobody can deny, but that the things that are seen are signs and figures, and those that are not seen, the Body and Blood of CHRIST. And that therefore the nature of this mystery is such, that when we receive the Bread and Wine, we also together with them receive at the same time the Body and Blood of CHRIST, which, in the celebration of the holy Eucharist, are as truly given as they are represented. Hence came into the Church this manner of speaking, 'The consecrated Bread is CHRIST'S Body.'

2. We put in the second rank those places that say, that the Bishops and Priests make the Body of CHRIST with the sacred words of their mouth, as St. Hierom speaks in his Epistle to Heliodorus, and St. Ambrose, and others. To this I say, that at the prayer and blessing of the Priest, the common bread is made Sacramental Bread, which, when broken and eaten, is the *Communion* of the Body of CHRIST, and therefore may well be called so, sacramentally. For the Bread (as I have often said before) doth not only represent the Body of our LORD, but also being received, we are truly made partakers of that precious Body. For so saith St. Hierom; "The Body and Blood of CHRIST is made at the prayer of the Priest;" that is, the Element is so qualified, that being received it becomes the Communion of the Body and Blood of CHRIST, which it could not without the preceding prayers. The Greeks call this, "To prepare and to consecrate the Body of the LORD." As St. Chrysostom saith well; "These are not the works of man's power, but still the operation of Him, who made them in the last Supper; as for us, we are only Ministers, but He it is that sanctifies and changeth them."

3. In the third place, to what is brought out of the Fathers, concerning the conversion, change, transmutation, transfiguration, and transelementation of the Bread and Wine in the Eucharist (wherein the Papists do greatly glory, boasting of the consent of Antiquity with them), I answer, that there is no such consequence. Transubstantiation being another species of change, the enumeration was not full, for it doth not follow, that because there is a conversion, a transmutation, a transelementation, there should be also a Transubstantiation; which the Fathers never so much as mentioned. For because this is a Sacrament, the change must be understood to be sacramental also, whereby common Bread and Wine become the Sacrament of the Body and Blood of CHRIST; which could not be, did not the substance of the Bread and Wine remain, for a Sacrament consisteth of two parts, an earthly and a heavenly. And so, because ordinary Bread is changed by consecration into a Bread which is no more of common use, but appointed by divine institution to be a sacramental sign, whereby is represented the Body of CHRIST, in whom dwelleth the fulness of the Godhead bodily, and being thereby dignified, having great excellencies superadded, and so made what it was not before, it is therefore said by some of the Fathers to be changed, to be made another thing. And truly that change is great and supernatural, but yet not substantial, not of a substance which substantially ceaseth to be, into another substance which substantially beginneth to be, but it is a change of state and condition which alters not the natural properties of the Element. This is also confirmed by Scripture, which usually describes and represents the conversion of men, and the supernatural change of things, as though it were natural, though it be not so. So those that are renewed by the Word, and Spirit, and Faith of CHRIST, are said to be regenerated, converted, and transformed, to put off the old man, and put on the new man, and to be new creatures; but they are not said to become another substance, to be transubstantiated; for men thus converted are still the same human body, and the same rational soul as before, though in a far better state and condition, as every Christian will acknowledge. Nay, the Fathers themselves used those words, Transmutation, Transformation, Transelementation, upon other occasions, when they speak of things whose substance is neither lost nor changed.

4. To the fourth head I refer what the Fathers say of our touching and seeing the Body of CHRIST, and drinking His Blood in the Sacrament; and thereto I answer, that we deny not but that some things emphatical, and even hyperbolical, have been said of the Sacrament by Chrysostom, and some others; and that those things may easy lead unwary men into error. That was the ancient Fathers' care, as it is ours still, to instruct the people not to look barely on the outward Elements, but in them to eye with their minds the Body and Blood of CHRIST, and with their *hearts lift up* to feed on that heavenly meat; for all the benefit of a Sacrament is lost, if we look no further than the Elements. Hence it is that those holy men, the better to teach this lesson to their hearers, and move their hearts more efficaciously, spake of the signs as if they had been the thing signified, and like orators said many things which will not bear a literal sense, nor a strict examen. Such is this, of an uncertain author under the name of St. Cyprian; "We are close to the Cross, we suck the Blood, and we put our tongues in the very wounds of our REDEEMER, so that, both outwardly and inwardly we are made red thereby." Such is that of St. Chrysostom; "In the Sacrament the Blood is drawn out of the side of CHRIST, the tongue is made bloody with that wonderful Blood." Again, "Thou seeth thy LORD sacrificed, and the crowding multitude round about sprinkled with His Blood; He that sits above with the FATHER is at the same time in our hands. Thou doth see and touch and eat Him. For I do not shew thee either Angels or Archangels, but the LORD of them Himself." Again; "He incorporates us with Himself, as if we were but the same thing. He makes us His Body indeed, and suffers us not only to see, but even to touch, to eat Him, and to put our teeth in His Flesh; so that by that food which He gives us, we become His Flesh." Such is that of St. Austin; "Let us give thanks, not only that we are made Christians, but also made CHRIST." Lastly, such is that of Leo; "In that mystical distribution, it is given us to be made His Flesh." Certainly, if any man would wrangle and take advantage of these, he might thereby maintain, as well that we are *transubstantiated* into CHRIST, and CHRIST'S Flesh into the Bread, as that the Bread and Wine are *transubstantiated* into His Body and Blood. But Protestants who scorn to play the sophisters, interpret these and the like passages of the Fathers, with candour and ingenuity (as it is most fitting they should). For the expressions of Preachers, which often have something of a paradox, must not be taken according to that harsher sound wherewith they at first strike the auditor's

ears. The Fathers spake not of any transubstantiated bread, but of the mystical and consecrated, when they used those sorts of expressions; and that for these reasons; 1. That they might extol and amplify the dignity of this mystery, which all true Christians acknowledge to be very great and peerless. 2. That communicants might not rest in the outward Elements, but seriously consider the thing represented, whereof they are most certainly made partakers, if they be worthy receivers. 3. And lastly, that they might approach so great a mystery with the more zeal, reverence, and devotion. And that those hyperbolic expressions are thus to be understood, the Fathers themselves teach clearly enough, when they come to interpret them.

5. Lastly, being the same holy Fathers who (as the manner is to discourse of Sacraments) speak sometimes of the Bread and Wine in the LORD'S Supper, as if they were the very Body and Blood of CHRIST, do also very often call them types, elements, signs, the figure of the Body and Blood of CHRIST; from hence it appears most manifestly, that they were of the Protestants, and not of the Papists' opinion. For we can without prejudice to what we believe of the Sacrament, use those former expressions which the Papists believe, do most favour them, if they be understood, as they ought to be, sacramentally. But the latter none can use, but he must thereby overthrow the groundless doctrine of Transubstantiation; these two, the Bread is transubstantiated into the Body, and the Bread also is the type, the sign, the figure of the Body of CHRIST, being wholly inconsistent. For it is impossible that a thing that loseth its being should yet be the sign and representation of another; neither can any thing be the type and the sign of itself.

But if without admitting of a sacramental sense the words be used too rigorously, nothing but this will follow; that the *Bread and Wine* are really and properly the very Body and Blood of CHRIST, which they themselves disown, that hold Transubstantiation. Therefore in this change, it is not a newness of substance, but of use and virtue that is produced; which yet the Fathers acknowledged with us, to be wonderful, supernatural, and proper only to GOD'S Omnipotency; for that earthly and corruptible meat cannot become to us a spiritual and heavenly, the Communion of the Body and Blood of CHRIST, without GOD'S especial power and operation. And whereas it is far above philosophy and human reason, that CHRIST from Heaven (where alone He is locally) should reach down to us the divine virtue of His Flesh, so that we are made one body with Him; therefore it is as necessary as it is reasonable, that the Fathers should tell us, that we ought with singleness of heart to believe the SON of GOD, when He saith, *This is My Body;* and that we ought not to measure this high and holy mystery by our narrow conceptions, or by the course of nature. For it is more acceptable to GOD with an humble simplicity of faith to reverence and embrace the words of CHRIST, than to wrest them violently to a strange and improper sense, and with curiosity and presumption to determine what exceeds the capacity of men and Angels.

Chapter 7
History of the Rise of the Romish Doctrine of Transubstantiation

We have proved it before, that the leprosy of Transubstantiation did not begin to spread over the body of the Church in a thousand years after CHRIST. But at last the thousand years being expired, and Satan loosed out of his prison, to go and deceive the nations, and compass the camp of the Saints about, then, to the great damage of Christian peace and religion, they began here and there to dispute against the clear, constant, and universal consent of the Fathers, and to maintain the new-started opinion. It is known to them that understand History, what manner of times were then, and what were those Bishops who then governed the Church of Rome; Sylvester II, John XIX and XX, Sergius IV, Benedictus VIII, John XXI, Benedict IX, Sylvester III, Gregory VI, Damasus II, Leo IX, Nicholas II, Gregory VII, or Hildebrand; who tore to pieces the Church of Rome with grievous schisms, cruel wars, and great slaughters. For the Roman Pontificate was come to that pass, that good men being put by, they whose life and doctrine was pious being oppressed, none could obtain that dignity, but they that could bribe best, and were most ambitious.

In that unhappy age the learned were at odds about the presence of the Body of CHRIST in the Sacrament; some defending the ancient doctrine of the Church, and some the new-sprung-up opinion.

Fulbert, Bishop of Chartres (A.D. 1010), was tutor to Berengarius, whom we shall soon have occasion to speak of, and his doctrine was altogether conformable to that of the Primitive Church, as appears clearly out of his Epistle to Adeodatus, wherein he teacheth, "That the mystery of faith in the Eucharist, is not to be looked on with our bodily eyes, but with the eyes of our mind. For what appears outwardly Bread and Wine, is made inwardly the Body and Blood of CHRIST; not that which is tasted with the mouth, but that which is relished by the heart's affection. Therefore," saith he, "prepare the palate of thy faith, open the throat of thy hope, and enlarge the bowels of thy charity, and take that Bread of life which is the food of the inward man." Again, "The perception of a divine taste proceeds from the faith of the inward man, whilst by receiving the saving Sacrament, CHRIST is received into the soul." All this is against those who teach in too gross a manner, that CHRIST in this mystery enters carnally the mouth and stomach of the receivers.

Fulbert was followed by Berengarius, his scholar, Archdeacon of Angers in France, a man of great worth, by the holiness both of his life and doctrine.

Berengarius stood up valiantly in defence of that doctrine which 170 years before, was delivered out of GOD'S Word and the holy Fathers, in France, by Bertram, and John Erigena, and by others elsewhere, against those who taught that in the Eucharist neither Bread nor Wine remained after the Consecration. Yet he did not either believe or teach (as many falsely and shamelessly have imputed to him) that nothing more is received in the LORD'S Supper, but bare signs only, or mere Bread and Wine; but he believed and openly profest, as St. Austin and other faithful Doctors of the Church had taught out of GOD'S Word, that in this mystery, the souls of the faithful are truly fed by the true Body and Blood of CHRIST to life eternal. Nevertheless it was neither his mind nor his doctrine, that the substance of the Bread and Wine is reduced to nothing, or changed into the substance of the natural Body of CHRIST; or (as some then would have had the Church believe) that CHRIST Himself comes down carnally from heaven. Entire books he wrote upon this subject, but they have been wholly supprest by his enemies, and now are not to be found. Yet what we have of him in his greatest enemy Lanfrank, I here set down; "By the Consecration at the Altar the Bread and Wine are made a Sacrament of Religion; not to cease to be what they were, but to be changed into something else, and to become what they were not;" agreeable to what St. Ambrose had taught. Again, "There are two parts in the Sacrifice of the Church (this is according to St. Irenæus), the visible Sacrament, and the invisible thing of the Sacrament; that is, the Body of CHRIST." *Item,* "The Bread and Wine which are consecrated, remain in their substance, having a resemblance with that whereof they are a Sacrament, for else they could not be a Sacrament." Lastly, "Sacraments are visible signs of divine things, but in them the invisible things are honoured." All this agrees well with St. Austin, and other Fathers above cited.

He did not therefore by this his doctrine exclude the Body of CHRIST from the Sacrament, but in its right administration he joined together the thing signified with the sacred sign; and taught that the Body of CHRIST was not eaten with the mouth in a carnal way, but with the mind, and soul, and spirit. Neither did Berengarius alone maintain this orthodox and ancient doctrine; for Sigibert, William of Malmesbury, Matthew Paris, and Matthew of Westminster, make it certain, that almost all the French, Italians, and English of those times were of the same opinion; and that many things were said, writ, and disputed in its defence by many men; amongst whom was Bruno, then Bishop of the same Church of Angers. Now this greatly displeaseth the Papal faction, who took great care that those men's writings should not be delivered to posterity, and now do write, that the doctrine of Berengarius, owned by the Fathers, and maintained by many famous nations, skult only in some dark corner or other.

The first Pope who opposed himself to Berengarius was Leo the Ninth, a plain man indeed, but too much led by Humbert and Hildebrand. For as soon as he was desired, he pronounced sentence of excommunication against Berengarius absent and unheard; and not long after he called a council of Verceil, wherein John Erigena and Berengarius were condemned, upon this account, that they should say, that the Bread and Wine in the Eucharist are only bare signs; which was far from their thoughts, and further yet from their belief. This roaring therefore of the Lion frightened not Berengarius; nay, the Gallican Churches did also oppose the Pope, and his Synod of Verceil, and defend with Berengarius the oppressed truth.

To Leo succeeded Pope Victor the Second, who seeing Berengarius could not be cast down and crushed by the fulminations of his predecessor, sent his legate Hildebrand into France, and called another Council at Tours, where Berengarius being cited, did freely appear, and whence he was freely dismissed, after he had given it under his hand, that the Bread and Wine in the Sacrifice of the Church, are not shadows and empty figures; and that he held none other but the common doctrine of the Church concerning the Sacrament. For he did not alter his judgment (as modern Papists give out), but he persisted to teach and maintain the same doctrine as before, as Lanfrank complains of him.

Yet his enemies would not rest satisfied with this, but they urged Pope Nicholas the Second, who (within a few months that Stephen the Tenth sate) succeeded Victor without the Emperor's consent, to call a new Council at Rome against Berengarius. For, that sensual manner of presence, by them devised, to the great dishonour of CHRIST, being rejected by Berengarius, and he teaching as he did before, that the Body of CHRIST was not present in such a sort, as that it might be at pleasure brought in and out, taken into the stomach, cast on the ground, trod under foot, and bit or devoured by any beasts, they falsely charged him as if he had denied that it is present at all. An hundred and thirteen Bishops came to the Council, to obey the Pope's Mandate; Berengarius came also. "And (as Sigonius and Leo Ostiensis say) when none present could withstand him, they sent for one Albericus, a Monk of Mount Cassin, made Cardinal by Pope Stephen:" who having asked seven days' time to answer in writing, brought at last his scroll against Berengarius. The reasons and arguments used therein to convince his antagonist are not now extant, but whatever they were, Berengarius was commanded presently without any delay to recant, in that form prescribed and appointed by Cardinal Humbert, which was thus: "I Berengarius, &c. assent to the Holy Roman and Apostolic See, and with my heart and mouth do profess, that I hold that faith concerning the Sacrament of the LORD'S Table which our Lord and venerable Pope Nicholas, and this sacred Council, have determined and imposed upon me by their evangelic and apostolic authority; to wit, that the Bread and Wine which are set on the Altar, are not after the consecration only a sacrament, sign, and figure, but also the very Body and Blood of our LORD JESUS CHRIST; (thus far it is well enough, but what follows is too horrid, and is disowned by the Papists themselves;) and that they (the Body and Blood) are touched and broken with the hands of the Priests, and ground with the teeth of the faithful, not sacramentally only, but in truth and sensibly." This is the prescript of the Recantation imposed on Berengarius, and by him at first rejected, but by imprisonment, and threats, and fear of being put to death, at last extorted from him.

This form of Recantation is to be found entire in Lanfrank, Algerus, and Gratian; yet the Glosser on Gratian, John Semeca marks it with this note; "Except you understand well the words of Berengarius," (he should rather have said of Pope Nicholas, and Cardinal Humbertus,) "you shall fall into a greater heresy than his was, for he exceeded the truth, and spake hyperbolically." And so Richard de Mediavilla; "Berengarius being accused, overshot himself in his justification:" but the excess of his words should be ascribed to those who prescribed and forced them upon him. Yet in all this we hear nothing of Transubstantiation.

Berengarius at last escaped out of this danger, and conscious to himself of having denied the truth, took heart again, and refuted in writing his own impious and absurd Recantation, and said, "That by force it was extorted from him by the Church of Malignants, the Council of Vanity." Lanfrank of Caen, at that time head of a Monastery in France, afterwards Archbishop of Canterbury, and Guitmundus Aversanus answered him. And though it is not to be doubted but that Berengarius, and those of his party, writ and replied again and again, yet so well did their adversaries look to it, that nothing of theirs remains, save some citations in Lanfrank. But it were to be wished that we had now the entire works of Berengarius, who was a learned man, and a constant follower of Antiquity; for out of them we might know with more certainty how things went, than we can out of what his profest enemies have said.

This sacramental debate ceased awhile because of the tumults of war raised in Apulia and elsewhere by Pope Nicholas the Second; but it began again as soon as Hildebrand, called Gregory the Seventh, came to the Papal chair. For Berengarius was cited again to a new Council at Rome, "where some being of one opinion and some another" (as it is in the acts of that Council, writ by those of the Pope's faction), his cause could not be so entirely oppressed but that some Bishops were still found to uphold it. Nay, the ringleader himself, Hildebrand, is said to have doubted, "whether what we receive at the LORD'S Table be indeed the Body of CHRIST by a substantial conversion." But three months space having been granted to Berengarius, and a fast appointed to the Cardinals, "that GOD would shew by some sign from heaven (which yet He did not) who was in the right, the Pope or Berengarius, concerning the Body of the LORD;" at last the business was decided without any oracle from above, and a new form of retraction imposed on Berengarius, whereby he was henceforth forward to confess, under pain of the Pope's high displeasure, "that the mystic Bread," (first made magical and enchanting by Hildebrand,) "is substantially turned into the true and proper Flesh of CHRIST;" which whether he ever did is not certain. For though Malmesbury tells us, "that he died in that Roman faith," yet there are ancienter than he, who say, "that he never was converted from his first opinion." And some relate, "that after this last condemnation having given over his studies, and given to the poor all he had, he wrought with his own hands for his living." Other things related of him by some slaves of the Roman See, deserves no credit. These things happened, ... in the year 1079; and soon after Berengarius died.

Berengarius being dead the orthodox and ancient doctrine of the LORD'S Supper which he maintained did not die with him (as the Chronicus Cassinensis would have it); for it was still constantly retained by St. Bernard, Abbot of Clairvaux, who lived about the beginning of the twelfth century. In his discourse on the LORD'S Supper, he joins together the *outward form of the Sacrament*, and *the spiritual efficacy of it*, as the shell and the kernel, the sacred sign, and the thing signified; the one he takes out of the words of the Institution, and the other, out of CHRIST'S Sermon in the sixth of St. John. And in the same place explaining, that Sacraments are not *things absolute* in themselves without any relation, but mysteries, wherein by the gift of a visible sign, an invisible and divine grace with the Body and Blood of CHRIST is given, he saith, "That the visible sign is as a ring, which is given not for itself or absolutely, but to invest and give possession of an estate made over to one." . . . . . Now, as no man can fancy that the ring is substantially changed into the inheritance, whether lands or houses, none also can say with truth, or without absurdity, that the Bread and Wine are substantially changed into the Body and Blood of CHRIST. But in his Sermon on the Purification, which none doubts to be his, he speaks yet more plainly; "The Body of CHRIST in the Sacrament is the food of the soul, not of the belly, therefore we eat him not corporally: but in the manner that CHRIST is meat, in the same manner we understand that he is eaten." Also in his Sermon on St. Martin, which undoubtedly is his also; "To this day," saith he, "the same flesh is given to us, but spiritually, therefore not corporally." For the truth of things spiritually present is certain also.

The thirteenth century now follows; wherein the world growing both older and worse, a great deal of trouble and confusion there was about religion . . . . . So that now there remained nothing but to confirm the new tenet of Transubstantiation, and impose it so peremptorily on the Christian world, that none might dare so much as to hiss against it. This Pope Innocent the Third bravely performed. He succeeding Celestin the Third at thirty years of age, and marching stoutly in the footsteps of Hildebrand, called a Council at Rome in St. John Lateran, and was the first that ever presumed to make the new-devised Doctrine of Transubstantiation an Article of Faith necessary to salvation, and that by his own mere authority.

In the fifteenth century the Council of Constance (which by a sacrilegious attempt took away the sacramental cup from the people, and from the Priests when they do not officiate) did wrongfully condemn Wiclif, who was already dead, because amongst other things he had taught with the Ancients, "That the substance of the Bread and Wine remains materially in the Sacrament of the Altar; and that in the same Sacrament, no accidents of Bread and Wine remain without a substance." Which two assertions are most true.

By these any considering person may easily see, that Transubstantiation is a mere novelty; nor warranted either by scripture or antiquity; invented about the middle of the twelfth century, out of some misunderstood sayings of some of the Fathers; confirmed by no ecclesiastical or Papal Decree before the year 1215, afterwards received only here and there in the Roman Church; debated in the schools by many disputes; liable to many very bad consequences; rejected (for there was never those wanting that opposed it) by many great and pious men, until it was maintained in the sacrilegious Council of Constance; and at last in the year 1551, confirmed in the Council of Trent, by a few Latin Bishops, slaves to the Roman See; imposed upon all, under pain of an anathema to be feared by none; and so spread too far, by the tyrannical and most unjust command of the Pope. So that we have no reason to embrace it, until it shall be demonstrated, that except the substance of the Bread be changed into the very Body of CHRIST, His words cannot possibly be true; nor His Body present. Which will never be done.

Reprinted March 25, 1834
The Feast of the Annunciation

TRACT 29: AD POPULUM

Christian Liberty
Or, Why Should We Belong to the Church of England?

BY A LAYMAN

> *He that receiveth you, receiveth Me; and he that receiveth Me, receiveth Him that sent Me. He that receiveth a prophet, in the name of a prophet, shall receive a prophet's reward; and he that receiveth a righteous man, in the name of a righteous man, shall receive a righteous man's reward.*
> —ST. MATTHEW 10:40-41

John Evans was walking along the lane between his own house and the common, when just at the place where the lane makes a turning, he suddenly met Dr. Spencer, the Rector of his parish. John was not particularly pleased at thus meeting his Pastor, for several reasons. He had formerly been a most regular attendant at the parish church, from which he had lately chosen to absent himself, with his family. Not that he stayed away from idleness, or from any intentional disregard of the commands of GOD; he felt, as he imagined, the same reverence for the Divine Will as ever; it was, indeed, rather a mistaken zeal than anything else, which had led to his change of conduct. He had been induced, one Sunday, by a friend who belonged to a dissenting congregation, to go with him to the meeting-house; and when he was there, there was something in the energy of the preacher's manner, in the vehement action by which his teaching was accompanied, and in his seeming earnestness in the holy cause of GOD, which, as it was quite new to John, was particularly striking to him. Compared with the fervour of this man, the quiet but sound discourses of his Rector seemed spiritless and tame; and John came out of the meeting under the influence of such enthusiastic feelings, as led him to resolve to visit it again the first opportunity. And thus he was led on to go again and again, till at last he made up his mind to become a regular attendant there. Thither he accordingly took his family, Sunday after Sunday; and deserted, of course, the old parish church, the venerable building in which he and his had received the holy rite of Baptism, in which, as each of them in turn outgrew their infancy, they had heard for the first time the solemn sound of congregational prayer, and in which those who had arrived at a proper age, had frequently received, from CHRIST'S authorized Ministers, the symbols of His sacred Body and Blood.

It will be seen from what follows, that in making this change upon such grounds as have been described, John Evans did not understand that he was disobeying the GOD whom he was trying to serve, and putting a slight upon that SAVIOUR, whose disciple he not only professed himself, but in good earnest desired to be. Yet though he did not enter into this view of the matter; though he knew not that he had shown disrespect to CHRIST in His Minister; still he felt as though he had not been behaving with perfect respect to the Doctor, whom he loved on his own account, as he had indeed every reason to do. So what with his fear of a rebuke on this ground (a rebuke which he dreaded the more from the mildness of the language in which he knew that it would be clothed); what with the irksomeness of having to avow opinions which must be disagreeable to one whom he so highly respected; and moreover, the suspicion which he could not help feeling, that in these new ways of his, so different from what he had been used to revere, and so suddenly taken up, he might *possibly* be wrong; for all these various reasons, he met his Pastor with a downcast and half-guilty look, very different from the open, honest smile with which he had till then ever greeted the good Clergyman.

Dr. Spencer, however, took no notice of the difference. "Well, John," said he, "I am glad to see you. I was on my way to have a little conversation with you, and should have been sorry to have missed you."

John thought it best to be bold, and come out at once with his defence of himself. "I believe, Sir," said he, "that I can guess what it is you were wishing to talk with me about. I have taken a step which I fear,...I know,...must be displeasing to you, Sir. I trust however, that in exercising my *Christian Liberty* in the choice of my spiritual teacher, and joining the meeting instead of going to Church, I shall not seem to have acted from respect to you, Sir, who have so long been a good friend to me and mine."

Dr.—By no means, John; do not suppose either that I feel personally offended by your conduct, or that I do not regard you with feelings as friendly as ever. But, as to the *Christian Liberty* you speak of, we perhaps understand that matter rather differently; and it was because I thought you were in some mistake about it, that I was coming to see you today. I have missed yourself and family for some Sundays past in Church, and understood you had joined the meeting. Is not this the case?

John.—It is. Sir; and, as I have already said, without the slightest notion of showing you disrespect.

Dr.—Say no more about that, John; I know you too well to suspect you for a moment of such a feeling as that. Speak to me, as to your sincere friend and well-wisher, in perfect candour; and do not fear that I shall be offended by anything you say, while you tell me fairly your reasons for this change in your conduct.

J.—I am sure, Sir, that in the old Church I never heard anything from you but what was good; and I never thought, till the other day, that I could pray better in any other words than in those of the Church Service. But there is something so fine in the prayers without book, as they are offered at meeting, and . . . . .

Dr.—And something perhaps in the manner and language of the preacher, who preaches there without book also? But let me ask, had you no other reasons than these, and such as these, for leaving the Church?

J.—None, Sir, but such as these; at least none that I am aware of.

Dr.—You did not consider that either the Church Prayer-Book, or my Sermons, taught doctrines contrary to the great truths revealed in GOD'S Word?

J.—GOD forbid, Sir.

Dr.—You had then, perhaps, some such notion as this; you thought that in the Church you could pray well, but at meeting you could pray rather better?

J.—Just so, Sir.

Dr.—And you thought that you were doing GOD service, then, by joining that worship which touched you most?

J.—And surely, Sir, I was right in that thought, at least.

Dr.—You would have been right, if GOD had not chosen a Minister for you. In that case perhaps you might have used your Christian Liberty, as you call it, and joined any congregation and worship you pleased. But

His having given a clear command alters the case, and makes that which would otherwise have been a matter of indifference, an act of disobedience and sin.

J.—But if I may be so bold as to ask, Sir, when did GOD give this command, and where is it to be found? I am not so ready with the Bible as learned people, yet I know it in my own way. That was the very thing I heard Mr. Tims, who preaches at the meeting, ask last Sunday. He said, "where is the Church of England spoken of in the Bible? name chapter and verse where we are bid belong to it." And then he went on to say, that the new heart is everything; and that we shall not be asked at the last day, whether we were Churchmen or Dissenters, but what the state of our heart is.

Dr.—We shall be asked at the last day, whether we have obeyed GOD'S commandments; now, one of those commandments is, that we should belong to the Church, as I will soon show you. But first you shall tell me what has been your reason, till lately, for going to Church.

J.—I was born of Church-going parents, and that made me a regular Church-goer in my youth. And when I grew up, I always, at least till the other day, thought that I had the best of reasons for keeping regular to Church. In the first place, the Church was the Law Church; and that of itself would be a reason, even if there were no other, for good subjects keeping to it; and then, I knew it had been in the country many, many years, whereas all the meetings about are (so to say) of yesterday, and in one sense upstarts. And then I had heard from you, Sir, that in former times it had Saints and Martyrs, such as were when our LORD was on earth. And I thought it therefore far more likely to be right, and had a stronger claim on me than any other religion; and especially since I was a pretty regular reader of my Bible, and never found the teaching which I heard at Church different from that which I thus picked up at home.

Dr.—All good reasons as far as they went; but I see that I was right in supposing the chief claim the Church has on all Christians, is unknown to you. Our Church is sprung from that very Church which CHRIST set up at Jerusalem when He came upon earth; and none of the sects have this great gift. It is a branch of that Holy Church, which CHRIST promised to be with, "even unto the end of the world." You must surely often have met in the Bible with mention of "the Church:" what did you suppose the word to mean?

J.—I do not know, Sir, that I had any very clear idea what it meant; but I rather thought it meant all sincere Christians in all parts of the world, to whatever Church or sect they might belong.

Dr.—Then it seems you did not understand the word "Church" to signify a body of men, bound by the same laws, acting together, speaking the same thing, attending the same worship, reverencing the same Pastors and Teachers, and receiving at their hands the Sacraments which Christ has ordained. Yet it is quite certain that this is what our LORD meant, when He spoke of His Church. He meant a Church such as the Church of England. This will be clear to you from Matthew 18:15-17. In these verses CHRIST speaks of the Church; in the last of them He bids His Disciples regard anyone who should in certain cases refuse to "hear the Church," as a heathen, and a publican; as an opposer of His authority, and an outcast from His sacred fold. Thus it appears the Church He speaks of, is not a mere number of good people scattered over the world, who may or may not have communion with each other (which was your notion of the word), but one public orderly body, consisting of Ministers and people, such as the Church of England. To be sure the Church of England happens to have wealth and honour, and that first Church had not; but this is but an accidental difference between them. If the Church of England were to lose its wealth and honour, it would not, could not cease to be a branch of the true Church. For the true Church, and the Church of England, as a branch of it, is founded on a rock, and against it the gates of hell will never prevail; as you may read, Matthew 16:18-19.

J.—If you would kindly write down these texts for me, I will turn them out of my own Bible, and think over them. There is one thing, however, Sir, which comes into my mind to ask you. Even supposing all Christians *ought* to join together in one, yet they *do not*. There are a good many religions among us, and how is a plain unlearned man like me to know which is the real Church, spoken of in these passages?

Dr.—The matter is not so difficult as you imagine, even to the most unlearned. The true Church of CHRIST must possess, as I will now show you, *certain marks;* to which not even a pretence is made by the numerous sects of Dissenters with which our country, from different unfortunate circumstances, abounds. Let me go back to the time when the Gospel was first preached, and converts made by the Apostles. Many of these believers, we find, acknowledged in the Apostles the authority which CHRIST had given them over the flock, and were followers of them even as they were of CHRIST (1 Cor 11:1), remembering them in all things, and keeping the ordinances which they had delivered to the congregation in each place; and for this conduct the Corinthians received the inspired praise of St. Paul (1 Cor 11:2). But there were others, who called themselves Christians, who caused divisions among the brethren (1 Cor 2:18-19), forming parties of their own, and setting at nought the Apostolical Authority. To these St. Paul spoke in vain, when he said, "I beseech you, brethren, by the name of our LORD JESUS CHRIST, that ye all speak the same thing, and that there be no divisions among you; but that ye be perfectly joined together in the same mind, and in the same judgment" (1 Cor 1:10). They slighted the LORD'S accredited Minister, and said that his bodily presence was weak, and his speech contemptible (2 Cor 10:10). Many of the sects which these men formed, fell, as was to be expected, into follies and heresies; but even without reference to this fact, even if we suppose them to have taught the great doctrines of Christianity with the same purity as the Apostles did, could a reasonable man entertain a moment's doubt, granting CHRIST had indeed founded a Church on earth, *which* that Church was; whether the name of Church belonged to the company of Christians which obeyed His Apostles; or, on the other hand, to any one of the sects which vilified and despised them?

J.—Certainly not; that is, there could be no doubt, as long as the Apostles were alive, that the Christians whom they governed must have made up the true visible Church of CHRIST.

Dr.—Sharply argued, John; but you shall not escape from me, notwithstanding. For at all events, is it not plain that there was great number of sects then as now? so that a man, who wished to do his duty, would have to look about him carefully, and would be in danger of doing wrong, if he joined the first body of so-called Christians, which he met with?—a great number of sects, I repeat, *in spite of the* Apostles being alive; so that it is not the mere circumstance of the Apostles being dead, which makes a search necessary to find the true Church.

J.—I see what you would say, Sir.

Dr.—Now then to proceed. You are disposed to doubt, whether one Church was truer than another after the Apostles' death. Surely is it not plain, that that Church would still be the true one, which they had governed? Now you will find that our LORD promised to be with His

Apostles in their character of teachers and baptizers of the nations, alway, even *unto the end of the world* (Matt 28:19-20). What did He mean by that?

J.—He could not mean that Peter, James, or John, or their brethren, were to live for ever on earth; for we know that they are long since dead.

Dr.—Certainly not; and we must therefore ascribe to His words the only other meaning which they can reasonably bear. As He could not have spoken of the *persons* of the Apostles, He must have spoken of their *offices*. He must have meant that though Peter, James, and John should be taken from the world, the true Church should never be left without Apostles, but be guided by their successors to the end of time.

John Evans had all this while been retracing with Dr. Spencer the way he had lately come, and had now arrived at the door of his own house. The good Clergyman thinking he had given him matter enough to cast in his mind, took this as a fit moment to break off the conversation, determining to resume it some early day. He therefore merely went into his parishioner's house to turn out for him the texts he had referred to, and then wished him good evening.

The next Sunday John was at Church; and after the Service was over, he kept lingering in the path which led to the Dr.'s house, in hopes of being overtaken by his Rector. He was not disappointed. Dr. Spencer soon joined him, and the argument between them was resumed.

J.—If, Sir, as you were saying, our LORD meant, that there should be teachers and rulers of the Church, to stand in the place of the Apostles after their death, how is it we hear nothing of these successors, so to call them, in Scripture?

Dr.—On the other hand I affirm, we hear a great deal about them in Scripture, as you will agree with me. Surely you recollect the Apostles solemnly laying their hands on others, or, as it is called, *ordaining* them, to act as their assistants and fellows; and this they did, when Christians became too numerous for them to attend to them all by themselves. Such a person was Timothy, whom St. Paul thus consecrated by the putting on of his hands (1 Tim 1:6), to bear rule over that branch of the Church which was established at Ephesus in Asia; Titus too, whom he left with authority over the Church in the island of Crete, "to set in order the things that were wanting" (Titus 1:5); and such Epaphroditus, whom he sent to the Philippians as his "brother, and companion in labour, and fellow-soldier, but their messenger," or *Apostle* (Phil 2:25). Now in the absence of the Apostles, what do you suppose would have been the conduct of all true Christians to these whom the Apostles had appointed?

J.—Of course they would have shown them all honour and obedience, in order to show their respect for the Apostles themselves.

Dr.—Certainly; as reverencing St. Paul, they would have attended to his plain doctrine; "Whether any do enquire of Titus, he is my partner and fellow-helper concerning you; or our brethren (i.e. Luke and another sent to act jointly with Titus) be enquired of, they are the *Apostles* of the Churches, and the glory of CHRIST. Wherefore show ye to them and before the Churches, the proof of your love, and of our boasting on your behalf" (2 Cor 8:23-24). On the other hand, how do you think these new Apostles would have been treated by those who slighted the authority of St. Peter and St. Paul.

J.—Those who set at nought the Apostles themselves, would also set at nought those who stood in their place.

Dr.—You see then, that had we lived in the days of the Apostles, we should have had one plain test among others, for discovering the true Church, in spite of all counterfeits of it. The true Church was that Christian body, which was governed by men *commissioned* by the Apostles; and those who were perverse towards St. Peter and St. Paul, would have been disobedient towards them. But let us now go a step further. Do you suppose that Timothy, for instance, ceased to be an Apostle, such as St. Paul had made him, on the death of St. Paul?

J.—I do not see why he should; but I should like to know whether there is proof from Scripture that he did not.

Dr.—When St. Paul was just going to be put to death for the sake of the Gospel, he writes thus to Timothy: "Preach the Word; be instant in season, out of season; reprove, rebuke, exhort with all long-suffering and doctrine. . . . . . Watch *thou* in all things, endure affliction, do the work of an evangelist, make full proof of thy ministry. For I am now ready to be offered, and the time of my departure is at hand. I have fought a good fight, I have finished my course" (2 Tim 4:2-7).

J.—From these words it is certainly clear that St. Paul intended Timothy, whom he had appointed to act as his brother and fellow-labourer while he lived, to act as his successor when he should be no more.

Dr.—And all true Christians, who had reverenced Timothy as if really St. Paul, when that Apostle was removed from them for a time by *distance*, would no less reverence him as such, when the Apostle was removed once for all by *death*.

J.—They could do no less.

Dr.—It follows then, that even when the Apostles had all entered into their rest, i.e. in the second age of the Gospel, we might still have used the test I have given, to distinguish the Church of CHRIST from sects falsely claiming that name. We should have found the one set of Christians reverently sitting at the feet of the successors of the Apostles; all the others so-called, openly rejecting their rightful authority.

J.—It is true; ever while these successors of the Apostles lived, all who professed to obey CHRIST, were bound to pay them, and would have paid them, a reverence which the false sects would not have paid; so that in those times there would certainly have been no difficulty in finding which was the Church, which it was our duty to join.

Dr.—And when Timothy, Titus, or Epaphroditus, as exercising the same full authority which had been exercised by St. Paul, themselves appointed fellow-labourers and successors, committing, as the Apostle had enjoined one of them to do, the things which they had heard to faithful men who might be able to teach others also (2 Tim 2:2); would not these faithful men be reverenced by all true Christians, for the very same reasons which led them to reverence those who appointed them?

J.—They would so, no doubt. As long as a direct line was continued from the Apostles themselves onwards, all consistent Christians must have paid them reverence. And such a succession might have gone on for a long while,—an hundred years or more.

Dr.—What if it have now gone on for eighteen hundred years? What if, by the good providence of GOD, the line which began with the Apostles Peter and Paul should have continued even to this very day? so that there are men who stand in the place of the holy Saints and Martyrs of Scripture up to this very hour, under the great and eternal Head of the Church? You look surprised, but such is the fact; and if such persons do really exist, and if we find one community of Christians acknowledging, and obeying, and ruled by them, while every other body of professing Christians in our island disclaims and rejects them, you will see that this test will enable the most simple-minded and unlearned person to discriminate between the true Church of CHRIST and the unauthorized sects which call themselves CHRIST'S followers now, almost as clearly as he could, had He lived in the days of the Apostles themselves.

J.—Yes; the body of Christians, which reverences and is guided by the successors of the Apostles must be the true Church of CHRIST. But who are these successors of the Apostles in our country? though, to be sure, I think I know that answer you will give me.

Dr.—The Bishops of the Church of England are they. There is not one of them who cannot trace his right to guide and govern CHRIST'S Church, and to ordain its Ministers, through a long line of predecessors, up to the favoured persons who were consecrated by the laying on of the holy hands of St. Peter and of St. Paul. This is a fact which dissenters from the Church of England do not, and cannot, deny: nor do they profess that the authority of those, whom they call their ministers, to teach and to administer the Sacraments, rests at all on such grounds as these.

J.—I understand you, Sir; but I have one remark to make, if you will please to hear it. Bishops do not work miracles, as the Apostles did; nor can you mean that we are to look upon their teaching and writings now, as dictated by immediate inspiration, and consequently infallible, like the New Testament. How then are they Successors of the Apostles?

Dr.—You are bringing me to a large subject, John; which we will discuss some other time, not on a Sunday evening, when you have your young ones at home, waiting to say their verses to you; and I had rather rest than argue after the Services of the day. We will have some further talk, when occasion offers; meanwhile, in answer to your enquiry, I will but bid you compare John 20 with Acts 2. The *miraculous* gifts were sent down upon the Apostles *on the day of Pentecost;* but the *commission to preach, teach, and ordain,* were given, quite independently of all such extraordinary endowments, *before our SAVIOUR ascended into heaven.* One word at parting.—You have had a good education; your mind has been opened to enter into arguments, to see objections, and answer questions; your understanding has been sharpened. This is a talent which may be used rightly, or abused; to the unwary all gifts are temptations. As riches betray men into selfishness and an evil security; so does a sharp wit tend to make them self-confident, arrogant, and irreverent. Look at the advantages which GOD has given you, not as a cause of boasting and self-gratification, but seriously and anxiously, as a treasure of which you are steward for GOD, and concerning which you must one day give account to Him.

JOHN WILLIAM BOWDEN
The Feast of the Annunciation
March 25, 1834

TRACT 30: AD POPULUM
Christian Liberty
Or, Why Should We Belong to the Church of England? (Continued)

BY A LAYMAN

> *He that receiveth you, receiveth Me; and he that receiveth Me, receiveth Him that sent Me. He that receiveth a prophet, in the name of a prophet, shall receive a prophet's reward; and he that receiveth a righteous man, in the name of a righteous man, shall receive a righteous man's reward.*
> —ST. MATTHEW 10:40-41

John Evans did not fail to look out in his Bible the texts to which Dr. Spencer had referred him; and he saw clearly that the miraculous powers with which it pleased GOD to endue the Apostles, were by no means necessarily connected with the commission which those Apostles had previously received from our LORD; the commission, we mean, to teach and baptize all nations.

John was seen again on the next Sunday, at his accustomed place in church. The Dr. preached from the text, Mark 16:17-18; "And these signs shall follow them that believe: in My name shall they cast out devils; they shall speak with new tongues; they shall take up serpents; and if they drink any deadly thing, it shall not hurt them; they shall lay hands on the sick, and they shall recover."

He pointed out to his congregation the beautiful regularity which pervades the works of GOD; the settled laws, the established order, with which our Maker guides the course of things around us; the certainty with which the stars rise and set, the moon waxes and wanes, the flower follows the bud, and the seed the flower. He reminded his hearers how truly, from the times of the flood, GOD'S promise has been fulfilled; and seed time and harvest, cold and heat, summer and winter, day and night, have not ceased

(Gen 8:8). "And surely," said he, "we see in these things the proofs that GOD is a GOD of order; that He would not lightly or without important reasons change the system which He has established, the laws which He has framed. If then we were to hear that the ALMIGHTY had on a certain occasion broken through these laws, and violated by miracles the established order of nature, we should have the strongest reasons to suppose, 1st, that He had only done so, in order to accomplish something which could not conceivably have been accomplished without such interpositions; and 2ndly, that He would discontinue these interpositions as soon as they became no longer necessary.

"Now both these conclusions," continued the Doctor, "we find to agree alike with the Bible and with the recorded history of mankind. It was necessary that the doctrines of Christianity should be known to be the infallible truth of GOD; that what the Apostles said or wrote on the subject should be received as the words of GOD Himself speaking to mankind. Now this authority, as far as we can see, can be given to mortal man only by GOD'S visibly interfering in his support; and such interferences are what we call miracles. We see then, that for the establishment in the world of Christianity, and of the authority of those sacred books which form the New Testament, miracles were necessary; and we find from Scripture, that miracles were then vouchsafed. But when the interference had been fully proved, when evidence of it could be handed down by ordinary means to following generations; and when no more divine truth was to be revealed, miracles were needed no longer; and the history of the world informs us, that they have ceased for seventeen hundred years."

And while the Dr., in conclusion, pointed out on the one hand the folly of expecting a recurrence of such marvels in our own days, an expectation which amounts to an acknowledgement that Christianity is as yet imperfect, and that we are to look for a more complete revelation; he dwelt with much earnestness on the danger of imagining that GOD'S peculiar protection of Christianity, GOD'S peculiar inward gifts to believers ceased with the cessation of the outward signs and wonders which at first accompanied the revelation of His Word.

John listened with great attention; and, when the Service was over, he thought long and deeply upon what had been said. He looked out also the different texts which the Dr. had mentioned in his Sermon; and in so doing, he came to one which rather puzzled him. It was John 14:16. "It is strange," said he to himself; "our LORD promised that the COMFORTER whom He would send should abide with His followers for ever; I really do not see why this promise should be given, if the greatest and most striking gifts which that COMFORTER was to bestow, were to cease at the end of one, or at most of two generations."

That evening, as he was strolling in the fine summer twilight along the banks of the river, he met the Dr., who had walked that way to enjoy the fineness of the season, and to refresh himself after the holy labours of the day. He told him his difficulty, nearly in the words in which we have expressed it; and the Dr., smiling good naturedly, thus replied.

Dr.—Are you quite sure, John, that you have stated your case aright? Is it perfectly certain that miraculous powers were the greatest gifts which the Eternal SPIRIT was commissioned to bestow upon mankind?

J.—It certainly appeared to me that they were; such marked, such striking instances of GOD'S favour were surely greater boons than anything else which we can conceive to be given to mortals in this present life. I think, Sir, that I have heard you yourself call these gifts of the SPIRIT, as opposed to others, His extraordinary gifts.

Dr.—You may very probably have heard me so call them; but "extraordinary" only means "unusual;" and it does not always follow that what is unusual is more important than what is of frequent occurrence. But tell me, John, in the case in which one thing is done in order to prepare for the doing of some other thing, which is the most important of the two? the first of these things or the last; the means or the end?

J.—The end, of course, is more important than the means; no man would venture to call the scaffolding which is raised that the house may be built, more important than the house itself.

Dr.—Now think a moment, John, before you answer me; why were the miraculous powers bestowed on the Apostles?

J.—To make men believers in CHRIST.

Dr.—To prepare the way, that is, for their receiving those inward gifts of the SPIRIT in which true believers now participate as fully as those who lived in the days of the Apostles.

J.—I see, Sir; the extraordinary gifts might be compared to the scaffolding, the ordinary ones to the house.

Dr.—Exactly so, John; marvellous and striking as were the signs and wonders of the Apostolic age, we should ever recollect that they were not greater gifts, or even gifts so great as those inward ones which are our evangelical inheritance, as well as that of the Primitive Christians. When the doctrine of the HOLY GHOST, and of His inward influence, was new to the world, it pleased GOD to confirm it, and to show that the influence was real, by permitting, in some cases, those on whom it descended to perform works which they could not have done, had not GOD been with them. Thus the real importance, even then, of these miraculous gifts consisted in their bearing witness to the inward and unseen ones which GOD still showers upon His Church.

J.—And which we dare not suppose to have ceased merely because the outward signs of them did, when GOD Himself had promised that they should last for ever.

Dr.—Well; the promise of support to the Apostles, in the performance of their Ministerial duties, was equally perpetual; CHRIST was to be with them, we have seen, as the teachers and baptizers of all nations, "alway, even unto the end of the world." The reality of their powers, and, among others, of their power of conferring the HOLY GHOST on others, was attested at first by miracles (Acts 3:17-18). But we have no more reason for supposing that the true powers of the Ministry ceased with the outward signs, in the case of the Apostles, than we have for supposing, in the case just mentioned of the gifts of common believers, that from the moment miracles were no longer vouchsafed, the HOLY SPIRIT withdrew Himself from the guidance of the Church for ever. That GOD has bestowed Apostolic gifts upon Apostles, and the regenerating influences of His HOLY GHOST upon other believers, we know from the recorded testimony of those who witnessed the miracles by which the reality of those gifts and influences was at first established. That those gifts and influences will be alike perpetual in the Church, we are bound to believe upon the solemn word of Him who gave them.

J.—Miracles, then, performed in one age, and handed down by history to others, form the standing proofs of the reality of those gifts which were given to the Church for ever; and one of those gifts was undoubtedly the Apostolic power; which we must believe, upon this evidence, to be still existing.

Dr.—Exactly so; and infallibility of doctrine, itself a miracle, ceased with miracles in general. We cannot see any reason for the continuance of such a gift to the successors of the Apostles, when the Apostles themselves have recorded all things necessary to salvation in those sacred Scriptures which have come down to our times, and to which we can all refer. Nor have we the slightest ground for doubting the permanence of those Apostolic privileges which were of perpetual necessity, merely because a miraculous gift, evidently no longer necessary, has been discontinued.

J.—This, Sir, I understand; but there is one difficulty which occurs to me. As the rulers of the true Church are no longer infallible, what is to prevent their all falling together into error, and thus leading astray the whole Church committed to their care?

Dr.—We may infer from Christ's promise already mentioned, that this will never happen to the whole Church at once; that some true Apostles will be found on earth in every age, until that last period of the world's history, which shall witness His coming. But that with regard to particular branches of His Church this may happen, and has happened, is a melancholy truth. There is one simple test, however, by which we may at once assure ourselves that the Church of England has not so fallen away, or, as it is called, apostatized from the faith of her Lord and Master.

J.—And what is that, Sir?

Dr.—As the eternal truth of GOD is contained in His revealed word, the Bible; no Church, whatever may be the errors of its individual members, can be said, as a Church, to have fallen away, and consequently to have lost her claim to the obedience of CHRIST'S true disciples, while she still reverences that Bible;—while she puts it into the hand of each of her followers, and bids him read it, and seek there and there only the proofs of the doctrine which she inculcates; and while she declares, as the Church of England does in her 6th Article, that "Holy Scripture containeth all things necessary to salvation; so that whatsoever is not read therein, nor may be proved thereby, is not to be required of any man that it should be believed as an article of the Faith, or be thought requisite or necessary to salvation."

J.—Then according to you, Sir, the Church of England is not only the true, but the original Church of CHRIST established in this kingdom.—Now Sam Jones, the Catholic, who attends the Popish Chapel in the next parish, tells me that his is the original Church, and that the Church of England is a new one.

Dr.—That which is truly the Catholic Church, is indeed the oldest; but though we in a common way call the Papists, or followers of the Pope,

Catholics, yet it is we who are the true Catholics; for the term only means members of CHRIST'S universal Church. The history of the Papists is this. Many centuries ago, strange and corrupt notions and practices prevailed in many of the churches in Europe. Among others, people thought that the Pope or Bishop of Rome was gifted with authority from Heaven to control all the branches of the Church on earth, and that his word was to be of more weight than even the Holy Scriptures themselves. But about three hundred years ago, the Bishops of the Church of England saw these errors in their true light; they saw that the Pope's authority was not founded on Scripture, and they consequently refused to acknowledge it, while they at the same time corrected, upon scriptural principles, the other errors and evil practices which I have alluded to. These changes did not make the Church of England a new church, nor prevent that body which was CHRIST'S true and original Church before, from being CHRIST'S true and original Church still. Some Bishops of that day, it is true, disapproved of these changes, and refused to accede to them; but as, when they died, they providentially appointed no successors, there has never since been any real ground for doubt which was the true Church of CHRIST in this favoured land. The Bishops of the Church of England, and they only, are the representatives by succession of those who, more than a thousand years ago, planted the Gospel on our shores.[1]

J.—But there are persons whom the Papists call their Bishops—whence do they come?

Dr.—They derive what they call their right from their appointment by foreign Bishops in an unauthorized manner. The Pope and his followers would by no means acknowledge the changes which had taken place in England; they declared that our Church had apostatized from the faith, and refused to communicate with us, till we should return to all our ancient errors. They have since, upon the alleged ground that our line of Bishops was extinct, given commission from time to time to different

---

[1] In the same manner it may be shown, that the established Church of Ireland alone represents that Church which the labours of St. Patrick, in the fifth century, planted in the island. Those who preside over the Romanists have received consecration from Rome at a very recent period. And the corruptions which prevail in their religion, and which distinguish it from ours, became prevalent long after the Saint's death. Our doctrines, therefore, approach more nearly to his than theirs do; and our Church is the true and original Church of CHRIST in Ireland, in every sense which the words will bear.

persons to exercise episcopal authority here; but as the ground was false, the commission was of course void. We acknowledge the Pope and his Bishops in foreign countries to be, by station, ministers of the Church, though we admit and lament the fact, that they have led the branches of it over which they preside into apostasy and shame; yet we feel that in sending their representatives hither, to act in defiance of the Church already established, they are exceeding the limits of their authority. We feel that GOD, who is not the author of confusion, but of peace, in all churches of the saints (1 Cor 14:33), cannot sanction the intrusion of one Bishop, however duly consecrated, into the See of another, with a view to the usurpation of his name and office, and to the organizing a systematic opposition to his authority. We are compelled therefore to regard those who are ordained, as Popish Priests are, by these intruding Bishops, as unauthorized and schismatical ministers of religion, and as violators, like the other dissenters around them, of the laws of CHRIST'S Church, and of the unity of His fold.

J.—I thank you, Sir, for giving me so good an answer to Sam when next I meet him. And I thank you too, deeply and sincerely do I thank you, for teaching me the nature of one great branch of Christian duty which I never understood before. I seem now to see that there is a sin of which a Christian may be guilty, of which I never before thought; the sin, I mean, of refusing obedience to the command of our REDEEMER to hear His Apostles; to demean ourselves as dutiful members of the Church which those holy persons founded, and over which He Himself, invisibly, presides; a sin, of which they are deeply guilty who separate themselves from that Church altogether, and join one or other of the many sects which reject her authority. Pray, Sir, by what name is such a sin properly called?

Dr.—It is called "schism," from a Greek word signifying "division." A man may forfeit the privileges enjoyed by him as a member of CHRIST'S Church in two ways:—either on account of "heresy," of his adopting opinions opposed to the great truths of the Word of GOD; or through schism, through a disregard of Church authority, and a notion that so long as his doctrine is pure, he may join what sect he pleases, or even set up one for himself. The exercise of such a privilege I have heard some people call "Christian Liberty."

J. (smiling.)—I understand you, Sir; but you shall hear me use the word in this improper sense no more. The true liberty, wherewith CHRIST has made us free, is theirs alone, who, in reverencing His ministers, walk in the way of His commandments. Admitting, as I now do, the force of what you have said; convinced, as I now am, that the Church of England is the Apostolic Church of CHRIST, established by our LORD Himself, I cannot but see that their sin is indeed great, who wilfully reject and despise it.

Dr.—Such persons would do well to consider our SAVIOUR'S words to those Ministers whose successors they slight. "He that despiseth you, despiseth Me; and he that despiseth Me, despiseth Him that sent me" (Luke 10:16).

J.—They would indeed, Sir; and I thank God that you have shown me the meaning of this text before I had completely separated myself from the Church to which my SAVIOUR has commanded me to belong. GOD knows, I meant to do no such thing when first my curiosity led me to the meeting.

Dr.—I know it, John; but let this show you the danger of making the first step, of yielding to the first temptation. Curiosity led you to a place, to which, if you understood your duty, you had no business to go; you were pleased, and tempted to repeat your visit, and might soon have been led to unite yourself entirely to that unauthorized congregation; in defiance, as I have now shown you, of the solemnly declared will of the ALMIGHTY.

J.—Well, Sir; I will, by GOD'S blessing, keep myself from such temptations for the future. I trust that on each succeeding Sunday, while life and health are spared me, I shall be found in my old accustomed seat at Church, and kneel in the sacred spot where my forefathers knelt before me; and GOD grant that no temptation may ever again lead me astray, or induce me to separate from the holy Church of my REDEEMER.

Dr.—It gives me, John, the sincerest pleasure to hear you express such sentiments as these. One good effect will, through GOD'S grace, result even from this your temporary wandering from the fold. You will now know better than you did what we mean when in the words of our Liturgy we pray for "the good estate of the Catholic Church;" and you will be enabled, I trust, to join more fully than heretofore in the beautiful prayer, "that it may be so guided and governed by GOD'S good SPIRIT, that all who profess and call themselves Christians may be led into the way of truth, and hold the faith in unity of spirit, in the bond of peace, and in righteousness of life."

J.—I hope, Sir, that I shall; I hope that I shall ever feel duly thankful for the blessing of being called into CHRIST'S Church, thus happily established among us; and I trust that when in the name of the congregation you put up the prayer for protection against "false doctrine, heresy, and *schism*," my heart and soul may accompany my lips in the response,—"Good Lord, deliver us!"

JOHN WILLIAM BOWDEN
March 25, 1834
The Feast of the Annunciation

TRACT 31: AD CLERUM
The Reformed Church

> *All the people shouted with a great shout, when they praised the Lord, because the foundation of the House of the Lord was laid. But many of the Priests and Levites, and chief of the fathers, who were ancient men that had seen the first House, when the foundation of this House was laid before their eyes, wept with a loud voice.*
> —EZRA 3:11-12

Some remarks may, perhaps, be profitably made on the following well known lines in Herbert's Church Militant, in which the text above quoted is applied to our own period:

> The second Temple could not reach the first,
> And the late Reformation never durst
> Compare with ancient times and purer years,
> But in the Jews and us, deserveth tears.
> Nay, it shall every year decrease and fade,
> Till such a darkness shall the world invade
> At CHRIST'S last coming, as His first did find;
> Yet must their proportions be assigned
> To these diminishings, as is between
> The spacious world and Jewry to be seen.

Surely there is a close analogy between the state of the Jews after the captivity, and our own; and, if so, a clear understanding and acknowledgment of it will tend to teach us our own place, and suggest to us our prospects.

    1. It is scarcely necessary to notice the general correspondence between the fortunes of the two Churches. Both Jews and Christians "left their first love," mixed with the world, were brought under the power of their enemies, went into captivity, and at length, through God's mercy, were brought back again from Babylon. Ezra and Nehemiah are the forerunners of our Ridleys and Lauds; Sanballat and Geshem of the disturbers of our Israel. Samaria has set up its rival temple among us.

2. The second Temple lacked the peculiar treasures of the Temple of Solomon, the Prince of Peace; such as the Ark, the visible glory of GOD, the tables of the Covenant, Aaron's rod, the manna, the oracle. In like manner the Christian Church was, in the beginning, set up in unity; unity of doctrine, or *truth,* unity of discipline, or *catholicism,* unity of heart, or *charity*. In spite of the heresies which then disturbed the repose of Christians, consider the evidences which present themselves in ecclesiastical history of their firm endurance of persecution, their tender regard for the members of Christ, however widely removed by place and language, their self-denying liberality in supplying their wants, the close correspondence of all parts of the body Catholic, as though it were but one family, their profound reverential spirit towards sacred things, the majesty of their religious services, and the noble strictness of their life and conversation. Here we see the "Rod" of the Priesthood, budding forth with fresh life; the "Manna" of the Christian ordinances uncorrupted; the "Oracle" of Tradition fresh from the breasts of the Apostles; the "Law," written in its purity on "the fleshly tables of the heart;" the "Shechinah," which a multitude of Martyrs, Saints, Confessors, and gifted Teachers, poured throughout the Temple. But where is our unity now? our ministrations of self-denying love? our prodigality of pious and charitable works? our resolute resistance of evil? We are reformed; we have come out of Babylon, and have rebuilt our Church; but it is Ichabod; "the glory is departed from Israel."

3. The Jewish polity was, on its restoration, so secularized, that the vestiges of a Theocracy scarcely remained in the eyes of any but attentive believers. That it really existed as before, is plain from the prophetic gift possessed by Caiaphas, wicked man as he was. Consider the anomaly of the political relation of the Jews towards the Ptolemies and Seleucidæ, their alliance with Rome, their dispersion over the Roman Empire, their disuse of certain of the Mosaic ordinances, the cruelties and blasphemies of Antiochus, the reign of Herod, and his virtual re-building of the Temple, a remarkable omen as regards ourselves. Turn to the restored Christian Church, and reflect upon the perplexed questions concerning the union of Church and State, to which the politics of the last three centuries have given rise; the tyrannical encroachments of the civil power at various eras; the profanations at the time of the Great Rebellion; the deliberate impiety of the French Revolution; and the present apparent

breaking up of Ecclesiastical Polity everywhere, the innumerable schisms, the mixture of men of different creeds and sects, and the contempt poured upon any show of Apostolical zeal.

4. Consider the following passages from the Prophets, after the Captivity, and see if they do not apply to present times.

Haggai 1:4-10: "Is it time for you, O ye, to dwell in your ceiled houses, and this house lie waste? Now therefore thus saith the LORD of Hosts, Consider your ways. Ye have *sown much*, and *bring in little;* ye eat, but ye have not enough; ye drink, but ye are not filled with drink; ye clothe you, but there is none warm; and he that earneth wages, *earneth wages to put it into a bag with holes,*" &c.

Malachi 1:6-13: "A son honoureth his father, and a servant his master; if then I be a Father, where is Mine honour? and if I be a Master, where is My fear? .... Ye say, The *table of the Lord is polluted*, and *the fruit thereof, even His meat, contemptible.* Ye say also, Behold what a *weariness* is it, ... and *ye brought that which was torn, and the lame, and the sick;* thus ye brought an offering; should I accept this of your hands, saith the LORD?"

Malachi 2:1-9: "And now, O ye Priests, this commandment is for you ... And ye shall know that I have sent this commandment unto you, that My covenant might be with Levi, saith the LORD of Hosts. My covenant was with him of life and peace, and I gave them to him, for the fear wherewith he feared Me, and was afraid before My Name. The Law of Truth was in his mouth, and iniquity was not found in his lips; he walked with Me in peace and equity, and did turn many away from iniquity. For the Priest's lips should keep knowledge, and they shall seek the Law at his mouth; for he is the messenger of the LORD of Hosts. *But ye are departed out of the way;* ye have caused many to stumble at the Law; *ye have corrupted the covenant of Levi,* saith the LORD of Hosts. *Therefore have I also made you contemptible and base before all the people.*" Does not the history of the times of Hoadley and such as he, and our present trials throw light upon the parallel?

Malachi 3: 8-9: "Will a man rob GOD? yet ye have robbed Me; but ye say, Wherein have we robbed Thee? *in tithes and offerings. Ye are cursed with a curse;* for ye have robbed Me, even this whole nation."

5. It is remarkable that, while the reinstated Jewish Church was so deficient in zeal, piety, and consistent obedience, and was punished by

failure and disorganization; yet it never fell into those gross and flagrant offences, which were the opprobrium of its earlier period. *It was clear of the sin of idolatry.*

6. Moreover consider the *parties*, unknown to the era of the Theocracy, which divided the Church after the captivity; the Pharisees, Sadducees, and the rest; the necessary consequence of a relaxation of the original principle of national union. The case is the same in this day; as if the Church were already dead, new forms of organization, multiplied varieties of life and action, show themselves within her.

7. Lastly. The following texts suggest hope to all true Christians. Haggai 2:5-9: "*According to the word that I covenanted with you, when ye came out of Egypt,* so MY SPIRIT REMAINETH AMONG YOU: fear ye not." He will be with us even in this base and grovelling age, as with St. Paul, St. Cyprian, and St. Athanasius.

> "Thou wilt; for Thou art Israel's GOD;
> And thine unwearied arm
> *Is ready yet* with Moses' rod," &c.

"The glory of this latter house SHALL BE GREATER THAN OF THE FORMER, saith the LORD of Hosts."

Strange it now seems before the event, how the Church should close both with glory and yet in unbelief; yet surely, as in the history of Jerusalem, so now both predictions will be at once fulfilled. "The day cometh that shall burn as an oven, and *all the proud,* yea, and *all who do wickedly, shall be stubble:* but *unto you that fear My name shall the Sun of Righteousness arise with healing in His wings"* (Mal 4:1-2).

And let it be remembered, that when our Lord seems at greatest distance from His Church, then He is even at the doors. Doubtless, when the Angel appeared in the Temple to Zacharias, the news of a miraculous interposition was as great a marvel to the world at large as if it were now noised abroad of one of our own Ministers in the course of his Christian Service.

JOHN HENRY NEWMAN
The Feast of St. Mark
April 25, 1834

TRACT 32: AD CLERUM
The Standing Ordinances of Religion

Most of us, perhaps, will find, upon examination, that we do not feel and act, as the Apostles and the early Church felt and acted, with regard to the Ordinances of our Religion. The reader is entreated to give this suggestion a *fair* consideration; not to hurry on, nor turn away from the recollection, that we shall all one day be judged, not merely by what we actually knew, but by what we *might* have known, respecting our duties to CHRIST and His Church. Let him consider, whether his own reason, and the Holy Scriptures, which were expressly written in order that we might possess full religious knowledge, do not say more on this subject than he has yet duly weighed and acted upon.

First, consider what *Reason* says; which surely, as well as Scripture, was given us for *religious* ends.

1. Can you possibly imagine any better method of *perpetuating doctrines*, than by ordinances, which live on like monuments? Consider, for instance, what is implied in Christian Salvation; remember whose property and subjects we are when we come into the world; and then endeavour, if you can, to estimate the value of those two Blessed Ordinances, which are the standing and definite publication, to every one of us, to our fathers, and our children, of the infinite mercies of GOD, as manifested in the Covenant of the Gospel. E.g. a generation of ungodly men (suppose) rise up and possess the earth; Satan, through their means, corrupts all that he can, in the world; but meantime, *something* is living

on, in the very midst of them, independent of the variable opinions of the human mind; something, which they cannot spoil, and which, after they are gone to their account, and all their wretched folly has spent itself upon their own head, will come forth pure and unsullied, full of sweetness and edifying comfort to the remnant which shall then rise up, who will feed upon it by faith, and form anew the living temple of the Holy Ghost, in their generation. Thus the consecrated Form of Religion will be like some fair statue, which lies buried for ages, but comes forth at length as beautiful as ever; they will be furnished with all requisites for teaching us those lessons, which the preceding age has been engaged in obliterating.

2. If it be true that our weak and carnal minds do not readily dwell upon, nor comprehend, spiritual things by themselves, can we conceive any thing more precious to us on earth, than the outward forms which GOD Himself has appointed to arrest our attention, to embody unseen realities, to serve as a kind of ladder between earth and heaven, between our spirit and the Spirit of Holiness? It is much to our purpose to observe, that Almighty God Himself directly declares that this is His design, in the institution of Forms and Ordinances. And the consideration of such passages of Scripture may perhaps set us on asking ourselves whether we can be really desiring the *end*, if we find ourselves at all irregular in seeking the means which He has appointed. (Vide Exod 12:26, 13:5-10 and 11-16; Lev 23:43; Josh 4:1-7.)

3. Further, religious ordinances are, to the consciences of individuals, a *recurring testimony against sin*. Can we conceive any thing more precious in an ungodly world, in the perverse world of our own heart? Dare we then suffer to decay, and go to nought, the means which GOD has provided for calling sinners to repentance, and even the best men to self-examination? Shall we suffer ourselves to think and speak lightly of them, and neglect to defend them when they are attacked? To remove a barrier against error, is in its measure to encourage and tempt men to it; and comes under the denunciation pronounced by our Blessed Lord, "Woe unto him through whom offences come; it were better for him that a millstone were hanged about his neck, and he cast into the sea, than that he should make to stumble one of these little ones" (Luke 17:1, 2).

Just the same care did GOD take of His peculiar people of old. "Write ye this song for you, and teach it the children of Israel; put it in their mouths, that *this song may be a witness for Me against the children of*

Israel. For when I shall have brought them into the land which I sware unto their fathers, that floweth with milk and honey, and they shall have eaten and filled themselves, and waxed fat; then will they turn unto other gods, and serve them, and provoke Me, and break My covenant. And it shall come to pass, when many evils and troubles are befallen them, that *this song shall testify against them as a witness;* for it shall not be forgotten out of the mouths of their seed" (Deut 31:19-21).

"Which of you," says Hooker, "receiveth a guest whom he honoureth, and whom he loveth, and *doth not sweep his chamber against his coming?* And shall we suffer the chambers of our hearts and consciences to lie full of vomiting, full of filth, full of garbage, knowing that Christ hath said, 'I and My Father will come and dwell with you?' ... Blessed and praised for ever and ever be His Name, who, perceiving of how senseless and heavy metal we are made, hath instituted in His Church a Spiritual Supper, and an Holy Communion, *to be celebrated often*, that we might thereby be occasioned often to examine these buildings of ours, in what case they stand. For sith God doth not dwell in temples which are unclean; sith a shrine cannot be a sanctuary to Him; and this Supper is received as a seal unto us, that we are His house and His sanctuary; that His Christ is as truly united unto me, and I to Him, as my arm is united and knit unto my shoulder; that He dwelleth in me as verily as the elements of bread and wine abide within me; which persuasion, by receiving these dreadful mysteries, we profess ourselves to have; a due comfort, if truly; and if in hypocrisy, then woe with us."

4. These arguments, in behalf of the duty of keeping to the Standing Ordinances of Religion, are strengthened by the consideration of the peculiar influence which old and familiar institutions exert over the affections. If Christianity were left to select and reject its ordinances, as one age succeeded to another, there would be no safeguard for the permanence and identity of the religious temper itself. God indeed might invisibly preserve it; but so He might (did He so choose) without ordinances of any kind. But, since He has vouchsafed to employ them, it is but judging according to the revealed course of His Providence, to say, that His purpose is more fully answered by their being of a standing than of a variable nature. Thus we find an argument from the reason of the case, for rigidly adhering to those which have been transmitted to us.

5. Consider for one moment what becomes of any of us, if we be not blest and supported with the Divine Grace; and then consider through what channels it is most *natural to expect*, and *safest to seek* this Grace: whether through *Standing* Ordinances, those to which the Church has ever had recourse as appointed by CHRIST and His Apostles, or those which we follow without inquiry as to their antiquity or acceptableness. The analogy of former dispensations leads us to the same conclusion. Abraham at Hebron seeks a sign (Gen 15:8, 9); Almighty GOD refers him to the *usual* ordinance of worship, sacrifice, and *therein* sends him a sign. So again, He might have revealed Himself to Moses in any place; but if Moses would find Him, it must be *in the Tabernacle*. Cornelius *prayed* and *fasted*, certainly not expecting a supernatural vision; but one was sent him, with the message of salvation. On the other hand, it is the peculiarity of false prophets and unsound teachers to seek *change* and *novelty* in the rites with which they approach GOD. "When Balaam saw that it pleased the LORD to bless Israel, he went not *as at other times* to seek for enchantments, but he set his face towards the wilderness" (Num 14:1). Accordingly he is obliged to speak with a wavering belief: "*Peradventure* the LORD will come to meet me."

So much for what *Reason* suggests to us. Now let us observe what GOD Himself has directly told us in *Scripture* concerning Standing Religious Ordinances.

1. He *positively* enjoins them. Turn to the Jewish ceremonies, and remember that they were,—(1.) Often unintelligible in their full import, yet positively enjoined, even on pain of death. E.g. Circumcision (Gen 17:14), the Passover (Exod 12:15; Num 9:13). And remember that our faith and obedience are chiefly tried in things not understood, as, for instance, in the prohibition of the tree of knowledge. (2.) They were afterwards found to be significant. See the Epistle to the Hebrews throughout. Just as wise teachers store the minds of children with things which they will not fully understand till a future day, so does our Divine Master admit us to the Symbols of that eternal worship and service of Him, which shall constitute the blessedness of the next life, a blessedness which it hath not entered into man's heart to conceive. (3.) The ordinances of the Christian Church are held in such high honour, that even to those whom He had first enriched with His miraculous gift, it was yet a farther and indispensable blessing to receive a solemn admission into

her sacred mysteries. Mark, for instance, St. Peter's converts, Acts 10:44-48. They had received the HOLY GHOST, and spake with other tongues: "Then answered Peter, Can any man forbid water, that these should not be baptized, which have received the HOLY GHOST as well as we? And he commanded them to be baptized in the name of the LORD." Vide also Acts 13:2, 3.

2. GOD provided that the Jews should be *able* to keep His ordinances; rather interrupting the course of nature, and controlling the feelings of whole nations, than that the ordinances of His service should be set aside on a single occasion. If He commands the observance of the Sabbath in the wilderness, He provides for the people a double store of manna on the day before, and miraculously preserves it from corruption (Exod 16:5, 24). If He directs that the land be allowed to lie fallow every seventh year, He sends a triple harvest in the sixth year (Lev 25:21). If He enjoins all the males to leave their homes, and appear before Him thrice in the year, He suspends all the jealous and hostile feelings of the neighbouring nations, and promises that they should not even "desire" the land of the Israelites (Exod 34:24).

3. We cannot dare to conjecture *how much evil may come from neglecting* positive ordinances. King Saul departed from the express command of God, respecting the way in which sacrifice should be made to Him. He could even make a plausible excuse for what he did; but turn to 1 Samuel 13:13, and see what it drew down upon him: "Thou hast done foolishly; thou hast not kept the commandment of the LORD thy GOD which He commanded thee; for now would the LORD have established thy kingdom upon Israel for ever. But now thy kingdom shall not continue; the LORD hath sought Him a man after His own heart, and the Lord hath commanded Him to be captain over His people, because thou hast not kept that which the LORD commanded thee." Think again of Nadab and Abihu; they did not *neglect* the worship of GOD; but they thought they might surely take the fire for the sacrifice from whence they would; "surely this was a *minor* point," as some among us are presumptuous enough to say. But He who gave laws to them and us, knows nothing of minor points. There can be no little sin, for there is no little authority to sin against. Nadab and Abihu were struck dead for offering with strange fire. This is agreeable to the analogy of the physical world, which is open to our senses. It is a simple and apparently harmless

thing to place a candle near gunpowder, or to bring certain gases together; but the result may cost us our life.

4. Such was the importance of observing positive ordinances in the Jewish Church. Surely the lesson delivered in the Old Testament is intended for us Christians. We have the same unchanging Father, who was the GOD of Israel, and who has given us the Scriptures that we may have the means of searching out His will. First consider the light in which He views in the law of Moses what we are apt to call "minor points." "Therefore shall ye abide at the door of the Tabernacle of the Congregation day and night, seven days, and keep the charge of the Lord, *that ye die not*" (Lev 8:35). After the death of Nadab and Abihu, the charge is given "unto Aaron, and unto Eleazar and Ithamar, his sons, uncover not your heads, neither rend your clothes, lest *ye die*, and lest *wrath come upon all the people*" (Lev 10:6). "Do not drink wine nor strong drink, thou nor thy sons with thee, when ye go into the Tabernacle of the Congregation, *lest ye die*" (Ibid.).

This was the uniform tone of the Divine Guardian of the Church then. Is the duty less urgent now? when, (1.) the added claim on our gratitude is all that the New Testament tells us: (2.) The Ordinances are so much fewer, and therefore, first, the *trouble* of them is so incomparably diminished; next, the *preciousness* of them (humanly speaking) so much more strikingly seen: they are the only jewels of this sort that we have left.

5. Remark may be made upon the very circumstance, that, in the Christian Covenant, Standing Ordinances are made the channels of its peculiar blessings. The first use of Ordinances is that of witnessing for the Truth, as above mentioned. Now their *sacramental* character is perfectly distinct from this, and is doubtless a great honour put on them. Had we been left to conjecture, we might have supposed, that in the more perfect or spiritual system, the gifts of grace would rather have been attached to certain high *moral* performances; whereas they are deposited in mere positive ordinances, as if to warn us against dropping the ceremonial of Christianity.

This last observation leads to the brief notice of an objection sometimes brought against the necessity of a Christian's attention to Ordinances, grounded on the notion of the *spiritual character* of Christianity. Now,—1. Are we quite sure that *we* are more spiritual, and more independent of the external helps of the Church, than Samuel,—

Hezekiah,—Josiah,—and Daniel?—2. What does our own experience say? Do we see the best and holiest of men becoming most independent and regardless of them, or the very reverse? 3. Are the feelings of love, affection, reverence, tender remembrance, which are entertained towards such places and things as are associated in our minds with the persons who are the primary objects of these feelings, *inconsistent* with spiritual-mindedness? Are not the Ordinances which Christ and His Apostles have appointed, the *bond of perpetuated unity* to the Church, a precious and mysterious medium for the "Communion of Saints" in all countries and ages? No one among us would think it a mark of weakness to cherish with attachment and respect a Bible which his father had used for half a century, from which he had learned the words of life and the way of salvation. And is it not a soothing and elevating privilege, to feel that we, even at this distant day, are allowed to come and walk in the very steps of all the holy men of old, the glorious company of the Apostles, and the noble army of martyrs, to take that narrow path, whose farther end they have now found to be in heaven? In walking over the very ground where the holy Apostles lived and walked as Bishops, or in following our LORD Himself into Gethsemane, along the beach of the sea of Gennesareth, or in pausing with Him on the Mount Olivet, as He weeps over Jerusalem, we find ourselves moved with something too deep and touching for words, and almost for thought; and is it no privilege, no blessing, to *think* with Him, to have our spirit admitted to move in the same path which His Holy Spirit has chosen; to be consecrated with Him and to Him in the water of Baptism, to eat the Holy Supper with Him, to fast with Him, to pray with Him in the very form and very thoughts which flowed from His divine mind and lips?

If these things are so, how can we hold up our heads, and dare to think of the way in which we have handled His Ordinances, handled that *Form* in which He has deigned to live on in the world, and to move before the eyes of His Church! If we can recollect the moment when we have been so dead in heart as to have found ourselves considering, not how often our Saviour would let us come and hold communion with Him, but how few times would satisfy Him,—whether "this one" omission would draw down His displeasure,—if there be one of us who lives in this spirit, "how dwelleth the love of God in him?"

Once more, if, when all times, all places, all forms, are in themselves alike, yet it has pleased the High and Lofty One that inhabiteth eternity, whose Name is Holy, to choose to Himself certain forms, places, and times, for His especial dwelling upon earth,—with what reverend and solemn feelings should we go to meet Him there, and approach His altar with our gift! We read that the GOD of Israel would admit no blemished creature to be sacrificed to Him (Lev 22:18, 25); nor will He now accept the offering of our hearts unless we cleanse ourselves from all unbelief, insincerity, and guile: "wash our hands in innocency, and so go to His altar."

CHARLES PAGE EDEN
The Feast of St. Mark
April 25, 1834

TRACT 33: AD SCHOLAS
Primitive Episcopacy

The first step towards evangelizing a heathen country in the early times, seems to have been to seize upon some principal city in it as a centre of operation; to place a Pastor, *i.e.*, a Bishop there; to surround him with a sufficient number of associates and assistants; and then to wait, till, under the blessing of GOD, this Missionary College was enabled to gather around it the scattered children of grace from the evil world, and invest itself with the shape and influence of an organized Church. The converts would, in the first instance, be naturally attracted to the immediate vicinity of the Missionary or Bishop, whose diocese, nevertheless, would extend indefinitely over the heathen country on every side, his mission being without restriction to all to whom CHRIST had never been preached. As he prospered in the increase of his flock, and sent out his clergy to greater and greater distances from the city, so would the homestead (so to call it) of the Church enlarge; other towns would be brought under his government, till at length he would find "the burden too heavy for him," and would appoint other Pastors to supply his place in this or that part of his diocese. To these he would commit a greater or lesser share of his spiritual power, as might be necessary; sometimes he would make them fully his representatives, or ordain them Bishops; at other times he would employ presbyters for his purpose. These assistants, or (as they were called) Chorepiscopi, would naturally be confined to their respective districts; and if Bishops, an approximation would evidently be made to a division of the large original diocese into a number of smaller ones connected with and subordinate to the Bishop of the metropolitan city. Thus, from the very Missionary character of the Primitive Church, there was a tendency in its polity to what was afterwards called the Provincial and Patriarchal system.

It is not, indeed, to be supposed that this was the only way in which the graduated order of sees (so to call it) originated; but, at least, it is one way. And there is this advantage in remarking it: we learn from it, that large dioceses are the characteristics of a Church in its infancy or weakness; whereas, the more firmly Christianity was rooted in a country, and the more vigorous its rulers, the more diligently were its sees multiplied throughout the ecclesiastical territory. Thus, St. Basil, in the fourth century, finding his exarchate defenceless in the neighbourhood of Mount Taurus, created a number of dioceses to meet the emergency. These subordinate sees may be called suffragan to the Metropolitan Church, whether their respective rulers were mere representatives of the Bishop who created them, *i.e.*, Chorepiscopi; or, on the other hand, substantive authorities, sovereign within their own limits, though bound by external ties to each other and to their Metropolitan. The most perfect state of a Christian country would be, that of a sufficient number of separate dioceses; the next to it, the system of Chorepiscopi, or Suffragan Bishops in the modern sense of the word.

Few persons, who have not expressly examined the subject, are aware of the minuteness of the dioceses into which many parts of Christendom were divided in the first ages. Some Churches in Italy were more like our rural deaneries than what we now consider dioceses; being not above ten or twelve miles in extent, and their sees not above five or six miles from each other. Even now (or, at least, in Bingham's time), the kingdom of Naples contains 147 sees, of which twenty are Archbishopricks. Asia Minor is 630 miles long, 210 broad; yet in this country there were almost 400 dioceses. Palestine is in length 160 miles, in breadth 120; yet the number of known dioceses amounted to 48. Again, in the province of Syria Secunda, the see of Larissa (*e.g.*) was about 14 miles from Apamea, Arethusa 16 from Epiphania. And so, again, in the West, though the dioceses were generally larger, as partaking more of a Missionary character, yet in Ireland there were at one time from 50 to 60 sees.

Such was the character of the Primitive Regimen, where Christianity especially flourished in the zeal and number of its professors. But, where the country was mountainous or desert, the inhabitants scanty, or but partially Christian, it was considered advisable to leave all to the management of one chief Pastor, who appointed assistants to himself according to his discretion, as the circumstances of the times required. The office of these Chorepiscopi, or country Bishops, was to preside over the country clergy, inquire into their behaviour, and report to their principal; also to provide fit persons for the inferior ministrations of the Church. They had the power of ordaining the lower ranks of clergy, such as the readers, subdeacons, and exorcists; they might ordain priests and deacons with the leave of the city Bishop, and administer the rite of confirmation; and were permitted to sit and vote in synods and councils. Thus their office bore a considerable resemblance to that of our Archdeacons; except, of course, that they had the power of ordination; whereas the latter are but presbyters. And, in matter of fact, by such presbyters (*visitors*, as they were called), they were superseded in the course of the fourth and following centuries, till at length the Pope caused the order to be set aside almost altogether in the ninth.

Little use was made of Suffragans during the middle ages; but, at the time of our Reformation, Archbishop Cranmer felt the deficiency of the English Church in respect of Bishopricks, and projected several measures to supply it. The most complete was that of increasing the number of dioceses; availing himself of existing circumstances, he advised the King to apply the Abbey lands to the founding of twenty additional sees. Bishop Burnet gives some of the particulars of this attempt in the following passage:—

"On the 23rd of May, in the session of Parliament, a bill was brought in by Cromwell for giving the king power to erect new bishopricks by his letters-patent.[1] It was read that day for the first, second, and third time; and sent down to the Commons. The preamble of it was, 'that it was known what slothful and ungodly life had been led by those who were called religious. But that these houses might be converted to better uses; that GOD'S word might be better set forth; children brought

---

[1] It is scarcely necessary to observe, that parliament was then the lay synod of the Church of England.

up in learning; clerks nourished in the universities; and that old decayed servants might have livings; poor people might have almshouses to maintain them; readers of Greek, Hebrew, and Latin, might have good stipends; daily alms might be administered, and allowance might be made for mending of the highways, and exhibitions for ministers of the Church; for these ends, if the king thought fit to have more bishopricks or cathedral churches erected out of the rents of these houses, full power was given him to erect and found them, and to make rules and statutes for them, and such translations of sees, or divisions of them, as he thought fit.' In the same paper, there is a list of the sees which he intended to found; of which what was done afterwards came so far short, that I know nothing to which it can be so reasonably imputed, as the declining of Cranmer's interest at court, who had proposed the erecting the new cathedrals and sees, with other things mentioned in the preamble of the statute, as a great mean of reforming the Church."[2] Some of the proposed additional dioceses are then enumerated; Essex, Hertford, Bedfordshire and Buckinghamshire, Oxford and Berkshire, Northampton and Huntingdon, Middlesex, Leicester and Rutland, Gloucestershire, Lancashire, Suffolk, Stafford and Salop, Nottingham and Derby, Cornwall. As to the means by which they were to be endowed, no opinion is here expressed on its lawfulness, as the present sketch is confined to the consideration of the spiritual part of the ecclesiastical system. It is scarcely necessary to add, that Cranmer's views were partly realised, in the subsequent creation of the dioceses of Chester, Bristol, Glocester, Oxford, and Peterborough.

The same prelate, whose episcopate has had so important an influence upon the constitution of our Church ever since, also projected with great wisdom, a system of suffragan bishops or Chorepiscopi, which he was able to bring into effect, and which lasted till the reign of King James. Twenty-six such bishops were appointed; the bishop of the diocese having the power of presenting two persons to the king, who might choose either of them, and present him to the archbishop of the province for consecration. These suffragans exercised such jurisdiction as their principal gave them, or as had formerly been committed to suffragans; their authority lasting no longer than he continued their commission to them. "These were believed," says Burnet, "to be the same with the Chorepiscopi in the

---

[2] Burnet, Hist. Reform. iii.

primitive church; which, as they were begun before the first council of Nice, so they continued in the Western Church till the 9th century, and then a decretal of Damasus being forged, that condemned them, they were put down every where by degrees, and now revived in England. The suffragan sees were as follows; Thetford, Ipswich, Colchester, Dover, Guilford, Southampton, Taunton, Shaftsbury, Molton, Marlborough, Bedford, Leicester, Gloucester, Shrewsbury, Bristol, Penrith, Bridgwater, Nottingham, Grantham, Hull, Huntingdon, Cambridge, Pereth, Berwick, St. Germain's, and the Isle of Wight."[3]

After the disuse of suffragans in the reign of James I there was a fresh project for establishing them on the Restoration. Charles, in one of his declarations, promises to increase the number of bishops, in accordance with Archbishop Usher's plan for episcopal government. However, his intention was not put into execution, doubtless owing to existing circumstances, which reasonably interfered with it.

The following extract is made from Bingham, Antiqu. ix. 8. "One great objection against the present diocesan episcopacy, and that which to many may look the most plausible, is drawn from the vast extent and greatness of most of the northern dioceses of the world, which makes it so extremely difficult for one man to discharge all the offices of the episcopal function . . . . . . The Church England has usually followed the larger model, and had very great and extensive dioceses; for at first she had but seven bishopricks in the whole nation, and those commensurate in a manner to the seven Saxon kingdoms. Since that time she has thought it a point of wisdom to contract her dioceses, and multiply them into above 20; and if she should think fit to add 40 or 100 more, she would not be without precedent in the practice of the Primitive Church . . . . In Ireland, there are not now above half the number of dioceses that there were before, and consequently they must needs be larger by uniting them together. In England, there are more in number than formerly, some new ones being created out of old ones, and at present, the whole number augmented to three times as many as they were for some ages after the first conversion. Besides that, we have another way of contracting dioceses in effect here in England appointed by law, which law was never yet repealed; which is by devolving part of the bishop's care upon the Chorepiscopi, or

---

[3] Hist. Reform. ii.

suffragan bishops, as the law calls them:—a method commonly practised in the ancient Church in such large dioceses as those of St. Basil and Theodoret, one of which had no less than fifty Chorepiscopi under him, if Nazianzen rightly informs us. And it is a practice, which was continued here all the reign of Queen Elizabeth, and even to the end of King James; and is what may be revived again, whenever any bishop thinks his diocese too large, or his burden too great to be sustained by himself alone."

To the above statements, may be subjoined the present number of souls, and the area of square miles, in certain of our dioceses, as given in a pamphlet lately published, which has come into the writer's hands since the foregoing was put on paper. (Vide Plan for a New Arrangement, &c. by Lord Henley.)

	Souls.	Square Miles.
Chester	1,806,722	4140
London	1,676,725	1942
York	1,526,288	5300
Lincoln	920,011	5775
Lichfield	978,655	3344

By this table, it is not here intended to insinuate the necessity of any immediate measure of multiplying the English sees or appointing suffragans (the expediency of which is to be determined by a variety of considerations, which it were unprofitable here to detail), but to show that the *genius* of our ecclesiastical system tends towards such an increase, and that it is but a question of time which has to be determined. These statements are also made with a view of keeping up in the minds of churchmen a recollection of the injury, which the Irish branch of our Church has lately sustained in the diminution of its sees.

JOHN HENRY NEWMAN
The Feast of St. Philip and St. James
May 1, 1834

TRACT 34: AD SCHOLAS
Rites and Customs of the Church

> Ὁ μὲν οὖν πιστὸς, ὡς χρὴ, καὶ ἐρρωμένος οὐδὲ δεῖται λόγου καὶ αἰτίας, ὑπὲρ ὧν ἂν ἐπιταχθῇ, ἀλλ' ἀρκεῖται τῇ παραδόσει μόνῃ.
>
> He who is duly strengthened in faith, does not go so far as to require reason and cause, for what is enjoined, but is satisfied with the *tradition* alone.
> —ST. JOHN CHRYSOSTOM,
> HOMILY 26 ON 1 CORINTHIANS

The reader of ecclesiastical history is sometimes surprised at finding observances and customs generally received in the Church at an early date, which have not express warrant in the Apostolic writings; *e.g.* the use of the cross in baptism. The following pages will be directed to the consideration of this circumstance; with a view of suggesting from those writings themselves, that a minute ritual was contemporaneous with them, that the Apostles recognize it as existing and binding, that it was founded on religious *principles*, and tended to the inculcation of religious truth. Not that any formal proof is attainable or conceivable, considering the brevity and subjects of the inspired documents; but such fair evidence of the fact, as may recommend it to the belief of the earnest and single-minded Christian. It is abundantly evident that the Epistles were not written to prescribe and enforce the ritual of religion; all then we can expect, if it existed in the days of the Apostles, is an occasional allusion to it in their Epistles as existing, and a plain acquiescence in it: and thus much we find.

Let us consider that remarkable passage, 1 Corinthians 11:2-16, which, I am persuaded, most readers pass over as if they could get little instruction from it. St. Paul is therein blaming the Corinthians for not adhering to the *custom* of the Church, which prescribed that men should wear their hair short, and that women should have their head covered during divine service; a custom apparently most unimportant, if any one ever was, but in his view strictly binding on Christians. He begins by implying that it is one out of many rules or traditions (παραδόσεις) which he had given them, and they were bound to keep. He ends by refusing to argue with any one who obstinately cavils at it and rejects it: "If any man seem to be contentious, we have no such custom, neither the churches of GOD." Here then at once a view is opened to us which is quite sufficient to remove the surprise we might otherwise feel at the multitude of rites, which were in use in the Primitive Church, but about which the New Testament is silent; and further, to command our obedience to such as come down to us from the first ages, and are agreeable to Scripture.

In accordance with this conclusion, is the clear and forcible command given by the Apostle, "Brethren, stand fast, and hold the traditions which ye have been taught, whether *by word*, or our epistle" (2 Thess 2:15).

To return. St. Paul goes on to give the *reason* of the usage, for the satisfaction of the weak brethren at Corinth. It was, he implies, a symbol or development (so to say) of the principle of the subordination of the woman to the man, and a memorial of the history of our creation; nay, it was founded in "*nature*," *i.e.* natural reason. And lastly, it had a practical object; the woman ought to have her head covered "*because* of the angels." We need not stop to inquire *what* this reason was; but it was a reason of a practical nature which the Corinthians understood, though we may not. If it mean, as is probable, "because she is in the sight of the heavenly angels" (1 Tim 5:21), it gives a still greater importance to the ceremonies of worship, as connecting them with the unseen world.

It would seem indeed as if the very multiplicity of the details of the Church ritual made it plainly impossible for St. Paul to write them all down, or to do more than *remind* the Corinthians of his way of conducting religious order when he was among them. "Be ye *followers* of me," he says, "I praise you that *ye remember me* in all things" (1 Cor 11:1-2). It is evident there are ten thousand little points in the working of any large system, which a present instructor alone can settle. Hence it is customary at present, when a school is set up, or any novel manufacture in trade, or extraordinary machinery is to be brought into use, to set it going by sending a person fully skilled in its practical details. Such was St. Paul as regards the system of Christian discipline and worship; and when he could not go himself, he sent Timothy in his place. He says in the 4th chapter: "I beseech you, be ye followers of me. *For this cause* have I sent unto you Timotheus, who shall bring you into remembrance *of my ways which be in Christ, as I teach every where in every Church*" (1 Cor 4:16-17). Here there is the same reference to an uniform system of discipline, whether as to Christian conduct, worship, or Church government.

Another important allusion appears to be contained in the 22nd verse of the chapter above commented on. "What have ye not houses to eat and drink in? or despise ye the *Church of God?*" (1 Cor 11:22). This is remarkable as being a solitary allusion in Scripture to *houses* of prayer under the Christian system, which nevertheless we know from *ecclesiastical history* were used from the very first. Here then is a most solemn ordinance of primitive Christianity, which barely escapes, if it escapes, omission in Scripture.

A passing allusion is made in another passage of the same Epistle, to the use of the word Amen at the conclusion of the Eucharistical prayer, as it is preserved after it and all other prayers to this day. Thus the ritual of the Apostles descended to minutiæ, and these so invariable in their use as to allow of an appeal to them.

In the original institution of the Eucharist, as recorded in the Gospels, there is no mention of *consecrating* the elements; but in 1 Corinthians 10:16, St. Paul calls it "the cup *of blessing, which we bless*." This incidental information, vouchsafed to us in Scripture, should lead us to be very cautious how we put aside other usages of the early Church concerning this sacrament, which do not happen to be clearly mentioned in Scripture; as *e.g.* the solemn offering of the elements to GOD by way of pleading his mercy through CHRIST, which seems to have been universal in the Church, till Popery corrupted it into a superstitious and blasphemous ordinance.

As regards the same Sacrament, let us consider the use of the word λειτουργούντων, *ministering* (Acts 13:2); a word which, dropt (so to say) by accident, and interpreted, as is reasonable, by its use in the services of the Jewish Law (Luke 1:23; Heb 10:11), remarkably coincides with the λειτουργία of the Primitive Church, according to which the offering of the Altar was intercessory, as pleading Christ's merits before the throne of grace.

Again, in 1 Corinthians 15:29, we incidentally discover the existence of persons who are styled "the baptized for the dead." Perhaps it is impossible to determine what is meant by this phrase, on which little light is thrown by early writers. However, any how it seems to refer to a *custom* of the Church, which was so usual as to admit of an appeal to it, which St. Paul approved, yet which he did not in the Epistle directly enforce, and but casually mentions.

In 1 Corinthians 1:16, St. Paul happens to inform us that he baptized the *household* of Stephanus. It has pleased the Holy Spirit to preserve to us this fact; by which is detected the existence of a rule of discipline for which the express doctrinal parts of Scripture afford but indirect warrant, viz. the custom of household baptism. (Vid. also Acts 16:15, 33.) This accidental disclosure accurately anticipates the after practice of the early Church, which urged the baptism of families, infants included, and gave a weighty doctrinal *reason* for it; viz. that all men were born in sin and in the wrath of God, and needed to be individually translated into that kingdom of grace, into which baptism is the initiation.

These instances, then, not to notice others of either a like or a different kind, are surely sufficient to reconcile us to the complete ritual system which breaks upon us in the writings of the Fathers. If any parts of it indeed are contrary to Scripture, that is of course a decisive reason at once for believing them to be additions and corruptions of the original ceremonial; but till this is shown, we are bound to venerate what is certainly primitive, and probably is apostolic.

It will be remarked, moreover, that many of the religious observances of the early Church are expressly built upon words of Scripture, and intended to be a visible memorial of them, after the manner of St. Paul's directions about the respective habits of men and women, with which this paper opened. Metaphorical or mystical descriptions were represented by a corresponding literal action. Our Lord Himself authorised this procedure when He took up the metaphor of the prophets concerning the fountain opened for our cleansing (Zech 13:1) and represented it in the visible rite of baptism. Accordingly, from the frequent mention of *oil* in Scripture as the emblem of spiritual gifts (Isa 61:1-3, &c.), it was actually used in the primitive Church in the ceremony of admitting catechumens, and in baptizing. And here again they had the precedent of the Apostles, who applied it in effecting their miraculous cures (Mark 6:13; Jas 5:14). And so from the figurative mention in Scripture of *salt*, as the necessary preparation of every religious sacrifice, it was in use in the Western Church, in the ceremony of admitting converts into the rank of catechumens. So again from Philippians 2:10, it was customary to bow the head at the name of Jesus. It were endless to multiply instances of a similar pious attention to the very words of Scripture, as their custom of continual public prayer from such passages as Luke 18:7; or of burying the bodies of martyrs under the altar, from Revelation 6:9; or of the white vestments of the officiating ministers, from Revelation 4:4.

Two passages from the Fathers shall now be laid before the reader, in order to the further illustration of our subject:

> "Though this observance has not been determined by any text of Scripture, yet it is established by custom, which doubtless is derived from Apostolic tradition. For how can an usage ever obtain, which has not first been given by tradition? But you say, even though tradition can be produced, still a written (Scripture) authority must be demanded. Let us examine, then, how far it is true, that an Apostolic tradition itself, unless written in Scripture, is inadmissible. Now I will give up the point at once, if it is not already determined by instances of other observances, which are maintained without any Scripture proof, on the mere plea of tradition, and the sanction of consequent custom. To begin with baptism. Before we enter the water, we solemnly renounce the Devil, his pomp, and his angels, in church in the presence of the Bishop. Then we are plunged in the water thrice, and answer certain questions over and above what the Lord has determined in the written gospel. After coming out of it, we taste a mixture of milk and honey; and for a whole week from that day we abstain from our daily bath. The sacrament of the Eucharist, though given by the Lord to all and at supper time, yet is celebrated in our meetings before day break, and only at the hand of our presiding ministers . . . . . We sign our forehead with the cross whenever we set out and walk, go in or out, dress, gird on our sandals, bathe, eat, light our lamps, sit or lie down to rest, whatever we do. If you demand a scriptural rule for these and such like observances, we can give you none; all we say to you is, that tradition directs, usage sanctions, faith obeys. That reason justifies this tradition, usage, and faith, you will soon yourself see, or will easily learn from others; meanwhile you will do well to believe that there is a law to which obedience is due. I add one instance from the old dispensation. It is so usual among the Jewish females to veil their head that they are even known by it. I ask where the law is to be found; the Apostle's decision of course is not to the point. Now if I no where find a law, it follows that tradition

introduced the custom, which afterwards was confirmed by the Apostle when he explained the reason of it. These instances are enough to show that a tradition, even though not in Scripture, still binds our conduct, if a continuous usage be preserved as the witness of it."[1]

Upon this passage it may be observed, that Tertullian, flourishing A.D. 200, is on the one hand a very early witness for the existence of the general doctrine which it contains, while on the other he gives no sanction to the claims of those later customs on our acceptance which the Church of Rome upholds, but which cannot be clearly traced to primitive times.

Basil, whose work on the HOLY SPIRIT, § 66, shall next be cited, flourished in the middle of the fourth century, 150 years after Tertullian, and was of a very different school; yet he will be found to be in exact agreement with him on the subject before us, viz. that the ritual of the Church was derived from the Apostles, and was based on religious principles and doctrines. He adds a reason for its not being given us in Scripture, which we may receive or reject as our judgment leads us, viz. that the rites were memorials of doctrines not intended for publication except among baptized Christians, whereas the Scriptures were open to all men. This at least is clear, that the ritual could scarcely have been given in detail in Scripture, without imparting to the Gospel the character of a burdensome ceremonial, and withdrawing our attention from its doctrines and precepts.

> "Of those articles of doctrine and preaching, which are in the custody of the Church, some come to us in Scripture itself, some are conveyed to us by a continuous tradition in mystical depositories. Both have equal claims on our devotion, and are received by all, at least by all who are in any respect Churchmen. For, should we attempt to supersede the usages which are not enjoined in Scripture as if unimportant, we should do most serious injury to Evangelical truth; nay, reduce it to a bare name. To take an obvious instance; which Apostle has taught us in Scripture to sign believers with the cross? Where does Scripture teach us to turn to the east in prayer? Which of the saints has left us recorded in Scripture the words of invocation at the consecration of the bread of the Eucharist, and of the cup of blessing? Thus we are not content with what Apostle or Evangelist has left on record, but we add other rites before and after it, as important

---

[1] Tertullian de Coron. § 3.

to the celebration of the mystery, receiving them from a teaching distinct from Scripture. Moreover, we bless the water of baptism, and the oil for anointing, and also the candidate for baptism himself . . . . . After the example of Moses, the Apostles and Fathers who modelled the Churches, were accustomed to lodge their sacred doctrine in mystic forms, as being secretly and silently conveyed . . . . This is the reason why there is a tradition of observances independent of Scripture, lest doctrines, being exposed to the world, should be so familiar as to be despised . . . . . We stand instead of kneeling at prayer on the Sunday; but all of us do not know the reason of this . . . . . Again, every time we kneel down and rise up, we show by our outward action, that sin has levelled us with the ground, and the loving mercy of our Creator has recalled us to heaven."

The conclusion to be drawn from all that has been said in these pages is this:—That rites and ordinances, far from being unmeaning, are in their nature capable of impressing our memories and imaginations with the great revealed verities; far from being superstitious, are expressly sanctioned in Scripture as to their principle, and delivered to the Church in their form by tradition. Further, that they varied in different countries, according to the respective founder of the Church in each. Thus, *e.g.*, St. John and St. Philip are known to have adopted the Jewish rule for observing Easter-day; while other Apostles celebrated it always on a Sunday. Lastly, that, although the details of the early ritual varied in importance, and corrupt additions were made in the middle ages, yet that, as a whole, the Catholic ritual was a precious possession; and if we, who have escaped from Popery, have lost not only the possession, but the sense of its value, it is a serious question whether we are not like men who recover from some grievous illness with the loss or injury of their sight or hearing;—whether we are not like the Jews returned from captivity, who could never find the rod of Aaron or the Ark of the Covenant, which, indeed, had ever been hid from the world, but then was removed from the Temple itself.

JOHN HENRY NEWMAN
The Feast of St. Philip and St. James
May 1, 1834

TRACT 35: AD POPULUM
The People's Interest in Their Minister's Commission

And I will give unto thee the keys of the Kingdom of Heaven: and whatsoever thou shalt bind on earth, shall be bound in heaven; and whatsoever thou shalt loose on earth, shall be loosed in heaven.
—THE GOSPEL OF ST. MATTHEW 16:19

In these words our blessed LORD delivers to St. Peter, the same commission, as we find Him, in chapter 18 of the same Gospel, giving to the rest of the apostles; the commission, power, and authority of chief shepherds, or pastors to the Church;—the commission to be the keepers and guardians of the revealed word, of GOD, and to have authority to teach the people out of it, what they must do to be saved, what course of faith and duty will admit them to heaven, through the sacrifice of CHRIST: and what will exclude them from all claim to the salvation which He has purchased for man. It is to this part of the commission that St. Paul alludes when he says, "As we have been allowed of GOD to be put in trust with the Gospel, so we speak not as pleasing men, but GOD which trieth our hearts" (1 Thess 2:4); and again he says, "we are ambassadors for CHRIST, as though GOD did beseech you by us" (2 Cor 5:20).

But something beyond the ministration of the Word, is committed to the care of the pastors, when our LORD speaks of "the keys of heaven," viz. the ministration of the sacraments. The sacrament of Baptism, by which souls are admitted into covenant with GOD, and without which none can enter into the kingdom of heaven (John 3:5); the sacrament of the Body and Blood of CHRIST, by which the souls of the faithful are strengthened for their LORD'S service, and brought into union with Him (1 Cor 10:16), and, without which they are, ordinarily speaking, cut off from union with Him, from communion with the faithful, and cast out of the Kingdom of Heaven. For it is expressly said, "Except ye eat the flesh of the Son of Man, and drink His blood, ye have no life in you" (John 6:53). St. Paul also tells us, that the ministration of these sacraments is entrusted to the pastors of the Church by this commission, when he says, "Let a man so account of us, as of the ministers of CHRIST, and stewards of the mysteries of God" (1 Cor 4:1).

This commission, which you find in chapter 16 given to St. Peter, and in chapter 18 given to all the Apostles,—which is made mention of in St. Luke's Gospel, where our SAVIOUR says to them, "I appoint unto you a kingdom, as my FATHER hath appointed unto Me" (Luke 22:29), and again in St. John's, where CHRIST says, "As my FATHER hath sent Me, even so send I you" (John 20:21);—this commission, I say, was left by the apostles to their successors, viz. those apostles or bishops whom they appointed to be their helpers in governing the churches during their lifetime, and to occupy their place when dead. And it has been handed down, by the laying on of hands, from bishops to bishops, and will so continue to the end of time, according to that promise, whereby our LORD engaged to continue with them always in the exercise of it, when He said to the apostles, "Lo, I am with you always, even unto the end of the world" (Matt 28:20). By virtue of this commission, each bishop stands in the place of an apostle of the Church; and discharges the important trust reposed in him, either in his own person, or by the clergy whom he ordains and gifts with a share of his authority.

Herein is the difference between the ministry of such persons as have received this commission from the bishop, and of those who have not received it;—that to the former, CHRIST has promised that His presence shall remain, "Lo, I am with you always, even to the end of the world:" and that when they minister the Word and Sacraments (which are the keys of the Kingdom of Heaven), what they do upon earth, in His name, according to His will, shall be ratified and made good in heaven. "Whatsoever thou shalt bind on earth, shall be bound in heaven; and whatsoever thou shalt loose on earth, shall be loosed in heaven" (Matt 18:18). But to those who have not received the commission, our LORD has given no such promise. A person not commissioned from the bishop, may use the words of Baptism, and sprinkle or bathe with the water, *on earth*, but there is no promise from CHRIST, that such a man shall admit souls to the *Kingdom of Heaven*. A person not commissioned may break bread, and pour out wine, and pretend to give the LORD'S Supper, but it can afford no comfort to any to receive it at his hands, because there is no warrant from CHRIST to lead communicants to suppose that while he does so here *on earth*, they will be partakers in the SAVIOUR'S *heavenly* Body and Blood. And as for the person himself, who takes upon himself without warrant to minister in holy things, he is all the while treading in the footsteps of Korah, Dathan, and Abiram, whose awful punishment you read of in the book of Numbers. (Compare Numbers 16 with Jude 5:11.)

It is of the utmost importance that you should know and understand that it is by virtue of this commission, that we Clergymen lay claim to your attention, when we minister the Word and the Sacraments. It is not because we have received an expensive education; it is not because we move in the station of what is called gentlemen; it is not because we have hitherto been encouraged by the State; it is not because we, most of us, have enough of this world's goods both to supply our own wants, and to impart to the necessities of others; it is not for these things that we dare to speak to you in the name of GOD. Time was when the clergy had them not; the time may come again when they shall not have them. Men may rudely and unjustly take away these things; may make us as poor as the poorest; may destroy what is called our station in society; may make us appear in the eyes of men a humbled and degraded class, as they did the Apostles; may "cast out our name as evil for the SON of MAN'S sake," as they did theirs. This cannot alter our position in spiritual things, nor the relation which we bear to GOD and CHRIST, and to your souls. Men cannot take away what CHRIST has given us,—I mean the Divine commission: they cannot set aside the trust which He has placed in our hands,—I mean "the ministry of reconciliation" (2 Cor 5:18), nor make void the promise He has made, that in the faithful exercise of this ministry, He is "with us always, even to the end Of the world."

Remember, then, that whether your pastors be rich or poor, honoured or despised by the world, it is only the having received this commission that makes us "bold in our GOD to speak unto you the Gospel of GOD" (1 Thess 2:2); and it is only this that can give you any security that the ministration of the Word and Sacraments shall be effectual to the saving of your souls. Learn, then, to cherish and value the blessing which GOD has vouchsafed to you, in having given you pastors who have received this commission. *The Dissenting teachers have it not.* They lay no claim to regular succession from the Apostles; and though the Roman Catholic clergy have indeed been ordained by the hands of Bishops, they are mere intruders in this country, have no right to come here, and besides, have so corrupted the truth of GOD'S word, that they are not to be listened to for a moment.

ARTHUR PHILIP PERCEVAL
The Feast of the Ascension
May 8, 1834

TRACT 36: AD POPULUM
Account of Religious Sects at Present Existing in England

> *I beseech you, brethren, mark them which cause divisions and offences contrary to the doctrine which ye have learned; and avoid them.*
> —ROMANS 17:17

It is conceived, that many members of the English Church, whom late events have awakened to a knowledge of the religious differences which exist in the world, are but insufficiently acquainted with the chief points which distinguish the various religious bodies which are among them; and may be anxious for information on the subject. The following statement, drawn up by a Clergyman at the request of a parishioner, is submitted to their consideration.

The English Church, which is a true branch or portion of the "One Holy, Catholic, and Apostolic Church" of CHRIST,[1] receives and teaches the entire Truth of GOD according to the Scriptures; the Truth, the whole Truth, and nothing but the Truth. This may be proved by reference to the Scriptures; in which no fundamental doctrine can be pointed out, which the Church does not teach: nor can it be shown that the Church teaches any thing, as necessary to salvation, but what is contained in the Scriptures, or can be proved by them,—this being the acknowledged rule of teaching set forth in the 6th Article of the Church.

The parties which are separated from, and opposed to, the Church, may be arranged into three classes. 1. Those who reject the Truth. 2. Those who receive and teach a *part*, but not the whole, of the Truth. 3. Those who teach more than the Truth.

---

[1] See Nicene Creed.

I. Those who reject the Truth.

Under this head are included all who deny that JESUS "is the CHRIST, the SON of the living GOD" (Matt 16:16), and that salvation is through His blood. Such are

1. SOCINIANS (so called from Socinus, a chief teacher of their error), who profess to receive the Old and New Testament, but reject these fundamental doctrines as there set forth, and reject also the doctrine of the Personality and operations of the HOLY GHOST.[2] These men commonly call themselves Unitarians.

2. JEWS, who profess to receive the Old Testament, but denounce our LORD as an Impostor. These contradict the Prophets of the Old Testament, to whose evidence our LORD appealed while fulfilling their prophecies (John 5:39, 46): and they forget the living witness they themselves afford to our SAVIOUR'S truth, who foretold concerning their Church and nation, the evils which have since happened, and under which they are now suffering.[3]

3. DEISTS (so called from professing to acknowledge merely a *Deity*), who reject both the Testaments, denying that GOD has ever revealed His will to men. Thus they contradict reason, which suggests that He would not leave the beings whom He created capable of happiness, without instruction how to attain that happiness: they contradict also the unanswerable evidence of history, miracles, and fulfilment of prophecy, which prove that He actually has revealed His Will, and that the Book which we call the Bible contains that Revelation.[4]

4. ATHEISTS (i.e. men "without God"), who deny altogether the existence of a GOD. These contradict the voice of nature, which, by the regularity of seasons, the succession, growth, and decay, of plants, of animals, and men, by the course of the planets and all its other wonderful works, attest the existence, power, and goodness of a Superior Being, who must have made all these things at the first, and now continues and preserves them.

These four Classes may be placed together, because to all four the same passage of St. John is applicable. "Whosoever denieth the SON, the

---

[2] On these points see "Churchman's Manual." Oxford, 1834, pp. 20-23.
[3] See Leslie's Short and Easy Method with the Jews.
[4] See Leslie's Short and Easy Method with the Deists.

same hath not the FATHER" (1 John 2:23), and of all four it may be truly said, "They have trodden under foot the SON of GOD, and counted the blood of the Covenant an unholy thing, and done despite to the SPIRIT of Grace" (Heb 9:29).

II. Those who receive and teach a part but not the whole of the Truth, erring in respect of one or more fundamental doctrines.

Under this head are included most of what are called "Protestant Dissenters." The chief of these are,—

1. PRESBYTERIANS, so called from maintaining the validity of ordination by *Presbyters* or Elders only, in other words, by the second order of the clergy, dispensing with and superseding the first.[5]

2. INDEPENDENTS, so called from being opposed to and *independent* of *all* ecclesiastical government.[6]

3. METHODISTS (subdivided into an immense variety of sects; the chief are Wesleyans, Whitfieldians, or Lady Huntingdon's, Ranters, or Primitive Methodists, Brianites, or Bible Christians, Protestant Methodists, Tent Methodists, Independent Methodists, and Kilhamites). These three do not receive or teach the Truth respecting the doctrine of "laying on of hands," which St. Paul classes among the fundamental doctrines of Christianity (Heb 6:2), and by which the Christian ministry receives its commission and authority to administer the Word and Sacraments. For they one and all reject the first (*i.e.* the Apostolic, or, as we now call it, Episcopal) order of clergy, who exercised that rite according to the New Testament, and without whom there is no warrant from Scripture for believing that the Clergy can be appointed, or the Sacraments be duly administered.[7]

4. BAPTISTS, who have departed from the Truth not only as concerns the doctrine "of laying on of hands," but also as concerns the doctrine of *Baptism;* another of the fundamental doctrines, according to St. Paul. For they refuse to permit their children to receive that sign of

---

[5] From this error have sprung all the Sects enumerated under this second head.
[6] See Hebrews 13:17.
[7] See "Churchman's Manual," pp. 5-15; Acts 14:23; 1 Timothy 5:22; Titus 1:5.

admission into the Christian covenant. Thus they contradict the Old Testament, for there we find that to the Christian Covenant, or Covenant in CHRIST, which GOD confirmed with Abraham (Gen 17:14), children were enjoined to be admitted; and those children whose parents withheld them from receiving the sign of the covenant, were counted by GOD to have broken His covenant (Gal 3:17). They contradict also the New Testament, for there our SAVIOUR says, "Suffer little children to come unto me, and forbid them not" (Mark 10:14); and St. Paul declares that where either parent is a believer, then "are the children holy," *i.e.* admissible to the covenant of grace (1 Cor 7:14).

5. QUAKERS, who reject altogether laying on of hands, and both the Sacraments.

Besides these are, especially in Wales, JUMPERS and SHAKERS, a chief part of whose religious worship consists in violent exercise and contortions of the body.[8]

III. Those who teach more than the Truth.

Under this head are included all who teach *besides* the Scriptures, something else as of equal authority with what is contained in them. The chief of these are,—

1. ROMANISTS, or PAPISTS, (so called because they are the followers of the *Pope* or Bishop of *Rome*), who teach that the images of GOD and of the Saints ought to be worshipped; that the Virgin Mary and other Saints ought to be prayed to; that in the LORD'S Supper, after consecration, the bread is no longer bread, the wine no longer wine; that all Churches owe obedience to the Pope of Rome, &c. &c.[9] They have at different times attempted to confirm these doctrines by pretended miracles.

2. NEW JERUSALEMITES, or SWEDENBORGIANS, so called from their leader, who pretended to have received a new revelation.

3. SOUTHCOTIANS: the followers of Johanna Southcote, who pretended to be a prophetess.

---

[8] The Moravians are purposely omitted: for they cannot well be said to be *opposed* to the Church. They lay claim also to an Apostolic or Episcopal Ministry, though it is believeD that they are unable to substantiate the succession.
[9] See "Churchman's Manual," pp. 15-19.

4. IRVINGITES; so called from one of their chief leaders, who pretend to have received a new Revelation, and a new order of Apostles, which, like the Papists, they attempt to confirm by pretended gifts of unknown tongues, prophecy, and miracles; like all under this head, a mixture of delusion and imposture.

Churchman, whosoever thou art, that readest the list of follies and errors in the 2d and 3d classes, into which the pride of man's heart and the wiles of Satan, have beguiled so many of those who call upon the name of the LORD JESUS CHRIST (1 Cor 1:2), first give to GOD your hearty thanks for having preserved you a member of the "One Holy, Catholic, and Apostolic Church," which teaches the way of God in truth (Matt 22:16), "neither handling the Word of GOD deceitfully," like the second class, nor following cunningly devised fables (2 Pet 1:16), like the third, but by manifestation of the truth, commending itself to every man's conscience in the sight of GOD (1 Cor 4:2). Next pray to Him for yourself, that you may have grace to walk worthy of your high calling and privilege; in repentance, faith, and holiness, and in close communion with the Church, especially by a frequent participation in the Eucharistic Sacrifice and Sacrament of the LORD'S Supper, which is at once the highest and most essential act of Christian worship, and the surest token of Church membership. Next pray to GOD for mercy upon all, both those who have gone beyond or fallen short of the Truth, and those who have altogether rejected it; that He may be pleased so to turn their hearts, and fetch them home to His flock, that they may be saved together with His true servants, and be made one fold under one Shepherd.

One word more. From each of these three Classes, which have been here considered, the Church in England has undergone persecution. 1st. In the 4th and 6th centuries, *from those who reject the Truth*, when they who denied that JESUS is the CHRIST, the SON of the living GOD, expelled and murdered those who believed in Him, and called upon His Name. 2nd. In the 16th century, *from those who teach more than the Truth*, when the Papists or Romanists burned alive those who rejected their corrupt additions to the Catholic faith. 3rd. In the 17th century, *from those who teach less than the Truth*, when the Protestant Dissenters expelled and barbarously treated the Clergy, shut up the Churches, and forbade the use of the English Liturgy. But on each occasion, though it pleased GOD for a while to try the faith and constancy of his servants by sufferings, He failed not finally to deliver His people, and to protect and strengthen His Church.

At the present time, these three Classes of opponents have united their forces; and unbeliever, Papist, and Protestant Dissenter, obeying Satan's bidding, are endeavouring to do that together, which they have failed to do singly, namely, to overthrow and destroy our branch of the Catholic and Apostolic Church. And it is not improbable that GOD, for our correction and improvement, or for the glory of His name, may again put the faith and constancy of His servants to the proof, by permitting them to suffer afflictions for His name's sake. But as He is "the same yesterday and today and for ever" (Heb 13:8), His power undiminished, His truth unchanged, we may rest assured, that if we will be true to Him, He will be true to us; and will protect the Church of His SON, which is "built upon the foundation of the Apostles and Prophets, JESUS CHRIST Himself being the Chief Corner-stone" (Eph 2:20), and concerning which Church, that SON has said, that "the gates of Hell shall not prevail against it" (Matt 16:15). Fear not, therefore, neither be faint-hearted; has not GOD commanded you? Be strong, and of good courage!

ARTHUR PHILIP PERCEVAL
The Feast of St. Barnabas
June 11, 1834

TRACT 37: AD POPULUM
Bishop Wilson's Form of Excommunication

It is well known that Bishop Wilson, who presided over the Church in the Isle of Man, from 1698 to 1755, was stirred up by Him who made him overseer, to revive the Primitive Discipline, and was remarkably blest in his undertaking. The principle of this discipline is, that no man who sinned openly, whether in creed or practice, should be allowed to remain in free and full communion with the Church; but should be censured, put to penance, suspended, or excommunicated, as the case might require. The following is the form he proposed to use, in inflicting the extreme punishment of excommunication.

My Brethren, and all good Christians here met together.
    We are met upon a very *unusual* and *mournful* occasion.
    We have hitherto (blessed be GOD) preserved, in some good measure, the ancient discipline of the Church; and notorious sinners have been prevailed upon to take shame to themselves in a public confession of their offences; and to desire the prayers of the Church for the grace that is necessary for a *true conversion.*
    I am sorry to tell you, that there is a person now under the censures of the Church, who utterly refuseth to submit to this wholesome

discipline; being more concerned for the shame that attends his censures, than he is for his salvation.

We have laid before you *his crimes;* and the Christian methods which have been made use of to bring him to a sense of *his guilt* and *danger,* and to oblige him to make what satisfaction he can for the scandal he hath given.

You will see how very long we have waited in hopes of bringing him to submit to the discipline of the Church; until at last our discipline begins to be slighted, as too weak for such offenders.

However, it ought not to repent us that we have waited with patience; when we consider with what mighty patience GOD himself waiteth to be gracious; and that the sentence of excommunications was never, in the primitive Church, executed hastily, nor until all other probable ways had been made use of *without effect.*[1]

Now, this being the last remedy which the Church can make use of for awakening obstinate offenders, the whole Church ought to be satisfied upon what grounds, and by what authority we pronounce this sentence; and what will be the effects of such a sentence when passed according to the will and appointment of JESUS CHRIST.

The Holy Scriptures tell us, that our LORD JESUS CHRIST, who came to seek and save his lost creatures, has appointed divers ordinances for the conversion and salvation of men.

For instance:—He has appointed *Preaching,*[2] to draw men to him; He has appointed the Sacrament of *Baptism,*[3] by which we are admitted into His household the Church; and that of the LORD'S Supper,[4] as a pledge of his love, and of our communion with Him. And lastly, He hath ordained *Godly Discipline,*[5] that such who do not live as becomes their Christian profession may be reproved, corrected, and amended, or else cast out of his Church.

And all these ordinances are committed unto His Ministers, who are called his *stewards;*[6] because to them He has committed the keys[7] of His house and kingdom, that is, the Church; that they may admit such as

---

[1] Matthew 18:15-17.
[2] Mark 16:15.
[3] Matthew 28:19.
[4] Luke 22:19; 1 Corinthians 11:26, 10:16.
[5] Matthew 28:15, &c.
[6] 1 Corinthians 4:1, 2; Luke 12:42.
[7] Matthew 16:19, 18:15, &c.; John 20:23; 1 Corinthians 5:4.

are worthy, and that they may shut out such as behave themselves disorderly in His family.

JESUS CHRIST, I say, committed this power to His Apostles, and they to their successors;[8] with this assurance from his own mouth, *He that heareth you, heareth Me, and he that despiseth you, despiseth Me, and Him that sent Me.*

So that you see, whosoever makes a jest of Church Discipline, makes a jest of an ordinance of GOD; and a man may as well despise the whole Christian Religion, as *this* power, which is as much the ordinance of JESUS CHRIST, as preaching, or the use of the Sacraments.

The most unlearned Christian will understand this, when he is asked, For what end he was baptized? He will answer, That he might thereby be made a member of CHRIST, a child of GOD, and an inheritor of the kingdom of Heaven.

But why does he believe that Baptism does give him a right to these blessings? Why; because JESUS CHRIST gave power to His Ministers to baptize all nations; that such as are baptized[9] into CHRIST, have put on CHRIST; that is, are members of CHRIST'S body, which is His Church.

Now, will not our LORD CHRIST, who has promised to own you for His children when His Ministers have admitted you into His Church by Baptism, will He not also disown you, when the same Ministers, *acting in His name*, shall by the same power of the keys, shut you out of His Church?

For if you believe that they receive you into CHRIST'S Church by *Baptism*, you must believe that they shut you out as effectually by *Excommunication*.

In short, every Christian, when he is baptized, is admitted into the Church upon a most solemn promise to live as a Christian ought to do; if he does not do so, those very Ministers who admitted him are bound to *exhort*,[10] to *rebuke* and to *censure* him; and if these methods will not do, to *excommunicate him*; that is, to cut him off from the body of CHRIST, and from GOD'S favour and mercy:—not that he may be lost for ever, but that he may see his sad condition, and repent, and be saved.

---

[8] Compare Matthew 10:40; Luke 10:16; and Titus 2:15, 3:10.

[9] Gal 3:27.

[10] 2 Timothy 4:2.

The form of excommunication made use of by the Apostles of our LORD, was, by *delivering offenders to Satan*.[11] Now, because this is laughed at by profane persons, who do not know the Scriptures, I will show you what that means. The Spirit and the Word of GOD has told us, that the devil has a kingdom and subjects, over whom he reigns; that is, *over the children of disobedience*.[12]

That JESUS CHRIST has also *His* kingdom and subjects; and when the Apostles gained over any of the subjects of Satan unto CHRIST, they are said *to turn them from darkness to light and from the power of Satan unto* GOD.[13]

Now, when any of CHRIST'S subjects become rebellious, and refuse to be governed by the laws of the Gospel, His Ministers are bound to admonish them of their sin, and of their danger; and if they refuse to obey their godly admonitions, then to turn them out of that society of which CHRIST is the head; and consequently, *such persons* fall under the power of Satan again, who useth his subjects like slaves. And GOD permits him to do so, that sinners, if they are not utterly lost, may with the prodigal, when he was forced to herd with swine, see the state they are fallen into, and repent; and desire to get out of the snare and power of the devil; and be restored to the favour of GOD.

So that excommunication is made use of, *not as a punishment only*, but *as a remedy;* that sinners, seeing the evil state they are in, being deprived of all hopes of salvation while they are out of the Church, may desire to be restored to GOD'S grace, from which they are fallen, that they may work out their salvation with more fear for the time to come.

But here I must take notice of one thing that often hinders the Discipline of the Church from having this good effect upon sinners. They are apt to say, *If I am shut out of this Church, I can go to another*. Why, has CHRIST more Churches than one?[14] Is Christ divided? saith the Apostle.[15] Do not all Christians profess to believe one *holy, Apostolic* Church?[16] And is not this Church a member of that holy Church? And have not the Ministers of CHRIST *here* the same authority from their LORD and

---

[11] 1 Corinthians 5:5 and 1 Timothy 1:20.
[12] Ephesians 4:2.
[13] Acts 26:18.
[14] Ephesians 4:4, &c.
[15] 1 Corinthians 1:13.
[16] Nicene Creed.

PRINCE, as any other Christian Bishop; namely, the authority of *binding*, and *loosing*? And will not our sentence, when we proceed according to the rules which CHRIST hath given us, be confirmed in Heaven? If so, what advantage will a sinner get by going to another society, if after all JESUS CHRIST shall confirm the sentence of his former Pastor? And for want of being reconciled by Him, shall shut him out of Heaven?

It is true, our LORD hath not given us any power to compel men by *outward force*, either to come into, or to continue in His Church; but will people for this reason despise the power which CHRIST has given us? They will hardly do so, if they know what St. Paul hath said upon this: "The weapons we use," saith he, "are not carnal, *but mighty through* GOD;"[17] that is, GOD can humble the stoutest sinner, and make the power of His ministers effectual, when they use their power for His glory, and according to His will.

You see, good Christians, that we take upon us no authority but what CHRIST has given us; what His Apostles exercised, and what we are bound by our most *solemn vows* to exercise.

Every Bishop, for instance, at his consecration, solemnly promises, *that he will correct and punish disobedient and criminous persons within his diocese, according to such authority as he has by* GOD'S *word*.[18] What authority he has by GOD'S Word, you have already heard; and all serious Christians must acknowledge, that we should become adversaries to ourselves, to our Church, and our country, if we should suffer CHRIST'S discipline to fall into decay, while we are warranted and bound, both by the laws of GOD and this land, to exercise it; especially when vices of this kind begin to grow upon us.

Only let us take care that we use *this authority* as the Apostle directs, *for edification, and not for destruction*.[19]

And if we must be forced to shut this unhappy person out of the Church, let it be with the same compassion and reluctancy that a father turns his rebellious son out of his house, not with a design that he should starve and be lost for ever; but that being made sensible of the misery of being out of his father's house, he may more earnestly desire to return and

---

[17] See 2 Corinthians 10:4.
[18] See Consecration Service.
[19] 2 Corinthians 10:8. See too the Service for the Consecration of Bishops, in the Prayer just before Consecration.

be received into favour, and become a more dutiful child for the time to come.

GOD has infinite expedients to bring back sinners that are gone away from Him. We know how the prodigal son was brought to a sense of his condition by the miseries he met with when he was from under his father's care.[20] How David's eyes were opened by a parable.[21] How Manasseh became an instance of repentance, when in bonds.[22] And we should not despair, but be confident rather that GOD will bless His own institutions in the hands of us His ministers, for the good of all such persons as draw these censures upon themselves. And it will be far from being severity to them, if by these means they may be brought to a sense of their evil condition, and *"their souls saved in the day of the* LORD JESUS.*"*[23]

This is the design of Church censures; and that they may have this good effect, the Apostle has given directions to all Christians not to accompany with such, that they may be ashamed.[24] And our holy Church in her Articles, as you will find it in the thirty-third Article of the Church of England, has declared in these words: *That person which by open denunciation of the Church is rightly cut off from the unity of the Church, and excommunicated, ought to be taken of the whole multitude of the faithful, as a heathen and publican, until he be openly reconciled by penance, and received into the Church by a judge that hath authority thereunto.*

Pursuant to which Article, the Church in the eighty-fifth Canon appoints, *that all persons excommunicated, and so denounced, be kept out of the church by the churchwardens.*

And in the sixty-fifth Canon directs, *That all such as stand lawfully excommunicated, shall every six months be openly denounced and declared excommunicate; that others may be thereby admonished to refrain their company and society, &c.*

As for any temporal penalties or incapacities which an excommunicate person may be exposed to; these do not properly belong to the Church; they are no part of our sentence; they are altogether in the

---

[20] Luke 15:17.
[21] 2 Samuel 12:1, &c.
[22] 2 Chronicles 23:12.
[23] 1 Corinthians 5:5.
[24] 2 Thessalonians 3:6, 14.

hands of the civil magistrate. Our sentence is purely spiritual; it is the sentence of JESUS CHRIST, and only concerns the good of the souls of those He has committed to our care. It is part of that ministry which we received by the imposition of hands, and which we most humbly pray GOD to enable us to exercise to *His glory*, to the putting a stop to the growing vices of the age, and to the edification of the Church of CHRIST, which He has purchased with his blood.[25] *Amen.*

The Sentence.

It is with great reluctancy, GOD is our witness, and after many prayers to GOD for their conversion, that we proceed to this *last remedy* which CHRIST has appointed for the conversion of sinners.

But we hope you are not shut out, that you may ever remain out of the Church; but that you may become sensible of your errors, and return with more zeal to your HEAVENLY FATHER.

In the mean time we must do our duty, and leave the event to GOD.

In the name of JESUS CHRIST, and by the authority which we have received from Him, we separate you from the communion of the Church, which He has purchased with His blood, and which is the society of all faithful people; and you are no longer a member of His Body, or of His kingdom, until you be openly reconciled by penance, and received into the Church by a judge that hath authority so to do.

When Persons excommunicated are received back into the Church.

I, an unworthy minister of JESUS CHRIST, by the same authority and power, even that of our LORD JESUS CHRIST; by which for thy obstinacy, and other crimes, thou hast been excluded from the communion of CHRIST'S Holy Church: By the same power, I do now release thee from that bond of excommunication, according to the confession now made by thee before GOD and this Church; and do restore thee again unto the communion of the Church of CHRIST: beseeching the ALMIGHTY to give

---

[25] Acts 20:28.

thee His grace that thou mayest continue a worthy member of the same unto thy life's end, through JESUS CHRIST our LORD. *Amen.*

Reprinted June 24, 1834
The Feast of St. John the Baptist

TRACT 38: AD SCHOLAS

Via Media, No. 1

Laicus.—Will you listen to a few free questions from one who has not known you long enough to be familiar with you without apology? I am struck by many things I have heard you say, which show me that, somehow or other, my religious system is incomplete; yet at the same time the world accuses you of Popery, and there are seasons when I have misgivings whither you are carrying me.

Clericus.—I trust I am prepared, most willing I certainly am, to meet any objections you have to bring against any doctrines which you have heard me maintain. Say more definitely what the charge against me is.

L. That your religious system, which I have heard some persons style the Apostolical, and which I so name by way of designation, is like that against which our forefathers protested at the Reformation.

C. I will admit it, *i.e.* if I may reverse your statement, and say, that the Popish system resembles it. Indeed, how could it be otherwise, seeing that all corruptions of the truth must be like the truth which they corrupt, else they would not persuade mankind to take them instead of it?

L. A bold thing to say, surely; to make the earlier system an imitation of the later!

C. A bolder, surely, to assume that mine is the later, and the Popish the earlier. When think you that my system (so to call it) arose?—not with myself?

L. Of course not; but whatever individuals have held it in our Church since the Reformation, it must be acknowledged that they have been but few, though some of them doubtless eminent men.

C. Perhaps you would say (*i.e.* the persons whose views you are representing), that at the Reformation, the stain of the old theology was left among us, and has shown itself in its measure ever since, as in the poor, so again in the educated classes;— that the peasantry still use and transmit their Popish rhymes, and the minds of students still linger among the early Fathers; but that the genius and principles of our Church have ever been what is commonly called Protestant.

L. This is a fair general account of what would be maintained.

C. You would consider that the Protestant principles and doctrines of this day were those of our Reformers in the sixteenth century; and that what is called Popery now is what was called Popery then.

L. On the whole: there are indeed extravagances now, as is obvious. I would not defend extremes; but I suppose our Reformers would agree with moderate Protestants of this day, in what they meant by Protestantism and by Popery.

C. This is an important question, of course; much depends on the correctness of the answer you have made to it. Do you make it as a matter of history, from knowing the opinions of our Reformers, or from what you consider probable?

L. I am no divine. I judge from a general knowledge of history, and from the obvious probabilities of the case, which no one can gainsay.

C. Let us then go by *probabilities*, since you lead the way. Is it not according to *probabilities* that opinions and principles should *not* be the same now as they were 300 years since? that though our professions are the same, yet we should not mean by them what the Reformers meant? Can you point to any period of Church history, in which doctrine remained for any time uncorrupted? Three hundred years is a long time. Are you quite sure we do not need A SECOND REFORMATION?

L. Are you really serious? Have we not Articles and a Liturgy which keep us from deviating from the standard of truth set up in the sixteenth century?

C. Nay, I am maintaining no paradox. Surely there is a multitude of men all around us who say the great body of the Clergy *has* departed from the doctrines of our Martyrs at the Reformation. I do not say I agree with the particular charges they prefer; but the very circumstance that they are made is a proof there is nothing extravagant in the notion of the Church having departed from the doctrine of the sixteenth century.

L. It is true; but the persons you refer to bring forward, at least, an intelligible charge; they appeal to the Articles, and maintain that the Clergy have departed from the doctrine therein contained. They may be right or wrong; but at least they give us the means of judging for ourselves.

C. This surely is beside the point. We were speaking of *probabilities*. *What* change actually *has* been made, if any, is a further question, a question of *fact*. But before going on to examine the particular case, I observe that change of opinion was *probable;* probable in itself you can hardly deny, considering the history of the universal Church; not extravagantly improbable, moreover, in spite of Articles, as the extensively prevailing opinion to which I alluded, that the clergy have departed from them, sufficiently proves. Now consider the course of religion and politics, domestic and foreign, during the last three centuries, and tell me whether events have not occurred to increase this probability almost to a certainty; the probability, I mean, that the members of the English Church of the present day differ from the principles of the Church of Rome more than our forefathers differed. First, consider the history of the Puritans from first to last. Without pronouncing any opinion on the truth or unsoundness of their principles, were they not evidently further removed from Rome than were our Reformers? Was not their influence all on the side of leading the English Church farther from Rome than our Reformers placed it? Think of the fall of the Scottish Episcopal Church. Reflect upon the separation and extinction of the Nonjurors, upon the rise of Methodism, upon our political alliances with foreign Protestant communities. Consider especially the history and the school of Hoadley. That man, whom a high authority of the present day does not hesitate to call a Socinian,[1] was for near fifty years a bishop in our Church.

L. You tell me to think on these facts. I wish I were versed enough in our ecclesiastical history to do so.

C. But you are as well versed in it as the generality of educated men; as those whose opinions you are now maintaining. And they surely must

---

[1] "It is true he was a Bishop, though a Socinian." —Bp. Blomfield's Letter to C. Butler, Esq. 1825.

be well acquainted with our history, and the doctrines taught in the different schools and eras, who scruple not to charge such as me with a declension from the true Anti-popish doctrine of our Church. For what the doctrine of the Church is, what it has been for three centuries, is a matter of fact which cannot be known without reading.

L. Let us leave, if you please, this ground of *probability*, which, whatever you may say, cannot convince me while I am able to urge that strong objection to it which you would not let me mention just now. I repeat, we have Articles; we have a Liturgy; the dispute lies in a little compass, without need of historical reading:—do you mean to say we have departed from them?

C. I am not unwilling to follow you a second time, and will be explicit. I reply, we *have* departed from them. Did you ever study the Rubrics of the Prayer Book?

L. But surely they have long been obsolete;—they are impracticable!

C. It is enough; you have answered your own question without trouble of mine. Not only do we not obey them, but it seems we style them impracticable. I take your admission. Now, I ask you, are not these Rubrics (I might also mention parts of the services themselves which have fallen into disuse), such as the present day would call Popish? and, if so, is not this a proof that the spirit of the present day has departed (whether for good or evil) from the spirit of the Reformation?—and is it wonderful that such as I should be called Popish, if the Church Services themselves are considered so?

L. Will you give me some instances?

C. Is it quite in accordance with our present Protestant notions, that unbaptized persons should not be buried with the rites of the Church?—that every Clergyman should read the Daily Service morning and evening at home, if he cannot get a congregation?—that in college chapels the Holy Communion should be administered every week?—that Saints' Days should be observed?—that stated days of fasting should be set apart by the Church? Ask even a sober-minded really serious man about the observance of these rules; will he not look grave, and say that he is afraid of formality and superstition if these rules were attended to?

L. And is there not the danger?

C. The simple question is, whether there is more danger now than three centuries since? was there not far more superstition in the sixteenth than in the nineteenth century? and does the spirit of the nineteenth move with the spirit of the sixteenth, if the sixteenth commands and the nineteenth draws back?

L. But you spoke of parts of the Services themselves, as laid aside?

C. Alas! . . . .

What is the prevailing opinion or usage respecting the form of absolution in the office for Visiting the Sick? What is thought by a great body of men of the words in which the Priesthood is conveyed? Are there no objections to the Athanasian Creed? Does no one stumble at the word "oblations," in the Prayer for the Church Militant? Is there no clamour against parts of the Burial Service? No secret or scarcely secret murmurings against the word *regeneration* in the Baptismal? No bold protestations against reading the Apocrypha? Now do not all these objections rest upon one ground: *viz.* That these parts of our Services savour of Popery? And again, are not these the popular objections of the day?

L. I cannot deny it.

C. I consider then that already I have said enough to show that the Church of this day has deviated from the opinions of our Reformers, and become more opposed than they were to the system they protested against. And therefore, I would observe, it is not fair to judge of me, or such as me, in the off-hand way which many men take the liberty to adopt. Men seem to think that we are plainly and indisputably proved to be Popish, if we are proved to differ from the generality of Churchmen now-a-days. But what if it turn out that they are silently floating down the stream, and we are upon the shore?

L. All, however, will allow, I suppose, that our Reformation was never completed in its details. The final judgment was not passed upon parts of the Prayer Book. There were, you know, alterations in the second edition of it published in King Edward's time; and these tended to a more Protestant doctrine than that which had first been adopted. For instance, in King Edward's first book the dead in CHRIST were prayed for (not of course as if there were a purgatory, but as if it were right to commemorate and hold communion with the saints in paradise);[2] in the second this commemoration was omitted. Again, in the first book the elements of the

---

[2] [This parenthetical phrase about purgatory was included in the 1834 collection of the *Tracts*, while it was omitted in the 1840 collection. –Ed.]

Lord's Supper were more distinctly offered up to God, and more formally consecrated than in the second edition, or at present. Had Queen Mary not succeeded, perhaps the men who effected this would have gone further.

C. I believe they would; nay indeed they did at a subsequent period. They took away the Liturgy altogether, and substituted a Directory.

L. They? the same men?

C. Yes, the foreign party: who afterwards went by the name of Puritans. Bucer, who altered in King Edward's time, and the Puritans, who destroyed in King Charles's, both came from the same religious quarter.

L. Ought you so to speak of the foreign Reformers? to them we owe the Protestant doctrine altogether.

C. I like foreign interference, as little from Geneva, as from Rome. Geneva at least never converted a part of England from heathenism, nor could lay claim to patriarchal authority over it. Why could we not be let alone, and suffered to reform ourselves?

L. You separate then your creed and cause from that of the Reformed Churches of the Continent?

C. Not altogether; but I protest against being brought into that close alliance with them which the world now a-days would force upon us. The glory of the English Church is, that it has taken the VIA MEDIA, as it has been called. It lies *between* the (so called) Reformers and the Romanists; whereas there are religious circles, and influential too, where it is thought enough to prove an English Clergyman unfaithful to his Church, if he preaches any thing at variance with the opinions of the Diet of Augsburg, or the Confessions of the Waldenses. However, since we have been led to speak of the foreign Reformers, I will, if you will still listen to me, strengthen my argument by an appeal to them.

L. That argument being, that what is now considered Protestant doctrine, is not what was considered such by the Reformers.

C. Yes; and I am going to offer reasons for thinking that the present age has lapsed, not only from the opinions of the English Reformers, but from those of the foreign also. This is too extensive a subject to do justice to, even had I the learning for it; but I may draw your attention to one or two obvious proofs of the fact.

L. You must mean from Calvin, for Luther is, in some points, reckoned nearer the Romish Church than ourselves.

C. I mean Calvin, about whose extreme distance from Rome there can be no doubt. What is the popular opinion now concerning the necessity of an Episcopal Regimen?

L. A late incident has shown what it is; that it is uncharitable to define the Catholic Church, as the body of Christians in every country as governed by Bishops, Priests, and Deacons; such a definition excluding pious Dissenters and others.

C. But what thought Calvin? "Calvin held those men worthy of anathema who would not submit themselves to truly Christian Bishops, if such could be had."[3] What would he have said then to the Wesleyan Methodists, and that portion of the (so called) Orthodox Dissenters, which co-operates, at present, with the Church? These allow that we, or that numbers among us, are truly Christian, yet make no attempts to obtain Bishops from us. Thus the age is more Protestant now than Calvin himself.

L. Certainly in this respect; unless Calvin spoke rhetorically under circumstances.

C. Now for a second instance. The following is his statement concerning the LORD'S Supper. "I understand what is to be understood by the words of CHRIST; that He doth not only offer us the benefits of His death and Resurrection, but His very body, wherein He died and rose again. I assert that the body of CHRIST is really (as the usual expression is), that it is truly given to us in the Sacrament, to be the saving food of our souls." . . . . . "The SON of GOD offers daily to us in the Holy Sacrament, the same body which He once offered in sacrifice to His Father, that it may be our spiritual food." . . . . . . "If any one ask me concerning the manner, I will not be ashamed to confess that it is a secret too high for my reason to comprehend, or my tongue to express."[4] Now, if I were of myself to use these words (in spite of the qualification at the end, concerning the *manner* of His presence in the Sacrament), would they not be sufficient to convict me of Popery in the judgment of this minute and unlearned generation?

---

[3] Vide the Churchman's Manual, p. 13.
[4] Vide Tracts for the Times, No. 27.

L. You speak plausibly, I will grant; yet surely, after all, it is not unnatural that the Reformers of the sixteenth century should have fallen short of a full Reformation in matters of doctrine and discipline. Light breaks but gradually on the mind: one age begins a work, another finishes.

C. I am arguing about a matter of fact, not defending the opinions of the Reformers. As to this notion of their but partial illumination, I am not concerned to oppose it, being quite content if the persons whom you are undertaking to represent are willing to *admit* it. And then, in consistency, I shall beg them to reproach me not with *Popery* but with *Protestantism*, and to be impartial enough to assail not only me, but "the Blessed Reformation," as they often call it, using words they do not understand. It is hard, indeed, that when I share in the opinions of the Reformers, I should have no share of their praises of them.

L. You speak as if you really agreed with the Reformers. You may say so in an argument, but in sober earnest you cannot mean to say you really agree with the great body of them. Neither you nor I should hesitate to confess they were often inconsistent, saying, at one time, what they disowned at another.

C. That they should have said different things at different times, is not wonderful, considering they were searching into Scripture and Antiquity, and feeling their way to the Truth. Since, however, they did vary in their opinions, for this very reason it is obvious I should be saying nothing at all, in saying, that I agreed with them, unless I stated explicitly at what period of their lives, or in which of their writings. This I do state clearly: I say I agree with them as they speak in the formularies of the Church; more cannot be required of me, nor indeed is it possible to say more.

L. What persons complain of is, that you are not satisfied with the formularies of the Church, but add to them doctrines not contained in them. You must allow there is little stress laid in the Articles on some points, which are quite cardinal in your system, to judge by your way of enforcing them.

C. This is not the first time you have spoken of this supposed system of ours. I will not stop to quarrel with you for calling it *ours*, as if it were not rather the Church's; but explain to me in what you consider it to consist.

L. The following are some of its doctrines: that the Church has an existence independent of the State; that the State may not religiously interfere with its internal concerns; that none may engage in ministerial works except such as are episcopally ordained; that the consecration of the Eucharist is especially entrusted to Bishops and Priests. Where do you find these doctrines in the formularies of the Church, so prominently set forth, as to sanction you in urging them at all, or at least so strongly as you are used to urge them?

C. As to urging them at all, we might be free to urge them even though not mentioned in the Articles; unless indeed the Articles are our rule of faith. Were the Church first set up at the Reformation, then indeed it might be right so to exalt its Articles as to forbid to teach "whatsoever is not read therein, nor may be proved thereby." I cannot consent, I am sure the Reformers did not wish me, to deprive myself of the Church's dowry, the doctrines which the Apostles spoke in Scripture, and impressed upon the early Church. I receive the Church as a messenger from Christ, rich in treasures old and new, rich with the accumulated wealth of ages.

L. Accumulated?

C. As you will yourself allow. Our articles are one portion of that accumulation. Age after age, fresh battles have been fought with heresy, fresh monuments of truth set up. As I will not consent to be deprived of the records of the Reformation, so neither will I part with those of former times. I look upon our Articles as in one sense an addition to the Creeds; and at the same time the Romanists added their Tridentine articles. Theirs I consider unchristian; ours as true.

L. The Articles have surely an especial claim upon you; you have subscribed these, and are therefore more bound to them, than other truths, whatever or wherever they be.

C. There is a popular confusion on this subject. Our Articles are not a *body of divinity*, but in great measure only protests against certain errors of a certain period of the Church. Now I will preach the whole counsel of God, whether set down in the Articles or not. I am bound to the Articles by subscription; but I am bound, more solemnly even than by subscription, by my baptism and by my ordination, to believe and maintain the *whole* gospel of Christ. The grace given at those seasons comes from the Apostles, not from Luther or Calvin, Bucer or

Cartwright. You will presently agree with me in this statement. Let me ask, do you not hold the inspiration of Holy Scripture?

L. Undoubtedly.

C. Is it not a clergyman's duty to maintain and confess it?

L. Certainly.

C. But the doctrine is no where found in the Articles; and for this plain reason, that both Romanists and Reformers admitted it; and the difference between the two parties was, not whether the Old and New Testament were inspired, but whether the Apocrypha was of canonical authority.

L. I must grant it.

C. And in the same way, I would say, there are many other doctrines unmentioned in the Articles, only because they were not then disputed by either party; and others, for other reasons, short of disbelief in them. I cannot, indeed, make my neighbour preach them, for he will tell me he believes only just so much as he has been obliged to subscribe; but it is hard if I am therefore to be defrauded of the full inheritance of faith myself. Look at the subject from another point of view, and see if we do not arrive at the same conclusion. A statesman of the last century is said to have remarked that we have Calvinistic Articles, and a Popish Liturgy. This of course is an idle calumny. But is there not certainly a distinction of doctrine and manner between the Liturgy and the Articles? And does not what I have just stated account for it, viz. that the Liturgy, as coming down from the Apostles, is the depository of their complete teaching; while the Articles are polemical, and for the most part only protests against certain definite errors? Such are my views about the Articles; and if in my teaching, I lay especially stress upon doctrines only indirectly contained in them, and say less about those which are therein put forth most prominently, it is because times are changed. We are in danger of unbelief more than of superstition. The Christian minister should be a witness against the errors of his day.

L. I cannot tell whether on consideration I shall agree with you or not. However, after all, you have said not a word to explain what your real differences from Popery are; what those false doctrines were which you conceive our Reformers withstood. You began by confessing that your opinions and the Popish opinions had a resemblance, and only disputed whether yours should be called like the Popish, or the Popish like yours. But in what are yours different from Rome?

C. Be assured of this—no party will be more opposed to our doctrine, if it ever prospers and makes noise, than that of Rome. This has been proved before now. In the seventeenth century the theology of the body of the English Church was substantially the same as ours is; and it experienced the full hostility of the Papacy. It was the true Via Media; Rome sought to block up that way as fiercely as the Puritans. History tells us this. In a few words then, before we separate, I will state some of my irreconcilable differences with Rome; and in stating her errors, I will closely follow the order observed by Bishop Hall in his treatise on "The Old Religion," whose Protestantism is unquestionable.

I consider that it is unscriptural to say with the Church of Rome, that "we are justified by inherent righteousness."

That it is unscriptural that "the good works of a man justified do truly merit eternal life."

That the doctrine of transubstantiation is profane and impious.

That the denial of the cup to the laity, is a presumptuous encroachment on their privileges as CHRIST'S people.

That the sacrifice of the mass is a mere corruption, without foundation in Scripture or antiquity; blasphemous and dangerous.

That the honour paid to images is dangerous in the case of the uneducated, that is of the great part of Christians.

That indulgences are a monstrous invention.

That the doctrine of purgatory is a wicked invention, at variance with Scripture, cruel to the better sort of Christians, and administering deceitful comfort to the irreligious.

That the practice of celebrating divine service in an unknown tongue is a great corruption.

That forced confession is an unauthorised and dangerous practice.

That the invocation of Saints is a dangerous practice, as tending to give, often actually giving, to creatures the honour and reliance due to the Creator alone.

That there are not seven Sacraments.

That the Romish Doctrine of Tradition is unscriptural.

That the claim of the Pope to be Universal Bishop cannot be maintained.

I might add other points in which also I protest against the Church of Rome, but I think it enough to make my confession in Hall's order, and so to leave it. And having done so, I will ask you but one question. Which uses the stronger language against Popery, the Articles or I? The only severe words in the Articles being, that "the Sacrifice of Masses" "were blasphemous fables and dangerous deceits;" whereas the "doctrines concerning Purgatory, Pardons, Worshipping, and Adoration, as well of Images as of relics, and also invocation of saints," is only called "a fond thing, vainly invented, and grounded upon no warranty of Scripture, but rather repugnant to the Word of God."

L. Thank you for this conversation; from which I hope to draw matter for reflection, though the subject seems to involve such deep historical research, I hardly know how to find my way through it.

JOHN HENRY NEWMAN
The Feast of St. James
July 25, 1834

TRACT 39: AD POPULUM
Bishop Wilson's Form of Receiving Penitents

After Morning Prayers, the person who is censured to penance standing in the accustomed place and habit, the Minister shall exhort him as follows:

BROTHER,

The Church being a society of persons professing to live in the fear of God, and expecting the judgments of God to fall upon them, if His laws are broken without calling the offenders to account; it is reasonable that every member of this society who has been guilty of any scandalous offence, should either openly confess his sins, and promise reformation for the time to come; or else should be cut off from the body of Christ, which is the Church.

Now, to awaken you to a true sense of your condition, I will set before you the Word of God; that you may certainly know what will be the end of a wicked life; and that knowing the terror of the Lord, you may speedily turn unto Him and make your peace.

Hear then what the Apostle St. Paul saith of great offenders:

Be not deceived: neither fornicators, nor adulterers, nor effeminate, nor thieves, nor covetous, nor drunkards, nor revilers, nor extortioners, shall inherit the kingdom of God (1 Cor 6:9).

Hear also what the same Apostle saith:

Now the works of the flesh are these, adultery, fornication, uncleanness, lasciviousness, witchcraft, hatred, variance, emulations, wrath, strife, seditions, heresies, envyings, murders, drunkenness, revellings, and such like: of the which I tell you before, as I have also told you in time past, that they which do such things shall not inherit the kingdom of God (Gal 5:19).

It is a fearful thing to fall into the hands of the living God, who can destroy both body and soul in hell; where the worm dieth not, and the fire is not quenched (Heb 10:31).

These being the very words of God, you will do well to consider into what a condition you have brought yourself; and, indeed, the only comfort you have is this, that you are yet alive, and that the day of grace and repentance is yet afforded you. Which that you may make use of, I must also let you know, what God has declared concerning such as repent and turn unto God, and bring forth fruits meet for repentance.

To the Lord our God belong mercies and forgivenesses, though we have rebelled against him (Dan 9:9).

If we confess our sins, He is faithful and just to forgive us our sins (1 John 1:9).

And our blessed Saviour, to show us what great compassion God has for him that has gone astray, and returns to his duty; He represents Him as a man, who having found his lost sheep, takes it upon his shoulders, rejoicing.

And in another parable, to make us understand the love of God for penitent sinners, he shows us how we may hope to be received, even as a compassionate father received his prodigal son, whenever he became humble and sensible of his faults; he embraced him, he clothed him, he rejoiced with his whole family. And such joy there is amongst the angels of God, when a sinner repenteth (Luke 15:10).

Such great encouragement you have to return to God. But then, you must do it sincerely; you must not only appear outwardly a penitent, but with a true penitent heart come before God and His Church. Which if you do, you will not look upon this as a punishment inflicted upon you by the Church, but as a wholesome medicine administered for the good of your precious soul. Without which, you might have gone on, adding sin to sin, until there had been no more space for repentance.

You will suffer yourself to be admonished; acknowledge your offence; and give glory to God, in owning his power to punish you in the next life, though you should escape in this.

You will testify to others that it is, indeed, an evil thing and bitter to forsake the Lord. And owning this so publicly, you will be ashamed to return to the sins you have repented of.

Then we shall all pray to God that He would, for Christ's sake, accept of your repentance; that He would enable you to live for the time to come in obedience to the laws of Jesus Christ, that your souls may be saved at the day of judgment.

These are the wholesome ends the Church proposes in her censures; following herein the Apostle's directions (2 Tim 2:25), in meekness instructing those that oppose themselves, that they may recover themselves out of the snares of the devil, who are taken captive by him at his will.

Therefore, dear brother, consider that you are in the presence of God—the searcher of hearts. You may, indeed, deceive this congregation with a feigned repentance, but you cannot deceive Him that made you; who, if you dissemble in this matter, will shut you out of heaven, though you continue a visible member of His Church here.

But that we may take all due caution, I must in the name of this congregation, ask you these questions:

Are you from your heart sorry for the sin you have committed?—*Answer.* I am.

Will you be more careful for the time to come; and by God's help, avoid all temptations to it?—*Answer.* I will.

Will you constantly pray to God to assist you to do so?—*Answer.* I will.

Do you desire the forgiveness of all good Christians whom you may have offended?—*Answer.* I do.

And do you desire that others, seeing your sorrow, may beware of falling into any grievous sin?—*Answer.* I do desire it.

Will you take patiently the admonition of such as, after a Christian manner, shall advise you, if they shall see you forget yourself and the promises you have now made?—*Answer.* I will.

Then shall the Minister say,

May the gracious God give you repentance to life eternal; receive you into his favour; continue you a true member of the Church of Christ; and bring you unto his everlasting kingdom, through the same Jesus Christ our Lord. *Amen.*

After which he shall speak to the congregation, as follows:

Seeing now, dearly beloved brethren, that this person is moved by the good Spirit of God to confess his sins, and to be afflicted for them; let us, that we may mourn with him as becomes good Christians, consider that we are all subject to sin, and to death eternal;

That there is nothing so vile and wicked which we should not run into, did not the grace of God prevent us;

That, therefore, we have nothing to value ourselves for above others, but what the good Spirit of God has given us.

Let him, then, as the Apostle advises, that thinks he stands, take heed lest he fall.

Let us ever remember the word of Christ, Watch and pray, that ye enter not into temptation; because our adversary the devil, as a roaring lion, walketh continually about, seeking whom he may devour.

Let us learn never to be ashamed to acknowledge our sins, but let us confess and forsake them, that we may find mercy. For it is far better to suffer shame here, than the wrath of God hereafter.

In a word; let us all with penitent hearts call our sins to remembrance, and judge ourselves, though we are not censured by the Church. Let us confess our sins unto God, who is most willing to pardon us, if we turn unto Him with all our hearts, stedfastly purposing to lead a new life. Which God grant we may all do, for Jesus Christ's sake. *Amen.*

Then shall he said distinctly the fifty-first Psalm, together with the Prayers appointed in the Commination service for Ash-Wednesday.

Reprinted July 25, 1834
The Feast of St. James

TRACT 40: AD POPULUM
Richard Nelson
III: On Baptism

> *Ye hear in the Gospel the express words of our Saviour Christ, that except a man be born of water and of the Spirit, he cannot enter into the kingdom of God. Whereby ye may perceive the great necessity of this Sacrament, where it may be had.*
> —Office of Baptism for those of Riper Years.

During the summer, after the conversation last related, in which, as the reader may remember, we had been speaking of the Athanasian Creed, I was called away to a distance from home by the unexpected illness of a near relation, which became serious, and lasted so long as to keep me absent for two or three Sundays. The time of year was about Midsummer, and it so happened that one of the Sundays was the eighth after Trinity. Thinking over the first morning lesson of the day, as I sat watching by my kinsman's bedside, I was forcibly struck by the awful way, in which it appears to impress upon men the duty of separating themselves, in some way or other, from unbelievers. "Eat no bread, nor drink water, neither turn again by the way that thou camest:" that is, "however tired, hungry, and thirsty you may be, and however kind and pressing they may be, have nothing at all to say to them: do not even return the same road, but make yourself as strange among them as ever you can." Long and deeply, with my Bible in my hand, did I muse upon this history, and the more I thought, the more I was convinced, putting every thing together, that such as I have said is its true moral and meaning. I must own, however, that the train of thought was not altogether agreeable to me. I could not disengage myself from an unpleasant, though not a very distinct, conviction that this material part of piety, separation from the enemies of God, had not been sufficiently pressed on my people, in my course of parochial instruction. The thought came across my mind, "What if any of them now should go astray for want of due warning on that point, and should come to a bad end?" And I secretly determined with myself, in the silence of the sick room, that I would endeavour for the future to supply this great deficiency, and that until Church discipline can be restored again (which the Prayer Book teaches us to wish and pray for), I would try to prevail on those who were most likely to be prevailed to act upon the principles of it, and establish something like it in their own houses: using a kind of holy reserve towards those who will not hear the Church. These thoughts occupied me that night during most of my waking hours; my patient happily sleeping soundly, and my anxiety about him of course growing less: and when towards morning I was relieved on my post as nurse, the same thoughts still haunted me in dreams. At last I settled into a sound slumber, and, as was not unnatural, overslept myself. I was awakened on the Monday morning, an hour after the usual time, by my friend's servant bringing a letter into my room, which I saw by the post-mark came from my own parish, but I could not at all recollect the hand writing. I opened it eagerly, not knowing what to expect, and read as follows:

"Honoured and dear Sir,

"I make bold to trouble you with a few lines, as I find on calling at the Parsonage that Mr. Mason is not yet well enough for you to leave him: which a little troubled me, for I wanted to ask your kind advice on a matter of some consequence, and I could do it much more comfortably by word of mouth. As it is, I must try and state my case to you by letter, hoping that I shall be able to make it plain, and knowing that you will excuse other defects, which will be many. The thing, Sir, is this: you have seen something of my nephew, young Philip Carey, the bricklayer of Amdale. For I remember, when he had some work in our parish, he went to you to buy a Bible, and you had some talk with him, and named him to me afterwards, seeming rather pleased with him; and indeed he is a steady, good tempered lad, though I say it that should not say it. Well, Sir, that Bible was intended for a present, he would not tell me then to whom, but I afterwards found that he had given it to a young woman named Vane, who was in service, where he last worked: and in short, there was a talk among the people, which I as a kinsman was one of the last to hear, that they were very soon going to be married. I was not very much surprised at this: but I own to you, Sir, I was more vexed than some of our people can well account for.

Not that I have any thing to say against the young woman's conduct; indeed I believe she has always borne a good character, and is, as the world goes, very respectable: but I knew very well that her father had been for many years unsettled in his thoughts on religion—more, as I believed, of a Baptist than any thing else: and I thought to myself, if Letitia (for that is her name) is not very different from her father, how can the Church's blessing go along with such an union? and without the Church's blessing, how can they expect to be happy? So I made it my business to see my nephew, and asked him quietly, if no scruple of this sort had ever come into his mind; and a good deal passed between us, which I need not at present tire you with. However, the upshot was, we parted good friends, but both of the same mind as when we met. And on the Sunday I walked over to Amdale, and called on my sister Lucy, Philip's mother (his father died last year), and we had a long discourse, in which she seemed to think me strange and bigoted: but yet I hoped that what I had said would keep them from going on quite inconsiderately. So much the more was I disappointed at receiving a note from my sister this morning, begging me to order my matters so as to be at Amdale church at 10 o'clock next Saturday, they having fixed on that day for the wedding, and wishing me to give the young woman away. I can see, they quite reckon upon it, and I fear they will be very much affronted should I refuse. I conclude they hardly thought me quite in earnest in what I said to them. But though it will be a great grief to me to have them look unpleasant at me (for next to my own family, I have always delighted in my sister's), I seem to have made up my mind, unless you, Sir, should think differently, not to have any thing to do with this marriage; and I cannot help thinking they will one day thank me for it. I shall not now intrude on you with my reasons; but one line just to say yes or no would greatly oblige,

"Honoured and dear Sir,
"Your obliged and humble servant,
"Richard Nelson."

When I had read this letter, though I was grieved to think that my friend Richard, who had always lived such a quiet life, and with whom I had sometimes talked of the great happiness we both enjoyed—a rare happiness in these times—of belonging, each of us, to a family undivided in religious opinions: though, I say, I was grieved to think of Richard's being thus disturbed, yet I was on the whole more pleased for the thing to have befallen him than if it had happened to any other man in the parish, for reasons which the reader will easily guess. I wrote to him as he desired, not a long letter, but such as to show him that I heartily approved of his principles, and trusted to his discretion for applying them in the most effectual way. While I stayed with my relation, I heard no more of the matter, but I thought of it day and night, and wondered how it would turn out. The middle of the next week, my relation having nearly recovered, I returned home; and the first thing I did was to contrive a little job of walling, that I might have an excuse for sending to Richard Nelson. I saw at once, when he came into the room, that he had been going through a good deal; he looked anxious, though very calm and cheerful. The following conversation, or something very like it, passed between us, after I had given my orders about the work:—

"And how goes on this wedding, Richard?"

"Pretty much as I expected, Sir: we have had a good deal to say to each other about it, I, and my sister, and Mr. Vane; but though I spoke very plainly to them, they would not believe I was in earnest, till the very day before that intended for the marriage. And when they saw that I meant what I said, they were forced to put off the marriage, till a friend of theirs can be written to, and come, with whom it seems they had made an old engagement, that he should be the father at their wedding, if any one was, out of their two families. In the mean time I am sorry to say they look rather black on me; and not only they, but a many of the neighbours, too. But luckily I had made up my mind to that beforehand."

"They must look black upon *me*, too, then. For I should have done just the same, according to what I understand of the case. But I suppose you told them on what ground you went?"

"I did, Sir, as well as I could, in my plain way. I saw them all at different times, Mr. Vane, and my sister, and the two young people, and told them all the same thing; viz., that I look on marriage as a sacred thing; that the Church never meant her sacred things to be made common; that such would be the case, were a person in Letitia's state (for do you know, Sir, she is not yet even baptized) to be admitted to Christian marriage; that the neglect of this rule is every day doing great mischief; and that, being as I am, Philip's Godfather, as well as his nearest relation, I was bound especially to do what I could to hinder him from the sin and the peril.

"And it was curious to me. Sir, in the midst of my vexation, to observe in what a different way the different persons I had to deal with received what I had to say. Each had his own objection, one to one part of my notions, and another to another. Mr. Vane thought it very strange that marriage should be made so purely a matter of Religion; my sister, I am sorry to say, was inclined to think very slightly of the difference between us and the Baptists; Philip was quite sure, that let him be once married, he should soon bring his wife to the same way of thinking as himself (for to do him justice, he has no thought of leaving the Church); and, as for the young woman, she said but little, but what she said, affected me more than all the rest; for she really seemed to think me unkind and cruel, in exposing and discrediting her, and making her out (so she said) to be no Christian."

"I do not much wonder," said I, "at the young people; but I own I am a little surprised that Mr. Vane should utter a thought which appears to me so very shocking, as that marriage need, not be sanctified by Religion at all."

"Why, Sir," replied Richard Nelson, "he has been of late much out and about, talking with all sorts of people; and then he meddles with politics and elections, all rather in a wild way, and it brings him into strange company, and sets him on reading strange books. So he has picked up this notion among others, which I understand the French are very full of, as well as our Frenchified newspapers. But I should not have thought of arguing with him about it, it seems so absurd and shocking of itself, if I had not been afraid of his doing my nephew some harm by it; for Philip was in the room with us, of course listening eagerly to what passed. But I do not know," (interrupting himself,) "why I am troubling you, Sir, with this conversation."

"By all means go on, I beg of you. I am a little inquisitive to know what he could have to say for such a notion."

"His fancy was, as far as I could make it out, that the peace and order of the country is every thing. And if, said he, people can go on well, and be faithful and happy in marriage without any public religious service, why should it be urged on them by the law?"

"To which I suppose you answered, that there is another world as well as this; and it does not follow that things will turn out well in that, because to our short and dim sight they seem to go on in peace and order here."

"To be sure, Sir, that is very plain; but I do not think I went so deep. I took him straight to Scripture; for in that way I thought Philip would attend to me most. I put it to him in this way: if marriage is a different thing to a Christian from what it would be to any one else; if it is not only one of the greatest earthly blessings, but also a special and holy token, appointed by God to signify unto us the mystical union that is betwixt Christ and his Church; then, to enter on it without prayer, or in any other but a religious way, must be almost as affronting to the Almighty, as if one profaned the Sacrament of His Son's body and blood. And again, since we are plainly told, that Christian men ought never to expect any blessing from God, except as members of His Son's body (that is, I take it, as parts of His Church), how can one help fearing to forfeit the whole of the blessing intended in matrimony, if one scornfully refuse it as offered by the Church? And I take it, that every man *does* reject it in God's sight, who, disliking it in his heart, submits to it merely because it is the law of the land. Thus I went on, not expecting to make any impression on Mr. Vane; indeed, I saw too clearly that he was sneering in his heart all the time, but he did not like to say much, for fear of turning Philip against him; who, as I rejoiced to perceive, entered very much into this part of my talk. And as we walked away to my sister's, he expressed to me some wonder that so pious a man as Mr. Vane should ever have approved of the notion of marrying by Justices of the Peace. 'But I assure you, uncle,' said he, 'that we none of us agree with him. My mother and Letitia would both of them be miserable if they thought the Church's blessing would be wanting on our union. And although I must acknowledge that I could wish some parts of the service omitted, yet it must be owned, on the whole, to be extremely beautiful; and I for my part,' he went on to say, 'never expect to see the day, when *I* shall take any dislike to the Church, for that or any other reason.'"

Here I interrupted Richard in his recital. "I do wish," I said, "that people who are so much wiser and more delicate than the Prayer Book, would look a little into their Bibles too. And when they have well reformed both, we shall see how purely the world will go on, the warnings of God being silenced, and the mistake corrected, which the Church has made, in speaking out plainly about fashionable and shameful sins."

My friend Richard smiled at my vehemence, and said, "To be sure, Sir, it is tolerably plain (what I have often thought of the warnings of the

Athanasian Creed also) that the very repugnance which many men feel towards repeating them, is rather a proof of their usefulness and necessity, supposing the substance of them to be true. For it is plain, that people who shudder so much at repeating them after the Church, would never have courage to deliver the like warnings for themselves. And the same kind of remark may be made on the passages you now allude to in the Office for Matrimony. And thus people might be left to perish unwarned, through false delicacy, or false good-nature. I must say, that if I was a Clergyman, and felt, as I suppose I should feel, that such warnings ought to be given, I should feel most deeply obliged to the Prayer Book for putting words into my mouth, and commanding me to speak them. I would much rather have it so, than be left to form words of my own. I should feel it less painful to myself, and probably less annoying to others. And now that we are upon this subject; permit me, Sir, just to ask you, do you not think it would do much good, and correct what may perhaps be justly called the *vulgar* objections to the Marriage Service, if men would try to enter a little more into the spirit of the household stories, and family scenes in the Old Testament? The book of Ruth especially—can any one read it reverentially, and not learn a great deal of the difference between True and False Delicacy? You will feel my meaning, Sir, at once."

"Indeed," said I, "I do; and although I am not aware that I ever before heard it said in so many words, yet, I should imagine it must have been silently experienced by every right-minded reader. And if it should turn out, that the spirit of that Book is exactly the same with the spirit of our Marriage Service, who would desire a more complete vindication of it? But pray let us go back to your story, which I beg pardon for having interrupted. You were on the way to your sister, Mrs. Carey's; and I think you told me, that you found it very hard to make her so much as understand your objection to the marriage, or how any one could possibly imagine Baptists, as such, to be aliens to the Church."

"Yes! she was quite positive at first, that I must have some view of my own, some worldly purpose, in 'setting my head' against the match. As long as she had this fancy, she would not even listen to my arguments: and as it was, I believe she did but half hear them. I did not indeed trouble her with many: for I thought that two or three plain texts, with the interpretation confirmed by a little unquestionable history, might and ought to be sufficient."

"Let me just guess, what line you probably took with her. I suppose you first pointed out to her, that our Saviour's praises are made to individuals, not simply as believing and repenting, but as joining themselves, by faith and repentance, to the Church which He was founding through his Apostles. For instance, you might perhaps put her in mind, that our Saviour in His prayer before His sufferings, in chapter 17 of St. John, plainly had an eye to the command he purposed to give them, when he was going to be taken out of their sight: which command we read in the last three verses of St. Matthew. The prayer was "not for the Apostles alone, but for all who should believe on Him THROUGH THEIR WORD: that they all might be one." For whom was this prayer offered? Not for all who any how should believe in Christ, but "for them who should believe on Him through the word of the Apostles:" *i.e.* for the very same persons described in the other text: "Go ye and teach (or, as it is in the margin, make Disciples, or Christians, of) all nations, baptizing them in the name of the FATHER, the SON, and the HOLY GHOST." Those whom he had before prayed for, he here in effect orders to be taught or made Disciples, by persons having Apostolical authority. But these very same Disciples are to be one and all baptized. For our Lord's words are quite express: "Make Christians of them by baptizing them;" so that if we are to go by these words, it is quite plain that persons unbaptized cannot properly be called Christians: and if we compare the same words with the other text, it seems very doubtful whether such persons are included in the meaning of our SAVIOUR's gracious intercession: which is surely a point to be deeply considered. Do you quite understand me, Richard?"

"Yes, Sir, I believe I do. Those are some of the places in Scripture, which I turned to and begged my sister Lucy to consider. But of course, Sir, I could not reason on them so exactly as you have now done. There was another place too, which I begged her to think a good deal of, which must needs, I think, sound very awful to those who are inclined to make light of Baptism: I mean what was said to Nicodemus, 'Except a man be born of WATER and of the Spirit, he cannot enter into the kingdom of GOD.' It seems to me, Sir, that in speaking those words, our Saviour, who knew what he would do, must have borne in mind his purpose of causing water to be what it is made in the Sacrament of Baptism, the outward and visible sign of our new birth, and admission into His Church. I put the substance of the two places side by side in this way.

St. John 3:5	St. Matthew 28:19
If you would enter into the kingdom of God, you must be born of water and of the Spirit.	If you would be a Disciple, or Christian, you must be baptized by Apostolical authority in the name of the Holy Trinity.

What made me stronger in this opinion, was observing the like argument in our Divine Master's language, when speaking of the other Holy Sacrament. As thus: for I wrote the four places down, to make my meaning plain to the very eye.

St. John 6:53	St. Matthew 26:28
If you would have life in you, you must eat the flesh of the Son of man, and drink his blood.	If you would eat Christ's body and drink his blood, you must take and eat the bread, and drink of the cup, blessed by those who have authority to bless it, in remembrance of Him.

"I hope, Sir, you will not think that I am using the Bible too freely: but I must own, to me it is very convincing, when I see one part of our SAVIOUR'S discourses thus pointing as it were to another, and both so thoroughly agreeing with the known customs of the early Church, as I have always understood these do.

"For it is now some few years, Sir, since I began to think on this subject, and what few doubts I had, were very much settled by a book which you kindly spared me from your Lending Library. I think it was called 'A conference of two men on the subject of Infant Baptism.' And it showed to my thinking most clearly, the opinion of the Church on that subject, in times when they must have known what the very Apostles used to do.

"These things, in my plain way, I tried to point out to my sister; and I was in hopes to have convinced her, that wilfully to remain unbaptized is a more grievous sin than the generality of Dissenters (aye, and a great many Churchmen) imagine. I thought, when our LORD so distinctly affirmed, that one MUST be born of water and the Spirit, before one could even "enter into GOD'S kingdom," it was not too much to ask of a Christian man, that he should not marry such a person, considering what the Holy Spirit has said by St. Paul to all Christians, that if they marry, they must marry "in the Lord;" that is to say, must select such persons as make part of the body of Christ, considering too what strict charges were given to the Israelites of old time, not to make marriages with the heathen and unbelievers. I thought to myself, and I put it strongly to my sister, how can I, with these convictions, with the Scriptures lying open before me, and as I think distinctly forbidding such things, how can I be helper to such a union? how can I come to GOD'S altar, and present my relation there to Him, and beg His blessing on an act which in my conscience I believe to be sinful, and most provoking to Him? In short, I told them it was out of the question; and if they would put themselves in my place for a moment, they would see that it must be so."

"I should like to know what the young man thought, as he stood by and heard all this."

"Oh, Sir, I could see that he was very uneasy; he made two or three endeavours to break in upon us with some remarks of his own: but I was steady in not permitting him till I had stated my own view, so as to give it a fair chance. When I had finished, and was going away, leaving my sister, as it seemed to me, more puzzled than convinced by what had been said, Philip came close up to me, and said, in the tone of a man more or less vexed, 'You mistake me quite, uncle, if you think I have any notion of leaving the Church, because I am proposing to marry one who is not yet a Churchwoman. I like the Church as well as ever. I was born and bred in it, and hope to die in it; nay, and by this very engagement of mine, I expect to do good service to the Church. For I shall be very much disappointed indeed, if Letitia be not very soon prevailed on to be baptized, and conform, after she becomes my wife.'

"I told him, if such was indeed her mind, the matter might in no long time be settled to the satisfaction of us all. He had only to wait till that happy change, which he so confidently looked for, had taken place, and I would most gladly attend him as he desired. At this he looked a little disconcerted, and it was plain enough that he had been mistaking what he only wished, for what was likely to happen. So I just asked him one question, whether he thought himself wiser and steadier than Solomon?

He very likely (said I), when he permitted himself first to form an attachment to a heathen, expected to bring her over to the faith and worship of the one true GOD; but it ended in his becoming himself an idolater. Indeed, GOD'S warnings to his ancient people, not to be unequally yoked with unbelievers, every where go upon the notion, that the corrupting side in such unions will be commonly too strong for that which was originally right. How can it be otherwise, while human nature is corrupt, and when the aid of Divine Grace is forfeited by men's presumptuously running themselves into a state of continual temptation? And, I added, what I have more than once heard from those who have read modern history, that the same kind of result is there also visible enough, attending on the like profane marriages among those who call themselves Christians. I ventured to mention one example, which had occurred to myself, in such little reading as I have had time for in that line—the example of one whom I deeply honour and reverence—you will guess that I mean King Charles the Martyr. I do not know whether I am right, but it has always seemed to me, that the one great error of his Majesty's life was his being "unequally yoked" with a person of another creed,—a person with whom I suppose he could not well pray, although, as we happen to know for certain, he prayed constantly for her conversion. His own faith to be sure was unstained; but we know what evil ensued to his family and kingdom; and perhaps many of his own calamities might be traced to the same cause. Now if that just and good king cannot be excused for such a marriage, what can be said for an ordinary Christian, should he run into the like danger? What is 'tempting GOD, if this be not?' Thus I ran on; but Philip evidently paid little attention to me. He seemed to be making up his mind that I was prejudiced, and that it was no use his listening at all. So I went away for the present, hoping before long to have an opportunity of speaking to him when he was more willing to hear."

"I thought," said I, "that you told me just now of your having conversed with the young woman herself: did I mistake you? or was that at another time?"

"That was just as I was going away: I passed by accident through the room where she was, and we had a very few words together. It was plain at once, by her manner, that she considered me personally unkind in what I had been saying of her to my sister. I begged her to bear with me, considering that I was so much older, and that I could have nothing at heart but my nephew's good; and I put her in mind of two or three things which had passed, such as I thought would be most apt to pacify and soothe her when she remembered them; and then I begged her seriously to consider, not at present whether I was right or no in my opinion of the necessity of Baptism, but, supposing I thought myself right, how could I act otherwise than I was doing? Which, I asked, is the truer charity? to let people go on unbaptized and unsanctified, for fear of paining them;—to treat them as if they were quite safe, when, if you will believe our SAVIOUR, you must believe they have not yet even entered into the Church and Kingdom of GOD,—or to show them that you feel in earnest for their danger; to remind them what sentence the Church would pass on them, should they die in their present condition? She would not, in that case, allow them Christian burial. Why? Evidently, because she thinks them not members of CHRIST'S body; not entitled by covenant to those promises, the rehearsing of which over the grave are in her mind a part of Christian burial. I believe and obey the Church; and if it was the nearest and dearest relation I have, I should count it kindness, not cruelty, to treat him as she would have him treated; to 'have compassion on him, making a difference,' and so try to bring him, with an humble and penitent heart, to our SAVIOUR'S Baptism in good time.

"This was the tone of what I said to her; but I had hardly time for so much as this: however, as she is naturally good tempered and candid, she seemed to take it pretty well."

"I should like to know," said I, "whether she has ever expressed any wish for Baptism. A person who thinks of it, but is as yet irresolute, may be regarded, I should think, in a different light from one who distinctly slights and disparages it; more like one of the beginners in Christianity, who were called in old time Catechumens. Whereas, those who indulge in scorn, and make themselves easy in such a condition, show the very temper of the worst heretics. Have you any notion to which of these two classes the young woman you are speaking of rather belongs?"

"I should not suppose she had ever thought much of the matter, until of late, that the question has been started by this proposed wedding. What thoughts she has, I should fear, are rather of the scornful kind. She has been used to hear people say, under breath, perhaps, but not the less emphatically for that, something like what Naaman the Syrian said, 'May

I not wash elsewhere and be clean?' with plenty of hints about superstition and Popery, and other words of the like sound."

"It is too likely; one has heard of late of too much of that kind among the Baptists, and among others who agree with them in slighting the ancient Church. And worse consequences even than the contempt of Baptism follow, I fear, too often. Persons become generally irreverent towards religion altogether. A proud common sense, as it calls itself, usurps the place of that humility which befits a creature and a sinner in judging of his duties towards GOD. Nothing is cordially believed which is not theoretically understood: nothing carefully and reverently practised, of which the *use* is not perceived. And thus the religion of our time is in danger of dwindling down to a wretched kind of political decency: and where, of all parties, is the change going on most rapidly? Among those who left the Apostolical Church because '*it was not spiritual enough*' for them!"

"And yet, Sir, is there any thing so strange in that? Our blessed Lord joined the two together,—the high, mysterious, and spiritual, doctrine of the Trinity, with the no less mysterious communication of grace by water Baptism. They who begin by being so bold as to despise the water, which He commanded to be used, it is very natural, as far as I see, that they should end by despising the word which He commanded to be spoken,—the sacred name of the FATHER, the SON, and the HOLY GHOST."

"It is indeed but too natural, like all the other steps which men make down the broad way which leads to perdition. But it is some kind of satisfaction to me to find, that quiet thoughtful laymen see the danger, as well as we who are of the clergy. And I suppose we shall be pretty well agreed upon the remedy, namely, to do what little we can towards reviving among men the knowledge and love of the ancient Church."

"Ah, Sir, if that might be! But a Christian must not despond about the Church, nor the meanest Christian of being made useful, in his place, towards the highest ends. I will not therefore indulge in forebodings; but will rather try again what I can do with the opportunity which Providence *has* put in my way. I certainly will do nothing to countenance this marriage; and if I cannot prevent it, at least some part of what I say may rise up in some of their minds some day, and may help them to truer and better thoughts. But you must help me, Sir, with your advice, and (may I be so bold?) with your prayers."

"It is my bounden duty, Richard," said I, as I shook him by the hand at parting. "And take this Scripture home for your comfort; that if a man humbly 'cast his bread upon the waters,'—if he trust his Maker with it in earnest, he shall 'find it after many days.'"

JOHN KEBLE
The Feast of St. James
July 25, 1834

TRACT 41: AD SCHOLAS
Via Media, No. 2

Laicus. I am come for some further conversation with you; or rather, for another exposition of your views on Church matters. I am not well read enough to argue with you; nor, on the other hand, do I profess to admit all you say: but I want, if you will let me, to get at your opinions. So will you lecture if I give the subjects?

Clericus. To lecture, as you call it, is quite beyond me, since at best I have but a smattering of reading in Church history. The more's the pity; though I have as much as a great many others: for ignorance of our historical position as Churchmen is one of the especial evils of the day. Yet even with a little knowledge, I am able to see certain facts which seem quite inconsistent with notions at present received. For my *practice*, I should be ashamed of myself if I guided it by any theories. Here the letter and spirit of the Liturgy is my direction, as it is of all classes of Churchmen, high and low. Yet, though I do not lay a great stress on such views as I gather from history, it is to my mind a strong confirmation of them, that they just account for and illustrate the conclusions to which I am led by plain obedience to my ordination vows.

L. If you only wish to keep to the Liturgy, not to change, what did you mean the other day by those ominous words, in which you suggested the need of a *second Reformation?*

C. Because I think the Church has in a measure *forgotten* its own principles, as declared in the 16th century; nay, under stranger circumstances, as far as I know, than have attended any of the errors and corruptions of the Papists. Grievous as are their declensions from primitive usage, I never heard in any case of their practice directly contradicting their services;—whereas, we go on lamenting once a year the absence of discipline in our Church, yet do not even dream of taking any one step towards its restoration. Again, we confess in the Articles that excommunication is a solemn duty of the Church under certain circumstances, and that the excommunicated person must be openly reconciled by penance, before he is acknowledged by the faithful as a brother; yet excommunication, I am told, is now a civil process, which takes place as a matter of course at a certain stage of certain law proceedings. Here a *reformation* is needed.

L. Only of discipline, not of doctrine.

C. Again, when the Church, with an unprecedented confidence, bound herself hand and foot, and made herself over to the civil power, in order to escape the Pope, she did not expect that infidels (as it has lately been hinted) would be suffered to have the absolute disposal of the crown patronage.

L. This, again, might be considered matter of discipline. Our Reformation in the 16th century was one in matters of *faith;* and therefore we do not need a second Reformation *in the same sense* in which we needed a first.

C. In what points would you say the Church's *faith* was reformed in the 16th century?

L. Take the then received belief in purgatory and pardons, which alone was a sufficient corruption to call for a reformation.

C. I conceive the presumption of the Popish doctrine on these points to lie in adding to the means of salvation set forth in Scripture. ALMIGHTY GOD has said His Son's merits shall wash away all sin, and that they shall be conveyed to believers through the two Sacraments; whereas, the Church of Rome has added other ways of gaining heaven.

L. Granted. The belief in purgatory and pardons disparages the sufficiency, first of CHRIST'S merits, next of His appointed sacraments.

C. And by "received" belief, I suppose you mean that it was the popular belief, which clergy and laity acted on, not that it was necessarily contained in any particular doctrinal formulary.

L. Proceed.

C. Do you not suppose that there are multitudes both among clergy and laity at the present day, who disparage, not indeed CHRIST'S merits, but the Sacraments He has appointed? and if so, is not their error so far the same in kind as that of the Romish Church—the preferring Abana and Pharpar to the waters of Jordan? Take the Sacrament of Baptism. Have not some denominations of schismatics *invented* a rite of dedication instead of Baptism? and do not Churchmen find themselves under the temptation of countenancing this Papist-like presumption?—Again, there is a well-known sect, which denies both Baptism and the Lord's Supper. A Churchman must believe its members to be altogether *external* to the fold of CHRIST. Whatever benevolent works they may be able to show, still, if we receive the Church's doctrine concerning the means "generally necessary to salvation," we must consider such persons to be mere heathens, except in knowledge. Now would there not be an outcry raised, as if I were uncharitable, did I refuse the rites of burial to such an one?

L. This outcry would not proceed from the better informed or the rulers of our Church.

C. Happily, we are not as yet so corrupted as at the era of the Reformation. Our Prelates are still sound, and know the difference between what is modern and what is ancient. Yet is not the mode of viewing the subject I refer to, a *growing* one? and how does it differ from the presumption of the Papists? In both cases, the power of CHRIST'S Sacraments is denied; in the one case by the unbelief of restlessness and fear, in the other by the unbelief of profaneness.

L. Well, supposing I grant that the Church of this day is in a measure faulty in faith and discipline; more or less, of course, according to the diocese and neighbourhood. Now, in the next place, what do you mean by your *Reformation?*

C. I would do what our Reformers in the 16th century did: they did not touch the existing documents of doctrine—there was no occasion—they kept the creeds as they were; but they *added* protests against the corruptions of faith, worship, and discipline, which had grown up round them. I would do the same thing now, if I could: I would not *change* the articles, I would *add* to them: add protests against the erastianism and latitudinarianism which have incrusted them. I would append to the Catechism a section on the power of the Church.

L. You have not mentioned any corruptions at present in *worship;* do you consider that there are such, as well as errors of faith and discipline?

C. Our Liturgy keeps us right in the main, yet there are what may be considered such, though for the most part occasional. To board over the altar of a Church, place an orchestra there of playhouse singers, and take money at the doors, seems to me as great an outrage as to sprinkle the forehead with holy water and to carry lighted tapers in a procession.

L. Do not speak so harshly of what has often been done piously. George the Third was a patron of concerts in one of our Cathedrals.

C. Far be it from my mind to dare to arraign the actions of that religious king! The same deed is of a different nature at different times and under different circumstances. Music in a Church may as reverentially subserve the feelings of devotion as pictures or architecture; but *it may not.*

L. You could not prevent such a desecration by adding a fortieth article to the thirty-nine.

C. Not directly: yet though there is no article directly condemning religious processions, they have nevertheless been discontinued. In like manner, were an article framed (to speak by way of illustration) declaratory of the sanctity of places set apart to the worship of God and the reception of the saints that sleep, doubtless Churchmen would be saved from many profane feelings and practices of the day, which they give into unawares, such as the holding vestries in Churches, the flocking to preachers rather than to sacraments (as if the servant were above the Master, who is Lord over His own house), the luxurious and fashionable fitting up of town Churches; the proposal to allow schismatics to hold their meetings in them; the off-hand project of pulling them down for the convenience of streets and roads; and the wanton preference (for it frequently is wanton) of unconsecrated places, whether for preaching to the poor, or for administering sacred rites to the rich.

L. It is visionary to talk of such a reformation: the people would not endure it.

C. It is; but I am not *advocating* it, I am but raising a *protest.* I say this ought to be, "because of the angels" (1 Cor 11:10), but I do not hope to persuade others to think as I do.

L. I think I quite understand the ground you take. You consider that, as time goes on, fresh and fresh articles of faith are necessary to secure the Church's purity, according to the rise of successive heresies and errors. These articles are all hidden, as it were, from the first, in the Church's bosom, and brought out into form according to the occasion. Such was the Nicene Confession against Arius; the English Articles against Popery: and such are those now called for in this age of schism, to meet the new heresy, which denies the holy Catholic Church—the heresy of Hoadley, and others like him.

C. Yes—and let it never be forgotten, that, whatever were the errors of the Convocation of our Church in the beginning of the 18th century, it expired in an attempt to brand the doctrines of Hoadley. May the day be merely delayed!

L. I understand you further to say, that you hold to the Reformers as far as they have spoken out in our formularies, which at the same time you consider as incomplete; that the doctrines which are wanting in the Articles, such as the Apostolical Commission, are the doctrines of the Catholic Church; doctrines which a member of that Church holds *as such* prior to subscription; that, moreover, they are quite consistent with our Articles, sometimes even implied in them, and sometimes clearly contained in the Liturgy, though not in the Articles, as the Apostolical Commission in the Ordination Service; lastly, that we are clearly bound to believe, and all of us do believe, as essential, doctrines which nevertheless are not contained in the Articles, as e.g. the inspiration of Holy Scripture.

C. Yes—and further I maintain, that, while I fully concur in the Articles, as far as they go, those who call one Papist, do not acquiesce in the doctrine of the Liturgy.

L. This is a subject I especially wish drawn out. You threw out some hints about it the other day, though I cannot say you convinced me. I have misgivings, after all, that our Reformers only *began* their own work. I do not say they saw the tendency and issue of their opinions; but surely, had they lived, and had the opportunity of doing more, they would have given into much more liberal notions (as they are called) than you are disposed to concede. It is not by producing a rubric, or an insulated passage from the services, that you can destroy this impression. Such instances only show they were inconsistent, which I will grant. Still, is not the genius of our formularies towards a more latitudinarian system than they reach?

C. I will cheerfully meet you on the ground you propose. Let us carefully examine the Liturgy in its separate parts. I think it will decide the point which I contended for the other day, viz. that we are more Protestant than our Reformers.

L. What do you mean by Protestant in your present use of it?

C. A number of distinct doctrines are included in the notion of Protestantism: and as to all these, our Church has taken the VIA MEDIA between it and Popery. At present I will use it in the sense most apposite to the topics we have been discussing; viz. as the religion of so-called freedom and independence, as hating superstition, suspicious of forms, jealous of priestcraft, advocating heart-worship; characteristics, which admit of a good or a bad interpretation, but which, understood as they are instanced in the majority of persons who are zealous for what is called Protestant doctrine, are (I maintain) very inconsistent with the Liturgy of our Church. Now let us begin with the Confirmation Service.

L. Will not the Baptismal be more to your purpose? In it regeneration is connected with the *formal* act of sprinkling a little water on the forehead of an infant.

C. It is true; but I would rather shew the general spirit of the services, than take those obvious instances which, it seems, you can find out for yourself. Is it not certain that a modern Protestant, even though he granted that children were regenerated in Baptism, would, in the Confirmation Service, have made them some address about the necessity of spiritual renovation, of becoming new creatures, &c.? I do not say such warning is not very appropriate; nor do I propose to account for our Church's not giving it; but is it not quite certain that the present *prevailing* temper in the Church would have given it, judging from the prayers and sermons of the day, and that the Liturgy does not? Were that day like this, would it not have been deemed formal and cold, and deficient in spiritual-mindedness, to have proposed a declaration such as has been actually adopted, that "to the end that Confirmation may be ministered to the more edifying of such as shall receive it . . . . none hereafter shall be confirmed, but such as can *say* the Creed, the Lord's Prayer, and the Ten Commandments," &c.; nothing being said of a change of heart, or spiritual affections? And yet, upon this mere external profession, the children receive the imposition of the Bishop's hands, "to *certify* them by this sign, of GOD's favour and gracious goodness towards them."

L. From the line you are adopting, I see you will find services more Anti-Protestant (in the *modern* sense of Protestant), than that for Confirmation.

C. Take, again, the Catechism. What can be more technical and formal (as the persons I speak of would say), than the division of our duties into our duty towards GOD and our duty towards our neighbour? Indeed, would not the very word *duty* be objected to by them, as obscuring the evangelical character of Christianity? Why is there no mention of newness of heart, of appropriating the mercies of redemption, and such like phrases, which are now common among so-called Protestants? Why no mention of justifying faith?

L. Faith is mentioned in an earlier part of the Catechism.

C. Yes, and it affords a remarkable contrast to the modern use of the word. Now-a-days, the *prominent* notion conveyed by it regards its properties, whether spiritual or not, warm, self-renouncing. But in the Catechism, the *prominent* notion is that of its *object,* the believing "*all* the Articles of the Christian faith," according to the Apostle's declaration, that it is "the substance of things hoped for, the evidence of things not seen."

L. I understand; and the Creed is also introduced into the service for Baptism.

C. And still more remarkably in the order for Visiting the Sick: more remarkably, both because of the season when it is introduced, when a Christian is drawing near his end, and also as being a preparation for the absolution. Most comfortable, truly, in his last hour, is such a distinct rehearsal of the great truths on which the Christian has fed by faith, with thanksgiving, all his life long; yet it surely would not have suggested itself to a modern Protestant. He would rather have instituted some more searching examination (as he would call it) of the state of the sick man's heart; whereas the whole of the minister's exhortation is what the modern school calls cold and formal. It ends thus:—"I require you to examine yourself and your estate, both toward GOD and man; so that, accusing and condemning yourself for your own faults, you may find mercy at our heavenly Father's hand for CHRIST's sake, and not be accused and condemned in that fearful judgment. Therefore, I shall rehearse to you the *Articles* of our Faith, *that you may know whether you believe as a Christian man should, or no.*"

L. You observe the Rubric which follows: it speaks of a further examination.

C. True; still it is what would now be called formal and external.

L. Yet it mentions a great number of topics for examination:— "Whether he repent him truly of his sins, and be in charity with all the world;" exhorting him to forgive, from the bottom of his heart, all persons that have offended him; and, if he hath offended any other, to ask them forgiveness; and, where he hath done injury or wrong to any man, that he make amends to the uttermost of his power. And, if he hath not before disposed of his goods, let him then be admonished to make his will, and to declare his debts, what he oweth, and what is owing to him; for the better discharging of his conscience, and the quietness of his executors." Here is an exhortation to repentance, charity, forgiveness of injuries, humbleness of mind, honesty, and justice. What could be added?

C. You will be told that worldly and spiritual matters are mixed together; and, besides, not a word said of looking to CHRIST, resting on Him, and renovation of heart. Such are the expressions which modern Protestantism would have considered necessary, and would have inserted as such. They are good words; still they are not those which our Church considers *the* words for a sick-bed *examination*. She does not give them the prominence which is now given them. She adopts a manner of address which savours of what is now called formality. That our Church was no stranger to the more solemn kind of language, which persons now use on every occasion, is evident from the prayer "for a sick person, when there appeareth small hope of recovery," and "the commendatory prayer;" still she adopts the other as her ordinary manner.

L. I can corroborate what you just now observed about the Creed, by what I lately read in some book or books, advocating a revision of the Liturgy. It was vehemently objected to the Apostles' Creed, that it contained no confession of the doctrine of the atonement, nor (I think) of original sin!

C. It is well to see persons consistent. When they go full lengths, they startle others, and, perhaps (please GOD) themselves. Indeed, I wish men would stop a while, and seriously reflect whether the mere verbal opposition which exists between their own language and the language of services (to say nothing to the difference of spirit), is not a sort of warning to them, if they would take it, against inconsiderately proceeding in their present course. But nothing is more rare at this day than *quiet* thought. Every one is in a bustle, being bent to do a great deal. We preach, and run from house to house; we do not pray or meditate. But, to return. Next, consider the first exhortation to the Communion: would it not be called, if I said it in discourse of my own, dark, cold, and formal? "The way and means thereto [to receive worthily] is,—First, to examine your lives and conversations by the rule of GOD'S *Commandments*, &c..... Therefore, if any of you be a *blasphemer* of GOD, an *hinderer* or *slanderer* of His word, an *adulterer*, or be in *malice*, or *envy*, or any other grievous crime, repent you of your sins," &c. Now this is what is called, in some quarters, by a great abuse of terms, "mere morality."

L. If I understand you, the Liturgy, all along, speaks of the Gospel dispensation, under which it is our blessedness to live, as being, at the same time, a moral *law;* that this is its *prominent* view; and that external observances and definite acts of duty are made the means and the tests of faith.

C. Yes; and that, in thus speaking, it runs quite counter to the innovating spirit of this day, which proceeds rashly forward on large and general views,—sweeps along, with one or two prominent doctrines, to the comparative neglect of the details of duty, and drops articles of faith and positive and ceremonial observances, as beneath the attention of a spiritual Christian, as monastic and superstitious, as forms, as minor points, as technical, lip-worship, narrow-minded, and bigotted.—Next, consider the wording of one part of the Commination Service:—"He was wounded for our offences, and smitten for our wickedness. Let us, therefore, return unto Him, who is the merciful receiver of all true penitent sinners; assuring ourselves that He is ready to receive us, and most willing to pardon us, if we come unto Him with faithful repentance; if we will submit ourselves unto Him, and *from henceforth walk* in His ways; if we will take *His easy yoke* and *light burden* upon us, to follow Him in *lowliness, patience,* and *charity,* and be *ordered* by the governance of His Holy Spirit; seeking *always His glory,* and *serving* Him duly in our vocation with thanksgiving: *This if we do,* CHRIST *will deliver us from the curse of the law,*" &c. Did another say this, he would be accused by the Protestant of this day of interfering with the doctrine of justification by faith.

L. You have not spoken of the daily service of the Church or of the Litany.

C. I should have more remarks to make than I like to trouble you with. First, I should observe on the absence of what are now called, *exclusively,* the great Protestant doctrines, or, at least, of the modes of expression in which it is at present the fashion to convey them. For instance, the Collects are *summaries* of doctrine, yet I believe they do not once mention what has sometimes been called the articulus stantis vel cadentis Eccelsiæ. This proves to me that, true and important as this doctrine is in a controversial statement, its direct mention is not so apposite in devotional and practical subjects as modern Protestants of our Church would consider it. Next, consider the general Confession, which prays simply that GOD would grant us "hereafter to live a godly, righteous, and sober life." *Righteous and sober!* alas! this is the very sort of words which Protestants consider superficial; good, *as far as they go,* but nothing more. In like manner, the priest, in the Absolution, bids us pray GOD "that the rest of our life hereafter may be *pure and holy.*" But I have given instances enough to explain my meaning about the Services generally: you can continue the examination for yourself. I will direct your notice to but one instance more,—the introduction of the Psalms into the Daily Service. Do you think a modern Protestant would have introduced them into it?

L. They are inspired.

C. Yes, but they are also what is called *Jewish.* I do certainly think, I cannot doubt, that, had the Liturgy been compiled in a day like this, at most, but a *selection* of them would have been inserted in it, though they were all used in the primitive worship from the very first. Do we not hear objections to using them in singing, and a wish to substitute hymns? Is not this a proof what judgment would have been passed on their introduction into the Service, by reformers of the nineteenth century? First, the imprecatory Psalms, as they are called, would have been set aside, of course.

L. Yes; I cannot doubt it; though some of them, at least, are prophetic, and expressly ascribed in the New Testament to the inspiration of the Holy Ghost.

C. And surely numerous other passages would have been pronounced unsuitable to the spiritual faith of a Christian. I mean all such as speak of our being rewarded according to the cleanness of our hands, and of our walking innocently, and of the LORD'S doing well to those that are good and true of heart. Indeed, this doctrine is so much the characteristic of that heavenly book, that I hardly see any part of it could have been retained, but what is clearly predictive of the Messiah.

L. I shall now take my leave, with many thanks, and will think over what you have said. However, have you not been labouring superfluously? We know all along that the *Puritans* of Hooker's time *did* object to the Prayer Book: there was no need of proving that.

C. I am not speaking of those who would admit they were Puritans; but of that arrogant Protestant spirit (so called) of the day, in and out of the Church (if it is possible to say what is in and what is out), which thinks it takes bold and large views, and would fain ride over the superstitions and formalities which it thinks it sees in those who (I maintain) hold to the old Catholic faith; and, as seeing that this spirit is coming on apace, I cry out betimes, whatever comes, it is that corruptions are pouring in, which, sooner or later, will need a SECOND REFORMATION.

JOHN HENRY NEWMAN
The Feast of St. Bartholomew
August 24, 1834

TRACT 42: AD POPULUM
Bishop Wilson's Meditations on His Sacred Office
No. 1—Sunday.

Question from the Office of Consecration.—ARE YOU PERSUADED THAT YOU BE TRULY CALLED TO THIS MINISTRATION, ACCORDING TO THE WILL OF OUR LORD JESUS CHRIST, AND THE ORDER OF THIS REALM?—*Ans.* I AM SO PERSUADED.

Almighty God, who by Thy Providence hast brought me into Thine immediate service, accept my desire of serving Thee; and grant that, in the sincerity of my soul, I may perform the several duties of my calling, and the vows that are upon me.

Blessed be Thy Good Spirit, that ever it come in my heart to become Thy minister. May the same Good Spirit make me truly sensible of the honour and danger of so great a trust, and of the account I am to give. And give me grace to make amends, by my future diligence, for the many days and years that I have spent unprofitably. And this I beg for JESUS CHRIST His sake.

He that doth not find himself endued with a spirit of his calling, hath reason to fear that God never called him. . . . . .

Marks of a True Pastor

St. John 10:1. "He that entereth not by the door into the sheepfold, but climbeth up some other way, the same is a thief and a robber. But he that entereth in by the door is the shepherd of the sheep." *A lawful entrance,* upon motives which aim at the glory of GOD and the good of souls. *An external call* and mission, from the Apostolic authority of Bishops.

"The sheep hear his voice;" that is, when he speaks to their hearts and to their capacities.

"He that calleth his sheep by name;" that is, he knows them so well, as to know all their wants.

"He goeth before them, and they follow him." He leads such a life, as they may safely follow.

"A stranger will they not follow;" that is, they ought not to follow such as break Catholic Unity.

"I am the door." It is by JESUS CHRIST, not by us, that the flock is kept in safety; without Him, we can do nothing; neither by our learning, our eloquence, or our labours:—This is to *rob* CHRIST of the glory of saving His sheep; and to enter into the ministry, only to plunder the Church of her revenues.

"The good shepherd giveth his life for the sheep;" either by spending it in the ministry; or suffering, if there be occasion; never sacrificing the flock to his own ease, avarice, or humours.

"The hireling careth not for the sheep." He lords it over them, makes what advantage he can of them, and counts them his own no longer than they are profitable to him. "He leaves them," that is, when dangers threaten. Then the good shepherd and the hireling are discovered.

Heb. 5:4. "No man taketh this honour unto himself, but he that is called of GOD, as was Aaron."

Heb. 5:2. . . . . . "High Priest, who can have compassion on the ignorant, and on them that are out of the way." A pastor, who is sensible of his own infirmities, will not fail to treat sinners with meekness and compassion.

Heb. 13:17. "They watch for your souls, as they that must give account." A most dreadful consideration this; insomuch as that St. Chrysostom said, upon reflecting upon it, "It is a wonder if any ruler in the Church be saved." It will be work enough for every man to give an account for himself; but to stand charged, and to be accountable for many others, who can think of it without trembling? O GOD! how presumptuous was I, to be persuaded to take upon me this charge!

Who will value himself upon ecclesiastical dignities, who considers that Judas was chosen to be an Apostle?

O Good Shepherd! I beseech Thee, for myself and for my flock, to seek us, to find us, to lead us, to defend us, and to preserve us to life eternal.

If GOD be satisfied with a pastor, it is of little importance whether he please or displease men.

Tit. 2:15. "These things speak, and exhort, and rebuke with all our authority. Let no man despise thee;" that is, for want of exercising ecclesiastical discipline.

The following are truths which cannot be preached too often: viz., the bondage of man by sin, the necessity of a Deliverer, the manner of our redemption, the danger of not closing with it, the power of grace to deliver us, &c. A pastor should do all this, and act with the dignity of a man who acts by the authority of God.

The Authority of Bishops

We are willing enough to desire to imitate JESUS CHRIST and his Apostles in their authority, without thinking of following them in their humility, their labours, self-denial, &c.

A Bishop is a Pastor set over other Pastors. They were to ordain Elders. They might receive an accusation against an Elder. They were to charge them to preach such and such doctrines, to stop the mouths of deceivers, to set in order the things that were wanting. And, lastly, this was the form of Church government in all ages, so that, to reject this, is to reject an ordinance of GOD.

Matt. 5:19. "Whosoever shall do and teach the commandments, the same shall be called great in the kingdom of GOD." It is in this the true greatness of a Bishop does consist, not in the eminence of his see, multitude of attendants, favour of princes, &c.

Bishops were called to sit in Parliament, to give their counsel according to *God's Law;* as the civil judges were to give their advice according to *the temporal laws* in matters of difficulty.

Mark 10:44. "Whosoever of you will be the chiefest, shall be servant of all." The greatest Prelate in the Church is he who is most conformable to the example of Christ, by humility, charity, and care of his flock, and who, for CHRIST'S sake, will be a servant to the servants of GOD.

O Sovereign Pastor of souls! renew in Thy Church, and especially in me, this spirit of humility; that I may serve Thee in the meanest of Thy servants. If I lie under the necessity of being served by others, let it be with regret, and let me exact no more service than is necessary.

Luke 10:3. "Behold, I send you forth as lambs among wolves." It belongs to Thee, O Lamb of GOD, to guard both me and my flock from wolves who assault us, either openly or in sheep's clothing. I depend entirely upon Thee, in whatever relates to my own preservation, or that of the people committed to my care.

Luke 19:20. "LORD, behold, here is Thy pound, which I have kept laid up in a napkin," O my SAVIOUR! I tremble to think how I have followed the example of this slothful servant; and what reason I have to dread his doom. Rest is a crime in one who has promised to labour all the days of his life; and in me, therefore, it is a great evil, not to be always doing good. Pardon me, my GOD, for what is past; and let me not imagine that, because I am free from gross and scandalous crimes, that, therefore, I lead a good life. O LORD, give me grace proportionable to the talents I have received, and to the account I am to give; that I may faithfully perform all the duties belonging to my state. Amen.

Whoever is associated in the Priesthood of CHRIST, ought, in imitation of Him, to sacrifice himself for the advantage of His Church, and for all the designs of God.

Luke 22:26. "But ye shall not be so; but he that is greatest among you, let him be as the younger; and he that is chief, as he that doth serve." A Bishop does not know his office in the Church, if he pretends to distinguish himself by power, imperiousness, and grandeur; or by any other way than by humility, and by a great concern for souls. Marks of distinction are rather a burthen, which he bears out of necessity, but complains of them secretly to GOD. He considers himself as the *servant*, not as the *Lord* of souls. Even JESUS CHRIST made Himself our pattern in this.

Translation of Bishops and Pastors

Self-love is too often at the bottom, and not the glory of GOD or the good of souls. When men's labours are attended with tolerable success, yet, because either they can better their temporal condition, or think that a more public station would be more suitable to their great capacities, they leave their station for one more full of dangers, without any prospect of being more serviceable to GOD or to His Church, and the souls of men; not considering that this is the voice of pride, self-love, and covetousness, and an evil example to others, to whom we do, or should, preach humility, as the very foundation of Christianity.

The greater share we have in the authority of JESUS CHRIST, the greater must we expect to have in His sufferings; the cross being the reward of faithful pastors.

To leave a clergy and a people to whom one is perfectly well known, to go to another to whom one is a stranger, and this for the sake of riches, which are supposed to have been renounced,—this was unknown to the first ages of Christianity.

He is but the vain image of a Pastor, an idle shepherd, who chooses to abandon his flock, and leave them to the conduct of those who have no concern for them, and entrust the salvation of those souls to others, for whom he himself is responsible to GOD. He may be learned, he may be employed, &c. but he cannot be a good shepherd. . . . .

Church Government

Col. 4:5. "Walk in wisdom toward them that are without, redeeming the time." Prudence is very necessary in dangerous times; it being no small fault to give occasion to the raising of storms against the Church and her ministers, for want of having a due regard to the times and to the passions of carnal men . . . .

Matt. 20:26-27. "Whosoever will be great among you, let him be your minister; and whosoever will be chief among you, let him be your servant; even as the Son of man came not to be ministered unto, but to minister." GOD give me a true and prudent humility; to have nothing of the air of secular governors, to attend the flock of CHRIST as a servant, to look on Him as my pattern, to study His conduct and spirit, to spend and be spent for my flock, that I may never desire to increase my burden, that I may be better qualified to be ministered unto, and that I may never strive to live at ease, in plenty, in luxury, repose, and independence. Amen.

The name of a *servant* ought to be esteemed honourable to the eye of faith, and a real privilege; since JESUS CHRIST took upon Him the nature of a servant.

Bishops and Priests (saith St. Ambrose) are honourable, on account of the sacrifice they offer. The power of the keys, and the exercise of that power; the due use of confirmation, and (previous to that) examination; a strict examination into the learning, lives, and characters, of such as are designed for Holy Orders, are matters of infinite and eternal concern....

A man may be ruined by those very means which were designed to enable him to discharge his duty with more convenience. And Bishops have too often been put into such easy circumstances, as to forget that they were Bishops....

Rev. 1:16. "And He had in His right hand seven stars." Make me, O JESUS, a shining star in Thy Church; support me by Thy right hand; guide and direct me by Thy light; let me never become a wandering star.

A primitive Bishop will be careful to avoid, as much as possible, worldly equipage and retinue, excess, pomp, and ostentation.....

Bishops are called angels in the Revelations, intimating that they should have no interest on earth at heart so much as that of the good of the Church and the honour of God.....

At the Lord's Supper

(Before the Service begins.)

May it please Thee, O GOD, who hast called us to this ministry, to make us worthy to offer unto Thee this sacrifice for our own sins and for the sins of Thy people. Accept our service and our persons, through our LORD JESUS CHRIST, who liveth and reigneth with Thee and the HOLY GHOST, one GOD, world without end. Amen.

O, reject not this people for me and for my sins!

(Upon placing the alms upon the Altar.)

All that we possess is the effect of Thy bounty, O GOD! Of Thy own do we give Thee. Pardon all our vain expences; and accept of this testimony of our gratitude to Thee, our benefactor, for the LORD JESUS' sake.

(Upon placing the Elements upon the Altar.)

Vouchsafe to receive these Thy creatures from the hands of us sinners, O Thou self-sufficient GOD!

(Immediately after the Consecration.)

We offer unto Thee, our King and our GOD, this bread and this cup. We give Thee thanks for these and for all Thy mercies; beseeching Thee to send down Thy HOLY SPIRIT upon this sacrifice, that He may make this bread the body of Thy CHRIST, and this cup the blood of Thy CHRIST; and that all we, who are partakers thereof, may thereby obtain remission of our sins, and all other benefits of His passion.

And, together with us, remember, O GOD, for good, the whole mystical body of Thy Son; that such as are yet alive may finish their course with joy; and that we, with all such as are dead in the LORD, may rest in hope and rise in glory, for Thy Son's sake, whose death we now commemorate. Amen.

May I adore Thee, O GOD, by offering to Thee the pure and unbloody sacrifice, which Thou hast ordained by Jesus Christ. Amen.

But how should I dare to offer Thee this sacrifice, if I had not first offered myself a sacrifice to Thee, my GOD? May I never offer the prayers of the faithful with polluted lips, nor distribute the bread of life with unclean hands.

I acknowledge and receive Thee, O JESUS, as sent of GOD, a Prophet, to make His will known to us, and His merciful purpose to save us; as our Priest, who offered Himself an acceptable sacrifice for us, to satisfy the Divine Justice, and to make intercession for us; and as our King, to rule, and defend us against all our enemies.

May I always receive the Holy Sacrament in the same meaning, intention, and blessed effect, with which JESUS CHRIST administered it to His Apostles in His last Supper.

Concerning Confirmation

By faith we receive the Spirit, which is of GOD. "I will put My Spirit within you, saith GOD."

We are truly Christians by receiving the Spirit of CHRIST.

This is the great blessing of the Gospel, the fellowship of the HOLY GHOST, with the desire of which we conclude our daily prayers, with the grace of our LORD JESUS CHRIST....

The Effect and Blessing of Confirmation

It is to convey the inestimable blessing of the Holy Spirit of God by prayer and the imposition of the hands of God's ministers, that He may dwell in you, and keep you from the temptations of the world, the flesh, and the devil.

Confirmation is the perfection of baptism. The Holy Ghost descends invisibly upon such as are rightly prepared to receive such a blessing, as at the first He came visibly upon those that had been baptized....

As the Holy Spirit is present in our baptism, to seal the remission of sins, and to infuse the seeds of Christian life; so is He present in confirmation, to shed further influences on those that receive it, for stirring up the gift of God bestowed in baptism, &c.

Prayer after Confirmation

Matt. 19:15. And He laid His hands on them.

O HOLY SPIRIT of grace! I make my humble supplication to Thee in behalf of those Thy servants on whom I have this day laid my hands. Be Thou their wisdom, to give them the knowledge of religion; their understanding, to know their duty; their counsel in all their doubts; their strength against all temptations; their knowledge, in what belongs to the state of life in which Thy Providence shall place them; their piety and godliness in all their actions; and be Thou their fear, all their life long, for JESUS CHRIST'S sake. Amen.

Reprinted August 24, 1834
The Feast of St. Bartholomew

TRACT 43: AD POPULUM
Richard Nelson
IV: Length of the Public Services

> *"What a weariness is it!"*
> —Malachi 1:13

> *"O, they be blessed that may dwell*
> *Within Thy house always:*
> *For they all times Thy facts do tell,*
> *And ever give Thee praise.*
>
> *Yea, happy sure likewise are they*
> *Whose stay and strength Thou art,*
> *Who to Thy house do mind the way,*
> *And seek it in their heart."*
> —Psalm 84:5, 6

Among all the boys of our Sunday-school, none have given me so much trouble as Absalom Plush, and two of farmer Yawn's sons. They are almost always behind their time: at school they are very inattentive, and at Church their conduct has been repeatedly so disgraceful that it even attracted the attention of one of the Churchwardens, who gave them a severe reprimand, and threatened to send for a constable; since which, they have conducted themselves rather more decently. Perhaps my readers may be inclined to ask why I suffer them to remain in the school, their behaviour having been so bad. My answer must be, that as they are but little boys (for Absalom is the eldest, and he is not more than eleven, if so much), I still hope they may improve; and if I were to put them out of the school, I fear I should lose all chance of gaining any influence over them. However, I have made up my mind that if they behave in this sort of way again, they shall go.

There is, too, another consideration which has rather disposed me to be sorry for these boys in the midst of my displeasure, namely, that if they had been well instructed, and a good example had been set them at home, they would, perhaps, have behaved differently at school and in Church. For young Plush does not want for sense, though he is so unruly; and as to the little Yawns, they are not naturally of bad dispositions, but so determinedly indolent and unwilling to make any exertion for their own improvement, that it is a great trial of one's patience to endeavour to teach them. I am, however, sorry to say, the examples they have before them at home are not such as to encourage them to turn to good account the instruction they may receive at Church or at the school. This I was fully aware of from the first, and, accordingly, as it is my usual custom when the children behave ill at school to take the first opportunity of mentioning it to the parents and friends, with the hope of throwing in a word which may be for *their* good too, I determined that I would do so in these instances.

An occasion soon offered itself of speaking to farmer Yawn, whose house is very near to mine. But before I state what passed between us, I should say that I had, that same morning, talked the matter over with my friend Richard Nelson, in whose class Absalom was, as well as the elder of the two Yawns.

"Sir," replied Richard, in answer to my question respecting the conduct of these boys, "as to Lawrence Yawn, I cannot say that he applies much to his book, or, as I think, ever means to do so. Indeed, I have heard that he should say he likes to be at the bottom of the class, because then he has a chance of leaning against the wall, or of resting on the corner of my chair. But Absalom Plush is much more untractable, and inclined to be impudent too. To give you an instance, Sir, what happened only last Sunday. He came in very late, as he frequently does, and when I spoke to him about it he only laughed, and said he could not come sooner, and under breath, as I thought, he *should not*, and he seemed to me occasionally to be humming to himself some kind of song."

"A song!" said I, "what in the school? that is something new indeed."

"However," proceeded Nelson, "according to your advice to us in such cases, I took no notice at the time: but in the evening, as he happened to come along the path by our garden, I said to him, 'Absalom, I do wish you would pay a little more attention at school, I really fancied today you were singing something of a song.' 'Well,' said he, 'suppose I was—what then? 'twas only a bit of a tune that a man was singing in at father's, one night last week; and father said, that altering the words a little, it would just suit us boys of the Sunday-school. There is no harm (he continued) in the words, I will tell you what they were.' But they seemed to me, Sir, to be part of a very mischievous ballad, signifying that instead of Churches and Prayer Books, people had better sit in public houses and study newspapers; that Church-going is time-wasting, and so forth. So it is plain that the boy is encouraged at home in his bad ways; and, as you ask me the question, Sir, I fear it is not much better with the two Yawns; for I dare say you must have observed that there are six or seven people, who always come late into Church, rain or shine, morning or evening, and amongst them Master Yawn comes in as regularly as possible just about the end of the first Lesson."

"Yes," I said, "I have observed it, and have long wished for an opportunity of inquiring into the cause of such a practice."

After some other observations we parted, and it happened, as I before observed, that on the same day my neighbour Yawn came to our house to borrow a milking bucket, which I very readily lent him, though not with my servant's good will, as such articles seldom returned from the farmer's in exactly as good a condition as they went.

Seeing him, then, go out of the yard with the bucket in his hand, I met him at the garden gate, and said to him at once, "I do wish, Mr. Yawn, you would speak to Lawrence and the little boy, for by their irregularity and extreme idleness, they vex me very much, and do harm to the other boys in the school."

"Sir," he replied, making a low bow, "I am very sorry indeed to come troubling again so soon for a bucket, but our people are so careless—" "O never mind about the bucket," I said, "only please let it be throughly cleaned—but I want you to tell me what will be the best way of treating that idle fellow, Lawrence, and his little brother."

"Sir," he answered, "I am very sorry indeed they should have done any thing to offend you, but you may depend on it they shall always for the future come to school in good time, and mind what is said to them; otherwise, their mother or I will *give them the stick* as sure as every Sunday morning comes round."

"Mr. Yawn," I replied, "I should be very sorry to have Sunday made the day for such unpleasing performances in your house or in any other. I do not at all wish any boys to come to the school against their will, especially if their friends only send them to please me."

"O Sir," he said, "I am sure it is not at all against *our* will—though, certainly, 'tis a longish while for the children to stay, from nine to half past twelve, or more; and I don't altogether wonder that the boys are tired. But they shall come for the future, and stay too, tired or not tired, for I should be very sorry we should do any thing to offend you, Sir."

"You have told me so now three times, Mr. Yawn," I answered, "so of course I ought to believe it. But at all events, I hope *I* shall not offend *you* if I take this opportunity to ask you, why you and Edward Gape, and two or three others, make a rule of treating our Church service in such a careless, and I must say scornful, way?"

"*Me* treat the Church with scorn!" he replied, "why, Sir, what can you be thinking of? Why I scarcely ever miss a Sunday. 'Twould be a good thing for you clergymen if every body else was as regular."

"As to that," I replied, "it makes no sort of difference to us whether people come or stay away, except so far as that we ought to be thankful when they do right, and grieved when they neglect their duty. In this respect, Mr. Yawn, *we* are the really 'independent' ministers. But what I allude to is, your strange unaccountable custom of coming into Church so late. I have been here now nearly six years, and in all that time, though by your own account you have come to Church regularly once every Sunday, yet I doubt if ever you have been within the walls till after I had begun reading the Lessons."

"Yes, Sir, I have," he said, "you are mistaken there."

"Come now," I said, "if I have been here five years and a half, I have been here 286 Sundays, and I think I may venture to say, that during all that time you have not been in Church time enough to hear *all* the first Lesson more than twenty times."

"Perhaps not," he said, "twenty is a good many."

"Well," I replied, "I will venture to say not more than *ten* times."

"I am not sure of that," he answered.

"But I am sure of it," I said, "sure that you have not been in by the time I mention, even *five* Sundays."

"I can remember at least *three* times," he answered, "once when I mistook the clock, and once when old Thomas Pout brought his new bassoon, and on the Fast-day I was in at the Psalms, I am confident. But I don't wish to make an argument about the matter; I will tell you, Sir, plainly, that I have a great deal to do on a Sunday morning, more than you think of, and that instead of finding fault with me for being so late, you should thank me for coming at all. Think, Sir, how many don't come at all, and there am I in the pew as regular, pretty near, as old Job the clerk, only half an hour later."

"Yes," I said, "you are very regular, in your irregularity. But, Mr. Yawn, let me ask you this one question,—do you come to Church to do any good to ALMIGHTY GOD, or to me, or to yourself? Is it any profit to the ALMIGHTY that you serve Him, if such an imperfect attendance as yours can be called service; or to me is it any profit of advantage in the way of worldly interest? You know full well, my friend, that yours is the danger, yours will be the loss, if you persist in thus dishonouring the holy, jealous GOD."

To this his only reply was, that he had been used to do it for a good way in forty years, and it was not to be expected he should alter now; and with this observation he walked slowly away with the bucket over his arm. But thinking, I suppose, that he had not been quite civil to me, he turned round with the intention, as I hoped, of making some sort of promise of amendment; but my hope was groundless, for he came back and said in rather a low voice, "I hope, Sir, nothing I have said will prevent you taking your butter of us as usual; and as to the boys, I promise you they shall be well punished every Sunday morning, and then, Sir, if they do behave ill, you know it will not be my fault, or my wife's."

I made no answer, but as I walked back to the house, I was led sadly to reflect on the tendency of a worldly and selfish spirit to deaden not merely all serious sense of Religion, but even the natural affection of a parent for his children.

Some few evenings afterwards, as I was returning homewards from a distant part of the parish, Nelson overtook me, when I told him of the conversation I had with my neighbour Yawn, adding that I had little hope his boys would ever come to any good, especially as their father seemed determined to keep to his bad habit merely because it *was* his habit, without giving any sort of reason or excuse for it.

"O Sir," replied Nelson, "he fancies he has a very fair reason, only he did not like to mention it to *you*. He thinks or at least pretends to think (for I do not imagine he puts his *mind* much to any thing) that the Church Service altogether is too long and tedious. And he and some others have of late been much encouraged in this their notion by a travelling man (whether he comes from Hull or Preston I am not sure), who quarters at Plush's occasionally, sometimes for a fortnight at a time, and is so kind as to offer to enlighten us in this dark corner of the world."

"I have heard of him," I said; "it seems then he dabbles in religion as well as in politics."

"Yes, Sir," replied Richard, "that he certainly does, for I had the whole account of him from a man who was working with me the week before last; you know him, Sir, I dare say, William Burnet."

"O yes, I know him," I said, "very well; any thing like the prospect of a change in religion or politics William dearly loves, without troubling himself much to inquire whether or not it is likely to be a change for the better in either case. But what did the wise man from Hull say about the Church Service?"

"Why," answered Nelson, "as I never was in company with the man myself, perhaps it will be the best way for me to tell you, Sir, if you like to hear it, what passed between Burnet and me on the subject. And indeed it is not Burnet only, but a good many others are of the same way of thinking, more than used to be formerly."

"Yes," said I, "their number increases, I fear, very rapidly, and if so, all who love Truth and the Prayer-book, ought to be on their guard. But now will you please to tell me how you answered Burnet's arguments?"

"Sir," he replied, "I will tell you as near as I can remember, what passed between us on this subject, though I do not promise to be able to repeat his exact words; and certainly nothing I said is worthy to be called an answer to arguments."

"Make no apologies," I said, "but proceed."

Well then, Sir, said Nelson, thus it was,—Burnet was constantly commending this friend of his, who was then lodging at Plush's, and wishing me to come along if it were but one evening, that I might judge for myself how *beautiful* he could talk and expound on any subject a person might choose to mention, politics, trade, agriculture, learning, religion, and what not.

But I said to him, "No, Will, I have something else to do of an evening than to sit in a beer-shop listening to your friend Tiptop (for that is the man's name). But I dare say you can give me some account of his wise sayings; what was he upon last night?"

"Last night, (said Will, after some little consideration,) last night he was lecturing about the Church Prayer-book, a subject that he has often spoken very well upon in my hearing, but never better than he did yesterday evening."

"What was his argument?" I asked.

"Judge by this," said Will, taking a printed paper out of his pocket, "it is one of Mr. Tiptop's *perspectuses,* as he calls them." (I have this paper with me, said Nelson to me, and with your leave, Sir, I will read some of the heads.) "*The Church Service lengthy, tedious, and prolix—in this respect lamentably prejudicious to the spread of vital religion—vast numbers of highly-talented individuals unable to devote their time and attention to these procrastinated forms—consequently compelled to neglect religion altogether—surprising effects, if the service was abbreviated at least one half—the churches immediately sure to be filled with crowds of devout worshippers—this with facility accomplished by merely shortening the lessons three-fifths, omitting all superstitious forms, such as the absolution, creeds, &c.—the Lord's Prayer repeated usque ad nauseum.*" (At this expression, Will said all the company expressed their approbation very vehemently, some even clapping their hands; but he did not like to ask what it meant, for fear of appearing ignorant): and so Mr. Tiptop finished with saying, that in his opinion, about a couple of pleasing hymns, a dozen verses out of the Testament, three or four prayers, and a sermon in quantity and quality according to the taste of the audience; this would be enough for *him* in all conscience, and he supposed for others too, and need not altogether take up more than thirty-five or forty minutes at the outside, allowing fifteen or twenty for the sermon.

"But Will," said I, "do you really and seriously imagine it would be well if such alterations as these were made in the Church Service?"

"To be sure I do," he answered, "and so do many other people, who understand these things better than I or you do. Indeed Mr. Tiptop told us that some gentlemen had actually taken the matter up, and that it would be brought before the parliament very speedily, and such alterations would be made as should suit the spirit of the age; above all, that the Service *must* be shortened, otherwise the Church would be entirely deserted, and the Establishment upset."

"GOD forbid," I said, "that the Church should be governed by the spirit of the times. I trust she is governed by a very different SPIRIT. I trust she may be willing to *be* (as you threaten) utterly deserted, rather than herself desert the station allotted to her by the Chief Shepherd. And as to the Establishment being in danger, it may be perhaps true, yet I am sure nothing more dangerous can befal it, than for our governors to hearken to the counsels of such orators as Tiptop, though encouraged by all the Plushes in England, each with a company of puffers and smokers about him."

"But Dick," said he to me, "what is the use of a Church, my friend, if people are tired of it, and won't go to it?"

To this I answered, "You might as well ask, what is the use of our SAVIOUR'S precepts, if people are tired of them and won't obey them? You will not, I suppose, say, that the holy rules of the Gospel ought to be publicly set aside, merely because they are so generally neglected?"

"No," he replied, "of course I do not mean that."

"Well then," said I, "neither should you affirm that it is the duty of the Church to withdraw or alter her rules, merely because people are weary of complying with them."

"That may be true," he answered, "but you must remember that the Church herself did not mean that the Service should be so long. What we have all at once, was formerly divided into two or three parts, as I have understood. Why should it not be so again?"

"What you say is, I believe, no more than the truth," I replied; "I have been lately reading a little book upon the subject, and from that I understood that there were first the early morning prayers—then, perhaps, after two or three hours, the Litany—and then again, after a short interval, the Communion Service, including a sermon of considerable length (an hour possibly) and afterwards the administration of the Sacrament. But this last service alone, would be much beyond Mr. Tiptop's limit of forty minutes; and in this way, 'the spirit of the age' would be more opposed even than it is now."

"O," he said, "I never thought of having the Sacrament administered every Sunday."

"Then," replied I, "you forgot one of the principal intentions of the Church in having the Services so divided. If the Bishops and clergy thought well, I do not deny that it would in many respects be edifying, if this ancient custom *in all its parts* could be revived; but yet I will tell you plainly, that I do not think it would have the effect you seem to imagine, of bringing more people to Church, for, to my knowledge, it was tried by a clergyman in a parish near Sheffield, and to his great surprise, many of his parishioners staid in consequence quite away from the Church. Some said, they should not think of going to hear half a service; others, who had a mile or two to come to Church, said they were scarcely allowed to rest themselves, but that as soon as they got in it was time to go back. So the clergyman thought it best to return to the old, or, rather I should say, the modern custom again, of uniting the services."

"And yet," said Burnet, "the American Church has shortened the Lessons very much, Mr. Tiptop told us."

"It may be so," I answered, "but it does not follow that it is a wise measure nevertheless, though far be it from me to say that it is otherwise. Still, of the two, the daughter should take pattern from the mother, rather than the mother from the daughter. And for myself I must say, that I have often been glad that the lessons are of considerable length, for two reasons especially."

"What are they?" he asked.

"The one is," I replied, "that in very short readings it is not so easy to discover the general meaning and argument; and the other, that if I have from any cause been inattentive in one part, I have not been so throughout. So also with respect to the Lord's Prayer, I have often and often been glad to have had a second and a third opportunity of joining in it with increased attention. Therefore, Will, I for one shall never give my vote to have the Service shortened in either of these ways; and as to Mr. Tiptop's fine *perspectus*, or what he calls it, I don't think it worth a rush."

To this Burnet answered, "that it was plainly of no use to reason with me, as he saw I was determined to keep to the old ways."

"That I am," said I, "and think I have pretty good authority for it, authority somewhat more to be depended on than Mr. Tiptop's opinion."

"But," continued Will, "I do still persist in affirming that great numbers of people *are* weary of the length of the Service, and that it would be but common kindness to see what can be done to relieve their grievance. And since nothing can be more easy than just to omit a few prayers and other old-fashioned forms, and shorten the lessons, it would be a shame not to try it, and when it is done, every body will be pleased, and the Church establishment will be greatly strengthened."

"Well," said I, "whatever effect such a measure might have on the *Establishment,* I am confident it would deeply injure the *Church*. And as to what you say about relieving a grievance, I wish you to consider this argument which I met with in a book of Sermons that was lent to me a few weeks ago. 'If people were weary merely of the *length* of the Service, they would be at least attentive at the *beginning,* and their weariness would come on by degrees; but we know it is not so. Of the two, they are often more tired in the early part of the Service than in the later.' I do not remember the exact words, but such is the meaning."

"Yes," he said, "that is because they care more about the sermon than they do about the Prayers and Lessons."

"Very well," I replied, "you have supplied me with a strong argument against your own views. For by whose opinion do you think the Church ought to be chiefly guided, that of the few (if they *be* few) who delight in the Prayers and Lessons, or that of the many (if they *be* many) who are weary of them even from the beginning?"

"Why," he replied, "I thought it was now almost universally agreed, that What most people think, is True—What most people determine, is Just—What most people like, is Good. Mr. Tiptop called these 'Three Grand Parliament Principles,' and we all admired them."

"But, Will," I said, "suppose it should happen that 'What most people like' might be to get rid of the restraints of Religion altogether, I reckon you would not consider this a safe and good principle to be guided by; and yet you may be sure that this, and nothing less than this, lies at the root of all these pretended Church Reforms. And as to the principal contriver of these deceits, the Great Reformer himself, I do not choose to mention his name to you, but I think you will find him spoken of, and his character awfully set forth, in the eighth chapter of St. John, and, if I recollect right, the 44th verse.

"But really now, Will," I continued, "will you be kind enough to tell me, what are people hindered from by the length of the Service? how comes it men's time is so much more precious now than it was formerly? and if the Service were made shorter, how would they be better employed than in hearing GOD'S holy word, and praying for His blessing on themselves and their friends?

"I say, Will, what do Farmer Yawn, and Ned Gape, and the rest of you do, who walk always so late into church; are you spending your time any better than as if you came into GOD'S house before the bell ceases?"

"As to that," said he, laughing, "we generally sit on the wall, at least when the weather is dry, and look at Ned's pigs, or talk over the news, or any thing, just to pass the time. But the farmer's rule is, to begin shaving just as the bells chime, and then he comes in at the first lesson as exact as clock-work, and we after him."

"Then," said I, "why should you and he trouble about having the Service shortened, for I suppose, whatever were its length or shortness, you would always come in twenty minutes after it had begun."

"That would be as we should please," he said. "However, I see plainly I shall never be able to reason you out of your bigoted old fashioned notions. I only wish I could bring you and Mr. Tiptop together. I think he would soon settle you and your arguments too; he would quickly turn the laugh against you, I can assure you, Master Nelson."

To this I answered, "that I had no reason to be afraid of Tiptop, his arguments, or his jests, but that I never would willingly go or stay in the company of persons who could make light of serious matters; and I told Burnet, that I was sure, sooner or later, he would allow that I was right in this resolution."

"This, Sir, was the substance of my conversation with Will; and if you should be disengaged next Sunday evening and disposed to see me, I should be glad to have a few more words with you on the same subject."

To this I readily agreed, so we parted at his garden-gate; and as I heard his door shut, I could not but say to myself, if happiness is to be found on earth it is in that cottage, and what is the precious secret whereby it has been attained? No secret at all (I answered myself), but simply the practice of "pure and undefiled religion," "patient continuance in well doing," with "glory, honour, and immortality" in view.

When he came to me into my study on the Sunday evening, according to appointment, he said that he really was anxious to know whether there was any truth in the report which Tiptop and others had so confidently spread about, that some alteration of the Prayer-book was intended, especially (as they said) for the purpose of making the Service more 'short and compact, and suitable to the taste of the times.'

I answered, "that of course it was out of my power to say what our governors in Church or State might wish, but that I feared that in Religion, as in other matters, there was some reason to apprehend too great regard might be paid to popular fancies, even by those who are as far as possible from approving of them."

"Sir," he replied very earnestly, "I hope and trust the Church Services will never be shortened one sentence, line, or word. Grown people, Sir, are but children in Religion. If once you begin to yield to their indolence and dislike of trouble, you sanction the bad feeling, and it will go on increasing till it has eaten out the very heart of piety."

"Yes," I replied, "I fully agree with you. And to say the truth, it is my firm opinion that if any alteration is necessary, it is the other way, that the Service should be longer instead of shorter. I mean, for instance, that the "Prayer for Christ's Church Militant" should be regularly used as appointed, after the morning sermon when there is no Communion; at least where it can be done without any great inconvenience, which possibly in some churches may not be the case. It is to my mind one of the most perfect of uninspired compositions, and it is greatly to be wished that it might be made familiar to every ear and every heart."

"Sir," said he, "I have often thought so. Still at the best our weakness is great: 'the corruptible body,' as the wise man says, 'presses down the soul;' and I suppose it is the case with all of us occasionally, and even when we would most earnestly deplore and strive against it, that our thoughts are apt to wander and our devotions to be cold. Whenever, therefore, I have found myself disposed to be weary of GOD'S house and service, or have heard others complaining of the tediousness of the Prayers and Lessons, I have said to myself,—if David, the Prince of Penitents, were here now, would he speak or think thus, he who desired to abide in GOD'S tabernacle for ever—who envied (as it were) the sparrows and the swallows their continual abode under the sacred roof—who, when shut out, or far away, longed, yea, even fainted for the courts of the LORD, as a hart thirsting for the water brooks! If holy Daniel, that greatest of statesmen, that real "man of business;" if he were among us now—he, who in a far distant land, and prime minister to the greatest of earthly kings, would yet let no day pass in which he would not thrice find or make leisure to offer solemn prayers to the GOD of his fathers, his windows being open in his chamber towards Jerusalem, where lay the temple of his GOD in ruins; that as he could not be there in person, he would be so in heart and mind, would *he* say that our Church Service is too long? If St. Paul, that most heroic, and (if there were such a word) that most *unselfish* of men,—if he were now among us, would he be weary of our Lessons, Prayers, and Creeds,—he, whose conversation and home was in heaven—who desired to depart and to be with CHRIST, and who calls on all true Christians to '*hold fast* the form of sound words,' in Christian faith and love! Or the beloved John, the last and greatest of prophets,—weary, not of his LORD'S service, but of being kept so long from His presence—would he, and all the other holy men of every age, prophets, apostles, martyrs, confessors, and saints, whether of the Patriarchal, Jewish, or Christian Churches, would they complain of our Services being TOO LONG?

"O no, Sir, that is not to be imagined. So neither ought we to complain, heirs with them of the same promises, and looking to meet them hereafter in our one great eternal Home."

"Richard," I replied, "you say true. As it is dangerous for an individual to take for his guidance any but a perfect pattern of Christian conduct, so is it dangerous for the Church to follow any but a perfect model of Christian worship, so far as perfection can be obtained. Her rules should be framed not according to what people *are*, but to what they *ought to be:* otherwise you must plainly see that a door will be at once opened for numberless errors as well in doctrine as in practice."

"Yes, Sir, I see it," he replied. "And, therefore, it seems to me, that when on such subjects popular opinion runs vehemently in a wrong direction (or if not wrong, at least questionable), that then it is not the best time, but the very worst possible, for yielding to its fancies. So that even if it should be, at any time, necessary or expedient (which I cannot think it ever will be) to shorten the Church Services, yet then is the very worst of all times to set about it, when there is the greatest demand for it."

"You are quite right," I said, "beyond all doubt. But I think it would be a great support to the good cause, that is, to the cause of GOD, and truth, the Church, and the Prayer Book; and also a great encouragement to such among us of the clergy as desire to stand in the old paths; if in every parish *a few* serious thinking persons would consider of drawing up and signing a solemn address to their respective Bishops, plainly saying that they utterly disapprove of all plans whatever for shortening the Church Service, unless some urgent cause should arise, stronger than they have ever yet heard; and that as churchmen they never can or will consent to any such plans of miscalled Church reform. For you know, Richard, *laymen* are quite as much part of THE CHURCH as the *clergy;* and it is your right and duty to stand up in its defence, as much as it is ours."

"Sir," he replied, "you may be sure I would gladly sign such a declaration as this you propose, and I think I know four or five more who would sign it also with all their hearts."

"That will be sufficient," I said, "for our parish, for no doubt the Bishops will estimate the value of such addresses, not by the quantity, but by the quality of those who sign them—not by the number of names, but by the worth of those who bear them, their honesty, piety, and truth."

So we agreed that an address of this kind should be prepared, and kept ready to be presented to the Bishop whenever circumstances should seem to require.

Not of course that we were so vain as to expect that *our* exertions could be of much avail; but still, as Richard said, "We cannot stand by and see the noble old Prayer Book pulled to pieces, just to humour a mob of Tiptops, Gapes, and Yawns."

THOMAS KEBLE
The Feast of St. Matthew
September 21, 1834

TRACT 44: AD POPULUM
Bishop Wilson's Meditations on His Sacred Office
No. 2—Monday.

Question from the Office of Consecration.—ARE YOU PERSUADED THAT THE HOLY SCRIPTURES CONTAIN SUFFICIENTLY ALL DOCTRINE REQUIRED OF NECESSITY TO ETERNAL SALVATION THROUGH FAITH IN JESUS CHRIST? AND ARE YOU DETERMINED, OUT OF THE SAME HOLY SCRIPTURES, TO INSTRUCT THE PEOPLE COMMITTED TO YOUR CHARGE, AND TO TEACH OR MAINTAIN NOTHING AS REQUIRED OF NECESSITY TO ETERNAL SALVATION, BUT THAT WHICH YOU SHALL BE PERSUADED MAY BE CONCLUDED AND PROVED BY THE SAME?—*Ans.* I AM SO PERSUADED AND DETERMINED BY GOD'S GRACE.

Question.—WILL YOU THEN FAITHFULLY EXERCISE YOURSELF IN THE SAME HOLY SCRIPTURES, AND CALL UPON GOD BY PRAYER FOR THE TRUE UNDERSTANDING OF THE SAME; SO AS YOU MAY BE ABLE BY THEM TO TEACH AND EXHORT WITH WHOLESOME DOCTRINE, AND TO WITHSTAND AND CONVINCE GAINSAYERS? *Ans.* I WILL DO SO BY THE HELP OF GOD.

O GOD, the fountain of all wisdom, enlighten my mind, that I myself may seek and be able to teach others, the wonders of Thy law; that I may learn from Thee, what I ought to think and speak concerning Thee; and that whatever in Thy Holy Word I shall profitably learn, I may in deed fulfil the same. Direct and bless all my labours. Give me a discerning spirit, a sound judgment, and an honest and a religious heart, that in all my studies my first aim may be to set forth Thy glory, by setting forward the salvation of men. And if, by my ministry, Thy kingdom shall be enlarged, let me, in all humility, ascribe the success, not unto myself, but unto Thy GOOD SPIRIT, which enables us both to will and to do what is acceptable to Thee, through JESUS CHRIST our LORD. Amen.

Acts 6:4. "But we will give ourselves continually unto prayer, and to the ministry of the word."

Luke 6:39. "Can the blind lead the blind? Shall they not both fall into the ditch?"

1 Tim. 4:13. "Give attendance to reading, to exhortation, to doctrine." Quesnelle says, Not to read, is to tempt GOD; to do nothing but study, is to forget the ministry. To read, in order to appear more learned, is a sinful vanity. But to read, in order to exhort, and to instruct with wholesome doctrine, this is according to GOD'S will and word.

James 1:5. "If any of you lack wisdom, let him ask of GOD, who giveth to every man liberally, and upbraideth not, and it shall be given him." Wisdom being the gift of GOD, and this gift the fruit of prayer, a prayer that is humble, earnest, and persevering, will assuredly be blessed with this excellent gift. O JESUS, cause *me* to read, to understand, to love, to practise, and to preach Thy Word.

John 7:17. "If any man will do (that is, is disposed, desires to do) His will, he shall know of the doctrine, whether it be of GOD, or whether I speak of myself." Light and truth discover themselves to such as desire to follow them.

Ps. 25:14. "The secret of the LORD is among them that fear Him, and He will shew them His covenant." It was the saying of a learned man, saith Dr. Lightfoot, that he got more knowledge by his prayers than by all his studies.

Matt. 11:25. "I thank Thee, O FATHER, LORD of heaven and earth, because Thou hast hid these things from the wise and prudent, and hast revealed them unto babes." My GOD and SAVIOUR, imprint on my heart the amiable characters of simplicity and humility, which are the marks of Thy elect, of such to whom Thou wilt reveal Thyself. It is a dangerous mistake to think that any man can have a right understanding of divine things, without being illuminated by divine grace, and without leading an holy life.

Ps. 119:19. "I have more understanding than my teachers, because I keep Thy commandments." There is a light arising from a sincere good life, which dispelleth all darkness, and is the best defence against error and sophistry.

Ps. 25:10. "All the paths of the LORD are mercy and truth unto such as keep His covenant and His Testimonies." That is; to such as do so, all the ways of GOD, and whatever He hath revealed, will appear to be the effect of infinite wisdom, goodness, justice, and truth. He giveth light and understanding unto the simple.

Matt. 5:8. "Blessed are the pure in heart, for they shall see GOD."

Luke 22:32. "When thou art converted, strengthen thy brethren." GOD grant that we may all of us consider the *absurdity* of going about to *convert others*, without being *converted ourselves*. To understand the Holy Scriptures aright, is to understand them as the Primitive Church did.

1 Sam. 3:9. "Speak, LORD, for Thy servant heareth." Speak to my *heart*, that I may obey Thy word. "Teach me to do Thy will, for thou art my GOD." It belongs to GOD, to give the true understanding of His own word.

Matt. 7:5. "Thou hypocrite, first cast out the beam out of thine own eye, and then shalt thou see clearly to cast out the mote out of thy brother's eye." That is, purify your own heart from all worldly aims; mortify your own passions, which are the cause of your blindness; study that Word which alone can enlighten you; and lay aside all prejudices which are contrary to piety. A Pastor should never undertake to teach a virtue which he has never practised himself.

Luke 5:5. "We have toiled all the night, and taken nothing." So does every preacher, who does not beg GOD'S blessing upon his labours. It is impossible for any man to *teach* well, who does not *live* well.

"My people perish for want of knowledge." The design of Religion being to lead men to GOD, how he is to be *served, appeased, attained;* the business of a preacher should be to show how all the parts of religion contribute to these ends. He that reads the Sacred Scriptures, and understands the things concerning the kingdom of GOD, and the way of conducting men thither, need not complain for want of learning. In preaching, we must speak to *the heart*, as well as to *the understanding* and to *the ear*. The end of preaching is, to turn men from sin unto GOD, that they may be saved. He that has not this in his view will do little good. A preacher should accustom himself to give a practical turn to every thing. He that leaves it to his hearers to apply what he has said, leaves to them the greatest part of his own duty. To be heartily in love with the truth one recommends, is the great secret of becoming a good preacher.

John 7:16. "My doctrine is not Mine, but His that sent Me." To preach *our own thoughts*, forsaking GOD'S word, is like an ambassador, who neglects his prince's instructions, and follows his own fancy. With what truth can it be said, that "the sheep hear his voice," when the shepherd speaks of things, or in such a manner, as is above their capacity? Grant, O LORD, that I may read thy word with the same spirit with which it was written. *Learning* does not always lead men to GOD; it often carries them from him. Indeed, when they study to *find out*, and correct their own *weakness*, their *folly*, and the *corruption of their nature;* to be convinced of the *evil of sin*, of the *vanity* of the world; to fill their souls with *heavenly wisdom* and *devout affections* towards GOD; and all this, that they may be better able to *convince* and *edify* their neighbour; such learning leads men indeed to GOD:—the rest is folly. Have mercy upon all that sit in darkness; and may the saving truths of the Gospel be received in all the world! He that sets his heart upon the world, is not in a capacity of understanding the Gospel. Give me that true wisdom which consists in knowing how to save myself and them that hear me. Remember, that a man may have the knowledge of the Word, without the Spirit.

Obscurity of the Scriptures

Serves to subdue the pride of man; to convince us, that to understand them, we have need of a light superior to reason, and that we may apply to GOD for help. May I ever understand the true language of thy Word, O LORD, and profit by it! Vouchsafe, O GOD, to give me a love for thy Sacred Scriptures, and a true understanding of them, that I may see therein the wonders of thy conduct, and thy love for us, thy miserable creatures.

Sermons

Should be instructions, not declamations, or displaying curious thoughts, which may amuse, but not edify Christians.

If GOD suffers even an holy pastor not presently to see the fruits of his labours, it is to convince him, that the success of his labours belongs to

GOD; that he ought to humble himself, and pray much, and fear lest the fault should be in himself.

Pride and irreligion meet with darkness in the midst of light; raise vain disputes, unprofitable reflections and inquiries; while humility attains to light, in the midst of darkness and difficulties.

Whenever GOD vouchsafes to open the heart, be the understanding and parts never so small, we see the reasonableness and beauty of His word, we taste the sweetness, and feel the power thereof.

John 12:16. "These things understood not His disciples at the first; but when JESUS was glorified, then remembered they that these things were written of Him, and that they had done these things unto Him." We often read the Scripture, without comprehending its full meaning; however, let us not be discouraged; the light, in GOD'S good time, will break out, and disperse the darkness, and we shall see the mysteries of the Gospel. Grant me, O LORD, a persevering love of Thy Word, and so much light, as is necessary for myself, and those that hear me.

John 12:30. "JESUS said, This voice came not for Me, but for your sakes." The way to profit by reading the Scriptures, is to apply to ourselves that which is spoken in general to all; this truth, this command, this threat, this promise, this intimation, is to me.

John 12:49. "I have not spoken of myself, but the FATHER which sent me gave me a command, what I should say, and how I should speak." He preaches with a well-grounded confidence, who advances nothing merely of his own head, but what he has received from GOD. He may then expect a blessing. But then, let him take care not to disguise it by a language foreign from GOD's Word. O HOLY SPIRIT of grace, cause me both to understand and love thy Word.

Acts 1:1. "The former treatise have I made of all that JESUS began both *to do* and teach." This is the whole of a Pastor's life. For a man to preach the Gospel *before* he has practised it, is to be a very bad imitator of the Prince of Pastors. LORD, grant that I may imitate thee by a life conformable to thine; by all ways becoming my station in the Church; and lay hold of all the opportunities which Thou shalt put into my hands. It is GOD who does all good by the labours of His ministers. To Him, therefore, must be all the praise. More sinners are converted by holy, than by learned men. Inflame my heart, O GOD, with an ardent love for Thy Word, an ardent zeal for Thy Glory, with a pure and disinterested love for

Thy Church, and with an hearty desire of establishing Thy kingdom. Who can say it is not owing to himself, that his flock are ignorant of their duty?

Rom. 2:21. "Thou, therefore, which teachest another, teachest thou not thyself?" Unhappy that person who has in his hands the rule of knowledge and of the truth, and makes no other use thereof, but to set up for a teacher of others, without applying to himself those truths with which his mind is filled. A mind full of light, and a heart full of darkness, how dreadful is that man's condition! "Without holiness no man shall see the LORD." In all our studies, we should take care to beg of GOD to preserve us from error, and to lead us to, and keep us in, all truths necessary to salvation, by His HOLY SPIRIT.

Col. 4:4. "That I may make it manifest (that is, the mystery of the Gospel) as I ought to speak." All preachers do not speak *as they ought*. A man may have the skill to give Christian truths a turn agreeable to the hearers, without affecting their hearts. Human learning will enable him to do this. It is prayer only that can enable him so to speak as to convert the heart. May I ever speak to the hearts, and to the capacities of my flock.

2 Tim. 4:1, 2, 3, &c. "I charge thee, before GOD and the LORD JESUS CHRIST, preach the Word. Be instant in season, out of season; reprove, rebuke, exhort, with all longsuffering and gravity. For the time will come, when they will not endure sound doctrine; and they shall turn away their ears from the truth. But watch thou in all things, endure afflictions, make full proof of (or fulfil) thy ministry." Preaching is a duty, but not the only duty of a Pastor. He is to take all occasions to *instruct* those that seek the truth; *refute* such as oppose it; *reprove* those that do not practise it; and *confirm* such as have embraced it. And the more we perceive the times of Apostasy approaching, the more zealous ought we to be to defend sound doctrine. We deceive ourselves, if we fancy that we have done our duty when we have given our people a sermon one day in seven: we must try all ways to gain a soul. It will be no comfort to a Pastor, that the world praises him for some one part of his duty, while GOD condemns him for the neglect of another.

1 Pet. 4:11. "If any man speak, let him speak as the oracles of GOD." That is, worthy of GOD, not weakening it by softening interpretations, nor altering it by human inventions, nor degrading it by a profane eloquence. If we find that people do not attend to the Sacred Scripture, as the Word of GOD, with eagerness and attention, we ought to fear that the

fault is in those that preach it after such a manner as is not proper or likely to make them believe it to be the Word of GOD. It is good to know what GOD has revealed, and to be ignorant of what he has not thought fit to make known to us.

Ejaculations Before Reading the Holy Scriptures

Give me, O GOD, a love for thy Scriptures, and a true understanding of them. O JESUS, open my understanding, cause me to love Thy Word, and to order my faith and life according to it. May I, O JESUS, love Thy Word, make Thy Gospel my delight, and continue in the practice of Thy law unto my life's end.

Reading Scripture

John 16:13. "The HOLY SPIRIT shall guide you into all truth." O HOLY SPIRIT, make me to understand, embrace, and love the truths of the Gospel. Give, O GOD, Thy blessing unto Thy Word, that it may become effectual to my conversion and salvation, and to the salvation of all that read or hear it. Give me grace to read Thy Holy Word with reverence and respect becoming the gracious manifestation of Thy Will to men; submitting my understanding and will to Thine. Let Thy gracious promises, O GOD, contained in Thy Word, quicken my obedience. Let Thy dreadful threatenings and judgments upon sinners, fright me from sin, and oblige me to a speedy repentance, for JESUS CHRIST His sake. Cause me, O GOD, to believe Thy Word, to obey Thy commands, to fear Thy judgments, and to hope in, and depend upon, Thy gracious promises contained in Thy Holy Word, for JESUS CHRIST'S sake. Grant, O LORD, that in reading Thy Holy Word, I may never prefer my private sentiments before those of the Church in the purely ancient times of Christianity. Give me a full persuasion of those great truths, which Thou hast revealed in Thy Holy Word. The Gospel will not be a means of salvation to him who reads or hears it only, but to him who reads, loves, remembers, and practises it by a lively faith. Cause me, O GOD, rightly to understand, and constantly to walk in the way of Thy commandments. Grant us in this world knowledge of Thy truth, and in the world to come life everlasting, for JESUS CHRIST'S sake. *Amen*. From hardness of heart and contempt of Thy Word, Good LORD deliver us. Give us all grace to hear meekly Thy Word, to receive it with pure affection, and to bring forth the fruits of the SPIRIT, to amend our lives according to Thy Holy Word.

Luke 24:45. "Then opened he their understanding, that they might understand the Scriptures." Unless Thou, O JESUS, openest our understanding, all our pains, all our learning, will signify little.

Matt. 13:36. "Declare unto us this parable." This should instruct us, that the knowledge of GOD'S Word, and the mysteries of the Gospel, are favours which we must always beg of GOD.

Reprinted September 29, 1834
The Feast of St. Michael

TRACT 45: AD CLERUM
The Grounds of Our Faith

Every system of theology has its dangers, its tendencies towards evil. Systems short of the truth have this tendency inherent in themselves, and in process of time discover it, and work out the anticipated evil, which is but the legitimate though latent consequence of their principles. Thus, we may consider the present state of Geneva the fair result on the long run of the system of self-will which was established there in the sixteenth century. But even the one true system of religion has its dangers on all sides, from the weakness of its recipients, who pervert it. Thus the Holy Catholic doctrines, in which the Church was set up, were corrupted into Popery, not legitimately, or necessarily, but by various external causes acting on human corruption, in the lapse of many ages. St. Paul's command of obedience to rulers, was changed into the tyrannical rule of *one* Bishop over *all* countries; his recommendation of an unmarried life, for certain religious objects, was made a rule of celibacy in the case of the clergy. Now, let us ask, what are the bad *tendencies* of Protestantism? for this is a question which nearly concerns ourselves. We are nearly 300 years from its rise in this country; have any evils yet shewn themselves from it? It is not here proposed to examine the question at large; but a hint on one part of the subject, may be made in answer to it.

At the Reformation, the authority of the Church was discarded by the spirit then predominant among Protestants, and Scripture was considered as the sole document both for ascertaining and proving our faith. The question immediately arose, "Is this or that doctrine in

Scripture?"—and in consequence, various intellectual gifts, such as argumentative subtilty, critical acumen, knowledge of the languages, rose into importance, and became the interpreters of Christian truth. Exposition lay through controversy. Now the natural effect of disputation is to make us shun all but the strongest proofs, those which an adversary will find substantial impediments in his line of reasoning; and, therefore, to generate a cautious, discriminative turn of thought, to fix in the mind a *standard* of proof simulating demonstration, and to make light of mere probabilities. This intellectual habit, resulting from controversy, would also arise from the peculiar exercises of thought necessary for the accurate scholar or antiquarian. It followed, that in course of time, all the delicate shades of truth and falsehood, the unobtrusive indications of God's will, the low tones of the "still small voice," in which Scripture abounds, were rudely rejected; the crumbs from the rich man's table, which Faith eagerly looks about for, were despised by the proud-hearted intellectualist, who (as if it were a favour in him to accept the Gospel) would be content with nothing short of certainty, and ridiculed as superstitious and illogical whatever did not approve itself to his own cold, hard, and unimpassioned temper. For instance, if the cases of Lydia, of the jailor, of Stephanas, were brought to shew our Lord's *wish* as to the baptism of households, the actions of his apostles *to interpret* his own commands, it was answered; "This is no satisfactory *proof*; it is not *certain* that every one of those households was not himself a believer; it is not *certain* there were any children among them:"—though surely, in as many as *three* households, the probability is on the side which the Church has taken, especially viewing the texts in connexion with our Saviour's words, "Suffer the little children," &c. Again, while the observance of the Lord's day was grounded upon the *practice* of the apostles, it was somehow felt, that this proof was not *strong enough* to bind the mass of Protestants: and so the chief argument now in use is one drawn from the Jewish law, viz., the direct Scripture *command,* contained in the fourth commandment.

Our Saviour has noticed the frame of mind here alluded to, in Mark 8:11, 12, where his feelings and judgment upon it are also told us:—"And the Pharisees came forth, and began to question with Him, seeking of Him *a sign from heaven,* tempting Him. And *He sighed deeply in His spirit,* and saith, Why doth this generation seek after a sign? Verily I say unto you, *There shall no sign be given unto this generation.* And He left them."

We are warned against the same hard, intractable temper in the book of Psalms:—"I will inform thee, and teach thee in the way wherein thou shalt go; *and I will guide thee with Mine eye*. Be ye not like to horse and mule, *which have no understanding;* whose mouths must be held *with bit and bridle*, lest they fall upon thee." Psalm 32:9, 10. This stubborn spirit, which yields to nothing but violence, is determined to *feel* Christ's yoke ere it submits to it, will not see except in broad day-light, and like the servant who hid his talent, is ever making excuses, murmuring, doubting, grudging obedience, and stifling docile and open-hearted faith, is the spirit of ultra-Protestantism, *i.e.* that spirit, to which the principles of Protestantism *tend,* and which they have in a great measure *realized*. On this subject the reader may consult Nos. 4, 8, and 19, of this series of Tracts.

Now to apply this to the doctrines, at present so much undervalued, which it is the especial object of these Tracts to enforce.

When a clergyman has spoken strongly in defence of Episcopacy, a hearer will go away saying, that there is much very able and forcible, much very eloquent and excellent, in what he has just heard; but after all, *there is very little about Episcopacy in Scripture*. This is the point to which a shrewd, clear-headed reasoner will resort,—*"after all;"* we come round and round to it; the doctrine advocated is plausible, useful, generally received hitherto;—granted,—*but* Scripture says very little about it.

Now it cannot be for a moment allowed, that Scripture *contains* little on the subject of Church Government; though it may readily be granted that it *obtrudes* on the reader little about it. The doctrine is in it, not on it; not on the surface. This need not be proved here, since the subject has been variously considered in former Numbers of this series. But it may be useful in a few words to shew how the state of the argument and controversy concerning Episcopacy, illustrates the above remarks, and how parallel it is to the state in which other religious truths are found, which no Churchman ventures to dispute.

1. Now in the first place, let us suppose, *for the sake of argument*, that Episcopacy is in fact not at all mentioned in Scripture: even then it would be our duty to receive it. Why? because the first Christians received it. If we wish to get at the truth, no matter how we get at it, *if* we get at it. If it be a fact, that the earliest Christian communities were universally

episcopal, it is a reason for our maintaining Episcopacy; and *in proportion to our conviction*, is it incumbent on us to maintain it.

Nor can it be fairly dismissed as a non-essential, an ordinance indifferent and mutable, though formerly existing over Christendom; for, *who* made us judges of essentials and non-essentials? *how* do we determine them? In the Jewish law, the slightest transgression of the commandment was followed by the penalty of death; vide Leviticus 8:35; 10:6. Does not its universality imply a necessary connexion with Christian doctrine? Consider how such reasonings would carry us through life; how the business of the world depends on punctuality in minutes; how "great a matter" a mere spark dropped on gunpowder "kindleth."

But, it may be urged, that we Protestants believe the *Scriptures* to contain the whole rule of duty.—Certainly not; they constitute a rule of *faith*, not a rule of *practice;* a rule of *doctrine*, not a rule of *conduct* or *discipline*. Where (*e.g.*) are we told in Scripture, that gambling is wrong? or again, suicide? Our Article is precise; "Holy Scripture containeth all things necessary to salvation, so that whatsoever is not read therein, &c. is not to be required of any man, that it should be *believed* as an article of *faith*." Again it says, that the Apocrypha is *not* to be applied "to establish any *doctrine*," implying that *this* is the use of the canonical books.

2. However, let us pass from this argument, which is but founded on a *supposition*, that Episcopacy is not enjoined in Scripture. Suppose we maintain, as we may well maintain, that it *is* enjoined in Scripture. An objector will say, that, at all events it is but obscurely contained therein, and cannot be drawn out from it without a great deal of delicate care and skill. Here comes in the operation of that principle of *faith* in opposition to *criticism*, which was above explained; the principle of being content with a little light, where we cannot obtain sunshine. If it is *probably* pleasing to Christ, let us maintain it. Now take a parallel case: *e.g.* the practice of infant baptism; where is this *enjoined* in Scripture? No where. Why do we observe it? Because the primitive Church observed it, and because the Apostles in Scripture *appear* to have sanctioned it, though this is not altogether certain *from* Scripture. In a difficult case we do as well as we can, and carefully *study* what is most agreeable to our Lord and Saviour. This is how our Church expresses it in the 27th Article: "The baptism of young children is in any wise to be retained in the Church, *as most agreeable* with the institution of Christ." This is true wariness and

Christian caution; very different from that spurious caution which ultra-Protestantism exercises. Let a man only be consistent, and apply the same judgment in the case of Episcopacy: let him consider whether the duty of keeping to Bishops, be not "*most agreeable* with the institution of Christ." If, indeed, he denies this altogether, these remarks do not apply; but they are addressed to waverers, and falsely moderate men, who cannot deny, that the evidence of Scripture is in favour of Churchmen, but say it is not strong enough. They say, that if Almighty God had intended an uniformity in Church Government among Christians, he would have spoken more clearly.

Now if they carried on this line of argument consistently, they would not baptize their children: happily they are inconsistent. It would be more happy still, were they consistent on the other side; and, as they baptize their children, because it is safer to observe than to omit the sacrament, did they also keep to the Church, as the safer side. The received practice, then, of infant baptism seems a final answer to all who quarrel with the Scripture evidence for Episcopacy.

3. But further still, infant baptism, like Episcopacy, is but a case of *discipline*. What shall we say, when we consider that a case of *doctrine*, necessary doctrine, doctrine the very highest and most sacred, may be produced, where the argument lies as little on the surface of Scripture,— where the proof, though *most conclusive*, is as indirect and circuitous as that for Episcopacy; viz. the doctrine of the Trinity? Where is this solemn and comfortable mystery formally stated in Scripture, as we find it in the creeds? Why is it not? Let a man consider whether all the objections which he urges against the Scripture argument for Episcopacy may not be turned against his own belief in the Trinity. It is a happy thing for themselves that men are inconsistent; yet it is miserable to advocate and establish a *principle*, which, not in their own case indeed, but in the case of others who learn it of them, leads to Socinianism. This being considered, can we any longer wonder at the awful fact, that the descendants of Calvin, the first Presbyterian, are at the present day in the number of those who have denied the Lord who bought them?

JOHN HENRY NEWMAN
The Feast of St. Luke
October 18, 1834

TRACT 46: AD POPULUM
Bishop Wilson's Meditations on His Sacred Office
No. 3—Tuesday.

Question from the Office of Ordination.—ARE YOU READY, WITH ALL FAITHFUL DILIGENCE, TO BANISH AND DRIVE AWAY ALL ERRONEOUS AND STRANGE DOCTRINE, CONTRARY TO GOD'S WORD; AND BOTH PRIVATELY AND OPENLY TO CALL UPON AND ENCOURAGE OTHERS TO DO THE SAME?—*Ans.* I AM READY, THE LORD BEING MY HELPER.

Blessed be the good providence of GOD, who, in great compassion for this Church and Nation, has hitherto preserved us from heresies and schisms.

O LORD, continue to us this great mercy, and grant that we, who are appointed to watch over Thy flock, may employ our learning and our time in promoting of true piety; that we may never grow secure and careless, but that we may endeavour to secure the *power*, as well as the *form* of godliness. Have pity upon all Christian Churches, that are distracted by contending parties, and reduce all that wander out of the way. Enable us to preserve this Church in peace and unity, by all means becoming the spirit of the Gospel. Keep us stedfast in the faith, that we may never be tossed about with any wind of doctrine, or the craft of men. Let the zeal and industry of those that are in error provoke us to be zealously affected in a righteous cause; in labouring to make men good, and in converting sinners from the error of their ways; which GOD grant for JESUS CHRIST'S sake.—Amen.

"But," the Bishop, "himself also, as his important affairs will permit him, shall use his best endeavour by instruction, persuasion, and all good means he can devise, to reclaim both them and all other within his Diocese so affected."—*Canon 66th.*

2 Tim. 4:3. "The time will come when they will not endure sound doctrine, but after their own lusts shall they heap to themselves teachers, having itching ears."

N.B. We are now in these sad times, and it behoves all faithful Pastors to know it. It is not the doctrine of the Gospel, if it favours men's lusts. They that will not receive, or who reject, the truth, are often judicially punished with a greediness to receive errors, falsehoods, and fables.

Ver. 5. "Watch thou in all things, endure afflictions, make full proof of (*or fulfil*) thy ministry." He that is wanting in any essential part, is wanting to his own salvation.

LORD, Thou art just in all the troubles which Thou hast brought upon this Church and Nation. Yet, O LORD, have mercy upon us, and restore to us that peace and unity which we once enjoyed.

Matt. 7:20. "By their fruits ye shall know them." This rule, though given by CHRIST himself, is seldom observed. The best fruits are counted as nothing, are overlooked, and often condemned by those who have none good to show. Hence, all the evils the Church suffers.

Matt. 13:25. "But while men slept, his enemy came and sowed tares among the wheat." O JESU, awaken the Pastors of Thy flock, and open their eyes, that they may perceive the tares which choke the seed,—the wolves which destroy Thy sheep.

A mixture of good and bad in the Church is necessary to instruct, exercise, purify, sanctify, and keep the righteous in humility.

Matt. 13:29. "Nay, lest, while ye gather up the tares, ye root up also the wheat with them." A zeal not regulated by this prohibition, allows no time to the good to grow strong in goodness, or to the wicked to forsake their evil ways; but chooses rather to destroy the good, provided they can but destroy the bad.

Rev. 2:14, 20. "I have a few things against thee, because thou hast there them that hold the doctrine of Balaam, who taught Balak to cast a stumbling-block before the children of Israel, to eat things sacrificed unto idols, and to commit fornication. Thou sufferest that woman Jezebel to teach and to seduce my servants to commit fornication." How dreadful is the government of the Church, wherein a man must answer for those sins which he does not hinder! To tolerate by silence those who favour and promote sin, JESUS CHRIST rebukes in the persons of these Bishops.

O my SAVIOUR! Thou who givest me this warning, enable me to profit by it. Assist me, in this day of trial, effectually to oppose and suppress that spirit of impurity, idolatry, profaneness, and irreligion, which is broken in upon us.

If for fear of offending men, or from a false love of peace, we forbear to defend the truth, we betray and abandon it.

Acts 28:29. "And when he had said these things,—the Jews had great reasonings among themselves." A preacher of the truth is not to be blamed for the contests which it gives occasion to carnal men to raise. Even CHRIST Himself could not preach without disturbing sinners;—and if He came not to bring peace on earth, but a sword of division, His Ministers ought to expect to do the same.

It is not by the heat of disputation, but by the gentleness of charity, that souls are gained over to GOD. And when controversy is necessary, as sometimes it is, let it never be managed with harshness, bitterness, or severity, lest it exasperate and harden, more than convert and edify. A prudent condescension has often prevailed upon the weak, and rendered them capable of hearkening to reason, when the contrary conduct would have removed them farther from the light.

We ought to avoid evil men and seducers, in order to shame them;—to deprive them of that credit, whereby they may do hurt;—to make them to return to a right mind;—and that we may avoid the snare ourselves.

Disputes

The primitive Fathers were ever modest upon religious questions. They contented themselves with resolving such questions as were proposed to them, without starting new ones; and carefully suppressed the curious, restless temper.

May I receive from Thee, O GOD, at all times, the rules of my behaviour on these occasions.

GOD judges otherwise than we do of these things. He knows the good He intends to bring out of evil,—either for the sanctification of the righteous,—conversion of the wicked, by His goodness in bearing with them,—or leaving them without excuse.

One single soul is worth the utmost pains of the greatest Minister of CHRIST. But, then, let us take care, when it is brought into the fold, that he be a better Christian than before,—that he be not two-fold more the child of hell than before.

Reprinted October 28, 1834
The Feast of St. Simon & St. Jude

Records *of* *the* Church

THE HOLY CHURCH THROUGHOUT
ALL THE WORLD DOTH ACKNOWLEDGE THEE

RECORD 1

Epistle of Ignatius to the Ephesians

St. Ignatius, Bishop of Antioch, and Martyr, is reported to have been the child whom CHRIST took into His arms, in order to give His disciples a pattern of Christian humbleness. But, however this was, he certainly was a disciple and friend of the Apostles, particularly St. Peter and St. John.

St. Peter and St. Paul are said to have laid on him their hands, and made him Bishop of Antioch. In A.D. 106, when he had been Bishop nearly 40 years, the persecuting Emperor Trajan came to Antioch; and on finding Ignatius resolute in confessing the faith of CHRIST, he ordered him to be carried prisoner to Rome, and there thrown to the beasts in the idolatrous heathen shows, a command which was strictly obeyed. During his journey, he wrote letters to various Churches, by way of taking leave of them, and to confirm them in Christian zeal, love, and unity; and these by GOD'S good providence are preserved to us. They are especially valuable to us at the present day, as shewing us how important it is, in the judgment of this blessed Martyr, to honor and obey our Bishops. They are as follows.—

Epistle of Ignatius, the Friend of St. Peter and St. John, on the Way to Martyrdom, to the Ephesians

Ignatius, also called Theophorus, to her who is blessed in the greatness and fulness of GOD the Father; to the predestinate before all worlds to be ever in marvellous glory unchangeable, united, and elect through the true Passion, through the will of the FATHER and JESUS CHRIST our God; to the truly beatified Church, which is in Ephesus of Asia, all health in JESUS CHRIST and in unspotted grace.

 I. I welcome in GOD'S behalf that well-beloved name, which ye have attained in all righteousness, according to the Faith and Love which is in JESUS CHRIST our SAVIOUR, for that being followers of GOD, and kindling the inward flame by the Blood of GOD, ye have perfectly accomplished the work that belonged to you, when ye heard that I came bound from Syria, for the common name and hope; trusting through your prayers to fight with beasts at Rome, that so by suffering I may become indeed the Disciple of Him "who gave himself to GOD, an Offering and Sacrifice for us." How many ye be, that be called by the name of GOD, I have heard from Onesimus, whose love is beyond all words, your Bishop according to the flesh; whom I beseech you, by JESUS CHRIST, to love, and that ye would all be like unto him. And blessed be GOD, who has granted unto you, who are so worthy of him, to enjoy such a Bishop.

 II. As to my fellow-servant Burrhus, who is your most blessed Deacon, in things pertaining to GOD, I pray that he may abide with you to the honour both of you and of your Bishop. And Crocus, also, worthy both of GOD and you, whom I have received as the sample of your love, has in all things refreshed me, as the Father of our LORD JESUS CHRIST shall also refresh him; together with Onesimus, and Burrhus, and Euplus, and Fronto, in seeing whom I have seen the love of you all. And may I always have joy of you, if I be worthy of it! It is therefore fitting that you should by all means glorify JESUS CHRIST, who hath glorified you: that by a uniform obedience, "Ye may be perfectly joined together in the same mind, and in the same judgment; and may all speak the same thing:" and that being subject to your Bishop, and his Presbytery, ye may be sanctified in all things.

 III. These things I prescribe to you, not as if I were somebody; for though I am bound for His name, I am not yet perfect in CHRIST JESUS. But now I begin to learn, and I speak to you as Fellow-Disciples together with me. For I ought to have been stirred up by you in Faith, in Admonition, in Patience, in Long-suffering. But forasmuch as Charity suffers me not to be silent towards you, I have first taken upon me to exhort you, that ye would all concur in the mind of GOD. For JESUS

CHRIST, our inseparable Life, is the Mind of the FATHER; like as the Bishops, appointed even unto the utmost bounds of the earth, are after the mind of JESUS CHRIST.

IV. Wherefore it will become you to concur in the mind of your Bishops, as also ye do. For your famous Presbytery, worthy of GOD, is knit as closely to its Bishop, as the strings to a harp. Therefore by your unanimity and harmonious love JESUS CHRIST is sung; and each of you taketh part in the chorus: that so being attuned together in one mind, and taking up the song of GOD, ye may with one voice, and in a perfect unity, sing to the FATHER by JESUS CHRIST; to the end that by this means He may both hear you, and perceive by your works, that ye are indeed the members of His Son. Wherefore it is profitable for you to live in blameless unity, that so ye may always have fellowship with GOD.

V. For if I in this little time have held such communion with your Bishop, I mean not earthly, but spiritual; how much more must I think you blessed, who are so joined to him, as the Church is to JESUS CHRIST, and JESUS CHRIST to the FATHER; that so all things may agree in the same unity? Let no man deceive himself; if a man be not within the ALTAR, he faileth of the BREAD of GOD. For if the prayer of one or two be of such force, as we are told, how much more that of the Bishop and the whole Church? He, therefore, that does not come together into the same place with it, is proud, and has already condemned himself. For it is written, "God resisteth the proud." Let us take heed therefore, that we do not set ourselves against the Bishop, that we may be set under GOD.

VI. And the more any seeth his Bishop keep silence, the more let him reverence him. For whomsoever the master of the house sendeth to his own household, we ought so to receive, as we would him that sent him. It is plain then that we ought to look to the Bishop, even as to the LORD himself. And truly Onesimus himself doth greatly commend your good order in GOD: in that ye all live according to the truth, and that no heresy dwelleth among you, but ye hearken to no man above JESUS CHRIST, speaking to you in truth.

VII. For some there are who carry about the name of CHRIST in deceitfulness, and do many things unworthy of GOD; whom ye must flee, as ye would wild beasts. For they are ravening dogs, which bite secretly; against whom ye must guard yourselves, as hardly to be cured. There is one Physician, both Fleshly and Spiritual; Begotten, not Made; God incarnate;

true Life in Death; both of Mary and of GOD; first made subject to suffering, then liable to suffer no more.

VIII. Wherefore let no man deceive you; as indeed neither are ye deceived, being wholly the servants of GOD. For inasmuch as there is no contention nor strife among you, to trouble you, surely ye live according to GOD'S Will. My soul be for yours; and I myself the expiatory offering for your church of Ephesus, so famous to all ages. They that are of the flesh cannot do the works of the spirit; neither they that are of the spirit the works of the flesh; as also faith cannot do the works of unfaithfulness; neither unfaithfulness the works of faith. But even those things which ye do according to the flesh are spiritual; forasmuch as ye do all things in JESUS CHRIST.

IX. Nevertheless I have heard of some who have gone to you, having perverse doctrine; whom ye did not suffer to sow among you; but stopped your ears, that ye might not receive those things that were sown by them: as being the stones of the temple of the FATHER, prepared for His building; and drawn up on high by the cross of CHRIST, as by an engine; using the HOLY GHOST as the line by which to ascend: your faith being your support, and your charity the way that leads you up unto GOD. Ye therefore, with all the companions of your way, are full of GOD, of His spiritual temple, of CHRIST, of the Holy One: adorned in all things with the commands of CHRIST; through whom also I triumph, in that I have been thought worthy by this present Epistle to hold converse with you; and to joy together, that having regard to the other life, ye love nothing but GOD only.

X. Pray also without ceasing for all men; for there is hope of repentance in them, that they may attain unto GOD. Suffer them therefore to learn from you, if only from your works. Against their raging, be ye mild; against their boasting, be ye lowly-minded; against their blasphemies, oppose your prayers; against their errors, be ye "stedfast in the faith;" against their cruelty, be ye gentle: not striving to imitate them again, let us be found their brethren in all kindness, but imitators of the LORD; if any one be more than other either injured, or defrauded, or despised; that so no plant of the devil be found in you, but ye may remain in all holiness and sobriety both of body and spirit, in CHRIST JESUS.

XI. The last times are come upon us: let us therefore be very reverent, and fear the long-suffering of GOD, that it be not to us unto condemnation. For let us either fear the wrath that is to come, or be thankful for present grace; one of the two; only to be found in CHRIST JESUS, unto true life. Besides Him, let nothing be worthy of you; for whom also I bear about these bonds, those spiritual jewels in which I would to GOD, that through your prayers, I might rise again; of which may I ever partake, that I may be found in the lot of the Christians of Ephesus, who have always agreed with the Apostles, through the power of JESUS CHRIST.

XII. I know both who I am, and to whom I write; I, a man condemned; ye, such as have obtained mercy: I, exposed to danger; ye, confirmed against danger. Ye are the passage of those that are killed for GOD; the companions of Paul in the mysteries of the Gospel; the holy martyr, the truly blessed Paul; in whose footsteps may I be found, when I shall have attained unto GOD; who, throughout all his Epistle, makes mention of you in CHRIST JESUS.

XIII. Let it be your care therefore to come oftener together, to give thanks and glory to GOD. For when ye meet often together in the same place, the powers of the devil are destroyed, and his mischief is dissolved by the unity of your faith. And indeed, nothing is better than peace; by which all war, both spiritual and earthly, is abolished.

XIV. Of all which nothing is hid from you, if ye have perfect faith and charity in JESUS CHRIST, which are the beginning and end of life: the beginning, faith; the end, charity. And these two joined together, are of GOD; and on them followeth all other goodness. No man, professing a true faith, goes wrong; neither does he who has charity, hate any. "The tree is made manifest by its fruit;" so they who profess themselves to be Christians, shall be known by what they do. For it is not now the time for profession, but for the power of faith, if a man be found faithful unto the end.

XV. It is better for a man to hold his peace, and be a Christian; than to say he is a Christian, and not to be. It is good to teach, if what he says, he does likewise. There is therefore one master "who spake, and it was done;" and even those things which he did without speaking, are worthy of the Father. He that hath the word of JESUS, is truly able to hear his very silence, that he may be perfect; and both do according to what he speaks, and be known by those things in which he is silent. There is nothing hid from GOD, but even our secrets are nigh unto Him. Let us therefore do all things, as becomes those who have GOD dwelling in them; that we may be

His temples, and He may be our GOD within us, as also He is, and will show Himself, before our faces, by those things for which we justly love Him.

XVI. Be not deceived, brethren; those that corrupt other, shall not inherit the kingdom of GOD. If therefore they who do this according to the flesh, have suffered death; how much more shall he die, who by his wicked doctrine corrupts the faith of GOD, for which CHRIST was crucified? He that is thus defiled, shall depart into unquenchable fire, and so also shall he that hearkens unto him.

XVII. For this cause did the LORD suffer the ointment to be poured on His head; that He might breathe the breath of immortality unto His church. Be not ye therefore anointed with the evil savour of the doctrine of the prince of this world; lest he lead you away captive from the life that is set before you. And why are we not all wise; seeing we have received the knowledge of GOD, which is JESUS CHRIST? Why do we suffer ourselves foolishly to perish; not considering the gift which the LORD has truly sent to us?

XVIII. My life be an offering for the doctrine of the Cross; which is indeed a stumbling-block to the unbelievers, but to us salvation and life eternal. "Where is the wise man? Where is the disputer?" Where is the boasting of those who are called wise? For JESUS CHRIST, our GOD, was according to the dispensation of GOD, conceived in the womb of Mary, of the seed of David, by the HOLY GHOST: was born, and baptized, that through his Passion he might purify water.

XIX. Now the virginity of Mary, and her delivery, was kept in secret from the prince of this world; as was also the death of our LORD; three most notable mysteries, yet done in secret by GOD. How then was our SAVIOUR manifested to the world? There shone a star in heaven above all other stars, and its light was unspeakable, and its strangeness wrought amazement. All the other stars, yea, the sun and moon also, were but its train; and it sent forth its light beyond them all. And there was trouble to think whence this unwonted strangeness might be. Hence all the power of magic was dissolved; and every bond of wickedness was destroyed; ignorance was taken away; the old kingdom was abolished; GOD himself appearing in the form of a man, for the renewal of eternal life. Moreover the full dispensation of GOD then took its beginning. From thenceforth all things were disturbed; forasmuch as he designed to abolish death.

XX. But if JESUS CHRIST shall give me grace through your prayers, and it be His will, I purpose in a second Epistle which I will shortly write unto you, to manifest to you more fully the dispensation (of which I have now begun to speak) unto the new man, which is JESUS CHRIST; both in his faith, and in his love, in his suffering and in his resurrection, especially if the LORD shall make it known unto me: that ye may all and each of you, by grace, concur in professing the name of one faith, and one JESUS CHRIST, who was of the race of David according to the flesh; the Son of man, and Son of GOD; that ye may obey your Bishop and the Presbytery with an entire affection; breaking one and the same bread, which is the medicine of immortality; our antidote that we should not die, but live for ever in CHRIST JESUS.

XXI. My soul be for yours, and for theirs whom ye have sent to Smyrna, to the glory of GOD; from whence also I write to you; giving thanks unto the LORD, and loving Polycarp even as I do you. Remember me, as JESUS CHRIST doth remember you. Pray for the church which is in Syria, from whence I am carried bound to Rome, being the least of all the faithful which are there; amongst whom I have been thought worthy to be found to the glory of GOD. Fare ye well in GOD the FATHER, and in JESUS CHRIST, our common Hope. Amen.

November 11, 1833

RECORD 2
Epistle of Ignatius to the Magnesians

Ignatius, which is also Theophorus, to the Church that is in Magnesia, nigh to Mæander, the blessed of GOD the Father through JESUS CHRIST our Saviour: in whom I salute it, and pray that it may have all joy, in GOD the Father and JESUS CHRIST.

I. Being aware how righteously ordered is your love and charity in GOD, the gladness which I feel has induced me to address you in the spirit of JESUS CHRIST. For, admitted as I am to the noblest of titles in the bonds which I bear about me, I make my song to the Churches, praying that they may possess a union of the Flesh and Spirit of JESUS CHRIST (who is our life evermore), and of Faith, and Charity which surpasseth all things, and, more than these, of JESUS and of the FATHER, through whom, when we have endured all assaults from the prince of this world, after we have escaped, we shall be with GOD.

II. Seeing now it is my privilege to behold you, through Damas your most holy Bishop, and your worthy Presbyters, Bassus and Apollonius, and your Deacon my fellow-labourer Sotion, toward whom I am tenderly affectioned, because he is subject to his Bishop as to a gracious gift from GOD, and to the Presbytery as to an institution of JESUS CHRIST, I determined to write unto you.

III. Your duty likewise is it, not to bear yourselves toward your Bishop with a freedom proportioned to his youth, but according to the power of GOD the Father, to concede to him all homage. As I am aware the holy Presbyters do, you take no occasion from his apparent youthfulness for the station, but as men wise in a godly wisdom submitting themselves to him; yet not to him, but to the FATHER of JESUS CHRIST, the Bishop of us all. Meet therefore it is, that for the honour of Him, who wills it, ye should present an obedience that is without guile; since in any delusion of your visible Bishop, you trifle rather with the Bishop invisible, and so the question is not with flesh, but with GOD who seeth the secrets.

IV. It is men's duty not merely to bear the name of Christians, but to be such likewise; whereas some there are, who profess to acknowledge the Bishop, yet do all without consideration of the office. To me such persons appear to be void of a good conscience, since they are a congregation of men not gathered together in strict conformity to the commandment.

V. Now, as all things have their end, two alternatives are laid before us, death, and life: and every man must go to his own place. For there are, as it were, two coins, one of GOD and one the world's: and each of these has its proper mark upon it; unbelievers the mark of this world, and they who in love believe, the mark of GOD the Father through JESUS CHRIST; through whom if we are not readily disposed to die after the likeness of His passion, neither have we His life in us.

VI. Seeing now that, through the persons aforenamed, I have seen you all gathered together in faith and love, take good heed, I charge you, that you do all things in a spirit of godly concord:—the Bishop holding presidency over you, in the place of GOD; and the Presbyters in the place of the Council of Apostles; and the Deacons, my well-beloved, entrusted with the service of JESUS CHRIST, who was with the FATHER before the worlds, and appeared in the last days. Assuming therefore all of you this scheme of godly unity, give heed one to another, and let no man regard his neighbour in a fleshly spirit, but love ye one another continually in JESUS CHRIST. Let there be in you nothing which can divide you; but be ye made one, in the Bishop, and in the Superiors, for an example and lesson of incorruption.

VII. As therefore our LORD, being united with the FATHER, did nothing without Him, neither of Himself, nor by His Apostles, so neither do you do any thing, apart from the Bishop and the Presbyters. Neither seek ye gratification in any thing to your own selfish judgment, but be there in the same place, one Form of prayer, one topic of supplication, one

Mind, one Hope, in love and joy reproachless. There is One JESUS CHRIST, who surpasseth all things; together therefore haste ye all, as to One Temple of GOD, as to One Altar, as to One JESUS CHRIST, who proceeded from One FATHER, and is in One, and to One returned.

VIII. Be not led astray by strange doctrines, nor by old fables, which are unprofitable. For if we still live under the Judaic Law, it is a confession that we have not received Grace. For in the faith of JESUS CHRIST the holy Prophets lived; wherefore also they were persecuted, being inspired with His grace, that unbelievers might be fully assured, that there is One GOD, who manifested Himself in JESUS CHRIST His Son, who is His Eternal Word (not proceeding from silence), who in all things well pleased Him who sent Him.

IX. If then they who lived under the old dispensation, have come to a newness of hope, superseding the Sabbatical system, with that rule of life which is according to the LORD'S Day, wherein our life has arisen through the LORD, and through His death which some deny (from which mystery we received our faith, and thence take patience, that we may be found Disciples of JESUS CHRIST our only Master); how shall we be able to have life except through Him? Whom the prophets also, being His Disciples, expected in spirit as their Master; and therefore He for whom they justly waited, did by His advent raise them from the dead.

X. Let us not then be insensible to His goodness; for, if He should imitate the way in which we act, we already have perished. Wherefore, becoming His disciples, let us live according to the religion of CHRIST; for whosoever is called by any other name but this, is not of GOD. Put aside therefore the evil leaven, which hath grown old and waxed sour, and be ye changed into the new leaven which is JESUS CHRIST. Be ye salted in Him, that none among you may be corrupted, inasmuch as by your savour shall ye be judged. The name of JESUS CHRIST cannot be joined with an adherence to Judaism. For the Christian faith goes not for its completion to the Jewish, but the Jewish goes to the Christian; that every tongue that believeth may be gathered to GOD.

XI. Beloved, it is my desire, not as knowing that any of you are so affected, but as setting myself below you, to guard you against these things, so that you fall not upon the hooks of vain doctrine, but be fully assured of the Birth, and Passion, and Resurrection, which took place in the time of the government of Pontius Pilate; which verily and surely are things done by JESUS CHRIST our Hope:—and from that Hope may none of you be turned away.

XII. May you be my joy in all things, if of that I be worthy; and bound though I am, I am above comparison with any of you who are loosed. I know that ye are not puffed up, for ye have JESUS CHRIST within you; and I know that from the abundance of my praise ye gather caution; as it is written, the just man accuseth himself.

XIII. Study therefore to be confirmed in the doctrines of the LORD and of the Apostles, that in all you do, you may be well advanced in flesh and spirit, in faith and love, through the SON, FATHER, and SPIRIT, the Beginning and the End; under your most excellent Bishop, and your Presbytery, a well twined spiritual garland, and the Deacons according to GOD: be ye subject to the Bishop, and one to another, as JESUS CHRIST to His FATHER according to the Flesh, and the Apostles to CHRIST, and to the FATHER, and to the SPIRIT, that your union may be of the flesh and of the spirit.

XIV. Knowing that GOD dwelleth in you richly, I have exhorted you in few words. Remember me in your prayers, that I may be joined to GOD. Remember also the Church which is in Syria (whereby I am not worthy to be called); for I require your united prayer and love to GOD, that the Church in Syria may be refreshed with dew through your Church.

XV. The Ephesians in Smyrna (whence I write to you) salute you; who now are here to the glory of GOD, like unto you, and have refreshed me in all things, together with Polycarp, Bishop of the Smyrnæans. Likewise the other Churches salute you in the honour of JESUS CHRIST. Be strong in the concord of GOD, possessing the Spirit indivisible, which is CHRIST JESUS.

November 16, 1833

RECORD 3

The Apostle St. John and the Robber
From the Church History of Eusebius

Listen to a tale, which is no mere tale, but a true story which has been handed down and kept in memory, of John the Apostle. For when the Roman Emperor was dead, and St. John had returned to Ephesus from his banishment in the island of Patmos, he went over the neighbouring countries; in some places to appoint Bishops, in some to establish new Churches, in others to separate to the Ministry some one of those whom the Spirit pointed out to him. At length he arrived at a city not very far from Ephesus, of which some even give the name; and after he had refreshed the brethren, he turned at last to the Bishop, whom he had appointed, and having observed a youth of goodly stature, comely appearance, and of an ardent spirit, "Here," he said, "is a deposit which I earnestly commend to your care, in the sight of CHRIST and the Church." And after the Bishop had accepted the charge, and had promised all that was required of him, he repeated the same request, and with the same solemn form of words. Accordingly the Elder, taking to his home the youth intrusted to him, bred, controlled, fostered, and at last admitted him to baptism. After this he relaxed somewhat of his constant care and watchfulness, as having placed upon him the seal of the Lord, that last and best preservative from evil. But the other, having thus obtained his liberty too early, was taken hold of by certain idle and profligate youths of his own age, themselves habituated to wickedness. At first they lure him on by expensive revellings, next they carry him along with them on a thieving expedition by night, and then they beg him to join them in some still greater crime. By little and little he became habituated to vice, and then through the hotness of his nature, starting like a hard-mouthed and spirited horse out of the right path, and taking as it were the bit into his mouth, rushed so much the more violently down the precipice. Finally despairing of the salvation which is by GOD, he was no longer contented with more petty offences; but, as he was now altogether lost, would fain do some great thing, and disdained to suffer but an equal punishment with the rest. He took therefore with him these same companions, and having got together a band of robbers, became their ready leader, and of all the most violent, the most bloody, the most cruel.

An interval elapsed; and upon some need falling out in the Church, the men of the city again called upon John to visit them. After he had set in order the things for which he came, "Come," said he to the Bishop, "give me back the deposit which I and CHRIST committed to thee in the sight of the Church over which you preside." The Bishop was at first amazed, for he thought that John was unjustly charging him with money which had not been really given him, and knew not either how to credit a demand for what he had never received, or how to discredit the Apostle. But when he said plainly, "It is the youth I demand of thee, the soul of a brother," the old man groaned from the bottom of his heart, and shedding a few tears at the thought, answered him, "He is dead." "How then did he die, and by what death?" "He is dead," he said, "to GOD, for he has ended in becoming wicked and abandoned, and to sum up all, a robber, and now instead of the Church, he has taken to the hills with an armed band of robbers like himself." Then the Apostle tore his garment, and uttering a loud wail, beat his head, and said, "A careful guardian truly, I left of the soul of my brother, but bring me a horse, and let me have some one to guide me on my way." So he rode away from the Church, just as he was, and when he came to the place, being taken, by the outposts of the robbers, he neither fled from them, nor asked for mercy, but cried out, "For this purpose came I, bring me to your chief." He in the mean time, in the armour he wore, waited for his approach. When, however, he recognized St. John, as he drew near, he was filled with shame, and turned and fled. But the Apostle followed after him with all his strength, forgetful of his years, and calling out, "Why do you fly from me, my son, me your father, unarmed, and stricken in years; pity me, my son, and fear me not. Thou hast yet hope of life. I will give account for thee to CHRIST; yea, if it be needful, I will willingly undergo the death for thee, even as our LORD the death for us. For thee will I render up my breath. Stay and believe; CHRIST hath sent me." But the young man, when he heard his words, first stood still, with eyes cast down to the ground; next threw away his arms, and then trembling, wept bitterly. And when the old man drew nigh to him, he threw his arms around him, and besought pardon, as best he could, with his groans, and was baptized as it were a second time, with tears, hiding only his blood-stained hand. But John, with promises and solemn protestations of his having obtained his pardon from the SAVIOUR, besought him, nay, knelt to him, and kissed the very right hand he had withheld from him, as already cleansed by change of heart; and so brought him back to the Church. Finally interceding for him, sometimes in frequent prayers, sometimes striving together with him in long continued fasts, and sometimes soothing his spirit with various holy texts, he departed not, so they tell us, till he had fully reinstated him in the Church, and had thus set forth a mighty example of true change of heart, and a mighty proof of regeneration, a trophy as it were of a visible resurrection.

ಆ

Here we see sinners baptized, taught, and brought to repentance by the Holy Church, at the hands of the Apostles, and the Bishops whom they have appointed.

Conduct of St. John the Apostle,
and His Disciple Polycarp, Bishop of Smyrna,
Towards the False Teachers Cerinthus & Marcion
In the Words of Irenæus, Bishop of Lyons, in France

When Polycarp visited Rome at the time Anicetus was Bishop there, he converted many heretics to the Church of GOD, declaring that he had received from the Apostles that one and only doctrine, which the Church has delivered to us. And there are those who heard him say, that John, the LORD'S Disciple, who lived at Ephesus, having gone to a bath, and finding

Cerinthus within, rushed out without bathing, with the exclamation, "Let us fly, lest the bath fall in, while Cerinthus, the enemy of the truth, is in it."

And Polycarp himself was once met and addressed by Marcion, in these words; "Do you acknowledge me?" "Yes," he replied, "I acknowledge you to be the first-born of Satan."

Such caution did the Apostles and their Disciples observe, lest they should hold intercourse even by word of mouth with any of those who adulterate the truth: as says St. Paul too; "A man that is an heretic, after the first and second admonition, reject; knowing that he that is such, is subverted, and sinneth, being condemned of himself."

ಎ

Hence we learn to avoid false teachers, after the pattern of the Blessed Apostle and his Disciple, even though it inconvenience us to do so.

November 22, 1833

RECORD 4

Epistle of Ignatius to Polycarp

Ignatius, called also Theophorus, to Polycarp, of the Church at Smyrna, Bishop and Superintendant: yea, rather himself superintended by GOD the FATHER, and the LORD JESUS CHRIST, All hail!

I. Welcoming thy disposition which is to GOD ward, founded as upon an immoveable rock, I glorify Him, in that I have been honoured by thy holy presence, and praying that I may rejoice in it through GOD. I beseech thee, by the grace of GOD, wherewith thou art invested, to press onwards in thy course, and to exhort all unto salvation. Maintain thy station in all diligence, both of body and soul; study to preserve that unity, than which nothing is better. Endure all men, as the LORD has also endured thee; continue, as thou dost, to bear with all men in love; devote thyself to prayer without ceasing; seek for more understanding than thou hast; watch with an unwearied spirit; speak unto every one as GOD shall enable thee: as a practised combatant, endure the weaknesses of all; for where labour abounds, there also abounds gain.

II. For in that thou lovest the good disciples, what thank hast thou? yea, rather with mildness bring into subjection the more mischievous. For every wound is not treated with the same application; but violent paroxysms are to be assuaged by emollient medicines. Be in all things "wise as the serpent, and harmless as the dove." For this end art thou formed of flesh and spirit, that thou mayest soften the things which are in thy sight: but pray that the things which are invisible may be revealed unto thee, that thou mayest want in nothing, but abound in every gift of GOD. The present season demands thee, as pilots the wind, as the storm-tost mariner his desired haven, that thou attain unto GOD. Be temperate, as GOD'S Champion; the reward is incorruption, and eternal life: in which also thy faith is firm. In all things, my soul is as thine, and so are my bonds which thou hast loved.

III. Be not dismayed at those who seem worthy of trust, and yet teach new doctrines: stand firm, as the anvil under the stroke, for he is a mighty champion, who though buffetted, yet overcometh. But above all, for the sake of GOD, we must endure all, that He also may endure us. Become more and more zealous: study the times; await Him who is above all time, the Eternal, the Invisible (who yet for us men became visible), the Impalpable, the Impassible: who yet for our salvation became subject unto suffering, and endured all things.

IV. Let not the widows be neglected, for thou under the LORD art their guardian; let nothing be done without thy sanction, neither thyself do any thing without the sanction of GOD; which thing indeed thy constancy suffers thee not to do. Let your assemblies be held more frequently. Seek out and address all by name. Slight not the slaves; yet suffer them not to be puffed up, but let them rather serve the more diligently unto the glory of GOD, that from Him they may obtain a more perfect freedom. Let them not seek to be emancipated at the public cost, lest they be found to be the slaves of their own desires.

V. Avoid evil arts; nay, rather mention them not at all. Speak unto my sisters, that they love the LORD, and be content, in will as in deed, with their husbands. Exhort also my brethren in the name of JESUS CHRIST, that they love their wives, even as the LORD loveth the Church. If any one can remain in chastity, to the honour of the flesh of our LORD, let him do so in all humility. If he boast, he is already lost; yea, if he reveal it to any one, save the Bishop, he is corrupted. It is fitting for those who purpose matrimony, to accomplish their union with the sanction of the Bishop; that their marriage may be godly, and not according to lust. Let all things be done to the honour of GOD.

VI. Hearken unto your Bishop, that GOD may also hearken unto you. My soul is as the soul of them who are in subjection to their Bishop, their Presbyters, their Deacons; and may my portion be with them in the LORD! Labour together, strive together, run together, suffer together, lie down together, rise up together, as the stewards, the ministers, and the servants of GOD. Seek to please Him, whose soldiers ye are, and whose wages ye receive. Let none of you be a deserter: let your baptism remain, for it is your armour; your faith, a helmet; your love, a spear; your long-suffering, a coat of mail. Let your deposits be your good works, that ye may finally receive the portion earned by your service. Be patient with one another in mildness, as GOD is with you. May I rejoice in you alway!

VII. But as it has been disclosed to me that the Church of Antioch in Syria, through your prayers, is at peace, I have rather been of good cheer in secure reliance on GOD (if through suffering I shall attain unto Him) that by your prayers also I may be found in the resurrection a true disciple. It is meet, O most blessed Polycarp, that thou shouldst call together a holy council, and choose some one, well-beloved and zealous, that he may be called GOD'S Messenger; and to appoint him to go into Syria, that he may make manifest your zealous love, to the glory of CHRIST. A Christian is not master of himself, but is devoted to GOD'S service. This work is GOD'S, and your's, when you have accomplished it. For I trust in the Grace which is in you, that ye are ready to every good work which appertaineth unto GOD; and therefore, as I know your zeal for the truth, my exhortation has been brief.

VIII. Since I have not been able to write to all the Churches, because I have been suddenly called upon to sail from Troas to Neapolis, do thou write to those which are nearest to thee, knowing that GOD'S will is that they shall do the same onwards, sending, if possible, messengers; if not, entrusting their Epistles to those whom thou shalt send, that ye may all be glorified for ever, as ye are worthy. I salute all by name; and especially the wife of Epitropus, with her household and family. I salute Attalus my beloved. I salute him who shall be chosen to go into Syria; that the grace of GOD may be with him alway in my prayer, through our GOD JESUS CHRIST; in whom may you continue in the unity of GOD, and under His protection. Salute Alce, my well-beloved. Farewell in the LORD!

November 26, 1833

RECORD 5

Epistle of Ignatius to the Trallians

Ignatius, which is also Theophorus, to the Holy Church that is in Tralles in Asia, beloved of GOD, the Father of JESUS CHRIST, chosen, godlike, having peace through the flesh and blood and passion of JESUS CHRIST (who is our hope in the following of His resurrection), which I salute in the plenitude of my Apostolic character, and pray that it may have all joy.

I. I know the reproachless spirit, and unfailing unanimity, that not by occasion, but habitually belong to you; which also were set forth to me by Polybius your Bishop, who, by GOD'S will and the will of JESUS CHRIST, was present in Smyrna, and so rejoiced with me in my bonds for JESUS CHRIST, that in his person you were all before my eyes. So that meeting with this godly kindness in him, I reckon on finding you (as I have also known you) the followers of GOD.

II. For in that you are subject to your Bishop as to JESUS CHRIST, you seem to me to be living not after the way of men, but according to JESUS CHRIST; who died for your sakes, that by believing in His death ye may from death escape. It is therefore your bounden duty, as it also is your practice, to do nothing apart from the Bishop. Be subject moreover to the Presbytery, as to the Apostles of JESUS CHRIST our hope: may we be found to have had our conversation in Him! It is requisite too, that they who are Deacons [ministers] of the mysteries of JESUS CHRIST, should be obliging to all men in every manner; for they are not ministers [deacons] of meat and drink, but servants of GOD'S Church: they must therefore guard against reproach as against fire.

III. Likewise let all men give heed to the Deacons, as to an institution of JESUS CHRIST; and to the Bishop, as to the image of GOD; and to the Presbyters as to the Council of GOD and the Company of Apostles. Without these the name of Church is not. On which points I am persuaded that you hold with me; for I found and retain with me a specimen of your love in the person of your Bishop; whose whole constitution of mind is an instructive lesson, and his meekness full of power. I suppose that even Atheists respect him. Though able to write on this point, thus far only I mean to do so, lest a convict such as I should be giving laws to you like an Apostle.

IV. GOD has granted to me the knowledge of many things; but I control myself, lest I perish in my boasting: for now I must be especially fearful, and hold off from them that puff me up. For they who make me their talk, inflict a persecution upon me. I am well contented to suffer, yet I know not that I am worthy to do so. My zeal, known but to few, is the more excited in myself. I have need therefore of that moderation, whereby the Prince of this world is brought to nought.

V. Am I unable to write to you of spiritual things? I am not unable, but fear lest I should bring an injury on infants such as you. Excuse therefore my doing so; lest from inability to receive my words, you be choked of them. For even I, prisoner as I am, am not enabled to behold the things that are in Heaven, the marshalling of the Angels, the stations of the celestial Powers, visible things and things invisible, but herein I am but a learner. For many things are placed beyond our capacity, lest we cease to have dependence on GOD.

VI. I exhort you, therefore (yet not I, but the love of JESUS CHRIST), to use only the Christian nourishment, and to abstain from the strange herb, which is heresy. For the heretics receiving credit on the score of worldly reputation, invest Christianity with poison; offering as it were their fatal drug in a sop; and he who knows it not, accepteth death with a ready and fatal welcome.

VII. From such men keep yourselves guarded. And guarded ye will be, if ye are not puffed up, nor separated from JESUS CHRIST our LORD, and from the Bishop, and from the rules laid down by the Apostles. He that is within the altar is pure: he that is without, whoever, namely, acts independently of the Bishop, the Presbytery, and the Deacons, is a man of unclean conscience.

VIII. I am not aware that there is aught of this kind in you, but, for the love I bear you, I put you on your guard, foreseeing as I do the snares of the Devil. Do you therefore, gathering a spirit of meekness, stablish yourselves in Faith, which is the flesh of the LORD, and in Love, which is the blood of JESUS CHRIST. Let none of you find a fault in his neighbour. Give no occasion to the heathen; lest, on the score of a foolish, the godly many be evil spoken of; for "woe unto him, because of whose levity My name is evil spoken of by any."

IX. Turn then a deaf ear to any man who departs in what he says from JESUS CHRIST, who was of the seed of David, and born of Mary; who verily was born, did eat and did drink; verily was persecuted, under Pontius Pilate; verily was crucified and died, being seen of them that are in Heaven, of them that are on earth, and of them that are under the earth; who verily also was raised from the dead, His FATHER raising HIM; in the likeness whereto, us also who believe in HIM shall His FATHER raise up through JESUS CHRIST, without whom the real life belongs not to us.

X. But if (as some godless men, which are unbelievers, assert) it was only His shade that suffered (whereas they are but a shade), how came I to be in bonds? and why do I rejoice in the prospect of "fighting with beasts?" In such case I perish to no purpose, and belie my LORD.

XI. Avoid then those mischievous offshoots, fruitful of death, the which if a man taste he shall die thereby; for these were not planted of the FATHER. For if they were, we should see them growing from the Cross, and their fruit would be unto eternal life; in accordance whereto He in His passion inviteth you under the title of His own Members. The Head and the limbs cannot therefore have a separate existence, for GOD hath promised their union, and Himself existeth therein.

XII. I send you my salutation from Smyrna, together with the salutation of the Churches that are here with me, which have "every way refreshed me, both in body and spirit. My bonds supply you with a lesson; for I bear them for JESUS CHRIST'S sake, praying that I may go to GOD. Continue in one mind, and assemble together for prayer; for it is right for every one of you, and for the Presbyters particularly, to refresh your Bishop's spirit, that so you may show honour to the FATHER, to JESUS CHRIST, and to the Apostles. I pray that you may hear me in love; and that I may not, by writing this, be made a testimony against you. Likewise do you for my sake pray (for I desire your love in the mercy of GOD), that I may be held worthy of that destiny which I press on to gain, and may not become a castaway.

XIII. The love of the Smyrneans and Ephesians saluteth you. Remember in your prayers the Church that is in Syria, whereby I am not worthy to be called, being last among them. Be strong in JESUS CHRIST; subject to your Bishop as to the commandment, and to the Presbytery likewise. Love one another, every one of you, with an undivided heart. My spirit saluteth you; not now only, but when I shall have gone to GOD. I have yet to fear for myself; but the Father is faithful in JESUS CHRIST, to fulfil my prayer and yours. In Him may you be found blameless!

N.D.

RECORD 6
Account of the Martyrs of Lyons and Vienne
From the Church History of Eusebius

In the seventeenth year of the Emperor Antoninus Verus, the persecution raged with fresh violence against us, in some parts of the world, by means of the attacks made on us by the populace of the several cities. We may conjecture, from what occurred in a single country, that myriads of martyrdoms took place throughout the earth. These are well worthy of immortal memory, and happen to have been transmitted to posterity in writing. The whole document, which contains the fullest account of them, is placed in my collection of Martyrs, containing a description which is not merely historical, but also instructive. As much, however, as is connected with my present purpose, I will select and insert here.

Others, in composing historical narrations, commit to writing victories in war, and trophies over the enemy, and the exploits of generals, and the valour of troops, stained with blood and endless slaughter, in defence of their children, their country, and their fortunes. But our narrative of the acts of a Divine Commonwealth, will rather seek to inscribe, on an everlasting monument, those most peaceful wars for the peace of the soul; and the Heroes who have fought in these, rather for the truth than for their country, and rather for religion than for the objects of their dearest affections. It will proclaim, for eternal memory, the perseverance, and the enduring valour of the combatants in the cause of Piety, and their trophies over devils, and their victories over unseen adversaries, and their crowns which followed.

Gaul [i.e. France] then was the place of the conflicts of which we speak. The principal cities of this country, remarkable and celebrated above others, are Lyons and Vienne, through both which runs the stream of the Rhone, which passes with a rapid course round that whole region. The account of the martyrdoms, transmitted by the Churches of chief note in these parts to those in Asia and Phrygia, thus describes the things done among them; and I will give their own words.

Letter of the Churches of Lyons and Vienne in the South of France to the Churches of Asia and Phrygia

The Servants of CHRIST, that sojourn at Vienne and Lyons in Gaul, to the Brethren in Asia and Phrygia, who have the same faith and hope of redemption with us, peace, and grace, and glory, from GOD the FATHER, and CHRIST JESUS our LORD. * * * * The greatness of the sufferings in this country, and the wonderful rage of the heathen against the Saints, and how much the blessed Martyrs endured, we are neither able accurately to declare, nor is it possible to be comprehended in writing. For the Adversary rushed down upon us with all his might, as already anticipating his future coming without control (Rev 20:3); and went through all possible means in preparing, and exercising his own beforehand, against the Servants of GOD. So that we were not only excluded from the houses, the baths, and the market; but it was even forbidden for any of us to shew himself, in any place whatever.

But the Grace of GOD took the lead in opposition to him; and, protecting the weak, set Firm Pillars in battle array against him, whose fortitude rendered them first to draw on themselves the whole violence of the Evil One; men who went forth to meet him, supporting patiently every kind of insult and torture, and counting the most he could do as little, were in haste to be with CHRIST; shewing, of a truth, that "the sufferings of this present time are not to be compared with the glory that shall be revealed in us."

And, in the first place, they nobly endured all the injuries heaped on them by the assembled populace, who hooted, beat, dragged about, plundered, stoned, and confined them; and did all such things, as are wont to be done by a furious mob to those, whom it hates and counts its enemies. And, lastly, when brought into the market-place by the commander of the troops and the authorities of the city, and questioned before the whole multitude, they confessed, and were shut up in prison till the arrival of the Governor.

And when afterwards they were brought before the Governor, and he shewed the utmost cruelty towards us, Vettius Epagathus, one of the brethren (full of love toward GOD and his neighbour, and of so exact and perfect a life, that, though a young man, he was equal to the testimony borne to the aged Zacharias, in that he "walked in all the commandments and judgments of the LORD blameless," and ready in every service to his neighbour, having great "zeal toward GOD," and "fervent in spirit"), this excellent man could not endure the unreasonable judgment, which was passing against us, but testified his indignation, and demanded to be heard himself in defence of the Brethren. And when those about the tribunal hooted him down (for he was a man of note) and the Governor would not allow the just claim he had put in on our behalf, but only asked if he too were a Christian, he confessed with a loud voice, and was himself taken, and so took his place among the number of the Martyrs; being called the Advocate of the Christians, and having in himself the "ADVOCATE" (or the Comforter, John 14:16), the SPIRIT, yet more than Zacharias (Luke 1:67). Which he also shewed by the fulness of his love, being ready to lay down his own life for the sake of defending his Brethren. For he was, yea, is, a genuine Disciple of CHRIST, "following the Lamb wherever He goeth."

Then also others began to be distinguishable; and the First Martyrs were conspicuous and prepared, fulfilling with all readiness the Martyr's confession. Those also might be discerned who were unprepared and unexercised, and still weak, unable to bear the strain of a great conflict. About ten of whom fell away; who also caused us much grief and unmeasured lamentation, and hindered the readiness of others, who were not yet arrested, and who, though suffering all possible indignities, were in attendance on the Martyrs, and did not desert them. Then, however, we were all greatly alarmed by the uncertainty of the confession; not fearing the cruelties that were inflicted, but looking to the end, and fearing that any one might fall away.

Those, however, who were worthy, were daily apprehended, filling up their number, so that there were taken up, from the two Churches, all the best men, and those, by whom things here were chiefly kept together. There were also taken up some heathen servants belonging to persons amongst our number, since the Governor ordered a public inquisition to be made after us all. And they, by a device of Satan, fearing the tortures which they saw the Saints endure, the soldiers urging them on, belied us as holding Thyestean feasts,[1] and guilty of impurities like those of Œdipus, and such things as it is not allowed us to mention, or even to think of, no, nor to believe that they ever existed among mankind.

But when these things were noised abroad, all were infuriated against us; so that, even if any had before shewn moderation on account of connections, even these were greatly enraged, and stung with malice (Acts 5:33) against us. And that was fulfilled which the LORD had foretold us, "the time shall come, when every one, that killeth you, shall think that he doeth GOD service" (John 16:2). Then afterwards the Holy Martyrs endured tortures beyond all description; Satan being ambitious of drawing some to blaspheme with their lips.

But most eminently did all the rage of the populace, the Governor, and the soldiers, light on Sanctus, a deacon of Vienne; and on Maturus, one newly enlightened, but a noble champion; and on Attalus, a Pergamene by birth, who had always been "a pillar and support" (1 Tim 3:15) of those in this neighbourhood; and on Blandina, by whom CHRIST shewed that the things which are lowly esteemed among men, and held by them mean and contemptible, are thought worthy of great honour with GOD, for that love of Him, which is shewed forth in power, and does not boast in a vain appearance.

For when we all were in fear, and her own mistress according to the flesh, (who also herself was one champion among the Martyrs,) was in agony for her, lest she should be unable to make even one bold confession, from the weakness of her body; Blandina was filled with such strength, that even those, who tortured her by turns in every possible way, from morning till evening, were wearied and gave it up, themselves confessing that they were conquered, having nothing more that they could do to her. And they wondered at her remaining still alive, her whole body being

---

[1] i.e. Eating human flesh, a calumny derived from the LORD's Supper.

mangled and pierced in every part; and declared, that any one kind of torture was enough to deprive her of life, not to say so many and so severe.

But that blessed woman, like a brave wrestler, renewed her strength in confessing; and it was to her recovery, and rest, and ease from her sufferings, to say "I am a Christian, and nothing vile is done amongst us."

Sanctus also, for his part, enduring exceedingly, and above every man, all the cruelties of men with a noble patience, when the wicked hoped that, by means of the continuance and severity of the tortures, they should hear something from him that ought not to be uttered, set himself against them with such firmness as not to mention even his own name, nor that of the nation or city whence he was, nor whether he were bond or free; but to all questions he answered in the Roman tongue, "I am a Christian." This he repeatedly declared to be to him instead of a name, instead of a country, and instead of a family; but no other word did the heathen hear from him. Whence also there was great strife both of the Governor and torturers against him; so that, when they had nothing left that they could do to him, at last they fastened red hot plates of brass on the tenderest parts of his body. But though his limbs were burning, he remained upright and unshrinking, stedfast to his confession, bathed and strengthened from Heaven with that fountain of living water, that springs from the well of CHRIST. But his body bore witness of what had been done, being one entire wound and bruise, and wrenched, and deprived of the external form of man. In whom CHRIST Himself suffering shewed forth great glory, confounding the adversary, and shewing, for an example to others, that nothing is terrible where is the love of the FATHER; nothing painful where is the glory of CHRIST. For when the ungodly again, after several days, tortured the Martyr, and thought that they should overcome him by applying the same torments while his wounds were yet swollen and sore, and could scarce bear the mere touch of the hand; or that by dying under the torture he would at least alarm the rest; not only did no such thing befal him, but also, contrary to all human expectation, his frail body recovered and was strengthened in his latter torments, and regained its former appearance, and the use of the limbs; so that, by the favour of CHRIST, his second torture was made to him no punishment, but a remedy.

And then the Devil, thinking he had already swallowed up one woman of the number of those, who had denied CHRIST, named Biblias, led her to the torture, to compel her to say impious things concerning us, as one now easily to be broken, and without courage. But she came to herself under the tortures, and awoke, so to speak, from a deep sleep; being reminded by temporal punishment of the eternal misery of hell; and declared, in contradiction of the blasphemers, "How should those devour children, with whom it is not allowed even to eat the blood of brute animals?" And from this time she confessed herself to be a Christian, and was added to the number of the Martyrs.

But, when these tyrannical cruelties were confounded by CHRIST through the patience of the Blessed Martyrs, the Devil imagined other devices, such as confinement in prison, in the darkest and most loathsome dungeon; and stretching their feet in the stocks, even to the fifth hole; and all other such insults, as the underkeepers, when enraged (and these same men filled with the Evil Spirit) are accustomed to put upon their prisoners; so that many were suffocated in the prison, those whom the LORD willed thus to escape, showing forth His glory. Some there were who had been bitterly tormented, so that it should have seemed that with all possible care they could scarce have lived, who stayed in prison; deprived indeed of human care, but revived and strengthened by the LORD in body and soul, and exciting and comforting the rest. But the young, and those newly apprehended, whose bodies had suffered no previous mangling, could not endure the pressure of this confinement, but died in prison.

But the blessed Pothinus, who was entrusted with the bishoprick of the Church in Lyons, above ninety years of age, and quite worn out in body, scarce able to breathe from his previous infirmity, but renewed in strength by the readiness of his spirit, in his earnest desire of martyrdom, himself also was dragged to the tribunal; his body worn out with age and disease; but his life being still kept in him, that CHRIST might triumph through it:—who, when brought by the soldiers to the tribunal, all the authorities of the city following him, and all the crowd, as though he had been CHRIST Himself, uttering all sorts of cries against him, bore a good testimony. And when asked by the Governor, who might be the GOD of the Christians? he said, "If thou be worthy, thou shalt know." After this he was dragged about without mercy, and suffered all kinds of buffeting, those who were near him insulting him with their hands and feet, without regard to his age; and those at a distance throwing at him whatever came to hand; and all thinking any one guilty of a great fault and impiety, who should be wanting in insolence towards him. For they considered that they should thus avenge their gods. And he was cast, scarce alive, into the prison, and died after two days. Here then there took place a remarkable dispensation of GOD, and an infinite compassion of JESUS was shown forth; a thing, which had rarely occurred in the brotherhood, but is not unsuited to the wisdom of CHRIST. For those, who denied at their first apprehension, were themselves also confined, and partook of our sufferings. At this time the denial of the faith was of no use to them; for those, who confessed what they were, were imprisoned as Christians, no further charge being brought against them; whereas these were still detained as murderers[2] and impure, suffering double the punishment of the rest. Those indeed the joy of martyrdom,[3] and the hope of the promises, and the love of CHRIST, and the SPIRIT of the FATHER, comforted; but these, conscience tormented with great vengeance; so that, in passing by, their countenances might be distinguished amongst all the rest. For the one went cheerfully, great glory and grace being mingled in their countenances; so that their very chains hung on them as a noble ornament, as on a bride adorned with robes embroidered and fringed with gold; at the same time, smelling so of the sweet odour of CHRIST, that some even appeared to have been anointed with earthly perfumes. But the others went abashed, and dejected, and wretched in their looks, and full of disgrace; and, moreover reproached by the very heathen as ignoble and unmanly; bearing indeed the charge of murder,[4] but having lost the honourable, and glorious, and life-giving Name. The rest, seeing these things, were confirmed; and those who were apprehended confessed, without hesitation, not even taking any thought of the reasonings of the Devil.

To conclude; their martyrdoms were distinguished by various kinds of death. For, having plaited a crown of different colours, and of all kinds of flowers, they offered it to the FATHER. It was needful, it seems, that these

---

[2] Vid. p. 438.
[3] Bearing witness.
[4] Namely, of eating human flesh, as above, p. 438.

noble champions, who had endured a varied conflict, and been greatly victorious, should receive the great and incorruptible crown.

Maturus, and Sanctus, and Blandina, and Attalus, were taken to the beasts in the public place, for a common spectacle to the inhumanity of the heathen; this day of wild-beast fighting being given on purpose to shew forth our Martyrs. And Maturus, and Sanctus, again went through, in the Amphitheatre, every torture, as if they had absolutely suffered nothing before. Rather, as having now in several combats foiled the Adversary, and engaged in the contest for the very crown, they supported again the courses of scourging usually inflicted there, and the dragging about by the beasts, and whatever else the mad populace shouted and demanded on this side and that, to have done to them; and above all, the iron seat, on which their bodies, being scorched, choked them with the smell. But their persecutors did not cease even with this; but were yet more outrageous, wishing to overcome their patience. And even thus they could hear nothing from Sanctus, beyond the words of confession he had been accustomed to use from the first. These then, their life holding out long through a severe conflict, were at last put to death; being by themselves, throughout that day, a spectacle to the world, instead of all the variety of single combats. But Blandina, hung up on a Cross, was placed to be devoured by the beasts that were turned in. She thus visibly hanging in the figure of a Cross, and engaged in earnest prayer, wrought great readiness in those who underwent the conflict; since they saw, in the midst of their sufferings, even with the outward eye, in their sister, Him who was crucified for them, to persuade those who believe in Him, that every one who hath suffered for the glory of CHRIST, hath for ever communion with the Living GOD. And, none of the beasts having at that time touched her, she was taken down from the cross, and carried up again to the prison, to be kept for another conflict; that, by conquering in yet more encounters, she might bring inexorable condemnation on the crooked Serpent; and, though by nature little, weak, and easily to be despised, yet having put on CHRIST, the great and invincible Champion, she might encourage the brethren; having overpowered the Adversary in many combats, and having won in the contest the incorruptible crown.

Next Attalus himself, being much called for by the multitude (for he was a well-known man) came in prepared for the combat by a good conscience, since he was truly exercised in the Christian discipline, and had always been amongst us a witness of the truth. He was led all round the Amphitheatre, with a tablet carried before him, on which was written in Latin, "This is Attalus the Christian." And the people being exceedingly enraged against him, the Governor, having understood that he was a Roman, ordered him to be taken back among the rest that were in the prison; concerning whom he sent to Cæsar, and waited for his decision. But the meantime was not idle nor fruitless to them, but through their patience the infinite mercy of CHRIST appeared. For the dead members were enlivened through the living; and the Martyrs shewed favour to those who were not martyrs, and there was great joy to the Virgin Mother, the Church, in receiving those again living, whom she had cast away as dead and abortive. For by those good men, the greater number of those, who had denied CHRIST were renewed, and reconceived, and rekindled; and learned to confess; and now, living and full of nerve, were brought before the tribunal;—GOD, who desireth not the death of a sinner, but sheweth goodness to repentance, granting them of His kindness to be again questioned by the Governor. For (Cæsar having ordered that these should be executed, but that if any denied, they should be released), when the public festival here began, which is numerously attended by persons, who come together to it from all nations, he brought the blessed Martyrs to the tribunal for a spectacle, and to make a show of them to the multitudes. Wherefore also he examined them again; and as many as appeared to have had Roman citizenship, he beheaded; but the rest he sent to the beasts. But CHRIST was greatly glorified in those who had denied before, but then confessed, contrary to the expectation of the heathen. For these were even separately examined, as on the idea that they were to be dismissed; but confessing, were added to the number of the Martyrs. But those remained without, who never had any trace of faith, nor a feeling of the bridal garment, nor a sense of the fear of GOD; but by their very manner of life brought scandal on the true way, that is, the sons of perdition. But all the others were united to the Church. And while they were under examination, one Alexander, a Phrygian by birth, and a physician by profession, who had lived many years in the provinces of Gaul, and was known almost by all, for his love to GOD, and boldness in declaring the word (for he was not without a share of the Apostolic gift), standing by the tribunal, and encouraging them by signs in their confession, was observed by those who stood round the tribunal, to be thus as it were in travail for them (Gal 4:19). But the multitude, being enraged at hearing these confess again, who had before denied, cried out against Alexander, as if he had been the cause of it. And the Governor turning upon him, and asking who he was, he answered "A Christian;" upon which the other, in a rage, condemned him to be given to the beasts. And next day he came in with Attalus. For the Governor, to please the people, gave up Attalus also again to the wild beasts. But they, in the Amphitheatre, having passed through all the instruments of torture, that ever were invented, and endured a most severe conflict, were at last put to death. Alexander without uttering a groan or a syllable, but conversing in his heart with GOD. But Attalus, when he was placed on the iron seat, and scorched, when the vapour went up from his body, said to the crowd, in the Roman tongue; "Behold this is man-eating, which yourselves do; but we neither eat men, nor do any other evil thing." And when asked what name GOD hath, he answered, "GOD hath not a name, as a man hath."

And after all these things, on the last remaining day of the combats, Blandina was brought in again, with a boy from Pontus, of about fifteen years old (who had been also brought in every day to see the tortures of the others); and were commanded to swear by their idols. And because they remained constant, and set them at nought, the multitude was enraged against them; so that they neither pitied the youth of the boy, nor respected the female; but they put them to all the most dreadful tortures, and made them pass through the whole course of inflictions, demanding of them again and again to swear (by the heathen gods), but unable to make them do so. For the youth of Pontus, encouraged by our sister, so that even the heathen saw that she was forwarding and confirming him, having nobly endured all his torments, gave up the ghost. But the blessed Blandina, last of all, like a noble mother, having stirred up her children, and sent them forward victorious to the king; and having herself gone through all the same conflicts with her children, hastened after them, rejoicing and exulting in her departure, as if called to a marriage supper, instead of being thrown to wild beasts. And after the scourging, after the wild beasts, after the scorching, at last she was placed in a basket, and thrown to a bull; and died, after having been much tossed about by the animal, having no feeling of her sufferings, through her hope and hold of those things which she believed, and her converse with CHRIST; even the heathen themselves confessing, that no woman ever among them bore such and so numerous tortures.

But not even thus could their madness, and cruelty to the Saints, be satisfied; for those fierce and barbarous tribes, stirred up by the Dragon, were hardly to be quieted. And they made another fierce attack on the bodies of the Martyrs, being not ashamed of their former defeat, because they had not the reasonable feeling of men; but it rather inflamed their anger, as though both Governor and people had been of some brute nature, shewing like unjust hatred toward us; that the Scripture might be fulfilled, "he that is ungodly, let him be ungodly still, and he that is righteous, let him be righteous still" (Rev 22:11). For they even threw those, who were stifled in the dungeon, to the dogs; watching them carefully night and day, lest any should be buried by us. And then having exposed what beasts and fire had left, partly torn, and partly burnt to a cinder, and the heads of the rest, with the headless bodies, they kept them in like manner unburied, with military observation and guard, many days. And some grinned and gnashed their teeth at them, seeking to wreak some further vengeance on them; others mocked and jested at them, glorifying their idols, and ascribing to them the punishment of the dead. Even the better sort, and those who seemed to have some compassion, uttered many reproaches, saying, "Where is their GOD, and what has His service profited them, which they chose before their own lives?" Such were the various doings of our enemies; but we were in great sorrow, for that we could not commit the bodies to the earth. For neither would night enable us to do it, nor would money persuade, nor entreaties shame them; but they guarded them in every way, as if they gained much in depriving them of burial.

The bodies of the Martyrs, when they had been publicly insulted and exposed in every way for six days, were at last burnt to ashes by the ungodly, and swept into the river Rhone, which runs by, that not a fragment of them might appear still on the earth. And this they did, as if they could overcome GOD, and deprive them of their resurrection; in order, as they said, that "these Christians may not have even that hope, of rising again, which persuades them to bring in upon us some strange and new worship, and to despise all terrors, coming readily and with joy to their death. Now let us see, if they will rise again; and if their GOD can help them, and take them out of our hands."

❧

Such were the sufferings of the Blessed Saints in early times for CHRIST their Saviour.

Hence we learn how CHRIST supports all who trust in Him; and how far we are below the Saints of early times in courage, patience, and love. We learn that our greatest troubles are very slight, compared with those which Christians then underwent, and underwent for their very virtue's sake; whereas now we often suffer only for our sins. And we learn beside, how blessed it is to suffer boldly in a good cause, for we encourage others to do the same; and we are reminded what a short time the fiercest sufferings last; for these cruel trials of the Christians of France took place so long ago, that it is as if they had never been; whereas ever since, and now, and so on for ever, these Martyrs have been rejoicing in heaven in the presence of GOD.

Moreover we learn how we ought to think of, love, and imitate good Christians, however far off. We are not so far from France, as France is from Asia. Now this letter was written to the Churches of Asia; which shows, how anxious the Christians in those parts were, to know about the trials of their brethren of France.

November 27, 1833

RECORD 7
Epistle of Ignatius to the Smyrnæans

Ignatius, who is called also Theophorus to the Church of GOD the FATHER and the beloved JESUS CHRIST, which is at Smyrna in Asia, mercifully blessed with every gift of GOD, fulfilled in faith and love, most acceptable in His sight, and fruitful in Saints, deficient in no one of His Gifts; Hail, in the HOLY SPIRIT and in the Word of GOD!

I. I glorify JESUS CHRIST, even GOD, who has made you thus wise unto salvation. For I have perceived that ye are perfected in immoveable faith, as though ye were nailed, both in body and soul, unto the cross of our LORD JESUS; and firmly stablished in love through the blood of CHRIST, most fully believing upon our LORD; who verily was of the race of David according to the flesh, but the SON of GOD according to the Will and the Power of GOD; truly born of a Virgin, baptized of John, in order that all righteousness might be fulfilled by Him, who for us was truly nailed to the cross in the flesh under Pontius Pilate and Herod the Tetrarch, of whose fruit are we, through His divine and blessed Passion; that He may by His resurrection raise a standard for ever for His faithful Saints, whether Jews or Gentiles, in one body of His Church.

II. For He suffered all these things for us, and for our salvation; and He verily suffered, as He in verity also raised Himself again; and not as some unbelievers say, that He suffered in appearance only, being themselves only an appearance; and according to their belief, so shall it be unto them, seeing that they are Phantastics and Demoniacs.

III. For I know, that even after the Resurrection He was in the flesh, and believe that He still is; and, when He came unto Peter and his companions, he said, "Take hold, handle me, and see, that I am not an incorporeal Spirit." And immediately they touched Him, and believed; being convinced both by His Flesh and His Spirit; through which conviction also they despised death, and were found to be superior to it. But after His Resurrection He in the flesh ate and drank with them, although being in the SPIRIT united to the FATHER.

IV. These things I exhort you, my beloved, knowing that thus also ye are disposed of yourselves. But I forewarn you against beasts in human shape; these you must not only not admit to your society, but if possible, not even come in their way. Only, pray for them, if by any means they may repent; which yet is a hard matter; but our LORD JESUS CHRIST, who is our true Life has power even for this. For if in appearance only these things were done by our LORD, then are my bonds also in appearance only. But wherefore have I given myself up unto death, to the fire, to the sword, to beasts? But if I am near the sword, I am near GOD; and if I am among beasts, I am with GOD also. Only, in the name of JESUS CHRIST I endure all: that I may suffer with Him, as He, who became perfect man, gives me strength.

V. Whom some, not knowing, deny: nay, rather are denied of Him, being the advocates not of truth but of death; whom neither the prophecies, nor the Law of Moses, nor even the Gospel up to this day, nor our individual sufferings have converted. For they think the same thing even concerning us. What availeth it to me, if any one praiseth me, but blasphemeth my LORD, denying that He came in the flesh? But he who denieth this, denieth Him altogether, being dead in Spirit. But the names of these men it hath not seemed good to me to write, seeing that they are in unbelief; nay, I would not that I should mention them at all, until they shall be turned to belief in His Passion, in which consists our Resurrection.

VI. Let no one deceive himself. Even heavenly things, and the glory of Angels, and Powers visible and invisible are condemned already, if they believe not in the blood of CHRIST. "He that is able to receive this, let him receive it." Let no one be puffed up by rank. For Faith and Love, to which nothing is preferable, are all in all. But consider those who hold other doctrines than the grace of GOD which has come unto us, how contrary they are to the will of GOD; who have no care for brotherly love, who take no thought for the widow, the orphan, or the oppressed, bond, or free, hungry, or thirsty.

VII. These abstain from the Sacrament, and from prayer; because they confess not that the Sacrament is the Body of our Saviour JESUS CHRIST, which suffered for our sins, which the FATHER in His mercy raised again. They then, denying the Gift of GOD, perish in their disputes. Well had it been for them to accept it rather with thankfulness, that through it they might rise again. From such then it is meet that you should abstain; and not even to speak concerning them, either in private or public. But attend diligently to the Prophets, and above all to the Gospel in which His Passion is made manifest to us, and His Resurrection perfected; but avoid divisions, as the beginning of evils.

VIII. Follow your Bishop, all of you, even as JESUS CHRIST the FATHER; and the body of Presbyters, as the Apostles. Respect the Deacons, as ye would the commandment of GOD. Let no one do any thing pertaining to the Church without the Bishop. Let that be esteemed a well-ordered celebration of the Sacrament, which is administered either by the Bishop, or by those to whom he has committed it. Where the Bishop is, there let the body of Believers be; even as where CHRIST is, there is the Catholic Church. Without the Bishop it is lawful neither to baptize, nor to celebrate the Communion; but whatever he judges right, that also is well-pleasing unto GOD, that all which is done be safe and firm.

IX. It is meet that we should return to a sober mind, and while we have yet time, repent and turn unto GOD. It is good to regard GOD, and the Bishop. Whoso honoureth the Bishop, he is honoured of GOD. But he that doeth any thing hidden from the Bishop, sheweth the Devil. May all things abound unto you in grace, for ye are worthy. In all things ye have refreshed me; even as JESUS CHRIST has refreshed you. Ye have loved me when I was present, and ye have loved me when I was absent. GOD reward you therefore, for whom ye endure all things; wherefore also ye will attain unto Him!

X. Ye have done well, in that ye have received as the servants of CHRIST, even of GOD, Philo, and Rhëus, and Agathopus, my followers in the word of GOD; who also bless the LORD for you, because ye have in every way refreshed them. None of these things shall perish. My soul be as your souls, and my bonds, which ye despised not, neither were ashamed of; wherefore He who was perfect Faith, even CHRIST JESUS, will not be ashamed of you.

XI. Your prayer has come unto the Church which is at Antioch in Syria; from whence coming in bonds, which are acceptable to GOD, I salute you all. Nor am I worthy to be called one of that Church, because I am the last of them. But by the will of GOD I was deemed worthy; not as being myself conscious thereof, but through the grace of GOD; which I pray may be given unto me perfectly, that through your prayers I may attain unto GOD. That therefore your work may be perfected, both on earth and in heaven, it is right for the honour of GOD; that your most sacred Church should elect some one to go into Syria to congratulate them that they are at rest, and that their numbers have been regained, and their body reestablished. It seems to me befitting, that you should send some one of your members with an Epistle, that he may with them glorify GOD for the quietness, which He has vouchsafed unto them; and for their having reached the harbour through your prayers. As ye are perfect, so let your sentiments be perfect. For to those who wish to do well, GOD is ready to vouchsafe it.

XII. The love of the brethren at Troas salutes you; from which place I send this Epistle by the hands of Burrhus, whom you sent with me, along with your Ephesian brethren, and who has in every way been a comfort to me. And would that all imitated him, as a pattern of GOD'S Ministry! The grace of GOD will fully reward him. I salute your holy Bishop, your most sacred Presbytery, and my fellow servants the Deacons, individually and together in the name of JESUS CHRIST, in His Flesh and Blood, His Passion and Resurrection, both of Body and Spirit, in the unity of GOD and of you. Grace be with you, mercy, peace, and patience evermore!

XIII. I salute the households of my brethren, their wives and children, the virgins and widows. Farewell through the SPIRIT. Philo, who is with me, salutes you. I salute the household of Tabia, and pray that she may be stablished, in body and soul, in Faith and Love. I salute Alce, my well-beloved, and the incomparable Daphnus, and Eutecnus, and all of you by name. Farewell in the grace of GOD!

November 30, 1833

RECORD 8
Epistle of Ignatius to the Romans

Ignatius, which is also Theophorus, to the Church which hath found mercy by the greatness of the supreme FATHER and of JESUS CHRIST His only Son, beloved and enlightened by the will of Him, who willeth all things, according to the love of JESUS CHRIST our GOD; and which is established in the place of the Romans, all-godly, all-gracious, all-blessed, all-praised, all-prospering, all-hallowed, enthroned in Love, with the name of CHRIST and with the name of the FATHER; salutation in the name of JESUS CHRIST, the Son of the FATHER; so that ye being united in flesh and spirit, according to all His will, ever filled with the grace of GOD, and cleansed from all outward pollution, may have a plenteous and blameless joy, through the LORD JESUS CHRIST our GOD.

I. Since, through prayer to GOD, it hath been granted unto me, to behold your godly countenances (an event I have very greatly desired), bound as I am in JESUS CHRIST, I have a hope of saluting you, if by GOD'S will I be deemed worthy to attain unto my end. For my progress has been begun successfully if I but find grace to come unto my consummation without hindrance. For I have fears from your love, lest even it should bring injury upon me; for to you it is easy to work your purpose; but there will be a difficulty in the way of my going unto GOD, if your affection interfere for me.

II. I desire that ye be not men-pleasers, but pleasers of GOD, which ye also are. For never shall I find such an opportunity of gaining the presence of GOD; nor can you have any deed reported of you more glorious, than your silence now. For if you abstain from interfering for my safety, I shall go unto GOD; but if you attach yourselves to my temporal welfare, I shall have to run my course anew. You can give me no better gift, than my immolation to GOD, while yet the altar is ready; that becoming a choir in love, ye may sing to the FATHER in JESUS CHRIST, for that it hath pleased GOD to call the Bishop of Syria out of the east, and that he should be brought into the west. It is well for me, in learning the world, that I should set unto GOD, that in GOD I may rise.

III. Ye have spoken evil of no man. Ye have taught others. It is my desire, that the lessons ye have given may find a firm foundation. Do ye only ask for me power from within and from without, that I may not only speak, but also feel; not only bear the name of Christian, but approve myself one; for if I approve myself one, I shall be entitled to the name, and shall be reckoned to have been faithful, when the world seeth me no more. For nothing visible is abiding; visible things are temporal; things invisible are eternal. For our GOD; which is JESUS CHRIST, assumes a more visible reality in His union with the FATHER. This is no time for holding peace. When Christianity is hated of the world, it calls for high exertions.

IV. I write to the Churches, and I charge you all, that I die willingly for GOD, unless you prevent me. I exhort you, not to shew me an unseasonable kindness. Suffer me to be devoured by wild beasts, for by their means I am permitted to go to GOD. I am food for GOD'S service. Let me be ground by the teeth of the wild beasts, that I may be found pure bread unto CHRIST. Yea, encourage ye them, that they may be my grave, and may leave no part of my body; so that, when I am fallen asleep, I may burthen no man. Then shall I be a true disciple unto CHRIST, when the world seeth my mortal body no more; pray ye to CHRIST for me, that by their instrumentality I may be found a sacrifice unto GOD. I make not my commands unto you, as though I were Peter or Paul; they were Apostles; I have been condemned; they were free; I, hitherto, am a slave: but if I suffer unto death, I shall become the freedman of JESUS, and shall have a resurrection unto liberty in Him. Now am I learning, while in my bonds, not to set my affections on any thing that is worldly and fallacious.

V. From Syria unto Rome I carry forward my sufferings, by land and sea, night and day; enchained of ten leopards, which are the soldiers ranked around me; who by kindness are made harsher. But I take a lesson from their misdeeds; yet not herein am I made perfect. I long for the wild beasts that are prepared for me. And I pray that they may be found ready; yea, I will encourage them quickly to devour me, and not to spare me with the timidity which they have shewn to others. If they do it not of their own will, I will put a force upon them. I claim of you to bear with me. I have discovered my true interest; I am just becoming a disciple. All things, whether seen or unseen, are tasteless to me, so that I go to CHRIST. Fire and Cross, the assault of beasts, the rending of my bones, the laceration of my limbs, the crushing of my whole frame, dire tortures of Satan, let them come upon me, so that I but go to CHRIST!

VI. In the enjoyments and the ambition of this present world, my hopes repose not; I had rather die in JESUS CHRIST, than reign unto the ends of the earth. For what shall it profit a man if he gain the whole world, and lose his own soul? I am seeking Him, who died for us; I am longing for Him, who rose for our sake. This is the gain which I have before me. Have pity on me, my Brethren. Do not prevent me from living. Do not wish for me to die, when I desire to live with GOD. Enter not into the sympathies of this world. Permit me my portion in the spotless light. For when I arrive thither, I shall belong to GOD. Suffer me to imitate the sufferings of my GOD. If any man hath Him in himself, let him perceive what are my wishes, and sympathize with me, knowing what it is "that constraineth me."

VII. The Prince of this world desireth to tear me away, and to corrupt the purpose that I have to God-ward. Let none of you, who are at my side, give him your help; adhere rather to my cause; it is the cause of GOD. Talk ye not of JESUS CHRIST, while your affections are set on the world. Let no hatred dwell within you. If, when I come among you, I claim of you to interfere for my preservation, yet listen not to me. Keep faith rather with the terms, in which I now write to you. I live, but while I am writing to you, I long to die. My affections are crucified. I have in me neither their flame, nor its fuel; but there is the living water, that speaketh in me, and saith from within, "Come hither unto the FATHER." I have no taste for corruptible food, or for the pleasures of this world. I long for the bread of GOD, heavenly bread, bread of life, which is the flesh of JESUS CHRIST the SON of GOD, who was of the seed of David in the latter days. And I long for the drink of GOD, His blood, which is Love without corruption, and Life for evermore.

VIII. I desire no longer to live after the manner of men; and no longer shall I live so, if you concede to me this favour. Favour me, therefore, that yourselves may find favour. I have written to you in few words. Place confidence in me. Surely JESUS CHRIST shall make this manifest unto you, that I have spoken truly; He is that mouth that cannot lie, whereby the FATHER spoke truly. Pray for me, that I may attain. I have written to you, not according to the flesh, but according to the counsel of GOD. If I suffer, let it have been with your good-will; if I am a castaway, let it have been at the expense of your regard for me.

IX. Remember in your prayers the Church that is in Syria, which hath GOD for its Shepherd instead of me. Its only Bishop now will be JESUS CHRIST, and your love. I feel unworthy to bear the name of my flock. I am the last among them. I am "one born out of due time." But, by the mercy of GOD, I shall be of some small account, if I go unto Him. My spirit saluteth you; as doth the love of the Churches, which received me in the name of JESUS CHRIST, not as a chance traveller; for even the cities, that lay not on my road, have in every instance forwarded me on this journeying of my outward man.

X. I write this unto you from Smyrna, by the hands of the truly blessed Ephesians. Crocus, a well-beloved name to me, and many others, are with me. I suppose you to be not unaware of those persons who have preceded me from Syria to Rome, to the glory of GOD. Make it known to them, that I am now at hand. They are all meet for GOD, and deserve your kindness; and you ought in every manner to assist them. I write this to you on the day preceding the 9th of the Kalends of September. Be strong unto the end, in the patience of JESUS CHRIST.

December 6, 1833

RECORD 9
The Martyrdom of Ignatius, Bishop of Antioch, at Rome

I. Not long after the accession of Trajan, Emperor of Rome, Ignatius, who had been the Disciple of St. John, the Apostle, and who himself shewn forth in his conduct all the features of the Apostolic character, was actively engaged in the task of superintending the Church of Antioch. He had been recently directing its affairs, when it was struggling through those frequent days of storm and persecution, which occurred during the reign of Domitian; and like a skilful Pilot, with rudder and with cable, he had borne up against the swelling and insurgent billows, by prayer, by fasting, by assiduous teaching, in dependence on the HOLY SPIRIT, as one who was deeply concerned that not one soul should perish, among the weak and the simple, that were entrusted to his care. It was not, therefore, without satisfaction, that he witnessed the calm which the Church enjoyed, during the temporary cessation of persecution; though, at the same time, for himself he had much misgiving, that he as yet fell short of the perfect love of CHRIST, and had not arrived at the highest elevation, which is offered to a Disciple's hopes. He felt that, were he to make the confession of Martyrdom, he would attain a more close similitude to his Divine Master. For the few succeeding years he continued at the head of the Church, a burning and shining light; and truly the expositions which he gave of the Holy Scriptures spread a bright reflection upon the hearts of all around him. At length he attained the object of his hopes.

II. It was in the ninth year of Trajan, when that monarch, elated with his recent victories over the Scythians, Dacians, and several other nations, appears to have regarded the pious brotherhood of Christians, as forming the only exception to the universality of his conquests; and he accordingly issued his threats of persecution against any person, who should refuse to perform the customary worship to the heathen gods; so that all who professed the Christian religion were either reduced by their fears to acquiesce in this worship, or were exposed to the prospect of death if they refused it. Alive to the danger which had fallen on the Church of Antioch, this valiant soldier of CHRIST permitted himself to be brought before Trajan, who was residing at the time in that city, and was on the eve of an expedition against Armenia and the Parthians. When brought into the imperial presence, he was thus addressed by Trajan.—"Who art thou," he said, "and what evil spirit is exercising its malice upon thee, that thou hast thus adventured to transgress the commands which I have given, and even to exercise such persuasion upon others, as has brought them to a miserable end?" Ignatius answered, "I bear the title of Theophorus; evil spirits cannot influence the acts of those who bear that name; the Servants of GOD are protected from the approach of Demons. But if, in supposing the malice of such beings towards me, you imply my hostility against them, I admit that you are not mistaken. For I am the subject of a Heavenly King, whose name is CHRIST, and by His help I bring to nought the counsels of the evil spirits." "What signifieth the title Theophorus?" enquired Trajan; "to whom belongs it?" "It belongs," replied Ignatius, "to all, who carry JESUS CHRIST in their bosoms." "Then," said Trajan, "do you think that we have not our gods in our minds, when we employ them to fight with us against our enemies?" Ignatius answered him; "You do wrong to designate as gods, the Demons whom the heathen worship. There is One God, who made the heavens and the earth, and all that is in them; and there is One JESUS CHRIST, the SON of GOD, the Only-begotten, of whose kingdom I am an expectant." "Do you mean," enquired Trajan, "that person, who was crucified in the time of Pontius Pilate?" "Him," replied Ignatius, "I mean, who nailed upon His Cross both the sins which I have committed, and the being that led me to commit them, and who has decreed that all spiritual craft and malice shall be put under the feet of them, who carry Him in their bosoms!" "Do you then," asked Trajan, "carry a crucified man within you?" Ignatius answered, "I do; for it is written, 'I will dwell within them, and I will walk among them.'" Trajan then issued this sentence. "We command that

Ignatius, who says that he carries about within him, one who has been crucified, be carried by soldiers in chains unto the great city of Rome, there to be devoured by wild beasts, for the public gratification." When the holy Martyr heard this announcement, he cried out with joy, "I thank Thee, O my Master, for that Thou hast permitted me to show forth, in the penalty I am to suffer, the perfect love I have toward Thee, and hast associated me with Thine Apostle Paul, in these iron bonds." So saying, he gladly put on the chains, and after offering up a prayer for the Church, and commending it with tears to the LORD, he was withdrawn like some leader of a goodly flock, the foremost of its associates in grace and stature, being destined, under the conduct of a harsh and savage soldiery, to become a prey for the wild beasts at Rome.

III. Maintaining a tone of mind thus elevated, and happy in the prospect of the closing scene, he travelled from Antioch to Seleucia, and proceeded forward by sea; and on arriving after a troublesome voyage at Smyrna, he gladly took the opportunity of disembarking to visit the holy Polycarp, who at that time was Bishop of the Smyrnæans, and who was his own fellow-disciple, both having at a former period received instruction from Saint John the Apostle. After having continued some time the guest of Polycarp, and having communicated with him in spiritual gifts, he declared the joy he found in his bonds, and invited him to give all diligence in assisting the main object of his desires; which was, that the wild beasts might make him an early prey; and so, retiring from the sight of this world, he might pass into the presence of CHRIST. To assist him in this object, he more particularly invited St. Polycarp. But he extended the request to the Church in general; for the Churches and cities of Asia had, through their Bishops, Presbyteries, and Deacons, received the holy man; and all were pressing forward to meet him, from their anxiety to partake in the spiritual gifts which he distributed.

IV. It was in terms like those which have been stated, that he gave evidence of the integrity of that love for his SAVIOUR, which was now leading him through a good confession to his heavenly inheritance; and he was assisted herein by the zealous prayers offered up by the persons who were with him, with a reference to the season of his trial. In repayment of the kindness shewn him by the Churches which received him on his journey, he sent by their rulers certain letters of thanks, which breathed forth the graces of a Christian spirit, in the language of supplication and warning. And, noticing what kindness of feeling was exhibited on all sides towards him, he began to fear, that now, while the glorious gate of martyrdom lay open before him, the affection of the Christian brotherhood would lead them to interfere with his devotion to the LORD; and he therefore addressed the Church of the Romans in an Epistle on the subject.[1]

V. Having, by that Epistle, engaged in his own view those of the brethren at Rome, whose intentions had been opposite, he left Smyrna, and proceeded on his voyage. The object of his military guard, in thus hurrying him forward, was, to arrive at Rome in time for the games, which are publicly held in that great city; so that the populace might see him, when he gained his Crown of Martyrdom, by being thrown to the wild beasts. He touched at Troas, and then crossed to Neapolis; and traversing Macedonia, by way of Philippi, advanced to the parts of Epirus near Epidamnus; here finding a vessel on the coast, he crossed the Adriatic, and entered the Tyrrhene sea. As he was coasting in sight of the various islands and towns, the city of Puteoli was pointed out to the holy man, and he expressed a strong desire to disembark there, in order that he might tread in the very footsteps of the Apostle Paul. But as the wind arose violently, and the vessel was running before it, he was prevented from doing so; and therefore passed straight onward, not without remarking how good and blessed a love was once exhibited by the brethren in that spot [Acts 28:13-14]. Taking advantage of the wind, which during the whole day and ensuing night continued favourable, we hurried forward; unwillingly ourselves, for we wept at the thought of that just man's separation from us; but he, on the other hand, was well satisfied with an early removal from this world, in the hope of being sooner joined unto the LORD he loved. We landed at the Roman Havens, nearly at the close of the unhallowed games. The soldiers expressed impatience at the tardiness of our arrival; and the Bishop was glad to acquiesce in their demand to hasten forward.

VI. The party was therefore hurried on from the place of landing called Portus; and, reports concerning the holy Martyr having gone before his arrival, he was met by certain brethren, whose minds were in a mingled state of fear and joy;—of joy, at being counted worthy to meet with him, whom the SAVIOUR had taken up in His arms, while at the same time they

---

[1] Vid. Records of the Church, No. 8.

shuddered at the thought of such a man being dragged away to death. To some of them he expressed a wish, that they should hold back from interference; as, in the ardour of their feelings, they declared an intention of inducing the populace to ask, that this good man might not be killed. Knowing this, he implored all, after saluting them, to show him a true love; expressing himself more largely on the point, than in his Epistle; and entreating them not to injure the prospects of one who was hastening to his LORD. And so, with all the brethren on their bended knees, he besought the SON of GOD for the Churches, that He would remove from them this persecution, and confirm the brotherhood in all mutual love. After which he was hurried off to the Amphitheatre, and straightway cast down into it, as the Emperor had ordered, nearly as the games were going to close. It was on that high day, which the Romans call the thirteenth, and multitudes were accordingly assembled. He was thrown to the wild beasts at a spot close to the temple; and so was speedily carried into effect the desire of this holy Martyr Ignatius, according to that which is written, "the desire of the righteous shall be granted." For thus he was a burthen to none of his brethren from the trouble of gathering up his remains; a consummation in correspondence with a wish, which he had previously expressed in his Epistle. The harder parts were alone left, and those were gathered up and carried to Antioch, where they were wrapped in a linen cloth, and deposited with the brethren of that Holy Church,—a treasure rendered invaluable, by the Christian graces, which had adorned the Martyr's life.

VII. This event took place on the thirteenth day before the Calends of January, that is, on the twentieth of December. The Consuls at Rome were Syrus, and Senecius for the second time. We personally witnessed every thing, and passed the following night within doors, in tears; and often knelt we down, and addressed to the LORD a prayer, that He would strengthen that reliance in Him, which the event of the day had tended to disturb. For a little time we reposed in sleep, and, on our doing so, some of us presently saw him, leaning over and embracing us; others saw our blessed Ignatius praying over us, as he had previously been doing; while to others he appeared with the marks of recent struggles and exertions upon him, but now come up, and standing before his LORD, his labours over, and rejoicing with exceeding gladness. After comparing the visions which thus presented themselves in our dreams, we sang an hymn to GOD, the

Giver of all good, and uttered the language of benediction over the departed Saint.

And now we make known to you the day and time at which this event occurred; that at the season of his Martyrdom we may gather together, and collect a portion of the spirit, which animated this courageous Champion and Martyr of CHRIST, who trod down Satan beneath his feet, and finished according to his hope his career of love and zeal, through JESUS CHRIST our LORD; to whom, with the FATHER and the HOLY GHOST, be glory and power throughout all ages! Amen.

ಌ

From this narrative, we learn to make the most of our time, wherever we are and however circumstanced. We are always on our trial, always have duties, always can be promoting GOD'S glory. Ignatius wrote his letters when he was a prisoner, travelling a weary way across a whole continent to his death. And of all his labours through forty years, these letters alone have been preserved to us. When then we are in pain, or trouble, and begin to despond, and think our labour has no fruit, let us think of this Blessed Martyr, praise GOD, and take courage.

December 6, 1833

RECORD 10

Epistle of Ignatius to the Philadelphians

Ignatius, which is also Theophorus, to the Church of GOD the FATHER, and our LORD JESUS CHRIST, that is in Philadelphia of Asia, that hath obtained mercy, and remaineth stedfast in godly concord, and exulteth continually in the Passion of our LORD; and hath in His Resurrection been richly furnished with all Mercy. Even this Church do I salute in the blood of JESUS CHRIST, which is our everlasting and abiding joy; especially if it be in Unity with the Bishop and his Fellow-Presbyters and Deacons, appointed after the mind of JESUS CHRIST; whom He hath according to His own Will established in all confidence, by His HOLY SPIRIT.

I. This your Bishop, I well know, hath obtained his public Ministry not of himself, or by the means of men, neither out of vain-glory, but in the Love of GOD the FATHER, and our LORD JESUS CHRIST. His moderation I do greatly admire; as he by silence doth more prevail, than others with their idle disputations; for he is exactly fitted to the commandments, even as a harp to its strings. Wherefore my soul esteemeth his mind toward GOD most happy; knowing it to be perfect in all virtue; as also his unmoved and dispassionate temper, according to the moderation of the Living GOD.

II. Do ye then, being children of light and truth, avoid division and corrupt doctrines; but where your shepherd is, thither follow ye as sheep. For there be many wolves, held worthy to be trusted, who captivate by corrupt pleasure those that are running a godly course; but in your Unity they shall have no place.

III. Abstain from the evil herbs, that CHRIST JESUS dresseth not; forasmuch as they are not the FATHER'S planting. I say not this because I have found you divided, but rather sifted from evil. For all that are of GOD, and JESUS CHRIST, these are with the Bishop; and all that shall repent and turn to the Unity of the Church, these also shall be of GOD, that they may live after the example of JESUS CHRIST. Be not deceived, Brethren; whosoever followeth one that createth schism, he inheriteth not the kingdom of GOD; whosoever walketh by another man's opinion, he consenteth not to the Passion of CHRIST.

IV. Endeavour therefore to use one and the same Eucharist; for there is but one Body of our LORD JESUS CHRIST; and one Cup; that His Blood may make us one. There is but one Altar; also there is one Bishop, together with the Presbytery and Deacons, my fellow-servants; that so whatsoever ye do, ye may do all according to the will of GOD.

V. My brethren, I abound in love toward you even to overflowing, and in my exceeding joy I fortify you; and yet not I, but JESUS CHRIST; for whom though I am in bonds, I have therefore the more fear, inasmuch as I am not yet made perfect. But your prayer to GOD shall make me perfect; that I may obtain that portion with which I was in mercy blessed; flying for refuge, to the Gospel as the Blood of CHRIST, and to the Apostles as to the Presbytery of the Church. Let us love the Prophets also, for that they have taught us, both to look with hope to the Gospel, and to await it; as they also believed in it and were saved, being in the Unity of JESUS CHRIST, holy men, worthy to be loved and had in wonder; who have received testimony from JESUS CHRIST, and have been reckoned in the Gospel of our common hope.

VI. Now should any one expound Judaism unto you, hearken not unto him; for it is better to hear Christianity from a man that hath circumcision, than Judaism from one that is uncircumcised. But if they speak, neither one of them, concerning JESUS CHRIST, they are unto me but as monuments and sepulchres of the dead, whereon is nothing written but the names of men. Fly therefore from the evil arts and snares of the Prince of this world; lest at any time, being oppressed by his devices, ye grow weak in love. But join all of you together with an undivided heart. I thank my GOD that I enjoy a good conscience toward you; and that no one can profess either privately or in public, that I have been burdensome to him in much or little; and I pray all, among whom I have spoken, not to entertain such profession as a testimony against me.

VII. For, though some would have deceived me according to the flesh, yet the spirit is not deceived, being of GOD; for it knoweth *whence it cometh and whither it goeth*, and reproveth all the secrets of the heart. I cried out while I tarried with you, spake with a loud voice; "Give heed to the Bishop, to the Presbytery, and the Deacons." Now some suspected, that I spake things, as knowing beforehand that among them was a spirit of division. But He is my witness, He for whom I am in bonds, that I knew it not from any living man; but the Spirit proclaimed, saying, "Keep your body as the Temple of GOD; love Unity; avoid divisions; be ye followers of JESUS CHRIST, even as He is a follower of His FATHER."

VIII. Wherefore I did my part, as a man fitted to the preserving of unity. For where is division and wrath, there GOD dwelleth not. The LORD therefore forgiveth all, when they repent, if in repentance they turn to godly Unity and the Council of the Bishop. I have faith in the grace of JESUS CHRIST, that He will loose you from every bond; and I exhort you to do nothing with contention, but according to the instruction of CHRIST. And this, I say; because I heard some affirm, that I have not faith in the Gospel, unless I find it written in the Records; and when I told them, It is so written; they answered, Nay, it doth not so appear. But my records are JESUS CHRIST. My uncorrupted records are His cross and death and resurrection, and the faith which is by Him; in the which I desire to be justified through your prayers.

IX. The Priests indeed are good; but far more excellent is the High-Priest, who hath received charge of the Holy of Holies; who hath alone received charge of the hidden things of GOD. He is the door of the FATHER, through which enter in Abraham, and Isaac, and Jacob, and the Prophets, and the Apostles, and the Church. All these things tend to godly unity; but the Gospel hath an especial gift, namely, the presence of our LORD JESUS CHRIST, with His Passion and Resurrection. For the beloved Prophets brought tidings of *Him;* but the Gospel is the fulfillment of Immortality. All things are good together, if ye have faith with love.

X. Now as I am told that, through your prayer, and the hearts ye bear in CHRIST JESUS, the Church which is in Antioch, of Syria, is in peace, it is fitting for you, as a Church of GOD, to elect a Deacon, who shall there exercise the office of GOD's ambassador; that so you may take part in their joy, when they are met together, and may glorify the name of GOD. Blessed in JESUS CHRIST is he, who shall be thought worthy of such a ministry; and ye also shall obtain glory. Now if ye be willing, it is not impossible to do this for the name of GOD; seeing that all the neighbouring Churches sent, some Bishops, some Priests and Deacons.

XI. Touching Philo, the Deacon from Cilicia, a man of good report, who serveth me even now in the word of GOD, together with Rheus Agathopus, one of the elect, who followelh me from Syria, having taken leave of life; these also do bear testimony unto you. And I thank GOD for your sakes, that ye received them, even as the LORD will receive you. But for those who shewed them dishonour, may they be redeemed through the grace of JESUS CHRIST. The brethren who are in Troas salute you with all love; whence also I write unto you by the hand of Burrhus, who was sent with me by the Ephesians and Smyrnaeans for respect's sake. Our LORD JESUS CHRIST will honour them, on whom they hope in body and soul, in faith, in love, in concord. Fare ye well in CHRIST JESUS, our common Hope.

December 10, 1833

RECORD 11

Account of the Martyrdom of St. James, the Apostle
From the Church History of Eusebius

The Church was delivered over to the Apostles, and especially to James, the LORD'S brother; who was surnamed the Just, by one consent, from the LORD'S time, even to our own. James was the name of many besides him; but this man was holy even from his mother's womb. He drank no wine, nor strong drink; neither did he eat any living thing; the razor came not on his head; he anointed not his body with oil, nor indulged in the luxury of the bath. He alone had leave to enter into the Holy place; his garment being not of woollen stuff, but of linen. So he used to go alone into the Temple, and was found continually kneeling on his knees, and praying for the forgiveness of the people; insomuch that his knees became hard, even as a camel's knees, because he was continually kneeling, worshipping GOD, and praying for the forgiveness of the people. Wherefore, by reason of his exceeding righteousness, he was called *Dicæus* and *Oblias;* which mean, being interpreted, the Just Man, and the Defence of the People, as the prophets declare concerning him.

It came to pass that certain of the seven sects of the people enquired of him, How JESUS was the door. And he said, That this JESUS was the SAVIOUR; whence some believed that JESUS was the CHRIST. Now the sects, whereunto the aforementioned persons belonged, believed neither in the Resurrection, nor that CHRIST should come hereafter to render to every man according to his works. But all who believe, believed through James. So when many of the Rulers also believed, there arose a disturbance of the Jews, and Scribes, and Pharisees, saying; "There is danger, lest all the people look to JESUS as the CHRIST." And when they were come together, they said unto James; "We pray thee, stop this people; for they have been deceived with regard to JESUS, as if He indeed were the CHRIST. We pray thee, therefore, persuade all people concerning JESUS, when they are come together on the day of the Passover. And this, we pray, because that all will be persuaded of thee; inasmuch as we and all the people bear witness to thee, that thou art a Just Man, and no respecter of persons. Do thou then persuade the multitude not to be deceived concerning JESUS; for also we and all the people are readily persuaded of thee. This do therefore; stand upon the pinnacle of the Temple, that thou mayst be conspicuous from on high, and that thy words may be well heard by all the people. For by reason of the Passover all the tribes are assembled, together with the Gentiles also." So the aforementioned Scribes and Pharisees set James upon the pinnacle of the Temple, and cried unto him, and said; "Thou just man, of whom we ought all to be persuaded, the people is deceived and followeth after JESUS which was crucified; do thou therefore declare unto us, how JESUS is the door." And he answered with a loud voice, and said; "Why ask ye me concerning JESUS, the Son of Man?—Behold, He sitteth on the right hand of Great Power, and He shall come hereafter upon the clouds of Heaven." And when many were fully convinced and believed on the testimony of James, and cried, Hosanna to the Son of David! Then came again those same Scribes and Pharisees, and said among themselves; "We have done ill, in that we have afforded such testimony to the name of JESUS. Come, let us go up, and cast him down, that the people may be afraid, and not believe his words." So they cried aloud, saying; "Oh! Oh! The Just One also hath been deceived!" And they fulfilled the word which is written in the book of Esaias; *Let us away with the Just One; because he is displeasing unto us; wherefore they shall eat of the fruits of their deeds.* Then went they up and cast down the Just One, and said one to another; "Let us stone James the Just." And they began to cast stones at him, because that after he was cast down, he died not, but turned and fell upon his knees, saying; "O LORD GOD FATHER, forgive them; they know not what they do." But while they were thus casting stones at him, one of the Priests, of the sons of Rechab, the son of Rechabeim, who have the witness of Jeremy the prophet, cried out, saying; "Cease ye; what are ye doing? Behold this Just Man prayeth for you." And one of them, of the company of Fullers, took the board with which he was wont to press the clothes, and struck therewith the head of the Just One; and thus James bore witness to the truth, even to martyrdom. And they buried him in that place; and his monument doth still remain, hard by the Temple. This man became a true witness and martyr, both to Jews and Gentiles, that JESUS is the Christ.

And straightway Vespasian besieged the city of the Jews, and carried them away captive.[1]

⁂

Hence we learn that even the holiest life will not shield good men from the envy and malice of those who hate their LORD and SAVIOUR; so that we must depend upon GOD alone, not upon an arm of flesh. The world admires true Christians for a while, and makes much of them; and then on a sudden turns round, and persecutes them. But they will calmly go through evil report and good report, for the name and cause of CHRIST; and be surprised neither when flattered nor evil intreated by sinners. They will make use of the good opinion the world has of them, while it lasts; but will fear to shrink ever so little from a bold Christian profession, in order to preserve it to them.

December 11, 1833

---

[1] Eusebius, it may be added, proceeds to declare, that among all intelligent Jews, an opinion prevailed, that the murder of James was the *cause* of the siege of Jerusalem, which so soon followed. "Josephus," says he, "scrupled not to assert directly in his History; 'These things happened to the Jews, in signal vengeance of the death of James the Just, brother to JESUS who was said to be the CHRIST. For notwithstanding his extraordinary character for justice, he was barbarously murdered by the Jews.'"

RECORD 12

The Martyrdom of Polycarp, the Disciple of St. John

Polycarp, Bishop of Smyrna, and Martyr, was a disciple of St. John; he was placed over the Church at Smyrna by the Apostle, and presided in it at least seventy years. Some persons have supposed that he was the "Angel," or Bishop, of Smyrna mentioned in Revelation 2:8-11. Shortly after St. John's death, he was visited by Ignatius, Bishop of Antioch, who had as well as himself attended the teaching of St. John, and was then on his way to martyrdom at Rome. It was from Smyrna that Ignatius wrote several of his Epistles, especially that to the Romans; and, when he had left the place, and got as far as Troas, he wrote his Epistles to Polycarp and the Church at Smyrna. We owe it to Polycarp that these important Epistles were preserved to after-ages.

    Among the disciples of Polycarp was Irenæus, who was Bishop of Lyons in France, after Pothinus, his predecessor, had been martyred in the great persecution there.[1] He gives the following account of his Master in one of his works. "I remember," he says, "what happened when I was a boy, more vividly than what takes place now; for what we learn in our youth grows up with us, and at last becomes part of our mind itself. Thus I can describe even the place, where the sainted Polycarp used to sit and discourse, and his goings forth, and comings in, and his manner of life, and his personal appearance, and his discourses to the people; and his account of what passed between him and St. John, and the other Disciples who had

---

[1] Vid. Records, No. 6.

seen the LORD; and his recollections of the sayings of those who were eyewitnesses of the Word of Life, of their account of His miracles, and His teaching, which was all agreeable to what is related in the Scriptures. To all this I used to listen with earnestness, through the mercy of God vouchsafed to me, recording them, not on paper, but in my heart; and through GOD'S grace I ever have them accurately in mind." Irenæus says this, when writing against a friend of his, who had been formerly taught by Polycarp, but had fallen away from the true faith into heresy. He adds; "I protest in the sight of GOD, that if that Blessed and Apostolical Elder had heard any such doctrine as thine, Florinus, he would have cried out, and stopped his ears, and said after his manner; 'O my GOD, unto what times hast thou reserved me, that I should hear such words!' and would have even fled the place in which he had heard them."

So far Irenæus. Now let us hear the account of Polycarp's Martyrdom, which took place under the Emperors Marcus Aurelius and Lucius Verus, A.D. 169.

Epistle from the Church at Smyrna to the Church at Philomelium

The Church of GOD which dwelleth in Smyrna to the Church of GOD which dwelleth in Philomelium, and all the members, in every place, of the Holy Catholic Church, mercy, peace, and love, from GOD the FATHER, and our LORD JESUS CHRIST, be multiplied.

We have written to you, brethren, the history of those who have been martyred, and more particularly of the blessed Polycarp, who closed the persecution, setting a seal as it were upon it by his own martyrdom. For almost all that happened before was done, that the LORD from on high might in him set forth to us this example of a true Christian confession. For he abode where he was, as also our LORD did, that he might be delivered up, in order that we too might be followers of him, and not look only to our own good, but to the good of our neighbours also; for it is the part of a sincere and stedfast charity for a man to desire not only his own salvation, but also of all the brethren.

Noble, therefore, and blessed are all those testimonies, which have been offered up according to GOD'S will (for to GOD must we with especial reverence attribute the power over all things); for who but must admire their nobleness, their endurance, their faithfulness to their LORD? For when torn with scourges, till their whole frame, even to the veins and arteries within, was laid open, they bore it so patiently, that the very bystanders pitied and bewailed them; yet they had attained to such a noble spirit, that not one of them uttered a cry or a groan *himself*, showing plainly to us, that in that hour of torment CHRIST'S witnesses were absent from the flesh, or rather that our LORD stood near and held converse with them; and they, intent on CHRIST'S favour, despised this world's torments, that they might by one hour's anguish purchase redemption from eternal chastisement. The fire of their cruel tormentors felt cold to them, for they had before their eyes the fleeing from the eternal fire that never shall be quenched, and with the eyes of their heart they looked to the good things reserved for them that endure; the things which ear hath not heard, nor eye seen, neither have they entered into the heart of man; but which were already half shown by the LORD to them, who were men no more, but already angels. In like manner also did those who were condemned to the wild beasts endure long time, in their confinement, fearful punishments; for they lay long stretched on sharp shells, and were buffeted with divers other torments, that, if he were able, the tyrant might by continued punishment turn them to a denial of the faith.

For many were the contrivances which the Devil wrought against them; but (thanks be to GOD) he prevailed not over them. For the heroic Germanicus gave courage to their fearfulness by the patient endurance that was in him; who fought with the wild beasts notably: for when the Proconsul endeavoured to persuade him, and besought him to compassionate his years, he provoked the animal, and drew it upon himself, wishing to be sooner freed from an unjust and lawless race. Upon this the whole multitude were struck with wonder at the Christians' noble love and devotion to their GOD, and shouted, "Away with the godless men, look for Polycarp."

But one Phrygian, Quintus by name, who had newly arrived from Phrygia, when he saw the wild beasts, played the coward; yet this was the man who had prevailed on himself and others to offer themselves voluntarily for apprehension. Him the Proconsul, after much urging, persuaded to take the oath and offer sacrifice: wherefore, brethren, we commend not those who give themselves up, since the Gospel doth not so teach.

Now the truly admirable Polycarp, when he first heard of these clamours, was nowise troubled, but wished to remain in the city. The greater part of us, however, persuaded him to withdraw, and he withdrew to a small villa, not far distant from the city, and there remained with a few brethren, doing nothing else, night and day, but praying for all men, and for the Churches throughout the world, as was his practice. And as he prayed, three days before his apprehension, he saw his pillow, in a vision, on fire. Turning therefore to those who were with him, he said prophetically, "I must be burnt alive."

His pursuers persevering in their endeavours, he removed to another villa; and immediately they came to the first place, and when they found him not, they took hold of two young slaves, one of whom being put to the torture confessed. And truly it was impossible that he should remain concealed, when they who betrayed him were his own servants: and the Irenarch,[2] who is also called the Distributor of lots, Herod by name, hastened to bring him to the theatre, that Polycarp might accomplish *his* lot, being made partaker of CHRIST; but they who betrayed him might undergo the penalties of Judas.

Taking therefore the lad with them, on the day of preparation, about the hour of supper, the search-officers and horsemen set forth with their ordinary weapons, as though they were pursuing a felon; and entering late in the evening, they found him lying down in a small chamber at the top of the house. From thence he might have got away to another place, but would not, saying, "The LORD'S will be done;" but, on hearing that they were come, he descended from his chamber, and conversed with them. And they who were there marvelling at his age and vigour, some said, "Was there such a mighty work about arresting an old man like this?" And he gave orders immediately to set before them meat and drink as much as they would, and besought them to give him an hour's free space to pray. And when they permitted him, standing up he prayed, being full of the grace of GOD, so that for two whole hours he could not cease; and they that heard him were astonished, and many repented that they had come out against such a divine old man.

---

[2] This office seems to have answered to that of Provost Marshal.

After he had done praying, having made mention of all with whom he had ever met, great and small, noble and obscure, and of the whole Catholic Church throughout the world; when the hour of going forth arrived, they set him on an ass, and led him into the city, it being the day of the great Sabbath. As he went, the Irenarch Herod and his father Nicetes, who were driving forth, happened to meet him, and transferred him into their chariot; and sitting by him argued with him, saying, "What harm is there in saying, Lord Cæsar? and in sacrificing, and so saving your life?" with the other usual sort of arguments. At first he gave them no answer: but on their persevering he only said, "I will not do what you counsel me." So they, when they found their endeavours to persuade him fruitless, railed at him, and pushed him down from the chariot so hastily, that in his descent his shin was laid open. But he, nowise moved, passed on readily and speedily as though he had received no injury, being led by the attendants to the theatre.

As he entered it, though the tumult there was so great that many heard not, a voice came to Polycarp from Heaven, "Be strong, Polycarp, and play the man."[3] Him that spake, not one of us saw; but the voice, those of ourselves who were present heard. On his being led to the tribunal, there was immense clamour at the news that Polycarp had been apprehended. At last, when he was brought near, the Proconsul asked him, if he were Polycarp; and, on his acknowledging it, he began to persuade him to deny the faith, saying, "Compassionate thine years;" and other similar expressions, which it is their wont to use. "Swear by the fortune of Cæsar; think better of the matter; say, Away with the godless men."[4] But Polycarp regarded with a sad countenance the whole multitude of lawless heathen in the theatre; and waving his hand towards them, groaned, and looking up to Heaven said, "Away with the godless men." And when the Governor urged him further, and said, "Swear, and I will dismiss thee; revile Christ;" Polycarp replied; "Eighty and six years have I been his servant, and he hath wronged me in nothing, and how can I blaspheme my King and my

---

[3] "Then they brought a faggot, kindled with fire, and laid the same down at Dr. Ridley's feet. To whom Master Latimer spake in this manner: '*Be of good comfort,* Master Ridley, *and play the man,* we shall this day light such a candle, by God's grace, in England, as I trust shall never be put out.'" —Fox's Book of Martyrs

[4] Literally, Atheists; for such, because they denied the heathen deities, the Christians were called; and such, because they denied the ONE TRUE GOD, Polycarp terms the unbelievers.

Saviour."[5] And on his pressing him again, saying, "Swear by the fortune of Cæsar," Polycarp replied; "If ye vainly suppose that I shall swear by Cæsar's fortune, as ye call it, pretending to be ignorant of my real character, let me tell you plainly, I am a Christian; and if ye wish to hear the Christian doctrine, appoint me a time, and hear me." The Proconsul answered, "Persuade the people." Polycarp replied, "To you I thought it right to give account, for we have been taught to give to rulers and the powers ordained of GOD such fitting honour as hurteth not our souls; but them I deem not worthy, that I should defend myself before them." The Proconsul said unto him, "I have wild beasts in readiness, to them will I throw thee, if thou wilt not change thy mind." But he said, "Bring them forth then, for the change of mind from better to worse I will never make. From cruelty to righteousness it were good to change." Again he said unto him, "I will have thee consumed by fire, since thou despisest the wild beasts, except thou change thy mind." Polycarp answered; "Thou threatenest me with a fire that burneth for an hour, and is speedily quenched; for thou knowest not of the fire of future judgment and eternal punishment reserved for the ungodly. But why tarriest thou? Bring what thou wilt."

As he spake these and other words, he was filled with confidence and joy, and his countenance was overspread with grace; so that not only was he not overthrown and confounded with what was said to him, but the Proconsul on the contrary was wonderstruck, and sent the herald to proclaim three times in the middle of the Stadium, that Polycarp had confessed himself to be a Christian. When this had been announced by the herald, the whole multitude, both of Gentiles and of Jews, who were settled in Smyrna, shouted with uncontrollable rage, and in a loud voice, "This man is the teacher of all Asia, the father of the Christians, who pulleth down our gods, who teacheth many neither to pay incense nor homage to them." With these words they called upon Philip, the Asiarch,[6] to let out a lion upon Polycarp. But he answered, he could not do that, as

---

[5] This must not be understood of his age (for then he could have been only seventeen when St. John died, and consequently could not have been consecrated Bishop by him, as is almost universally believed), but of his conversion to Christianity.

[6] Not the Proconsul, for his name was Quadratus, but as it appears below, the Pagan High Priest, to whom it had fallen to provide the wild beasts, and shows of gladiators, on that occasion.

the show of wild beasts was concluded. Then it occurred to them with one accord, to demand that he should burn Polycarp alive. For it was necessary that the vision which had been shewn to him upon his pillow should be fulfilled; when he saw it on fire as he prayed, and turned to the believers who were with him, and prophetically declared, "I must needs be burnt alive."

This, therefore, was no sooner said than done, for the multitude collected immediately wood and faggots from the shops and the baths, the Jews especially, as is their wont, being very zealous in assisting to this end. But, when the pile was ready, without any aid he laid aside his garments, and after unloosing his girdle, endeavoured to unbind his sandals too, a thing he had never done before, because that each of the faithful was ever pressing to be the first to touch his person. For he had ever been highly honoured on account of his virtuous conversation, even before his head had grown hoary.

Straightway then they arranged about his person all that was requisite for the pile.[7] But when they were about also to nail him to the stake, he said, "Leave me as I am, for He who giveth me to endure the fire, will also give me power, without the security of your nails, to remain untroubled upon the pile." They forbore, therefore, to nail him, but only bound him with cords. He therefore placed his hands behind him, and being bound to the stake even as the chief ram taken from a large flock, to be a burnt offering acceptable to GOD, lifted up his eyes to heaven, and said, "O LORD GOD ALMIGHTY, Father of Thy well-beloved and blessed Son JESUS CHRIST, through whom we have attained to the knowledge of Thee; Thou GOD of Angels and of Powers, and of every creature, and of the whole generation of the just who live before Thee; I bless Thee that Thou hast accounted me worthy of this day and hour, that I might receive my portion in the number of thy witnesses, and drink of the cup of Thine Anointed,[8] unto the resurrection of both body and soul unto eternal life through the incorruption of the HOLY SPIRIT; amongst which blessed martyrs may I be accepted before Thee this day for a rich and acceptable

---

[7] That is, probably, the shirt besmeared with pitch and tar, in which we elsewhere learn it was usual to clothe the Christian confessors, the stake to which they were fastened, and the cords used so to fasten them.

[8] Matthew 20:22, 23; 16:39, 42; John 18:11.

sacrifice, even as Thou hast foreordained, foreshewn, and now accomplished, the true and unfailing GOD. For this and for all Thy doings I praise Thee, I bless Thee, I glorify Thee, through the eternal High Priest, JESUS CHRIST, Thy well-beloved Son, through whom be glory to Thee with Him in the HOLY SPIRIT, both now and for evermore. Amen."

And when he had pronounced in a loud voice his Amen, having finished his prayer, they whose office it was kindled the fire, and a great flame flashed forth; and we, to whom the sight was vouchsafed, beheld truly a mighty marvel, who have been to this end preserved, that we might declare to the rest the things which were done. For the fire taking the shape of a dome, like the sail of a ship when filled with wind, compassed all round the body of the martyr; and he appeared in the middle, not like burning flesh, but like gold and silver tried in the furnace. Yea, we perceived too such a sweet odour as from the breath of frankincense, or some other precious perfume.

In the end, therefore, when the ungodly saw that his body could not be consumed of the fire, they commanded an executioner to go near to him, and thrust his sword into him. Which when he had done, there issued forth such a stream of blood, that it quenched the fire; and all the multitude marvelled that there was such a difference between the unbelievers and the elect. Of them was this man one, and the most remarkable in all our time, being Bishop of the Catholic Church that is in Smyrna, and an Apostolic and prophetic Teacher. For never word came from his mouth, but it has been, or shall be fulfilled.

But the envious and wicked Adversary of the generation of the righteous, when he saw the mightiness of his testimony, and his blameless conversation from the first, and how that he was now crowned with the crown of immortality, and had borne away a prize that could not be spoken against, contrived that his poor body might not be obtained by us, though many much desired to secure it, and to communicate over his holy remains.[9] For some suggested to Nicetes, the father of Herod, and brother of Alce, that he should persuade the governor not to give up his body, "lest," said he, "they leave the Crucified and take to worshipping this

---

[9] That is, probably, to meet for prayer and the celebration of the Eucharist with the body in their sight. The same feeling has shewn itself almost in all ages, in the interment of the dead in the church and churchyard.

fellow." And these things they said, as instigated and supported by the Jews, who even watched us when some of us were about to take his body from the fire, for they little knew how impossible it was for us either to forsake the worship of CHRIST, who suffered for the salvation of the whole world of them that be saved, or to pay worship to any other. For to Him truly we pay adoration, forasmuch as He was the Son of GOD; but the martyrs, as the disciples and followers of the LORD, we revere as they deserve, for their incomparable loyalty to their King and Master, praying that we may be made their partners and their fellow-disciples.

Then the centurion, seeing the earnestness of the Jews, laid out the body and burnt it, as was their custom; and so we afterwards gathered up his bones, more valued than stones of much price, and purer than fine gold, and laid them up in a fitting treasure-house. There assembling, as we may, in joy and in triumph, the LORD shall grant unto us to celebrate the birth-day of his martyrdom,[10] both to the remembering of them who wrestled before in the cause, and the training and preparing of those that shall come after.

Such is the story of the blessed Polycarp, who, being (with them of Philadelphia) the twelfth who has given his testimony in Smyrna, is made alone the especial subject of all men, so that even by the Gentiles is he spoken of in every place, having been not only a notable teacher, but also a chief witness; whose confession, rendered as it was according to the Gospel of CHRIST, all men desire to imitate. For by his patient endurance he triumphed over the unjust ruler, and thus having won the garland of immortality, and rejoicing with the Apostles, and all Saints, he glorifieth GOD and the FATHER and blesseth our LORD, who is both the Governor of our bodies, and the Shepherd of the Catholic Church throughout the world.

Ye requested, therefore, that these circumstances should be detailed to you at length, and we have now briefly signified them through our brother Marcus. Therefore after ye have understood these things, send our

---

[10] The Church always celebrated the day of martyrdom as that on which the Saint was truly born, and not what we call the birth-day. The following translation from an old writer may serve to explain this view. "We celebrate not the day of birth, since it is the entrance to sorrow and all trials; but it is the day of death we celebrate, as the lying down of all sorrows, and the escape from all trials. We celebrate the day of death, because these die not when they seem to die." —Comment. in Job. Lib. 3.

letter about to our brethren also in the regions beyond you, that they too may glorify the LORD, who maketh choice out of His own servants, who is able by His grace and free gift to bring all of you unto His eternal kingdom, through His only begotten SON JESUS CHRIST, to whom be glory, honour, dominion and greatness, for ever. Amen. Salute ye all the Saints. They that are with us salute you; and Evarestus, who hath written this, with all his house.

The blessed Polycarp gave his testimony on the 2nd of the month Xanthicus, on the 26th of March, on the Great Sabbath,[11] at the eighth hour. He was apprehended by Herod, in the High Priesthood of Philip of Tralles, in the proconsulship of Stratius Quadratus, in the everlasting reign of JESUS CHRIST, to whom be glory, honour, greatness, and a throne eternal, from generation to generation. Amen.

We pray you brethren to be strong, walking by the Gospel of JESUS CHRIST (with whom be glory to GOD, both FATHER and HOLY SPIRIT, for the salvation of the elect Saints), even as the blessed Polycarp suffered, in whose steps may we be found in the kingdom of JESUS CHRIST.

॰

This letter Gaius took from Irenæus, the disciple of Polycarp, being himself also a friend of Irenæus.

॰

And I Socrates, of Corinth, have transcribed it from the copy of Gaius. Grace be with all men.

॰

And I, again, Pionius have copied from the above written, Polycarp himself in a vision having shewed me where the manuscripts were, as I shall declare in the sequel, after I had long sought for them; and so I gathered

---

[11] There is some doubt what this great sabbath was; but it seems most probably that it was that which came between the days of our LORD'S passion and resurrection, a fitting time for His followers to enter into His rest.

them, when now by length of time almost worn out, that so the LORD JESUS CHRIST may gather me also with his elect; to whom be glory, with FATHER and HOLY GHOST, for ever and ever. Amen.

※

Thus ends this ancient history. It appears that one Pionius suffered martyrdom at the same place Smyrna, in the Decian persecution, which happened eighty years after this in which Polycarp suffered. The name and death of this martyr are mentioned by Eusebius in connection with that of Polycarp, and it seems probable that the full account of his sufferings was appended to the MS. which has been here translated. We may therefore infer, that this was the man, who had so diligently and faithfully transcribed the history of his fellow-countryman, and that having carefully conned his sacred lesson, and thus given courage to his fearfulness, and strength to his weakness, he at length by GOD'S grace was enabled to withstand the like tortures, "not accepting the deliverance, that *he* might obtain a better resurrection."

December 17, 1833

RECORD 13: AD POPULUM

Justin Martyr on Primitive Christian Worship

Justin, surnamed the Martyr, was born at Sichem in Samaria, where was Jacob's well. His parents were heathens, and he grew up to man's estate, ignorant of the true GOD, yet dissatisfied with what the wise men of this world taught on the subject of religion. He was of an inquiring turn, and successively attached himself to various sects of philosophers, beginning with the Stoics, who are mentioned in Acts 17:18. At length he fancied he was making progress in the discovery of the unseen world, when one day he wandered out by the sea-side to enjoy his meditations undisturbed. To his surprise he found himself joined by an old man of grave but mild countenance. Justin stopped and steadily gazed on him. The other asked him if he knew him, that he eyed him so earnestly. On Justin's expressing surprise at meeting any one in so solitary a place, the old man accounted for the accident, and then fell into conversation with him, which ended in his preaching to him JESUS CHRIST, and Justin's receiving impressions which led to his conversion to the true faith. This took place, A.D. 132, about thirty years after St. John's death. About eighteen years after he fixed his abode at Rome, where he employed himself in various writings in defence of the Gospel. At length he was called upon to die for it, under circumstances which are detailed in the following ancient account.

Narrative of the Martyrdom of Justin the Philosopher, A.D. 167

While the persecution raged against the Christians for their refusing to sacrifice to the idols, the holy men (Justin and his companions) were arrested and brought before Rusticus, the Prefect of Rome, who bade Justin believe in the gods and obey the Emperor. He answered, "It is safe and unexceptionable to obey the commands of our SAVIOUR JESUS CHRIST." The Prefect asked, "What department of learning do you pursue?" Justin answered, "I have essayed all, but I have attached myself to that true philosophy which the Christians profess, however displeasing it may be to mistaken reasoners." "Miserable man," said Rusticus, "is that your learning?" The other replied, "Yes, verily, I profess it in all truth of doctrine." "What doctrine?" "A reverent acknowledgment of the GOD of the Christians, whom we account to be the One original maker and framer of the whole world, visible and invisible; and of the LORD JESUS CHRIST, the Son of GOD, who was foretold by the prophets as the herald of salvation, and the instructor of dutiful disciples. For myself, mortal as I am, I cannot hope to speak adequately of His infinite majesty, which is a gift peculiar to the prophets. For they foretold His coming, whom I have declared to be the SON of GOD."

The Prefect said, "Where is your place of meeting?" Justin answered, "Where each chooses, and is able to come. Do you think that we all meet at the same place? Not so, for the Christian's GOD is not bounded by space, but though invisible fills both heaven and earth, and every where receives the homage and praise of the faithful." The Prefect Rusticus replied, "Tell me where ye meet together, in what place thou assemblest thy disciples." Justin answered, "that he lodged near one Martinus, at the baths called Timiotine; that this was the second time he had sojourned in Rome, that throughout the whole period he had known no other place of meeting, that he had communicated the words of truth to any one who chose to visit him." Rusticus said, "Art thou not in short a Christian?" Justin answered, "Yea, I *am* a Christian."

Then the Prefect said to Charito, "Say, thou too, Charito,—Art thou a Christian?" Charito answered, "By GOD'S command I am a Christian." He then said to Charitina, "And what sayest thou, Charitina?" She answered, "By GOD'S gift I am a Christian." He next addressed Evelpistus, and said, "And what art thou?" He, being a slave of Cæsar's, made answer, "I too am a Christian, being made free by Christ, and am partaker by Christ's favour of the same hope." The Prefect said to Hierax, "And art thou a Christian?" Hierax said, "Yea, I am a Christian, for I reverence and adore the same God." Rusticus said, "Hath Justin made you

Christians?" Hierax answered, "I was a Christian, and I will continue one." Then Pæon stood up and said, "I too am a Christian." The Prefect said, "Who was he that taught thee?" Pæon answered, "From my parents I received this good confession." Evelpistus said, "I too, though I have listened gladly to the preaching of Justin, was taught of my parents to be a Christian." Rusticus said, "And where are thy parents?" Evelpistus answered, "In Cappadocia." The Prefect asked Hierax where his parents were. Hierax made answer in these words: "CHRIST is our true father, and faith in Him our true mother. My earthly parents are dead, and I myself have been brought hither from Iconium in Phrygia." The Prefect Rusticus addressed Liberianus: "And what dost thou say?—art thou a Christian?—art thou too an unbeliever?" Liberianus said, "I too am a Christian, for I am a believer and a worshipper of the only true God."

The Prefect said to Justin, "Listen thou, who art accounted an orator, and supposest thyself skilled in true doctrine; if I should have thee scourged and beheaded, what is thy belief?—that thou wouldest ascend into heaven?" Justin said, "I do trust that if I endure these things, I shall receive rewards from Him, for I know that for them who have so lived, there remaineth the divine gift, till the times of the consummation of all things." The Prefect Rusticus said again, "Dost thou imagine, that thou shalt go up into heaven, and there receive a recompense?" Justin answered, "I imagine it not; for I know and am entirely persuaded that I shall." Rusticus said, "It remains then that we come to the matter in hand, which presseth us. Come, therefore, all of you together, and with one mind do sacrifice to the gods." Justin answered, "No man of right judgment falleth from religion to irreligion." Rusticus answered, "If ye will not obey me, ye shall be tortured without mercy." Justin replied, "We ask in prayer, that we may be tortured for the name of our LORD JESUS CHRIST and be saved; for this shall be our salvation and our confidence, at that more terrible tribunal whereat all the world must appear, of our King and Saviour." In like manner said the other martyrs also. "Do what thou wilt, for we are Christians and do no sacrifice to idols."

Then the Prefect Rusticus gave sentence, saying, "Let such as refuse to do sacrifice to the gods, and to obey the decree of the Emperor, be scourged, and then led away to capital punishment, in pursuance of the laws." So the holy martyrs, giving glory to God, were led forth to the accustomed place, and were beheaded, giving full completion to their testimony by the confession of the SAVIOUR. And certain of the faithful, when they had secretly taken up their bodies, deposited them in a meet place, the grace of our LORD JESUS CHRIST working with them, to whom be glory for ever and ever. Amen.

Justin's Account of Baptism, the Lord's Supper, and the Public Worship of God

We will state in what manner we are created anew by CHRIST, and have dedicated ourselves to GOD.—As many as are persuaded and believe that the things which we teach and declare are true, and promise that they are determined to live accordingly, are taught to pray, and to beseech GOD, with fasting, to grant them remission of their past sins, while we also pray and fast with them. We then lead them to a place where there is water, and there they are regenerated in the same manner as we also were; for they are then washed in that water in the name of GOD the FATHER and LORD of the universe, and of our SAVIOUR JESUS CHRIST, and of the HOLY SPIRIT. For CHRIST said, "Except ye be born again, ye shall not enter into the kingdom of heaven;" and that it is impossible that those who are once born should again enter into their mothers' wombs, is evident to all. Moreover, it is declared by the prophet Isaiah, in what manner they who have sinned and repent may escape the punishment of their sins. For it is said, "Wash you; make you clean; put away the evil from your souls; learn to do well; do justice to the fatherless, and avenge the widow: and come, and let us reason together, saith the LORD. Even if your sins should be as scarlet, I will make them white as wool: and if they should be as crimson, I will make them white as snow. But if ye will not hearken unto Me, the sword shall devour you: for the mouth of the LORD hath spoken these things."

The Apostles have also taught us for what reason this new birth is necessary. Since at our first birth we were born without our knowledge or consent, by the ordinary natural means, and were brought up in evil habits and evil instructions, in order that we may not longer remain the children of necessity or of ignorance, but may become the children of choice and judgment, and may obtain in the water remission of the sins which we have before committed, the name of GOD the FATHER and LORD of the

Universe is pronounced over him who is willing to be born again, and hath repented of his sins; he who leads him to be washed in the laver of baptism, saying this only over him:—for no one can give a name to the ineffable GOD; and if any man should dare to assert that there is such a name, he is afflicted with utter madness. And this washing is called illumination, since the minds of those who are thus instructed are illuminated. And he who is so illuminated is baptized also in the name of JESUS CHRIST, who was crucified under Pontius Pilate; and in the name of the HOLY SPIRIT, who by the prophets foretold all things concerning JESUS.   *   *   *

We, then, after having so washed him who hath expressed his conviction and professes the faith, lead him to the brethren, where they are gathered together, to make common prayers with great earnestness, both for themselves and for him who is now illuminated, and for all others in all places, that having learned the truth, we may be deemed worthy to be found men of godly conversation in our lives, and to keep the commandments, that so we may attain to eternal salvation. When we have finished our prayers, we salute one another with a kiss. After which, there is brought to the brother who presides, bread and a cup of wine mixed with water. And he, having received them, gives praise and glory to the FATHER of all things, through the name of the SON and of the HOLY SPIRIT, and gives thanks in many words for that GOD hath vouchsafed to them these things. And when he hath finished his praises and thanksgiving, all the people who are present, express their assent, saying Amen, which means in the Hebrew tongue, "So be it." He who presides having given thanks, and the people having expressed their assent, those whom we call deacons give to each of those who are present a portion of the bread which hath been blessed, and of the wine mixed with water, and carry some away for those who are absent. And this food is called by us the Eucharist (thanksgiving); of which no one may partake unless he believes that what we teach is true, and is washed in the Laver, which is appointed for the forgiveness of sins and unto regeneration, and lives in such a manner as CHRIST commanded. For we receive not these elements as common bread or common drink; but even as JESUS CHRIST our SAVIOUR, being made flesh by the word of GOD, had both flesh and blood for our salvation, even so we are taught, that the food which is blessed by prayer, according to the word which came from Him (by the conversion of which into our bodily substance our blood and flesh are nourished) is the Flesh and Blood of that JESUS who was made flesh. For the Apostles, in the Memoirs composed by them, which are called Gospels, have related that JESUS thus commanded them; that, having taken bread, and given thanks. He said, "Do this in remembrance of Me—this is My Body;" and that, in like manner, having taken the cup, and given thanks, He said, "This is My Blood;" and that He distributed them to these alone . . . . . After these solemnities are finished, we afterwards continually remind one another of them. And such of us as have possessions assist all those who are in want; and we all associate with one another. And over all our offerings we bless the Creator of all things, through His SON JESUS CHRIST, and through the HOLY SPIRIT.

And on the day which is called Sunday, there is an assembly in one place of all who dwell either in towns or in the country; and the Memoirs of the Apostles or the writings of the Prophets are read, as long as the time permits. Then, when the reader hath ceased, the head of the congregation delivers a discourse, in which he reminds and exhorts them to the imitation of all these good things. We then all stand up together, and put forth prayers. Then, as we have already said, when we cease from prayer, bread is brought, and wine, and water; and our Head, in like manner, offers up prayers and praises with his utmost power; and the people express their assent by saying Amen. The consecrated elements are then distributed and received by every one; and a portion is sent by the deacons to those who are absent.

Each of those also, who have abundance, and are willing, according to his choice, gives what he thinks fit; and what is collected is deposited with him who presides, who succours the fatherless and the widows, and those who are in necessity from disease or any other cause; those also who are in bonds, and the strangers who are sojourning among us; and, in a word, takes care of all who are in need.

We all of us assemble together on Sunday, because it is the first day in which GOD changed darkness and matter, and made the world. On the same day also JESUS CHRIST our SAVIOUR rose from the dead.[1]

April 25, 1834
The Feast of St. Mark

---

[1] Mr. Chevallier's translation has been generally adhered to in this extract.

RECORD 14: AD POPULUM
Irenæus on the Rule of Faith

Irenæus was Bishop of Lyons in France. He is supposed to have been a native of Asia; he was born, at latest, about forty years after St. John's death, and died A.D. 202. The following is his account of the *faith* of Christians, and of the *Church* as the pillar and ground, the appointed witness of that faith.

The Church, although extended through the whole world, even unto the ends of the earth, has received from the Apostles and their Disciples the belief in One GOD, the Father Almighty, Maker of heaven, and earth, the seas, and all that is in them;—and in one CHRIST JESUS, the Son of GOD, who was made flesh for our salvation; and in the HOLY GHOST, who by the Prophets proclaimed the merciful dispensation, and the coming, and the birth from a virgin, and the passion, and the resurrection, and the ascension into heaven, in our flesh, of the Beloved, CHRIST JESUS our Lord, and His appearing from heaven in the glory of the FATHER, to gather together all things in one, and to raise from the dead all flesh of human kind; that to CHRIST JESUS our Lord and God, and Saviour, and King, according to the good pleasure of the Invisible FATHER, every knee may bow, of things in heaven, and things in earth, and things under the earth, and every tongue may confess Him, and that He may recompense just judgment upon all, sending into everlasting fire wicked spirits and angels that transgressed and became apostates, and irreligious, unjust, lawless, and profane men, but upon the just and holy, who have kept His commandments, and persevere in His love, whether serving Him from the first, or turning by repentance, may bestow immortality by the free gift of life, and secure for them everlasting glory.

This is the message, and this the faith, which the Church has received (as was said above); and which, though dispersed throughout the whole world, she sedulously guards, as though she dwelt but in one place; believes as uniformly as though she had but one soul and the same heart; and preaches, teaches, hands down to posterity, as harmoniously as though she had but one mouth. True it is, the world's languages are various, but the power of the Tradition is one and the same. There is no difference of Faith or Tradition, whether in the Churches of Germany, or in Spain, or in Gaul, or in the East, or in Egypt, or in Africa, or in the more central parts of the world; but as the sun, God's creature, is one and the same in all the world, so also the preaching of the Truth shineth every where, and lighteth every one who will come to the knowledge of the Truth. Among the rulers of the Church, neither he who is powerful in word speaks other doctrine (for no one can be above his Master), nor does the weak in the word diminish the Tradition. For, whereas the Faith is one and the same, neither he who has much to say concerning it, hath any thing over, nor he who speaketh little any lack.

❧

What a lesson does this passage furnish to the inquiring Christian of this day! Irenæus was the disciple of Polycarp, the friend of St. John. Here then is a witness, only one remove from the Apostles, for the Catholic Faith, such as we hold it, such as we declare it in Church unto this day. Wanderers and disputers, perplexed inquirers, and weak brethren! come home to this true doctrine of CHRIST, clearly conveyed to us from CHRIST Himself and His Apostles.

And observe this holy Bishop tells us, that it was received as such, preached as such, delivered as such, *all over the world*. There is no room for disputing, it is one and the same Truth, as CHRIST is One, and as the HOLY SPIRIT in the Church is One. Yes! and as the Church itself is one. The one faith is held in the one Church. Wanderers come home to it! come home to the Church Catholic, of which Irenæus spoke, which is still upon earth; of which the English Church, with its Bishops, Priests, and Deacons, is a true and living branch. And, at all events, even if you are not persuaded to this suitable religious deed, yet at least you cannot refuse to take up a humbler judgment of the Christianity of this day than is generally taken. For is not unity the chief blessing which CHRIST prayed His Church might possess? Was it not, as the above extract shows, marvelously instanced in the state of the Primitive Church? Is it not lost now? Surely this is undeniable. Whatever our knowledge, our exertions, our various gifts, Christians *have lost* their peculiar privilege, have transgressed their peculiar duty, "that they all should be one, as CHRIST and the FATHER are One."

Anecdote of the Great St. Basil, Archbishop of Cæsarea in Cappadocia

The Holy Basil visited one day a sacred brotherhood; and, after such discourse as was fitting, said to the Head of it, "Hast thou a brother here who has the grace of obedience?" and he answered him, "My Lord, we be all thy servants, and are endeavouring after salvation." Basil said a second time, "Yea hast thou one so gifted?" And he brought unto him a brother. Then the Holy Basil employed him to minister to him as he dined. After he had eaten, the other brought him water to wash; but Basil said, "Come hither, and I too will give thee water to wash." And the other suffered the Bishop to pour out the water upon his hands. Then said Basil, "When I enter into the chancel, come before me, and I will make thee a Deacon." And afterwards he made him Priest, and took him with him to his own house on account of his *obedience*.

April 25, 1834
The Feast of St. Mark

RECORD 15: AD POPULUM
The Temporal Condition of the Church
From the Epistle to Diognetus

The writer of the Epistle to Diognetus was either Justin Martyr, or some disciple of the Apostles themselves, a contemporary of Justin Martyr, *i.e.* about A.D. 130.

Christians differ not from other men in country, or language, or customs. They do not live in any peculiar cities, or employ any particular dialect, or cultivate characteristic habits of life. The truths which they hold result not from the busy ingenuities of human thought; the counsels of man in them possess no champion. They dwell in cities, Greek and barbarian, each where he finds himself placed, and while they submit to the fashion of their country in dress and food and the general conduct of life, they yet maintain a system of interior polity, which beyond all controversy is full of admiration and wonder. The countries they inhabit are their own, but they dwell like aliens; they take their part in all privileges, as being citizens; and in all sufferings they partake as if they were strangers. In every foreign country they recognise a home; and in their home they see the place of their pilgrimage. They marry like other men, and exclude not their children from their affections: their table is open to all around them; they live in the world, but not according to its fashions; they walk on earth, but their conversation is in heaven. They obey the established laws, but in their lives transcend all law; they love all men, and are persecuted by all; they are unknown, and yet are condemned. Death to them is life; of their poverty they make many rich, and in the extremity of want they still possess all things. They are treated with dishonour, and by dishonour are made glorious; their integrity is insured by the insults which they suffer; when cursed they bless, and reproaches they pay with respect. When doing good they are punished as evil-doers; and when they are punished they rejoice as men that are raised unto life. By Jews they are treated as aliens and foes, by Greeks they are persecuted; and none of their enemies can state a ground for their enmity.

In good truth, Christians are to the world what the soul is to the body. The soul is transfused through the members of the body, and Christians through the cities of the world: the soul dwells in the body, but is not of the body; and Christians dwell in the world, but are not of the world. The soul unseen is treasured up in the visible body; and Christians visibly are in the world, but their faith is a guest unseen in it. The flesh hates the soul, and wars against it without provocation, because it forbids the enjoyment of its pleasures; and the world hates Christians without provocation, because they are at enmity with its enjoyments. The soul loves that flesh and those limbs that hate it; and Christians love all that hate them. The soul is shut up in the body, but itself is to the body a protector; and Christians are included in the world as in a prison house; and yet they are the guardians of the world. The immortal soul resides in a mortal tabernacle; and Christians dwell amidst corruption, but are waiting for incorruption in heaven. By loss of meat and drink the soul is strengthened; and Christians abound more and more, though suffering every day. Such is the station in which GOD has planted them, and it is not lawful for them to retire from it.

I have already said, that their faith was not a discovery of this world. It is not a human counsel which they support with this anxiety; nor are they entrusted with the stewardship of mysteries which proceed from man; but GOD Himself, the Almighty and Invisible Creator, has sent down from heaven to men His holy and incomprehensible Truth and Word, and fixed it in their hearts; not, as might, perhaps, be anticipated, sending any minister to man, angel, or principality (whether of those whose functions belong to the earth, or of such as are engaged in the economy of Heaven), but Him, who was the very Maker and Builder of all: by whom He built the heavens, and marked the bounds of the ocean; whose mysterious ordinances the elements all faithfully obey; from whom the sun receives the measure of its daily career, and at whose will the obedient moon puts forth her mighty lustre, with the stars that move attendant on her course. He is the universal Counsellor, and Lawgiver, and Monarch; His are the heavens, and all that is in heaven; His the earth, and all in the earth; the sea, and all that is in the sea; fire, air, and depth; the height above, and the deep beneath; all are His. Him GOD sent to man: but was it, as man might anticipate, to overrule, to terrify, and to strike? Not so; but in meekness and in mercy. He sent Him, as a king might send his royal son: as GOD He sent Him; as a Messenger and a Saviour to mankind, to persuade, but not to compel. Violence is not an attribute of GOD. He sent Him in love, not in judgment: in judgment He will hereafter send Him, and who will bear His coming? . . . . . See you not how Christians are cast to the beasts, that they may be made deny their Lord, and are not overcome? See you not how they abound, in proportion with the increase of their sufferings? These things seem not like the work of man; but they are the power of GOD, and indications of His presence.

What mortal man could tell what GOD was, before He came among us? Would you admit the vain and trifling fables of such empty philosophers, as say that the DEITY is composed of fire (calling that a Deity, to which themselves are tending); or of water, or of any other of those elements which GOD has created? And yet, if any of these fables is admissible, each and every of the creatures might similarly be called a God. These things are the trickery and deceit of impostors. Man had never seen or known Him, but He manifested Himself. He manifested Himself by faith, by which alone it is possible to see GOD. For that GOD, who is the Master and Architect of all, who made all things, and disposed them in their place, was found not only benevolent, but also patient. Such, indeed, He always has been, and is, and will be,—kind, and good, and mild, and true: and only He is good; and having conceived that great and unspeakable counsel, which He communicated to His SON alone, so long as He retained the project of His wisdom, and reserved it in concealment, He seemed to be without care or consideration for us; but when, through his beloved SON, He revealed and made manifest the things which, from the beginning, were prepared, He at once presented to us all the scheme, so that we partake and behold His benefits. Who among us could conceive these things? But He, in Himself, and with His Son, foreknew the course of His Providence.

For the time past, therefore, He suffered us to be borne along as we would by irregular impulses, led astray by pleasures and desires; not that He feels complacence in our sins, but He permits them, from no gratification in the times of unrighteousness, but because He is working out the purposes of His justice:—that, during the time past, convicted by our own works of unworthiness to enter into life, we might now be rendered worthy through the goodness of GOD; and being proved of ourselves unable to enter into the kingdom of GOD, we might, by the power of GOD, be made able. But when our unrighteousness was assured, and it was clearly manifested that the wages of sin is punishment, and death was before our eyes, then came the time, which GOD foreordained for the manifestation of His goodness and power, forasmuch as, in the abundance of His beneficence, love was alone displayed; He hated not, nor rejected us, nor remembered our guilt; but showed Himself long-suffering, and forbearing, and, in His own words, bare our sins. He gave His own SON as a ransom for us, the just for the unjust, the guileless for the guilty, the righteous for the wicked, the incorruptible for the corrupt, the immortal for the dying. For what other thing, except His righteousness, could cover our guilt? In whom was it possible for us lawless sinners to find justification, save in the SON of GOD alone? Oh, sweet exchange! Oh, counsel untraceable, and mercies out of thought!—that the guilt of many might be covered by one that was righteous, and the righteousness of one might justify many who were guilty. Having, then, in the times past, ensured the incapacity of our nature for the attainment of life, and sending a SAVIOUR afterwards, who is able to save those who of themselves are incapable of salvation, He has pleased, from both these truths, to make us rely on His goodness, and regard Him as our Guardian, our Father, our Teacher, our Counsellor, our Physician, our Mind, our Light, our Honour, and Glory, and Strength, and Life; and so take no thought for raiment or for food.

If, then, you are anxious to know and accept this Faith, first learn that God has love for mankind, and for their sake made the world, and gave them dominion over all things in it: He gave them reason and perception; them only He permits to look upward towards Himself, and made them in His own image, and sent to them His only-begotten Son, announcing a kingdom in Heaven, which He will give, if they love Him. When you learn this, with what joy, think you, will you be filled, or how will you love one who first loved you so well? And if you love Him, you will imitate His kindness. Nor wonder that man can be an imitator of GOD; by GOD'S gift, he can; for happiness does not rest in the possession of authority over others, or in aiming at advantages which others possess not, or in wealth or superior power: in these things it is not possible for man to imitate GOD; but he who bears a brother's burden, and shares of his abundance to them that want, does the work of God towards those, who at his hands receive what GOD had given him: and that man is an imitator of GOD. Thus shall you discover, while you dwell on earth, that GOD works His purposes in Heaven; you will begin to tell of the hidden things of GOD, and will love and admire those who are punished for refusing to deny Him; you will discern the deceitfulness and crafts of the world: for you will learn truly to live in Heaven, and despise that seeming death here, when you are afraid of the very death, which is kept for those who are condemned to eternal fire, the endless punishment of all who are cast to it; and you will esteem such as endure this world's fire for righteousness sake, and reckon them happy, when you know of the other fire.

I deal not in vain or foolish questions: but, whereas I was a disciple of the Apostles, I teach the Gentiles: I administer those doctrines which have been granted to all worthy disciples of the truth. For what man who has been taught aright and nurtured in the kindly word, does not feel an increasing desire clearly to know those things, which by the Word were directly spoken to the disciples, and which He manifested fully to them?—not being understood by unbelievers, but explaining them to His disciples; for they were reckoned worthy by Him to learn the mysteries of the Father. And for this cause the Word was sent forth, that He might be manifested to the world; and when His nation rejected Him, He was believed in by the Gentiles through the preaching of the Apostles. This is He that was from the beginning, and appeared in the latter days; and His advent is continually renewed in the hearts of His saints. This is He that is from everlasting, the Son this day declared: and of His riches the Church receives; for His expansive grace is shed abundantly among the saints, conferring wisdom, declaring mysteries, enouncing the times, rejoicing with the faithful, and giving to all that ask: and these break not the rule of faith, nor transgress the rule of the fathers. And thus the fear of the Law is proclaimed, and the inspiration of the Prophets acknowledged, and faith in the Gospels confined, and the Apostles' tradition secured; and the

Church rejoices in her grace: wherefore if you grieve not that grace, you shall be taught the truths which the Word communicates by those whom He chooses in His own good time. For those things which we have been moved to declare by the will of the Word commanding us, we will with all diligence communicate to you, because we love the lessons which have been revealed to us.

Ye then who are admitted to these truths, and accept them with a ready heart, shall learn what GOD has prepared for them that truly love Him, how that they grow into a paradise of pleasure, and lift within themselves a rich luxuriant tree, adorned with many fruits. It is in such ground that the tree of knowledge and the tree of life are planted; and knowledge is not that which brings death, but disobedience in the way of gaining it. For we are taught in plain words, that God in the beginning planted the tree of life in the midst of Paradise, showing that knowledge is the way to life; and they who did not use it aright at first, were robbed by the deceits of the serpent. For life cannot be separate from knowledge; nor can any knowledge be perfect, unless the true life be with it. For this cause they were planted side by side; and the Apostle perceiving this intent, and condemning all knowledge that is pursued otherwise than with a view to discovering the conditions of eternal life, says: knowledge puffeth up, but love edifieth. For he who thinks that he knows any thing, apart from the true knowledge which is attested by having the life within it, is without knowledge, deceived by the serpent, and a hater of life. But he who learns with fear, and studies to attain unto life, plants in hope, and may look for the fruit. Let your heart be a heart of knowledge, and in life perceive that understanding is granted, true and simple; its tree shall rise within you, and of its fruit you shall be filled with those enjoyments which are in the hand of GOD: which the serpent never touches, nor does any deceit come nigh: no Eve betrays them, but she to whom they are committed is the Virgin Church. Hereby is salvation manifested, and hence the Apostles find wisdom; while the Easter-feast of our Lord is solemnized, and congregations are gathered together in decency and order, and the Word, by whom the Father is glorified, teaches His saints with joy. To whom be glory everlasting. Amen.

May 8, 1834
The Feast of the Ascension

RECORD 16: AD SCHOLAS
Address of St. Clement of Alexandria to the Heathen

The HOLY SPIRIT says, "Despise not thou, my son, the training of the LORD, nor faint when thou art rebuked of Him." What surpassing condescension! How gently does He deal with us; not as a teacher with his disciples, nor as a master with his servants, nor as a GOD towards His creatures, but as a father instructs his sons! Moses confessed that he exceedingly feared and quaked when he heard concerning the word of GOD; but thou, who hearest that Word Himself, hast thou no dread, no distress of mind? no reverence, and earnestness withal to learn the truth? earnestness for salvation, fear of his wrath, delight in his promises, anxiety for acceptance, to rescue thee from condemnation? Come ye, O come, my band of young ones! Young ones, I say, for unless ye be born again as children, regenerated, as Scripture says, ye will not receive Him who is your own Father, nor will ever at any time gain entrance into the kingdom of heaven. To a stranger this is impossible; but when he has been enrolled by name and made a citizen, and submits to a new Father, then shall he be in the number of that Father's sons; then shall he be thought worthy of the inheritance. Thus is formed the first begotten Church, being made up of many holy children. These are "the first-born, whose names are written in heaven," who hold their "general assembly" with "an innumerable company of angels." Such are we, the nurslings of our GOD, true "friends" by kindred of the First-Begotten, as being the first of all men, to have discerned ALMIGHTY GOD, saved ourselves from sin, and abjured the Devil . . . . .

This is his sole work, to save man. Therefore he cries aloud, as urging us himself, "The kingdom of heaven is at hand." He converts men by means of fear. His apostle, in like manner, exhorting the Philippians, takes up his holy tidings, and repeats them. "The LORD is at hand," he says, "see well that we be not found wanting." But, alas! ye are all so fearless, nay, unbelieving, that ye listen neither to the LORD, nor to holy Paul, though he prays you in CHRIST'S stead to taste and see that CHRIST is God. It is faith that must bring you in, experience must teach you, and the Scripture must lead you on in knowledge, according to its word: "Come, ye children, hearken to me; and I will teach you the fear of the LORD." Then it briefly addresses those who have already believed: "What man is there who lusteth to live, who would fain see good days?" We make answer, It is we; who worship him who is our happiness, and who copy those who are like him. Hear, then, both ye who afar off, and ye who are nigh. The word is hid from no one; it is a light in common; it lighteth every man; in it there is no darkness. Let us hasten to our salvation, even to our regeneration, so that, many though we be, we may be brought close together by one love, according to that oneness which the one GOD imparts. Let us hasten, as having received a benefit; as seeking out our sole happiness. Let us follow after unity, till from many voices, loud and scattered to and fro, one divine harmony arises, led by one guide and teacher, the Divine Word, finding rest and fulness in the truth itself, and saying, Abba Father.

"Ye who thirst, come ye to the water," says the LORD; "all ye that have no silver, come and buy, yea, drink without silver." Thus does he exhort men to the holy bath, to their salvation, to their illumination, almost crying out to them, "Child, I give unto thee earth, and sea, and heaven; yea, all that is therein, I freely grant to thee: only, O my child, thirst for thy Father's presence. GOD will reveal himself to thee without price; truth is not dealt out as by a trader. He gives thee all things that fly, and swim, and walk the earth; all these things has thy Father framed for thy enjoyment, so take and be thankful. Those who are but spurious born are forced to buy their possessions with silver; sons of perdition, willing slaves of mammon. But into thine hands he gives thine own." Thus speaks he to his true seed, to him who loves his Father, for whose sake he worketh still, to whom alone he pledges, that the earth shall be given as a lasting foundation, which is not promised to corruption: "For mine is all the earth;" it is thine, if thou receive thy GOD; and therefore Scripture proclaims as good tidings, to those who have believed, "The saints of the LORD shall inherit the glory of GOD, and his power."

"Hope in him," it is written, "all the assembly of the people; pour out your heart before him." He speaks to those who have newly turned from wickedness. He pities and fills them with righteousness. Trust, O mortal, in him who is both GOD and man; who suffered and is worshipped, even a living GOD. Ye servants, put your trust in him who was dead; yea, all men, trust in him who out of all men alone is GOD. Believe and receive salvation as your reward; seek out GOD, and your soul shall live . . . . . The most sublime philosophers could but guess, and speak darkly about wisdom, but the disciples of CHRIST have seen and proclaimed it. Nay, and CHRIST in all portions of him (so to say) is one and the same undivided; so that there is neither barbarian, Jew, nor Greek, male, nor female, but one new man refashioned by the HOLY GHOST . . . I do but ask you to accept salvation. What does CHRIST desire, but freely to give you life? But who is he? The Word of truth, the builder of the inward temple, that GOD may dwell with men. Sanctify that temple; pleasures and comforts, leave them, as flowers of the day, to the wind, and to the fire . . . . . The Word of GOD shall guide thee, and the HOLY SPIRIT settle thee in the peaceful dwelling of the heavens. There thou shalt enjoy the presence of the Christian's GOD, and be initiated in his holy mysteries. Come, O heathen reveller, lean not on thy thyrsus,[1] bind not on thine ivy. Cast away thy turban, and thy fawnskin; put off folly. I will show to thee the Word of GOD, and his mysteries, accommodating my account to thine own fashions. Here is the mount, beloved of GOD, not the scene of tragic miseries, as Cithæron,[2] but a stage for truth to act upon, a holy mount, overshadowed with chaste and temperate groves. No Bacchantes revel here, with cruel rites, but the daughters of GOD hold festival, the pure, the gracious, divine songstresses of the awful mysteries of the Word, with their modest band of worshippers. That band are the just ones: the song is a hymn in honour of the Almighty King. Virgins are singing it, angels are heralding it, prophets are repeating it. The chant sounds abroad; those

---

[1] A spear or staff, surrounded with garlands of ivy and vine leaves, carried by the heathen revellers.
[2] A mountain where the heathen revels were held.

who are called hurry to the gathering, they hasten on, desiring to regain their Father. Thou, too, aged one, thou too must join us, leaving thy Thebes, abjuring thy sooth-saying; put out thy hand, and let us lead thee to the truth. Hasten, O Tiresias,[3] believe. He shall shine upon thy blind eyes more cheerily than the sun, through whom the eyes of the blind see. O mysteries of truest holiness! O unsullied Light! The sacred torches go before me, while I am brought into the presence of the heavens and GOD himself; my initiation places me among the holy ones. The LORD instructs me in his sacred rites; he seals his teachers with his illuminating guidance, and delivers over such as trust him to his Father, to be preserved for ever. He is everlasting, JESUS the one SAVIOUR, the Great High Priest of the one GOD his Father, who intercedes for men, and who is their teacher.

June 29, 1834
The Feast of St. Peter

---

[3] A heathen prophet.

RECORD 17: AD SCHOLAS
Tertullian's Account of the Rule of Faith

Tertullian was born at Carthage, in Africa, a heathen; but when he grew up he was converted to Christianity. At length he became a priest, either of the Church of Carthage, or of Rome; it is uncertain which. That is, it is uncertain whether, as we now speak, he *took orders* in Carthage or Rome; whether he was *ordained* by the Bishop of Carthage or of Rome. For at that blessed time the *whole extent* of Christendom was as closely united as the different parts of England are; so that it was all one from which of the bishops of the Church Catholic a Christian was ordained for the ministry. Rome was at that time not more divided from Carthage, or from Corinth, or from Ephesus, or from Jerusalem, than Winchester from London, or Durham, or Oxford, or Norwich. It was natural, indeed, for many reasons, that a man should receive orders from the Church in which he lived; but on fitting reasons a Carthaginian, like Tertullian, might receive his commission from the Bishop of Rome, just as now a native of London, for instance, may become a priest of the Church of Oxford.

This one Christian body, called sometimes *Christendom* (which means the kingdom of Christ), sometimes *the Church Catholic* (which means the incorporate society of Christians in all lands, as descended from the Apostles, and governed by the bishops, their representatives), consisted in the early times of two great portions, those who spoke Greek, and those who spoke Latin, which are sometimes familiarly called the Greek and the Latin Churches. Not that they were really divided, more than the Welsh Dioceses are from the English, but for convenience-sake they were considered as two, according to their respective languages. Writers, from whose works extracts have as yet been made in these Records, all spoke *Greek*, or (as it is said) were of the Greek Church; Ignatius, Polycarp, Justin, and the rest: as to the Christians of Lyons, &c. they were Greeks living in France, at that time a barbarous country. But Tertullian is a writer of the *Latin* Church; indeed he is the oldest of those whose works have come down to us, having been born about A.D. 160, only sixty years after St. John's death.

Tertullian's works, which have come down to us, are partly defences of Christianity and of the orthodox faith, and partly moral treatises. They are chiefly valuable, as *witnesses* of the state of the Church so short a time after the Apostles; as witnesses of what the Church then believed, taught, observed; as witnesses to the Creed as we hold it at this day, to Episcopacy, the Apostolical Succession, the Ceremonial of Religion, &c. *His own* authority indeed is small; for though very powerful as a writer, he was not a sound divine; was extravagant, nay even heterodox, in some of his opinions, and at length fell away into one of the heresies of his time. But all this, of course, does not interfere at all with the value of his writings as bearing testimony to *facts*, to the existing condition of the Church. And, moreover, as he writes ably, he is instructive on particular subjects, even though he is not a safe guide on the whole.

The work, from which an extract follows, was written when he was about forty years old, and may be called in English, "The Church's Plea (or Demur) against Dissenters." Tertullian's argument is this. "You who dissent from the Church," he says, "are confuted by the very *novelty* of your doctrine. The true doctrine must be *old*, and cannot be *new;* now the Church and its doctrines, which you despise, are much older than all your sects and their respective doctrines. Nay, the Church is as old as the Apostles; it was founded all over the world by the Apostles; and transmits down, from age to age, the doctrines which it received from them. But *from whom* did you receive your doctrine? Not from the Church, for you have gone out of it. Trace it up even for a few years, if you can; much less can you trace it up to the Apostles. In truth, your doctrine *began* with you, or at least with your immediate teachers: where was it before? Was it *hidden* from the Church, that doctrine which Christ commanded should be set up on high among the faithful, like a light within a house? Impossible: it plainly *began* with you: we can put our finger on the date of its birth; and *therefore* it is false: for Christ and His Apostles "*planted*" (1 Cor 3) the true Gospel, according to the will of the Father; and he says, 'Every plant, which my heavenly Father hath not planted, shall be rooted up.'" Such is the argument of the work from which the following passages are extracted; which obviously contain an instructive lesson for this day.

1.

> [The Separatists of Tertullian's age urged the words of our Lord, "Seek, and ye shall find," in proof that they might allowably strike out their own views (though novel) from the sacred text: he says upon this:—]

"Let us grant it has been said to all, 'Seek and ye shall find;' yet even as to these very words it is convenient to discuss their meaning with some guide of interpretation. No divine saying is so vague and extended, that its mere words are to be adhered to, and their real drift not determined. Now, in the first place, I lay down this proposition: that doubtless some one certain faith was instituted by Christ, which the nations ought by all means to believe; and, in seeking to find it, to seek with the purpose of believing when they had found it. The inquiry after one certain definite appointment (of God) must surely have an end some where or other. You are to seek *until* you find, and believe *when* you have found. After this, there is no more to do, but to *keep* what you have believed; this being in fact one part of your belief, viz. that there is nothing farther to be believed, nor therefore to be sought; inasmuch as you have found and believed that which was appointed by Him, who does not set you to seek any thing else but what he has appointed. I will presently make good, to the satisfaction of all doubters, that *we* have that in our possession which was appointed by Christ. In the mean time, from confidence in the proof, I anticipate so far as to admonish certain persons that they have nothing to seek *beyond* what they have already accepted; that *that* is what they were bound to seek: so that they must not interpret without consideration of the import of the words, 'Seek, and ye shall find.'

"But the import of this saying is determined by three particulars; the matter, the time, the manner: by the matter, that you should consider *what* is to be sought; by the time, *when* it is to be sought; by the manner, *how far*. Now that is to be sought, *which Christ instituted;* then, of course, *when you do not find it*, so long, of course, *until you find it*. But you have found it, when you have attained to belief, for you would not have believed, if you had not found; as neither would you have sought, unless that you might find. For where shall inquiry come to an end? where faith take her stand? where discovery gain her discharge? With Marcion? nay, Valentinus also sets up 'seek, and ye shall find.' With Valentinus? nay, Apelles too will beset me with the same declaration: and Hebion, and Simon, and all, one after another, have nothing else but this same text, by which to insinuate themselves into my approbation, to bind me to their cause. I shall therefore come to no result, while I meet on every side, 'seek, and ye shall find.'

> [To understand the above argument, it must be borne in mind that at baptism the Creed was committed to and accepted by the new Christian. Thus *the time of belief* was a certain definite date, to which Tertullian refers. It must be observed also, that the persons he speaks to were Separatists, who had been baptized *in the Church*, not regular hereditary Dissenters.]

2.

"Although we were to be for ever inquiring, yet *where* ought we to seek? Among heretics, where all is extraneous and adverse to the truth we hold, whom we are forbidden to approach? What servant expects food from one who is a stranger, not to say an enemy to his master? What soldier looks for presents and pay from unallied, not to say hostile princes, unless he be a downright deserter and rebel? Even she who sought diligently, sought her piece of money in her own house; he who asks for loaves, knocks at a friend's, not a stranger's door; and the widow interceded with a hard judge, but not an enemy. Let us then seek at home, and from those who are our own, and of that which is our own; and inquire respecting that only which may be called in question without injury to the Rule of Faith."

"But the Rule of Faith (that we may now profess what we mean to defend) is this:—That there is One only God, and no other Creator of the world beside, who brought all things out of nothing by His own Word sent forth before all things: that this Word, called His Son, appeared in the name of God to the Patriarchs in different ways; was always heard in the

Prophets; and at last conveyed by the Spirit and power of God the Father into the Virgin Mary, became flesh in her womb, and lived as her Son Jesus Christ; afterwards proclaimed a new law, and a new promise of the kingdom of Heaven, wrought miracles, was crucified, rose again on the third day, was taken into heaven, and sat down at the right hand of the Father; sent the power of the Holy Spirit in His stead, to guide believers; will come with glory to take His saints to the enjoyment of eternal life and His heavenly promises, and sentence the profane to eternal fire, bringing to life again good and bad, together with the resurrection of their flesh. This Rule, instituted, as it shall be proved, by Christ, has no questions raised about it among us, except such as heresies introduce, and such as constitute men heretics . . . . O novice, it is better to be ignorant, lest you should learn what you ought not, now that you know what you ought. 'Thy faith,' he says, 'hath made thee whole;' not a perverse troubling of the Scriptures. Faith has for its object THE RULE. The law of life is given you; keep it, and you are made whole: but this cross-examining of Scripture springs from restlessness; pursue it, and it brings, not salvation, but mere credit for cleverness. Let restlessness yield to faith; fame among men to salvation of the soul."

3.

[Next, he shows the futility of arguing with men who mutilate and alter the Scriptures; but this topic does not so nearly concern us at this day: though we cannot tell what is coming upon us. He then proceeds as follows, to show that there is nothing *gained* in arguing from Scripture, when God has given us so clear a guide in the Rule of Faith, *i.e.* the Creed preserved in the Church; for, though that Rule *is* also contained in Scripture, and may be proved from it, yet heretics will say it cannot; whereas they cannot deny the Creed came from the Apostles.]

"But for that person, if there be such, for whose sake you descend to a comparison of Scriptures, to confirm him when in doubt, will he incline to truth, or rather to heresies? Influenced by the very fact, that he sees you have hitherto gained no ground, and stand even with your adversary in denying this point and defending that, he will undoubtedly leave this even contest in still greater uncertainty, not knowing which he is to judge to be heresy. For surely nothing can hinder them retorting upon us, if they are minded, the charges we bring against them. Nay, they must, in self-defence, say that *we* rather introduce corruptions of Scripture, and false expositions, inasmuch as they claim truth for themselves. Therefore I do not advise appeal to the Scriptures: it is a ground in which there can be either no victory, or a doubtful one, or one as good as doubtful. For although the comparison of Scripture did not end so as to place either party on an equality, the order of things requires that this point should be first advanced, which is now the only question: viz. *To whom* belongs the faith itself? *Whose* are the Scriptures? *By whom*, and *through whom*, and *when*, and *to whom* was that system of instruction committed, by which men are made Christians? For there, wherever the truth of Christian instruction and faith shall be proved to be, *there* will be the truth of the Scriptures, and of expositions, and of all Christian traditions."

> [This ground of the truth is of course the Church. Tertullian does not mean to decry arguing from Scripture; he only says, it will not *silence* a subtle and perverse disputant; whereas the Rule of Faith *must* silence them, it is so clear. Again he argues, Were not the Scriptures *committed* to the Church? *therefore* the Church is the appointed *interpreter* of them. Since his time, the Church has gone wrong; but what he says is quite true of the *primitive* Church. And this is the rule of the Church of England, to interpret Scripture *according to the usage of the first centuries*.]

September 21, 1834
The Feast of St. Matthew

RECORD 18: AD SCHOLAS
Tertullian's Account of the Rule of Faith
Continued

4.

[By the "*Rule* of Faith" is sometimes meant the canon, or document containing the faith, (*e.g.* Scripture, or *ascertained* Apostolical tradition,) sometimes the collection of articles of faith, as in a confession, or, (as it is sometimes called) the Summa Fidei. In the former sense of course the Rule is the *authority*, in the latter it is the very doctrine to be proved. Tertullian uses the word in both senses in this treatise.]

CHRIST JESUS our Lord—whatever is His nature, (so to express myself) whatever is that GOD who is His Father, in whatever way He is GOD and man, whatever His doctrine, whatever His reward,—certainly declared all this, Himself, during His sojourn on earth, His present and pre-existent nature, His Father's will which He was fulfilling, His commands to man; declared it either openly to the people, or apart to His disciples, of whom He had especially selected twelve as His companions, and the destined teachers of the nations. Accordingly, on His departure to His Father, after His resurrection, He gave them their commission (*i.e.* the eleven, for one had fallen away) and bade them, Go teach the nations, baptizing them in the name of the FATHER, and of the SON, and of the HOLY GHOST. They then without delay, Apostles as they were called, or Missionaries, chose a twelfth by lot, according to the direction of the prophetic Psalm; and, when they had been visited by the promised Spirit of miracle and tongues, first preached faith in Jesus Christ, and founded churches throughout

Judea; next went forward into the wide world, publishing the same doctrine to the Gentiles, and establishing Churches in every city. From these in turn the faith has been, and still is, propagated continually for the creation of new churches, which, as well as the first founded, are called Apostolic, as being the offspring of those which were really such. Every family must be referred to its first original: therefore these Churches, many though they be and flourishing, yet are but one, that one original which the Apostles established, and from which they all spring. So they are all original, and all Apostolic, all being one. That oneness is evidenced by their loving inter-communion, and the name of brotherhood, and the interchange of hospitality; and these common rights are secured solely by their unanimous tradition of one and the same sacred covenant.

From this point, therefore, we begin our plea against all who preach a new doctrine. If the Lord Jesus Christ sent the Apostles to preach, it follows that no other preachers are to be received, but those whom Christ appointed, because "no one knoweth the Father but the Son, and he to whom the Son hath revealed Him." And it seems that the Son has revealed Him to no others than the Apostles, whom He sent to preach that doctrine, of course, which He revealed to them. But what they preached, that is, what Christ revealed to them, I shall here also plead should be proved in no other way, than by means of those same Churches, which the Apostles themselves founded, by preaching to them, as well as by word of mouth, as afterwards by Epistles. If these things are so, it follows immediately that all doctrine that agrees with those Apostolical Churches, the depositaries and sources of the faith, is to be reckoned for truth, preserving, as they doubtless do, what they received from the Apostles, the Apostles from Christ, Christ from God. But that every other doctrine is to be presumed false, that savours of contradiction to the truth of the Churches, and of the Apostles, and of Christ, and of God.

It only remains then to prove, whether this our doctrine, the rule of which we have given above, is to be considered of Apostolic tradition; and from this very fact, whether the rest come not of falsehood. Now our very inter-communion with the Apostolical Churches, which is matter of fact, is an evidence that our doctrine does not differ from theirs. This is the witness of the truth.

5.

[To get rid of the above plain argument, the Separatists used to urge that the Apostles had a private doctrine over and above that which they taught in open church; or again, that they were not fully instructed in Christian truth, alleging, *e.g.* St. Peter's error in *conduct* at Antioch, &c. The following passage is in answer to the former of these suppositions.]

Sometimes they maintain, not that the Apostles were ignorant or discordant in their preaching, but with a like wildness, that they did not reveal all things to all: for that they entrusted some truths openly to all, but some secretly to a few. Now St. Paul uses this expression to Timothy: "O Timothy, keep that which is committed to thee;" and again, "keep the good thing committed to thee." What is this thing committed, so proper to be assigned to some different doctrine? Is it of that declaration, of which he says, "This charge I entrust with thee, son Timothy." Also of that precept of which he says, "I charge thee before God, who giveth life to all things, and Jesus Christ, who witnessed before Pontius Pilate a good confession, that thou keep the precept." But what precept, and what charge? It will be understood from what is written before and after, that there is not any thing secretly pointed out by this expression relating to more abstruse doctrine, but that rather a charge is given concerning, not admitting any besides that which he had heard from himself, and I think openly. He says, "Before many witnesses." Who these many witnesses were, supposing they do not choose to understand *the Church,* makes no difference; since nothing can have been secret that was brought out before many witnesses. As to his admonishing him to "commit these things to faithful men, who are fit to teach others also;" this is not to be interpreted as any proof of some hidden gospel. For when he says "these things," he says it of those of which he was at present writing; but concerning hidden things, as concerning things not mentioned, and but tacitly understood, he would have said not "these," but "those."

His direction about committing "to faithful men," did not imply a secresy, but of course care to choose such men for the commission as would preach the Gospel with judgment and discrimination; not casting pearls to swine, or holy things to dogs, as the Lord speaks. Our Lord himself spoke forth openly, without the least hint of any hidden covenant.

He himself had ordered, that if they had heard any thing in darkness and in secret, they should proclaim it in the light, and on the house-top.

If, then, it is incredible that the Apostles either were ignorant of the fulness of the Gospel message, or abstained from publishing it to all in its completeness, let us next see whether, though the Apostles spoke with plainness and fulness, yet the Churches, by their own fault, received otherwise than the Apostles declared. You may find all such means of exciting scruples put forward by heretics. They take hold of the correction of the Churches by the Apostles: "O foolish Galatians, who hath bewitched you?" and "Ye did well, who hath hindered you?" and the very beginning, "I wonder that ye are so soon departed from him, who called you into grace, to another gospel;" of that too written to the Corinthians, that they were yet carnal, who ought to be fed with milk, and not yet fit for meat, as they thought they knew something, when as yet they knew nothing as it ought to be known. But, surely, the *fault found* with the Churches, which is their very objection, is a ground for believing it was *corrected*. Besides, let them also recollect those in whose faith and knowledge and conversation the Apostle rejoices, and gives thanks to God; which, be it observed, to this day share the rights of the one instituted body with those that were then blamed. However, grant all have erred; grant even an Apostle has been so mistaken as to impart his message only to a few; grant that the Holy Spirit has not vouchsafed to lead any Church into the truth, though for this cause sent by Christ, and for this cause asked of the Father, that He might be a teacher of the truth; grant that the steward of God, the vicegerent of Christ, has neglected his office, suffering the Churches meanwhile to understand and to believe otherwise than He himself declared by the Apostles:—is it likely that so many and so large Churches should have run by mistake into one belief? Different courses have different issues: the teaching of the Churches must then have varied in their form: but what we find the same throughout many, is not a mistake, but a tradition. Let a man then be bold, and say, that they erred who first delivered it. But, however the error arose, I suppose it reigned on as long as heresies were unknown. Truth awaited her release by some Marcionites and Valentinians; meanwhile the Gospel was preached amiss, men believed amiss, so many thousands were baptized amiss, so many works of faith were done amiss, so many miracles, so many spiritual gifts were wrought amiss, so many priesthoods, so many ministries discharged amiss; finally, so many martyrdoms crowned amiss. Or, if not altogether amiss, and in vain, what a thing is it, that the cause of God should be in progress before it was known of what God?—that there should have been Christians before Christ was found?—heresy before true doctrine? Nay, but in all things the truth precedes the image, the likeness comes after the reality; but it is absurd enough to suppose heresy to have come first in that teaching, even because it is that same teaching which foretold that there should be heresies. It was written to a Church holding that doctrine, yea, the doctrine itself writes to its Church: "And if an angel from heaven preach another Gospel to you, beside that we have preached, let him be accursed."

6.

[He next proceeds to show more fully that Apostolicity is the test of truth.]

But if any heresies dare to place themselves in the Apostolic age, that they may seem therefore to have been delivered by the Apostles, because they existed under the Apostles; we may say, Let them then show the rise of their churches, let them unroll the line of their Bishops, so running down by successions from the beginning, that their first Bishop may have had for his authority and predecessor some one of the Apostles, or such Apostolic men, as continued to hold with the Apostles. For in this manner the Apostolic Churches deduce their lines; as the Church of the Smyrnæans produces Polycarp appointed by John; as that of the Romans, Clement in like manner ordained by Peter; and as the others, in like manner, point to those who were appointed as Bishops by the Apostles, to deliver down for them the Apostolic seed. Let the heretics forge any such records. For what is unlawful for them after blasphemy? But though they should have forged them they will gain nothing. For their doctrine itself compared with that of the Apostles, will declare by its own diversity and contrariety, that it has neither any Apostle nor any Apostolic man for its author: because as the Apostles would not have taught different things among themselves, so neither would the Apostolic men have put forth things contradictory to the Apostles, excepting such men as revolted from the Apostles, and preached otherwise. This is the challenge they will receive from those Churches, which though they can show none of the Apostles, or Apostolic men, for their authority, as being much later, those even that are rising every day; yet conspiring in the same faith, are held no less apostolical on account of their kindred doctrine. Thus let all heresies, challenged by our Churches to either trial, prove themselves Apostolic in whatever way they think right. However they are not so, nor can prove themselves what they are not, nor are they received into peace and communion by Churches in any sense Apostolical: forasmuch as for the difference of their faith, they are in no wise Apostolic . . . . . .

Let all heresies, challenged and convicted by us on these terms (whether such as are later than, or contemporary with the Apostles, so that they differ from them; whether generally or specially marked by them, so that they have been condemned beforehand by them) dare to offer in answer any similar plea against our system. For if they deny the truth of it, they ought to convict it of heresy, by the same method by which themselves are convicted; and to show at the same time where that truth is to be sought, which is now sufficiently proved not to be with them. That which we maintain is not later: nay, it is before all others. This will be the testimony to the truth, as every where having the precedence in time. What, in fact, is not condemned, nay, is defended by the Apostles, this carries proof of its being theirs. For what they do not condemn, who condemn every alien system, they show to be their own, and, therefore, even maintain.

Come now, you that wish to turn this restlessness to profit in the search after salvation; run over the Apostolic Churches, in which the very chairs of the Apostles still hold place of honour, in which the very letters they wrote are recited, echoing the voice, and imaging the person of each of them. Is Achaia nearest to you? You have Corinth. If you are not far from Macedonia, you have Philippi, you have the Thessalonians. If you can reach Asia, you have Ephesus. But if you are in the neighbourhood of Italy, you have Rome, whence we also draw our own authority. How happy is that Church! where the Apostles poured forth their whole doctrine together with their blood; where Peter is likened in suffering to the Lord; where Paul is crowned with an end like the Baptist's; where the Apostle John, having been plunged in heated oil and suffered nothing, was banished to his island. Let us see what this Church has learned, what she has taught, what tokens she has sent of doctrine to the African Churches.

She knows One God, the Creator of the universe, and Christ Jesus of the Virgin Mary, the Son of the Creator, and the resurrection of the flesh: she unites the law and the prophets with the Evangelical and Apostolical writings, and thence brings her faith. This she signs with water, clothes with the Holy Spirit, feeds with the eucharist, encourages by martyrdom, and therefore will acknowledge no one who opposes it. This is the teaching, I say not now which foretold future heresies, but out of which heresies have arisen, though they ceased to be scions of it from the time that they opposed it. Even from the kernel of the mild rich and serviceable olive, a harsh wild olive springs; even from the seed of the most delicious and sweetest fig, a wayward and barren wild fig-tree arises. Thus, also, heresies are from us, not of us, degenerate from the stock of truth, and running into weeds of falsehood.

October 18, 1834
The Feast of St. Luke

Appendices

APPENDIX 1

Thematic Index of the Tracts, Volume 1

I. LITURGICAL

3. Thoughts Respectfully Addressed to the Clergy on Alterations in the Liturgy 10
9. On Shortening the Church Service 52
13. Sunday Lessons.—The Principle of Selection 84
37. Bishop Wilson's Form of Excommunication 323
39. Bishop Wilson's Form of Receiving Penitents 343

II. ON ORDINANCES

14. The Ember Days 96
16. Advent 113
18. Thoughts on the Benefits of the System of Fasting, Enjoined by Our Church 126
21. Mortification of the Flesh a Scripture Duty 163
25. Bishop Beveridge on the Great Necessity and Advantage of Public Prayer 199
26. Bishop Beveridge on the Necessity and Advantage of Frequent Communion 207
27. Bishop Cosin on the Doctrine of the Eucharist 227
28. The same continued 244

32. The Standing Ordinances of Religion 292
34. Rites and Customs of the Church 306

III. ON THE APOSTOLICAL SUCCESSION

1. Thoughts on the Ministerial Commission, Respectfully Addressed to the Clergy 1
4. Adherence to the Apostolical Succession the Safest Course 18
7. The Episcopal Church Apostolical 44
10. Heads of a Week-day Lecture, Delivered to a Country Congregation in ——shire 55
17. The Ministerial Commission a Trust from Christ for the Benefit of His People 120
24. The Scripture View of the Apostolic Commission 189
33. Primitive Episcopacy 300
35. The People's Interest in Their Minister's Commission 313
42. Bishop Wilson's Meditations on his Sacred Office, Number 1: Sunday 372
44. Bishop Wilson's Meditations on his Sacred Office, Number 2: Monday 394
46. Bishop Wilson's Meditations on his Sacred Office, Number 3: Tuesday 407

IV. ON THE DOCTRINE OF THE CHURCH

2. The Catholic Church 6
5. A short Address to His Brethren on the Nature and Constitution of the Church of Christ, and of the Branch of It Established in England. By a Layman 26
11. The Visible Church. Letters I. and II. 60
20. The same continued. Letter III. 156

23. The Faith and Obedience of Churchmen, the Strength of the Church 185
29. Christian Liberty; or, Why Should We Belong to the Church of England? By a Layman 268
30. The same continued 279

V. ON THE HISTORY OF THE CHURCH

15. On the Apostolical Succession of the English Church 102
31. The Reformed Church 288
36. Account of Religious Sects at Present Existing in England 317
38. Via Media.—No. I 331
41. Via Media.—No. II 361

VI. ON THE ARGUMENT FOR THE CHURCH

6. The Present Obligation of Primitive Practice 40
8. The Gospel a Law of Liberty 48
19. On Arguing Concerning the Apostolical Succession 152
45. The Grounds of Our Faith 402

VII. RICHARD NELSON

12. Bishops, Priests, and Deacons 69
22. The Athanasian Creed 168
40. Baptism 347
43. Length of the Public Service 380

VIII. RECORDS OF THE CHURCH

1. Epistle of Ignatius to the Ephesians 413

2. Epistle of Ignatius to the Magnesians 420
3. The Apostle St. John and the Robber 424
4. Epistle of Ignatius to Polycarp 428
5. Epistle of Ignatius to the Trallians 431
6. Account of the Martyrs of Lyons and Vienne 435
7. Epistle of Ignatius to the Smyrnæans 447
8. Epistle of Ignatius to the Romans 451
9. The Martyrdom of Ignatius at Rome 455
10. Epistle of Ignatius to the Philadelphians 461
11. Account of the Martyrdom of St. James the Apostle 465
12. The Martyrdom of Polycarp 468
13. Justin Martyr, on Primitive Christian Worship 479
14. Irenæus on the Rule of Faith 485
15. The Temporal Condition and the Principles of Christians, from the Epistle to Diognetus 488
16. Address of Clement of Alexandria to the Heathen 494
17. Tertullian on the Rule of Faith 498
18. The same continued 504

APPENDIX 2
Works Upholding the Doctrine Inculcated in the Tracts

This list of theological works was often printed alongside individual Tracts with this note:

The following Works, all in single volumes, or pamphlets, and recently published, will be found more or less to uphold or elucidate the general doctrines inculcated in these Tracts.

Bp. Taylor on Repentance, by Hale.—*Rivingtons*.

Bp. Taylor's Golden Grove.—*Parker, Oxford*.

Vincentii Lirinensis Commonitorium, *with translation*.—*Parker, Oxford*.

Pusey on Cathedrals and Clerical Education.—*Roake and Varty*.

Hook's University Sermons.—*Talboys, Oxford*.

Pusey on Baptism (*published separately*).—*Rivingtons*.

Newman's Sermons, 4 vols.—*Rivingtons*.

Newman on Romanism, &c.—*Rivingtons*.

The Christian Year.—*Parker, Oxford*.

Lyra Apostolica.—*Rivingtons*.

Perceval on the Roman Schism.—*Leslie*.

Bishop Jebb's Pastoral Instructions.—Duncan.

Dodsworth's Lectures on the Church.—*Burns*.

Newman on Suffragan Bishops.—*Rivingtons*.

Keble's Sermon on Tradition.—*Rivingtons*.

Memoir of Ambrose Bonwick.—*Parker, Oxford*.

Hymns for Children on the Lord's Prayer.—*Rivingtons*.

Law's first and second Letters to Hoadly.—*Rivingtons*.

Bp. Andrews' Devotions. Latin and Greek.—*Pickering*.

Hook's Family Prayers.—*Rivingtons*.

Herbert's Poems and Country Pastor.

Evans's Scripture Biography.—*Rivingtons*.

Le Bas' Life of Archbishop Laud.—Rivingtons.

Jones (of Nayland) on the Church.

Bp. Bethell on Baptismal Regeneration.—Rivingtons.

Bp. Beveridge's Sermons on the Ministry and Ordinances.—*Parker, Oxford*.

Bp. Jolly on the Eucharist.

Fulford's Sermons on the Ministry, &c.—*Rivingtons*.

Rose's Sermons on the Ministry.—*Rivingtons*.

A Catechism on the Church.—*Parker, Oxford*.

Russell's Judgment of the Anglican Church.—*Baily*.

Poole's Sermons on the Creed.—*Grant, Edinburgh*.

Sutton on the Eucharist.—*Parker, Oxford*.

Leslie on the Regale and Pontificate.—*Leslie*.

Pusey's Sermon on November 5.—*Rivingtons*.

Bishop Wilson's Sacra Privata.—*Parker, Oxford*.

The Cathedral, a Poem.—*Parker, Oxford*.

Palmer's Ecclesiastical History.—*Burns*.

Larger Works which may be profitably studied.

Bishop Bull's Sermons.—*Parker, Oxford.*

Bishop Bull's Works.—*University Press.*

Waterland's Works.—*Do.*

Wall on Infant Baptism.—*Do.*

Pearson on the Creed—*Do.*

Leslie's Works.—*Do.*

Bingham's Works.—*Straker, London.*

Palmer on the Liturgy.—*University Press.*

Palmer on the Church.—*Rivingtons.*

Hooker, ed. Keble.—*Do.*

APPENDIX 3
H.P. Liddon's Table of Tracts and Authors
for Volume 1

The following table is from H.P. Liddon's Life of Edward Bouverie Pusey, *Volume 3. London: Longman, Green, 1894, pp. 473-476. As Liddon notes, "It was intended that each volume should contain the Tracts issued in an Academical year."*

Tract	1833		
I	Sept. 9.	Thoughts on the Ministerial Commission. 4 pp., *Ad Clerum*.	[J. H. Newman].
II	Sept. 9.	The Catholic Church. 4 pp.	[J. H. Newman].
III	Sept. 9.	Thoughts respectfully addressed to the Clergy on alterations in the Liturgy. The Burial Service. The Principle of Unity. 8 pp.	[J. H. Newman].
IV	Sept. 21.	Adherence to the Apostolical Succession the safest course. On Alterations in the Prayer-book. 8 pp., *Ad Populum*.	[J. Keble].
V	Oct. 18.	A short address to his Brethren on the Nature and Constitution of the Church of Christ, and of the Branch of it established in England. By a Layman. 15. pp.	[J. W. Bowden].

VI	Oct. 29.	The Present Obligation of Primitive Practice. A sin of the Church. 4 pp., *Ad Populum*.	[J. H. Newman].
VII	Oct. 29.	The Episcopal Church Apostolical. 4 pp.	[J. H. Newman].
VIII	Oct. 31.	The Gospel a Law of Liberty. Church Reform. 4 pp.	[J. H. Newman].
IX	Oct. 31.	On Shortening the Church Services. Sunday Lessons. 4 pp., *Ad Populum*.	[R. H. Froude].
X	Nov. 4.	Heads of a Week-Day Lecture, delivered to a Country Congregation. 6 pp.	[J. H. Newman].
XI	Nov. 11.	The Visible Church. Letters I and II. 8 pp., *Ad Scholas*.	[J. H. Newman].
XII	Dec. 4.	Richard Nelson. No. 1 Bishops, Priests, and Deacons. 16 pp.	[Thos. Keble].
XIII	Dec. 5.	Sunday Lessons. The Principle of Selection. 11 pp., *Ad Populum*.	[J. Keble].
XIV	Dec. 12.	The Ember Days. 7 pp., *Ad Populum*.	[Alfred Menzies].
XV	Dec. 13.	On the Apostolical Succession in the English Church. 11 pp.	[W. Palmer, revised and completed by J. H. Newman].
XVI	Dec. 17.	Advent. 8 pp., *Ad Populum*.	[B. Harrison].
XVII	Dec. 20.	The Ministerial Commission: A Trust from Christ for the Benefit of His People. 7 pp., *Ad Populum*.	[B. Harrison].
XVIII	Dec. 21.	Thoughts on the Benefits of the System of Fasting enjoined by our Church. 28 pp.	[E. B. Pusey].
XIX	Dec. 23.	On arguing concerning the Apostolical Succession. On Reluctance to confess the Apostolical Succession. 4 pp.	[J. H. Newman].

XX	Dec. 24.	The Visible Church. Letter III. 4 pp., *Ad Scholas*.	[J. H. Newman].
	1834		
XXI	Jan. 1.	Mortification of the Flesh a Scripture duty. 4 pp., *Ad Populum*.	[J. H. Newman].
XXII	Jan. 6.	Richard Nelson. No. II. The Athanasian Creed. 18 pp.	[Thos. Keble].
XXIII	Jan. 6.	The Faith and Obedience of Churchmen the strength of the Church. 4 pp.	[A. P. Perceval].
XXIV	Jan. 25.	The Scripture View of the Apostolical Commission. 11 pp., *Ad Populum*.	[B. Harrison].
XXV	Jan. 25.	The great Necessity and Advantage of Public Prayer (extracted from Bishop Beveridge's Sermon on the subject). 8 pp., *Ad Populum*. A reprint.	
XXVI	Feb. 2.	The Necessity and Advantage of Frequent Communion (extracted from Bishop Beveridge's Sermon on the subject). 23 pp. A reprint.	
XXVII	Feb. 24.	The History of Popish Transubstantiation (by John Cosin, Bishop of Durham). 16 pp. A reprint.	
XXVIII	Mar. 25.	The same, concluded. 24 pp.	
XXIX	Mar. 25.	Christian Liberty, or, Why should we belong to the Church of England? By a Layman. 11 pp., *Ad Populum*.	[J. W. Bowden].
XXX	Mar. 25.	The same, continued. 8 pp., *Ad Populum*.	[J. W. Bowden].
XXXI	Apr. 25.	The Reformed Church. 4 pp., *Ad Clerum*.	[J. H. Newman].

APPENDIX 3: LIDDON'S TABLE OF TRACTS | 523

XXXII	Apr. 25.	The Standing Ordinances of Religion. 8 pp., *Ad Clerum*.	[C. P. Eden].
XXXIII	May 1.	Primitive Episcopacy. 7 pp., *Ad Scholas*.	[J. H. Newman].
XXXIV	May 1.	Rites and Customs of the Church. 8 pp., *Ad Scholas*.	[J. H. Newman].
XXXV	May 8.	The People's Interest in their Minister's Commission. 4 pp., *Ad Populum*.	[A. P. Perceval].
XXXVI	June 11	Account of Religious Sects at present existing in England. 7 pp., *Ad Populum*.	[A. P. Perceval].
XXXVII	June 24.	Bishop Wilson's Form of Excommunication. 8 pp., *Ad Populum*. A reprint.	
XXXVIII	July 25.	Via Media. No. I. 12 pp., *Ad Scholas*.	[J. H. Newman].
XXXIX	July 25.	Bishop Wilson's Form of Receiving Penitents. 4 pp., *Ad Populum*. A reprint.	
XL	July 25.	Richard Nelson. No. III. On Baptism. 15 pp., *Ad Populum*.	[John Keble].
XLI	Aug. 24.	Via Media. No. II. 12 pp., *Ad Scholas*.	[J. H. Newman].
XLII	Aug. 24.	Bishop Wilson's Meditations on his Sacred Office. No. I, Sunday. 15 pp., *Ad Populum*. A reprint.	
XLIII	Sept. 21.	Richard Nelson. No. IV. Length of the Public Service. 16 pp., *Ad Populum*.	[Thos. Keble].
XLIV	Sept. 29.	Bishop Wilson's Meditations on his Sacred Office. No. II, Monday. 4 pp. (2nd ed. 8 pp.), *Ad Populum*. A reprint.	
XLV	Oct. 18.	The Grounds of our Faith. 6 pp., *Ad Clerum*.	[J. H. Newman].

| XLVI | Oct. 28. | Bishop Wilson's Meditations on his Sacred Office. No. III, Tuesday. 4 pp., *Ad Populum*. A reprint. | |
| XLVII | Nov. 1. | The Visible Church. Letter IV. 4 pp., *Ad Clerum*. | [J. H. Newman]. |

A Note on the Text

In editing the first volume of the *Tracts for the Times*, I have consulted two editions: first, the *Tracts* as they were collected and printed in 1834 by J.G. & F. Rivington of London and J.H. Parker of Oxford; second, the 1840 edition produced by the same publishers, though by that date the former press had changed its name slightly to J.G.F. & J. Rivington. The text of individual tracts can vary from printing to printing. With this in mind, I developed several principles of selection as I assembled the present edition. In general, if there was a difference between an earlier and a later version of the text, I almost always included the earlier variant. This earlier variant was typically more controversial, and later editing attempted to moderate its claim. By choosing the earliest and more controversial variants, I hoped that readers would better understand why these tracts initially provoked such extreme reactions from both supporters and critics.

Yet I occasionally broke with my preference for the earlier variant if a tract was considerably expanded in a later edition and if this expansion had more to do with a fuller presentation of the subject than it did with moderating an earlier, controversial claim. This will be especially evident in the second volume of the *Tracts*, where I have included the much longer version of Tract 65.

That said, I want to acknowledge the fact that I did not set out to create an authoritative, critical edition of the *Tracts*. Rune Imberg remains the central authority on the text-critical issues of the *Tracts*—and the issues are indeed plentiful.¹ Establishing the dating and authorship of individual tracts continues to be an incredibly difficult enterprise, and no printing of the complete *Tracts* has fully integrated Imberg's research into the variations that occur in different printings. Imberg, for instance, has traced Tract 1 through seven different editions between 1833 and 1840, and among these editions, there are at least three sentences that were significantly revised.

I have made very few changes to the *Tracts* as they were printed in the editions that I consulted. For instance, references to scriptural citations are now given in Arabic, rather than Roman, numerals. In the editions consulted, the use of small caps—for words like GOD and LORD—were highly variable, sometimes with the same word being capitalized in one part of a sentence but not in another. I have attempted to preserve this idiosyncratic method of capitalization.

I have also inserted the name of an author at the end of every tract, using H.P. Liddon's table as a guide if the tract was originally published anonymously. Occasionally, the original publication included an attribution, sometimes merely the author's initials (e.g. E.B.P.); I have tried to note where this is the case through an editorial footnote. In general, the *Tracts* in this volume were published anonymously. Again, it should be noted that the authorship of individual tracts is a matter of scholarly debate, despite the fact that Liddon's table is so often referenced as the standard authority. As Imberg points out, Liddon attributes twenty-nine tracts to Newman, but Newman himself claimed that he wrote only twenty-three—"Is Liddon or Newman to be trusted?"²

As always, if you believe you have found an error, please send an email to seminarystreetpress@gmail.com; corrections will be incorporated into a future printing.

This project required the support and help of many. I would like to especially thank Fr. Patrick Raymond and Fr. Bob Petite of the Church of the Ascension in Chicago and Fr. Richard Wall and Dr. John Orens of St.

---

[1] See Rune Imberg, *In Quest of Authority: The "Tracts for the Times" and the Development of the Tractarian Leaders, 1833-1841*, Bibliotecha Historico-Ecclesiastica Lundensis 16 (Lund: Lund University Press, 1987); Rune Imberg, *Tracts for the Times: A Complete Survey of All the Editions*, Bibliotecha Historico-Ecclesiastica Lundensis 17 (Lund: Lund University Press, 1987).
[2] Imberg, *In Quest of Authority*, 37.

Paul's Parish, K Street in Washington, D.C. Both of these parishes inducted me into the Anglo-Catholic tradition, where I have found the beauty of holiness in abundance. I would also like to thank the people and priests of St. Paul's Episcopal Church in Peoria, Illinois and St. Augustine's Episcopal Church in Creede, Colorado. I would not have been able to bring this project to completion without the encouragement of many friends and teachers, particularly the Rev. Dr. Patricia Lyons, the Very Rev. Dr. Ian Markham, Dr. Hannah Matis, the Rev. Dr. Katherine Sonderegger, Arthur Clement, Harold and Janelle Cochran, Elma Ling Hoffman, Clare Kemmerer, William Pounds, Laura Ruth Venable, my parents, and the entire Virginia Theological Seminary community. Finally, I want to thank my wife, Gina Franco, for all her kindness—again and again, she has given me the gift of a life centered around words and the Word.

CHRISTOPHER POORE
September 14, 2021
Feast of the Holy Cross

The Library of Anglican Theology

No. 1   **Perfective Unction: A Discourse of Confirmation**
         Jeremy Taylor

No. 2   **The Incarnation of the Son of God**
         Charles Gore

No. 3   **Early Sermons from the African Episcopal Church of St. Thomas, Philadelphia**
         Absalom Jones & William Douglass

No. 4   **The Ministry of Consolation: A Guide to Confession *and* The Shadow of the Holy Week**
         Felicia Skene

No. 5   **Tracts for the Times**
         Volume One: Tracts 1–46 and Records of the Church 1–19

Made in the USA
Coppell, TX
28 October 2021